Knowlton School of Architecture,
The Ohio State University

The Light Construction Reader

Todd Gannon, Editor

SOURCE BOOKS
IN ARCHITECTURE

2

Series Editors
Todd Gannon and Jeffrey Kipnis

THE MONACELLI PRESS

First published in the United States of America in 2002
by The Monacelli Press, Inc.
10 East 92nd Street, New York, New York 10128

Library of Congress Cataloging-in-Publication Data

The Light Construction Reader / Todd Gannon, editor.
p. cm.—(Source books in architecture; 2)
A collection of 28 essays that explore themes and issues
surrounding the 1995 exhibition "Light Construction,"
held at the Museum of Modern Art, New York.
Includes bibliographical references.
ISBN 1-58093-105-7
1. Light in architecture. 2. Lighting, Architectural and
decorative. 3. Glass construction. 4. Architecture,
Modern--20th century. I. Gannon, Todd. II. Series.

NA2794.L54 2002
721'.04496—dc21
                                            2002022664

Printed and bound in Singapore

Designed by Lorraine Wild and Robert Ruehlman

Following the example of music publication, Source Books in Architecture offers an alternative to the traditional architectural monograph. If one is interested in hearing music, he or she simply purchases the desired recording. If, however, one wishes to study a particular piece in greater depth, it is possible to purchase the score— the written code that more clearly elucidates the structure, organization, and creative process that brings the work into being. This series is offered in the same spirit. Each Source Book focuses on a single work by a particular architect or a special topic in contemporary architecture. The work is documented with sketches, models, renderings, working drawings, and photographs at a level of detail that allows complete and careful study of the project from its conception to the completion of design and construction.

The graphic component is accompanied by commentary from the architect and critics that further explores both the technical and cultural content of the work in question.

Source Books in Architecture was conceived by Jeffrey Kipnis and is the product of the Herbert Baumer seminars, a series of interactions between students and seminal practitioners at the Knowlton School of Architecture at The Ohio State University. Based on a significant amount of research on distinguished architects, students lead a discussion with the architects that encourages them to reveal their architectural motivations and techniques. The students then record and transcribe the meetings, which become the bases of these Source Books.

The seminars are made possible through a generous bequest of Herbert Herndon Baumer. Educated at the Ecole des Beaux-Arts, Baumer was a professor in the Department of Architecture at The Ohio State University from 1922 to 1956. He had a dual career as a distinguished design professor who inspired many students and a noted architect who designed several buildings at The Ohio State University and other Ohio colleges.

ACKNOWLEDGMENTS
Todd Gannon

Jeffrey Kipnis first suggested the idea for this book to me six years ago, while I was a student at the Knowlton School of Architecture. Had I been able then to see the difficulties ahead, I would no doubt have immediately run screaming. That I did not owes entirely to his unwavering encouragement and support.

I have enjoyed the good fortune of working with a number of incredible people in the course of preparing this book. I would like to thank all of the writers, architects, artists, and photographers who generously allowed their works to be reproduced here as well as the publishers, agents, and archivists who assisted in our acquiring them.

Terence Riley of the Museum of Modern Art has generously supported the project from its inception. Robert Livesey, director of the Knowlton School of Architecture, and Mike Cadwell, head of the Architecture Section, have also offered continual encouragement. George Acock and my colleagues at Acock Associates Architects tolerated my occasional absence and inattention, and Ann Bremner of the Wexner Center for the Arts offered excellent advice at exactly the right time.

Friends and colleagues, including Mitch Acock, Bhakti Bania, Bharat Baste, Dave DiMaria, Jeremy Duval, Evan Filipek, Tracy Gannon, Jackie Gargus, Doug Graf, Jon Guldenzopf, Frank Giorlando, Carolyn Hank, Eric Hofmann, Chris Jahn, Mike Meehan, Rujuta Mody, Joe Moss, Jane Murphy, Ted Museliewicz, José Oubrerie, Ryan Palider, Manoj Patel, Andrew Rosenthal, Chris Shrodes, Michael Silver, and Tim Welsh, as well as the participants in my seminars at the Knowlton School, have helped to focus my understanding of the material. Mike Cadwell, Jeff Kipnis, and Terry Riley were kind enough to comment upon early drafts of the introductory text.

The seemingly endless work on the illustrations was carried out by Dawn Thornton, Laura McCoy, Bhakti Bania, and Laurie Gunzelman. They, with Elizabeth Kugler, Andrea Monfried, and Steven Sears of the Monacelli Press and graphic designers Lorraine Wild and Robert Ruehlman, turned a ragged pile of photocopies into the elegant object before you.

Finally, special thanks go to Nicole Hill, who had a hand in every phase of this book's production and patiently endured my neglect along the way.

Grateful acknowledgment is made to the following
for permission to reprint copyrighted material:

Terence Riley, "Light Construction," reprinted by
permission from *Light Construction*, by Terence Riley.
Copyright © 1995 by The Museum of Modern Art,
New York.

Herbert Muschamp, "Buildings That Hide and Reveal,"
reprinted by permission from *The New York Times*,
Sept 22, 1995. Copyright © 1995 by The New York Times,
New York.

Cynthia Davidson, "Reflections on Transparency:
An Interview with Terry Riley," reprinted by permission
from *ANY* Magazine #9. Copyright © 1994 by Anyone
Corporation, New York.

Bernard Tschumi, et al., "Light Construction Symposium,"
reprinted by permission from *Columbia D* #6.
Copyright © 1995 by Columbia University, New York.

Colin Rowe and Robert Slutzky, "Transparency: Literal
and Phenomenal, Part 1," reprinted by permission
from *Perspecta* 8: The Yale Architectural Journal.
Copyright © 1964 by Yale University, New Haven.

Colin Rowe and Robert Slutzky, "Transparency: Literal
and Phenomenal, Part 2," reprinted by permission
of the authors and publisher from *Perspecta* 13/14:
The Yale Architectural Journal. Copyright © 1971 by Yale
University, New Haven.

Rosemarie Haag Bletter, "Opaque Transparency,"
reprinted by permission from *Oppositions* 13, summer
1978. Copyright © 1978 by MIT Press, Cambridge.

Robert Somol, "Oublier Rowe," reprinted by permission
of the publisher from *ANY Magazine* 7/8: *Formwork:
Colin Rowe*. Copyright © 1994 by Anyone Corporation,
New York.

Detlef Mertins, "Transparency: Autonomy and
Relationality," reprinted by permission from
AA Files 32. Copyright © 1996 by the Architectural
Association, London.

Jeffrey Kipnis, "P-Tr's Progress," reprinted by permission from *Eleven Authors in Search of a Building*.
New York: The Monacelli Press. Copyright © 1996
by Jeffrey Kipnis.

Rosalind Krauss, "Death of the Hermeneutic Phantom:
Materialization of the Sign in the Work of Peter
Eisenman," reprinted by permission from *Houses
of Cards*, by Peter Eisenman. New York: Oxford
University Press. Copyright © 1987 by Peter Eisenman.

Jacques Derrida and Peter Eisenman, "An Exchange
between Jacques Derrida and Peter Eisenman," reprinted
by permission from *Assemblage* 12. Copyright © 1990
by MIT Press, Cambridge.

Richard Feynman, "Photons: Particles of Light,"
reprinted by permission from *QED: The Strange Theory
of Light and Matter*. Princeton University Press.
Copyright © 1985 by Richard P. Feynman.

Jean Starobinski, "Poppaea's Veil," reprinted by permis-
sion from *The Living Eye*. Cambridge: Harvard University
Press. Copyright © 1989 by Harvard University Press,
Cambridge.

The Light Construction Reader

PREFACE: GIVE IT A NAME

Jeffrey Kipnis

In the matter of glass, generally, we proceed upon false principles. Its leading feature is glitter — *and in that one word how much of all that is detestable do we express! Flickering, unquiet lights, are* sometimes *pleasing — to children and idiots always so — but in the embellishment of a room they should be scrupulously avoided.*
Edgar Allan Poe, The Philosophy of Furniture, *1850*

Two weeks ago on *The Simpsons,* I watched as Moe commissioned an architect to transform the facade of his bar from Walmart-Tudor to floating glass plate à la Gigon & Guyer. It occurred to me that if the influence of "Light Construction" has already made its way to cartoonland's Springfield, perhaps the time for this reader has past. Soon after "Light Construction" opened, I suggested to Todd Gannon, then a promising graduate student, that he pursue his initial enthusiasm for Terry Riley's exhibition by assembling for study the full text of every reference cited in the catalog essay. I never imagined he would show up a couple of months later with the task complete, his loose-leaf binder bulging with source texts and others of interest. When he did, the idea occurred of quickly publishing a reader in the hope of forestalling a facile, stylistic consumption of the exhibition at the expense of its deeper ideas. Most of the labor was done, we thought, how long could it take? Six months, a year tops? Neither of us grasped just how viscous was the tar pit Todd was about to dive into, that Bleak House called academic publishing.

Now, six years later, is it too late? Most certainly, in terms of the project's initial ambition. As *The Simpsons* attests, every production office has worked out its own secret recipe for "doing neo-modern." My favorite: assemble 3 parts orthogonality, 2 parts transparency, 1 part translucency, 1 part opaque surface effect; layer a little, but do not shake or stir. Chill. Curses, foiled again! Commodification rules; if only this book had been there to stop it.

On the other hand, I believe issues arising in the discourse of architecture since the exhibition make this reader all the more timely, its depth of reflection all the more probative. For some time now, architecture has been revisiting the problem of its own specificity. What, if any, are the effects architecture alone can engender, effects resistant to paraphrase in any other medium or practice? For the three decades prior to "Light Construction," such questions were either scattered to the wind, discredited by the powers of post-structuralist intertextuality, or exiled to the esoteric netherland of phenomenology. "Light Construction," with its straightforward concern for material effects, for scale, and for the palpable consequences of construction methods, contributed in large measure to wresting these questions from their languor and exile.

In lieu of a lengthy explication, allow me merely to suggest by example the shape of recent discussions, which echo old materialist arguments loosened from categorical or essentialist allegiances. To attain the stark, blinding glare in the desert shots of the film *Three Kings*, Director of Photography Newton Thomas Sigel employed a new lab technique called ski-bleach processing of color negative film stock, which artificially exaggerates contrasts and desaturates color. The light in that film is an effect specific to film that can only be seen in film—not in video, dvd or hdtv—and most certainly not in any desert. It is therefore an original, irreducible, filmic light, though not part of any "essence of film." Neither is it representational, even if it is entangled in a differential (semiotic) dialogue with other lights. Along similar lines, the so-called light, whether in painting, music, or film, sheds its apologetic quotations to take its stand as an authentic, materially specific, original light in its own right, open to research, development, and evolution by trial and error. If everything is always already copy, does it not follow that everything is also always already original? Thus can a logic of re-presentation give way to a medium-specific discourse of re-origination.

And architecture's light, its Natural Light? For all of architecture's celebration of that stuff, are we certain that we know what we mean when we invoke its name? If we simply mean light from the sun, then we face no difficulties. If, on the other hand, we want to invoke a more precious light unsullied by artifice, a light connected immediately and intimately to a particular place and time, then strictly speaking, there is no such thing, especially for architecture. Long before a beam of light passes through a pane of glass and glances off a facing wall, it is chosen by the building, which then colors, filters, dims, shapes, and otherwise manipulates it. Thus, a building echoes the very processes Earth herself uses to calm the unbearable electromagnetic insults hurled at us by the Sun.

From its beginning and as one of its most potent talents, architecture stirs the brute materiality of raw light into a poignant potion. Of course, we cannot claim for architecture exclusive license to brew this subtle elixir. Planning and Landscape, for example, each apothecary a variety of Natural Lights, from wholesale and quotidian to rare and intimate. But as poets and painters and filmmakers attest, architecture crafts a most exquisite achievement in that stuff. From holy shafts to shimmering shadows to hypnotic washes, architecture's light whispers to our souls. We mount no resistance to it as it rouses in us divine awe or abject horror, lascivious sensuality or transcendent repose.

What else can, in the time of a breath, detect a pair of headlights moving down a road at night, capture its beams and the tree shadows they subtend, stretch, reflect, refract and double these, blend in more ingredients— silhouettes of furniture, dancing shadows of drapes and blinds—and then project this ghostly ballet onto a bedroom wall? Most of us have been enthralled by these night-light visitations. They hold such allure for us that we each nurture a personal version of them as one of our most enduring memories. These are the Light Constructions whose thought, I believe, remains current in this volume, which is why I also express my fondest gratitude to my friends and colleagues Todd Gannon and Terry Riley for allowing me a part in this project.

INTRODUCTION
Todd Gannon

Identifying movements in architecture is a tricky business, and it is clear why most approach the task with trepidation. Unlike the historian, whose subject has ceased production and offers at least the illusion of stasis, definers of emerging tendencies face a subject in constant, unpredictable flux. A difficult process, this, hampered as much by the whims of fashion as by the limitations of established critical techniques, a process that in the end leaves its product to the critics, eager to point out obvious flaws, errors, and omissions. Worse, contemporary culture seems uninterested in such definitions in the first place. Today, the possibility of exception interests us much more than the rules.

Despite the obvious perils, the Museum of Modern Art in New York has undertaken this task at key moments during the twentieth century. In 1932, the exhibition "The International Style," and the accompanying book of the same title, crystallized our understanding of modern architecture by outlining simple principles of volume, regularity, and decoration. The show was a success, and mainstream architectural practice quickly absorbed the tendencies laid out by Philip Johnson and Henry-Russell Hitchcock. Sixty years later, Johnson and Mark Wigley attempted a similar definition of style with "Deconstructivist Architecture."

The 1995 exhibition "Light Construction" took a different, less aggressive tack. With a diverse collection of projects featuring an array of surfaces and materials, curator Terence Riley set out to investigate the vague characteristics of an "emergent sensibility" rather than the specific components of a style.

Subtle differences between the two words are important. Derived from the Latin *stilus* (a writing instrument) and, more distantly, from the Greek *stylos* (a pillar or column), style implies an exclusive set of formal traits shared by certain objects. Sensibility, on the other hand, has to do with the disposition of people. Its Latin root is the verb *sentire*, meaning to perceive, to know, or to feel. By organizing "Light Construction" in terms of sensibility rather than style, Riley has shifted our attention away from form and organization into the realm of perception, emotion, and effects.

This shift does not, however, oblige us to denounce objects altogether. "Light Construction" is full of beautiful ones. It simply suggests that the object alone cannot tell the whole story. While certainly interesting in their own right, these works produce effects that point beyond themselves to a broader social and historical context. They suggest that architecture can contribute to contemporary discourse on its own terms, that it does not have to operate at the service of symbol or meaning, and that its greatest strengths may lie outside the pale of configuration.

The thirty-eight essays collected here, by writers from within and outside the discipline, explore the themes and issues surrounding this important exhibition. Drawing on a wide range of influences including electronic media, architectural history, literary theory, and quantum physics, these writings provide a basis for understanding the emerging architecture of the twenty-first century.

Perhaps the defining characteristic of "Light Construction" is its fascination with glass and other translucent materials. The transparency and lightness of these materials reinforce progressive design tendencies just as masonry construction, clear about its chthonic weight and stability, underpins the most conservative practices. These materials introduce myriad technical and conceptual challenges to both design and construction. Structure, detailing, and environmental controls call for specific tectonic solutions, while the design process demands a similar specificity in terms of representation and conceptualization.

Strangely, the original popularity of glass did not derive from its transparency. Clear glass was in fact quite difficult to produce until the nineteenth century. Glass vessels instead became popular during the Roman period because they did not impart a taste or smell to the substances they contained.[1] This simultaneous presence and absence allows glass to assume its crucial role as architectural prophylactic. In a window, for example, one enjoys both visual connection to and physical protection from the exterior. Roles reverse in art framing, where the interposed membrane allows the viewer visual intimacy while protecting the work from the dangers this promiscuous contact might entail.

But for glass, as for any prophylactic, complete sensual absence remains elusive. As shown by physicist Richard Feynman, glass always reflects back some of the light cast upon it, giving away its physical presence.[2] This ubiquitous physicality may have led Mies van der Rohe to the experimental garden facade at the Tugendhat house. The glazing retracts into the wall below, allowing an unimpeded connection with the garden beyond. A stunning feat indeed, yet one Mies never attempted again. Technical difficulties and financial constraints aside, perhaps he was disappointed with the effect of total connection. With the interposed glass absent, so were the inherent relational complexities it affords.[3]

It is through these physical effects that glass comes to support the most radical architectural practices. And whether in the cathedrals of the twelfth century, the train sheds and exhibition halls of the nineteenth or the skyscrapers of the twentieth, this conceptual radicality relies upon comparable tectonic innovation. Working with progressive structural engineers and advanced materials, today's architects are again pushing the limits of glass architecture and greatly expanding its repertoire of effects.

Structural advances in the field parallel technological progress in the studio. New technology not only allows the description and construction of complex forms with relative ease, it also enables designers to study the effects of materials and lighting as never before, enriching even the simplest formal arrangements and making the difference between abstract representation and concrete construction increasingly difficult to distinguish.

Younger practitioners have all but abandoned the traditional techniques of the discipline. Forsaking the pencil and drafting table, we design with formZ and Photoshop. While the significance of these new tools is easily hyperbolized, certain differences are difficult to ignore. The opaque marks of ink and graphite no longer dominate the design process. Today, we work in the virtual space of the computer, and the medium we employ is light itself. To suggest that contemporary designers are simply enamored with light and glass, that we are witnessing nothing more than a passing fashion trend, fails to appreciate the pervasiveness of these materials. We simply cannot avoid it: today, every project begins behind a layer of glass.

A reconsideration of the conceptual techniques that ground architectural thinking echoes these technical innovations. In place of the fragmentary strategies of postmodernism, in place of deconstruction and collage, today's architects are looking toward new methods that reflect a more pluralist, media-savvy millennium.

Collage was the dominant technique of twentieth-century artistic production. The most celebrated practitioners—Corbusier, Duchamp, Koolhaas, Rauschenberg—relished the rich configurations produced through the juxtaposition of disparate objects and contexts. The vocabulary of collage peppered the language of twentieth-century critics and titled much of their propaganda. Recall, for example, *Assemblage*, *Oppositions*, and *Collage City*.[4] Collage was imported into architectural thinking from the cubist canvases of Pablo Picasso and Georges Braque through the influential writings of Colin Rowe and Robert Slutzky. Their two-part essay "Transparency: Literal and Phenomenal," introduced compelling analytical techniques that inspired a generation of postmodern practitioners.[5]

Rowe and Slutzky's argument relies on a linguistic ambiguity: "Transparency may be an inherent quality of substance—as in a wire mesh or glass curtain wall, or it may be an inherent quality of organization." As their argument plays out, it becomes clear that they favor organizational (phenomenal) transparencies over material (literal) ones. Intent upon uncovering configurational ambiguities, they disparage the "haphazard superimpositions provided by the accidental reflections of light playing upon a translucent or polished surface." What a building is made of is of little consequence to the argument; any material will do as long as it can be unequivocally categorized as solid or void. Although their work provides a rich platform from which to discuss configuration, certain shortcomings have become apparent to a number of critics.

Included in this volume are "Opaque Transparency" by Rosemarie Haag Bletter, "Oublier Rowe" by Robert Somol, "Transparency: Autonomy and Relationality" by Detlef Mertins, and two essays as much about Colin Rowe as their purported subject, Peter Eisenman: "Death of the Hermeneutic Phantom" by Rosalind Krauss and "P-Tr's Progress" by Jeffrey Kipnis.[6] While these writings differ greatly in content and character, certain affinities percolate to the surface. All are bound up with the problem of legibility, of architectural form as a language or code; all take issue with Rowe and Slutzky's object bias and with their insulation of those objects from the particularities of experience, temporality, and mood; and all criticize their tendency to play favorites—to stack the deck in favor of cubism, Le Corbusier, formalism, typology, political neutrality, and, ultimately, historicism. These writings are included here not to debunk Rowe and Slutzky, but rather to expand the possibilities of transparency as a critical tool, to increase its ability to come to terms with the diversity of contemporary architecture.

"Light Construction" calls for a wholesale reexamination of not just transparency, but of architectural effects in general. To this end, Riley cites in his catalog essay a number of writers, including Jean Starobinski, Italo Calvino, and Anthony Vidler, who explore these effects from novel vantage points. These writings are included here, as well as work by Gianni Vattimo and Eeva-Liisa Pelkonen that further explores the significance of direct experience to artistic understanding. For these writers, art objects do not passively await the contemplation of connoisseurs; instead, they act out dramatically, engaging experts and laypersons alike on material, emotional, and conceptual levels.

These essays are inflected by the immersion of contemporary culture in the media, information, and images. As critic Sanford Kwinter points out, "Images make up the true lingua franca of commerce, politics, and psyche . . . [The twentieth century] is the first century in a millennium to have left a larger and more constitutive record of itself in images than in words and ledgers."[7] And with this abundance of imagery comes an over-stimulation that can lead to new forms of artistic engagement.[8] Perhaps the clearest example is the motion picture: its significance springs not from the individual images that comprise it but rather from their collective effect. In today's media-saturated world, our attention often takes a similar turn away from objects themselves toward their impact upon us. In Vattimo's words, "The focal point for art corresponding to this excitability and hypersensitivity is no longer the *work*, but *experience*."[9]

These new methods of theorizing design have spawned revisionist readings of architectural history. The reappraisals of the expressionists, Pierre Chareau, and Mies van der Rohe collected here expand upon the orthodox histories of modernism and reveal as much about contemporary practice as they do of our modernist lineage.[10]

Perhaps no critic worked more ferociously to expand the canon of orthodox modernism than the late Reyner Banham. Included here are his explications of Paul Scheerbart and Pierre Chareau, two important figures of the period who were nonetheless marginalized by its first historians. By exploring exactly those idiosyncratic tendencies that got them written out of the canon in the first place, Banham set the stage for the wholesale rewrite of modernism by historians such as Manfredo Tafuri, William J. R. Curtis, and Colin St. John Wilson.[11] His writings here are paired with the complete text of Scheerbart's utopian treatise *Glass Architecture* and an essay by Kenneth Frampton in which Chareau's Maison de Verre finds an ally in the equally difficult-to-categorize *Grand Verre* by Marcel Duchamp.

From the biographical studies of Franz Schulze and Fritz Neumeyer to last year's exhibitions at the Museum of Modern Art and the Whitney Museum, recent scholarship reveals in no uncertain terms that Ludwig Mies van der Rohe stands as the modern patriarch of "Light Construction."[12] Yet ours is not the tidy, orthodox Mies of Giedion, Hitchcock, or Johnson. We, and the essays by Robin Evans and K. Michael Hays included here, refer instead to a newly formulated, contemporary Mies whose work is difficult and contradictory—at once honest and deceitful, sober and theatrical—a Mies ruthlessly idealistic yet fully immersed in the contingencies of materiality and perception.

But to characterize "Light Construction" as a simple realignment with the tendencies of modernism, even the more inclusive version offered here, disregards crucial differences. While architects then as now worked in the wake of radical technological innovation, our machines—phones and faxes, televisions and computers—offer little correlation between form and function. The information age has replaced the heroic machines of the past with pocket-sized gadgets and glass-faced boxes that grow more inconspicuous with increased ubiquity. Telephones hide in handbags, the latest laptops are less than one inch thick, and plasma technology has reduced televisions, once sturdy pieces of furniture, to near nothing, leaving behind an unadorned yet ever-changing surface.

Where does all this leave architects? Where, if not to these uncooperative items, are we to look for inspiration? In a world of digital surfaces, where is the place of the architectural object?

"Light Construction" points to one possibility. Rather than retreat to the empty historicism of a lost past or to an arcane theoretical position available only to the initiated, these architects face the information age head-on. While traditional practice remains hampered by the hegemony of the object, a growing number of avant-garde firms are experimenting with the production of effects. In doing so, these architects are formulating general principles and techniques that can, unlike many avant-garde experiments of the late twentieth century, affect the direction of mainstream practice in the twenty-first.

1 David Whitehouse, "Looking through Roman Glass," *Archaeology Online,* http://www.archaeology.org/online/features/roman/roman.html.

2 See "Photons: Particles of Light," on page 205 of this volume.

3 I am indebted to Jeffrey Kipnis for this observation.

4 It is interesting to note that the first major architectural journal of the information age bore the much more inclusive title *ANY*.

5 Although Colin Rowe plays a key role in the theorization of collage in architecture, the roots of the technique go much deeper. One might trace them through the fragmentary taxonomies of the Enlightenment to the facades of Fisher von Erlach, Alberti, and many others. See Alberto Perez-Gomez, *Architecture and the Crisis of Modern Science* (Cambridge: MIT Press, 1983).

6 It might seem strange that the architecture of Peter Eisenman would figure so strongly here. Profoundly influenced by the formalist doctrine of Rowe and Slutzky, Eisenman's oeuvre traces a distinct shift from an investigation of legible signs to visceral effects. As such, his career, and the criticism it has generated, can be read as a specific illustration of the general trends that the present collection attempts to identify.

7 Sanford Kwinter, "The Gay Science (What is Life?)," in Bruce Mau, *Life Style* (London: Phaidon, 2000), 37.

8 As observed by Walter Benjamin in his 1936 essay "The Work of Art in the Age of Mechanical Reproduction," in W. Benjamin, *Illuminations* (New York: Schocken Books, 1985).

9 Gianni Vattimo, *The Transparent Society* (Baltimore: Johns Hopkins University Press, 1992), 58. A portion of Vattimo's book is reprinted in this volume starting on page 257.

10 Yet it is not to modernity alone that these new works refer. In her erudite treatment of expressionist architecture, Rosemarie Haag Bletter not only broadens our understanding of early-twentieth-century architecture, but also traces its roots much further, exposing a distinguished if little known heritage in religion, literature, and myth.

11 See M. Tafuri and F. dal Co, *Modern Architecture* (New York: Abrams, 1979), W.J.R. Curtis, *Modern Architecture since 1900* (Oxford: Phaidon, 1992), and C. Wilson, *The Other Tradition of Modern Architecture* (London: Academy Editions, 1995), as well as K. Frampton, *Modern Architecture: A Critical History* (New York: Thames and Hudson, 1985).

12 See F. Schulze, *Mies van der Rohe: A Critical Biography* (Chicago: Univ. of Chicago Press, 1985), F. Neumeyer, *The Artless Word* (Cambridge: MIT Press, 1991), B. Bergdoll and T. Riley, eds., *Mies in Berlin* (New York: The Museum of Modern Art, 2001), and P. Lambert, ed., *Mies in America* (New York: Abrams, 2001). Other pertinent studies include J. Zukowsky, ed., *Mies Reconsidered* (New York: Rizzoli, 1986), D. Mertins, ed., *The Presence of Mies* (New York: Princeton Architectural Press, 1994), and J. Quetglas, *Fear of Glass* (Basel: Birkhäuser, 2001).

LIGHT CONSTRUCTION
Terence Riley

In recent years a new architectural sensibility has emerged, one that not only reflects the distance of our culture from the machine aesthetic of the early twentieth century but marks a fundamental shift in emphasis after three decades when debate about architecture focused on issues of form. In projects notable for artistic and technical innovation, contemporary designers are investigating the nature and potential of architectural surfaces. They are concerned not only with their visual and material qualities but with the meanings they may convey. Influenced by aspects of our culture, including electronic media and the computer, architects and artists are rethinking the inter-relationships of architecture, visual perception, and structure.

Represented in this survey are some thirty projects, created in response to commissions and competitions in ten countries. As the majority of the works have been or are being built, they engage their environments on materi-al as well as theoretical levels. This essay situates the projects in a broad, synthetic context, addressing both their cultural and aesthetic dimensions. Priority is given to the visual encounter with a structure, a choice that is not meant to imply a hierarchy of importance but to recognize that the appearance of architecture provides not only the initial but frequently the most defining contribution toward its eventual comprehension.

The sensibility expressed in these projects refers, but does not return, to the visual objectivity embraced by many early modernists, particularly as it is expressed in their fascination with glass structures. Ludwig Hilberseimer's 1929 essay "Glasarchitektur" represents that rationalist outlook and serves as a historical antipode to contemporary attitudes. For him the use of glass in architecture furthers hygienic and economic goals; he dis-cusses its formal properties only insofar as they enable the architect more clearly to express the structural system. Aesthetic concerns are essentially negated: "Glass is all the fashion today. Thus it is used in ways that are frequent-ly preposterous, having nothing to do with functional but only formal and decorative purposes, to call attention to itself; and the result, grotesquely, is that very often glass is combined with the load-bearing structure in such a way that glass's characteristic effects of lightness and transparency become completely lost."[1]

Hilberseimer's *sachlich* approach contains its own understated implications for an aesthetic vision. Describing the Crystal Palace (figs. 59 and 60), which "for the first time showed the possibilities of iron and glass structures," Hilberseimer writes, "It obliterated the old opposition of light and shadow, which had formed the proportions of past architecture. It made a space of evenly distributed brightness; it created a room of shadowless light."[2] The extensive use, in contemporary architecture, of semitransparent glazing materials (such as frosted or mottled glass), translucent plastic sheathings, double layers of glass (which, even if clear, produce enough reflections to function as screens), and an apparently infinite number of perforated materials, results in spaces very different from Hilberseimer's "room of shadowless light." Indeed, recent projects point to the possibility that "transparency" can also express the shadows of architecture.

The literary critic Jean Starobinski begins his essay "Poppaea's Veil": "The hidden fascinates."[3] His title refers to a passage in Montaigne's essay "That Difficulty Increases Desire," where the philosopher examines a complicated relationship between Poppaea, who was Nero's mistress, and her admirers: "How did Poppaea hit on the idea of hiding the beauties of her face behind a mask if not to make them more precious to her lovers?"[4] Starobinski analyzes the veil: "Obstacle and interposed sign, Poppaea's veil engenders a perfection that is immediately stolen away, and by its very flight demands to be recaptured by our desire."[5] To describe the action of the viewer, Starobinski rejects the term *vision,* which implies an immediately penetrating certitude, in favor of *gaze:* "If one looks at the etymology, one finds that to denote directed vision French resorts to the word *regard* [gaze], whose root originally referred not to the act of seeing but to expectation, concern, watchfulness, consideration, and safe-guard."[6] Starobinski's metaphor is literary, but it easily translates into architectural terms: the facade becomes an interposed veil, triggering a subjective relationship by distancing the viewer of the building from the space or forms within and isolating the viewer within from the outside world.

Created by streams of water running over light-gauge metal fencing in frigid weather, Michael Van Valkenburgh's elegantly simple Radcliffe Ice Walls (fig. 1) gives the metaphor substance: like Poppaea's veil, the walls interpose between the viewer and the landscape an ephemeral material (a frozen cloud) and an image (the fence) signifying protection or obstacle. Another germane example is the Ghost House by Philip Johnson (fig. 2), also made of chain-link fencing, which recalls both Frank Gehry's buildings made from off-the-shelf materials and Robert Irwin's diaphanous landscape projects. This minimalist rendition of the archetypal house was designed as a nursery, a latter-day lath house, for growing flowers. The chain-link surfaces not only render the house and its interior as a spectral form but prevent foraging deer or other inquisitive visitors from reaching the flower beds: a most succinct representation of Poppaea's distanced perfection, a literal expression of the watchful and concerned gaze.

A similarly mediated relationship between the viewer and a distanced space within can be seen in larger, more complex projects such as the Saishunkan Seiyaku Women's Dormitory by Kazuyo Sejima (figs. 3 and 4) and Fumihiko Maki's project for a new Congress Center in Salzburg (figs. 5 and 6). The dormitory's heavily screened facades, finely perforated like a sieve, provide maximum blockage with the fewest of hints of the interior spaces. Inside, these spaces are relatively free and open, with light filtering through the facades and descending from above. Still, various screened materials used throughout the project impose physical limitations on vision. The Congress Center's facades are more open, but the distance between the viewer and the space within is no less rigorously maintained. As in a Russian doll, the spaces nest one inside another, farther and farther removed from the viewer's grasp.

In these projects and others, the distance created between the viewer and the space within suggests, on some level, a voyeuristic condition made explicit in a gymnasium designed by Charles Thanhauser and Jack Esterson (New York City, 1993). In place of typical locker rooms for showering and changing are four freestanding cubicles within the training area, partially enclosed in frosted glass. From various perspectives, the obscured images of ath-letes dressing and undressing can be observed, accentuating the sensual aspects of physical culture. As in Alfred Hitchcock's *Rear Window,* the anonymity and detachment of the images enhance sensuality; in Montaigne's words, they "entrap our desires and . . . attract us by keeping us at a distance."[7]

That all of the preceding projects might be referred to as "transparent" suggests a newfound interest in a term long associated with the architecture of the modern movement. Yet the tension between viewer and object implied by the use of the architectural facade as a veiling membrane indicates a departure from past attitudes and a need to reexamine the word *transparency* as it relates to architecture. The presence of a new attitude is confirmed by a brief glance at such projects as the Goetz Collection by Jacques Herzog and Pierre de Meuron (figs. 8 and 189), the Cartier Foundation for Contemporary Art by Jean Nouvel (figs. 9, 53, and 54), or the ITM Building by Toyo Ito (fig. 184). The Goetz Collection, whose supporting structure is enclosed between the frosted surfaces of a double-glass facade, appears ghostlike, a complete reversal of the structural clarity of the so-called Miesian glass box (figs. 7 and 8). Seen through a freestanding, partially glazed palisade, the frame structure of the Cartier Foundation is more explicit and the use of clear plate glass more extensive than in the Goetz Collection. Even so, the Cartier Foundation achieves extreme visual complexity—"haze and evanescence" in the words of the architect—due to the overlapping buildup of views and multiple surface reflections. Transparency in the ITM Building and the Cartier Foundation is not created simply by applying a glass curtain wall to the exterior of the building's frame. Rather, the idea of transparency is present deep within the structures; one seems to be suspended within multiple layers of transparency, not only vertical wall surfaces but horizontal surfaces such as the translucent floor panels of Nouvel's project and the reflective floor and ceiling materials of the ITM Building. About the latter, the critic Yoshiharu Tsukamoto has noted: "The result is an interior bleached of all sense we customarily associate with the materials, sublimated into an experience of 'weightlessness,' in Ito's own terminology."[8]

Hilberseimer's ideal of shadowless light is difficult to see in the banal office towers and residential blocks erected in the postwar building boom. The depredations of the debased International Style of those years provided fertile ground for critics of both the modern rationalists and their latter-day followers. The antipathy of the architectural historian Colin Rowe for the kind of architecture proposed by Hilberseimer was buttressed by a distaste for the technological, anticlassical ethos of the glass curtain wall, which he felt was bereft of the intellectual complexities to be found in the traditional facade. In his critique of the purported objectivity of the early modern rationalists, Rowe found an ally in the painter Robert Slutzky, a former student of Josef Albers. Slutzky's interest in Gestalt psychology had led him to question the claims to objectivity of some modern painters. Together, they wrote in 1955–56 the essay "Transparency: Literal and Phenomenal," which was first published in 1963 and was widely read in the 1960s, influencing several generations of American architects. In it they state: "[The observer] may enjoy the sensation of looking through a glass wall and thus be able to see the interior and the exterior of the building simultaneously; but, in doing so, he will be conscious of few of those equivocal emotions which derive from phenomenal transparency."[9] They propose "phenomenal transparency" as an abstract, theoretical sense of transparency, derived from skillful manipulation of the architectural facade, viewed frontally, as opposed to the more straightforward "literal transparency" that they ascribe to the curtain-wall architecture of the modern rationalists.

Rem Koolhaas's 1989 Bibliothèque Nationale de France project (figs. 10 and 14), a massive, glass-enclosed cubic structure, offers a kind of transparency that appears to fall entirely outside Rowe and Slutzky's scheme: a building with the visual complexity they sought, which nevertheless rejects the traditional facade that Rowe ultimately defended. It is a building in which transparency is conceived, in the words of the architectural historian Anthony Vidler, "as a solid, not as a void, with the interior volumes carved out of a crystalline block so as to float within it, in amoebic suspension. These are then represented on the surface of the cube as shadowy presences, their three-dimensionality displayed ambiguously and flattened, superimposed on one another in a play of amorphous densities." Vidler also takes us a step further toward understanding the new direction of contemporary architecture: "The subject is suspended in a difficult moment between knowledge and blockage."[10]

The visual experience described by Vidler is certainly not the type that Rowe and Slutzky disparage as literal. But does the viewer's ambiguous perception of the building's interior volumes evoke those "equivocal emotions" that derive, those authors argue, from phenomenal transparency? The word *ambiguous* plays an important role both in their writings and in the more recent ones of Koolhaas; but it is not enough to think that all things ambiguous are necessarily related. The distinction between the experience of Koolhaas's design, as Vidler describes it, and the terms of analysis proposed by Rowe and Slutzky can best be understood if we look to the passage in which they use paintings by Pablo Picasso and Georges Braque to provide a "prevision," as they call it, of literal and phenomenal transparency.[11] They see Picasso's *Man with a Clarinet* of 1911 (fig. 63) as an example of literal transparency, "a positively transparent figure standing in a relatively deep space"; only gradually does the observer "redefine this sensation to allow for the real shallowness of the space." Braque's *The Portuguese* of the same year (fig. 64) reverses this experience: the painting's "highly developed interlacing of horizontal and vertical gridding . . . establishes a primarily shallow space"; only then does the viewer "become able to invest this space with a depth."

At this point it seems necessary to separate Rowe from Slutzky, whose concerns led him into a deep investigation of the relationship between the fine arts and the psychology of perception.[12] While admiring Slutzky's analysis, Rowe ultimately is concerned with how the cubist paintings might support his conviction that modern architecture represents nothing more than a formal evolution out of, rather than a break with, the architecture of the classical past. Disregarding the fundamental differences between traditional perspectival construction and synthetic cubism, and setting aside for the moment the differences between *Man with a Clarinet* and *The Portuguese* on which Rowe and Slutzky focus, we can identify three aspects of the paintings that made them useful to Rowe for architectural analysis: their frontality, analogous to that of the traditional facade; their figure-ground relationships, which privileged formal discernment; and their synthetic spatial depth, which suggested to Rowe an affinity with the compositional elements of the classical orders. Thus, the analytical tools developed by Slutzky to undermine rationalist objectivity in painting ironically serve Rowe to defend the objective viewpoint of the architectural connoisseur. In an extended comparison of Gropius's Bauhaus workshop wing (figs. 70 and 73), displaying literal transparency, and Le Corbusier's Villa Garches (figs. 71, 72, 74, and 75), representing phenomenal transparency, Rowe and Slutzky even criticize Gropius for "relying on the diagonal viewpoint," rather than the fixed, orthogonal viewpoint of Le Corbusier's work and, for that matter, the canvases of Picasso and Braque.[13] In so doing, they continue, Gropius "has exteriorized the opposed movements of his space, has allowed them to flow away into infinity."

Regardless of their ultimate positions, Rowe and Slutzky's ideas about transparency rest on the premise that the viewer has visual access to the object, either by penetrating to it directly or by constructing a visual path through the shallow space of the cubist grid. Vidler's term *blockage* has no function in a discussion of penetrating the spaces created by Picasso and Braque (or Rowe's architectural exemplar, Le Corbusier), but the term strongly resonates with the work of Marcel Duchamp, particularly his *Large Glass* of 1915–23 (fig. 11). For Duchamp the surface of *The Large Glass* is a kind of threshold, distinct from the object itself, suggesting a subjective tension between the viewer and the object like that created by Poppaea's veil; it is to be "looked at rather than through," in the words of the architecture critic Kenneth Frampton.[14] Another way of describing the effect on the viewer is suggested by Octavio Paz; whereas Picasso's work represents "movement before painting," Paz explains that "right from the start Duchamp set up a vertigo of delay in opposition to the vertigo of acceleration. In one of the notes in the celebrated *Green Box* he writes, 'use *delay* instead of "picture" or "painting"; "picture on glass" becomes "delay in glass."'"[15]

Frampton's comments on *The Large Glass* are made in an essay in which he compares Duchamp's great work to Pierre Chareau's 1932 Maison de Verre, a long-neglected masterpiece of prewar architecture, which ran completely against the grain of modern rationalist thought (figs. 12, 145–48). It was sheathed in layers of transparent and translucent materials, which alternately obscured and revealed a sequence of views—"ambiguous characteristics," Frampton notes, which "would surely have been anathema to the fresh air and hygiene cult of the mainstream Modern Movement."[16] Though the glass architecture of the Maison de Verre might have been dismissed by the rationalist Hilberseimer, it remains resistant to the visual delectation espoused by Rowe. Frampton points out that it served as both a private residence and gynecologist's office, a combination of functions richly analogous to the division of *The Large Glass* into the Bride's domain above and that of the eroticized Bachelor Apparatus below. Frampton writes, "The works are unclassifiable in any conventional sense; they are 'other' in the deepest sense of the word and this 'strangeness' is a consequence of their opposition to the mainstream of Western art after the Renaissance."[17] Frampton's writings, which underpin many of the thoughts expressed here by myself and others, point to the relationship between delay in glass and a potential delay in architecture that this essay attempts to establish.

These modes of delay resist the kind of classification that inevitably results from visual objectivity's fixed point of reference. Herzog and de Meuron's 1989 project for a Greek Orthodox Church in Zurich (fig. 190) and Ben van Berkel's ACOM Office Building renovation (fig. 13) provide examples of "delay in architecture." The church is a volume of glass and translucent marble enclosing a second volume of translucent alabaster, which is the sanctuary. On the alabaster are ghostlike photo-etched images of ancient icons, which act as filters, interposing faith, history, and memory, "delaying" the headlong rush of visual perception into the interior. The new facades surrounding the ACOM Office Building similarly provide a visual threshold, revealing the "memory" of the preexisting structure, built in the 1960s and now subsumed. Van Berkel employs translucent materials and perforated screens to hinder visual penetration, creating the greatest possible distance between the interior and exterior membranes.

Like Poppaea's veil, these facades have a positive presence and, in distancing the viewer, a specific function: they are something inserted *between*. The facades of Koolhaas's library not only transmit the shadowy presences of forms within but acknowledge equally amorphous forms *without,* specifically clouds, whose generic shapes are etched on the Paris and Périphérique facades (fig. 14). In this respect as well as in acting as thresholds, Koolhaas's facades have a certain affinity with *The Large Glass,* whose upper panel is dominated by the image of a cloud. The cloud is an appropriate symbol of the new definition of transparency: translucent but dense, substantial but without definite form, eternally positioned between the viewer and the distant horizon. Koolhaas describes the library's facades: "transparent, sometimes translucent, sometimes opaque; mysterious, revealing, or mute. . . . Almost natural – like a cloudy sky at night, like an eclipse."[18]

The "mysterious" facades mentioned by Koolhaas and the "haze and evanescence" that Nouvel sees in the Cartier Foundation originate in conditions Rowe and Slutzky somewhat derisively refer to as the "haphazard superimpositions provided by the accidental reflections of light playing upon a translucent or polished surface."[19] But the architects' words are not simply poetic, and the effect they describe is not haphazard, as a brief excursion into quantum electrodynamics may suggest. Transparent and translucent materials allow some photons (particles of light) to pass through them while they partially reflect others. This activity in the surface of the transparent membrane can account for the reflection of as much as 16 percent of the light particles that strike it, creating visible reflections and, frequently, a palpable luminescence.[20] The doubling of the glass found in many of the projects here increases the potential for the glass surface to cast back photons: up to 10 percent of those that pass through the outer layer are reflected by the inner one; still others ricochet between the two. The dynamics of light passing through transparent surfaces is described as a "slowing" of light by physicist Richard Feynman.[21] The similarity of his term to Duchamp's "delay in glass" provides a striking bridge between the languages of the physicist and the artist.

While Feynman's writings apply specifically to the passing of light through materials, the D. E. Shaw and Company Offices by Steven Holl (figs. 15 and 16) demonstrate a "slowing of light" as it reflects off opaque surfaces. In this project, natural light enters through the building's windows, strikes screen walls back-painted in various colors, and ricochets into the interiors, suffusing them with reflected colored light recalling the soft, pervasive glow of James Turrell's sculptures. The contrast between a classic modernist project and recent works illustrates the difference between today's attitudes toward the architectural surface and earlier conceptions of transparent and translucent skins. While capable of creating a remarkably complex surface, Mies van der Rohe intended in his Tugendhat House (figs. 47 and 48) to achieve the greatest transparency. To realize this aim, Mies employed the simplest kind of skin. The house was sheathed floor to ceiling by the largest sheets of plate glass produced in Europe up to that time. Ironically, given its expense, he hoped that the glazing would be essentially nonmaterial; in fact, a mechanism allowed the glass walls to be lowered into the basement, removing them altogether.

The projects presented here rarely display a skin that could be called nonmaterial; instead, they exploit the positive physical characteristics of glass and other substances. As opposed to the fraction of an inch by which the windows of the Tugendhat House separated its interior from the exterior, these newer projects frequently have very complex sections comprising a variety of materials, with discrete spaces between. This gives the surfaces a depth that is sometimes slight, as in the tightly bound sheathing of the Signal Box auf dem Wolf by Herzog and de Meuron (figs. 17 and 191), and sometimes more pronounced, as in Peter Zumthor's Kunsthaus Bregenz (fig. 18), currently under construction, whose interior and exterior are separated by layers of translucent shingles, a passable air space, and an interior wall. Such built-up sections increase emphasis on the architectural surface and reveal a desire for greater complexity, visual and otherwise, in the structure's skin. The reasons for multiple layers of material frequently include reducing the transmission of heat and cold, but the aim of insulating the structure is not solely a technical one. As does Poppaea's veil, layers of transparency define the viewer's relationship to the world, creating not only insulation but a notable isolation—removal from the continuum of space and experience implied by the nonmaterial surfaces of the Tugendhat House.

Architecture—though it may be read as a text with definite relationships to literature, philosophy, the fine arts, and so on—is a specific kind of text with its own critical tools. The section, a conceptual device with little application outside architecture, can be used to develop details, like the elements of a structure's surface, or even the building as a whole. The section of Harry Wolf's proposed ABN-AMRO Head Office Building (fig. 19) is analogous to details of the structure's curtain wall: each represents a volume of space suspended between glazed surfaces. Section views of the Leisure Studio (figs. 20 and 21) by Kaako, Laine, Liimatainen, and Tirkkonen, the Neues Museum extension (Berlin, 1994) proposed by David Chipperfield, and other projects all show a dense volume surrounded by open, unprogrammed space, itself enclosed by a glazed skin. Analogous to thermally efficient double-glazed walls, these designs isolate activities from light, sound, or heat. Yet the extravagance of these efficiencies reminds us that isolation is not simply a functional goal in these structures, but a visual and ultimately cultural one.

The tension between viewer and object engendered by the use of veil-like built-up membranes parallels a tension between architectural surface and architectural form that is evident in many of the works presented here. The art historian Hubert Damisch has written at length about the invention of perspective drawing, one of the principal design tools since the Renaissance, and its inherent bias toward form: "Perspective is able to comprehend only what its system can accommodate: things that occupy a place and have a shape that can be described by lines."[22] Damisch further notes that the limitations of perspective's ability to describe visual experience were apparent even at its inception. He cites Brunelleschi's 1417 experiment in which he tested the accuracy of his perspective drawing of the Baptistery of San Giovanni, seen from the door of the Cathedral in Florence. The drawing on a panel was held by the observer, who peered through a small hole in the back of it toward the Baptistery while holding at arm's length a mirror that reflected the right half of the panel, thus allowing him to compare the actual view of the structure with the reflection of Brunelleschi's drawing of it (fig. 22). Damisch notes that the architect attempted to compensate for the limitations he clearly saw in his drawing system. Having rendered the Baptistery and the surrounding square, Brunelleschi added a layer of silver leaf to the upper area of the panel to mirror the sky and the clouds, those aspects of the actual view that escaped his system of perspective. Brunelleschi's addition of silver leaf not only "manifests perspective as a structure of exclusion, the coherence of which is based upon a set of refusals," but, by reflecting the formlessness of the clouds, must "make room . . . for even those things which it excludes from its system."[23]

Many of the projects presented here exhibit a similarly compensatory attitude, an attempt to "make room" for that which neither perspective nor Cartesian space can describe. Dan Graham, in *Two-Way Mirror Cylinder inside Cube*, a component of his Rooftop Urban Park Project at the Dia Center for the Arts, New York (fig. 23), recognizes the usefulness of geometry, plan organization, and systemization of the structure while refusing to assign them a transcendent, defining role. The environment, endlessly reflected, literally superimposes formlessness on the structure's architectural surfaces, easily overcoming the certitude of the structurally framed view and the idealized abstraction of the circle and the square that create its plan, dissolving their Platonic forms in contingent perceptions. Similarly, the transparent surfaces, flickering video screens, and tilted volume of the Glass Video Gallery by Bernard Tschumi (figs. 25, 56, and 57) counteract the ability of a structural grid and perspective vision to determine the overall image of architecture. As Tschumi explains, "The appearance of permanence (buildings are solid; they are made of steel, concrete, bricks, etc.) is increasingly challenged by the immaterial representation of abstract systems (television and electronic images)."[24]

Rosalind Krauss has recently described a phenomenological reading of minimalist sculpture on the part of certain architecture critics, which effects a shift in meaning that closely parallels the shift from form to surface evident in the projects presented here. She writes, "Far from having what we could call the fixed and enduring centers of a kind of formulaic geometry, Minimalism produces the paradox of a centerless, because shifting, geometry. . . . Because of this demonstrable attack on the idea that works achieve their meaning by becoming manifestations or expressions of a hidden center, Minimalism was read as lodging meaning in the surface of the object, hence its interest in reflective materials, in exploiting the play of natural light."[25] This interpretation of minimalist sculpture's tendency to shift the meaning of the object from its form to its surface has broad implications for architecture. Jean Nouvel expresses a similar idea when he describes the architecture of his Cartier Foundation as one whose rules consist in "rendering superfluous the reading of solid volumes in a poetry of haze and evanescence."[26]

The position that Krauss describes need not be limited to a building with polished, reflective surfaces that record "actual, contingent particularities of its moment of being experienced."[27] For example, the "contingent particularities" of the Goetz Collection do not lie solely in the subtle reflections of the birch trees surrounding it. The project achieves a specific rather than universal character in its construction as well: it "reflects" its site in the laminated birch veneer panels of the facade. And even though the surfaces of the minimalist gymnasium by Iñaki Abalos and Juan Herreros (fig. 24) are much less transparent or translucent, that project also resists being perceived as an abstract formal exercise, insisting on its site-specificity, reflecting the character of the walled Spanish hill town of Simancas.

In telling contrast to the ultimate importance given to architectural form in both historicist postmodernism and deconstructivism, many of these projects exhibit a remarkable lack of concern for, if not antipathy toward, formal considerations. In fact, most of the projects could be described by a phrase no more complicated than "rectangular volume." Commenting on one of his recent projects, Koolhaas explains the logic of this formal restraint: "It is not a building that defines a clear architectural identity; but a building that creates and triggers potential."[28] The tension between surface and form in contemporary architecture is not limited to relatively simple forms: the overall silhouettes of Renzo Piano's Kansai International Airport (fig. 26), Frank Gehry's Frederick R. Weisman Art Museum (fig. 27), and Nicholas Grimshaw and Partners' Waterloo International Terminal (fig. 28), for example, are far too complex to be characterized as minimalist. Kansai Airport's sheer scale prevents us from grasping its form, and the extent of the new Waterloo terminal can only be seen from the air. Yet even when experiencing parts of Kansai Airport, we realize that its silvery, undulating skin is more critical to its design than is its formal composition; equally, the form of the Waterloo International Terminal reflects peculiarities of the lot lines of existing rail yards rather than any preconceived formal conceit. In both projects, the overall form is complex but indefinable, specific but nonrepresentational.

None of the above projects, nor any of the less articulated ones previously considered, displays interest in "timeless, unchanging geometries," and all of them complement the diminished importance of overall form by an increased sensitivity to the skin. And while the large projects may seem not just indifferent to but fundamentally estranged from the geometric rigors of perspectival construction, what impresses the viewer of a project such as Toyo Ito's Shimosuwa Municipal Museum (fig. 29) is not that its form is difficult to grasp, which it is, but that it simultaneously appears so precise. In effect, it suggests a new conception of measure and order. Brunelleschi perceived an unbridgeable gap between the measurable (the Baptistery) and the immeasurable (such as a cloud). Similarly, Leonardo da Vinci identified two kinds of visible bodies, "of which the first is without shape or any distinct or definite extremities. . . . The second kind of visible bodies is that of which the surface defines and distinguishes the shape."[29] Leonardo's distinction is essentially false, however, determined by the inability of Renaissance mathematics to describe complex surfaces. Fractal geometry has shown that there is no such fundamental distinction between the Baptistery and the cloud, only a difference in the manner of calculating their physical characteristics.

The computer has diminished the realm of the immeasurable in architectural design. In describing the uniquely shaped panels that compose the skin of the Shimosuwa Museum, Ito noted that without computer technology their cost, relative to that of standardized panels, would have been prohibitive. The use of extensive computer modeling in the design of Kansai Airport and Waterloo Terminal further demonstrates the extent to which technology has overcome the "problem" of structure, once a primary focus of design, whose "solution" subsequently defined, visually and otherwise, all other aspects of a project. This relativization of structure can be seen in various ways in the projects presented here; for example, Nagisa Kidosaki, writing about the Shimosuwa Museum, explains: "Thin membranes meant a thin structural system."[30]

The use of sophisticated computer modeling is only one sign of the impact of technology on the architectural surface. The incorporation of electronic media into contemporary structures may result in the transformation of a building's skin, which literally becomes a screen for projection in Herzog and de Meuron's 1993 Olivetti Bank project. A more architectonic synthesis of the electronic media can be seen in those projects in which electronic technology is not simply grafted to the structure but transformed into material and spatial qualities. The flattening of objects and activities projected onto translucent glazing gives a facade or interior surface the aura of a flickering electronic screen. On a small scale, this phenomenon is evident in the Thanhauser and Esterson gymnasium, where the athletes' silhouettes are projected onto the surfaces of dressing room cubicles (each cubicle has splayed walls, as if to suggest projection). On a larger scale, the farmhouses and elements of the natural landscape outside Ito's ITM Building collapse, in effect, as they are projected onto the surface glazing of the triple-height atrium. In Tod Williams and Billie Tsien's portable translucent set for the play *The World Upside Down* (fig. 30), projections actually became part of the performance as actors' silhouettes were cast onto screens and magnified by manipulation of the lighting. Jacques Herzog writes of "these surfaces for projection, these levels of overlapping, the almost-identity of architecture."[31]

Despite the ambiguous, equivocal, and at times even erotic undertones of many of the projects discussed here, it would be incorrect to assign them to a world of smoke and mirrors, where all is illusion, indecipherable and unattainable. Rather, they realign or rethink a nexus of ideas that has fueled much of architectural development since the Renaissance: perspectival vision, Cartesian space, and, by inference, the structural grid. Inherent in the works presented here, particularly Joel Sanders's studied Kyle Residence project (fig. 31), is the possibility of a position that includes the certitude of objective vision and the equivocal nature of the gaze; these works recognize the efficacy and the utility of perspectival construction without subordinating all else to its language of measure and order. The fusion of the two might be best understood in the designers' attitude toward structure, for centuries the most evident expression of the theoretical coincidence of perspectival vision and Cartesian thinking. Many of these projects share a common approach to the relationship between the structure and the skin: the structural members, rather than framing and therefore defining the point of view, are lapped over by single and double layers of translucent sheathing, as in the interior partitions of the Cartier Foundation, the clerestory of the Goetz Collection, and Annette Gigon and Mike Guyer's Kirchner Museum Davos (fig. 32). The structure, while providing support in a straightforward manner, has a diminished potential to determine the appearance of the building. Other projects here virtually erase the boundary between support and surface: the Glass Video Gallery makes no material distinction between the glass ribs that give it stability and the glass sheathing that encloses the space. The monocoque design of the Phoenix Art Museum Sculpture Pavilion by Williams and Tsien (fig. 33) similarly merges structure and sheathing. The pavilion's translucent resin panels, ranging from one-half to one inch thick and connected only with stainless steel clips, are self-supporting and stabilizing.

It could be argued that these self-effacing but critical details relativize the role of the structure in a more self-confident way than deconstructivist ploys such as tilted columns, destabilized surfaces, and structural redundancies, which, though meant to undermine the role of structure, frequently achieve the opposite: the specter of the displaced rises up endlessly to haunt the architecture. More fundamentally, such detailing can be unambiguous about creating ambiguity. Italo Calvino expresses this idea well: "Lightness for me goes with precision and determi-nation, not vagueness and the haphazard."[32] In "Lightness," one of Calvino's *Six Memos for the Next Millennium,* he writes, "I look to science to nourish my visions in which all heaviness disappears"; and further, "the iron machines still exist, but they obey the orders of weightless bits."[33] Calvino reminds us that just as the current conception of transparency is distant from that held by early modern rationalists, these contemporary expressions of lightness are distinct from earlier conceptions of lightweight architecture: they imply a seeming weightlessness rather than a calculation of relative weight.[34] Calvino's balance between iron machines and weightless bits is also seen in Starobinski's prescription for the "reflexive gaze," which incorporates the wisdom associated with vision, yet "trusts in the senses and in the world the senses reveal."[35]

The subject of Starobinski and Calvino is literature, but their observations have numerous implications for understanding the aesthetics of the architecture presented here, as well as its broader cultural context.[36] Calvino refers to Guido Cavalcanti as a poet of "lightness," which he defines as follows: "(1) it is to the highest degree light; (2) it is in motion; (3) it is a vector of information."[37] Ito's Tower of Winds (fig. 34) practically begs to be analyzed in these terms. Relatively nondescript in daylight, the structure was brought to life at night by thousands of computer-controlled light sources whose constantly changing patterns responded to sounds and wind. In the architect's words, "The intention was to extract the flow of air (wind) and noise (sound) from the general flow of things in the environment of the project and to transform them into light signals, that is, visual information. Simply put, it was an attempt to convert the environment into information."[38]

It is not surprising that the pervasive presence in contemporary culture of film, television, video, and computer screens, representing a unique sensibility of light, movement, and information, should find its way into architec-ture. Koolhaas's composition for the Karlsruhe Zentrum für Kunst und Medientechnologie (figs. 49 and 50) is perhaps the most provocative configuration of the electronic screen and the architectural facade, but the proposed display of financial quotations on the facade of Herzog and de Meuron's Olivetti Bank project is no less explicit and is equally convincing, given its program. Among built projects, Ito's Egg of Winds, Tschumi's Glass Video Gallery, and Mehrdad Yazdani's CineMania Theatre (1994) represent more restrained uses of electronic imagery but still demonstrate the ability of the architectural object to be transformed by the dull glow and flickering image of the electronic media. The effect, as Ito has described it, is to render urban space as a "phenomenal city of lights, sounds, and images . . . superimposed on the tangible urban space of buildings and civil engineering works."[39]

The architects' interest in electronic media is neither an expression of technological fantasy nor simply a fasci-nation with the aesthetic allure of low-voltage luminescence. It is rooted in the ability of these electronic modes of communication to portray the immediacy and the poignant transience of contemporary life. Their works bring to mind Ludwig Wittgenstein's observation: "It seems as though there is nothing intangible about the chair or the table, but there is about the fleeting human experience."[40] Dennis Adams's installation *Bus Shelter IV* (fig. 35) narrows the gap between the tangible and the intangible. Adams transforms an ordinary bus shelter into the setting for an urban drama in which commuters find themselves both observers and observed. Interposed between enlarged backlit transparencies, they find their own images projected and reflected by a highly manipulative visual environment.

The many images here that portray the architecture at night, lit from within, suggest that Ito is not alone in seeking an architecture that "is to the highest degree light." In Zaha Hadid's 1994 proposal for the Cardiff Bay Opera House, the nocturnal view is not simply the inverse of the building's daylight appearance. Indeed, the drawings prepared for the competition indicate that the design was conceived as a nighttime phenomenon. *Floor Plan,* an installation by Melissa Gould (fig. 36), equally depends on darkness, literally and metaphorically, to convey its message. The project consisted of a nearly full-scale outline of the plan of a Berlin synagogue destroyed during the Nazi terror. The ghost building was evoked by lights in shallow trenches, which traced the configuration of the synagogue's walls and columns. Photographs document the poignant dramatic character of the project: we see eerily lit faces of visitors moving through the installation. More tragically, the work can disappear at the flick of a switch. Gould's project demonstrates unequivocally that "lightness" should not be confused with frivolity.

The current fascination with the architecture of lightness in many ways depends on recent technological developments. It also manifests a persistent theme in Western culture. Describing his proposed ABN-AMRO Head Office Building, Harry Wolf refers to the "longstanding concern for light in the Netherlands; that is, the association of luminosity, precision, and probity in all matters." However, notwithstanding the philosophical associations of light with the Enlightenment, illumination, and so on, the attempt to magnify the presence of natural light in northern European projects is primarily a response to the immediate setting—also a longstanding concern. Wolf recalls "Vermeer's preoccupation with subtle modulations of light through a window."[41] Jan Vermeer's emphasis on ambient light is, among other things, an attempt to magnify its diminished presence in northern latitudes; a similar motive led to the gilding of architectural features, from the cupolas of New Haven's churches and the Goldene Dachel of Munich's imperial residence to the reflective sheathing of Gehry's Weisman Art Museum. The Kirchner Museum's principal galleries are lit by a clerestory level, capturing light from all directions in a plenum and diffusing it through the galleries' frosted-glass ceilings. This sensitivity to low levels of natural light also may be a response to the flattening of the shadowless landscape, particularly during the winter months.

Herzog usefully observes: "Le Corbusier . . . wrote, 'Architecture is the scientific, correct, and wonderful game of volumes assembled under light.' What, however, if architecture is not a game at all, especially not a scientific and correct one, and if the light is often clouded over, diffuse, not so radiant as it is in the ideal southern landscape?"[42] Steven Holl's Helsinki Museum of Contemporary Art (figs. 37 and 38) traps this diffuse northern light within its section in order to introduce it, both directly and by reflection, into the lower parts of the building—suggesting, perhaps, an architectural antithesis of Le Corbusier's *brise-soleil,* a shield from Mediterranean sunlight. Oriented to maximize exposure to the sun, which is low on the horizon most of the year, the museum incorporates a reflecting pool as an extension of nearby Töölo Bay. In Holl's words, "The horizontal light of northern latitudes is enhanced by a waterscape that would serve as an urban mirror, thereby linking the new museum to Helsinki's Töölo heart, which on a clear day, in [Alvar] Aalto's words, 'extends to Lapland.'"[43]

In climates far removed from the idealized, sun-filled landscape of the Mediterranean, which Le Corbusier encountered in his youthful *voyage en Orient,* the longing for light may conflict with another more recent cultural concern. The past two decades have seen an increasing consciousness of architecture's environmental implications, particularly the energy consumption of buildings. Two approaches, both of which avoid or minimize mechanical heating and cooling systems dependent on fuel consumption, attempt to balance environmental concerns with the widespread use of glass and other thermally inefficient materials.

The first approach is essentially passive, in the technical sense of employing nonmechanical systems to heat and cool structures and often electing to forgo optimal climate control. Williams and Tsien's Phoenix Art Museum Sculpture Pavilion is to have no mechanical air-conditioning system; instead, it will employ a low-technology cooling device based on commonsense thermodynamics. Approximately twenty feet above the viewing area, scores of nozzles emit a fine mist of cool water, which evaporates before reaching ground level. The heat exchange that occurs during the evaporation process lowers the air temperature by ten to twenty degrees, and this heavier air then descends to cool visitors in the open pavilion. The simple principles behind this low-technology approach are equally useful in the colder climate of Munich, where the Goetz Collection is enclosed by a double layer of glass that not only contributes to the "slowing" of light but acts as a sort of a duct, like a chimney. As heat accumulates in the lower floor (which is below grade and therefore has a more stable temperature), it escapes into the space between the layers of glass and rises to the upper floor, providing a secondary source of heat. The Leisure Studio and Glass Video Gallery reject systems requiring high energy consumption to compensate for low thermal efficiency; users must simply accept constraints imposed by the climate: diminished comfort or restricted use when temperatures reach seasonal extremes. This attitude should not be perceived as a kind of obliviousness to the reality of climatic conditions but as a value judgment: a conscious decision reflecting a deep-rooted preference for the enhancement of available light, for one particular kind of comfort instead of another.

The second approach uses higher technology to achieve energy efficiency. Just as the computer has rendered the problem of structure less fundamental, limitations on the efficiency of mechanical heating and cooling are being overcome by technological advancements. Norman Foster's Business Promotion Center (Duisburg, Germany, 1993) is a building with an insulated glass facade wrapped in another layer of glass (fig. 39). A continuous air space between the two layers rises from the ground to the top of the structure. Large buildings, in contrast to smaller ones such as the Goetz Collection, absorb too much heat. To control heat intake, the air space in the Duisburg project has translucent louvers that can admit light but deflect heat, which can then be exhausted upward before entering the interior glazing. Within this system, there is an attempt to address microenvironmental differences between interior spaces. Even though the louvers adjust themselves automatically to the position of the sun, office workers can readjust them. Occupants may also open windows in the inner glazing to ventilate offices from the air moving through the twenty-centimeter gap between the inner and outer glazing.

Just as lightness offers a way to understand much of contemporary architecture in terms other than formal ones, cultural concerns with light and the environment are not limited to glass structures. The shimmering skin of metal tiles that covers Kansai Airport not only evokes the architect's stated goal of "lightness," but acts as a huge umbrella, protecting the structure from heat gain as well as rain. The building's undulating wave shape is, borrowing Calvino's words, "to the highest degree light," but it also interestingly embodies his emphasis on movement. Its shape expresses the flow of passengers across the structure from the "landside" to the "airside," as they move from check-in to departure, and it is also calculated to channel streams of air. The voluptuous interior ceiling carries ribbonlike channels, their shape derived from computer models of the flow of air, which guide heated and cooled air through the length of the building without the use of enclosed air ducts.

Such applications of innovative solutions to environmental problems bespeak a confidence in technology that has become discredited in some quarters. But the dismissal of a technological approach as evidence of an unjustified faith in the myth of progress is refuted by the successes of Foster, Piano, Peter Rice, and many other architects and engineers. Much of their research seeks to justify the ongoing use of glazed structures, so it is not surprising that their attention often focuses on glazing materials. While this research, like that devoted to conversion of solar energy, has limited application today, new glazing materials are on the edge of wide use. "Superwindows" with various coatings and gas-filled cavities have already proven to have better insulation properties than today's thermally efficient opaque materials.

Perhaps more intriguing than this new class of high-performance but essentially static systems are what Stephen Selkowitz and Stephen LaSourd call "smart" glazings, which react to changing conditions. These include "photochromic glass, which reversibly changes optical density when exposed to light," and "thermochromic glazings, which become translucent when a preset thermal threshold is reached."[44] The former, used in sunglasses, is not yet sold for architectural use, but the latter, according to the authors, will become more widely available in the near future. A third type of smart glazings, called electrochromic, consists of multilayer assemblies through which a low-voltage electric current can be passed, causing ions to move to the outer layer where they may reflect heat-producing ultraviolet light but transmit visible wavelengths.

To speak of the technological attitudes of the projects discussed here as cultural phenomena requires further scrutiny, particularly given the prominence of glass structures over the course of this century. Glass architecture is not, however, unique to our time; a centuries-long fascination with it is evident in Jewish, Arabic, and European literature and mythology. As the architectural historian Rosemarie Haag Bletter has demonstrated, the "glass dream" that inspired these cultures has ancient roots, traceable to the biblical accounts of King Solomon's temple having reflective floors made of gold.[45] The glass dream was sustained through the Mozarabic culture of medieval Spain, principally in literary form, but it also found built expression in small metaphorical structures such as garden pavilions. "Because an actual glass or crystal palace was not technically feasible, the semblance of such a building was attained through allusion: water and light were used to suggest a dissolution of solid materials into a fleeting vision of disembodied, mobile architecture."[46] In the Gothic period, the glass dream found greater expression in built form, in the soaring cathedrals with their expansive walls of colored glass, as well as in literary sources, particularly the legends of the Holy Grail. In Wolfram von Eschenbach's *Parzifal,* the sought-for grail is symbolized by a glowing crystal hidden in a cave. The association between the image of a crystal or jewel and glass architecture is enduring. Zaha Hadid, describing her design for the Cardiff Bay Opera House, refers to the overall organization as an "inverted necklace" that strings together the various service elements, which she calls the "jewels" of the program.[47] Similarly, Harry Wolf speaks of his attempts to "create a heightened sense of transparency, just as light reflected and refracted in a gem seems more compelling and brilliant."[48]

This literary and architectural motive continued through the Renaissance, emerging as a central theme of Francesco Colonna's widely read *Hypnerotomachia Poliphili* of 1499. An expression of the romantic aspect of the Renaissance fascination with the ruins of classical antiquity, it invokes images of structures with transparent alabaster walls and floors of highly polished obsidian, so mirrorlike that viewers thought they were walking through the reflected sky. While the Enlightenment was characterized by a fascination with light and the scientific investigation of optics, its architectural expressions were not as poetic. The Crystal Palace might seem equally rationalist, though it is hard for us to imagine the impact of this first extensively glazed large structure, envisioned as the stage for a global event, and the spectacle created by its construction and dismantling. Furthermore, the glass fountain at its crossing was an understated but direct reference to the fantastic Mozarabic structures described by Bletter.[49]

As Bletter has demonstrated, the association of crystalline architecture with the transcendent (and its counterpart, the association of opaque materials with the profane) is central to the glass dream in all of its manifestations. The expressionist movement in the twentieth century added to the spirituality, fantasy, transformation, and utopianism with which glass architecture had historically been identified. In the aftermath of the First World War, expressionists such as architect Bruno Taut were seeking not only new forms but a new society. Bletter notes, "The crystalline glass house [fig. 40] . . . concretizes for Taut the kind of unstructured society he envisions. Glass is here no longer the carrier of spiritual or personal transformation but of a political metamorphosis."[50]

In an essay published in 1984, K. Michael Hays proposes the possibility of a "critical architecture" that is perceived as a cultural phenomenon, as a readable text, without forgetting that it is a particular kind of text with specific references to its own history, "a critical architecture that claims for itself a place between the efficient representation of preexisting cultural values and the wholly detached autonomy of an abstract formal system."[51] If the architecture presented here can claim to occupy such a position, one might ask, Where is that place? Of what exactly is this contemporary architecture critical?

First and foremost, it is a critique of the canonical history of modern architecture. The historian Reyner Banham writes, "The official history of the Modern Movement, as laid out in the late Twenties and codified in the Thirties, is a view through the marrow-hole of a dry bone. . . . The choice of a skeletal history of the movement with all the Futurists, Romantics, Expressionists, Elementarists and pure aesthetes omitted, though it is most fully expressed in [Siegfried] Giedion's *Bauen in Frankreich,* is not to be laid to Giedion's charge, for it was the choice of the movement as a whole. Quite suddenly modern architects decided to cut off half their grandparents without a farthing."[52]

The modern past is reconfigured by many of the projects discussed here in that they offer a chance to reconsider the reputations of certain figures whose work was largely ignored in the postwar period. Fritz Neumeyer uses terms strikingly similar to Starobinski's when describing Otto Wagner's 1904–6 Postal Savings Bank in Vienna: "Like the then floating garment that clothes the female body in ancient Greek sculpture, revealing as much beauty as it conceals, Wagner's treatment of the structure and construction exploits a similar kind of delicate, sensuous play that was probably only evident to a connoisseur of a certain age and experience. Exactly this principle gives the interior of the [Postal Savings Bank] its quality of silk-like transparency. The glass veil is lifted up on iron stilts that carefully cut into its skin and gently disappear."[53]

Paul Nelson's "technosurrealist"[54] Suspended House (fig. 41), a glazed volume with free-floating forms suspended within, provides a model for a number of projects, from Sejima's Women's Dormitory to Maki's Congress Center project and Manfred and Laurids Ortner's proposed Museum of Modern Art for Vienna's Museum Quarter (fig. 42). Describing his unbuilt project of 1938, Nelson said, "Suspension in space . . . heightens the sense of isolation from the outside world."[55]

The Maison de Verre by Pierre Chareau, largely ignored by modern historians until the publication of Kenneth Frampton's monograph on Chareau in 1969, looms large in any discussion of lightness.[56] Recognized in its time as having transcended the then ossifying parameters of the International Style, it was referred to as having a "cinematographic sense of space," a description that invokes much of the imagery employed here to describe contemporary architectural synergy.[57] In its visual complexity, the coyness with which it reveals its interior space, and its willful subordination of structural clarity, the facade of the Maison de Verre could serve as a précis for Starobinski's notion of the gaze as a reflexive act. Vidler's description of facades that reveal "shadowy presences" could equally be applied to Chareau's masterwork or the Johnson Research Laboratory Tower by Frank Lloyd Wright, the great American architect whose contribution to modern architecture was frequently marginalized by European historians.

Oscar Nitzchke's seminal project of 1935, La Maison de la Publicité (fig. 43), was similarly neglected by modern historians, whose interests were more focused on the machine metaphor than on populist expressions of modern culture such as cinema and advertising.[58] Yet the project offers an early example of the current fascination with electronic media and the nocturnal transformation of architecture. Recalling Calvino's triad of light, movement, and information, Nitzchke's project assumes a prophetic aura. Louis Kahn's decision to use glass for its specific material qualities in his projected Memorial to the Six Million Jewish Martyrs (1966–72), instead of regarding it as a nonmaterial, is unusual for its time, and dECOi's 1991 Another Glass House (fig. 44) is a recent project that transforms its inspiration, Philip Johnson's 1949 Glass House, by emphasizing glass's materiality, which Johnson implicitly denied.

In postmodernism's caricature (ironically based largely on Giedion) of modern history, the wholesale devaluation of buildings such as Gordon Bunshaft's 1963 Beinecke Rare Book and Manuscript Library at Yale University (fig. 45) has further obscured the roots of a number of works presented here. The Beinecke's section within a section—an outer layer of translucent alabaster enclosing a glazed, climate-controlled rare books library—is revived in various ways in Peter Zumthor's Kunsthaus Bregenz, David Chipperfield's proposed extension of the Neues Museum in Berlin, and the Herzog and de Meuron Greek Orthodox Church project.

Besides representing an attempt to recapture lost figures in modern architectural history, the projects here also reflect the current reevaluation of the canonical masters. As a result of the historical parody of "glass boxes" offered by postmodern critics, a new generation is rediscovering an architecture of the not so recent past. Charles Jencks's dismissal of the work of Mies van der Rohe exemplifies postmodernist criticism: "For the general aspect of an architecture created around one (or a few) simplified values, I will use the term univalence. No doubt in terms of expression the architecture of Mies van der Rohe and his followers is the most univalent formal system we have, because it makes use of few materials and a single, right-angled geometry."[59] Detlef Mertins's writings are among recent, less hostile appraisals: "Could it be that this seemingly familiar architecture is still in many ways unknown, and that the monolithic Miesian edifice refracts the light of interpretation, multiplying its potential implications for contemporary architectural practices?"[60] Mertins could well be speaking of Koolhaas's Two Patio Villas (fig. 46), in which the use of clear, frosted, green-tinted, and armored glass recalls not the nonmaterial of the Tugendhat House but the rich surfaces and the multiplicity of perceptions evident in Mies's Barcelona Pavilion (figs. 161–68, 172, 173, 175, 179, 180, and 182).

Although the expressionists were rejected by rationalist architects such as Hilberseimer and effectively written out of the history of modern architecture by Giedion and others, the influence of Taut and his followers, referred to as the Glass Chain, is evident in the work of a number of canonical modern masters, including Mies's glass skyscrapers of about 1920. Walter Gropius, in his manifesto for the Bauhaus, was influenced by Taut's expressionist utopianism: "Together let us desire, conceive, and create the new structure of the future, which will embrace architecture and sculpture and painting in one unity and which will one day rise toward heaven from the hands of a million workers like the crystal symbol of a new faith."[61] Frampton, Banham, and others have noted that standard modern histories frequently underestimate the important relationships between what have come to be perceived as irreconcilably opposed tendencies.

The success of Rowe and Slutzky in awakening a generation of American, and to a lesser extent European, architects from the "glass dream" over the course of four decades depended on establishing a more narrow dialectic than the fundamental one between transparency and opacity described by Bletter. Given Rowe's nostalgia for the classical facade and his antipathy toward technological imagery, that longstanding relationship was enormously inconvenient. Rowe and Slutzky inverted the dichotomy by equating the literal transparency of glass structures with materiality and the phenomenal transparency of Le Corbusier with the higher functions of intellectual abstraction: "A basic distinction must perhaps be established. Transparency may be an inherent quality of substance—as in a wire mesh or glass curtain wall, or it may be an inherent quality of organization . . . a phenomenal or seeming transparency."[62]

If much of the architecture herein can be seen as a critical response to Giedion and the "room of shadowless light" that he helped canonize, it also represents a critique of the formalism espoused by Rowe in the course of devaluing glass architecture. The facades seen here express not only a post-Rovian sense of transparency but the rejection of the frontally viewed classical facade and its "structure of exclusion," its "set of refusals." While there is a common interest in maintaining a level of ambiguity, in limiting the overreaching certitude of architectural expression, this recent architecture goes beyond evoking the "equivocal emotions" that Rowe and Slutzky found in the presence of architectural form, investigating the possibility of rethinking, and investing with meaning, the architectural skin. As membranes, screens, and filters, the surfaces of this architecture establish a vertigo of delay, blockage, and slowness, upending the "vertigo of acceleration" that has dominated architectural design since the invention of perspectival drawing.

In a contemporary context, the critique of Rowe's Epicureanism represented by the projects here need not be taken as endorsement of a new *sachlich* architecture of shadowless light, an expression of the renewed puritanism of our time. Just the opposite: this recent architecture, trusting in "the senses and in the world the senses reveal," can be described as beautiful—a word infrequently heard in architectural debates. Indeed, academic rationalists enjoyed such success in establishing the basis for architectural discussions that architects have been called "secret agents for beauty." As a group, the projects here have a compelling visual attraction, undiminished by close reflection, that implicitly criticizes Hilberseimer's rejection of the aesthetic dimension. They likewise reject the strictures of postmodernism, which have alternated between invoking, as inspirations for architecture, a suffocating supremacy of historical form and arid philosophical speculation. Of the latter Koolhaas writes, "Our amalgamated wisdom can be caricatured: according to Derrida we cannot be Whole, according to Baudrillard we cannot be Real, according to Virilio we cannot be There—inconvenient repertoire for a profession helplessly about being Whole, Real, and There."[63]

In Tony Kushner's play *Angels in America,* part two opens with Aleksii Antedilluvianovich Prelapsarianov, the World's Oldest Living Bolshevik, haranguing the audience: "What System of Thought have these Reformers to present to this mad swirling planetary disorganization, to the Inevident Welter of fact, event, phenomenon, calamity?"[64] Prelapsarianov's taunts remind us that the already muddied waters of the postmodern debate, played out over the last thirty years, are further roiled by the approaching millennium, with its own set of critical references. Even so, without claiming an overreaching system of thought, it is possible to see in the current architectural synergy further evidence of a renewed adherence to the spirit of the century, a spirit that most often expressed itself as one of invention and idealism. In response to the "inconvenient repertoire" of poststructuralism, Koolhaas imagines a "potential to reconstruct the Whole, resurrect the Real, reinvent the collective, reclaim maximum possibility."[65]

Beyond his own work, Koolhaas's words resonate in projects at vastly different scales, though, as is often the case, they can be most distinctly seen in smaller projects, where simpler programs allow for more direct expression. Despite its modest scale, the Leisure Studio eloquently fits Hays's definition of a critical architecture, but it is also an expression of an idealism too easily dismissed in a cynical age. Designed by an architectural collaborative as a *contre-projet* in response to an official housing exhibition, it is currently used as an informal meeting place where artists and architects socialize and exchange ideas. In contrast to standard professional practice, the structure was built and paid for by the architects themselves. Tod Williams and Billie Tsien's mobile, translucent stage set evokes the choreographer's theme of societal transformation, and in doing so reminds us that the realm of the aesthetic has social dimensions. Graham's *Two-Way Mirror Cylinder inside Cube,* a work which clearly occupies a position "in between," consciously refers to the history of glass architecture. (Bletter's commentary on expressionist design could well be applied to it: "Those very aspects . . . that appear on first glance to be its most revolutionary ones—transparency, instability, and flexibility—on closer examination turn out to be its most richly traditional features."[66]) But Graham's work, too, transcends a purely aesthetic approach. By incorporating it into his Rooftop Urban Park Project, which he characterizes as a "utopian presence" in the city, he elevates the work from the status of mere formal abstraction. His contemporary urban park—which, like its traditional counterparts, seeks to reintegrate alienated city dwellers with their environment while providing a contemplative place apart—restores the aesthetic dimension of the glass dream and points toward the idealism that sustained it.

I would like to thank Kenneth Frampton, Michael Hays, Rem Koolhaas, Guy Nordenson, Joan Ockman, Jean Starobinski, Bernard Tschumi, and Kirk Varnedoe for their suggestions and comments. I also thank Christopher Lyon for his dedication and insights during the editorial process, and Pierre Adler, Bevin Howard, Lucy Maulsby, Vera Neukirchen, and Heather Urban for research and translation assistance.

[1] Ludwig Hilberseimer, "Glasarchitektur," *Die Form* 4 (1929): 522. Translated by Vera Neukirchen.

[2] Hilberseimer, "Glasarchitektur," 521.

[3] Jean Starobinski, "Poppaea's Veil," in *The Living Eye* (Cambridge: Harvard University Press, 1989), 1. Reprinted in this volume starting on page 231.

[4] Michel de Montaigne, *The Essays of Michel de Montaigne,* trans. and ed. M. A. Screech (London: Allen Lane, Penguin Press, 1991), 697. The passage continues: "Why do women now cover up those beauties—right down below their heels—which every woman wants to display and every man wants to see? Why do they clothe with so many obstacles, layer upon layer, those parts which are the principal seat of our desires—and of theirs? And what use are those defense-works with which our women have started to arm their thighs, if not to entrap our desires and to attract us by keeping us at a distance?"

[5] Starobinski, "Poppaea's Veil," 1–2.

[6] Starobinski, "Poppaea's Veil," 2.

[7] Montaigne, *Essays,* 697.

[8] Yoshiharu Tsukamoto, "Toyo Ito: An Opaque 'Transparency,'" in *JA Library* 2, special issue of *The Japan Architect* (Summer 1993): 154.

[9] Colin Rowe and Robert Slutzky, "Transparency: Literal and Phenomenal," in Rowe, *The Mathematics of the Ideal Villa and Other Essays* (Cambridge: MIT Press, 1976), 171. The essay is reprinted in this volume starting on page 91.

[10] Anthony Vidler, *The Architectural Uncanny: Essays in the Modern Unhomely* (Cambridge: MIT Press, 1992, 221). A section of Vidler's book is reprinted in this volume starting on page 267.

[11] Rowe and Slutzky, "Transparency," 163–64. Reprinted in this volume starting on page 91.

[12] In a recent communication with the author, the architectural historian Joan Ockman summarized the elements of phenomenal transparency as "free play in the object, the extension of 'aesthetic time,' and oscillating readings or meanings that are ultimately unresolvable." Her description clearly shows that a foundation of Gestalt psychology, provided by her husband Robert Slutzky, supported the concept of phenomenal transparency.

[13] Rowe and Slutzky, "Transparency," 171. Reprinted in this volume starting on page 91.

[14] Kenneth Frampton, "Pierre Chareau: An Eclectic Architect," in Marc Vellay and Frampton, *Pierre Chareau, Architect and Craftsman, 1883–1950* (New York: Rizzoli, 1985), 243. Reprinted in this volume starting on page 375.

[15] Octavio Paz, *Marcel Duchamp, or The Castle of Purity*, trans. D. Gardner (London: Cape Goliard Press, 1970), 1–2. I am indebted to Peter Eisenman for suggesting that I look at Paz's discussion of transparency.

[16] Frampton, "Pierre Chareau: An Eclectic Architect," 242. Reprinted in this volume starting on page 375.

[17] Frampton, "Pierre Chareau: An Eclectic Architect."

[18] Rem Koolhaas and Bruce Mau, *S, M, L, XL* (New York: Monacelli Press, 1995), 654.

[19] Rowe and Slutzky, "Transparency," 166. Reprinted in this volume starting on page 91.

[20] Richard P. Feynman, *QED: The Strange Theory of Light and Matter* (Princeton: Princeton University Press, 1985), 69. I thank Guy Nordenson for suggesting Feynman's writings. Feynman's essay is reprinted in this volume starting on page 205.

[21] Richard P. Feynman, *QED*, 109.

[22] Hubert Damisch, *Théorie du nuage* (Paris: Editions du Seuil, 1972), 170. Translated by Pierre Adler. I owe to Rosalind Krauss my introduction to Damisch's book, to which she refers in the essay cited in note 25.

[23] Hubert Damisch, *Théorie du nuage*.

[24] Bernard Tschumi, "Groningen, Glass Video Gallery, 1990," in *Event-Cities* (Cambridge: MIT Press, 1994), 559.

[25] Rosalind Krauss, "Minimalism: The Grid, The/Cloud/, and the Detail," in *The Presence of Mies*, ed. Detlef Mertins (Princeton: Princeton Architectural Press, 1994), 133–34.

[26] Jean Nouvel, "The Cartier Building," architect's statement, n.d.

[27] Krauss, "Minimalism," 133.

[28] Koolhaas and Mau, *S, M, L, XL*, 1261.

[29] Leonardo da Vinci, *The Notebooks of Leonardo da Vinci*, arr., trans., and intro. E. MacCurdy (New York: George Braziller, 1939), 986–88.

[30] Nagisa Kidosaki, "Shimosuwa Municipal Museum," in *JA Library 2*, special issue of *The Japan Architect* (Summer 1993): 27.

[31] Jacques Herzog, architect's statement, n.d.

[32] Italo Calvino, "Lightness," in *Six Memos for the Next Millennium* (New York: Vintage International, 1993), 16. Reprinted in this volume starting on page 241.

[33] Italo Calvino, "Lightness," 8.

[34] The linguistic relationship between *lightness* and *lightweight* exists principally in English.

[35] Starobinski, "Poppaea's Veil," 6. Reprinted in this volume starting on page 231.

[36] For further analysis of Calvino and lightness in architecture, see Cynthia Davidson and John Rajchman, eds., *ANY Magazine* 5 (March/April 1994).

[37] Calvino, "Lightness," 13.

[38] Toyo Ito, "A Garden of Microchips: The Architectural Image of the Microelectronic Age," in *JA Library 2*, special issue of *The Japan Architect* (Summer 1993): 11–13. Reprinted in this volume starting on page 421.

[39] Toyo Ito, "A Garden of Microchips," 11.

[40] Quoted in Ray Monk, *Ludwig Wittgenstein: The Duty of Genius* (New York: Penguin Books, 1990), 355. The passage is from notes taken by Rush Rhees of Wittgenstein's 1936 lecture "The Language of Sense Data and Private Experience – I."

[41] Harry Wolf, "ABN-AMRO Head Office Building," architect's statement, n.d.

[42] Jacques Herzog, "The Hidden Geometry of Nature," *Quaderns* 181–82 (1989): 104.

[43] Steven Holl, "Museum of Contemporary Art, Helsinki," architect's statement, n.d.

[44] Stephen Selkowitz and Stephen LaSourd, "Amazing Glass," *Progressive Architecture* 6 (June 1994): 109.

[45] Rosemarie Haag Bletter, "The Interpretation of the Glass Dream: Expressionist Architecture and the History of the Crystal Metaphor," *Journal of the Society of Architectural Historians* 40, no. 1 (March 1981): 20. Reprinted in this volume starting on page 311.

[46] Bletter, "Glass Dream," 25.

[47] Zaha Hadid, "Cardiff Bay Opera House Architectural Competition," architect's statement, n.d.

[48] Wolf, "ABN-AMRO Head Office Building."

[49] Prince Albert Saxe-Coburg, the royal patron of the Crystal Palace, commissioned Edward Lorenzo Percy to design a centerpiece based on literary accounts of a fountain in the Alhambra. See Hermione Hobhouse, *Prince Albert: His Life and Work* (London: Hamish Hamilton Limited/The Observer, 1983), 103 (caption).

[50] Bletter, "Glass Dream," 37.

[51] K. Michael Hays, "Critical Architecture: Between Culture and Form," *Perspecta* 21 (1984): 15. Reprinted in this volume starting on page 389.

[52] Reyner Banham, "The Glass Paradise," *Architectural Review* 125, no. 745 (February 1959): 88. Reprinted in this volume starting on page 337.

[53] Fritz Neumeyer, "Iron and Stone: The Architecture of the Grosstadt," in *Otto Wagner: Reflections on the Raiment of Modernity* ed. H. F. Mallgrave (Santa Monica, Calif.: Getty Center for the History of Art and the Humanities, 1993), 134f.

[54] Kenneth Frampton, "Paul Nelson and the School of Paris," in *The Filter of Reason: Work of Paul Nelson*, eds. Joseph Abram and Terence Riley (New York: Rizzoli, 1990), 12.

[55] Paul Nelson, interviewed by Judith Applegate, *Perspecta* 13–14 (April 1971): 75–129.

[56] Kenneth Frampton, "Maison de Verre," *Perspecta* 12 (1968): 77–326. For further discussion of the relationship between Nelson and Chareau, see Abram and Riley, eds., *The Filter of Reason: Work of Paul Nelson* (New York: Rizzoli, 1990).

[57] Paul Nelson, "La Maison de la Rue Saint-Guillaume," *L'Architecture d'aujourd'hui*, 4ème année, ser. 3, vol. 9 (Nov.–Dec. 1933): 9.

[58] For an interesting but somewhat incomplete account of the relationship between Nitzchke, Nelson, and Chareau, see Sean Daly, "Composite Modernism: The Architectural Strategies of Paul Nelson and Oscar Nitzchke," *Basilisk* [journal online] 1, no. 1 (1995), available at http://swerve.basilisk.com.

[59] Charles Jencks, *The Language of Post-Modern Architecture* (New York: Rizzoli, 1977), 15.

[60] Detlef Mertins, "New Mies," in *The Presence of Mies,* ed. Mertins (New York: Princeton Architectural Press, 1994), 23.

[61] Quoted by Bletter, "Glass Dream," 38.

[62] Rowe and Slutzky, "Transparency," 161.

[63] Koolhaas and Mau, *S, M, L, XL,* 969.

[64] Tony Kushner, *Angels in America: A Gay Fantasia on National Themes, Part II: Perestroika* (New York: Theater Communications Group, 1994), 13-14.

[65] Koolhaas and Mau, *S, M, L, XL,* 510.

[66] Bletter, "Glass Dream," 43.

BUILDINGS THAT HIDE AND REVEAL

Herbert Muschamp

"Light Construction," the new architecture show at the Museum of Modern Art, is a painfully frustrating muddle. Excellent projects are on view, they are handsomely presented, and an intriguing presence hovers in the air. But for a show that deals in large part with the themes of transparency and luminescence, "Light Construction" is unforgivably dim: poorly focused, capricious in its choices of projects, and lax in its grasp of the history in which it sites them.

This is the first international survey organized by Terence Riley, chief curator of the Modern's department of architecture and design, since he took over the department's helm three years ago. Despite its flaws, this is an important reading of contemporary architecture. Mr. Riley has done much to restore the department's luster as the country's premiere design showcase, and "Light Construction" is the most ambitious display of contemporary work he has put in that showcase.

The show's title is loaded. It harks back to the avant-garde Russian Constructivists and the premium they placed on built work. Unlike "Deconstructivist Architecture," the museum's blazing fizzle a few years back, this exhibition of more than thirty projects does not rely on academic theory to prop up its importance. Nor does it presume to announce a new style. Instead, it attempts to document the "emerging sensibility" that Mr. Riley discerns in a wide range of projects designed in the last decade.

The core of the show is a group of stunning buildings clad with skins of glass: clear glass, translucent glass, often a combination of both, occasionally combined with visually porous panels of perforated metal. Sometimes a plastic skin is used in place of glass. It is a show about the richness of surfaces, about the extraordinary range of visual possibilities that is possible in two dimensions, using materials usually valued for their power to disappear.

Fumihiko Maki's design for the Salzburg Congress Center (figs. 5 and 6); Jean Nouvel's Cartier Foundation in Paris (figs. 9, 53, and 54); Toyo Ito's Tower of Winds in Yokohama (fig. 34); Ben van Berkel's ACOM Office Building in Amersfoort, the Netherlands (fig. 13); the Goetz Collection, a private museum in Munich designed by Herzog and de Meuron (figs. 8 and 189): these are just a few of the outstanding designs with which Mr. Riley demonstrates that contemporary architects are far from exhausting the expressive potential of classic modern materials. He also demonstrates, once again, his eye for good work. And Mr. Riley's design for the installation, which incorporates models, drawings, and large color photographs, surpasses even the high standard he has already set in previous shows.

What links these projects, apart from their transparent and translucent skins, is that the building's skin is used not to reveal but to veil. Instead of exposing structure and interior volume, like the classic Miesian glass curtain wall, these surfaces tease the eye with no more than hints and glimpses of the building's inner life. They have the magical effect of theater scrims: appealing in themselves, they also have the potential to dematerialize, revealing interiors within, or to serve as shadow screens for fleeting movement. In Mr. Riley's view, this signals a fundamental shift from the objectivity of the modern building toward a more subjective state of awareness. Today's architects place minds over machines.

While it's debatable whether modernism was ever that purely rational, a good case can be made that in recent years architects have taken their cue more from psychology than from technology. Where Le Corbusier and Mies expressed the hard facts of technological society, architects like Mr. Herzog and Mr. de Meuron are exploring the subjective ground of emotions and relationships. Their concern is not with the traditional preoccupation with the security of the shelter but with the relatively provisional nature of shelter in a shifting, mobile society. They're exploring the subtle relations between observers and observed, solitude and society, distance and intimacy, between enabling dependence and ennobling participation.

This preoccupation, too, may reflect a technological impact: the shift from machine production to electronic communication. In any case, Mr. Riley offers a persuasive reading of designs that might otherwise be dismissed as a mere return to the International Style. Unfortunately, he has included many projects that dilute rather than reinforce his reading.

Things start to go fuzzy with the inclusion of artworks: outdoor sculpture, installation, and performance art. Dennis Adams's bus stop (fig. 35) provides welcome seating for museum-goers, and its display poster of Klaus Barbie affords a whiff of political awareness. But "light construction" it is not. Compared with the average New York City bus stop, it's a tank.

Dan Graham is a very good artist, but his urban park on the roof of the Dia Foundation in Chelsea (fig. 23) is at best an interesting failure, its play of light and reflection scarcely emphatic enough to justify the project's ambitious scale. *Radcliffe Ice Walls*, by the landscape artist Michael Van Valkenburgh (fig. 1), is another extraneous work. Made of curved segments of chain-link fence encrusted with ice, the work resembles some dubious offspring of Richard Serra's *Tilted Arc* and the St. Paul Winter Carnival.

Why was it necessary to include art? It is useful that the show's catalogue refers to other art forms, but why not movies? Why not mention the shower scene in *Psycho*? But putting them into the gallery itself makes it harder to grasp what architects are up to. Since most viewers are inclined to see art as a form of subjective expression, these projects make it harder to register the subtlety with which contemporary architects have drawn closer to the artist's traditional domain.

But some of the buildings make things even murkier. The steel facade of the Frederick R. Weisman Art Museum in Minneapolis (fig. 27), by Frank O. Gehry, does do wonderful things with reflected light, but the facade is not a membrane. Rather, the building is what Robert Venturi would call a "decorated shed." A more suitable Gehry entry might have been the Edgemar complex in Venice, California, where a suspended cage of chain-link fence veils the exterior staircase within what looks like a shower of industrially produced light.

Philip Johnson's Ghost House in New Canaan, Connecticut (fig. 2), an homage in chain-link to Mr. Gehry, is also a weak entry, certainly compared with the architect's famed Glass House, where doubly reflected trees create a stunning veil effect. Of course, the inclusion of a 1949 icon would have undermined the premise of an "emerging" trend.

With other projects, the focus slips away entirely, and we seem to have stumbled into another show altogether. With projects like Renzo Piano's Kansai International Airport in Osaka, Japan (fig. 26), and Nicholas Grimshaw's Waterloo International Terminal in London (fig. 28), the emphasis is on elegant engineering. While it's true that these structures show admirably "light construction," there is no veiling of structure. Indeed, both buildings turn structure into ravishing balletic spectacle. There's poetry to these projects, but there was to Nervi's buildings as well, and also to works by Santiago Calatrava, Richard Rogers, and Rafael Viñoly.

There are other problems. The word *emerging* places these projects in time; it implies a history. But the show omits much of the background from which the work emerges. It makes no sense, for instance, to include the Kyle Residence in Houston by Joel Sanders, and to omit the uncompleted Slow House on Long Island by Diller and Scofidio, to which it is heavily indebted. Diller and Scofidio's Kinney House in upstate New York also deserves at least a catalogue mention. It was one of the first projects to introduce voyeuristic distance as a design motif.

Other omissions are also troubling. It is perverse to find room for Bernard Tschumi's video pavilion in Groningen, the Netherlands (figs. 25, 56, and 57), a tilted glass box on concrete piers, and not for Dominique Perrault's Grande Bibliothèque Nationale in Paris, where wood, glass, and steel mesh are woven into the single most monumental example of the genre celebrated by the show. SITE's interior remodeling of its New York City offices, which feature walls made of unplastered metal lath, demonstrates a brilliant use of cheap materials to create the impression of veils. The fog-shrouded, reflective Mylar dome EAT designed for the 1970 Osaka World's Fair is another overlooked precursor.

The problem with this show begins with the word *sensibility*. Many museum curators today shy from the idea of endorsing movements. They fear the taint of the cultural marketplace. They know that in these pluralistic times, a movement is likely to be more significant for what it excludes than for what it embraces. But the term *sensibility* evades rather than grapples with these problems.

I happen to be powerfully drawn to the esthetic represented by many of the projects in this show. But I wouldn't call it my sensibility. I'd call it my taste. If called upon to explain it, I'd say something like this: I'm mildly repressed, and also a bit of a slob. I have too much stuff. I dream of a bare space, but not a cold modern white one. I'd like mine suffused with warm golden light, like afternoon on a California beach. I'm fascinated by the potential of glass for voyeuristic/exhibitionistic play.

Naturally, I don't expect everyone to share my taste. But I assume there are enough of us bobbing around in the same psychological boat that it would not embarrass me to invite people over. And if somebody said, oh, this is just warmed-over Minimalism, or "Swiss fascist" taste, then we could talk about it. We could slug it out.

While I respect Mr. Riley's desire to avoid imposing his taste on his times, my stronger instinct is to shout out: "Impose away! Dictate!" Shape taste, if you can. Because it's actually been some time since the Modern enjoyed the role of arbiter. Postmodernism flourished well enough without the Modern's seal of approval, while the museum's "Deconstructivist Architecture" show sounded a death knell for a movement that had not yet peaked.

Precision of content, not promotion of form: that's the real reason "Light Construction" needed sharper focus. In taking on a theme of subjectivity, Mr. Riley has gotten hold of a great topic. There are few issues more important in architecture now than the question of how buildings shape and define our relations to others. That's what links these buildings to contemporary life. The interplay of our mutual narcissistic projections, the way we relate our thoughts and actions to the world "out there," our dual identities both as acting subjects and passive objects: these ideas define a new field for architecture to explore.

"Light Construction" pulls together the remarkable results of the explorations some architects have already made. Then the show loses its way. To paraphrase the century's master of glass architecture, Mies van der Rohe, less "Light Construction" would have been a whole lot more.

ANY Magazine 9 (1994)

REFLECTIONS ON TRANSPARENCY:
AN INTERVIEW WITH TERENCE RILEY

Cynthia Davidson

Cynthia Davidson: Before we discuss different notions of transparency, let us attempt to establish some definitions. Do you define transparency as literal versus phenomenal?

Terence Riley: That is Colin Rowe's definition. In the dictionary, as in art, in photography, in all sorts of media, transparency implies an entire range of screened images, of somewhat translucent images, or any manner of perceptions that are neither opaque nor literally transparent, neither figure nor ground. This is what interests me.

CD: What is the relationship of translucency to transparency?

TR: One has to consider the transparent/opaque, figure/ground dualities that are very much a part of this discussion about architecture. Most people who are interested in visual phenomena do not use the word *translucency*, in part because transparent is not an absolute term for them. But architects frequently use the word *translucency* to mean that sort of intermediate zone between the dualities. Translucency, as opposed to absolute transparency, is when the transmission of the image breaks down, yet light is still passing through.

CD: I am interested in the differences between the transparency of modernity and that of postmodernism, especially in terms of the work of Rem Koolhaas because he appears to be a postmodern modernist. Yet by virtue of his work, his attitude toward transparency appears to be different from what we have discussed.

TR: The key project in understanding transparency as Mies van der Rohe understood it is the Tugendhat House (figs. 47 and 48). This was the most expensive house built in Europe in the 1930s due not only to the huge sheets of plate glass surrounding the main space, but also to an incredible mechanism that lowered them into the basement so that in good weather there was in fact no glass there. What Mies really wanted, which doubled the luxury, was nothing there. Glass was a surrogate for nothingness. If the glass isn't there, there is only the frame, the structure as definer. Mies was trying to establish a continuum of space between interior and exterior that confounds the presence of glass. Real space is thus inside and outside: the ultimate sense of transparency. Rem's work backs away from this.

Today there is a fascination with new possibilities of nonliteral transparency. There is an architectonic diagram, which Mies attempted, where the glass disappears and one is left with the frame. The architect is principally the designer of the frame and the glass is a surrogate, a stand-in, a weatherproofing, and not really part of the schema. The real schema is the frame. What is interesting now, and this is happening principally in Europe, is that architects are dealing with issues of transparency as an attitude toward detail. The glass is detailed to overlap or hide the frame so that no Miesian frame is established. Whatever reflections or illusions or screening that might occur with the glass extends not only to the reality behind it but to the frame itself.

CD: You are suggesting that the architectural frame is now something that is screened. Screen is another word we can consider in relationship to transparency.

TR: Screen is a very important concept because it links transparency to the electronic; you literally go from a screen wall, as opposed to a curtain wall, to Rem's idea of a media wall. This is a matter of different kinds of vision, the reliability of vision, and the sources of vision. For example, Mies's notion of vision was to produce clarity, to produce a lack of obstruction, in effect to replicate architecturally the continuum of space that is evident in nature or is natural. The postmodern world is not so convinced of this nature of vision. Jean Starobinski speaks of a veiled vision as opposed to a space of an implied continuum, or even an implied authenticity, because the continuum of space is vision. In this other space there is a certain authenticity between the viewer and what is viewed. Real time and real space are principally defined by vision. But once this veil that Starobinski speaks of is "inserted," it breaks this continuum; there is less of a guarantee of authenticity of what's behind the veil. At the same time, there is in Starobinski's work an increasing sense of desire because of this separation. This is what film and television are all about. Film has been much more central to the culture of the twentieth century than the theater because the proscenium of the theater is not a strong enough veil for the late twentieth century.

Surrealism's photographic background makes it difficult to separate it from the appearance of the camera. Why and how modern architecture has consistently limited and marginalized the role of the camera, both photographic and moving images, from itself as opposed to accepting the machine, which has always been given a superior role in defining architecture in the late twentieth century, is problematic.

CD: Rem is one of the few architects today who is influenced by surrealism. How do you think this is evident in his work?

TR: I think it has to do with the ethos of surrealism. Was it Braque or Léger who proposed that the most surreal expression of architecture was the revolving door? He remarked on seeing revolving doors and being amazed how people would disappear into a little cylinder and then pop out the other side, in classic surreal chronological disjunction. You can see a lot of things in Rem's work that contain that disjunction. It's a little like the magician's trick of sawing the lady in half. The shock is in the unexpected, the unexplainable disjunction in the body's "real" figure. Sections of the ZKM Media Center for Karlsruhe (figs. 49 and 50) are somewhat similar to the magician's trick. You expect more continuity than there is. The gesture or impulse, both in terms of plan and section, continuously produces leaps from one to the next.

CD: But do you relate that more to a surrealist gesture or is that something that we can also think of as conceptually translucent or conceptually transparent?

TR: There are elements of both, although there is a strong argument for seeing it as conceptually "translucent," particularly in the relationship between the ZKM and the Kunsthal. The Kunsthal in Rotterdam and ZKM were in production at the same time. Rem's heart was really in the ZKM project, and the Kunsthal just moved along in its shadow. The terrible thing is that ZKM was not built. However, it is interesting that the Kunsthal, which was built, seems to be expressive of a lot of what was going into ZKM, only on a much smaller scale, though in the end you can't call it a small building conceptually. It swallows whole some of ZKM's big concepts and expresses them in a spectacular way. There is no big media wall but there is a constructed tower that juts up from the mass of the building onto which images are projected. It is receptive to different kinds of light projection. It is not about projection in a literal electronic way, but it actually functions as projection—you can see that throughout the building. There are places where you can see somebody walking behind these structural glass planks. It is neither phenomenal nor literal transparency because you cannot really see through them, nor is there an abstract sense of transparency as in cubism. It is not real space anymore because you do not know how far back or how close their features are; they start to become two-dimensional. By collapsing the space and the forms behind it onto the surface of this veil, it starts working like a media wall.

CD: This is the issue of transparency or translucency that I'm interested in, the breaking down of hierarchies of space as deep or shallow.

TR: It is fascinating that this kind of projection on a screen is rendered two-dimensionally, like much of what was called phenomenal transparency, but it is actually real space. So it is not a compromise. It is in the middle—in the center of certain definitions of what transparent might mean.

What I find interesting about the media wall is its technology. How would you build it? One could imagine that it would indeed be possible to do something like that, but in five years would it look like yesterday's Walkman? The media wall is not so much a technological problem as a new kind of ideal vision. Rem thoroughly enjoys the idea of confounding the outside of a building, which is in this sense considered as a transmissible membrane or skin.

CD: Also its form and its frame. You begin to see a kind of formlessness of the form; Rem doesn't make form.

TR: What is interesting about the screenness of the wall is that it goes from edge to edge of the building. It obliterates the frame. It is not like a Miesian pavilion or even a television that has a box or frame around it. By stretching from edge to edge it becomes the form, and without the frame there is indeed a formless quality to the building. In this instance the detailing is very important, and it is typical of the current flexibility of thinking about transparency as being something between issues rather than as an absolute. The project would have been diminished if there had been a frame. Instead the screen takes over the structure.

CD: Tony Vidler has an essay in *The Architectural Uncanny* called "Transparency," in which he talks about the grands projets of Paris and a kind of "good" modernism that is now a transparent modernism—he refers to I. M. Pei's pyramid at the Louvre, which "disappears." Then he talks about Rem's Bibliothèque de France project as an example of transparency becoming translucency due to a ghosting of what he calls the "biological interior." Vidler calls this the "blurring of limits." There is a lack of hierarchy—you do not know quite what you are looking at. Do you think that is a good or acceptable definition of translucency?

TR: If we use the word *translucency* in Vidler's sense, I think that is true. However, it is becoming a fugitive term. Translucency literally means letting light through. One could say that plate glass is translucent, but in the received notion translucent means something in between absolutely transparent and absolutely opaque. It is not something that can be attributed to simple formal inversions of long-held canons.

Take the Bibliothèque Sainte Geneviève. Though it is opaque, it is conceptually transparent: all the column bays read through on the exteriors. Between the column bays are the stacks; between the stacks are windows. All of this reads on the exterior. In fact, where the stacks are is where the names of all the great men are inscribed. The Bibliothèque de France is completely different. Its idea of knowledge is not that of the self-assured, great-men view. Here the issue of translucency points to the lack of cohesion in contemporary culture, its indefinable outlines.

CD: As you talk, it seems clear that the modernist notion of transparency, whether literal or phenomenal, was conceptually clear, but since poststructuralism the concept has become blurred; thus translucency seems to be a more appropriate term than transparency, even if they mean the same thing, because translucency implies a more blurred condition.

TR: I am struck by the image of Goethe on his deathbed. As he is dying and his faculties are slipping away, particularly his sight, he calls out, "Mehr Licht!" (More light!) There now seems to be an interest in more light, and less in more vision. There seems to be a real problem about the issue of vision. As Vidler pointed out about the Bibliothèque, it is more defined by translucency than by the notion of vision. With this in mind you can reconsider the terms *poststructural modernist* and *postmodern modernist*. The modern derives, in a broad sense, a good deal of its justification from the relationships between vision and light. In the best sense this signals a kind of hope. As T. S. Eliot says, "Wait without hope, for that hope would be to hope for the wrong thing." That is, you cannot hope for something unless you have mentally described what you believe the solution to be, so it is better to "wait" than to "hope." The notion of maintaining light without vision is about hoping, but it is not formulating or prescribing, it is not about making a frame, for it leaves open possibilities—it is open-ended. It puts the modern in the poststructuralist modern: it is still accessible to the notions of the future, rather than a historically determined present.

The following essays were presented at a symposium held at Columbia University in conjunction with the Museum of Modern Art exhibition on September 22, 1995.

Introduction
Bernard Tschumi

"Light Construction" is simultaneously about vision and construction. In the last decade, significant investigations in psychoanalysis, the visual arts, and cinema studies have examined our inherited paradigm of vision, putting into question our common view of a self-possessing subject who sees. We are not dealing here with a simple subjectivity, or with a visual perspective. In a corresponding manner, we might say that certain new modes of architecture that increasingly focus on a vocabulary of glass and screens are a way of problematizing representation as well as our assumptions regarding structure. Glass, in light construction, might become a medium to think through these new relationships to structure. Another dimension of light construction is, of course, construction, and more precisely, the role of the construction industry in the making of architecture. In many ways, all of us who build, or who try to build in America, are confronted with this reality. Do we, as architects, determine how things are constructed, as we see in many of the examples shown in the MoMA exhibition, or do we conform to the standards and habits of a very conservative regional and building manufacturing industry? Today architecture could very well be at a juncture between a new understanding of visuality and a new approach to construction technology.

Terence Riley

As the curator of the exhibition "Light Construction" I have probably been given enough opportunity to talk and write about the topic. The one substantial addition I can make is to comment on the background of the show, to provide a personal dimension to its development, that is, how I got to the point where "Light Construction" came to be hanging in the galleries.

First, I would like to change the most likely perceptions that may exist of my relationship to the work exhibited. I feel uncomfortable being perceived as some sort of ambassador from a powerful cultural institution, with little attachment to architecture other than a lofty critical stance. Before working at the Museum of Modern Art or at the Columbia Architecture Galleries, I was in private practice with John Keenen, who also graduated from Columbia's Graduate School of Architecture, Planning, and Preservation. While my position at the Museum of Modern Art may be higher in profile, the practice of architecture has always been a very important part of my life.

I'd like to describe how "Light Construction" emerged out of, and away from, what had been personal architectural explorations. My first thoughts on an exhibition about contemporary architecture were very much related to the work I was producing with Keenen; my working title was "Architectonics." Essentially this was going to be a show that would collate buildings related along architectonic lines. I separated buildings according to materials as a way of looking at them, and I noticed that this approach worked for metal, wood, fabric, and so on. But the projects I was considering that been constructed out of glass seemed somehow resistant to being characterized strictly by material. They really consisted of an anti-material—one with no fixed character—a somewhat empty image. It was a material that wanted to be something that it couldn't necessarily be by itself. At that point, I renamed the exhibition, focusing on the glass projects, and for a while was referring to it as "Transparencies."

The first notion that sparked the transformation from "Architectonics" to "Transparencies" was, of course, an interest in the simultaneous immateriality and materiality of glass. The reason for the plural, "transparencies," was the realization that the term transparency typically had had a singular definition in the modern period: it was the inverse of opacity. There was one absolute sense of transparency. What I found happening today was that there was an architecture that was somewhat recognizable in terms of its forms and its intentions, which appear to recall the language of high modernism, but that there was no longer a conception of transparency as simply the opposite of opaque. That's when the exhibition acquired the name "Transparencies." But even "Transparencies," which I wrote about in ANY just about a year ago, was rather limiting.*

In that article I was investigating certain visual phenomena that were still wholly related to the physical condition of glass. The critical changes in my research had to do with understanding "Light Construction's" cultural rather than physical qualities. Those cultural dimensions are extremely varied: philosophy, history, physics, and so on. I need to admit first and foremost that I'm neither a philosopher nor a historian. This approach implies a certain intellectual promiscuity, yet I think it is the sort of approach most suited to the polyvalent meanings to be read into "Light Construction."

One of the historical studies that influenced me, in terms of going from "Transparencies" to "Light Construction," was Rosemarie Haag Bletter's essay "The Interpretation of the Glass Dream: Expressionist Architecture and the History of the Crystal Metaphor,"** in which she lays out a two-thousand-year history of the search for a transparent architecture, starting with the apocryphal temple of King Solomon, which reportedly had highly polished floors, so polished that a visitor would feel as if he were falling through the floor as the light was reflected from it. Bletter traces a whole tradition that includes Mozarabic glass fountains, glass domes that were transformed into Gothic cathedrals and the Parsifal legends—with the image of the grail as a glowing crystal. Bletter's rendering of this incredible history continues through Bruno Taut, who associates glass architecture with the spiritual, the transcendent—both personal transformation and societal transformation. Bletter's historical thread extends into the 1930s in the work of Ludwig Hilberseimer and the Functionalists; a poignant quotation of Hilberseimer refers to the Crystal Palace and its foretelling of rooms of "shadowless light."

Contemporary ideas regarding transparencies are part of this historical continuum and are as culturally derived as those discussed previously. The Swiss literary critic Jean Starobinski touches on many of the contemporary issues surrounding transparency in his essay "Poppaea's Veil."*** Poppaea was a mistress of the emperor Nero who, with a number of other women, was vying for the emperor's attention. To distinguish herself from her competitors, she adopted the strategy of wearing a veil. The thesis is that the insertion of the veil, the presence of the thing between, sets up a certain subjective relationship between the viewer and the object; a very different relationship from the objective notion of vision implied by the classic modernist glass house, which opens up, expanding to the horizon, suggesting a continuum between the viewer and the world.

    * See "Reflections on Transparency: An Interview with Terence Riley," starting on page 47 of this volume.
  ** See pages 311–35 in this volume.
 *** See pages 231–39 in this volume.
**** See pages 241–55 in this volume.

Unlike the notion of absolute transparency is one of mediated transparencies, establishing a totally different kind of relationship, a visual relationship that in French, Starobinski points out, is more properly called a "gaze." I found the etymology of the word quite interesting for its potential link to the architecture in "Light Construction." Whereas vision has very well known limits and very well known associations, "to gaze" in French is *regarder,* which comes from root words that mean "to safeguard," to "protect."

In a similar vein, many of the projects that are made out of fencing display a resonance with safeguarding, but with the idea of a veil—putting something between someone and something else. Bernard Tschumi summarized earlier what is at the heart of this whole issue: a definite and very important shift in terms of meaning is occurring from the form of the object to its skin. In reading through some of Hubert Damisch's work it is instructive to note his ideas about perspectival vision and how it creates form. Like Starobinski, he questions the certitude that has been coupled with form through this particular conception of vision.

What is interesting about Starobinski is that he also comes back to something he calls the reflexive gaze in which, in his words, the world is not all smoke and mirrors, but in which there is the possibility of oscillating between the wisdom associated with vision and the "real" world while protecting the less rationally defined world the senses reveal. So it's neither a clear endorsement one way or the other; it's actually a very common-sense sort of attitude: accepting the kind of wisdom associated with vision and its various benefits, without allowing that vision to overcome or overpower the notion of a different way of seeing or a different way of thinking.

The repeated use of the terms *light* and *lightness* in recent critical and popular publications demonstrates the importance of the root *light* as a key word in contemporary architectural discussions: light, lightness, lightweight. John Rajchman's important reading of Italo Calvino's essay "Lightness"**** permanently put the word into the consciousness of architects. In a parallel use of the term Renzo Piano used "light" to describe his Kansai International Airport (fig. 26), built on a man-made island. When he first went to see the site, there was none, as it hadn't been built yet. The island was to be made out of "soup" and then transformed into something as hard as possible. Then, a not only incredibly lightweight, but lightly conceived structure was set down on it, with the architect knowing full well that the building would sink and continue to sink for fifty years. When the surveyors went to stake out the building, the contractors had to proceed with work immediately, as the stakes in the ground on the island would begin to move and they would no longer be in relationship with each other as the island shifted and settled. This is an architecture that has no terra firma. This is an architecture that is conceived as existing in a moving matrix. And it does so in an incredibly elegant and important way.

Calvino's forecast for the millennium, in which *lightness* will be a key word, is becoming evident all around us. For architecture it will no doubt play the same important role that the word *constructive* played in the earlier part of this century, during the Machine Age. *Construct, construction,* and *constructivist* all possessed a root concept that did not need to be defined at that time. It was so essential, it pervaded everything. Similarly, *light* is one of those words that is so pervasive it almost absorbs its own meanings. "Light Construction" is an intersection of the two key words of the architecture of our time, an architecture that is increasingly drawn to the light, even as it is still tethered, for the time being, to the mechanical world of the early part of this century.

I've said a number of times recently that "Light Construction" is not an "ism." (The last thing that the twentieth century needs in its final five years is the introduction of a movement.) Nor is it a beauty contest. And maybe the world is not innocent enough anymore to believe this, but there are no architects in the show, only buildings. It's not an attempt to resolve those various issues that a museum exhibition cannot well resolve. It's an attempt to capture a moment in which what was is ceasing to be even as it only seems to know what it wants to become. It's also very good architecture. "Light Construction" represents an architecture at a moment of enormous transference. What appears to be happening now is that architects are absorbing, both literally and sometimes by osmosis, much of the computer world: a world where, in Calvino's words, the iron machines still exist but now are controlled by weightless bits.

Henry-Russell Hitchcock was one of the first American historians to write about modern architecture. He did so most articulately in a very thoughtful, very literate, very well developed book called *Modern Architecture.* Alfred Barr, the first director of the Museum of Modern Art, reviewed it and though he generally praised it, spent much of his review telling Hitchcock to be more definitively critical, to cut out who's out and to bring in who's in. The result was that Hitchcock rewrote the book with Philip Johnson as *The International Style,* with its famous three rules regarding volume, regularity, and lack of ornament. At this point in time, as Le Corbusier's idealized concept of Mediterranean sunlight recedes, so too do the forms upon which that light played so magnificently. The flicker of a new light reveals less-defined forms. The question remains: Is the old set of rules being replaced by a new set, or are the new rules as vague as the new forms?

It was quite discouraging this morning to read that the *New York Times*'s architecture critic believes so strongly in the former. It seems to me that today's new forms are developing quite well without a defined set of rules. Is it really the exhibition curator's task to create a path where none is necessary? After reading Herbert Muschamp's review of "Light Construction," I picked up the section containing the book reviews and read the first paragraph, which I found to be an interesting rebuttal to Muschamp's arguments regarding the importance of style. I'm speaking of a review by Christopher Lehmann-Haupt of Milan Kundera's new book of essays, in which he notes: "One of the main points Kundera insists on most strenuously in his stimulating new nonfiction work is Nietzsche's injunction that we should neither corrupt the actual way our thoughts come to us nor, in Kundera's paraphrase, should we turn our ideas into systems." That's not a completely unproblematic idea, and I'm aware that we live in a problematic time. However, I do believe ours is a time unlike Hitchcock's and Johnson's: we should resist the impulse to make a new set of three rules, resist the impulse to make new systems.

I'd like to read a few lines from the play *Angels in America* by Tony Kushner. The words of the character Aleksii Antedilluvianovich Prelapsarianov, "the World's Oldest Living Bolshevik," point to some of the issues I've spoken about, issues that define our transitional times: "And Theory, how are we to proceed without Theory. What System of Thought have these reformers to present to this mad swirling planetary disorganization, to this evident welter of fact, events, phenomena, calamity?" Having previously referred to his countrymen as vipers, he continues, "If a snake sheds his skin before a new skin is ready, naked he will be in the world, prey to the forces of chaos. Have you, my little serpents, a new skin?" In Kushner's play, Prelapsarianov speaks of the need for theory and uses "the skin" as its metaphor. In "Light Construction," I have considered architecture's skin, looking to it not as a metaphor for a new architectural theory but as its herald.

Mark C. Taylor

Oh those Greeks! They knew how to live. What is required for that is to stop courageously at the surface, the fold, the skin, to adore appearance, to believe in forms, tones, words, in the whole Olympus of appearance. Those Greeks were superficial—out of profundity.
    Nietzsche

The deepest thing in man is his skin.
    Paul Valéry

Skin. Surface. What is so deep about skin? What is so profound about surface?

Though it seems obvious, it is no longer clear . . . clear that we know what surface is. Nor is skin any longer transparent. We must, therefore, begin by asking about the point at which we all begin . . . and end: the skin. What is skin? As is always the case, the positive emerges through the negative and vice versa. Thus, we might rephrase the question: What is not skin?

In the beginning, it is a question of skin. Not yet a question of bones but of skin—dermal layers that hide nothing . . . nothing but other dermal layers. Humpty Dumpty need not to have fallen to be faulted, for every fertilized egg is always already divided between vegetal and animal poles. The process of embryonic development involves cellular division and further differentiation. Through a quasi-cybernetic process governed by preprogrammed DNA, the pluripotentiality of the ovum is limited in ways that allow for the articulation of different organic structures and functions. Cells multiply by division to create a hollow ball called a blastomere. This sphere eventually invaginates to form a lined pocket comprised of two layers known as the mesoderm. The mature organism develops from these three dermal layers. Since the organism as a whole is formed by a complex of dermal layers, the body is, in effect, nothing but layers of skin in which interiority and exteriority are thoroughly convoluted.

The phrase *light construction*, so ably defined and explored by Terry Riley, reflects such dermal convolution. The result is a transfiguring of the very architecture of skin and surface. Surface, for the architects whose work is included in this exhibition, is no longer what it was for classical modernists. In his catalogue essay, Riley writes: "That all of the preceding projects might be referred to as 'transparent' suggests a newfound interest in a term long associated with architecture of the modern movement. Yet the tension between viewer and object implied by the use of the architectural facade as a veiling membrane indicates a departure from past attitude and a need to reexamine the word *transparency* as it relates to architecture." Riley develops his reexamination of transparency by contrasting it with translucence through a series of binary oppositions: e.g., clarity/ambiguity, penetration/delay, etc. Drawing on Starobinski's interpretation of the gaze, Riley concludes that a new, very unmodern surface emerges: "The facade becomes an interposed veil, triggering a subjective relationship by distancing the viewer of the building from the space or forms within and isolating the viewer from the outside world."

As a way of advancing debate, I would like to make three observations about Riley's analysis. First, there is a closer relationship between transparency and translucence than Riley suggests. Though not immediately evident, it is precisely transparency that leads to translucence. It is important to realize that the polarity of surface and depth is isomorphic with the polarity of interiority and exteriority. When depth becomes transparent, it is another surface; and when interiority becomes transparent, it is exteriorized. As everything becomes transparent, depth and interiority vanish. Paradoxically, the result of such radical transparency is not lucidity but translucence. In a certain sense, depth and interiority—even when they remain hidden—secure or ground surface and exteriority. If depth is surface and interiority is exteriority, then the very proliferation of surface renders it not only opaque but enigmatic. This enigma is what renders surface profound.

Second, the profundity of surface and superficiality of profundity make it necessary to rethink both surface and depth. When depth and interiority disappear, surface is transformed. Surface, in other words, no longer can be conceived as it was when it was the opposite of depth and interiority; it becomes something different, something other. Riley offers a gesture toward this insight when he introduces the notion of the veil and, by extension, emphasizes the *between*—or, I would prefer, the liminal character of surface. But no sooner does he offer this notion than he reinscribes it within precisely the opposites it undoes. The veil, we are told, distances the viewer from the space or forms within and isolates the viewer within the outside world. If, however, it's surface all the way down, then does the membrane any longer separate in this way? I would suggest that we must rethink surface as interface, or, more precisely, interfacing.

Third, interfaces must be read in terms of information processes. With this observation, I return to the question of skin with which I began. Though we usually think of skin as the sack that envelops the body's organs, it is actually the largest organ of the body. This organ is not only the interface where body meets world but, like the organs that develop from it, is the interface of the so-called material and the so-called immaterial. This interface, I noted, is a quasi-cybernetic process governed by preprogrammed DNA. The skin, in other words, is an information process in which material realities appear to be immaterial processes. If, however, the entire organism develops from dermal layers, then all of the organs—even the skeleton itself—are transparently information processes. Information processes are not merely displayed on the screen of the skin but pervade the very depths of the organism. In this play of data, surface and depth, as well as exteriority

and inferiority, are reinscribed. Riley is right when he argues that veils veil other veils. But, I believe, he is wrong when he insists that veils separate rather than interface.

To summarize: transparency that becomes translucence; surfaces that become interfaces; interfaces that are informational processes. Herein lies the depth of skin.

Hugh Dutton

There are two kinds of lightness in light architecture. First, lightweight construction, and second, light itself. In light architecture, both are important. We can define a building as structure, which supports it, and skin, which keeps the weather out. Lightweight structures allow the skin, through transparency or luminous surfaces, to respond to light itself. As regards structure, technological advances in the building industry and developments in structural engineering have removed structure from walls and surfaces. High-performance materials such as reinforced concrete, steel, and, more recently, composites have allowed a concentration of structure. Developments in structural engineering skills have further contributed to "lightweightness," with a greater understanding of how buildings behave, as has the recent use of computers in analyzing complex, interactive, and statically indeterminate structures like the dome of the Seis de Jeneval in Paris, which the engineering firm of Peter Rice, Martin Francis, and Ian Ritchie (RFR) has just completed.

One project in the development of nonlinear analysis that allows large tensile structures to be understood is Richard Rogers's Channel Four Headquarters in London, in which the glass is stabilized by purely tensile cable nets. The cable net is curved in two directions, with each direction of the cable's tension against the other. In regard to skin, the gradual removing of structure has allowed the skin to become more ephemeral—first transparent, then translucent—because it no longer has to hold up the building. This allows light itself to play a larger part in the architectural composition.

Recent developments in curtain-wall technology have created new possibilities, not only in glass, but also in architectural fabrics. Fritting is a process of baking paint onto glass in which the paint actually becomes part of the glass surface. One can also manufacture glass with a translucent film that has been sandwiched between two sheets of glass and a laminate. A special treatment for glass also allows it to be used on a floor, so one can actually walk on a translucent floor. Printed glass technology has been around for a long time but is now much improved with technology. There is also the possibility of laminating stone; recent technology has permitted the lamination of very thin stone, down to about 1 millimeter thick, onto glass. And there is another quite simple technique of putting a perforated steel mesh between two sheets of glass and a laminate. This process permits a reflectivity on the outside of the metal. From the inside, because of the relative light values, it is still very transparent.

Examples of projects affected by different technologies being developed in Japan include liquid crystal glass, which, when an electronic current is passed through it, changes from a transparent to a translucent state. In its translucent state, it can be used as a source of image projection. There is also thermochrome glass, which, when the glass is heated, becomes opaque and translucent.

In insulated glass, different treatments allow reflectivity and limit heat absorption while affecting the quality of the light that comes through the glass. Most of this technology was developed at RFR with Peter Rice. With the facade of the Banque Populaire de l'Ouest et d'Armorique (1989) in Rennes, HDA actually pulled the wind-bracing structure two meters away from the glass. The little sticks are actually the only connection between the glass surface and the structure. So the structure is completely outside, and the glass surface is on the inside.

HDA just finished a project in Paris that exploits the structural capacity of transparent glass, allowing us to create a transparent corner and a transparent roof. In the Pyramide Inversée (inverted pyramid) for the Louvre (1991), designed by I. M. Pei, the reflective nature of the glass is exploited to its full potential. This entails a mixture of architectural fabric and glass fiber with a Teflon coating on it, which has a translucent quality; mixed with glass, it produces a luminous, translucent surface. A project that we did with Peter Rice at La Villette, the Cité des Sciences et de l'Industrie by Adrian Fainsibler, is one of the first projects to really exploit what I think is important in the use of glass surface—its own structural capacity. In this case, all of the glass is suspended; each piece hangs from the one above it. The key detail is a ball bearing, which guarantees that there is no bending or twisting effect on the glass. The glass is loaded purely along its axis, where it is strongest.

I would like to close with an example of a project we finished in Paris, an office development at 50 Avenue Montaigne, which I think takes lightness to an extreme. This applies not only to the supporting structure, which in this case is a fan of cables pulled back to the concrete structure, but also to the structural capacity of the glass itself (we have quite big pieces of toughened glass, spanning up to 3.80 meters). The glass is fritted, which creates a diffuse light source at nighttime and disperses the view through it during the day. The glass is suspended 24 meters high (each piece suspended from the one above it) and is 60 meters wide.

Eeva-Liisa Pelkonen

Just after I received the invitation to attend this symposium, I saw a documentary on Finnish television called *Jean Nouvel—The Man in Black*. In presenting his work, Nouvel clarified his approach to making architecture. His remarks are helpful in locating the tendency in contemporary architecture toward "light constructions" on the map of the intellectual and artistic culture of the postwar era.

Most important, Nouvel emphasized the need for a particular problem-solving attitude in each design task, as opposed to the application of preexisting formal solutions; only then can architecture have any social significance. He also discussed the need for realization; that is, architecture cannot exist as a mere idea but must engage a particular social, economic, and political situation as well as a site condition. His final comment was perhaps the most telling—that he can never stop thinking about the future.

In contemporary European architecture Nouvel is not alone in believing that architecture can and should become engaged in the society at large. This belief is the main premise of the twentieth-century avant-garde: art and architecture are integrally linked to the social and the political and can therefore enhance transformation and change.

Like his predecessors within the avant-garde tradition, Nouvel actively participates in the intellectual culture of his time. It comes as no surprise that, nourished by the rarefied milieu in France from the 1960s onward, Nouvel is disposed toward Existential Marxism, particularly the ideas of Henri Lefebvre. Nouvel's belief that architecture should result from working with a complex set of factors related to a particular architectural task; that is, of a certain critique, recalls Lefebvre's *Critique de la vie quotidienne* (Critique of everyday life).

The book illustrates the main premise of Existential Marxism as a social theory suited to comprehending the conditions and contradictions of advanced industrial

society. Nouvel's notion of the particular also comes close to Lefebvre, who emphasized the concrete and the everyday—the analysis of the human situation. What is important is that critique is not simply a *knowledge* of everyday life, but a knowledge of the means to transform it. Therefore, just as Existential Marxism can be essentially understood as a "philosophy of action," Nouvel's approach to architecture might likewise be called an "architecture of action." As Nouvel's comment about the future reveals, like Lefebvre, he remains an eternal optimist anticipating utopian possibilities.

What interests me in the context of our theme is how the material condition of "light construction" corresponds to such an approach to making architecture. The obsession with glass in contemporary architecture helps us understand this correlation between "lightness" and a certain "tone" behind the work. We should remember that the typical building types that have been made with glass architecture—the glass house, the railway station, the exhibition hall, and the commercial arcade—are all sites for the ultimate modern experience: urban drifting, a moment in which we willingly surrender ourselves to the sensuous stimulus of the crowds. As the theorist Susan Buck-Morss has pointed out, these building types were meant for "transient purposes" and to be experienced by the masses rather than to be used for individual contemplation. Important for our discussion is that since glass architecture has always been "engineered" architecture, the following historical analogy exists: materiality and structure took formal strategies just as the mass experience took over mere contemplation. I would argue that it is exactly this correspondence between "tectonics" and "experience" in the Benjaminian sense that makes contemporary architecture so interesting. Therefore, I would like to oppose "lightness" as a material condition to the formal (classical) approach to architecture. Lightness emphasizes temporality rather than a static notion of space; active engagement rather than passive contemplation.

Such a move away from formal strategies toward the emphasis of material and structure has parallels in postwar art: the tendency of the European avant-garde has been to reject the kind of abstraction inherent in the classic heritage of modernism. According to the Danish painter Asger Jorn, the non-"materialist art" aimed to engage the particular human condition rather than be a mere object of contemplation. Jorn, who was a member of CoBrA and later the Situationist International, an international avant-garde group strongly influenced by Lefebvre, held that European art was corrupted by its classical heritage, its metaphysical overvaluation of reason and the idea. The new materialist attitude toward art and life must involve the expression of natural rhythms and passions, rather than seek to subordinate activity to a sovereign meaning.

Similarly, by means of a heightened sensibility toward materiality and structure, contemporary architecture, particularly in continental Europe—Nouvel provides a good example—enhances engagement by fighting the hegemony of form and meaning in Western architectural tradition—hence lightness. Through "lightness," and "light constructions," contemporary architecture has discovered its potential to convey a character and ambience that makes architecture resistant both to the metaphysical abyss as well as to the pessimistic traits of postwar thought. What I mean by character and ambience is a certain tone and ethos of the work. More subtle and elusive than meaning can ever be, ethos tells us about the disposition of the author without making any final judgments. Similarly, on a material level, lightness can be opposed to the formal approach to architecture: while form and meaning aim to fix things, "lightness," as I understand it, is about letting things loose, which manifests the utopian impulse within the work.

Guy Nordenson

In the early 1970s America was introduced to deconstruction via the works of, among others, Paul de Man and Harold Bloom—in particular, their books *Blindness and Insight* and *Anxiety of Influence,* respectively, through which many people were first exposed to the ideas of Jacques Derrida. This was the period during which Peter Eisenman's Institute of Architecture and Urban Studies was active, when Rem Koolhaas published his *Delirious New York,* and when the Vietnam War came to an end. I mention all this here to propose that we consider that the work which Terence Riley has put together in this exhibition has developed from seeds sown around that time. I believe that this is a body of work that closely reflects the ideas current at the time, and those of Derrida in particular. In his essay "Structure, Sign, and Play," presented at Johns Hopkins University in 1966, Derrida reviewed Levi-Strauss's works in detail and questioned the structuralist idea that totalization is impossible because the field of inquiry is too vast, rather than, as Derrida argued, because while the field is finite it is elusive because of a lack of determined origin and its nature of constant play. Here Derrida aligns himself with the critique of the Enlightenment—from Isaiah Berlin to Werner Heisenberg. If the Enlightenment was inspired by Newton's successes, our own era, not surprisingly, has undergone a sea of change as the consequences of the new sciences of relativity, quantum electrodynamics and particle physics work their influence through the culture.

This brings us back to the subject of light and construction, or light and matter. There is a wonderful book by the late physicist Richard Feynman called *QED: The Strange Theory of Light and Matter.*[*] In a footnote Feynman points out that Heisenberg's principle of uncertainty is a vestige of determinism. If we accept the probabilistic nature of matter and light's interaction,

* See Feynman's essay "Photons: Particles of Light," first published in *QED* and reprinted starting on page 205 of this volume.

then there is no problem of uncertainty. Rather, events are the product of probability amplitudes.

This is a difficult thing to accept and convey. Italo Calvino describes this world as one "of minute particles of humors and sensations, a fine dust of atoms like everything else that goes to make up the ultimate substance of the multiplicity of things."

I would like to offer a few concepts about light that, from my perspective, are relevant to the exhibition. First I propose that as "light" refers to the light of our sun, we are particularly interested in the strange facts of the interaction of light and matter. The light inside a building is radiated by the "matter" of construction. Light on glass sets off an interaction (scattering) and the glass emits a spectrum of light-energy. Light and matter or light and structure are always interacting, absorbing, emitting, and intermingling. Second, there is the lightness of bits, the universe of digital representation and the pattern of chaos revealed in the new telescope of the computer. This relates, of course, to chance, to Marcel Duchamp and John Cage, and back to quantum physics. But most of all, it reveals the mysterious beauty and order of turbulence and upheaval. Third, there is that lightness championed by Buckminster Fuller. Fuller, our twentieth-century Emerson, promised in 1969 that "the ever acceleratingly dangerous impasse of world-opposed politicians and ideological dogmas would be resolved by the computer." He identified and promoted that digital ephemeralization. For him, the lightest touch was best, as in Jean Prouvé's Tropical House and his own Dymaxion House. It is the lightness of nomads at home on Spaceship Earth. Fourth, and related to Fuller's ideas, there is a lightness of frugality. It is interesting to note that the visual imagery in many of the projects recalls the space and light of television and film.

If we consider the critic John Berger's description of perspectival space as a safe and transpose it to television and computer media, we can perhaps better recognize the continuity that exists in the business of capturing and preserving wealth. Facades are still in the art and business of containing and projecting economic value. Perhaps instead, as in a Bedouin tent or Prouvé's Tropical House, our interest could extend not to the representation of wealth but to the preservation of commonwealth through building lightness and frugality. Fifth, and finally, there is the lightness of being. Think of Duchamp, Cage, Milan Kundera, and countless others.

In closing, I would like to recount a little Zen story called "No Water, No Moon." When the nun Chiyono studied Zen under Bukko Engaku, she was unable to attain the fruits of meditation for a long time. At last, one moonlit night, she was carrying water in an old pail bound with bamboo. The bamboo broke and the bottom fell out of the pail. At that moment, Chiyono was set free. In commemoration, she wrote a poem:

In this way and that I tried to save
the old pail
since the bamboo strip was weakening
and about to break,
until at last, the bottom fell out.
No more water in the pail.
No more moon in the water!

K. Michael Hays

I would like to push the discussion out a little bit, as I think Eeva Pelkonen and Guy Nordenson have already begun to do, and think more about the larger cultural and historical context of some of the work in this exhibition. Terence Riley himself begins his catalogue essay with a kind of comparison between current interests in the psychological implications of diverse glazing surfaces and Ludwig Hilberseimer's perception of modernity's rationalist uses of glass. What Riley does not mention is that Hilberseimer's kind of modernism also had a psychological correlate. Siegfried Kracauer writes about the psychological correlate of modern architecture, the logic of the repetition and transparency of modern architecture. In his essay "The Mass Ornament," he uses the Tiller Girls (fig. 55), an American dance troupe similar to the Rockettes that performed in Berlin in the 1920s, as a kind of mock psychological paradigm for what could be thought of as Hilberseimer's architecture: "When they formed an undulating snake, they radiantly illustrated the virtues of a conveyor belt. When they tapped their feet in fast tempo, it sounded like 'business . . . business.' When they kicked their legs high with mathematical precision, they joyously affirmed the progress of rationalization. And when they kept repeating the same movements without ever interrupting their routine, one envisioned an uninterrupted chain of autos gliding from the factories into the world."[1]

I am trying to get at a kind of model of the logic of the series. On the other side of this kind of ecstatic psychological model is Georg Lukács's reminder of the relentless and unfruitful repetitive labor of the proletariat. Modernism had a depth model—Hilberseimer's model—of psychological experience that was a correlate of the formal research. When Riley talks about the shift from the logic of repetitive series, or the formal logic, to a logic of surface, what is the corresponding psychological model and where does it come from? Let's call

it "depthlessness" or "lightness." Where does that mode of perception come from? Eeva Pelkonen has already suggested the 1960s; Nordenson, the 1970s. I'll go back one more decade and suggest that this model actually had its roots in the urban developments of the 1950s when, for example, electronic advertising was used in American commercial cities on a scale previously unknown. Large-scale color printing on billboards, as we know from people like Peter Blake and Robert Venturi, began to be the primary surfaces seen. It was also at this time that television became available to a large number of people. The decentralization of the distribution of goods from urban centers out into the suburbs fundamentally began to change the mode of perception from a depth model—a spatial model, a formal model—to the logic of the perception of surfaces. What we are seeing may need to be tied historically to a development that was well under way in America in the 1950s.

Jean Baudrillard captures something when he suggests that instead of the logic of the series, our psychological investment is now in a nonreflecting surface, an immanent surface on which operations unfold, the smooth operational surface of communication. Baudrillard further says that with the television image—television being the ultimate and perfect object for this new era—our own body and the whole surrounding universe become a controlled screen. My point is to suggest that popular culture—a kind of absent, or partially absent, cause—and some of the projects in the exhibition, or their "sensibility," as Terence Riley describes it, are also symptoms of shifts and developments in the mode of perception given by popular culture. It's not an indictment of the work to say that it collapses into popular culture. Rather, I think we see now what is becoming a kind of salvage operation that is trying to redeem most perceptions in popular culture—media, music, video, television—in new kinds of surfaces.

This is important because some of the fundamental critical models, like Marxism or even deconstruction, will therefore have to be revised. Those that engage popular culture, such as Marxism, critical theory, and deconstruction, have been primarily negational models. We have two specific and powerful models. One is Kenneth Frampton's notion that architecture has an inertia or a resistance to popular culture. This model will necessarily be modulated by some of the works in the exhibition to allow for their redemptive stance toward popular culture. The other model, Bernard Tschumi's poststructuralist "De-, Dis-, Ex," will have to be modified to acknowledge reappropriation, reconstruction, redemption, and this kind of salvaging operation, which is a much more affirmative stance relative to popular culture.

Greg Lynn

The exhibition allows multiple threads to be pulled through the work because as Terence Riley has said, there are enough issues, without condensing things into a style or movement, to allow for multiple readings. Some of the organizational and formal research in the projects might constitute a kind of "light underground," meaning that a building can be conceived and conceptualized as light without necessarily being lightweight. This can be seen as a *concept* of lightness, as opposed to a *phenomenon* of lightness, which moves toward transparency and dematerialization. As an initial provocation, one of the most overrated and undercriticized concepts in architecture is the persistent myth that buildings must stand up. A number of projects in the exhibition "Light Construction" do not stand up but explore alternative concepts of structure—such as

leaning, hanging, and suspension—that are fundamental formal principles related to the concept of lightness, and do not look to gravity as a single force emanating from the earth. There is a kind of subterfuge in saying that transparency is the only interpretation of lightness and that lightweight and light are identical. It is necessary at this point to back up from the experiential questions of what would make a building *light* and reconsider concepts on which we could found or ground light architecture, instead of formulating a light architecture as a resistance to gravity, which is what our discipline has been founded on. Lightness suggests that we might suspend strategies based on notions of simple gravity and look toward multiple gravities.

Three projects in the exhibition propose complex responses to multiple gravities: Rem Koolhaas's Bibliothèque Nationale de France in Paris (fig. 14), in the catalogue text is described as a floating object held behind a transparent screen. But before that tectonic articulation was ever developed, there had to be a concept of an overstructuring, in an almost Corbusian manner, of the building so that these volumes could be suspended conceptually in the space. Likewise, in Bernard Tschumi's Glass Video Gallery in Groningen, the Netherlands (figs. 25, 56, and 57), a very lightweight structure is developed, but the ground on which that structure is supported is sloped. Finally, in Toyo Ito's Sendai Mediathèque in Japan (fig. 58), the columns, instead of being seen as solid structural elements, are conceived as towers of latticework in the center. These are all new concepts of structure and support, what I consider light concepts. I do not want to oppose the *conceptual* light to the *phenomenal* light because in each one of these projects, I think there is a very strong sense of invention as to what lightweight materials can do.

Toyo Ito

At one time the architect's main project was to create an architecture and an urban space that fluidly utilized and integrated the local topography and natural forces such as wind, water, and light. But during the modern period, architecture's relationship with nature ended and the urban as architectural space became a rigidly "geometric," artificial space. Today, however, through the penetration of various new forms of media, fluidity is regaining validity. As more urban and architectural space is controlled by the media, it is becoming increasingly cinematic and fluid. It has become a transparent kind of space. Therefore, I think we are now forced to admit more openness and flexibility to this closed and artificial urban and architectural space, combining the fluidity created by the media with the fluidity of nature.

This fluidity was the major focus of our installation in London. Two of the structural components we used were liquid crystal and glass. For me, these materials refer metaphorically to similar things in our physical bodies. On the one hand, our material bodies are a primitive mechanism, taking in air and water and circulating them. On the other hand, there is another kind of body that consists of circulating electronic information—the body that is connected to the rest of the world through various forms of media, including computer microchips. Today, we are being forced to think about how to architecturally combine these two different bodies and how to find an appropriate space for the emerging third body. This is why I have been completely focused on the idea of lightness in architecture.

In the Tower of Winds (fig. 34), there were two major concerns. One had to do with the skin of the structure, which is made with perforated aluminum panels. It represents the constantly changing quality of skin over time. The other concern was the visualization of daily urban phenomena, such as traffic, noise, or wind.

We also built a small museum on a lakeside. Although the building itself has a specific formal configuration, our main concern was how to present the building as a reflection of other phenomenal conditions such as fog or rainbows on the surface of the water. We conceived the aluminum surface as a reflective device operating between the town and its natural surroundings. The exterior, a linenlike skin, is produced and manipulated with the aid of a computer.

Although not exhibited in "Light Construction," our Mediathèque project, located in Sendai (fig. 58), north of Tokyo, is effective in illustrating my theories. The program combines an art gallery and a library. The building consists of seven horizontal slabs supported by twelve structural tubes. The structure is made of meshed steel. The inside of the tubes can be utilized as a transportation system, for other mechanical services such as plumbing and electricity, or for circulating information. The larger tubes, which look like three stems, are open as void spaces. The natural light from above flows into those vertical voids. The tubes do not formally connote a tree; rather, the interior space evokes the inside of a tree, in terms of the circulation of water and other activities. The tubes are covered by translucent glass. The lighting devices are placed discreetly underneath the bottom of the tubes and when lit, the tubes become illuminated from the inside out. The exterior skin is composed of glass, which is reflective at the top, becoming gradually more transparent toward the bottom. During the day, the glass reflects the outside on its surface; at night, it reveals what is going on inside.

Joan Ockman

I'd like to begin by commenting on Herbert Muschamp's review of this provocative exhibition that appeared in the *New York Times* this morning. Like Muschamp, we all naturally will wish to quibble one way or another with Terence Riley's inclusions and exclusions, and I would agree that less might have been more in this instance. However, I want to take issue with the review's main thrust. Muschamp suggested that the exhibition is ultimately about taste. Now while, historically speaking, MoMA has a long record of architectural taste-making, I do not necessarily believe that taste is the primary issue here. And that is why I wish a few of the projects in the exhibition had not been included. If a more succinct articulation of the show's thesis had been provided, critics would not be able to suggest that "Light Construction" is a matter of taste-making.

But if the exhibition does not merely reflect a current taste for the sophisticated use of glass and a penchant for lightweight building technology, then what is it about? Riley speaks of an "emerging sensibility" in his introduction. It's not clear to me what a sensibility is in this context, let alone an emerging one. Maybe "tendency" or "style" would have been a better characterization. But the main reason I don't believe that "Light Construction" can be dismissed as a matter of taste is that these buildings lay claim to being connected, at least potentially, to a new mode of production—a new mode of construction and a new relationship between architecture and the city. As Walter Benjamin writes in his essay "Paris, Capital of the Nineteenth Century," "Construction fills the role of the unconscious." In this vein Benjamin interpreted the arcade as a crystallization of nineteenth-century culture, a building type key to the advent of modernity. Are the buildings in the current exhibition comparable today with respect to postmodernity? Can an architecture of "light construction"

be said to be—for example—a materialization of the advancing forces of dematerialization in our culture?

I found Hugh Dutton's presentation quite suggestive. I'm not a technical expert, so it raised many questions for me. I'm eager to know how extraordinary, how extravagant all these new ways of treating glass are. To paraphrase Buckminster Fuller, how much do these new glass surfaces weigh? Are they *really* light? Are they environmentally "correct"? Are these technologies at all likely to become normative; do they have the potential to supersede current building practice? Bernard Tschumi mentioned the construction industry's resistance to accepting new ways of building. Are the new treatments of glass we are seeing strictly haute couture, or will they trickle down to the mainstream of building construction? It is worth recalling that the development of architectural glass—going back several hundred years—was directed up until about the first quarter of this century toward transparency, toward the perfection of an ever larger plate of glass to a point of perfect clarity. But now that transparency as a see-through characteristic has been technologically mastered, it's hardly surprising to find that it is no longer the issue. The mastery of the transparent glass plane makes way for more complex and interesting uses of this marvelous material.

Historically speaking, we can discern two seemingly antithetical points of inception for the glass or transparent dream with respect to modern architecture culture. Certainly the Crystal Palace (figs. 59 and 60), designed by Joseph Paxton and erected in 1851, is one such point. It constitutes the canonical beginning of modern architecture in Sigfried Giedion's *Space, Time, and Architecture* as well as in most other classic modernist historiographies. In its day the Crystal Palace was not just a building but an event. Its reception was sensational. People made pilgrimages from all over Europe to see this large glass building derived from the typology of the greenhouse conjoined with the railway shed and built for the first great international trade fair. A very common perception was a sense of dematerialization, of dissolution. The interior of the building was painted mostly blue, a color that blended into the blue of the sky. In its vastness the building seemed to "melt into air," to evoke Marx's famous words, to become a kind of dream landscape. A contemporary called it "a spectacle, incomparable and fairylike." It inaugurated a new optics.

Symbolically, the Crystal Palace stood for a world that was progress-oriented, scientific, and practical. Constructed in record time from economical, modular, and demountable parts, it was the epitome of rational engineering. At the same time, however, like the contemporary arcade buildings, it housed the proliferating products of a nascent consumer capitalism. The clarities and lucidities of structure were dissolved not only by the building's new optical scale, but also by its phantasmagoria of endless goods. Rationalism yielded to spectacle and surreality.

Now let's jump a hundred years, to 1958 to be precise. Peter and Alison Smithson had just returned from a first trip to the United States having witnessed the array of new curtain-wall buildings springing up on Park Avenue (the first of them, Lever House, fig. 61, had been completed six years earlier, in fact precisely on the centenary of the Crystal Palace). The Smithsons made the following observation: "Glass and metal-faced buildings give the maximum light reflection into the street. And this in itself is a contribution to the city. And there are, moreover, magical distortions when two straight up and down buildings are opposite one another. A blue glass city, no matter how organizationally banal, is never optically boring."

What had changed in the course of a century? One may say that Park Avenue represents the transformation of the Crystal Palace into a normative urban phenomenon: the glass building as a metonymic emblem of the modernist city rather than as a singular spectacle in a park. The postwar International Style turned the Crystal Palace inside out, so to speak, and multiplied it. And now, another half century later, we may ask the same question with respect to the glass buildings of our own day. What has changed? What distinguishes the most exciting buildings in "Light Construction"—buildings like Toyo Ito's Tower of Winds (fig. 34), Jean Nouvel's Cartier Foundation (figs. 9, 53, and 54), and Jacques Herzog and Pierre de Meuron's Goetz Collection (figs. 8 and 189)—from their progenitors? Certainly one of the things that the exhibition reveals is that we are still bedazzled, thrilled, hypnotized by the paradoxical optics of glass, by reflective and transparent and translucent and changeable luminous surfaces. But what innovation has postmodernity contributed to this tradition? Is it just refinement, or are there new constructional principles—technical and cultural—operative in these contemporary buildings?

There is a second glass paradigm to be found at the origins of modernity, and this one brings us closer to the more metaphysical connotations of the word *light* on which Riley plays in his exhibition title. If the Crystal Palace was a profane and secular dream, then the Crystal Cathedral—the one, for example, in Lyonel Feininger's woodcut (fig. 131) accompanying the founding proclamation of the Bauhaus, or in the imagery of Mies's two early glass skyscrapers (figs. 154–57)—represents a new religion of modern architecture. The Crystal Cathedral is a vehicle of visionary and utopian thought, and as such a privileged icon of the early modern avant-garde. Unlike the Enlightenment tradition of glass, that of the Crystal Cathedral has to do with the spiritual mission of architecture as art, with introverted as much as extroverted experience. It harks back to the "lightness" of Gothic architecture, to stained glass and highly attenuated structure. In this tradition glass tends to be associated with crystalline substances and jewel-like stones, with the alchemical transformation of base materials into precious ones—the basic recipe for glass, remember, is little more than sand plus lime plus heat. It thereby embodies mystical and transcendental meanings. We should recall that Paul Scheerbart's book *Glass Architecture** and the apocalyptic projects of Bruno Taut's Glass Chain call for colored light and magical effects, not for transparency and lucidity.

Actually, Scheerbart's idiosyncratic little book is not crystal clear, so to speak; it combines the most sublime and poetic prophecy with utterly pragmatic and down-to-earth observation, for example, on the way glass architecture promotes hygiene, overcoming the problem of vermin and dirt in dark, dank buildings. In fact, both of our paradigms are ultimately ambiguous: the rationalism of the Crystal Palace is inflected by capitalist surreality and spectacle, while the expressionism of the Crystal Cathedral, born in the apocalyptic atmosphere of World War I Europe, comes to coexist, especially in the work of Mies, for one, with a *sachlich* view of the world. Perhaps it's not surprising that such a paradoxical material as glass should come to thrive on internal contradictions.

Likewise in the work on exhibit, these two impure paradigms of the culture of glass persist, although in even more blurred or merged forms. In Nicholas Grimshaw's Waterloo International Terminal (fig. 28)—painted blue like the Crystal Palace—it is, in fact, the rationalism of computer design that allows for an extra-

ordinarily expressive "organic" form. Nouvel's billboard facade for Cartier operates schizophrenically, outwardly spectacularizing the city while inwardly maintaining the building's privacy and discretion. Tod Williams and Billie Tsien's Phoenix Art Museum Sculpture Pavilion (fig. 33) aspires to be a metaphysical space of contemplation while addressing in an ingeniously practical way the climatic problems of a desert building. These complexly negotiated architectural concerns—technical, psychological, environmental—are, it seems to me, what mark these buildings as absolutely contemporary even as they also place the culture of "light construction" within a 150-year-old tradition.

To conclude, I'd like to invoke the Russian tradition of glass architecture—the pre-Constructivist tradition. (Marshall Berman writes beautifully about this in his book *All That Is Solid Melts into Air.*) Fyodor Dostoyevsky went to see the Crystal Palace shortly after it was built. Actually, by the time he saw the building, it had already been moved from Hyde Park to Sydenham Hill, where it was reerected in a more elaborate configuration, one that bears a good deal of resemblance to some of our postmodern shopping malls and suburban office parks. And he hated it. Or at least he dreaded it. Dostoyevsky had been trained as an engineer and architectural draftsman, but he rebelled against this background. He became deeply antipositivist, increasingly suspicious of Western rationalism and materialism. In his book *Notes from the Underground,* the protagonist-narrator rails against a building that you

* See Scheerbart's *Glass Architecture* starting on page 345 of this volume.

can't throw stones at—that you can't stick your tongue out at, as the character puts it. In part Dostoyevsky's novel was a polemic against his contemporary Nikolai Chernyshevsky, who had written a book called *What Is to Be Done?* a year earlier. Chernyshevsky anticipates Le Corbusier's Radiant City by seventy years, describing, through the dream vision of one of his characters, a utopian society whose inhabitants live blissfully in glass towers spaced far apart in acres of greenery. But Dostoyevsky (speaking through his Underground Man) prefers to remain more earthbound and urban; his character says that a building made of glass is one in which you can never be at home. He declares that it may be fine for engineers to design such buildings, but he remains deeply skeptical about whether it is possible actually to live in one.

With respect to this critique, it's interesting to discover that in late-nineteenth-century Russian parlance, the term *Crystal Palace* came to be a synonym for the millennium. The current exhibition at the Museum of Modern Art is suggesting something similar, it seems. In other words, the Crystal Palace will be soon upon us. The question is, can a dematerialized architecture of dazzling surface qualities house our physicality as effectively as our fantasies? And is lightness really an emerging mode of construction—and being—or just an old mode with some new imagery, a past vision of the future? On the threshold of the millennium, we may well throw a few stones at the new palaces and cathedrals.

[1] Siegfried Kracauer, "The Mass Ornament," in *The Mass Ornament: Wiemar Essays,* trans. and ed. Thomas Y. Levin (Cambridge, Mass., and London: Harvard University Press, 1995), 69–70.

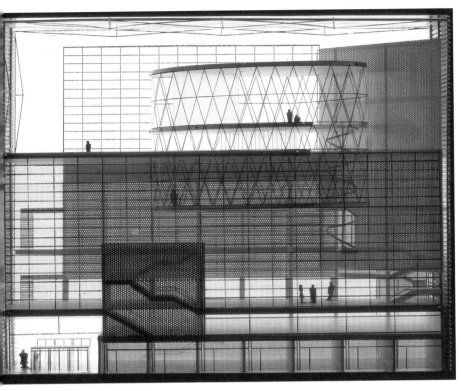

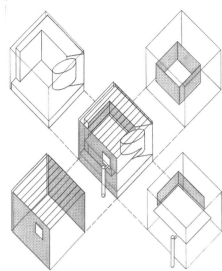

6

Michael Van Valkenburgh, Radcliffe Ice Walls, Cambridge, Mass., 1988. View.

Philip Johnson, Ghost House, New Canaan, Conn., 1986. View.

3 Kazuyo Sejima, Saishunkan Seiyaku Women's Dormitory, Kumamoto, Japan, 1991. Interior view.

4 Kazuyo Sejima, Saishunkan Seiyaku Women's Dormitory, Kumamoto, Japan, 1991. Exterior view.

5 Fumihiko Maki, Congress Center (competition proposal), Salzburg, Austria, 1992. View of model.

6 Fumihiko Maki, Congress Center (competition proposal), Salzburg, Austria, 1992. Axonometric.

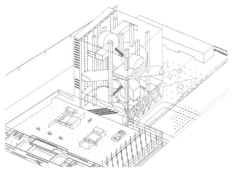

7 Ludwig Mies van der Rohe, Farnsworth House, Plano, Ill., 1946–52. Exterior view.

8 Herzog and de Meuron, Goetz Collection, Munich, Germany, 1992. Exterior view.

9 Jean Nouvel, Cartier Foundation for Contemporary Art, Paris, France, 1994. Exterior view.

10 Rem Koolhaas–OMA, Bibliothèque Nationale de France (competition proposal), Paris, France, 1989. Axonometric.

11

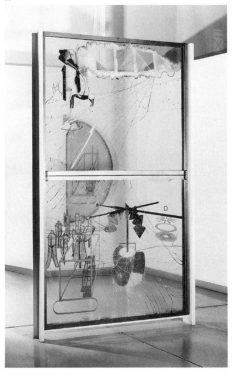

12

13

11 Marcel Duchamp, *The Bride Stripped Bare by Her Bachelors, Even (The Large Glass)*, 1915–23. Oil, varnish, lead foil, lead wire, and dust on two glass panels (cracked), each mounted between two glass panels, with five glass strips, aluminum foil, and a wood-and-steel frame. Philadelphia Museum of Art.

12 Pierre Chareau, Maison de Verre, Paris, France, 1932. Exterior view.

13 Ben van Berkel and Caroline Bos, ACOM Office Building, Amersfoort, the Netherlands, 1993. Exterior view.

14 Rem Koolhaas–OMA, Bibliothèque Nationale de France (competition proposal), Paris, France, 1989. Périphérique facade.

15 Steven Holl, D.E. Shaw and Company Offices, New York, N.Y., 1991. Diagram showing daylight infiltration.

16 Steven Holl, D.E. Shaw and Company Offices, New York, N.Y., 1991. Interior view.

17 Herzog and de Meuron, Signal Box auf dem Wolf, Basel, Switzerland, 1995. Exterior view.

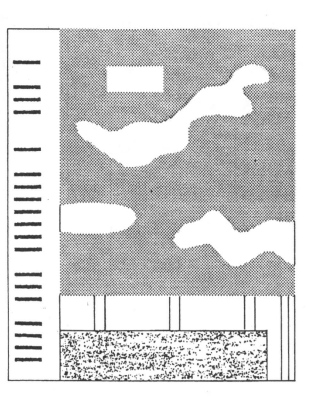

17

15

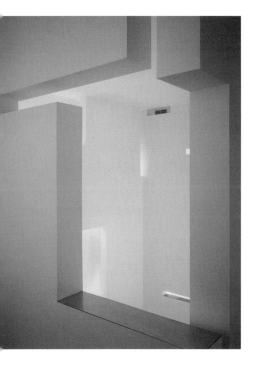

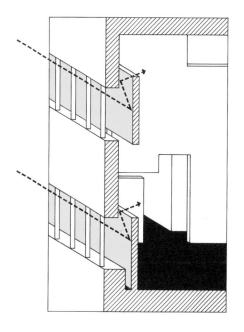

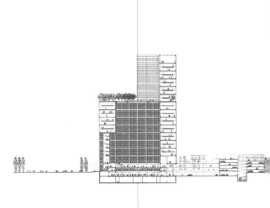

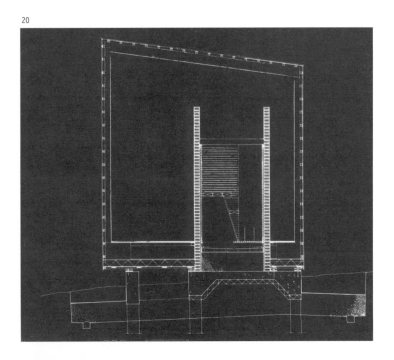

18 Peter Zumthor, Kunsthaus Bregenz, Bregenz, Austria, 1991. Exterior view.
19 Harry C. Wolf, ABN-AMRO Head Office Building (competition proposal),
Amsterdam, the Netherlands, 1992. Section.
20 Kaako, Laine, Liimatainen & Tirkkonen, Leisure Studio, Espoo, Finland,
1992. Section.

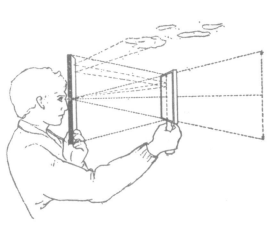

23

Kaako, Laine, Liimatainen & Tirkkonen, Leisure Studio, Espoo,
and, 1992. Exterior view.
Reconstruction of Brunelleschi's perspective experiment, 1417.
Dan Graham, *Two-Way Mirror Cylinder inside Cube*, New York,
, 1991. Exterior view.

24 Abalos and Herreros, Municipal Gymnasium, Simancas, Spain,
1991. General view of Simancas, with municipal gymnasium at right
and cathedral above.
25 Bernard Tschumi, Glass Video Gallery, Groningen, the Netherlands,
1990. Interior view.
26 Renzo Piano Building Workshop, Kansai International Airport,
Osaka, Japan, 1994. Exterior view.
27 Frank Gehry, Frederick R. Weisman Art Museum, Minneapolis,
Minn., 1993. Exterior view.
28 Nicholas Grimshaw and Partners, Waterloo International Terminal,
London, England, 1993. Interior view.
29 Toyo Ito, Shimosuwa Municipal Museum, Shimosuwa, Japan, 1993.
Exterior view.
30 Williams and Tsien, *The World Upside Down* (stage set),
Amsterdam and New York City, 1990–91. View.

b

c

31

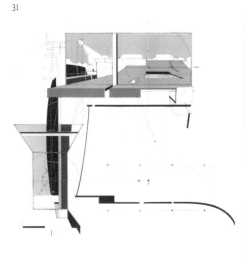

32

33

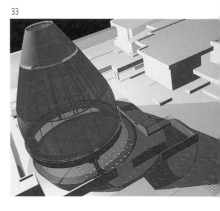

34

35

31 Joel Sanders, Kyle Residence (project), Houston, Tex., 1991. Composite drawing, incorporating views
from living room through corner (left); and toward back of house, showing projection apparatus
and tilted-up grass-covered roof.

32 Gigon and Guyer, Kirchner Museum Davos, Davos, Switzerland. Exterior view.

33 Williams and Tsien, Phoenix Art Museum Sculpture Pavilion, Phoenix, Ariz., 1990. Computer rendering.

34 Toyo Ito, Tower of Winds, Yokohama, Japan, 1986. Exterior views.

35 Dennis Adams, *Bus Shelter IV*, Münster, Germany, 1987. View.

36 Melissa Gould, *Floor Plan*, Linz, Austria, 1991. View.

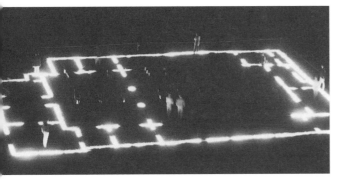

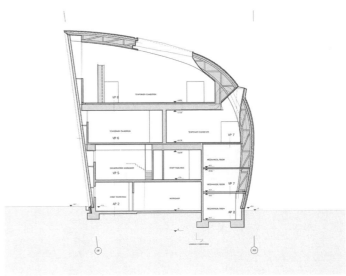

39

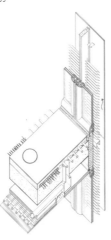

40

Steven Holl, Helsinki Museum of Contemporary Art, Helsinki, Finland, 1993.
tion.
Steven Holl, Helsinki Museum of Contemporary Art, Helsinki, Finland, 1993.
rior view.
Lord Norman Foster and Partners, Business Promotion Center, Duisburg,
many, 1993. Axonometric cutaway of layered glass cladding and floor slab.
Bruno Taut, Glass Pavilion, Cologne, Germany, 1914. Exterior view.

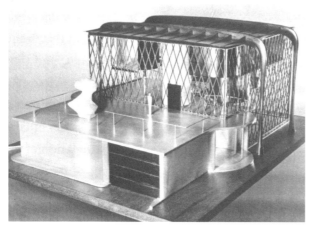

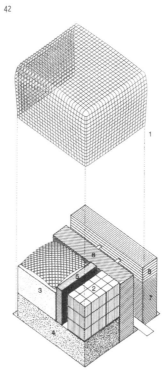

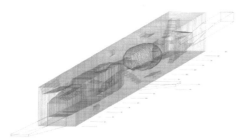

41 Paul Nelson, Maison Suspendue (project), 1938. View of model.
42 Manfred and Laurids Ortner, The Museum of Modern Art,
Museumquartier (competition proposal), Vienna, Austria, 1990.
Axonometric.
43 Oscar Nitzchke, Maison de la Publicité, Paris, France, 1935.
Perspective, Gouache and photomontage.
44 dECOi, Another Glass House (competition proposal), 1991.
45 Gordon Bunshaft–SOM, Beinecke Rare Book and Manuscript
Library, Yale University, New Haven, Conn., 1963. Interior view.

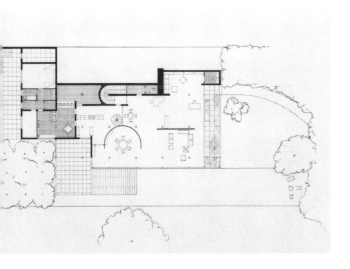

46 Rem Koolhaas–OMA, Two Patio Villas, Rotterdam,
the Netherlands, 1991.
47 Ludwig Mies van der Rohe, Tugendhat House, Brno, Czech
Republic, 1928–29. Exterior view.
48 Ludwig Mies van der Rohe, Tugendhat House, Brno, Czech
Republic, 1928–29. Main level plan.

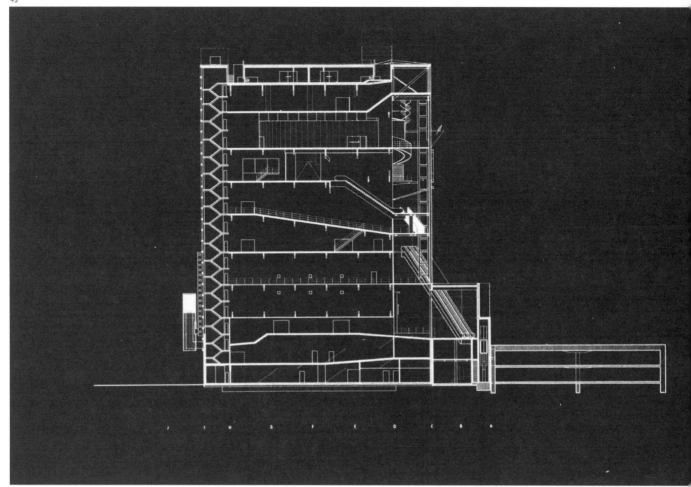

49 Rem Koolhaas—OMA, Zentrum für Kunst und Medientechnologie
(competition proposal), Karlsruhe, Germany, 1989–92. Section.
50 Rem Koolhaas—OMA, Zentrum für Kunst und Medientechnologie
(competition proposal), Karlsruhe, Germany, 1989–92.
View of model.

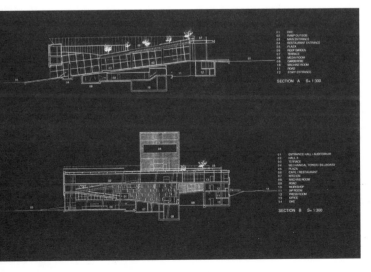

51 Rem Koolhaas–OMA, Kunsthal II, Rotterdam, the Netherlands, 1992. Sections.
52 Rem Koolhaas–OMA, Kunsthal II, Rotterdam, the Netherlands, 1992. Interior view.

53

54

53 Jean Nouvel, Cartier Foundation for Contemporary Art, Paris, France, 1994. Exterior view.

54 Jean Nouvel, Cartier Foundation for Contemporary Art, Paris, France, 1994. Exterior view.

55 *Girls at Rehersal*, from Siegfried Kracauer, *The Mass Ornament*.

56 Bernard Tschumi, Glass Video Gallery, Groningen, the Netherlands, 1990. Exterior view.

57 Bernard Tschumi, Glass Video Gallery, Groningen, the Netherlands, 1990. Section.

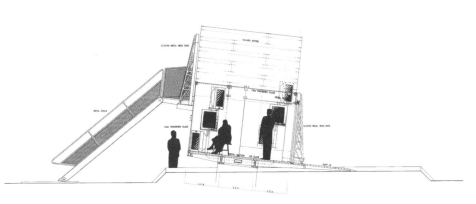

58

59

58 Toyo Ito, Sendai Mediathèque, Sendai, Japan, 1995–2001.
View of model.
59 Joseph Paxton, Crystal Palace, London, England, 1851. Exterior vi

61

Joseph Paxton, Crystal Palace, London, England, 1851.
Interior view.
Gordon Bunshaft–SOM, Lever House, New York, N.Y., 1951–52.
Exterior view.

m *Perspecta* 8: The Yale Architectural Journal
64)

Colin Rowe and Robert Slutzky

Transparency *1591 1. The quality or condition of being transparent; diapheneity; pellucidity 1615. 2. That which
is transparent 1591. b.* spec. *A picture, print, inscription or device on some translucent substance, made visible
by means of light behind 1807. c. A photograph or picture on glass or other transparent substance intended
to be seen by transmitted light 1874. 3. A burlesque translation of the German title of address Durchlaucht 1844.*

Transparent *1. Having the property of transmitting light, so as to render bodies lying beyond completely visible,
that can be seen through. b. Penetrating, as light 1593. c. Admitting the passage of light through interstices
(rare) 1693. 2.* fig. *a. Open, candid, ingenuous 1590. b. Easily seen through, recognized, or detected; manifest,
obvious 1592.*

"Simultaneity," "interpenetration," "superimposition," "ambivalence," "space-time," "transparency": in the literature of contemporary architecture these words, and others like them, are often used as synonyms. We are all familiar with the manifestations to which they are applied—or assume ourselves to be so. These are, we believe, the
specific formal characteristics of contemporary architecture; and, as we respond to these, we rarely seek to analyze
the nature of our response.

It may indeed be futile to attempt to make efficient critical instruments of such approximate definitions.
Perhaps any such attempt can only result in sophistries. Yet it also becomes evident that, unless the evasive nature
of these words is examined, we could be in danger of misinterpreting the forms of lucid complexity to which they
may sometimes refer; and it is for this reason that here some attempt will be made to expose certain levels of
meaning with which the term *transparency* has become endowed.

By the dictionary definition the quality or state of being transparent is a material condition—that of being pervious to light and air, the result of an intellectual imperative—of our inherent demand for that which should be easily detected, perfectly evident; and an attribute of personality—the absence of guile, pretence, or dissimulation;
and thus the adjective *transparent*, by defining a purely physical significance, by functioning as a critical honorific,
and in being dignified by far from disagreeable moral overtones, is a word, from the first, richly loaded with the
possibilities of both meaning and misunderstanding.

But, in addition to these accepted connotations, as a condition to be discovered in a work of art, transparency has become involved with further levels of interpretation which, in his *Language of Vision,* are admirably defined by György Képes:

If one sees two or more figures overlapping one another, and each of them claims for itself the common over-lapped part, then one is confronted with a contradiction of spatial dimensions. To resolve this contradiction one must assume the presence of a new optical quality. The figures are endowed with transparency: that is, they are able to interpenetrate without an optical destruction of each other. Transparency however implies more than an optical characteristic, it implies a broader spatial order. Transparency means a simultaneous perception of differ-ent spatial locations. Space not only recedes but fluctuates in a continuous activity. The position of the transpar-ent figures has equivocal meaning as one sees each figure now as the closer, now as the further one.[1]

Thus, there is now introduced a conception of transparency quite distinct from any physical quality of sub-stance and almost equally remote from the idea of the transparent as the perfectly clear. In fact, by this definition, the transparent ceases to be that which is perfectly clear and becomes, instead, that which is clearly ambiguous. Nor is this definition an entirely esoteric one; and when we read (as we so often do) of "transparent overlapping planes" we sense that more than a physical transparency is involved.

For instance, while László Moholy-Nagy in his *Vision in Motion* constantly refers to "transparent cellophane sheets," "transparent plastic," "transparency and moving light," "Rubens' radiant transparent shadows,"[2] a careful reading of the book might suggest that for him such literal transparency is often furnished with certain metaphori-cal qualities. Some superimpositions of form, Moholy-Nagy tells us, "overcome space and time fixations. They transpose insignificant singularities into meaningful complexities. . . . The transparent qualities of the superimpo-sitions often suggest transparency of context as well, revealing unnoticed structural qualities in the object."[3] And again, in commenting on what he calls "the manifold word agglutinations" of James Joyce, on the Joycean "pun," Moholy-Nagy finds that these are "the approach to the practical task of building up a completeness by an ingenious transparency of relationships."[4] In other words, he seems to have felt that, by a process of distortion, recomposi-tion, and *double entendre,* a linguistic transparency—the literary equivalent of Képes's "interpenetration without optical destruction"—might be effected and that whoever experiences one of these Joycean "agglutinations" will enjoy the sensation of looking through a first plane of significance to others lying behind.

Therefore, at the beginning of any inquiry into transparency, a basic distinction must perhaps be established. Transparency may be an inherent quality of substance—as in a wire mesh or glass curtain wall, or it may be an inherent quality of organization—as both Képes and, to a lesser degree, Moholy-Nagy suggest it to be; and one might, for this reason, distinguish between a real or *literal* and a *phenomenal* or seeming transparency.

Possibly our feeling for literal transparency derives from two sources, from what might be designated as machine aesthetic and from Cubist painting; probably our feeling for phenomenal transparency derives from Cubist painting alone; and certainly any Cubist canvas of 1911–12 could serve to illustrate the presence of these two orders or levels of the transparent.

But, in considering phenomena so baffling and complex as those which distinguish Cubist painting, the would-be analyst is at a disadvantage; and, presumably, it is for this reason that, almost fifty years after the event, dispassionate analysis of the Cubist achievement is still almost entirely lacking.[5] Explanations which obscure the pictorial problems of Cubism are to be found in abundance, and one might be skeptical of these, just as one might be skeptical of those two plausible interpretations which involve the fusion of temporal and spatial factors, which see Cubism as a premonition of relativity, and which in this way present it as little more than a "natural" by-product of a particular cultural atmosphere. As Alfred Barr tells us, Apollinaire "invoked the fourth dimension . . . in a metaphorical rather than a mathematical sense";[6] and, rather than attempt to relate Picasso to Minkowski, it would, for us, be preferable to refer to less disputable sources of inspiration.

A late Cézanne such as the *Mont Sainte-Victoire* of 1904–6 (fig. 62) in the Philadelphia Museum of Art is characterized by certain extreme simplifications: most notably, by a highly developed insistence on a frontal viewpoint of the whole scene; by a suppression of the more obvious elements suggestive of depth; and by a resultant contracting of foreground, middleground, and background into a distinctly compressed pictorial matrix. Sources of light are definite but various; and a further contemplation of the picture reveals a tipping forward of the objects in space, which is assisted by the painter's use of opaque and contrasted color and made more emphatic by the intersection of the canvas provided by the base of the mountain. The center of the composition is occupied by a rather dense gridding of oblique and rectilinear lines; and this area is then buttressed and stabilized by a more insistent horizontal and vertical grid which introduces a certain peripheric interest.

Frontality, suppression of depth, contracting of space, definition of light sources, tipping forward of objects, restricted palette, oblique and rectilinear grids, propensities toward peripheric development are all characteristics of Analytical Cubism; and, in the typical compositions of 1911–12, detached from a more overtly representational purpose, they assume a more evident significance. In these pictures, apart from the pulling to pieces and reassembly of objects, perhaps above all we are conscious of a further shrinkage of depth and an increased emphasis which is now awarded to the grid. We discover about this time a meshing of two systems of coordinates. On the one hand an arrangement of oblique and curved lines suggests a certain diagonal spatial recession. On the other, a series of horizontal and vertical lines implies a contradictory statement of frontality. Generally speaking, the oblique and curved lines possess a certain naturalistic significance while the rectilinear ones show a geometricizing tendency serving as a reassertion of the picture plane. But both systems of coordinates provide for the orientation of the figures simultaneously in an extended space and on a painted surface, while their intersecting, overlapping, interlocking, their building up into larger and fluctuating configurations, permits the genesis of the typical Cubist motif.

But, as the observer distinguishes between all the planes to which these grids give rise, he becomes progressively conscious of an opposition between certain areas of luminous paint and others of a more dense coloration. He distinguishes between certain planes to which he is able to attribute a physical nature allied to that of celluloid, others whose essence is semi-opaque, and further areas of a substance totally opposed to the transmission of light. And he may discover that all of these planes, translucent or otherwise, and regardless of their representational content, are to be found implicated in the manifestation which Képes has defined as transparency.

The double nature of this transparency may be illustrated by the comparison and analysis of a somewhat atypical Picasso, *Man with a Clarinet* (fig. 63), and a representative Braque, *The Portuguese* (fig. 64), both of 1911. In each picture a pyramidal form implies an image; but then, while Picasso defines his pyramid by means of a strong contour, Braque uses a more complicated inference. Picasso's contour is so assertive and independent of its background that the observer has some sense of a positively transparent figure standing in a relatively deep space, and only subsequently does he redefine this sensation to allow for the real shallowness of the space. But with Braque the reading of the picture follows a reverse order. A highly developed interlacing of horizontal and vertical gridding, created by gapped lines and intruding planes, establishes a primarily shallow space, and only gradually does the observer become able to invest this space with a depth which permits the figure to assume substance. Braque offers the possibility of an independent reading of figure and grid. Picasso scarcely does so. Picasso's grid is rather subsumed within his figure or appears as a form of peripheral incident intended to stabilize it.

The differences of method in these two pictures could easily be overemphasized. At different times they will appear to be dissimilar and alike. But it is necessary to point out that there are present in this parallel the intimations of different directions. In the Picasso we enjoy the sensation of looking through a figure standing in a deep space; whereas in Braque's shallow, flattened, laterally extended space, we are provided with no physically perspicuous object. In the one we receive a prevision of literal, in the other, of phenomenal transparency; and the evidence of these two distinct attitudes will become much clearer if a comparison is attempted between the works of two such slightly later painters as Robert Delaunay and Juan Gris.

Delaunay's *Simultaneous Windows* of 1911 and Gris's *Still Life* of 1912 (figs. 65 and 66) both include objects which are presumably transparent, the one windows, the other bottles; but, while Gris suppresses the literal transparency of glass in favor of a transparency of gridding, Delaunay accepts with unrestrained enthusiasm the elusively reflective qualities of his superimposed "glazed openings." Gris weaves a system of oblique and curved lines into some sort of shallow, corrugated space; and, in the architectonic tradition of Cézanne, in order to amplify both his objects and structure, he assumes varied but definite light sources. Delaunay's preoccupation with form presupposes an entirely different attitude. Forms to him—e.g., a low block of buildings and various naturalistic objects reminiscent of the Eiffel Tower—are nothing but reflections and refractions of light which he presents in terms analogous to Cubist gridding. But, despite this geometricizing of image, the generally ethereal nature of both Delaunay's forms and his space appears more characteristic of impressionism; and this resemblance is further reinforced by the manner in which he uses his medium. In contrast to the flat, planar areas of opaque and almost monochromatic color which Gris invests with such high tactile value, Delaunay emphasizes a quasi-impressionistic calligraphy; and, while Gris provides explicit definition of a rear plane, Delaunay dissolves the possibilities of so distinct a closure of his space. Gris's rear plane functions as a catalyst which localizes the ambiguities of his pictorial objects and engenders their fluctuating values. Delaunay's distaste for so specific a procedure leaves the latent ambiguities of his form unresolved, exposed, without reference. Both operations might be recognized as attempts to elucidate the congested intricacy of Analytical Cubism; but, where Gris seems to have intensified some of the characteristics of Cubist space and to have imbued its plastic principles with a new bravura, Delaunay has, perhaps, been led to explore the poetical overtones of Cubism by divorcing them from their metrical syntax.

When something of the attitude of a Delaunay becomes fused with a machine-aesthetic emphasis upon materials and stiffened by a certain enthusiasm for planar structures, then literal transparency becomes complete; and perhaps it is most appropriately to be illustrated by the work of Moholy-Nagy. In his *Abstract of an Artist,* Moholy-Nagy tells us that around 1921 his "transparent paintings" became completely freed from all elements reminiscent of nature, and, to quote him directly, "I see today that this was the logical result of the Cubist paintings which I had admiringly studied."[7]

Now whether a freedom from all elements reminiscent of nature may be considered a logical continuation of Cubism is not relevant to the present discussion, but whether Moholy-Nagy did succeed in emptying his work of all naturalistic content is of some importance; and his seeming belief that Cubism had pointed the way toward a freeing of forms may justify us in the analysis of one of his subsequent works and its parallel with another post-Cubist painting. With Moholy-Nagy's *La Sarraz* of 1930 (fig. 67) might reasonably be compared a Fernand Léger of 1926, *Three Faces* (fig. 68).

In *La Sarraz* five circles connected by an S-shaped band, two sets of trapezoidal planes of translucent color, a number of near horizontal and vertical bars, a liberal splattering of light and dark flecks, and a number of slightly convergent dashes are all imposed upon a black background. In *Three Faces* three major areas displaying organic forms, abstracted artifacts, and purely geometric shapes are tied together by horizontal banding and common contour. In contrast to Moholy-Nagy, Léger aligns his pictorial objects at right angles to each other and to the edges of his picture plane; he provides these objects with a flat, opaque coloring, setting up a figure-ground reading through the compressed disposition of highly contrasted surfaces; and, while Moholy-Nagy seems to have flung open a window onto some private version of outer space, Léger, working within an almost two-dimensional scheme, achieves a maximum clarity of both "negative" and "positive" forms. By means of restriction, Léger's picture becomes charged with an equivocal depth reading, with a phenomenal transparency singularly reminiscent of that to which Moholy-Nagy was so sensitive in the writings of Joyce, but which, in spite of the literal transparency of his paint, he himself has been unable or unwilling to achieve.

For, in spite of its modernity of motif, Moholy-Nagy's picture still shows the conventional pre-Cubist foreground, middleground, and background; and, in spite of a rather casual interweaving of surface and depth elements introduced to destroy the logic of this deep space, Moholy-Nagy's picture can be submitted to only one reading. But the case of Léger is very different. For Léger, through the refined virtuosity with which he assembles post-Cubist constituents, makes completely plain the multifunctioned behavior of clearly defined form. Through flat planes, through an absence of volume suggesting its presence, through the implication rather than the fact of a grid, through an interrupted checkerboard pattern stimulated by color, proximity, and discreet superimposition, he leads the eye to experience an inexhaustible series of larger and smaller organizations within the whole. Léger's concern is with the structure of form; Moholy-Nagy's with materials and light. Moholy-Nagy has accepted the Cubist figure but has lifted it from out of its spatial matrix: Léger has preserved and even intensified the typically Cubist tension between figure and space.

These three comparisons may clarify some of the basic differences between literal and phenomenal transparency in the painting of the last forty-five years. Literal transparency, we might notice, tends to be associated with the *trompe l'oeil* effect of a translucent object in a deep, naturalistic space; while phenomenal transparency seems to be found when a painter seeks the articulated presentation of frontally aligned objects in a shallow, abstracted space.

But, in considering architectural rather than pictorial transparencies, inevitable confusions arise. For, while painting can only imply the third dimension, architecture cannot suppress it. Provided with the reality rather than the counterfeit of three dimensions, in architecture, literal transparency can become a physical fact; but phenomenal transparency will be more difficult to achieve—and is, indeed, so difficult to discuss that generally critics have been entirely willing to associate transparency in architecture exclusively with a transparency of materials. Thus György Képes, having provided an almost classical explanation of the phenomena we have noticed in Braque, Gris, and Léger, appears to consider that the architectural analogue of these must be found in the physical qualities of glass and plastics, that the equivalent of carefully calculated Cubist and post-Cubist compositions will be discovered in the haphazard superimpositions provided by the accidental reflections of light playing upon a translucent or polished surface.[8] And, similarly, Siegfried Giedion seems to assume that the presence of an all-glass wall at the Bauhaus (fig. 70), with "its extensive transparent areas," permits "the hovering relations of planes and the kind of 'overlapping' which appears in contemporary painting"; and he proceeds to reinforce this suggestion with a quotation from Alfred Barr on the characteristic "transparency of overlapping planes" in Analytical Cubism.[9]

In Picasso's *L'Arlésienne* (fig. 69), the picture which provides the visual support for these inferences of Giedion's, such a transparency of overlapping planes is very obviously to be found. There Picasso offers planes apparently of celluloid through which the observer has the sensation of looking; and, in doing so, no doubt his sensations are somewhat similar to those of an observer of the workshop wing at the Bauhaus. In each case a transparency of materials is discovered. But then, in the laterally constructed space of his picture, Picasso, through the compilation of larger and smaller forms, also offers limitless possibilities of alternative interpretation. *L'Arlésienne* has the fluctuating, equivocal meaning which Képes recognizes as characteristic of transparency; while the glass wall at the Bauhaus, an unambiguous surface giving upon an unambiguous space, seems to be singularly free of this quality; and thus, for the evidence of what we have designated phenomenal transparency, we shall here be obliged to look elsewhere.

Almost contemporary with the Bauhaus, Le Corbusier's villa at Garches (figs. 71 and 72) might fairly be juxtaposed with it. Superficially, the garden facade of this house and the elevations of the workshop wing at the Bauhaus (fig. 73) are not dissimilar. Both employ cantilevered wall slabs and both display a recessed ground floor. Neither admits an interruption of the horizontal movement of the glazing and both make a point of carrying this glazing around the corner. But further similarities are looked for in vain. From here on, one might say that Le Corbusier is primarily occupied with the planar qualities of glass and Gropius with its translucent attributes. By the introduction of a wall surface almost equal in height to that of his glazing divisions, Le Corbusier stiffens his glass plane and provides it with an overall surface tension; while Gropius permits his translucent surface the appearance of hanging rather loosely from a fascia which protrudes somewhat in the fashion of a curtain box. At Garches one may enjoy the illusion that *possibly* the framing of the windows passes behind the wall surface; but, at the Bauhaus, since one is never for a moment unaware that the slab is pressing up behind the window, one is not enabled to indulge in such speculations.

At Garches the ground floor is conceived of as a vertical surface traversed by a range of horizontal windows; at the Bauhaus it is given the appearance of a solid wall extensively punctured by glazing. At Garches it offers an explicit indication of the frame which carries the cantilevers above; at the Bauhaus it shows somewhat stubby piers which do not automatically connect with the idea of a skeleton structure. In this workshop wing of the Bauhaus one might say that Gropius is absorbed with the idea of establishing a plinth upon which to dispose an arrangement of horizontal planes, and that his principal concern appears to be the wish that two of these planes should be visible through a veil of glass. But glass would hardly seem to hold such fascination for Le Corbusier; and, although one can obviously see through his windows, it is not here that the transparency of his building is to be found.

At Garches the recessed surface of the ground floor is redefined upon the roof by the two freestanding walls which terminate the terrace; and the same statement of depth is taken up by the glazed doors in the side walls which act as conclusions to the fenestration. In these ways Le Corbusier proposes the idea that, immediately behind his glazing, there lies a narrow slot of space traveling parallel to it; and, of course, in consequence of this, he implies a further idea—that bounding this slot of space, and behind it, there lies a plane of which the ground floor, the freestanding walls, and the inner reveals of the doors all form a part; and, although this plane may be dismissed as very obviously a conceptual convenience rather than a physical fact, its obtrusive presence is undeniable. Recognizing the physical plane of glass and concrete and this imaginary (though scarcely less real) plane that lies behind, we become aware that here a transparency is effected not through the agency of a window but rather through our being made conscious of primary concepts which "interpenetrate without optical destruction of each other."

And obviously these two planes are not all, since a third and equally distinct parallel surface is both introduced and implied. It defines the rear wall of the terrace and is further reiterated by other parallel dimensions: the parapets of the garden stairs, the terrace, and the second-floor balcony. In itself, each of these planes is incomplete or perhaps even fragmentary; yet it is with these parallel planes as points of reference that the facade is organized, and the implication of all is that of a vertical layerlike stratification of the interior space of the building, of a succession of laterally extended spaces traveling one behind the other.

It is this system of spatial stratification which brings Le Corbusier's facade into the closest relationship with the Léger we have already examined. In *Three Faces* Léger conceives of his canvas as a field modeled in low relief. Of his three major panels (which overlap, dovetail, and alternately comprise and exclude each other), two are closely implicated in an almost equivalent depth relationship, while the third constitutes a *coulisse* which both advances and recedes. At Garches, Le Corbusier replaces Léger's picture plane with a most highly developed regard for the frontal viewpoint (the preferred views include only the slightest deviations from parallel perspective); Léger's canvas becomes Le Corbusier's second plane; other planes are either imposed upon or subtracted from this basic datum; and deep space is then contrived in similar *coulisse* fashion, with the facade cut open and depth inserted into the ensuing slot.

These remarks, which might infer that Le Corbusier had indeed succeeded in alienating architecture from its necessary three-dimensional existence, require qualification; and, in order to provide it, it is now necessary to proceed to some discussion of the building's internal space. And here, at the very beginning, it may be noticed that this space appears to be a flat contradiction of the facade, particularly on the principal floor (fig. 75) where the volume revealed is almost directly opposite to that which might have been anticipated. Thus, the glazing of the garden facade might have suggested the presence of a single large room behind it; and it might have further inspired the belief that the direction of this room was parallel with that of the facade. But the internal divisions of the space deny any such statement, disclosing, instead, a major volume whose primary direction is at right angles to the facade; while, in both the major volume and in the subsidiary spaces which surround it, the predominance of this direction is further conspicuously emphasized by the flanking walls.

But the spatial structure of this floor is obviously more complex than it at first appears, and ultimately it compels a revision of these initial assumptions. Gradually the lateral nature of the cantilevered slots becomes evident; and, while the apse of the dining room, the position of the principal stairs, the void, the library, all reaffirm the same dimension, by means of these elements the planes of the facade can now be seen to effect a profound modification of the deep extension of the internal space, which now comes to approach the stratified succession of flattened spaces suggested by the external appearance.

So much might be said for a reading of the internal volumes in terms of the vertical planes; and a further reading in terms of the horizontal planes, the floors, will reveal similar characteristics. Thus, after recognizing that a floor is not a wall and that plans are not paintings, we might still examine these horizontal planes in very much the same manner as we have the facade, again selecting *Three Faces* as a point of departure. A complement of Léger's picture plane may now be offered by the roofs of the penthouse and the elliptical pavilion, by the summits of the freestanding walls and by the top of the rather curious gazebo—all of which lie on the same surface (fig. 74). The second plane now becomes the major roof terrace and the *coulisse* space becomes the cut in the slab which leads the eye down to the terrace below; and similar parallels are very obvious in considering the organization of the principal floor. For here the vertical equivalent of deep space is introduced by the double height of the outer terrace and by the void connecting living room with entrance hall; and here, just as Léger enlarges spatial dimensions through the displacement of the inner edges of his outer panels, so Le Corbusier encroaches upon the space of his central area.

Thus, throughout this house, there is that contradiction of spatial dimensions which Képes recognizes as characteristic of transparency. There is a continuous dialectic between fact and implication. The reality of deep space is constantly opposed to the inference of shallow; and, by means of the resultant tension, reading after reading is enforced. The five layers of space which vertically divide the building's volume and the four layers which cut it horizontally will all, from time to time, claim attention; and this gridding of space will then result in continuous fluctuations of interpretation.

These possibly cerebral refinements are scarcely so conspicuous at the Bauhaus; indeed they are attributes of which an aesthetic of materials is apt to be impatient. In the workshop wing of the Bauhaus it is the literal transparency which Giedion has chiefly applauded, at Garches it is the phenomenal transparency which has engaged our attention; and, if with some reason we have been able to relate the achievement of Le Corbusier to that of Léger, with equal justification we might notice a community of interest in the expression of Gropius and Moholy-Nagy.

Moholy-Nagy was always preoccupied with the expression of glass, metal, reflecting substances, light; and Gropius, at least in the 1920s, would seem to have been equally concerned with the idea of using materials for their intrinsic qualities. Both, it may be said without injustice, received a certain stimulus from the experiments of *De Stijl* and the Russian Constructivists; but both apparently were unwilling to accept certain more Parisian conclusions.

For, seemingly, it was in Paris that the Cubist "discovery" of shallow space was most completely exploited; and it was there that the idea of the picture plane as uniformly activated field was most entirely understood. With Picasso, Braque, Gris, Léger, Ozenfant, we are never conscious of the picture plane functioning in any passive role. Both it, as negative space, and the objects placed upon it, as positive figure, are endowed with an equal capacity to stimulate. But outside the school of Paris this condition is not typical, although Mondrian, a Parisian by adoption, constitutes one major exception and Klee another. But a glance at any representative works of Kandinsky, Malevich, El Lissitzky, or Van Doesburg will reveal that these painters, like Moholy-Nagy, scarcely felt the necessity of providing any distinct spatial matrix for their principal objects. They are apt to accept a simplification of the Cubist image as a composition of geometrical planes, but are apt to reject the comparable Cubist abstraction of space; and, if for these reasons their pictures offer us figures which float in an infinite, atmospheric, naturalistic void, without any of the rich Parisian stratification of volume, the Bauhaus may be accepted as their architectural equivalent.

Thus, in the Bauhaus complex, although we are presented with a composition of slablike buildings whose forms suggest the possibility of a reading of space by layers, we are scarcely conscious of the presence of spatial stratification. Through the movements of the dormitory building, the administrative offices, and the workshop wing, the principal floor may suggest a channeling of space in one direction (fig. 76). Through the countermovements of roadway, classrooms, and auditorium wing, the ground floor may suggest a movement of space in the other (fig. 77). A preference for neither direction is stated (fig. 80); and the ensuing dilemma is resolved, as indeed it only can be resolved in this case, by giving priority to diagonal points of view.

Much as Van Doesburg and Moholy-Nagy eschew Cubist frontality, so does Gropius; and it is significant that, while the published photographs of Garches tend to minimize factors of diagonal recession, almost invariably the published photographs of the Bauhaus tend to play up just these factors. And the importance of these diagonal views of the Bauhaus is constantly reasserted—by the translucent corner of the workshop wing and by such features as the balconies of the dormitory and the protruding slab over the entrance to the workshops, features which require for their understanding a renunciation of the principle of frontality.

In plan, the Bauhaus reveals a succession of spaces but scarcely "a contradiction of spatial dimensions." Relying on the diagonal viewpoint, Gropius has exteriorized the opposed movements of his space, has allowed them to flow away into infinity; and, by being unwilling to attribute to either one any significant difference of quality, he has prohibited the possibilities of a potential ambiguity. Thus, only the contours of his buildings assume a layerlike character; but these layers of building scarcely act to suggest a layerlike structure of either internal or external space. Denied, by these means, the possibility of penetrating a stratified space defined either by real planes or their imaginary projections, the observer is also denied the possibility of experiencing those conflicts between one space which is explicit and another which is implied. He may enjoy the sensation of looking through a glass wall and thus be able to see the interior and the exterior of the building simultaneously; but, in doing so, he will be conscious of few of those equivocal emotions which derive from phenomenal transparency.

But to some degree, since the one is a single block and the other a complex of wings, an extended comparison between Garches and the Bauhaus is unjust to both. For, within the limitations of a simple volume, it is possible that certain relationships can be inferred which, in a more elaborate composition, will always lie beyond the bounds of possibility; and, for these reasons, it may be more apt to distinguish literal from phenomenal transparency by a further parallel between Gropius and Le Corbusier.

Le Corbusier's League of Nations project of 1927 (figs. 78 and 79), like the Bauhaus, possesses heterogeneous elements and functions which lead to an extended organization and to the appearance of a further feature which both buildings have in common: the narrow block. But it is here again that similarities cease: for, while the Bauhaus blocks pinwheel in a manner highly suggestive of Constructivist compositions (fig. 80), in the League of Nations these same long blocks define a system of striations almost more rigid than is evident at Garches.

In the League of Nations project lateral extension characterizes the two principal wings of the Secretariat, qualifies the library and book stack area, is reemphasized by the entrance quay and foyers of the General Assembly Building, and dominates even the auditorium itself. There, the introduction of glazing along the side walls, disturbing the normal focus of the hall upon the presidential box, introduces the same transverse direction. And, by such means, the counterstatement of deep space becomes a highly assertive proposition, chiefly suggested by a lozenge shape whose major axis passes through the General Assembly Building and whose outline is comprised by a mirror image projection of the auditorium volume into the approach roads of the *cour d'honneur*. But again, as at Garches, the intimations of depth inherent in this form are consistently retracted. A cut, a displacement, and a sliding sideways occur along the line of its minor axis; and, as a figure, it is repeatedly scored through and broken down into a series of lateral references—by trees, by circulations, by the momentum of the buildings themselves—so that finally, by a series of positive and negative implications, the whole area becomes a sort of monumental debate, an argument between a real and deep space and an ideal and shallow one.

We will presume the Palace of the League of Nations as having been built and an observer following the axial approach to its auditorium. Necessarily he is subjected to the polar attraction of its principal entrance which he sees framed within a screen of trees. But these trees, intersecting his vision, also introduce a lateral deflection of interest, so that he becomes successively aware, first, of a relation between the flanking office building and the foreground *parterre,* and second, of a relation between the crosswalk and the courtyard of the Secretariat. And once within the trees, beneath the low umbrella which they provide, yet a further tension is established: the space, which is inflected toward the General Assembly Building, is defined by, and reads as, a projection of the book stack and library. And finally, with the trees as a volume behind him, the observer at last finds himself standing on a low terrace, confronting the entrance quay but separated from it by a rift of space so complete that it is only by the propulsive power of the walk behind him that he can be enabled to cross it. With his arc of vision no longer restricted, he is now offered the General Assembly Building in its full extent; but since a newly revealed lack of focus compels his eye to slide along this facade, it is again irresistibly drawn sideways—to the view of gardens and lake beyond. And should the observer turn around from this rift between him and his obvious goal, and should he look back at the trees which he has just abandoned, he will find that the lateral sliding of the space becomes only more determined, emphasized by the trees themselves and the cross alley leading into the slotted indenture alongside the book stack. While further, if our observer is a man of moderate sophistication, and if the piercing of a volume or screen of trees by a road might have come to suggest to him that the intrinsic function of this road is to penetrate similar volumes and screens, then, by inference, the terrace upon which he is standing becomes, not a prelude to the auditorium, as its axial relationship suggests, but a projection of the volumes and planes of the office building with which it is aligned.

These stratifications, devices by means of which space becomes constructed, substantial, and articulate, are the essence of that phenomenal transparency which has been noticed as characteristic of the central post-Cubist tradition. They have never been noticed as characteristic of the Bauhaus. For obviously there completely different space conceptions are manifest. In the League of Nations project Le Corbusier provides the observer with a series of quite specific locations: at the Bauhaus the observer is without such points of reference. Although the League of Nations project is extensively glazed, except in the auditorium, such glazing is scarcely of capital importance. At the Palace of the League of Nations corners and angles, as the indices of spatial dimension, are assertive and definite. At the Bauhaus, Giedion tells us, they are "dematerialized." At the Palace of the League of Nations space is crystalline; but at the Bauhaus it is glazing which gives the building a "crystalline translucence." At the Palace of the League of Nations glass provides a surface as definite and as taut as the top of a drum; but at the Bauhaus glass walls "flow into one another," "blend into each other," "wrap around the building," and in other ways (by acting as the absence of plane) "contribute to that process of loosening up which now dominates the architectural scene."[10]

But we look in vain for "loosening up" in the Palace of the League of Nations. There is no evidence there of any desire to obliterate sharp distinction. Le Corbusier's planes are like knives for the apportionate slicing of space. If we could attribute to space the qualities of water, then his building is like a dam by means of which space is contained, embanked, tunneled, sluiced, and finally spilled into the informal gardens alongside the lake. While by contrast, the Bauhaus, insulated in a sea of amorphic outline, is like a reef gently lapped by a placid tide.

The foregoing, no doubt an overextended discussion of two schemes, the one mutilated, the other unbuilt, has been a necessary means toward clarifying the spatial milieu in which phenomenal transparency becomes possible. It is not intended to suggest that phenomenal transparency (for all its Cubist descent) is a necessary constituent of modern architecture, nor that its presence might be used as a piece of litmus paper for the test of architectural orthodoxy. It is simply intended to serve as a characterization of species and, also, as a warning against the confusion of species.

[1] György Képes, *Language of Vision* (Chicago: Paul Theobold and Company, 1944), 77.

[2] László Moholy-Nagy, *Vision in Motion* (Chicago: Paul Theobold and Company, 1947), 88, 194, 159, and 157.

[3] Moholy-Nagy, *Vision in Motion*, 210.

[4] Moholy-Nagy, *Vision in Motion*, 350.

[5] Among the exceptions are studies such as those by Alfred Barr, publications such as Christopher Gray's *Cubist Aesthetic Theories* (Baltimore: John Hopkins University Press, 1953), and Winthrop Judkins's "Towards a Reinterpretation of Cubism," *Art Bulletin* 30, no. 4 (1948).

[6] Alfred Barr, *Picasso: Fifty Years of His Art* (New York: The Museum of Modern Art, 1946), 68.

[7] László Moholy-Nagy, *The New Vision* and *Abstract of an Artist* (New York: Wittenborn and Company, 1946), 75.

[8] Képes, *Language of Vision*, 79, 117, and elsewhere.

[9] Siegfried Giedion, *Space, Time, and Architecture* (Cambridge, Mass.: Harvard University Press, 1954), 490 and 491.

[10] Giedion, 489, and Siegfried Giedion, *Walter Gropius: Work and Teamwork* (New York: Reinhold, 1954), 54–55.

Perspecta 13/14: The Yale Architectural Journal
71)

TRANSPARENCY: LITERAL AND PHENOMENAL
PART II

Colin Rowe and Robert Slutzky

In a previous article we elaborated, through a discussion of several Cubist and post-Cubist paintings, certain meanings which have attached themselves to the word *transparency*. With the Bauhaus, Garches, and Le Corbusier's project for the Palace of the League of Nations serving as primary points of architectural reference, two kinds of transparency were investigated. They were distinguished as literal and phenomenal. Literal transparency, it was stipulated, could be experienced in the presence of a glazed opening or a wire mesh; but no definite conclusions as to the prerequisites of phenomenal transparency were presented. However, the examples of Garches and the League of Nations at least suggested circumstances which might be the cause of this manifestation; and thus it was implied that phenomenal transparency might be perceived when one plane is seen at no great distance behind another and tying in the same visual direction as the first. Consequently, it was further implied that among the causes (or, if one prefers it, the by-products) of phenomenal transparency there might be found a preference for shallow space, or where such space was not possible, for a stratification of deep space, so that the phenomenal as opposed to the real space could be experienced as shallow. But some of these suppositions are of so tendentious and so arguable a nature that in this present article it is proposed to consign them to temporary oblivion, and to concentrate attention, not upon the three-dimensional or spatial aspects of phenomenal transparency, but as far as possible upon its two-dimensional manifestations—upon phenomenal transparency as pattern.

Substituting the United Nations Building for the Bauhaus and Le Corbusier's Algiers Skyscraper project for his villa at Garches, we might arrive at a parallel between the two former roughly approximate to the parallel which was maintained between the two latter. Thus the Secretariat of the United Nations may stand as a monumental example of literal transparency; and the Algiers Skyscraper may represent almost a textbook example of that other transparency which György Képes defines as the capacity of figures to interpenetrate without optical destruction of each other.[1]

The published drawings of the Algiers block (fig. 82) show a tower whose organization may be apprehended in a variety of ways:

1. The eye may be engaged by the three horizontal bands which divide the structure into four definite areas.
2. If these are overlooked or become recessive the eye may become absorbed with the cellular pattern of the *brise soleil* and this pattern will gradually be felt to extend itself behind the horizontal bands.
3. As the disruption of the *brise soleil* pattern to the left of the facade becomes apparent, the observer will construct a further figure which, in mediating the two *brise soleil* grids, appears as a kind of channel cutting open the facade and connecting the *pilotis* of the lower floors with the incidents upon the roof.
4. When this new figure is discovered to be interwoven with the three central floors of the building, the eye (or the mind) is compelled to provide further explanation and the observer comes to see the composition as a kind of E-shaped overlay imposed upon the "neutral" background provided by the *brise soleil*.

These four variations are presented, not necessarily in the order in which they might be experienced, nor as excluding further interpretations to which they give rise, but simply with the object of establishing the basic figures whose presence a quite naive individual might detect.[2]

With the United Nations Building and the Algiers Skyscraper as almost classic exemplars of literal and phenomenal transparency, it would surely be possible to sustain a classification of modern architecture according to the absence or presence of these qualities, but to do so would involve unnecessarily tedious analysis. The two interpretations which have been laid upon the word *transparency* become apparent from the comparison of these two buildings, and only in order to reinforce this distinction of meaning does it seem necessary to include a further parallel—one between Pietro Belluschi's Equitable Life Insurance Building in Portland, Oregon (fig. 83), and I. M. Pei's Mile High Center in Denver, Colorado (fig. 84).

The former is evidently an instance of literal transparency. Direct, matter of fact, a kind of lucid academic critique of the Chicago architecture of the 1980s, it shows few of those characteristics which Képes lists as those of (phenomenal) transparency. It barely exhibits either overlapping or interpenetrating figures, perhaps little contradiction of spatial dimensions; nor does it offer the observer a means of "simultaneous perception of different spatial dimensions";[3] and, except for its surface flatness, it is without equivocal meaning.

On the other hand, the Denver building, which displays a comparable regard for the structural frame and which is equally transparent in the literal sense, exhibits all of the foregoing ambiguities. Confronted with the Mile High Center the observer perceives:

1. The vertical and horizontal gridding of a black structural frame.
2. A further system of gridding provided by a blue sub-frame which is constituted by the window mullions and the horizontal transoms or sill members.
3. That each of these frames provides a visual reinforcement of the other and that their overlapping leaves some doubt as to where the floor levels of the building actually are to be found.

Further discrimination leads to the awareness that the black structural frame lies entirely in one vertical plane and thus to the color black a specific spatial depth is attributed. Concurrently, an attempt is made to attribute a similar specific spatial depth to the color blue—only to reveal that the horizontal members of the blue sub-frame pass behind the black frame, while its vertical members pass in front. Hence, an equivocal contradiction of spatial dimensions results from this interweaving or overlapping of two figures which are simultaneously apprehended; and in order to explain this situation, first the black frame and then the blue will become dominant for the observer. At one time he will accept the existence of the blue frame in the two distinct spatial layers which it occupies, but at another he will seek to interpret its color according to the logic of color displayed in the black frame. Thus he will come to suppress the modeling of the blue frame and attempt to see it as entirely flat, but in doing so he will be obliged to see either the horizontal or vertical members of the black frame as pressed forward, or pressed back, or warped by the tension which has been introduced.

This building is presumably an exceptionally succinct statement of a phenomenal transparency, but to certain types of mind the elegant post-Miesian achievement which it represents will suggest not only Chicago but also Italy. It is undoubtedly indiscreet to pluck such a building as the Farnese villa at Caprarola (fig. 85) from out of its cultural background and to propose that it may be examined face to face with this recent office building from Denver. The functions of the two buildings are not similar; their structural systems could scarcely be more unlike; the social context, the technology, the economy, the content which each implies can scarcely be related. But for the present we are concerned neither with function nor structure (as generally understood), nor with the social context, technology, economics, or content; but simply with the manifestations which reveal themselves to the eye.

Presented with one of the two identical garden facades of Caprarola, the observer recognizes a building organized in terms of two major stories and he is quite shortly aware of:

1. the primary articulation of the wall which the orders and their respective entablature establish.
2. a further articulation of the wall which is effected by means of a sort of lattice of flat stone strips.

This stone lattice work which forms a visual insulation between the pilasters and the plastic activity of the windows functions in two primary manners—as a subsidiary pilaster which serves the "real" pilasters and confirms the vertical punctuation of the facade, and as a frame which serves the bay, indicating a system of paneling and providing the facade with a number of horizontal emphases of an importance almost equal to that of the lower entablature.

Thus the imposition of pilasters upon lattice leads (as at Denver) to an uncertainty as to the floor level and to an ambiguity as to the basic unit of the facade. By implication of the pilasters there are two major horizontal divisions; by implication of the projecting window heads below and window sills above, both of which may be read as lattice, a tripartite division of the facade is deduced. The overlapping and interlacing of these two systems and the fluctuations of significance to which each gives rise can pass without comment, for at Caprarola, as at Denver, it is apparent that the observer finds himself in the presence of an architectural tapestry whose warp and woof are immediately apparent to the eye, but whose invisible threads his organizing instinct mentally reconstructs.

Now if Caprarola as well as Denver shows phenomenal transparency, we are obliged to conclude that, after all, it is neither a new, nor even a post-Cubist manifestation; and perhaps if we were to trace back the evolution of literal transparency down the long route leading from the United Nations Building via such conspicuous monuments as the Bauhaus and the Crystal Palace, to the great glass and stone cages of the later Middle Ages, we might also discover in these buildings some evidence of phenomenal transparency in the nave of St. Denis (fig. 86), for instance, where the triforium rather than appearing as an independent unit will seem to be an intersection of the clerestory and the nave arcade, sometimes being subsumed within the first, and on other occasions presenting itself as a projection of the second.

Thus almost any medieval or quattrocento Venetian palace will reveal similar attributes to a greater or a lesser degree, and the organization, although not the asymmetry, of the Ca d'Oro (fig. 88) may be considered representative of the type. In the Ca d'Oro a basically bipartite facade is presented, where one center is determined by the loggias to the left, and the other by the cutting of three square windows through the plane of the wall surface to the right. Each of these two centers is invested with the control of sharply contrasted, clearly defined, and apparently symmetrical areas, which are isolated from each other by a thin, almost embroidered pilaster providing visual support for a heraldic trophy displayed on the second floor. But almost immediately after one recognizes this trophy, one proceeds to question it. It coordinates the space around itself and compels a symmetrical interpretation of the two windows between which it is placed, so that these windows are read together, and hence by means of this reading, the pilaster becomes, not the frontier between two opposed units, but the spine of an element straddling these units and demanding a revision of one's initial assumption as to the nature of each.

Once perceived, the uncertain valency of this pilaster quite undermines the primary response to the Ca d'Oro facade; and, as the element which it has now produced receives further attention, this becomes even more problematical. Since it is symmetrical on the second floor, one is predisposed to believe this element to be symmetrical on the first; and when discovered not to be the case, when the two windows flanking the pilasters on this floor are discovered to be unequal, then further figural variations are automatically sponsored. Now, an attribution of symmetry to any one unit of the facade is discovered to be unwarranted, and each of the two major units acquires the ability to enlarge itself by absorbing this third; so that while the right-hand and left-hand sections of the facade are constantly augmented and diminished, infinitely more subtle relationships are now constructed, and, activating these, one might notice the schema provided by the rhythm of the projecting balconies and also the elaborating frilling of the cornice which, as a kind of arpeggio to the facade, provides a system of notation serving to intensify the polyvalent activity of the wall below. By these and other means, horizontal and vertical, and L- and T-shaped configurations are finally precipitated within the intricate formal meshwork, so that first one element and then another comes to function as a kind of gear, the apprehension of which sets in motion whole systems of reversible mechanics.

The permutations inherent in a structure of this kind are identical with those which issue from less eccentric Venetian facades, and of these the sixteenth-century Palazzo Mocenigo (fig. 87) might be considered reasonably characteristic. Here, in a facade vertically divided into three, each division in itself is symmetrical, and the symmetry of each is reinforced in the center by triply repeated arches and in the sides by the elaborately mounted heraldic displays which are compressed between the windows of the *piano nobile*.[4] However, under sustained observation these apparently clear divisions of the facade begin to change. First, it is noticed that the central division enjoys the capacity to extend itself at the expense of the other two; and secondly, that the sides show a certain tendency to infiltrate, to slide in behind the outer bays of the central motif; while, following these initial realizations, the constituents of the facade enter into a successive series of relationships. At one stage the outer windows become isolated slots emphasizing the extremities of the wall; at another this same quality of slot is transferred to the central arched windows; and, presently, the heraldic trophies assume essential significance as the bonding element between these peripheric and central developments. At this stage the facade is dominated by a system of double H's; but, as its underlying structure becomes elucidated, this composition is displaced by a cruciform element which is implied by the plastic development of the principal floor and the association of the superimposed central arches. But the process of subtraction and addition continues, and as the upper and lower stages of the palace are now noticed to show a paneling of the wall, and as the *piano nobile* does not sustain the paneling, by this discontinuity of elements, another figure is raised into significance. Just as formerly the heraldic trophies effected a bridge between the center and extremities of the facade, now the central windows of the principal floor become the bridging element which integrates the two areas.

These different readings abstracted from the Palazzo Mocenigo by no means exhaust the possibility of still further ones; but they are in themselves a sufficient exposition of the functional multiplicity with which each and every part of the design is endowed. Substantially the building is of Venetian origin; but the presence of certain features obliges one to presume the possibility of other influences also; and thus, on the top floor, because some Michelangelesque origin might be suspected for the profiles of the window pediments, one might also believe that something of the explicit nature of the overlapping and interlocking of figures derives from the same source.

Certainly in both the model and drawings of Michelangelo's proposed facade for San Lorenzo (figs. 89 and 90) everything that the traditional Venetian nuances of the Palazzo Mocenigo might obscure becomes clarified and exposed; and for this reason San Lorenzo requires little introductory comment. A wall surface modeled in low relief is articulated by means of a skeletal organization of columns and pilasters, by suites of moldings, string courses, architraves, and a pediment.

So much is obvious; but it now becomes necessary to note the transpositions to which this skeletal organization proceeds to lend itself. Thus, to allow the eye to travel sideways across the design, four vertical elements—the coupled pilasters and columns—might be seen as contributing to the existence of a grid and as defining three larger spatial intervals (fig. 91a). But, almost immediately this information is then subjected to "correction." These three spatial intervals, while they can appear identical in width, are, in reality, far from being so. The central is distinctly narrower than the flanking ones; and as a result, and in collaboration with the central pediment, a subversion of the initial reading is instigated. The inner sets of pilasters and columns now disengage themselves from the outer. They cease to participate in the apparent and "neutral" grid. Instead they begin to appear as subservient to a hierarchical and centralized situation; and thus, in place of the quadripartite interpretation of the facade, there develops a tripartite division (fig. 91b).

Likewise, if the eye travels up and down this surface there is something comparable which happens. Here to be noted is an elementary contrast between a low and a high relief. Columns below turn into pilasters above, and, thereby, a basic horizontal division becomes enforced (fig. 91c). But this, again, becomes an interpretation which cannot be sustained. The areas of emphatically high and emphatically low relief are separated by a contested territory (Is it the attic to the one or the pedestal to the other?) which progressively insists upon its autonomy and which, accordingly, compels yet further revision (fig. 91d).

But so intimate and manifold are the interrelationships of figure inherent within this organization that seriously to insist upon any initial or dominant interpretation is to be quite arbitrary; and therefore, rather than try to impose a private version of the continuous oscillations of appearance which San Lorenzo provides, it might be more expedient simply to allude to some of the more notable figures which it displays. These include:

1. a fluctuating series of H-shaped figures, which are promoted by the intersections of the narrow bays and the "attic-pedestal" (fig. 91e).
2. a further H-shaped figure provided by the lateral banding of niches, plaques, and central aedicule—"window"—in the upper wall, and by the equivalent banding and gapping of doors and panels in the lower wall (fig. 91f).
3. an expanding series of cruciform figures which are derived from the intersection of the "attic-pedestal" and the central bay (fig. 91g).

4. a checkerboard reading which is created by three segmental pediments of the outer doors and of the upper "window" (fig. 91h).

5. an inverted checkerboard which overlaps the preceding one and which is derived from the two circular plaques with their connected niches (fig. 91i).

6. a T-shaped figure generated by the impact of the pediment above and the high relief development below which comprises some kind of reflection of the volume of the building lying behind and is presumably a residue of earlier studies (fig. 91j).

A quite random observation of San Lorenzo discloses the immanence of at least such configurations as these; but a more discriminating examination can discover more concealed and subtle modulations. The segmental pediments of the upper "window" and outer doors may again be noticed. These establish a triangle of interest; and, since the visual elements comprising this triangle are almost alike, there is a tendency to attribute to them a corresponding size. However, since one of these elements is smaller than the other two, there is a further tendency to assume it to be located at a greater distance from the eye; and thus, when seen in conjunction with the two doors below, the remarkable under-scaling of the central "window" (together with the under-structure of its immediate vicinity) introduces a curious tension between the readings of the horizontals and verticals in the wall plane. Providing an implication of depth, this under-scaling suggests that beyond this vertical plane and visible through it there lies a perspective recession or an inclined surface to which each of these three elements is attached (figs. 91k, 91l).

With this last and almost Cubist transparency which Michelangelo has introduced, specific analysis of San Lorenzo need not be carried further. It should be apparent that these phenomena which we have examined are of an order closely comparable to those which we might find in many modern paintings—for instance in the later paintings of Mondrian; and although to erect a parallel between a Michelangelo facade and a Mondrian painting may at first appear as frivolous as a comparison between Caprarola and the Mile High Center, almost any representative of Mondrian's Boogie Woogie series might justify such a parallel. Thus, whoever chooses to examine with any care the incomplete *Victory Boogie Woogie* of 1943–44 (fig. 92) will be obliged to extract from it a series of transparencies—of triangles, cross shapes, T's and U's which the composition may be said to spill over in a manner similar to San Lorenzo.[5]

Obviously dissimilar as regards their content and their more overt formal manifestations, both *Victory Boogie Woogie* and San Lorenzo are at least alike in defying any accurate description of what they are. In San Lorenzo a lucidly symmetrical, monochromatic composition is saturated with alternative readings. In *Victory Boogie Woogie* an asymmetrical composition derives qualities of excitement from color, congestion, and the symmetrical nature of its individual parts. The readings of San Lorenzo are for the most part explicit; those of *Victory Boogie Woogie* are less expressed. The fluctuations of Michelangelo's facade are sudden; those of Mondrian's painting are less violent. In *Victory Boogie Woogie* the different areas of white gradually *congeal* to provide the central cruciform figure; and this figure slowly *dissolves* before a further interpretation in which the vertical axis provides a dominant element. But in both painting and facade there might be noticed a tendency of the different elements to build, to coordinate themselves, to amalgamate by means of proximity or common contour into larger configurations. Thus in *Victory Boogie Woogie*, while areas of red and areas of blue distributed throughout the canvas offer two alternative constellations, adjacent reds and blues show a tendency to withdraw from these systems and to unite into a series of larger wholes. In San Lorenzo these same propensities may be noticed. There, where a constellation of rectangular areas and columns and a rival constellation of circular and quasi-circular elements are to be found, coalitions are constantly formed between the contiguous representatives of each system.

Again the facade and painting both show a disposition of frontally aligned objects which are arranged within a lightly compressed space; both show these objects functioning as a series of relief layers for the further articulation of this space; and both show a framework syncopated by a staccato punctuation—in the one case of conventional architectural elements, in the other of small colored squares. In Michelangelo's design the wall plane which provides the mount, i.e., the "negative" background upon which these individual elements are displayed, has the ability to assume an opposite role, i.e., to become in itself a "positive" element or a series of "positive" elements; and in Mondrian's picture one is conscious of the white areas behaving in the same manner. Thus in any primary interpretation of *Victory Boogie Woogie* the white rectangles will appear to designate a basic ground, a rear surface which supports the yellows, reds, blues, and grays; but, like Michelangelo's wall, Mondrian's white plane can cease to be recessive and, by exerting a pressure on the figures which initially it appeared to subsume, it can become as highly charged an element or series of elements as they.

By not permitting the eye to penetrate any far removed space, this rear plane prohibits a resolution of *either* composition in depth, and thus in each case its presence may be said to disturb the possibilities of central locus. In each case by investing the space of canvas and facade with a lateral structure, this plane functions as a generator of peripheric emphasis and replaces any one focal point by a series of differentiated episodes. By these means it acquires an overall surface tension, becoming a kind of tightly stretched membrane which acts upon the different elements it supports and in turn is reacted upon by them. Imbued by these elements with tautness, it presses them further forward; and thus, by reason of the spatial constriction which it creates, this rear plane serves both as the catalyst and as the neutralizer of the successive figures which the observer experiences.

Comparisons, parallels, and analyses such as these could be prolonged almost indefinitely, but possibly enough has been said to indicate the constancy of the manifestation which in contemporary works Moholy-Nagy and Képes have recognized as transparency.[6] In all instances their transparency—our phenomenal transparency—has taken place within a highly abstracted and intellectualized work of art; and in every case it has been the product of the most undeviating regard for formal structure, of the most remorseless and sophisticated visual logic. So much for the general context in which phenomenal transparency seems to appear; but for Moholy-Nagy the transparency of meanings to which he responds in the writings of James Joyce is a method of building up a rich and manifold completeness. It is the literary analogue of the transparency revealed by Cubism—and this transparency, whether literal or phenomenal, is conceived by him to be a kind of symbol of space-time, which is mystically validated by the discoveries of science, and which, as unique means of achieving cultural integration, is assumed to be inherent to the whole ethos of the twentieth century. But, if there is any substance to the preceding investigations, then transparency is not the exclusively post-Cubist development which he supposed; it is independent of either modern physics or Minkowski; it is not characteristic of the twentieth century alone; and it has no necessary correlation with any impending integration of culture. In fact, almost the reverse could be claimed; and San Lorenzo, the Palazzo Mocenigo, Caprarola, at least, could be presented as the evidences of a Mannerist malaise, as the illustrations of "a self-conscious dissenting, frustrated style," as the indices to "a period of tormenting doubt, and rigorous enforcement of no longer self-understood dogma," as the external effects of mental disquiet, disequilibrium, schism.[7]

Now, that these two widely separated interpretations of closely related phenomena—the one insisting on the virtues, the other on the dubieties, of phenomenal transparency—should exist side by side without any public embarrassment need not be hard to understand. In the first case, the mental block of so many modern architects against history is notorious; and, in the second, the unwillingness of so many art historians to enter into serious criticism of contemporary achievement is one of the more patent limitations of that species. But if we can allow that in all the instances discussed, the method of raising fluctuating figures into ambiguous prominence is a common denominator which all share, then it becomes a matter of some urgency to know how, in the face of two such radically different evaluations of this common denominator, any justice can possibly be done to it.

One may of course propose that a common method of organization does not necessarily predicate an identity of psychic content; that the pursuit of phenomenal transparency may be sane, creative, and responsible (a received idea of modern architecture); or that it may be deranged, capricious, and delinquent (a received idea of Mannerism); but, if this proposition is unacceptable, then we are faced with a serious critical dilemma.

The temptation is to escape it; and several attractive routes of escape do suggest themselves. Thus, we might, for instance:

1. choose to deny the existence of phenomenal transparency as a visual manifestation;
2. stigmatize the perception of phenomenal transparency as a product of hyper-aesthetic sensitivity, or assert that its pursuit is no more than a formalistic sidetrack of contemporary painting and architecture;
3. attribute a proto-modernity to Michelangelo, Vignola, and the rest, or suggest that the contemporary architect who uses phenomenal transparency is Mannerist in spite of himself.

Escape route 1 is a congested road. Escape route 2 is a kind of spiritual *autobahn* which permits its travelers the pleasing illusion that in some sequestered *cul-de-sac* Picasso, Braque, Gris, Léger, Mondrian, and Le Corbusier are all involved together in some esoterically purposeless rite. Escape route 3 drags us on a sinuous detour through a linguistically picturesque terrain. The use of the first we might condemn as irresponsible and myopic; the use of the second we might dismiss as philistine; while of the third we might say it is of no use. It is a kind of conquest of the problem by definition, that is, no conquest at all, for if we are at the liberty to attribute a proto-modernity—or a deutero-Mannerism—to all and sundry, then we make nonsense of the notion of modernity and whimsically subvert the categories of history. With all these escape routes ultimately closed, the problem therefore remains unilluminated, unsolved—at least in its wider implications. However, in its narrowest implications the mere *existence of the problem* at least suggests that phenomenal transparency does have a basis in common vision, and does imply, on our part, some kind of archetypal response toward it.

In considering phenomenal transparency in this way, entirely at a perceptual level, it has not been possible to overlook gestalt psychology, since the gestalt psychologists, in their analysis of perception, seem to have been preoccupied with just those questions which are central to any examination of the problem. "Configuration," "figure-ground," "field," "common contour," "proximity," "constellation"—sometimes inadvertently and sometimes consciously our vocabulary has been saturated with the gestalt phraseology, precisely because of the adequacy of its terms. Quite briefly, the Algerian Skyscraper, the Denver building, Caprarola, the nave of St. Denis, the Ca d'Oro, the Palazzo Mocenigo, San Lorenzo, *Victory Boogie Woogie* look like some elaborate orchestrations of the rather curious little diagrams which are to be found so profusely scattered through any treatise on gestalt;[8] and, if in the presence of these diagrams we can overcome our primary amusement at what seems to be a discrepancy between a highly intellectual psychology of perception and its highly ingenuous visual examples, we might recognize these as exhibiting, in the most primitive form, the crucial circumstances which permit the development of the more complicated structures we have examined.

Thus, if we are not deterred by the combination of art nouveau and believe-it-or-not characteristics displayed by figure 94, it might be accepted as a representation of a basic figural ambiguity which has been consistently encountered. "Normally one sees a plain vase; it is only after a period of fixation that the profiles of two figures spring forth. What was once ground becomes figure and vice versa."[9] Similarly in figure 93 identical conditions are induced. One sees a black Maltese cross imposed upon a white octagon; but, by reason of the spatial quality of the eight constituent triangles, one's experience of this diagram inevitably reverses itself.

The possibilities of such "transfiguration" are illustrated with rather more subtlety and perhaps with rather more direct architectural relevance in figure 95. In figure 95 a group of rectangles is presented but "the figure may also be seen as two H's with certain intervening lines." These H's exist, but it is an effort to see them; and figure 95 in fact was set up by the gestaltists to prove precisely this—that in spite of the existence of the H's, "despite our extensive past experience of the letter H, it is nevertheless, the articulation of the presented object (i.e., the rectangles) which determines what we shall see.[10]

But with certain minor modifications of figure 95 the co-existence of the H's and the rectangles can become quite explicit, so that in part A of figure 95, we are conscious of both. In part A of figure 95, by tripping off the top and bottom closures of the rectangles, the H-figures become completely exposed, but the rectangles themselves survive as unavoidable inferences which the observer constructs by reason of identical length, proximity, and similarity of their ingredient elements. Preoccupation with the rectangles in part A of figure 95 leads to a fixation upon the four lines which constitute their horizontal axis; and, because of their identity of direction, ultimately these are seen as the visible parts of one continuous line which is presumed to pass behind a solid matter whose area concurs with that of the three rectangles. Thus, by reason of the breaking of this line, not only is an implication of depth introduced into a two-dimensional surface, but also the presumption as to the existence of the rectangles receives confirmation.

In part B of figure 95, a further modification of the same figure, all these activities become rather more manifest. In this diagram the behavior of the horizontal lines becomes much clearer. The observer is either disposed to see four horizontal lines each of which functions as the crossbar of an H and is therefore led to complete two further H figures; or, alternatively, he is led to see one interrupted horizontal line which appears as a split running through the middle of a background plane; but, in each case, through an automatic interpretation of the presented object, he is led to provide it with a ground or to frame it within a field. Inside this field H's simultaneously function as the disengaging elements between dominant rectangles and also as the dominant figures themselves; while, as the observer's sensitiveness to the organization increases, it becomes apparent that minor rectangles must also be built up and that further H-shaped figures with double vertical members must be accepted (part C of figure 95). It is not necessary to say more in order to demonstrate the applicability of this last diagram to the facade of San Lorenzo or to that of the Algiers Skyscraper; it is equally evident that the kind of perceptual activity which this diagram involves is of the same order as that which is exercised at a much higher level, with longer periods of fixation, in a painting by Léger or Mondrian; and in all these cases the figure-ground phenomenon which is exemplified may be said to be the essential prerequisite of transparency.

According to gestalt, while figure is generally seen as figure by reason of its greater closure compactness, density, internal articulation, and while ground is generally seen as ground by reason of its lack of these qualities, in the figure-ground relationship the ground, although it may at first appear anonymous, is neither subservient nor passive. As an environment imposing a common relationship on all that happens, it is also an enclosure containing figures which it lifts into prominence; and these, by reason of the prominence with which they become endowed, react upon the ground and provide it in turn with a figural significance. There is thus in figure-ground a double function inherent to each of the components. Each can be itself and its opposite; so that any specific instance of figure-ground is a condition of being of which the components are at once the product and the cause, a structure which becomes significant by reason of reciprocal action between the whole and its parts, and—one might say— an area of reference, qualified by and at the same time qualifying the objects which are referred to it.

In complicated examples of figure-ground such as those we have examined, the ground obviously contains several figures, and these in themselves also function as subsidiary grounds supporting further configurations. Gestalt maintains that the observer organizes these discrete visual stimuli according to certain laws, which are stated as factors, of proximity, similarity, direction, closure, experience, "good curve," "good gestalt," "common fate," "objective set," and the untranslatable "prägnanz."[11] "Gestalt theory," it is stated, "does not hold that the senses carry amorphous material on which order is imposed by a receiving mind," but attributes powers of discrimination to the senses, refusing "to reserve the capacity of synthesis to the higher faculties of the human mind," and emphasizing instead "the formative powers . . ." "the intelligence of the peripheral sensory processes."[12] In other words gestalt conceives the act of perception not as a simple Stimulus-Response reaction but as a process which might be characterized as follows: *"Constellation of Stimuli–Organization–Reaction to Results of Organization."*[13] Further, gestalt supposes that mental activity and organic behavior are subject to the same laws, "that 'good shape'" is a quality of nature in general, inorganic as well as organic," so that "the processes of organization active in perception somehow do justice to the organization outside in the physical world."[14]

But supposing the senses are endowed with "intelligence," with powers of discrimination, with organizing capacity; and supposing physical and psychical processes to be governed by the same rule. In themselves these hypotheses really seem to have very little to do with what appears to be the inordinate gestalt interest in phenomenal transparency, which it recognizes under a variety of names as "phenomenal identity," "double representation," "duo formation."[15] One is apt at first to consider this interest to be no more than a reflection of an intellectual style which has characterized the first half of the twentieth century, to regard it for instance as parallel to the critical literary interest in ambiguity disclosed by such studies as William Empson's *Seven Types of Ambiguity,* to the art historical interest suggested by the reinterpretation of the sixteenth century, to the artistic interest implied by analytical cubism and so much of modern architecture. But although the preliminary gestalt researches into figural ambiguities do date from the years during which analytical cubism made of phenomenal transparency a principal method of composition, it must be recognized that something of the gestalt "taste" for figural ambiguities is related to its emphasis upon field.

For gestalt the existence of a field is a prerequisite of all perceptual experience. Consciousness of field, it is assumed, must precede consciousness of a figure; and figure in itself is inconceivable in isolation. In this article attention has been directed toward visual fields alone, and gestalt does seem to have favored visual illustration of field; but obviously field as such must vary with the nature of the objects and/or perceptions involved. For instance, in the case of our apprehension of a tree the field may be provided by a mountain, or a lake, or the wall of a house, or any number of things; in the case of our apprehension of a poetic metaphor–n itself a field–the larger field may become a sonnet; in history a given epoch may endow with "field properties" the idiosyncrasies of the various figures which it supports. But in all these cases the field is assumed to be more than the sum total of the elements which it embraces. Genetically it is prior to them. It is the condition of their quality and the reason for their behavior.

It may now become possible to see that the gestalt interest in ambiguity is not merely arbitrary. The unstable, equivocal figure-ground phenomenon, whose fluctuations may be either sluggish or volatile, brings the supporting matrix, the field, into high prominence. Figure-ground is figure-field keyed up to a pitch of maximum contrast. It is field revealed as positive; and thus for gestalt it is the ultimate summary, the classic condensation of the field idea.

[1] György Képes, *Language of Vision* (Chicago: Paul Theobold and Company, 1944), 77.

[2] "Intervention of the plastic sensibilities. All seemed to be implaca-bly controlled by the succession of rational requirements . . . . The plan was rigorously symmetric. But by a further tracing of the Golden mean the posture of the facade becomes asymmetric. The form seems to swell to the left then shift to the right. It is responding to the double call of the site. The cliff, the sea." Le Corbusier and Francis de Pierrefeu, *The Home of Man* (London: Architectural Press, 1948). It is in these terms that Le Corbusier describes the fluctuating figures which the Algiers Skyscraper provides.

[3] György Képes, *Language of Vision.*, 77.

[4] It is interesting to notice that the facade of the Palazzo Mocenigo (a refacing of an older medieval structure), although symmetrical in all its parts, is not in itself symmetrical.

[5] The diamond is a result of a rotated square whose diagonals, formerly tending to be read as vectors inducing recessional perspective, now become an ideal right-angle armature stiffening that plane and investing the points, rather than the edges, with the capacity to act as terminals to the scanning eye. In this performance, a "gravity-free" buoyant and thoroughly frontalized plane is established, exerting pressure from behind to any chromatic figuration placed upon it.

[6] László Moholy-Nagy, *Vision in Motion* (Chicago: Paul Theobold and Company, 1947), 350. György Képes, *Language of Vision*, 77.

[7] For these quotations see Nikolaus Pevsner, "The Architecture of Mannerism" in *The Mint* (London: Routledge and Kegan Paul, 1946), 132 and 136. They may be regarded as reasonably representative of a received idea.

[8] K. Koffka, *Principles of Gestalt Psychology* (London: Routledge and Kegan Paul, 1935). W. Köhler, *Gestalt Psychology* (New York: H. Leveright, 1929). G. Hartmann, *Gestalt Psychology* (New York: The Ronald Press Company, 1935). W. D. Ellis, *A Source Book of Gestalt Psychology* (New York: Harcourt, Brace, 1938).

[9] Hartmann, *Gestalt Psychology*, 25.

[10] Ellis, *A Source Book of Gestalt Psychology*, 58.

[11] See Wertheimer, *Laws of Organization in Perceptual Forms*, in Ellis, *A Source Book of Gestalt Psychology*, 71.

[12] R. Arnheim, *Gestalt and Art, Journal of Aesthetics and Art Criticism* 11, no. 8 (1943): 71.

[13] Hartmann, *Gestalt Psychology*, 100.

[14] Arnheim, *Gestalt and Art*, 73.

[15] "Phenomenal identity": Ellis, *A Source Book of Gestalt Psychology*, 147; "double representation": Koffka, *Principles of Gestalt Psychology*, 178; "duo formation": Koffka, 178.

Oppositions 13 (1978)

OPAQUE TRANSPARENCY

Rosemarie Haag Bletter

In 1963 Colin Rowe and Robert Slutzky published the first of their essays, "Transparency: Literal and Phenomenal," in *Perspecta* 8, the Yale architectural journal. The same essay appeared in German in 1968 under the title "Transparenz" as the first number of Le Corbusier studies published by the Institut für Geschichte und Theorie der Architektur of the Eidgenössische Technische Hochschule, Zurich. This version contains, aside from an extensive commentary by Bernhard Hoesli, footnotes which reproduce sections in English that had been deleted from the original manuscript for the *Perspecta* article. The *Perspecta* version of this essay was, finally, published a third time in 1976 as part of Colin Rowe's collected essays, *The Mathematics of the Ideal Villa*. The second part of "Transparency" appeared in *Perspecta* 13/14 in 1971, eight years after the publication of the first essay. Part II was not republished anywhere, however, not even in Rowe's collected essays. Why part II presented a less forceful statement than part I will be considered below, but the more important concern here is to discuss the interesting and influential attempt in part I to redefine the language of architectural criticism, particularly criticism of Le Corbusier's works.

All three versions of part I are textually identical, with only inconsequential additions to the illustrations in the later publications. (The footnotes of the Swiss pamphlet resurrecting deleted portions of the English manuscript would be of interest if we were dealing with the genesis of Rowe and Slutzky's particular position, but since these cuts were never used in the English-language versions of "Transparency" and since they appear as English footnotes to the German text, their general import to the overall argument is negligible.)

The object of this review is to question not all the conclusions of "Transparency" but the specific methodology used by the two authors. Briefly, Rowe and Slutzky find Sigfried Giedion's association of the kind of transparency that occurs in the Bauhaus buildings at Dessau with the "transparency of overlapping planes" in analytic Cubism (from *Space, Time, and Architecture*) unconvincing. To refine Giedion's use of the term, they turn to György Képes's definition of an apparent transparency as one which offers "a simultaneous perception of different spatial locations" (*Language of Vision*). Then using both Giedion and Képes, they assume two forms of transparency to exist: the one described by Giedion is called "literal" (actual) and the one alluded to by Képes becomes "phenomenal" (illusionistic) transparency. These two varying concepts of transparency are then buttressed by comparisons among a number of paintings. Typically, a Constructivist work by Moholy-Nagy (fig. 67) exhibiting literal transparency is contrasted with a Cubist painting by Léger (fig. 68) in which the ambiguous, spatially fluctuating form of phenomenal transparency can be discerned. And, by extension, a similar differentiation is drawn between the Constructivist-influenced Bauhaus and Le Corbusier's Villa Stein at Garches, which owes something to Cubist spatial perception.

The question that must be raised is the following: Does such a categorization into two concepts of transparency become a useful critical instrument, as the authors claim? Are these categories universal enough to tell us more than the obvious, that the architecture of Gropius is different from that of Le Corbusier? Can the notion of literal and phenomenal transparency be applied to modern architecture in general, as Giedion had clearly intended with his terminology?

Since the classification used by Rowe and Slutzky is established by means of painting first, it is necessary to start with an examination of their argument in this area. On the surface a grouping of Gropius with Constructivism and of Le Corbusier with Cubism makes sense. But a comparison between a painting by Moholy-Nagy and one by Léger would seem to be loaded in favor of Cubism from the start—Moholy-Nagy's strength was as a conceptual artist, not as a painter. In general, the authors seemed to find the gridded, shallow space associated with phenomenal transparency more interesting than the static, two-dimensional space used to convey literal transparency. This is probably so because of the obvious architectonic qualities of phenomenal transparency—their claim at the end of the essay that no value judgments are implied by such categories to the contrary. Whenever the two classes of transparency are contrasted, literal transparency is treated, however inadvertently, in a rather negative tone. Writing about Moholy-Nagy and Gropius, the authors tell us that "Both . . . received a certain stimulus from the experiments of De Stijl and the Russian Constructivists; but both were apparently unwilling to accept certain more Parisian conclusions." "Unwilling to accept" sounds like an artistic deficiency when in fact Constructivist and De Stijl artistic intentions were quite different, and could not possibly have been explored together with Cubist spatial solutions. The comparisons are, then, not entirely fair because other styles are merely used as a foil for Cubism, while their own unique and positive aspects are not brought out. In a similar vein, Rowe and Slutzky write that "a glance at any representative work of Kandinsky, Malevich, El Lissitzky, or Van Doesburg will reveal that these painters, like Moholy-Nagy, scarcely felt the necessity of providing any distinct spatial matrix for their principal objects. They are apt to accept a simplification of the Cubist image as a composition of geometrical planes, but are apt to reject the comparable Cubist abstraction of space; and . . . for these reasons their pictures offer us figures which float in an infinite, atmospheric, naturalistic void, without any of the rich Parisian stratification of volume." Again, the reader is informed only in what way these artists do and do not adhere to Cubism. Such a Francophile analysis clearly prevents the creation of any objective system of classification.

For instance, the work chosen by Moholy-Nagy (his *La Sarraz* of 1930) exhibits literal transparency, to be sure, but it is not altogether characteristic of his *oeuvre*. If his *Large Railway Painting* (1920), *AXI* (1923), or a large number of his photograms of the 1920s had been used, his work would have had to be grouped with that of Léger. The same is true of the work of Kandinsky and Malevich: no tight grouping with literal transparency is possible. Be that as it may, even if we grant that Moholy-Nagy's *La Sarraz* is representative of his work, there are other aspects of the Cubist/Constructivist comparison that do not ring true. This is the authors' categorization of the spatial qualities of Constructivist works as naturalistic and of Cubist works as abstract. Diagonals, as they are used in Moholy-Nagy's and many Constructivist paintings, are assumed to be vestigial referents to a naturalistic, spatial recession: "Generally speaking, the oblique and curved lines possess a certain naturalistic significance, while the rectilinear ones show a geometrizing tendency which serves as a reassertion of the picture plane." Perhaps diagonal lines in Futurist works retain this vestige of naturalism—the Futurists called them "lines of force"—and they represented, therefore, actual movement through an illusionistic space. In Suprematist and Constructivist painting, however, the mechanistic Futurist conception of the diagonal became transformed to stand for far more abstract ideas, spiritual and revolutionary force, respectively. Thus, diagonals in Constructivism cannot be seen as reference points to specific loci in space. In fact, they reassert the picture plane more consistently than do Cubist works.

Other aspects of Constructivist painting are similarly interpreted by Rowe and Slutzky as naturalistic. Literal transparency is associated with "the *trompe l'oeil* effect of a translucent object in a deep, naturalistic space . . ." and the absolutely undefined background of Moholy-Nagy's *La Sarraz* is said to fling open "a window onto some private version of outer space. . . ." While it is true that Kandinsky, Malevich, and De Stijl artists were interested in portraying a cosmic, universal space, this never took the form of anything so literal as "outer space," not even in Moholy-Nagy's second-generation Constructivist works. Ironically, of all of the major early-twentieth-century movements, it is only in Cubism that palpable, naturalistic forms such as glasses, bottles, knives, cigarettes, newspapers, etc., are still discernable no matter how fragmented their portrayal. To refer to Cubism as abstract and to Constructivism as naturalistic, then, is a somewhat arbitrary classification which does not inspire a great deal of confidence. Without ever clarifying this point sufficiently, the two authors seem to prefer in Cubist painting precisely the suggestion of a naturalistic space, its layers of grids which exist in a shallow space. This adherence to structured form within a spatial matrix in Cubism would be of interest to an architectonic conception, but Constructivism's near-total abstraction is not so easily applicable to built form.

Their particular and rather unorthodox interpretation of Cubism and Constructivism really makes sense only if it is restricted to a purely *formal* analysis. The Cubist works given by Rowe and Slutzky as examples of phenomenal transparency are ones in which conventional notions of "in front of" and "behind" are depicted ambiguously through the deformation of objects and surrounding space into a shallow, oscillating zone. It is probably this confusion of object and its matrix which leads them to see these works as abstract. In the Constructivist paintings cited, the coherent representation of abstract objects against a background is seen as naturalistic because, even though the content of such works is entirely abstract, the naturalistic convention of "in front of" and "behind" is employed. Again, as was stated earlier, even such a formalistic interpretation of their categories does not manage to encompass Cubist and Constructivist painting in general. In any case, the completely formal and perceptual basis of their system of classification is not stated clearly enough at the outset of their argument, leading to much unnecessary confusion.

Phenomenal and literary transparency are categories that are not style-specific and they are, therefore, poor organizing tools in a discussion that attempts to contrast Cubism and Constructivism. And if these concepts rest on such a shaky foundation in painting, is it then meaningful to transfer them to architecture?

Rowe and Slutzky's main comparison between Le Corbusier's Villa Stein at Garches (figs. 71 and 72) and Gropius's Bauhaus (figs. 70 and 73) without any doubt does give us a new awareness of Le Corbusier's spatially complex architecture. But here also (as with painting, because the critical categories are limited) the comparison is turned into a procedure that resembles a contrasting of apples and oranges where we are told that an apple is better than an orange. The Bauhaus becomes a foil for the villa at Garches in the same way that Moholy-Nagy's painting functioned as a foil for Léger's. Rowe and Slutzky in their concluding statement say that "It is not intended to suggest that phenomenal transparency (for all its Cubist descent) is a necessary constituent of modern architecture, nor that its presence might be used like a piece of litmus paper for the test of architectural orthodoxy." Nevertheless, in the actual comparison the absence of phenomenal transparency is treated as a default: "Relying on the diagonal viewpoint, Gropius has exteriorized the opposed movements of his space, has allowed them to flow away into infinity; and by being unwilling to attribute to either of them any significant difference of quality, he has prohibited the possibilities of a potential ambiguity." The Bauhaus's association with Constructivist principles rests precisely in its unfocused massing, which gives this group of buildings an anti-monumental abstract aspect having no conventional "facades." As regards phenomenal transparency at the garden facade of the Villa Stein, it can only be fully appreciated if the observer is centered in front of the facade, i.e., at Garches if he stands in the garden at some distance from the house. Because phenomenal transparency is seen by the authors as a formal problem of perception and as an extension of Cubism, the naturalistic background such an approach requires is not brought out: the garden facade at Garches functions like a pre-Cubist picture plane which presumes a fixed, frontal point of view. Where the point of view in a Cubist painting hardly matters because the shallow space is all projected onto a flat plane, similar devices in architecture, no matter how shallow the space, become occluded with a shifting point of view because of the effects of parallax. Thus, the frontal approach Le Corbusier prefers is in many ways still tied to Renaissance rather than Cubist spatial perception, and may derive directly from his interest in Beaux Arts planning, especially the use of the highly directional *enfilade*. An examination of Le Corbusier's work in terms of phenomenal transparency, then, gives us useful insights about some aspects of his working procedure, but this perceptual system of analysis does not allow us to see the full richness of his *oeuvre* (for instance, that together with some obvious Cubist notions of spatial organization much more traditional Beaux Arts ones could be retained as well). The differences between Cubist painting and Le Corbusier's architecture are hardly examined, and the Constructivist/naturalistic Cubist/abstract categories, though wrong to begin with, can now be shown to be not very meaningful in any case. For, even if we assume Cubist space to be abstract, Le Corbusier applies Cubist principles within a naturalist context.

The point of this analysis, it must be emphasized, is not to show that Gropius was dealt with unfairly—few would question today Le Corbusier's superior status—but to show that the two classifications of transparency have yielded useful critical results only for some aspects of Le Corbusier's work. Further questions that are raised by the methodology of Rowe and Slutzky are these: Does phenomenal transparency characterize most of Le Corbusier's works of the 1920s? Would a comparison between literal and phenomenal transparency have seemed as interesting if Le Corbusier's street facade at Garches had been contrasted with the work of a somewhat stronger architect than Gropius, say, of Mies? In any case, the inclusion of Constructivism in Rowe and Slutzky's analysis does not add very much to the discussion. A more detailed critique of Le Corbusier might have yielded more lucid results. The concepts of phenomenal and literal transparency are at once too general and too circumscribed to be useful in the categorization of anything. And though they claim in their summary that the essay is to "give a characterization of species," they never make entirely clear what sort of species we end up with when architecture is divided Last Judgment-style into the blessed (phenomenal transparency) and the damned (literal transparency).

The answer to several puzzling aspects of "Transparency: Literal and Phenomenal," can be found in part II, which was published in *Perspecta* in 1971. This appeared too late to have been included in the Swiss publication, but it was also not included in Rowe's collected essays of 1976. Did he regard it as a weak link in the argument? Whatever the reasons for the exclusion, part II is, nevertheless, important in understanding Rowe and Slutzky's method. It exposes the specific attitudes that determined their basic definitions in the first essay.

Here the reader is told that "it would surely be possible to sustain a classification of modern architecture according to the absence or presence of (literal and phenomenal transparency), but to do so would involve unnecessarily tedious analysis." This then is an admission that the two forms of transparency are quite universal. While in part I phenomenal transparency was primarily paired with Cubism, there is in part II finally an awareness that there is nothing uniquely Cubist about it. The authors have discovered its presence in Gothic and Mannerist architecture as well. There follows a lengthy analysis of Michelangelo's proposed facade for San Lorenzo (figs. 89 and 90). Without explanation, though, the definition of phenomenal transparency of part I (a gridded space within a shallow *three*-dimensional zone which is perceived in fluctuating, ambiguous patterns) is shifted slightly to refer to ambiguous readings within an essentially *two*-dimensional space. The facades of the Villa Farnese and San Lorenzo do indeed elicit ambiguous readings (figs. 85 and 91), but they are not developed in depth. Thus the original definition of phenomenal transparency taken from György Képes (a simultaneous perception of different spatial locations) no longer has the full implications it did at Garches.

Finally, toward the end of this second essay, Gestalt psychology is invoked as an explanation both of the authors' analytical procedure and of phenomenal transparency. Since this interest in Gestalt psychology elucidates their emphasis on perceptual, formal organization in painting and architecture, it might have been of greater service at the beginning of the first essay. To explain the notion of phenomenal transparency, the authors point to some of the better-known Gestalt figures in which an ambiguous figure-ground relationship produces two separate readings (for instance, the vase which can also be interpreted as two facing profiles). The authors mistakenly conclude from such examples that ambiguity is a basic ingredient of perception, that ambiguous perception is, in effect, archetypal. Not only is this a misconception of Gestalt psychology, but if phenomenal transparency were indeed archetypal, it could then not also be used as a category in the classification of very particular architectural species. If the argument against the general usefulness of literal and phenomenal transparency is not yet convincing, the claim by the authors that ambiguous perception is archetypal would seem to be the final act of hara-kiri.

But to come back to Rowe and Slutzky's faulty understanding of Gestalt psychology: Gestalt psychology does not at all deal with ambiguous perception *per se*, as is implied in their essay. Gestalt psychology (not to be confused with the more recent Gestalt therapy) is a branch of normal psychology and as such covers the study of ordinary perception. The example of the vase/profiles figure cited by Rowe and Slutzky as an instance of ambiguous vision does not show anything of the kind (fig. 94). On the contrary, this figure, and others like it, is used by Gestalt psychologists to show precisely the opposite: that the mind attempts to maintain a coherent image at all costs. For the vase/profiles are not seen simultaneously: the mind takes in either one or the other. Even after both images are comprehended, their perception is sequential, not simultaneous. Gestalt psychology, therefore, cannot be called upon to explain ambiguities in Le Corbusier's architecture.

To make this point clearer, other figures can be used to show that the mind in its normal state tends to choose the most economical, efficient, and rational explanations.

For example, note the square with a missing corner (fig. 96). Since our language does not possess a word for such a figure, to make sense of it a mental comparison is made with similar known figures, i.e., squares. To justify calling this a square, however, the "missing corner" must be filled in. Hence, though no square is really shown, the near-universal description of this figure is that it is a "square with a corner missing." We might call this procedure an act of mental comprehension. Gestalt psychology is further concerned with how the mind organizes and retains complex images. Let us take, for instance, the figure of a hexagram (fig. 97). Though a comparatively simple image, it can in reality be drawn in a great number of different sequences. That most people choose to draw it as two superimposed triangles illustrates that the mind tends to rely on the most economical forms in the selection of efficient mnemonic ideograms. Gestalt psychology, rather than being concerned with ambiguous images, deals with the mental ordering of perceptions which may or may not be ambiguous. The mind also selects from a chaotic visual field those groupings which make the most sense, which are meaningful. Thus the seeing of randomly organized images depends to some extent on one's experience if meaningful associations are to be made. Perception is, thus, not the completely sensory act Rowe and Slutzky claim it to be. The senses and the mind constantly interact to understand the millions of stimuli the eyes receive. Rowe and Slutzky write that the images are organized, among other things, according to what they call the "untranslatable 'prägnanz'" (sic). "Prägnanz" is in fact translatable and means "significance" or, literally, the state of being pregnant as in "pregnant with meaning." The eye does perform on the sensory level a certain amount of organization, but such organization depends on what psychologists see as a kind of field perception—no meaning derives from this sort of seeing. Significant seeing can only occur when there is an interaction between immediate sensory experience and long-range cognitive experience.

The authors finally propose that a natural affinity between Gestalt principles and Cubist perception exists because both are inventions of the early twentieth century. There are obviously certain cultural links between Gestalt psychology and Cubism, but to propose Gestalt notions as a critical tool particularly for that style is not entirely convincing. This is like saying that nineteenth-century naturalism should be analyzed in terms of material-istic theory. Our methods of critical analysis can and even ought to be outside that of the system examined.

Be that as it may, no ideological or formal relationship exists between Cubism and Gestalt psychology. To wit, Gestalt psychology, which had its beginnings in Germany, could be more readily linked with Gropius and Moholy-Nagy (in fact, Gestalt psychology was taught at the Bauhaus). Rowe and Slutzky's curious application of Gestalt ideas is then carried to a strange literal conclusion by Bernhard Hoesli in his commentary on "Transparenz" in the Swiss publication of this essay. Hoesli proposes exercises for students of architecture that incorporate phenomenal transparency. It had been comforting for some to believe that good architecture might result from the application of the golden section, or the Modulor: Hoesli uses phenomenal transparency as yet another recipe.

Phenomenal transparency is, then, quite useful in helping us comprehend some works of Le Corbusier, but the overall analysis of Rowe and Slutzky is too erratic to make for workable categories of architectural examination. While we may not agree with Giedion's definitions of modern architecture, literal and phenomenal transparency in no way provide us with a new general definition.

OUBLIER ROWE

Robert E. Somol

The smallest qualifiers find their way into the slightest interstices of meaning; clauses and chapters wind into spirals; a magisterial art of decentering allows the opening of new spaces (spaces of power and of discourse) which are immediately covered up by the meticulous outpouring of Foucault's writing. . . . Foucault's discourse is no truer than any other. No, its strength and seduction are in the analysis which unwinds the subtle meanderings of its object, describing it with a tactile and tactical exactness, where seduction feeds analytical force and where language itself gives birth to the operation of new powers. . . . Foucault's therefore is not a discourse of the truth but a mythic discourse in the strong sense of the word, and I secretly believe that it has no illusions about the effect of truth it produces. That, by the way, is what is missing in those who follow in Foucault's footsteps and pass right by this mythic arrangement to end up with the truth, nothing but the truth.

Jean Baudrillard, *Forget Foucault*

I. CASES AND CONTROVERSIES

Almost fifty years after the publication of "The Mathematics of the Ideal Villa," an old and forever premature question returns: What does one make of Colin Rowe and the reception to which his work has become subject? This issue becomes more complicated because to cite Rowe is already to invoke both more and less than a specific subject; it is to confront a form of discursivity. Ultimately, this Rowe effect constitutes the very possibility of discussing architecture today, or at least architecture as a particular kind of signifying regime. Recalling the initial impasse—while remaining necessarily within the terms of its forms as well as those established by the previous contents of this publication—one must ask, is the event of this issue an act of memory or prophecy? Indeed, it has been precisely around these two poles that *ANY* has previously organized its themes: while the second issue (on Seaside) was a debate between these ostensible obstacles, and the third (on James Stirling) was a memorial, the remaining numbers have explicitly configured themselves as manifestos (on writing, electrotecture, the feminine, and lightness). While it may be fortuitous that this issue organized around Rowe falls between numbers on Tadao Ando and Rem Koolhaas—and thereby between certain contemporary versions of tradition and utopia—this does not completely relieve the tension and sense of disquiet.

Given the fact that Rowe's voice has been directly associated with the two "memorial" issues, and that his discourse has been apparently captured by what could be called the camp of retrospection (but which often goes by the ironic name of the new urbanism), it is initially hard to imagine how Rowe could escape the fate of being remembered. Moreover, this fate seems absolutely guaranteed by the fact that, at first glance, the prophetic or prescriptive manifestos of *ANY* represent a systematic dismantling of Rowe's formalist version of modernism. The specific materialities and contingencies activated by the thematics of writing; the deobjectification, loss of boundaries, and elevation of technology and program associated with electrotecture; the gendered subjectivities and new bodies announced by the feminine; and the multiple statics, subversion of the ground datum, and fall of vertical decidability proposed by lightness—all these, and others too, would seem an unbearable assault on the abstract, apolitical, and objective language form articulated by Rowe and his associates after the war. It has been suggested that with the emergence of these issues the entire project of an architectural semiotics has become obsolete. That in short, work on form has been suspended.

In large measure, of course, this narrative is persuasive as the trajectory of the postwar period has seemed to consist of a shift in focus from the interiority of the object to the exteriority of effects. In other words, while the first generation of the neo-avant-garde in the early 1960s began to investigate the *semiotics of form*, its progeny (specifically, the generation that came of age after the events of May 1968) have indulged a *diagrammatics of function and structure*. This being stipulated, however—and precisely in the name of those later parties—one must still make a plea for the case of language or of form (though on different grounds), and for several reasons. First, to do otherwise would be to reinstate the dialectical form-substance opposition on which the initial high modernist (formalist) version of architectural language was constructed, and which allowed it to claim a political neutrality or, at least, objectivity. In other words, hierarchical arrangements, such as the well-known distinction made by Rowe between *physique*-flesh and *morale*-word, cannot simply be inverted. Rather, the linguistic or semiotic field needs to be expanded, as it were, in order to be limited to a particular model of language (or, alternatively, compelled to renounce language-form).

Gilles Deleuze and Félix Guattari (who follow Louis Hjelmslev in this matter) propose one potential model for this expansion in which a double articulation exists between expansion and content, but one where each term is doubled again by its own form and substance traits (for example, there is an expression-*substance* as well as an expression-form; a content-*form* as well as a content-substance).[1] This expanded model—which cannot be fully explicated here—begins to explain what could otherwise be understood only as a fundamental contradiction in the options posed by formalism and its more recent (material) discontents. In other words, it accounts for the real complicity between Rowe's distinction among phenomenal and literal transparencies and the related distinction made repeatedly in *ANY* (no. 5) between lightness and the merely lightweight. Far from having exhausted the linguistic model, then, we remain within a more complex version of it as recognized by the editors of the lightness issue, who (quite reasonably) desire a notational and conceptual aspect to the condition of "lightness" and not simply structures that are literally lightweight or suspended.

In addition to the fact that, as seen above, the semiotics of the object and the diagrammatics of force are related (and, in any case, could not be distinguished except by assuming the limited model of language that the latter position rejects), there are other contemporary and historical reasons for working through this tradition. First, and despite whatever animosity or suspicions either side may have in the matter, today, more than ever, work on form and form as work, broadly speaking theory and design practice, stand or fall together. Despite Rowe's individual testimony in this matter—"I find myself scarcely of the intellectual chic to cope with the choicest of recent critical confections from Paris and Frankfurt which are, to me, so hopelessly arcane"—it remains the case, prima facie, that formal experimentation and theoretical research are being systematically and jointly repressed in various academic, commercial, and social settings by the combined forces of the behavioral and building sciences, and, along a different axis, by the strange political alignment of developer architects (who nominate themselves to speak for the real world) and social reformers (who predetermine the limits of authentic critique). One implication of this diagnosis is that advanced theory—which has done so much to free itself from a particular version of language and has thereby been able successfully to recuperate from tradition such formerly taboo topics as program, structure, materials, the body, context, and, most recently, the earth, the ground, and gravity itself—must figure a way to rethink the discourse on form. Meanwhile, those previous definers and defenders of that discourse may be surprised that the most robust programmatics of form will emerge from where they least expect it, from the arcane realm of theory. But of course, historically, this has always been the case.

Despite the fact that the legacy of American formalism, particularly in its trajectory from central Texas to upstate New York over the last forty years, may have derived its most visible doctrines from traditional, historicist, or postmodern followers of Rowe (the party of the truth and nothing but the truth), it seems that the most vigorous research into the predicaments and possibilities of form has emerged within neo-avant-garde production. In this regard, the complementary extension and critique of Rowe's work found in the diverse developments of his early colleagues and protégés John Hejduk and Peter Eisenman are exemplary. The establishment and institutionalization of work on form as a discourse are inseparable from the vicissitudes of the postwar avant-garde, a cultural formation that, reciprocally, is inconceivable without the presence of Colin Rowe. Beginning slowly with the insights and blindness of Rowe's model (with, for example, Hejduk's study of Piet Mondrian and the diagonal and Eisenman's work on rotation and transformation in Giuseppe Terragni), each has developed a radical alternative to the limited way in which modernism was institutionalized after the war, simultaneously expanding and evacuating the categories of postwar formalism while opening the way for recovery and investigation of historical avant-garde paradigms and procedures to follow. In their blasphemy they have perhaps remained the most faithful.

In their dispute with the manner in which modernism was received, the subject of Hejduk's and Eisenman's "anxious influence," to borrow Harold Bloom's model, was first and foremost a strong critic rather than a strong poet. In other words, all of their productive misreadings of modernist European predecessors can be understood as a swerve within and against the production of Rowe's formalism, and it is this swerve that allows them to develop other possibilities suppressed within that tradition. It is in the spirit of this prescriptive or projective chance offered by the swerve that the present issue on Rowe and form is undertaken. Moreover, the method of the swerve, or forms of misreading, may also allow the reconfiguration of Rowe's temporal opposition of memory and prophecy, an opposition that he seems committed to, provided that it presents the opportunity to perform the role of disinterested fulcrum. It is precisely this dialectic, inspired (and required) by his own discourse, that allows Rowe to be baffled by—or to express a distanced "interest, amusement, and ever renewed amazement" in—current architectural debates. However, in his silence or through his more active yet still critically distant apologetics (the voice of reasoned disinterest which begins with his negative defense of the New York Five and returns twenty years later as the identical brief employed in the name of Duany and Plater-Zyberk in *ANY* (no. 3), there resides an increasingly vehement ambivalence in Rowe's tone. While Rowe's work may not directly propose a content (expression) as is often assumed to be the case by proponents of *Collage City*, neither is his method, with its model of the critic as adjudicator, apolitical. For otherwise, with pluralism running rampant and debate proceeding apace, why would one need to enter the fray to defend and articulate diversity? Unless, that is, as happened with postwar American political discourse, a procedural formalism (the establishment a set of rules and languages) would also emerge as a normative ideal, as an end state vision. To put the matter somewhat perversely, for Rowe literal pluralism was simply never enough and, as always suspected, the physique-form has been implicated with a morale-word all along. Shot through with value choices and questions of power, the rules of formalist discourse (with its modes of categorizing facts as well as its flexibility in capitulating to or distinguishing precedents) have always been involved with the boundary of maintenance of the political. Moreover, while Rowe's formalism (and he and others would no doubt dispute the "ism") was expected to avoid the ideological and therefore could never explicitly legislate a particular style, successful forms (or good gestalts) nevertheless had to demonstrate that choices, indeed, were at once made and continuously possible. Ultimately this approach underwrites forms that obey a logic of substitution (from which historical reference is merely option). It is from this pluralist bias that the proliferation of postmodern "kit of parts" strategies derive. In other words, each object must make evident the preexisting system through which choices (or options) are available. In the end, the descriptive and prescriptive realms are subtly elided, creating a situation in which only forms that are themselves internally pluralist are allowed to participate in the debate. The differences presumably promoted by the formal-proceduralist model, then, are predetermined and limited by those recognized in the structure of the system, a previous whole or identity.

Perhaps the most explicit texts that both describe and enact a deviation in the aesthetics (and politics) of formalist modernism are two essays by Eisenman, one ostensibly on Michael Graves (but at least as much about Rowe) and the other a reflection on Philip Johnson (and equally about himself).[2] As the two strong poet-critics of modernism in America projected through Eisenman's lens, Rowe and Johnson begin to appear as the original odd couple of postwar architecture. While both have been sponsors of the neo-avant-garde (bracketing, for example, the *Five Architects* publication), traditional readings of both have seemed to dominate, regardless of whether they are reviled or celebrated for their supposed apostasy and rejection of the modernism they were once imagined to have introduced. Representing mirror formalisms—one objective, the other subjective—Rowe's tactic of deferral begins to appear Socratic (as "certainty in doubt"[3]), whereas Johnson's consumption and exhaustion of specific forms can be understood, perhaps, as sophistic ("the simulacral being, the satyr or centaur, the Proteus who intrudes and insinuates himself everywhere"[4]). Here, through varied degrees of irony and sophistication, one can begin to perceive counter formal programs, one vaguely Platonic and the other Nietzschean, which coexist uncomfortably but necessarily within the discourse on form and, in the case of Rowe, begin to account for his peculiar mixture of skepticism and belief.

It is precisely these Platonic or Cartesian dialectics within Rowe's thought that must be exposed and realigned if an alternative version of formalism is to be solicited and engaged, one which, in the name of future work, swerves from the current catalogue of Rowe effects. In one way or another, these antinomies perpetually recur in gestalt science, cubist aesthetics, and liberal politics, the three primary disciplines whose collusion provided all the salient features for a formalist discourse within postwar American modernism. While this discourse privileged the now familiar notions of balance, ambiguity, framed boundaries, reason, proportion, analogy, the distinguishing of species, and part-to-whole compositional economies, it may be possible to work the status form (and, of course, necessarily politics) through a different semiotic regime with distinct implications for the production, evaluation, and teaching of architecture. In various idioms, the essays that follow wager that, through an investigation of new sciences, aesthetics, and politics, or via alternative rearrangements of private subjects and public objects, a deviationist formalism may be approached. While this endeavor will inevitably be provisional and undoubtedly foreign to the politics of form as it has been practiced to date, it will at least save Rowe from those always too faithful and anxious to commemorate, bury, and dismiss.

II. THE LAW OF THE COLON: FACILITY AND *LA VASE*

How to be intelligible without involving retrospection?; and, without being unduly sententious, it should be enough to observe that except in terms of retrospection, in terms of memory upon which prophesy itself is based, upon recollections of words with meaning, mathematical symbols with values and physical forms with attendant overtones, it is difficult to see how any ideal of communication can flourish.
   Colin Rowe

As constructed after the war, the discourse of formalism was related to a broader intellectual, cultural, and political agenda which sought to found social arrangement on relativist grounds, to disinfect and therefore protect forms from any political (ideological) connotations in the name of freedom (autonomy) and diversity (heterogeneity). In this view, content (meaning) would resist capture by any particular value system only by remaining in a constant state of debate or dialectic or ambiguity. In this way, the new (difference) was contained and domesticated by being available only by reference to precedence, the economy of the same and the like—a previous identity located both in a form of communication and a community form. Thus, the attempts to correlate or align architecture and language in the postwar period would establish the possibility (however contradictory that goal would become) for an architecture of both *autonomy* and *heterogeneity* against the modern (read: European and ideological) rhetoric and experience of anonymous and homogeneous building. It is within this context that Rowe would escort American architecture into the realm of the symbolic (the realm, for Julia Kristeva and Jacques Lacan, of the law and language) through the device of the colon: that which establishes relation, balance, parity, ratio, proportion, analogy, and reason. The colon legislates both linguistic-visual analogies (Corbusier : Palladio :: Late Corb : Schinkel) and the mathematical ratios (3:5::5:8), and it was largely on this dual basis that physique-flesh came to be severed from morale-word. In the meantime, the question as to the proper articulation between form and word—variously figured as vertical-image and horizontal-text, practice and theory, design and criticism—has remained as one of the principal themes that has characterized architectural production and discussion for the last thirty years.

The initial distinction, of course, was not intended to oppose form and language, but rather to elevate form *as its own language*, to make it unnecessary to refer to, or be co-opted by, what were thought to be external languages, ideologies, or rationales. As suggested earlier, the particular expression-substance privileged by Rowe consisted of the optical analogs of cubist aesthetics as articulated by the insights of gestalt psychology and filtered through the vision of a liberal polity. As with other arenas in the postwar formalization of politics, apparently objective procedures and forms of communication (whether linguistic or legal) came to assume and require a specific image of society or community. The relativist account of liberal democracy emerged as the only remaining normative ideal. In other words, form became its own morale.[5]

While the empirical was rapidly emerging as the normative in postwar America, the attempt to articulate a language of architectural form came to rely on a set of clear, almost Cartesian, distinctions between mind and body, idea and fact, intentionality and anonymity, universal and particular, abstract and real, utopia and tradition, collective and individual, prescriptive and descriptive. Throughout Rowe's writings these hierarchical oppositions are often identified with particular places, namely Europe and America. In his essay on the frame structure, for instance, Rowe argues that the frame in Chicago existed technically as a "reasonable fact" developed to solve a particular "practical problem" in response to "commercial speculation."[16] In contrast, the gridded structure in Europe was, first and foremost, an "essential idea" and "theoretical statement" that served as a polemic for the "universal problem of architecture" (rather than the specific problem of the office building), one that expressed a deep "moral revolt." As further evidence, Rowe opposes Mies van der Rowe's Glass Tower, *which is something that it does not profess to be,*" to Daniel Burnham's Reliance Building, which "*is what it is*"—the duplicity of glass and the dependability of reliance conveniently serving as proper names for their respective formal conditions. Here, the development of a strong (and contained) language of architecture requires distinguishing mere (literal) building (largely American) from phenomenal acts of architecture (European), and it is by virtue of this proposal for an architectural sign distinct from its referent that the postwar formalist (and later structuralist) research into the *language* of architecture evolves.

The fate of the frame is repeated, in its return trip across the Atlantic in the 1930s and 1940s, when the ideology of the European modern movement is repressed by the production and repression of the so-called International Style in the United States. It is largely as a subtle response to this translation, in his apologetic for the New York Five, that Rowe articulates a linguistic capacity for form itself, divorced from any outside social or political referent that would, in any case, be impossible in the liberal American context.

For in the United States the revolution was assumed to have already occurred—in 1776, and it was further assumed to have initiated a social order which was not to be superseded by subsequent developments. In other words, with the revolutionary theme divested by circumstances of both its catastrophic and futuristic implications, with the theme rendered retrospective, legalistic and even nationalist, an indigenous modern architecture in America deployed connotations quite distinct from its European counterparts.

Colin Rowe, Introduction to *Five Architects* [emphasis added]

Again suggesting the dichotomy between American matter and European mind, Rowe nonetheless opens the possibility for those architects who will follow in his wake to begin to invent a new conceptual and theoretical project despite (or more likely, due to) their repetition of continental architecture's *physique*-flesh. In an incredibly powerful sleight of hand Rowe steals the idea for subsequent American postwar practice precisely by demonstrating its resistance to ideology. In other words, the American neo-avant-garde, protégés, and successors of Rowe would find themselves at the forefront of architectural ideas that would finally consider the "universal problem of architecture" (i.e., a self-reflective language of architecture) in a peculiarly Anglo-American idiom. Beginning with Rowe, the diverse series of ideal villas and collage cities proposed by this tradition represented a sustained reflection on the form and content of individual and collective arrangements, and an investigation into varied compositional and associative laws in the relation of part to whole.

The analogy that could begin to satisfy the need for an explicitly nonideological basis for form was located, not surprisingly given the American reconstruction of both modernism and Europe after the war, in the law. Based on the radical subjectivity of value, the goal of liberalism is individual liberty, an ideal middle term situated between tyranny and license, or totalitarian structure and anarchic event. And it is the neutral instrumentality of the law that will presumably mediate the complex (but articulate) contradictions constructed through this liberal vision of personality and politics. Rowe's collage urbanism, for instance, is constituted through the balance between structure and event (or scaffold and exhibit), a balance (or collage) founded on the significantly political and eminently reasonable model of the law. As Rowe and Fred Koetter write in *Collage City*, "It is the notion of the law, the neutral background which illustrates and stimulates the particular . . . which equips itself with both empirical and ideal . . . it is this very public institution which must now be gainfully employed in commentary upon the scaffold-exhibit relationship."[7] For Rowe, the "elementary and enlivening duplicities of the law" along with "the idea of free trade" serve as emblems for the "balancing act" of structure and event as well as the techniques of collage. As forces opposed to his promotion of this legal-capitalist (contractual) economy, Rowe dismisses "accident" and "gifts of chance," which he associates with debtorship and theft, violations of the entrepreneurial demands of the private law system. In order to begin to develop a deviationist formalism one would first have to separate the notion of repetition from the generality of the law. While generality invokes "the qualitative order of resemblances and the quantitative order of equivalences" (or as suggested above, analogy and ratio), another model of repetition would advance "non-exchangeable and non-substitutable singularities." As an explicit alternative to the privileged terms of Rowe's liberal model of the law of collage, Deleuze suggests that "if exchange is the criterion of generality [i.e., the order of laws], theft and gift are those of repetition."[8] Rowe's collage, then, with its vision of heterogeneity as contained pluralism, ultimately maintains the arrangements of self and society. This political and legal theme finds its first explicit site for articulation in the solitary, unrelenting landscape of central Texas and, not surprisingly, it is here aligned with the question of unified or multiple subjectivity.

It is in the town of Lockhart, Texas, that Rowe and Hejduk find a specific representative of the American courthouse town, an urban type which itself was adduced earlier in their article as "a more representative illustration" of settlement patterns in the west than, for example, the mining town. Through layers of representation and exemplification, a typical situation is described that by necessity avoids the bizarre or the random.

This is a town dedicated to an idea, and its scheme is neither fortuitous nor whimsical. The theme of centralized courthouse in central square is—or should be—a banal one. And it is in fact one of great power. . . . Here it is the law which assumes public significance; and it is around the secular image of the law, like architectural illustrations of a political principle, that these towns revolve. In each case the courthouse is both visual focus and social guarantee; and in each square the reality of government made formally explicit provides the continuing assurance for order. . . . Urbanistic phenomena they palpably are, but they are also emblems of a political theory. A purely architectural experience of their squares is therefore never possible. Within these enclosures the observer can never disentangle his aesthetic response from his reaction as a social animal.

Colin Rowe and John Hejduk, "Lockhart, Texas"

It is with regard to this theme of the political theories and implications of the city, the polis, to which Rowe and Hejduk have continually returned over the succeeding thirty years in their urban thought, twin practices that form a real debate over the liberal-legal vision of the city and modernism. While Rowe would emphasize the reasonable, judicious, orderly, and decisive aspects as the preconditions for an exemplary urbanism, Hejduk, for example, has recovered other traits with very different political, social, and formal implications. It is not simply at the more obvious scale of the city, however, that Rowe's formalism finds alliance with a liberal-legal version of language and an individualist mode of exchange.

In drawing attention to James Stirling's Staatsgalerie in his essay "Losing Face," Anthony Vidler begins to suggest the central importance of the pair "face-language" for Rowe's discussion and evaluation of architectural phenomena. In Deleuze and Guattari's terms, Rowe's formalism relies on a signifying regime constructed through "faciality," an assemblage constituted by the articulation of the "white wall" of significance and the "black hole" of subjectification. It is this faciality aspect of Rowe's formalism that would seek to establish a modern *architecture parlante* that serves to reveal the specific connections of cubism, gestalt, and liberalism. Despite the inevitable plan orientation of architectural discourse, the optical bias of the formalist discipline (or, more precisely, the disciplines through which it constructed itself) has persistently committed its version of language to the vertical, the visual, and the frontal, or what Rosalind Krauss has identified as the dominant "fronto-parallel" relations of high modernism. And it is precisely within the terms of that discourse that Rowe escapes the horizontality of the plan datum and inscribes a new set of visual-optical signifying possibilities. As he and Robert Slutzky flatly admit: "After recognizing that a floor is not a wall and that plans are not paintings, we might still examine these horizontal planes in very much the same manner as we have the facade, again selecting *Three Faces* as a point of departure."[9] Despite typology's apparent commitment to the horizontal plan, it is first conceived as vertical, as *facialized*. Like the faciality machine of Deleuze and Guattari, typological analysis with high formal discourse operates as a "deviance detector," sorting out, distinguishing, and establishing degrees of deviation. The development of an articulate architectural language through fronto-parallel relations is not limited to Rowe, of course, but can also be seen in the early writings and work of Robert Venturi, who also alludes to the practices and terms established by high modern painting.

Returning to Rowe's discussion of Stirling's Staatsgalerie, one can locate many of the principles of postwar formalism, including the bounded relation of writing to form (or critic to architect), the necessary conditions of a vertical faciality, and the requirement of an integrated and singular individual subjectivity. In attempting to account for his previous impasse in considering the Staatsgalerie, Rowe confesses: "It must have been the relative absence of this concern in Stirling [in the vertical surface] that arrested my writing in 1973 and remains my reservation about Stuttgart."[10] Here, then, the architect must provide a face in order for the critic to write, a quid pro quo, a vertical surface in exchange for a horizontal one, a physique for a word. Without the frontal, vertical of the object, there is apparently no consideration, and no contract is possible between critic and architect, word and form. In a perhaps more revealing observation earlier in this same essay, Rowe associates his inability to write with the fact that there were too many Stirlings: "For in 1973, just *how many* Stirlings were there?" Somehow the lack of face corresponds to a multiplicity which induces the blockage of language, or at least of a linguistic order that requires an identifiable individual liable to the authorial codes of liberal-legalism. As Deleuze and Guattari remark, "The face is a politics." Consequently, "losing face," or the vis-à-vis of faciality, obliterates not simply the fronto-parallel attributes of cubism, but also the recognizable whole shapes of gestalt, the face to face that establishes the vase (as containment), the reciprocal vision that installs the subject, ensures proper form, and forestalls *la vase* (i.e., the slime, ooze, and mud that might be associated, via Krauss, with Bataille's *bassesse* or *informe*).

Of course, the trajectories of the postwar avant-garde have largely abandoned Rowe's requisite model of faciality as the basis for a humanist or liberal version of modernism, starting with techniques of defacing as rotation (Eisenman's early axonometric studies), masking (Hejduk), and bodybuilding (Gehry), to more recent experiments in programming the skin (Tschumi) and the development of postliberal "probeheads" (Koolhaas's Zeebrugge Maritime Terminal). While Rowe required the abstract individual (of the standard "reasonable man" variety posited by the law) for his construction of postwar formalism, Hejduk pursues the hyperspecific (and no longer generalizable) subject, and Eisenman suspends the autonomy of the individual altogether. Both directions have had the effect of eroding a legal formalism: in Hejduk, there emerges a type for every individual, whereas for Eisenman there exists no individual against which to specify a type. While the former would ultimately have the event-figure form a new structure, a new field (as in the masques), the latter would have structure itself become an event-figure (evident, for example, in the folds of Rebstock as well as the Max Reinhardt Haus). In this way, Hejduk has advanced the black hole (figure) of subjectivity *en abime*, while Eisenman exhausts the white wall (field) of signification. This dissolution of Rowe's particular version of formalism (generated by the face-language pole) does not (nor can it) end all semiotic projects, but simply serves to dispossess the optical model with its requirements for the vertical, grounded, necessary, and framed. The white wall/black hole (figure-ground) system of the faciality machine eliminated other semiotic regimes which now become open for investigation, as evidenced by a variety of contemporary practices that have already begun to consider the signifying potential of "the base" in terms of materiality, the body, use, structure, etc. Only now, after the prerequisite construction of Rowe's formwork of faciality, is it possible to recognize the "mud" of *la vase*.

The solicitation of the base or *informe* constitutes one aspect of a deviationist or expanded formalism, a virtual project impossible to imagine before Rowe's elevation of an articulate architectural poetics and its development and involution by subsequent neo-avant-garde initiatives. This program for the pursuit of a pure difference (difference thought neither in terms of a previous identity nor in simple contradiction to the same) allows and requires a new consideration of time as well. The two formalisms (classical and deviationist) produce not simply alternative models of difference, but contrary notions of time, or modes of repetition, as well. As Roberto Unger has critically observed of traditional doctrinal development in his own attempt to elaborate a deviationist practice: "A doctrinal practice that puts its hope in the contrast of legal reasoning to ideology, philosophy, and political prophecy ends up as a collection of make-shift apologies."[11] This begins to clarify the experience that Rowe's discourse—though attempting to poise itself between memory and prophecy—ended, more often than not, rejecting prophecy and serving as a form of apologetic for existent practices, where the empirical became the normative through default. In place of the strong narrative times of utopia and tradition, Rowe attempted to argue for the eternal present of formalism, the "forever now," but since its model of difference was entirely dependent on the identification of preexisting ideal types, this timeless model was ultimately co-opted by historicism.

By invoking the precedent of language (conceived as requiring a particular form of repetition), Rowe constrains difference to an internal and framed articulation within a system, a previous identity, rather than a process of perpetual differentiation (which might, as Rowe correctly feared, also imply a continual becoming identical). In classical formalism, repetition can only be thought in terms of a particular language model, the law of generality and representation. In the work of both Rowe and Michael Fried, for instance, the same critique of literal representation is made: of Walter Gropius's Bauhaus, where movements "flow away into infinity," and the endlessness of Donald Judd's "one thing after another." Today, however, it may be possible to conceive repetition as producing difference rather than ensuring resemblance. As a procedure of the new, repetition, by setting in motion divergent series, would operate as a kind of difference machine (rather than an identity machine). Unlike Rowe's liberal-legal formalism, this repetition would not operate by a logic of the substitution or displacement of parts that always maintain the integrity of the established kit, but through a condensation where a continuous whole-part would perpetually provoke new "kits." In place of Rowe's timeless formalism (which attempted to balance both prophecy and memory), this deviationist formalism would effect the untimely, a simulacral both and neither approach in relation to precedence and utopia. Rather than choosing between or balancing preservation and "erase and replace" strategies, for example, this expanded formalism would operate to maintain and subvert. Formal identity would emerge only as a function of a previous disparity, a differing repetition—the event of the untimely. Finally, anticipating Paulette Singley's portrait of Rowe's *interior parlante* with its undecidable irony, the tenets of classical formalism might themselves begin to unravel from within through the operation of this nonbinary formalism. As ventured by Deleuze in "Plato and the Simulacrum": "The final definition of the Sophist leads us to the point where we can no longer distinguish him from Socrates himself: the ironist operating in private by elliptical arguments. Was it not inevitable that irony be pushed this far? And that Plato be the first to indicate this direction for the overthrow of Platonism?" And, one might further inquire, that Rowe be the first to indicate the overthrow of formalism? A program of repetition without recognition: the amnesia of form.

1 For a full account of this model see Gilles Deleuze and Félix Guattari, See *A Thousand Plateaus*, trans. Brian Massumi (Minneapolis: University of Minnesota Press, 1987), 40–110.

2 See Peter Eisenman, "Postscript: The Graves of Modernism," *Oppositions* 12 (Spring 1978): 21–26; and his "Introduction" in *Philip Johnson: Writings* (New York: Oxford University Press, 1976), 10–25.

3 See Anthony Vidler, *The Architectural Uncanny* (Cambridge, Mass.: MIT Press, 1992), 192.

4 Gilles Deleuze, "Plato and the Simulacrum," *October* 27: 47.

5 This observation is related to Serge Guilbaut's remark that, with regard to "advanced" art after 1950, "the depolitization of the avant-garde was necessary before it could be put into political use.

6 Colin Rowe, "Chicago Frame," in *The Mathematics of the Ideal Villa and Other Essays* (Cambridge, Mass.: MIT Press, 1976), 93–106.

7 Colin Rowe and Fred Koetter, *Collage City* (Cambridge, Mass.: 1978), 146.

8 See Gilles Deleuze, *Difference and Repetition*, trans. Paul Patton (New York: Columbia University Press, 1994): "It is in repetition and by repetition that Forgetting becomes a positive power."

9 See *The Mathematics of the Ideal Villa and Other Essays*, 169.

10 Colin Rowe, "James Stirling: A Highly Personal and Very Disjointed Memoir," in *James Stirling: Buildings and Projects*, ed. Peter Arnell and Ted Bickford (New York: Rizzoli, 1984), 23.

11 Roberto Unger, "The Critical Legal Studies Movement," *Harvard Law Review* (January 1983).

m *AA Files* 32 (1996)

TRANSPARENCY: AUTONOMY
AND RELATIONALITY

Detlef Mertins

The binary distinction announced by Colin Rowe and Robert Slutzky's well-known essay of 1964, "Transparency: Literal and Phenomenal," has been deeply absorbed within American architectural culture.[1] It continues to be reiterated and reformulated by teachers, critics, and even historians grappling with the shift from orthodox mid-century modernism to post-modern and post-structural problematics—grappling all the more for now recognizing that contemporary preoccupations have emerged out of, as much as in reaction to, modernism in its various guises.[2]

Without meaning to detract from the brilliance of Rowe and Slutzky's essay or to diminish the productive role that their distinguishing between two "species" of modernism has played in architecture, I would like to suggest that this setting-apart was more complex and unstable than it is usually taken to have been. Elsewhere I have suggested that the literal transparency of machine aesthetics—as much American as German in its conception[3]—is inadequate to the ideal of transparency promoted by Sigfried Giedion and László Moholy-Nagy, for which Rowe and Slutzky mobilized the term.[4] As early as 1978, in a largely overlooked critique, Rosemary Haag Bletter observed that Rowe and Slutzky's analysis was "too erratic to make workable categories," and their "unorthodox" interpretation of cubism and constructivism was sensible only in formal and not in historical terms.[5] Just as Rowe and Slutzky believed that post-cubist transparency was not as simple as seeing clearly through glass, so too did Giedion and Moholy-Nagy. Their concept of transparency was likewise based on a phenomenology of spatial perception, albeit a four-dimensional one in which the boundaries between inside and outside, subject and object, were dissolved for an observer assumed to be moving freely in space and time. In contrast, Rowe and Slutzky invoked a two-dimensional phenomenology that fixed the observer in a position on axis with the plane of the facade as if viewing a painting. And, while Rowe and Slutzky characterized Giedion as championing Walter Gropius and the Bauhaus at Dessau, in fact Giedion too took the experiments of cubism as the origins of a transparency whose ultimate exemplar in architecture was Le Corbusier's Purism.[6] Dividing the avant-garde into two *opposing* camps and favoring one over the other, Rowe and Slutzky staked their distinctive claim to the legacy of cubism, the architecture of Le Corbusier, and the phenomenology of space, while dismissing the parallel claims of their opponents and reducing the ambition of their enterprise to something they characterized as simple and "literal."

Considered today, however, Rowe and Slutzky's claim should be recognized as based (perhaps unconsciously) on assumptions and *topoi* of the late nineteenth century whose reiteration at the end of the twentieth may be of limited strategic value. Reviewing the formal characteristics that underpinned the categories of literal and phenomenal transparency, one cannot help but be struck by their correspondence to those deployed by Heinrich Wölfflin in forging a distinction between linear and painterly styles, so important for his theory of historical change in art. Wölfflin had inaugurated this influential polarity in *Renaissance and Baroque* of 1888 and later systemized it in his *Principles of Art History* of 1915.[7] While Wölfflin's binary had recast Friedrich Nietzsche's portrayal of the conflict between Apollonian and Dionysian impulses[8] in more psychological, formal, and historical terms, Rowe and Slutzky's interpretation of the phenomenal eschewed the issue of historical change and with it the strategic potential of tensions between the formed and the formless. Their preference for the (classical) architectonics of Fernand Léger and Juan Gris displaced the (baroque) movement, disintegration, and participation of László Moholy-Nagy and Robert Delaunay as a model for modernism. Instead, they argued for a self-contained form whose underlying theory of spatial and aesthetic perception privileged stasis, flatness, and the self-reflexive autonomy of the aesthetic object.[9]

Where Giedion considered modern space to be four-dimensional, indivisible from time and the perception of a subject moving freely in the same space as the object—he called it "relational space"—Rowe and Slutzky conceived of space as emphatically two-dimensional. For them time, like the viewer, effectively stood still. To be more precise, time was consumed in a movement internal to the eye, for the eye's oscillation between layered planes was thought to generate a thick spatiality. This phenomenal space was considered to be purely optical, in the sense suggested in the late nineteenth century by the aesthetician Konrad Fiedler when he speculated on the possibility of extracting "pure visibility" as an autonomous element in respect to the object, leaving its tactility behind.[10] The planar model of spatial perception on which Rowe and Slutzky's interpretation rested sought an objective congruence between the physiological optics considered inherent to sight and the self-referentially inscribed form of the building. On this basis, they assumed a new kind of cognition and a new kind of pleasure as the building attempted to present itself in ideal visual terms, faced nevertheless with the limitations of material appearances.

Although Rowe and Slutzky's portrait of the garden facade of Le Corbusier's Villa Stein de Monzie at Garches (1926–27) is well known (figs. 71 and 72), I would like to rehearse it here in order to trace the resonance of its very particular terms with the theory of artistic perception that underlies it. To begin, the authors ask the reader to imagine the villa—they use the classical term *facade* and not the modernist *elevation*—as a delaminated version of Fernand Léger's painting *Three Faces* of 1926 (fig. 68). They present the building as an analogous "system of spatial stratification" and "a field modeled in low relief" in which the impression of depth is generated by fluctuations in figure-ground relations among flat, highly contrasting shapes tied together by horizontal bands and common contours. In other words, they ask the reader to suspend conventional understanding long enough—or to step back far enough—to consider the cubic volume and internal spatial order of the buildings as operating exclusively on a two-dimensional surface. As well, they ask the reader to "enjoy the sensation that *possibly* the framing of the windows passes behind the wall surface," to follow the hint provided by the side walls (set back from the principal plane of the facade) in order to recognize there "a narrow slot of space traveling parallel to it," and to imagine that, "bounding this slot of space, and behind it, there lies a plane of which the ground floor, the freestanding walls, and the inner reveals of the door all form a part." The authors present this "imaginary (though scarcely less real) plane that lies behind" as a "conceptual convenience," instrumental in achieving the cognitive effect of "our being made conscious of primary concepts which 'interpenetrate without optical destruction of each other.'" They draw the reader's eye to other parallel planes, both in front of and behind this slot of space, planes that are incomplete yet contribute to the organization of the facade in such a way as to imply "a vertical layerlike stratification of the interior space of the building, a succession of laterally extended spaces traveling one behind the other."[11]

While the three-dimensionality of the building may not actually be in question, what concerns Rowe and Slutzky is that, from a point deep in the garden and aligned with the central axis of the building, it is possible to entertain an analogy with Purist painting and to construct an imaginary model of the entire building in the mind's eye. It was in relation to this capacity of Purist architecture to stimulate the imaginative participation of the viewer—configuring a virtual representation of the building which Rosalind Krauss aptly termed a "hermeneutic phantom"—that Rowe and Slutzky drew on György Képes's Gestalt-based theories of visual communication in *Language of Vision* (1944) to set themselves apart from both Giedion and Moholy-Nagy. Yet Képes's book abounds in examples of Moholy-Nagy's work, and Giedion's introduction to it reads like a synopsis of his own *Space, Time, and Architecture* (1941)—which was after all the central object of Rowe and Slutzky's critique.[12] Rowe and Slutzky's use of Képes at the expense of his friends and allies was made possible by the way Képes expounded on the principles of cubism and post-cubism through the lens of Gestalt theory. Although Moholy-Nagy and Giedion placed considerable emphasis on the role played by cubism in the history of modern art and architecture, Képes's debt to Gestalt theory and its debt in turn to nineteenth-century psychophysiology served to distinguish his interpretation from theirs. Yet Rowe and Slutzky could not have considered Képes's account to be an "almost classical explanation" of paintings by Georges Braque, Juan Gris, and Fernand Léger had it not been precedented within early Purism, which presented its linear architectonics as an extension of and a corrective to cubism.

Although Rowe and Slutzky did not refer to them, the early Purist paintings of Jeanneret and Ozenfant were implicitly the point of reference for their characterization of post-cubism in terms of precise spatial locations (fig. 101). It should be recognized, however, that where these paintings compressed and layered the purified objects that they depicted into a two-dimensional space, subsequent Purist paintings slid out from under the rigor of architectonic objectivism into the fluid, perhaps even oceanic, space that Robert Slutzky later described so eloquently.[13] It was these paintings that Giedion (following Jeanneret or Ozenfant) described in terms of the *mariage des contours*, for they internalized the opposition of linear and painterly qualities, in a play of perception, illusion, and cognition engendered by the simultaneous assertion and denial of volumes. Where Giedion (once again following Le Corbusier) recognized that achieving the effect of Purist paintings in architecture required the manipulation of form and color for observers moving in psychophysiological space (fig. 100),[14] Rowe and Slutzky, adopting Képes's language of ambiguity, insisted on the primacy of the flat image.[15]

Introducing their notion of "phenomenal" transparency, Rowe and Slutzky quoted the following passage from *The Language of Vision*, which appears under the heading "Transparency, interpretation":

If one sees two or more figures partly overlapping one another, and each of them claims for itself the common overlapped part, then one is confronted with a contradiction of spatial dimensions. To resolve this contradiction, one must assume the presence of a new optical quality. The figures are endowed with transparency; that is, they are able to interpenetrate without an optical destruction of each other. Transparency however implies more than an optical characteristic; it implies a broader spatial order. Transparency means a simultaneous perception of different spatial locations. Space not only recedes but fluctuates in a continuous activity. The position of the transparent figures has equivocal meaning as one sees each figure now as the closer, now as the further one.[16]

What Rowe and Slutzky did not cite, however, were the theories of vision and representation that underlay Képes's argument and the role these played in his polemic, which was aimed at renewing the language of vision. They did not, for instance, note the subject of Képes's book—modern graphic design, not architecture—or the fact that he associated transparency with the *mariage des contours*. Nor did the examples presented by Rowe and Slutzky even approach the diversity of those presented by Képes in support of his argument.[17]

For Képes (echoing Moholy-Nagy and Giedion as well as Ozenfant and Jeanneret) modern vision needed to be resynchronized to the conditions of modern technology, which had, he suggested, finally succeeded in breaking down the old system of perspectival representation. He believed that new technologies of photography and film had opened up an opportunity to renew a mode of visual representation that was more congruent with what he took to be the biological conditions of human perception—a form of representation on a flat surface, similar to non-Western and pre-perspectival painting, as well as the naïve drawings made by children.

Képes's opening section on "plastic organization" laid the theoretical foundation (interpolated from Gestalt theory[18]) for his claim that these other forms of representation—at once more primitive and more modern—were also more natural. He suggested that, like the anatomist, the perspectivalist achieved knowledge as well as the optical and scientific mastery of nature only at the expense of the living, moving aspects of the body, "the flux of the innumerable visual relationships that the visible world has for the spectator." For Képes, perspective "froze the living, fluctuating wealth of the visual field into a static geometrical system, eliminating the time-element always present in the experiencing of space, and thus destroying the dynamic relationships in the experience of the spectator."[19]

Within Képes's two-dimensional post-perspectival theory of spatial representation, images played a number of interrelated roles. They mediated between the inner and the outer world, not in the fixed, unequivocal, and absolute manner of perspective, but rather in engaging the viewer's participation. This, he thought, occurred in several ways. Because both the eye and the picture plane have a limited ability to register depth and space, Képes held that the viewer's perceptual apparatus was constantly engaged in resolving contradictory information.[20] He believed that such material deficiencies required that the observer take an active role in forming the object, or at least its virtual Gestalt. "Every experiencing," Képes wrote, "is a forming; a dynamic process of integration, a 'plastic experience.'"[21] Equivocal images such as overlapping planes or the "marriage of contours" provide opportunities for the spectator to engage in the natural process of integrating space with knowledge of the objects depicted at the level of apperception or habit. Képes argued that visual images should achieve this kind of dynamic interaction between tension and balance,[22] attraction and repulsion,[23] figure and ground, creating "not a facade but a living, flowing space"—a space-time that offers opportunities for "wider and deeper human experiences."[24] Such images were thought to transform the two-dimensionality of the surface into a spatialized field that nevertheless retained its two-dimensionality even as it integrated the third and fourth dimensions.

Rowe and Slutzky's reading of Képes's treatise was selective in ways that side-stepped his preoccupation with living, flowing space—even in two-dimensional graphic design—which they associated with the "literal" machinist and constructivist "species" of modernism. While not immune to the claims of Gestalt to be an absolute perceptual science or to Képes's aspiration to modernize vision in objective terms, they focused instead on his notion that contradiction, ambiguity, and tension in visual representation—the oscillation of figure and ground, near and far, inside and outside generated by overlapping planes—were essential to achieving a balanced ecology of human perception. For Rowe and Slutzky such contradictions were a source of aesthetic pleasure: the pleasures of space released in the tension of perception that weaves disconnected elements into a unified yet ambiguous and unstable two-dimensional image.

As Képes acknowledged, the roots of Gestalt theories of perception and psychology lie in the late-nineteenth-century psychophysiological research of figures such as Wilhelm Wundt, Hermann von Helmholtz, and Theodor Lipps. These theories had already combined science and philosophy into several kinds of "scientific aesthetics," which in turn had served artists seeking to reground their practice on a supposedly objective basis as a response to the critique of imitation, naturalism, and perspective. In this respect, Képes's book belongs to a series of theoretical-historical treatises written by artists and informed by art historians and aestheticians—a series that would include writings by August Endell, Wassily Kandinsky, Johannes Itten, Paul Klee, László Moholy-Nagy, as well as Ozenfant and Le Corbusier. It is nevertheless curious to find the optical theories of Helmholtz so explicitly foregrounded in Képes's book, some sixty years after they were first formulated and long after their scientific authority had been eclipsed. Képes cited Helmholtz directly, not only in setting out his understanding of spatial perception as a function of muscular movements in the eye (compensating for inherent limitations such as the two-dimensionality of the retinal image[25]), but also in discussing color theory and after-images,[26] the origins of linear perspective,[27] and the importance, for physiological optics, of studying the paintings of great masters.[28]

In his own time Helmholtz's theory of artistic vision as fundamentally two-dimensional had been of great consequence to the sculptor and theorist Adolf von Hildebrand, who together with Konrad Fiedler and the painter Hans von Marées was part of a well-known and influential trio of formalists.[29] In his much-read treatise of 1893, *The Problem of Form in the Fine Arts*,[30] Hildebrand explained that the aim of art was to bring nature into relation with the visual faculties,[31] which he understood, following the theories of vision by Helmholtz (whose work he read and whose bust he sculptured), Salmon Sticher, and Wilhelm Wundt,[32] as fundamentally two-dimensional. While he acknowledged the importance of stereoscopic vision for life in three dimensions, he favored two-dimensional monocular vision for art. "The painter," he wrote, "gives on a plane a visual impression of three-dimensional form, while the sculptor forms something three-dimensional for the purpose of affording a plane visual impression."[33] Only in this way could what he called "effective form," as distinct from "inherent form," be created, and a clear comprehension of the values of spatial form as such be achieved.[34] These categories may be understood as one of the *topoi* below the surface of Rowe and Slutzky's later distinction between phenomenal and literal transparency. For Hildebrand, the problem of form in relief focused on how the different planes of the image, representing different objects at different distances, work together within an effective system. Such a system presents objects as coherent surface images, their spatial form evoked by means of an attraction of the eye into depth. Movement into depth was also thought to require a background, a surface against which the figure stands out coherently. The double demand for unified surface image and movement into depth was to be resolved by the technique of superimposition, which conceals at the same time as it connects, thereby enhancing surface unity without sacrificing the distinctions of distance.[35]

Not surprisingly, Hildebrand privileged relief sculpture, especially that of ancient Greece, which he declared to be paradigmatic for the presentation of three-dimensional impressions. His own sculptures as well as the paintings of von Marées, with their overlapping compositional structures and relief built up with pigment, demonstrated how the effect of spatial depth could be achieved while maintaining the integrity of the two-dimensional surface (figs. 102 and 103).[36] In introducing the concept of relief, Hildebrand reiterated his proposition that with "an ever more concentrated juxtaposition of objective surface effects" the sculptor was able to achieve "a simple idea of volume, that is, of a surface that extends into depth."[37] To illustrate this principle he drew the following analogy, which bears a striking correspondence to Rowe and Slutzky's imaginary slot of space at the Villa Stein—so striking as to render explicit the theoretical assumptions implicit in the critics' reading:

Imagine a figure placed between two parallel planes of glass, positioned in such a way that the figure's outermost points touch the glass. The figure then occupies and describes a space of uniform depth, within which its component parts are arranged. Seen from the front through the glass, the figure is coherent, first as an identifiable object within a uniform planar stratum, second as a volume defined by the uniform depth of the general volume. The figure lives, so to speak, in a planar stratum of uniform depth, and each form tends to spread out along the surface, that is, to make itself recognizable. Its outermost parts, touching the panes, continue to lie on a single plane, even if the panes are taken away.[38]

For Hildebrand the true artistic object was "a planar stratum of uniform depth" and the total volume of the picture was produced by "a number of such imaginary strata placed one behind another in a series." The distinctive achievement of an artist working in this way was to create an image of space and form which in actuality was a compound of countless kinaesthetic images in which "what remains is a surface impression that strongly suggests the idea of depth: one that the calmly observing eye is able to take in without any kinaesthetic activity."[39] "Visual perception," Hildebrand believed, occurred when the eye at rest took in a "distant view," as it was inclined to do, while "kinaesthetic perception" was concerned with the "near view," in which the eye engaged in a series of movements in order to grasp the object as a whole. To perceive spatial depth, he believed, there was a need for a particular type of movement in the eye that would coordinate the two modes of vision in an "effective form" which conformed to the truth of perception. The idea of truth to nature was of no consequence to Hildebrand, for whom the purpose of art was to create a distinct and autonomous world of perception—a world constituted specifically for the aesthetic pleasure of humanity.

Yve-Alain Bois has suggested that a profound fear of space motivated this instance by Hildebrand on the autonomy of the domain of art, a "fear of seeing the sculptural object lose itself in the world of object, fear of seeing the limits of art blur as real space invaded the imaginary space of art."[40] The sculptor had condemned the nineteenth-century panorama, the figures in waxworks, and the tombs of Canova, all of which played with the ambiguous boundaries between "real" space and "representational" space. According to Bois, Hildebrand's conception of sculpture as painting, reiterated in the postwar period by the American formalist critic Clement Greenberg in his interpretation of Picasso's cubist constructions as well as sculptures by David Smith[41]—like Rowe and Slutzky's conception of architecture as painting—aimed at safeguarding art from the terrifying prospect of the dissolution of the distinction between the autonomous space of the art object and real space. This fear had been absorbed within a bourgeois art in the nineteenth century, which was withdrawing from the destabilizing experience of industrialization, modernizing, and metropolitanization into the autonomous self-referential interior of artistic forms and practices—knowable, controllable, and secure.[42] Like Greenberg, the critic Michael Fried was fearful of the emergence of a relational conception of art, the greatest threat of which he identified in Minimalism, or what he called "literalist" art.[43] Robert Somol has already commented on the correspondence of terms and critiques between Rowe and Fried, and has even pointed to a possible way of revaluing the category of the "literal" in architecture through the notion of repetition.[44] Here, however, I would like to expand this to suggest that the relationality of the "literal" prefigures certain aspects of contemporary theory. Just as Rosalind Krauss began her reading of Minimalist art by revaluing what Fried feared about it—recognizing its "theatricality," or its being in the space and time of the observer, as the basis of its strategic contribution to the history of post-Formalism and the early history of post-Modernism—so I would like to point to Giedion and Moholy-Nagy for their pre-Minimalist (although still idealist) conception of relational space, which was likewise opposed to formalist autonomy and was already engaged in the concrete historical conditions of the space occupied by both the work of art and the observer.[45]

The aesthetic effect that interested Rowe and Slutzky was not the dissolution of substance into the particles of space, which had underpinned Alois Riegl's "Impressionist" reading of late Roman artworks, or the following *Raumgestaltung* of Moholy-Nagy's constructivism, or the formlessness of van Doesburg's quest for a "cubist" four-dimensional architecture. Rather, they sought the hermeneutic pleasure of an almost complete self-referentiality—one that absorbed doubt without compromising cognitive efficacy. Enjoying the play of Gestalt ambiguities that was characteristic of Purist paintings—figure and ground, object and matrix, space and surface—Rowe and Slutzky's game of assertion and denial accepted the experience of doubt, ambiguity, and contradiction, which accompanied the emergence of subjective aesthetics, only by internalizing, aestheticizing, and neutralizing its potential to destabilize cognitive certainty. Based still on an objective aesthetics of perceptive reception (Hildebrand), itself based on an outdated objectivist optics (Helmholtz), their appreciation of Purist still lifes and Le Corbusier's Villa Stein limited the game to the frame of the two-dimensional plane charged with the obligation of representing the spatial structure of the building for an observer aligned perspectivally on axis. Just as Hildebrand privileged relief sculpture out of a fear that introducing the subject's gaze into the construction of the art object would dissolve its autonomy into the uncontrollable space occupied by the observer,[46] so Rowe and Slutzky pulled back from the implications for architecture of the potentially uncontrollable ambiguities and contradictions of the *mariage des contours*—of the object dissolved into a liquid field of unstable yet constitutive relationships. They reasserted the pictorial facade as the guarantor of self-reflective transparency. Notwithstanding her admiration for the formalist tradition with which she associated Rowe, it was this move that prompted Krauss, in her essay of 1980, to reject formalism in favor of structuralism. She argued that the formalists' demand for "examining the ground of its own access to knowledge"—which earlier she had valued for turning transparency into opacity—simply resulted in a second-order transparency, still grounded in the proposition of an intelligence which is transparent to itself.

While Giedion was likewise motivated by the desire for unity, control, and consciousness, he nevertheless attempted to rethink the possibility of achieving such conditions through an analysis of the structural and material conditions of modernity. He recognized that synthetic cubism, collage, and montage marked a turn from the determinate representation of a self-positing consciousness toward a "new optics" of indeterminate biotechnic constructions hovering contingently without ground in a relational space that is as historical and concrete as it is virtual and ineffable. Beyond the label of literal, the ideal of transparency that Giedion and Moholy-Nagy sought to articulate in the 1920s, 1930s, and 1940s was phenomenal and perceptual, after all, in its confrontation with the machine, or more precisely with modes of production and reception in the modern industrial era. As such, it may yet figure in our understanding of the prehistory of preoccupations in our own time with systems of meditation, on the one hand, and the immediacy of formlessness on the other.

The author would like to thank Alan Colquhoun, George Baird, and Georges Teyssot for their comments on earlier versions of this essay.

[1] Colin Rowe and Robert Slutzky, "Transparency: Literal and Phenomenal," *Perspecta* 8 (1964): 45–54. The extent to which Gestalt psychology informed this essay is more explicit in its sequel, "Transparency: Literal and Phenomenal, Part II," *Perspecta* 13/14 (1971): 287–301. Both essays are reprinted in this volume, starting on page 91 and 103, respectively.

[2] The most considered critical treatments of the distinction between literal and phenomenal transparency are by Rosalind Krauss, "Death of a Hermeneutic Phantom," *Architecture + Urbanism* 112 (January 1980): 189–219; Anthony Vidler, "Transparency," *The Architectural Uncanny* (Cambridge, Mass.: MIT Press, 1992), 218-19; Terence Riley, *Light Construction* (New York: Museum of Modern Art, 1995); and Robert Somol, "Oublier Rowe," *Formwork: Colin Rowe, ANY* 7/8 (1994). [All of these essays are reprinted in the present volume.] These critics have understood the issue of transparency in cognitive as well as visual terms—of the modern subject believing that ideas, forms, and interpretations can be transparent to the mind that thinks them.

[3] See for instance Alfred H. Barr Jr.'s influential exhibition "Machine Art" of 1934 at the Museum of Modern Art. Exhibition catalogue: *Machine Art* (New York: Museum of Modern Art, 1934).

[4] See Detlef Mertins, "Anything but Literal: Sigfried Giedion and the Reception of Cubism in Germany," in *Architecture and Cubism*, ed. Nancy Troy and Eve Blau (Cambridge, Mass.: MIT Press, forthcoming). See also D. Mertins, "System and Freedom: Sigfried Giedion, Emil Kaufmann, and the Constitution of Architectural Modernity," in *Autonomy & Ideology: Positioning an Avant-Garde in America*, ed. Robert Somol (New York: Monacelli Press, 1997).

[5] See Rosemary Haag Bletter, "Opaque Transparency," *Oppositions* 13 (Summer 1978): 121–26. Reprinted in this volume starting on page 115.

[6] See Sigfried Giedion, *Space, Time, and Architecture* (Cambridge, Mass.: Harvard University Press, 1941).

[7] See Heinrich Wölfflin, *Renaissance und Barok: Eine Untersuchung über Wesen und Entstehung des Barockstils in Italien* (Munich: Theodor Ackermann, 1988), partially trans. Kathrin Simon as *Renaissance and Baroque* (Ithaca, N.Y.: Cornell University Press, 1964). See also H. Wölfflin, *Kunstgeschichtliche Grundbegriffe. Das Problem der Stilentwicklung in der neueren Kunst* (Munich: Hugo Bruckmann, 1915), trans. M. D. Hottinger as *Principles of Art History: The Problem of Development of Style in Later Art* (New York: Dover, 1950). For the sources of Wölfflin's categories and the significance of Jacob Burckhardt, who also taught Nietzsche, see Joan Goldhammer Hart, "Heinrich Wölfflin: An Intellectual Biography" (unpublished dissertation, University of California, Berkeley, 1981), 139–211. For an interpretation of Wölfflin's categories in relation to Nietzsche's Apollonian and Dionysian, see Jan Bailostocki, "'Barok': Stil, Epoche, Haltung," in *Stil und Ikonographie* (Dresden: 1965), 80.

[8] Friedrich Nietzsche, "The Birth of Tragedy: Out of the Spirit of Music," in *The Birth of Tragedy and the Case of Wagner,* trans. Walter Kaufmann (New York: Vintage Books, 1967).

[9] For a post-structural analysis of Rowe's thought in relation to issues of autonomy and form, see R. E. Somol, "Oublier Rowe," *Formwork: Colin Rowe (Any* 7/8), 1994. Reprinted in this volume starting on page 123.

[10] See Konrad Fiedler, "Über den Ursprung der künstlerischen Tätigkeit" (1887), in K. Fiedler, *Schriften zur Kunst*, vol. I, ed. Gottfried Boehm (Munich: Wilhelm Fink, 1971), 183–367. While Giedion also emphasized vision (the "new optics"), it was the embodied vision of an observer moving in space and time that he had in mind, just as he often used corporeal metaphors to characterize buildings.

[11] Rowe and Slutzky, "Transparency," 49.

[12] György Képes, *Language of Vision* (Chicago, Ill.: Paul Theobald and Company, 1944). Képes was much younger than Moholy-Nagy and settled in Berlin in 1931 under the latter's influence. He then followed Moholy-Nagy to London, where they worked together, and then later to Chicago, where Képes taught in Moholy-Nagy's New Bauhaus. See Krisztina Passuth, *Moholy-Nagy* (London: Thames and Hudson, 1985), 60, 65, 69, 70. If Képes initially drew Moholy-Nagy and Giedion, Giedion's later thought on transparency in primitive as well as modern art bears traces of Képes's *Language of Vision*. See S. Giedion, "Transparency: Primitive and Modern," *Art News* 51, no. 4 (June–August 1952): 47–50, 92–96.

[13] Robert Slutzky, "Aqueous Humor," *Oppositions* 19/20 (Winter/Spring 1980): 29–51; see also R. Slutzky, "Après le Purisme," *Assemblage* 4 (October 1987): 95–101, in which he turns to the *mariage des contours* as the basis of what he called a new poetic imagination, which he tracks to Le Corbusier's Ronchamp and La Tourette, "two structures that encapsulate the subliminal and the sublime." Slutzky writes, "With Le Corbusier, the constraints of Purist aesthetics, of compositional literalness, will be radically loosened, giving way to more ambiguous space and content and allowing the artist's psychic energies to overflow into his work."

[14] For a detailed reconsideration of Giedion's interpretation of the relationship between Le Corbusier's architecture and his Purist paintings, see D. Mertins, "Anything but Literal," in *Architecture and Cubism*. An earlier version of this was published in D. Mertins, "Open Contours and Other Autonomies," *Monolithic Architecture*, ed. Rodolfo Machado and Rodolphe el-Khoury (New York: Prestel, 1996), 36–61.

[15] Le Corbusier's fascination with perception in motion is well known. What remains less well known, however, is the explicitness with which he linked his notion of the architectural promenade to the perceptual play of volumes and colors. See D. Mertins, "Anything but Literal."

Underlying Giedion and Moholy-Nagy's concern for the moving spectator was the theory of *Raumgestaltung* (space forming) developed by the art historian August Schmarsow. See A. Schmarsow, "The Essence of Architectural Creation" (1893), in *Empathy, Form, and Space*, ed. and trans. Harry Francis Mallgrave and Eleftherios Ikonomou (Santa Monica, Calif.: Getty Center for the History of Art and the Humanities, 1994), 281–97; and Mitchell Schwarzer, "The Emergence of Architectural Space: August Schmarsow's Theory of *Raumgestaltung*," *Assemblage* 15 (1991): 50–61.

In 1919, Fritz Hoeber invoked Schmarsow's theory of the cognition of objects by an observer in motion in a critique of Hildebrand, in order to emphasize that the plastic arts were not configurations merely for the eye, but rather for the "entire organism," the "experiencing soul." See Fritz Hoeber, "Die Irrtümer der Hildebrandschen Raumästhetik," *Der Sturm* 9, no. 12 (March 1919): 157–58.

[16] Képes, *Language*, 77.

[17] Képes, *Language*, 76–85. Képes grouped together, for instance, a study of Képes, *Language*, transparency by his student Clifford Eitel, a fifteenth-century German painting of the Last Supper in association with a diagram of overlapping planes, Picasso's portrait of Kahnweiler, a still life by Ozenfant, a photograph of a layered view through a house by G. F. Keck, a space construction of 1930 by Moholy-Nagy, a photomontage made by Képes himself and one by Jack Waldheim, a double portrait drawing by Le Corbusier, and numerous examples of advertising including images by Képes, William Burtin, Paul Rand, Frank Barr, Cassandre, E. McKnight Kauffer, and Fernand Léger.

[18] Képes begins his acknowledgments in *Language of Vision* with the following statement: "First of all the author wishes to acknowledge his indebtedness to the Gestalt psychologists. Many of the inspiring ideas and concrete illustrations of Max Werthiemer, K. Koffka, and W. Kohler have been used in the first part of the book to explain the laws of visual organization." Képes, *Language*, 4.

[19] Képes, *Language*, 86.

[20] Képes, *Language*, 68.

[21] Képes, *Language*, 15.

[22] Képes, *Language*, 35.

[23] Képes, *Language*, 32, 60.

[24] Képes, *Language*, 66.

[25] Képes, *Language*, 34, 171.

[26] Képes, *Language*, 35.

[27] Képes, *Language*, 86.

[28] Képes, *Language*, 161.

[29] See Christian Lenz, ed., *Hans von Marées*, (Munich: Prestel, 1987), and Alfred Neumeyer, "Hans von Marées and the Classical Doctrine in the Nineteenth Century," *Art Bulletin* 20 (1938): 291–311. Von Marées's paintings were included in Paul Fechter's *Expressionismus* (1914) along with cubist paintings by Picasso and Braque, and later in Paul Küpper's *Kubismus* (1921). This was a sign not only of the extent to which the German discourse of expressionism sought to absorb the whole of modern painting but also of the fluid reciprocity between expressionism and cubism in the German scene at the time. Julius Meirer-Graefe, in *Hans von Marées* (Munich: R. Piper and Co., 1920), celebrated von Marées as the equal of Paul Cézanne.

[30] Adolf Hildebrand, "The Problem of Form in the Fine Arts, 1893," in *Empathy, Form and Space*, 227–79. For a discussion of the relationship of Alois Riegl's thought to that of Hildebrand, see Margaret Iversen, *Alois Riegl: Art History and Theory* (Cambridge, Mass.: MIT Press, 1991), 73–76.

[31] Hildebrand, "The Problem of Form," 232.

[32] See Hildebrand, "Introduction," in *Empathy, Form and Space*, 36; and Iversen, *Alois Riegl*, 73, (note 3).

[33] Hildebrand, "Problem of Form," 232.

[34] Hildebrand, "Problem of Form," 236.

[35] Hildebrand, "Problem of Form," 247.

[36] On Hildebrand's technique, see Helmut Börsch-Supan, "Zur Herkunft der Kunst von Marées," in *Hans von Marées*, ed. Lenz, 25–32.

[37] Hildebrand, "Problem of Form," 251.

[38] Hildebrand, "Problem of Form," 251.

[39] Hildebrand, "Problem of Form," 252.

[40] Hildebrand, "Problem of Form," 75.

[41] See Clement Greenberg, "Review of the Exhibition Collage" (1948; reprint in *Clement Greenberg: The Collected Essays and Criticism*, vol. 2, ed. John O'Brian Chicago, Ill.: University of Chicago Press, 1986, pp. 259–63); and C. Greenberg, "The New Sculpture" (1949; reprint in O'Brian). For a more detailed reading of these issues in relation to Greenberg, Fried, and Krauss, see D. Mertins in *Monolithic Architecture*.

[42] For the relationship between autonomous art and avant-garde art, see Peter Bürger, *Theory of the Avant-Garde*, trans. Michael Shaw (Minneapolis: University of Minnesota Press, 1984), and the forward by Jochen Schulte-Sasse, "Theory of Modernism versus the Theory of the Avant-Garde." It was against this fear among the bourgeoisie that the avant-gardes, especially the Dadaist-Constructivist axis in Germany, mounted their campaign after the war, to reengage art in social praxis, moving from painting to architecture.

[43] Michael Fried, "Art and Objecthood" (1967). Reprinted in *Minimal Art: A Critical Anthology*, ed. Gregory Battcock (New York: E. P. Dutton, 1968), 116–47.

[44] See. R. Somol, "Oublier Rowe," in *Formwork: Colin Rowe*, 15. Reprinted in this volume starting on page 123.

[45] See Rosalind Krauss, *Passages in Modern Sculpture* (Cambridge, Mass.: MIT Press, 1977), 201–42. Of course the distinction Krauss made in this text between the theatricality of Moholy-Nagy's *Light Space Modulator* of 1923–30 and that of Picabia's stage set for *Relâche* of 1924 is still significant. See also R. Krauss, "Sculpture in the Expanded Field," *October* 8 (Spring 1979); and R. Krauss, "Overcoming the Limits of Matter: On Revising Minimalism," in *American Art of the 1960s*, ed. John Elderfield (New York: Museum of Modern Art, 1991), 123–41 (especially 138–39).

For an interpretation of space-time in the relational aesthetics of art during the 1990s, see Nicholas Bourriaud, "An Introduction to Relational Aesthetics," in *Traffic*, exhibition catalogue (Bordeaux: Cap Musée d'Art Contemporaine, 1966), n.p.

[46] Yve-Alain Bois has discussed Hildebrand's fear of space—of art leaping from the two-dimensional surface of representation into the three-dimensional world (a fear, he argues, that Clement Greenberg shared but that Henry-Daniel Kahnweiler and Carl Einstein considered a key limitation of Western art). See Y.-A. Bois, "Kahnweiler's Lesson," in *Painting as Model* (Cambridge, MA: MIT Press, 1990), 65–97.

P-TR'S PROGRESS
Jeffrey Kipnis

PROLOGUE

Theory helps those of us who do practical work to determine the direction, to see the future clearly, to be resolute in action and to have confidence in the success of our work.
    Joseph Stalin

Night and day I dream of having my actions recorded in history. The most dishonorable way to win a name for oneself is through scholarly compositions, but at the moment it is the only way I know. . .
    Ho Chi Minh

Whatever its merits as a work of architecture, the Aronoff Center for Design and Art (figs. 104–7) confirms Eisenman's talent in another crucial area of the discipline, the construction of a professional persona. He has cultivated an Elmer Gantry character that enables him to persuade his clients to invest in nothing more than, but nothing less than, form. "But that is architecture!" he intones.

The genius of Eisenman's professional craft lies not only in his abilities to convince his clients of his difficult designs, but also in his will to guide them—the designs and the clients—through the protracted dissonance they encounter on the way to realization. Many, when they first confront the Aronoff Center, will quip that it is amazing that the architect gets such things built. Few will realize that they have said something important.

Eisenman honed his professional skills in the classrooms of Princeton, Harvard, The Cooper Union, and elsewhere. Always controversial, he nevertheless emerged as one of a generation's legendary teachers. In each class he could be heard to declare, "But that is architecture," as he urged students into an obedient awe of form.

"But that is architecture." Even today, Eisenman continues to mesmerize all comers with that passionate trope—so effective because it forecloses dissent even as it claims to deepen the discussion. It is not difficult to imagine why few of his students found a way to the measured reply, "No architecture is more than form."

1. PHENOMENAL TRANSPARENCY

Of course, long before he took to the lectern, Eisenman had himself been inducted into the formalist creed by Colin Rowe. In passing and on the way to outlining a deeply conservative position, Rowe opened the door to a post-Wölfflinian formalism that, despite his best efforts, he could not hold in check. "The Mathematics of the Ideal Villa," "Transparency: Literal and Phenomenal" (with Robert Slutzky), and his precocious attention to certain modern masters (Le Corbusier and Terragni)—albeit a perverse attention bent on subsuming these architects into his antiprogressivist project—earned for Rowe the bizarre status of the intellectual progenitor of the American avant-garde.

In the two mentioned essays, Rowe employed clever gimmicks to make his formalist case persuasive. Consider, for example, the hyperbolic titles. Given that architects are congenitally terrified that their art is merely superficial, who among them could resist Rowe's ponderous promises of profundity. No matter that the "Mathematics of the Ideal Villa" turned out to be a couple of cubes on grass or that "Phenomenal Transparency" ended up nothing more than a catchy *bon mot* for an interesting formal effect. The titles were their own guarantors, their own source of depth.

But Rowe's best trick was his canny use of examples. To ensure that the then-fashion for glass, lamentable to his retrograde tastes, fell short of more traditional solid materials, he pitted a modest Gropius against a Corbusian tour de force, remaining silent about Mies's considerably more convincing use of glass. To indemnify his an-historical formal comparisons in "Mathematics," he invoked two masterworks, each of consummate quality in its use of material, construction, detail, program, light and shadow, siting space, etc., allowing the issue of form to be artificially foregrounded.

The technique was simple but effective sophistry: twist the fact that great architecture often has intricate formal properties into an argument that intricate formal properties constitute great architecture. Most understood the distortion as rhetorical device; even if they followed Rowe's emphasis on form, they kept an eye on the balance of their architectural palette. Though Eisenman, a formidable critic early on, no doubt recognized the device as well, he embraced formalism with apostolic fervor.

Yet, let us not assume Eisenman's ecstatic tunnel vision doomed his architecture du jour. Though it has shackled his work with limitations, limitations that reach a critical point in the Aronoff Center, it has also allowed him to produce architectural effects never before imagined. These, too, reach a frenzied peak in Cincinnati, a peek at the brink of madness.

Virtually all of Eisenman's inventions derive from the Rowe/Slutzky treatment of Phenomenal Transparency. Despite the authors' effort to edify their terminology with dictionary quotations, their use of the term *phenomenal* is nonsensical,[1] notwithstanding its remarkable cachet. Nevertheless, Phenomenal Transparency has become the proper name for an important formal effect: the use of formal relations to express on opaque facades the increasingly complex sections made possible by modern construction. The transparency thus achieved is conceptual. It is not seen, but read; it belongs not to the senses, but to the mind.

It is doubtful that Le Corbusier sought to achieve the particular effect as described by Rowe and Slutzky; its availability at Garches is more likely an artifact of the architect's general bent for coherence. No matter; the authors' convincing account of the effect gave birth to its possibility as an explicit project. With their analysis, the authors introduced a new stage in the textualization of architectural form and gave momentum to the transformation of contemporary architecture from the sensual to the intellectual, a transformation that mirrored processes well under way in the other arts.

2. PHENOMENAL TRANSLUCENCY

The Rowe/Slutzky argument transfixed Eisenman.[2] According to the architect's own account, his preoccupation with their expanded textualization of formal relations was immediate and powerful. He saw in it the possibility of fulfilling architecture's long-lived, but long deferred ambition to achieve full status as a critical cultural apparatus. With such sophisticated formal effects, he argued, architects would be able to write cultural commentary in architecture.

For years, Eisenman meticulously cultivated the Phenomenal Transparency effect into an entire repertoire of formal devices. As he proceeded through his twelve houses (I–X, El Even Odd, Fin D'Out Hous) and through such projects as the Canneregio Housing and Wexner Center, he slowly mastered the technique of using process to coordinate ensembles of formal effects into increasingly ambitious and complex texts. In these designs, whether the textual subject matter was discursive or fictional, the architect remained faithful to the premise of a legible perspicacity of formal relationships fundamental to the original Rowe/Slutzky notion.

With those early works, Eisenman also went out of his way to broadcast his unconditional commitment to formal relationships over all other architectural values. He exalted in ignoring material traditions, using any expedient material as long as it allowed him to construct, and afford to construct, his forms. He systematically choreographed his form-texts to encroach on function. Whenever he published a project he included a complete exposition of the formal processes; if the publication was of a building, he chose photographs that confirmed the formal achievements. No images of people enjoying their homes, no pleasant views, no atmospheric interiors. Just Form.

At some point, beginning perhaps with the Romeo and Juliet project and certainly in full flower by the La Villette garden, a transformation occurred: Eisenman began to elaborate the formal intricacy of his designs well beyond the point of legibility. While he maintained an unfailing rigor in his deployment and annotation of formal relationships in these projects—thus preserving, in principle at least, the possibility of a correct reading—the sheer number of devices, repeated at several scales, and an increasing tendency to compel these devices to intersect and superpose, made legibility a practical impossibility.

In Eisenman's hands, the effect so cherished by Rowe, that is, the directed transmission of interior formal relationships through the facade by way of the eye to the mind of a discerning subject, gave way to mind-boggling spectra of formal reflections, refractions, and diffractions no longer obeying any simple sense of origin or directionality. Dazzling disarray supplanted tasteful clarity as the architect entangled his viewer in a web of formal counterparts to mirrors and veils, driving beyond Phenomenal Transparency to an entirely new architectural effect: Phenomenal Translucency.

3. PHEROMONAL TRANSLUCENCY

This new music frustrates me. . . . Its composers seem to think rather than feel.
   Sergei Rachmaninoff

The point of critique is not justification but a different way of feeling, another sensibility.
   Gilles Deleuze

A cursory survey of the architect's explication of the Aronoff Center will confirm what every visitor will intuit whether or not they understand his processes and arguments, indeed whether or not they know or care anything about formal relationships in architecture. The Center is, beyond doubt, a stunning achievement of Phenomenal Translucency: divaricating iterations of the Z form of the original buildings dance across a conceptual axis implied by the deviation of one leg of the Z from its ideal; the undulating contour of the site abstracts into an S form, internally reflects to generate a rope of superposed boxes, and then hangs like a necklace on the Z group so that the two organizing systems (Z and S) and the box elements of each blur into one another to create a fabulous, bewildering spectacle. However intriguing one may find the mechanisms of the design—its processes and notations—these offer nothing to account for the building's visceral impact.

The Center is everywhere discomforting, and it is no accident that once you are inside it, the sensation it most elicits is that of being immersed in the mise-en-abyme of reflections in an immense, mirrored room. But it is on the exterior where the darkest consequences of the transition from Phenomenal Transparency to Phenomenal Translucency first erupt.

The sequence of facades grips you with a fulsome ambivalence; as you move around the building, you experience incessant waves of fascination and dread. You confront a badly dissected harlequin splayed open to reveal alien organs, piebald and swollen. Unable to take your eyes off this macabre scene, you discover the xeno-vitals to be but real organs transected and recombined into a delirious fugue. You realize your first intuition was wrong. Far from being the result of incompetence, it is an expert work by a master surgeon, one driven to operate at the limit of technique but wearied of the traditions and values of his art. When you leave it, the building clings to you, not as a memory, but as an odor, partly erotic, partly necrotic.

An obtuse description, no doubt. But that speaks to a crucial change or register magnified by the Center's perfection of Phenomenal Translucency. Even as the design of the building claims to be a conceptual enterprise, its unfathomable complexity silently underwrites a certain reaffirmation of sensation over intellection. Eisenman had discovered early on that some of the most interesting aspects of his buildings were the unexpected experiences they produced, such as the giant, layered perspectival tubes generated by the grid-lattice at the Wexner Center. As sensations rather than understandings, these unintended effects did not properly belong to the formal readings the architect set out to embody.

Yet neither could they be simply detached from those readings; the latter established a receptive field, the milieu of sensibility for the new experiences. The Wexner's perspectival tunnels, for example, would not have felt the same, perhaps would not even have been noticed, had the lattice appeared at the Wexner Center as a traditional figure, e.g., a trellised pergola, rather than as but a moment in an elaborate scheme of grid notations suffusing the whole building and its site. Directed toward reading, toward interpretation, most of those notations were experientially flat. Thus, the encounter with the perspectival tunnels offered a particular shock.

At first Eisenman treated these experiential aspects of his designs as just deserts, as interest earned on a cerebral design process. But as the designs grew more complex and the possibility of reading receded, these effects gained increased importance, overtaking the status of interpretation. Formal textuality and process stopped being ends in themselves and became techniques by which unusual sensibilities were achieved. Once desperate to leave behind the pre-critical realm of architectural sensibilities in order to achieve a critical architecture, Eisenman now steered a post-critical turn toward new sensibilities, new feelings.

To distinguish post-critical from pre-critical sensibilities and to call attention to the fact that the emotional impact of the work emanates not from the representations of the architecture but from the formal structures themselves, Eisenman termed these new sensations collectively as "affects."[3] Thus, while the original objective of Eisenman's architecture was reading, its ultimate objective became affect. And the Aronoff Center is nothing if not a seething cauldron of affects.

As the consummation of this change in objective, the Center also completes Eisenman's two-decade-long reconstruction of Rowe's ideal modern subject, the patient, reflective connoisseur, into a contemporary subject who is never quite ideal, who, perpetually agitated and buffeted by irrepressible appetites, cannot simply see or read, but watches, gawks, gazes, and stares, a schizo-voyeur. The Center is a limit condition, an extreme case. Not merely Phenomenal Translucency, then, but something more promiscuous. Pheromonal Translucency?

Or, given the rupture wrought by the Viconian return of Eisenman's architecture to feelings and sensibilities, a return driven not by retreating from arcane form, but by driving form beyond the arcane, by driving form crazy, perhaps the Center is best considered a case of—

4. PHEROMONAL TRANSLUNACY

"pher-o-mone (fêr•e•môn), n. 1. Animal Behav. Any chemical substance released by an animal that serves to influence the sexual behavior of another member of the same species. 2. Chemicals whose physical form induces changes in behavior or affect in animals and are able to act at remote distances from the source. [1959. Gk.]" [emphasis added]

The best thing about Peter's buildings is the insane spaces he ends up with. That's why he is an important architect. All that other stuff, the philosophy and all, is just bullshit as far as I'm concerned.
    Frank Gehry

Eisenman's plunge into an architecture of post-critical sensibilities brings into focus certain chronic limitations of his technique. The most conspicuous at the Center is the inadequacy of his formal procedures to conceptualize and deploy materials in roles richer than providing shape and notation. This despite the fact that, with the exception of light and shadow, perhaps no other aspect of a building is so saturated with affective expectation.

Without doubt, architects have made the best use of material effects in buildings and provided the most color-ful meditations on them—consider, for example, Louis Kahn's conversation with a brick. Nevertheless, the materiali-ty of buildings is by no means a topic exclusive to architecture. The fundamental insinuation of material affectivity across many cultures has long been in evidence well beyond the boundaries of architecture, in art, literature, mythology, and elsewhere. Even the three little pigs and the wolf knew of it.

At the onset of his design career Eisenman used his radical formalism as an opportunity to neuter architecture's venerated tradition of evocative materiality, which he saw as irremediably sentimental and therefore pre-critical. As a result, all of his works to date are built in non-emotive materials used strictly to make forms and to code for-mal relations; that is, to support the textuality of the design. In the early projects in particular, materiality, albeit under erasure, was intrinsic to the architect's theoretical position.

As affect became increasingly important in his work, however, Eisenman's position on materiality quietly slipped from the purely theoretical. By the time he was building the Aronoff Center, the architect, aware of the affective potential of materiality, attempted belatedly to recapture it for his project. The finishing material for the exterior, for example, was originally a far more convincing Italian tile.

The Center, however, was designed strictly as a formal exercise; material considerations entered the design only as a desirable appurtenance, a rendering tool without any necessary, intrinsic relationship to the project's con-ception. Thus, when financial considerations imposed the inevitable Sophie's Choice between materials and form, Eisenman had no convincing alternative but to sacrifice materials.

Had the architect not broached the question of affect, his material technique may never have posed a serious problem. But with the onset of his move toward post-critical sensibilities, it is proving a handicap—in part because of a lost affective opportunity, in part because his material choices undermine the potential powers of his forms. At the Center, the consequences are most acutely evident on the exterior.

The facades of the Center are rendered in pigmented EIFS, a synthetic stucco that is the architectural equiva-lent of food coloring and gruel. Nontectonic and void of any intrinsic qualities, this faux-material and others like it are often chosen today for large, difficult forms because they are inexpensive, highly plastic, and easy to use. As such, they are typically found in the construction of pseudo-historical buildings, theme parks, and miniature golf courses. Like theater sets, however, these constructions need only suspend disbelief, an effect dependent on the generous receptivity of an audience. To achieve its full potential as a work of architecture, a building must not depend on generosity. It must surpass the suspension of disbelief, insisting itself on all constituencies by looking and feeling, by being real.[4]

As other contemporary architects have discovered, materials need not be traditional, precious, or valorized to meet a standard of insistence. But the facades of the Aronoff Center are less than materially insistent and suffer the repercussions. Many persons, for example, have found fault with Eisenman's choice of exterior colors. The colors are indeed jarring, but, on the other hand, they contribute substantially to the disturbing effect. It is not the colors, per se, but the use of irresolute materials that causes those colors to be problematic.

Whatever weaknesses the Aronoff Center suffers in materiality are more than overshadowed by the success of its exotic interior spaces. Circulating through the halls and rooms, one is overwhelmed by a masterpiece of Eisenman's interior style: staggered and shifting streams of pastel elements—columns, beams, walls—merge into and emerge from one another, intriguing windows puncture walls according to an order other than the traditional relationship to light or views, and so forth. To this signature palette the Center contributes a braided organization that snakes in plan and section like a giant caduceus, abandoned and on the verge of going feral.

As one moves through the building, again and again one comes upon astonishing spaces, moments in the building where all modes of interest—its elaborate formal relationships, its displacing affects, its twining plan and layered section, even its neutered materiality—converge and coalesce into an operatic chorus whose swells of assonance and dissonance are more transporting than any of its individual voices. While these dramatic moments occur in the primary voids of the building, e.g., the central triple-height atrium and the main theater, they are also found in less conspicuous locales, such as the entry to the building from the campus parking lot and the umbilical foyer that joins the navels of the old and new buildings.

The network of hyperactive spaces at the Center is far superior to those achieved in Eisenman's previous built works and are more convincingly linked throughout the building by the connective tissues of his stylistic palette. As a whole, the interiors absorb and agitate and push the visitor to multiple edges: to the edge of vertigo, to the edge of confusion, to the edge of credibility.

The interiors alone ensure that the Center will assume the status of the finest of Eisenman's work to date. Indeed, it is difficult to imagine that the architect could possibly squeeze any more surprises out of his textual-formal techniques. Hence, one suspects that, wherever the architect takes design from here, the Center will also stand as the culminating achievement of this line of his inquiry.

The Aronoff Center, however, is not just a work within Eisenman's oeuvre; it is one of the crowning achievements of a period of architectural research, taking its place alongside such buildings as Daniel Libeskind's Jewish Museum in Berlin and Frank Gehry's Guggenheim Museum in Bilbao. For the last two decades, these architects and others have concentrated their various efforts on an architecture of radical singularity; that is, the design of buildings that neither follow any other building as a prototype nor offer themselves as new prototypes.

This eschewal of prototypical ambition has its roots in a reaction against the stultifying Corporate Modernism enabled, if not authorized, by the explicitly prototypical researches of the early modernists. This prototypical intent continues in full force today in the work of the neo-historicists and certain new modernists. Over time, however, the architecture of radical singularity has tried to outgrow its initial formulation as a mere refusal and/or rejection of dominant architectural principles. Architects and theorists have been attempting to formulate an alternative body of ideas intended to construct radical singularity as a positive social, cultural, and political project for architecture; that is, as a continuously viable mode of practice.

As is to be expected, radical singularity has met with the same predictable uneasiness from the public as all other new and unusual ideas, though it has earned wide attention in academic circles. However extraordinary their results, with only a relatively few exemplary buildings to assess, it is far too early to determine the larger significance of this model of architectural practice. It may well be that radical singularity will cast a permanent pall on prototypical practices, or it may be that its avoidance of prototypical research may ultimately prove a dereliction. In retrospect, the Aronoff Center may be seen as a pivotal work in a new era of architecture or a climactic work of a fascinating period consigned to the irrelevant because it broached no enduring influence.

Whatever its ultimate impact on the future of architecture, there can be no doubt that the Aronoff Center will enjoy a well-deserved period of study and attention. Outrageous scion of a coupling between a house of cards and a hall of mirrors, the Center is fun house become work of art. No small achievement.

[1] Strictly speaking, what Rowe and Slutzky named "literal transparency" is a phenomenal effect, and their "phenomenal transparency" is an interpretive, and therefore literary, effect. Yet, despite possible appearances, I do not offer this observation as pedantry; to the contrary, I admire and subscribe to the authors' preference for rhetorical effect over scholarly rigor. I am particularly grateful to them for the term in question, whose (eisen) manic transformations structure this essay.

[2] Unlike Rowe's argument for formal typology in "Mathematics," which Eisenman virtually ignored. That essay argues the persistent viability of a limited catalogue of formal types across history, providing the linchpin for Rowe's conservative attack on zeitgeist theories. It was, therefore, anathema to Eisenman's avant-gardist ambitions. Eisenman recognized both the persuasive power of typological arguments and their threat to his position. He initially attempted to outflank typological theory with a deep structure argument for architectural form, following Noam Chomsky. The benefits of such a formulation to Eisenman's project are still apparent. 1. It would reinforce the configuration of architecture as a textual (intellectual) system. 2. It would allow for persistent formal types, analogues to specific languages, without making these the foundation of architectural knowledge, much as Chomsky's work accounted for particular languages without making any specific language or ur-language the basis of linguistic theory. 3. Finally and most importantly, it would emphasize the open-endedness of design. Chomsky had already shown that an infinite number of statements, most of which would be new, were enabled by the finite number of rules of his generative grammar.

However promising this approach was, it was quickly proved intractable for architects. He soon settled for appropriating formal types into his manipulations by reducing them to signs. While this approach allows him to acknowledge typology without obligating his architecture to its restrictive regimens, it ultimately skirted the key conservative claim that all received formal types embody persistent patterns of use and meaning, and that all persistent patterns of use and meaning have already engendered formal types. Eisenman's failure to confront typology head-on has left his work vulnerable to the criticism, particularly from the old-left, that it constitutes mere indulgence in fashion, rather than an authentic avant-garde.

[3] Eisenman's theoretical treatment of affect derives somewhat circuitously from Freud, who used the term to accent the mobility of expressed emotions and their independence from expressed representations. For example, in a dream one may report seeing a pleasant scene but experiencing an inappropriate feeling such as fear. In this case, an affect had moved from its original source and attached to the pastoral representation.

[4] It is important to note that the "material reality" of a building is not a natural outgrowth of some unchanging phenomenological essence of particular materials—wood, stone, steel—but an architectural effect whose persuasiveness, like any special effect, is open to the vicissitudes of changing contexts, attitudes, and techniques. Along this line, it is interesting to observe how some materials, e.g., marble or teak, once revered in architecture and revisited in the last decade by some architects, are today so extravagant that their use in a building renders it farcically irreal (cf. London's Canary Wharf).

DEATH OF A HERMENEUTIC PHANTOM:
MATERIALIZATION OF THE SIGN IN THE WORK
OF PETER EISENMAN

Rosalind Krauss

Cultures change; and whether we read those changes as growth or diminishment depends on our perspective—political, intellectual, aesthetic. Since the late 1950s, we have been witnessing, living through, and shaping such a change, which only now that it is fully wrought becomes distinct for us. One simple way of naming the cultural present, the one that now surrounds us, is to say that it is post-modernist. But by that term we are merely asserting that it is somehow different from the main thrust of Western culture in the first half of the twentieth century, a culture for which modernism serves as the most convenient name. To isolate and define that change is the general subject of this essay.

At least it is the explicit subject. The implicit one is the architecture of Peter Eisenman. And given the somewhat unorthodox—not to say oneiric—procedure of generating this kind of manifest and latent content, I need to preface my remarks with an explanation. For one might wonder why a discussion of this nature would be included in a book devoted to the specialized work of a single architect; and further, why I—who have no particular competence in architectural criticism—would be the one to do it.

The most direct answer is that Peter Eisenman and I lived through our own experience of this cultural shift, which is to say experienced the last ten or dozen years in critical, intellectual tandem. This relationship has less to do with whether the two of us came together for direct discussion (which, intermittently, we did), than with the fact that our two careers—his as an architect and architectural theorist, mine as an art critic and theorist—ran on parallel intellectual tracks. For both of us began by locating ourselves within the modernist tradition through its central analytical model, which is formalism. As formalists—self-professed and extremely determined—we were each involved in developing a set of what we then thought were logical elaborations to the initial model.

What we did not know in those years, from the mid- through the late 1960s, was that those elaborations were *logically* foreign to the soil of formalism, and could only really take root in a quite different domain. We had both, of course, read a description of our situation; but since we did not yet experience it as problematic, we did not internalize what we had read. In *The Structure of Scientific Revolutions*, Thomas Kuhn depicts the circumstances that precede what he calls a paradigm shift—that is, the moment when one set of theories or explanations is about to be supplanted by another. During this time the working scientist experiences physical behavior that, within the reigning paradigm, is anomalous. In order to account for these anomalies, the scientist must append sub-theories or qualifications to the major paradigm, ones that substantially begin to cut its efficiency as explanation. It is only a new paradigm that can—under an entirely new vision of lawlike behavior—effortlessly account for what had seemed awkward or unruly under the old one.

As a formalist, Eisenman exhibited anomalous behaviors by insisting on introducing a linguistic model into his work and criticism. At the time he did not see this as running against the grain of formalism, only as somewhat attenuating or dilating its normal categories of analysis. What is formalism, he reasons, if not a particular type of reading, and if so how can linguistics be foreign to it?

The kind of reading formalism demanded was one that converted transparency into opacity; one that both acknowledged the work of art itself and insisted that it force or promote that conversion. Transparency is used here in the sense that Sartre invokes it to speak of prose writing as something the gaze looks *through* toward a meaning. For the prose writer, words "are prolongations of his meanings, his pincers, his antennae, his eyeglasses. He maneuvers them from within."[1] Against this, Sartre distinguishes the language of the poet as opaque: the phrase-object; the work turned thing. Quoting two lines from Mallarmé,

To flee, to flee there, I feel that birds are drunk
But, oh, my heart, hear the song of the sailors.

Sartre speaks of "this 'but' which rises like a monolith at the threshold of the sentence," by means of which the poet (or reader) "tastes for their own sake the irritating flavors of objection, of reserve, of disjunction. He carries them to the absolute. He makes them real properties of the sentence, which becomes an utter objection without being an objection *to* anything precise."[2] The word turned monolith is the word become opaque, through which the disjunction—"but"—can be experienced sensuously as though it were a smooth pebble held in the hands, or the shiny skin of an apple.

But it is not merely toward the sensuous properties of the word/thing that the poem drives us. For even as the word is isolated out as object, it is transformed into a special type of thing: a cognitive object, one that forces us to reflect upon how it is we know something. As Sartre adds, "The ensemble of the words chosen functions as an *image* of the interrogative or restrictive nuance." Positioned usually as the shear between two lines of verse, the word *but* reinforces its meaning spatially by becoming an image of disjunction.

For the formalist a distinction between transparency and opacity was crucial to the differentiation between everything that was not art and everything that was. In this sense the formalist would oppose Sartre's inclusion of prose writing (the novel, the short story) in the category of transparency and claim that insofar as it was literature, prose writing had to have recourse to devices that dam up the reader's effortless flow toward the fiction's subject. In an often quoted passage the Russian formalist Viktor Shklovsky refers to a page from Tolstoy's journals to argue for the ethical necessity of this damming up, this thickening of experience: "I was cleaning a room," Tolstoy wrote, "and, meandering about approached the divan and couldn't remember whether or not I had dusted it. Since these movements are habitual and unconscious, I could not remember and felt that it was impossible to remember, so that if I had dusted it and forgot—that is, had acted unconsciously—then it was the same as if I had not. If some conscious person had been watching, then the fact could be established. If, however, no one was looking, or looking on unconsciously, then such lives are as if they had never been."[3] To lives that were routinized or mechanized by ordinary commerce with words and things, the work of art offered a renewal of perception. Against the threat of lives that "are as if they had never been," art could force a coming into consciousness through what Shklovsky termed "defamiliarization" or "making strange." It was its capacity to do so that rendered the work of art a cognitive object, one that had the power to cause in its reader or viewer reflection upon the modes of consciousness.

Shklovsky's analysis presents a taxonomy of strategies of defamiliarization within the novel form itself: retardation, double plotting, episodic composition, and "baring of the device"—that is, forcing the reader's attention to the actual procedures of writing, or narrating, directly exhibiting the technical substructure of the story. In writing about the visual arts, particularly painting, the critic Clement Greenberg addresses himself to this same opposition between the transparent–"Realistic, illusionistic art had dissembled the medium, using art to conceal art"–and the opaque–"Modernism used art to call attention to art."[4] For Greenberg the strategies of establishing the painting as a cognitive rather than a merely mimetic object are ones of locating the defining or limiting norms of painting, and displaying these as constitutive aspects of the medium: "the flat surface, the shape of the support, the properties of pigment." To force the viewer to encounter the picture as *first of all* a flat object, is for the painter what Shklovsky's "baring of the device" is for the writer. In its insistence on opacity (or flatness), and perforce its denial of illusionism, the modernist painting becomes a cognitive object insofar as it is internally coherent, inwardly referential to its own laws or norms, and logically distinct from everything that is not itself painting. For it is the first law of this type of analysis that the devices to be bared–the use of art to reveal art–must be distinct for the separate arts.

It would seem the easiest thing in the world to apply the same kind of analysis or systematization to architecture. And, indeed, during the heroic period of the Modern Style, architects did produce a startling kind of opacity. Stripping their buildings of ornament, they confronted the viewer/user with material surfaces denuded of their expected references to classical or picturesque style; they forced him to experience the material *tout court*: glass, concrete, steel, . . . as such. There were as well strategies of defamiliarization, as these materials infiltrated his home or his office with new sets of references: to the factory, the grain silo, the steamship, the industrial shed.

Yet there was something about this procedure that was inconsistent with the grounds of modernism. For, while we might find it attractive and up-to-date to model a house on a ship rather than a chateau, taking satisfaction in the aptness of the set of associations wrought by such a metaphor–associations to efficiency, ease of maintenance order–there is no logical necessity in the production of this model. It is no more *essentially* about the nature of the dwelling than if we were to say that a house is like a cave, or a nest, or a part of a hive. The likening of a house to a machine may, that is, produce a temporary opacity, but it does not necessarily produce a cognitive object. It does not force reflection about the nature of architecture in the same way that Mallarmé's "but" forces reflection, at an abstract level, about a certain terrain of language.

It is the same when we turn to the naked display of materials, which at first we might liken to Shklovsky's "baring of the device." For while to experience glass as glass may yield certain sensuous satisfactions, it does not drive those sensations back onto the cognitive ground of understanding which collates and connects them. And if we are told that glass-as-such or steel-as-such are merely the conduits to the direct experience of the building as *structure*, the pure perception of it as a support system, we may still feel that the exposure of the building as structure is not the same as the "baring of the device" of *structuring* as a fully cognitive procedure.

It was a corrective to this misplaced focus of architectural modernism that the formalist critic Colin Rowe published a series of essays that stressed architecture as a form of text to be read.[5] Not surprisingly, two of Rowe's central essays concerned themselves with the issue of transparency, differentiating a false from a true kind, on formal grounds. The false kind he termed "literal transparency," by which he meant a literal use of glass (or any other kind of opening) to permit one to see through to the structure. The other he called "phenomenal transparency," and with this term he wished to indicate–for architecture–the transparency turned into opacity of Mallarmé's "but."

Defining that type of transparency as the coexistence of phenomena that "interpenetrate without optical destruction of each other," Rowe concerns himself with architectural form as "a continuous dialectic between fact and implication."[6] For the facts of physical organization can be presented with enough in-built ambiguity so that they induce a reading of those facts in terms of several, alternate constructs. Rowe demonstrates this in an analysis of the garden facade of *Les Terraces*, the house by Le Corbusier at Garches, concluding that "the reality of deep space is constantly opposed to the inference of shallow; and by means of the resultant tension, reading after reading is enforced. The five layers of space which, vertically, divide the building's volume and the four layers which cut it horizontally will all, from time to time, claim attention; and this gridding of space will then result in continuous fluctuations of interpretation."[7] Through these "fluctuations" the building's surface is experienced, then, not as a thing—a mute object of stone or concrete—but as a ground of meanings, multiple, changing, addressing itself to the process of cognitive differentiation. This is a sense of surface that Rowe analogizes to the surface of cubist painting, the picture plane seen as a "uniformly active field," which "serves both as the catalyst and as the neutralizer of the successive figures which the observer experiences."[8]

The split between literal and phenomenal transparency can be likened, then, to the difference between what can be called an actual and a virtual object. The real or actual object—fossilized in time and space—is one thing, while the virtual object—a function of the viewer/reader's capacity to organize and reflect—is another. Insofar as the architectural critic wishes to make discriminations along this virtual/actual axis, he works in tandem with the other formalists in their efforts to distinguish literary from ordinary language or art objects from objects of common use. But to the extent that in order to make this distinction he must construct a hermeneutic phantom—a set of readings or interpretations that he substitutes for the real object—his activity veers away from theirs. In pointing to the instance of Mallarmé's "but" Sartre ties the reader more closely than ever to the absoluteness of that word—its actual location on the page as the carrier of opposition by virtue of its initiation of a new line, its sensuous properties as explosive and disarticulated sounds. But when Rowe essentializes the facade of a building as the sum of many alternate interpretations, he is suppressing the facade itself in favor of another edifice: the facade as a pretext of stimulus for a set of mental figurations, the creation of a transcendental object. Or, when Greenberg speaks of modernist painting as tying all perceptions back into the primary datum of the picture's flatness he is pointing to a physical fact as the condition or norm for meaning within the convention of painting. But Rowe, in analogizing the reading of buildings to the reading of paintings, transforms what is physically true of buildings—that they exist in three-dimensional space and are therefore experienced through time—and makes them instead a series of pictures, framing temporal experience as a set of static images.

That these might be the problems of applying formalism to architecture was not particularly obvious in 1963, the year when Rowe's first installment on the subject of transparency was published. To Eisenman, who was a student and colleague of Rowe, the analysis was extraordinarily liberating. It was of great importance to him that the kind of reading Rowe was advocating was fundamentally different from the kind of iconographic interpretation of architectural meaning that had been practiced in earlier forms of analysis. The building was not read in reference to underlying classical systems or ideal geometries, nor to sets of fundamental building types for which the present one became a newly elaborated or invented metaphor. Rowe was suppressing these kinds of meanings—to which Eisenman applied the general term *semantic*—in favor of a more abstract and generalized idea of organization. And insofar as that organization could be perceived regardless of specific content (the grain silo, the classical column, the villa type), it seemed appropriate to think of it as a species of syntax.

For Eisenman, formalism meant this replacement of semantics (or content) with syntax. And two practices seemed to follow, logically, from this changeover. The first was to embrace a notion of "Cardboard Architecture," the second was to insist on treating every part of a given building as a marker or sign.

"Cardboard Architecture" was an epithet first applied to the work of Le Corbusier in the late 1920s when it seemed that his buildings, with their smooth white surfaces and their flush detailing, were the cardboard models produced in architectural offices, peculiarly inflated to full scale. It had the connotations of insubstantiality and a strange insouciance with respect to issues of structure. But it was for precisely those reasons that Eisenman appropriated that kind of architectural *facture*. He wanted to unload the physical envelope of all function (this column "means" support) and all semantic associations (brick "means" warmth, stability, etc.). In place of these he welcomed the associations of the "model": that is, as a way of generating form, of exploring ideas, quite apart from the necessities of a real structure or the properties of real material. " 'Cardboard Architecture,' " he once wrote, "is a term which questions the nature of the reality of the physical environment; 'Cardboard Architecture' is a term which attempts to shift the focus from the existing conceptions of form to a consideration of form as a signal or a notation which can provide a range of formal information; 'Cardboard' is a means for an exploration into the nature of architectural form itself, in both its actual and conceptual states."[9]

THE BEGINNINGS OF A LINGUISTIC MODEL

In Eisenman's thinking, architecture would only really be perceived as "syntax" through a "consideration of form as a signal or notation." As an example of this we might think of what it would be like to enter a space in which there are regularly placed columns supporting the ceiling plane, and then encounter one column that supports nothing. Since the anomalous column does not function as structure, it can only make sense to use it in terms of some other function, and what that might be would obviously depend on its context. This example, which on an extremely simple level represents this procedure that Eisenman followed in House I, House II, and House III, brings us back to the remark made earlier—namely, that from the outset Eisenman was attempting logically to connect formalism and linguistics. Obviously his choice of terms—*semantics*, *syntactics*—begins to broach this subject. But more crucially, his notion that a thing is perceived as a sign only from within a field of differences attaches his thinking to that of structural linguistics. "What we have learned from Saussure," writes Merleau-Ponty, "is that, taken singly, signs do not signify anything, and that each one of them does not so much express a meaning as mark a divergence of meaning between itself and other signs. Since the same can be said for all other signs, we may conclude that language is made of differences without terms; or more exactly, that the terms of language are engendered only by the differences which appear among them."[10]

To understand this we might take a case that Saussure introduces in his *Course on General Linguistics*, a case drawn from a lever that seems so elementary that it had always been thought of as pre-linguistic. This case concerns phonology for which the letters in the alphabet of a given language seem to stand as basic units—though not yet units of meaning or signification. What Saussure endeavors to show is that if we take the letter *p*, in isolation, we are left with an abstraction that has no relation whatever to language. For *p* divides itself, linguistically, into implosive (*p* as in the word *up*) and explosive (*p* as in the word *put*) sounds. Thus the choice of the implosive *p* already differentiates itself from another possibility—the explosive sound; and because of this distinction, that choice is already fully laden with significance.[11]

If we return to the instance of the nonsupporting column, we can see its theoretical relationship to the two types of *p*. First, it is not being handled as an isolated symbol (the ionic column, say, which equals femininity, or the column set free from the wall as "sculpture"); but, rather, it locates itself within the simple binarism of supporting/nonsupporting. Second, that binarism implies that there is already in place a field of meaning within which the perception of that choice will be intelligible. The nonsupporting column is understood as a signifier ("a signal or notation") whose significance depends, at least in part, on the knowledge of everything that it is not. In the actual practice of House I (fig. 108), House II, and House III (fig. 109), Eisenman relied on the principle of redundancy to establish this binarism, to make it fully recognizable. Nonstructure can only be apparent in contrast to structure. And so, in those buildings the viewer is confronted with two parallel systems: one that holds the building up physically and another that obviously does not. So the point of that second system—its meaning—must derive from something else. The referent of "system II" cannot be to physical structure but must be to some alternate level of organization. (It should be mentioned here that the sophistication of design in these houses is such that identifying system I and system II is not a simple matter, and that given alternative readings and perspectives, the elements that make up the one or the other keep changing places.)

But what, we might ask, *is* the referent of this alternate system? To which the simplest answer is that it is the house that is not there, or rather, the house that is there only cognitively. As an example, we could take House III, in which the markings are the traces of a process of generating the building, through a 45-degree rotation. If we imagine two boxes set one inside the other, which begin with their sides in alignment, and then imagine that the inner one is made to go through a quarter turn, a procedure which rips open the closed sides of the outer box, we will have a simplified mental image of this process. Lest this seem like an absurdly arbitrary thing for someone to do, we might reflect that buildings ordinarily get designed by shifting spaces around: the room that no longer "works," located left of the entry, is moved, on paper, to the right, or its axis is changed, or its doorway is displayed. The designer does not understand these changes as arbitrary because he makes them in response to exigencies of the budget, or the program, or the site. When he is finished these changes no longer appear as *changes*, for they are now incorporated into the fixed structure of the completed object. In House III Eisenman makes the fact of these changes—that it evolved step-wise through time—a perceptual datum, and further, the "changes" themselves do not refer to the traditional rationalizations, which Eisenman sees as arbitrary in the extreme. They arise from a geometrical logic, which is itself apparent due to the fact that it is marked or signaled through what we are calling system II. Therefore, the complex of phenomena that surrounds one, in this building, is seen to be reducible to something simpler, even though that simple, originating order cannot be physically experienced.

The referent of system II is, then, a conceptual house, conceptual on three counts. First, because it is a virtual object, one that is "present" in conception rather than in fact. Second, because it is the indicator of a set of laws that generated it, a process of moving from hypothesis to conclusion through a series of predetermined rules of behavior, the deductive nature of which can itself be termed conceptual.[12] Third, because along the way it presents aspects of architecture from within a set of normative statements. For example, if we ask what, normatively, is the nature of a window, we realize that the answer is not this or that shaped opening in the surface of a wall, but, more generally, the lesion of a plane. In presenting the two-box analogue to House III, I said that the rotation would cause the sides of the outer box to split or rip, and thus the superimposition of the two systems leads to the production of wall openings as *lesions* rather than as "windows" formed by the arbitrary puncturing of the wall surface.

I am stressing this word *conceptual* partly because it was used by Eisenman himself to distinguish between his own practice and more traditional notions of design.[13] But I am using it as well because it helps us to locate what I said at the beginning of this essay about the ambivalence of his initial position—half in and half out of formalism. The potential for moving away from or beyond formalism, and therefore beyond modernism itself, issues from the contemplation of the linguistic model, a question to which we will soon turn. But the condition of still being inside the formalist/modernist system is signaled by the word *conceptual*.

This is because in focusing on a rift between object and idea, conceptualism favors the latter over the former. In Eisenman's mind it was the conceptual or virtual house that should take precedence in the viewer's experience of his building. In that sense, it was only the latter that was the *real* building. The relationship this bears to Rowe's "hermeneutic phantom" is obvious: the experience of the physical forms of the house is to be subsumed by a reading of them as alternate, ideated forms. Reality is to be excavated mentally, until one is able to unearth a kind of transcendental object lying beneath it. It is the house-as-idea that will rescue the architectural work from being no more than a house-as-object, a setting for Tolstoy's lives lived "as if they had never been."

In his theoretical text on the subject of conceptual architecture, Eisenman aligns his own position with that of a generation of artists who had been producing conceptual and minimalist sculpture. Relying on what had been the usual modes of describing this work in the art criticism of the 1960s, he speaks of the way this art calls for a replacement of physicality by a mental conception. One example of this, although it is not one Eisenman himself referred to, is the standard analysis of the significance of an untitled work by the sculptor Robert Morris, which is made up of three very large, identical, L-shaped beams, each of them separately disposed within their space of exhibition. Given the fact that one is up-ended, the second is lying on its side, and the third is poised on its two ends, this analysis proposes that the meaning of the work addresses the way the viewer can mentally correlate the three forms, seeing each as a physical instance of a single master idea. Thus the L-beams suggest "a child's manipulation of forms, as though they were huge building blocks. The urge to alter, to see many possibilities inherent in a single shape, is typical of a child's syncretistic vision, whereby the learning of one specific form can be transferred to any variation of that form."[14]

Actually, the meaning of this work by Morris is quite different from the one suggested above. Morris is surely calling on us to see that in our experience those forms are *not the same*. For their placement visually alters each of the forms, thickening the lower element of the up-ended unit, or bowing the sides of the one posted on its ends. Thus no matter how clearly we might *understand* that the three Ls are identical (in structure and dimension), it is impossible to see them as the same. Therefore, Morris seems to be saying, the "fact" of the objects' similarity belongs to a logic that exists *prior* to experience; because at the moment of experience, or *in* experience, the L's defeat this logic and are "different." Their "sameness" belongs only to an ideal structure—an inner being that we cannot see. Their difference belongs to their exterior—to the point at which they surface into the public world of our experience. The "difference" is their sculptural meaning; and this meaning is dependent upon the connection of these shapes to the space of experience.

It is because of this fact that one would want to place this work of Morris's within a post-modernist tradition. Because what this sculpture is rejecting is the notion of the perceiver as the privileged subject who confers significance on reality by recourse to a set of ideal meanings of which he himself is the generator. It refuses, that is, to allow the work to appear as the manifestation of a transcendental object in some kind of reciprocal relationship to its viewer/reader, understood as a transcendental ego or subject.

The further point to be made brings us back to the phonological instance of the stressed and unstressed *p*. Saussure had rejected the unqualified *p* as an abstraction that suggested that the applied *p*s (as in *up* or *put*) were merely inflections of some kind of prior ideal or norm. What he was insisting was that language is not to be found in that notion of priority, but only in the application by which the meaning of a choice arises from its difference from the not-chosen. With the L-beams, the variety of positions are like the *p*s as they exist in the spoken chain. They are thus a set of differences that call on us to acknowledge them as we encounter them, but not to reduce them to a prior, ideated figure: the L floating gravity-free in the mind. With this art, the cognitive project is therefore redirected. It is not about the intuition of the object as a goad to or confirmation of the viewer's capacities to initiate meanings. Rather, it confronts him with a multiple set of meanings that are already in place at the time at which he encounters them.

POST-FORMALIST STRUCTURES

With Eisenman's House VI one finds a similar redirection of the cognitive project away from the production of ideated figures or conceptual unities. Intuitively we are made to feel this from an exterior view of the house, where the formal strategy of layering, as in Rowe's analysis of *Les Terraces*, is perversely applied. Both front and back facades are constructed of lateral planes that step back in space to the "relief-ground" of a master plane—a large fin wall that expresses itself as the organizing vertical center of the structure. Yet the lack of symmetry on either facade, or between the two facades, undoes the cognitive task of such a central ground or spine. That is, the master plane seems to speak of or mark a center without performing the cognitive ordering that this form would normally provide.

When we enter the house it is once more to experience the center as marker, again with the enormous sensuous immediacy; the middle of the house is riven by a double staircase, one that creates a visual axis diagonally across the interior space. The staircase is made of two solid volumes, for both are freestanding, their sides filled in from the horizontal planes from which they spring up to the profiles of their steps and risers. They are extremely noticeable not only because they are the only volumes in an otherwise totally planar structure, but also because, within a house wholly neutrally colored, they are red and green. They are also noticeable because although the green one rises normally from the ground to the second floor, the red one "goes" nowhere. It is an upside-down stair, dropping perversely from the ceiling of a double-height space to a point that would be the level of the second story if there were access to a second story there.

The nonfunctionalism of the second stair secures the identity of both as signal or notation of some kind. The fact of this signaling is underscored by the use of color. We understand that we are in the presence of a notation, but it is one that marks a system which resists the kind of decoding that House III had both called for and satisfied. Strong centrality implied some kind of symmetrical unfolding about that center. Throughout the model of House VI we would expect a conceptual structure to exfoliate around this axis. It does not; or at least it does not for the ordinary viewer. For House VI was designed by recourse to topological analysis. And it is topologically symmetrical about a diagonal axis that runs through its center. This system, which is coded in the forms of the house, would be perfectly intelligible to a topological geometer. That it is not to us does not thereby drive it back into the realm of the hermeneutic phantom. For the hermeneutic phantom is intelligible (for us). It is simply not physical. House VI is physical. Its difficulty arises from its being the partial articulation of a language which is unfamiliar, although that language described the functions of the real world and was wholly in place before either Eisenman or we encountered it. The analysis of this house cannot proceed then by means of a reduction of the complex to the simple. It is more like the translation of one complex language into another, or rather, the intuition—by means of a relatively simple system of markings—of a larger, more complex totality, one that exceeds our intuitive grasp.

In House VI the operation of coding or marking has therefore changed from what it had been in Eisenman's earlier houses. We are not involved with a set of physical notations (the form of the building) that produce a conceptual object (the virtual, nonphysical structure) as their "meaning." This is because the architectural elements in House VI articulate a system rather than an object; the referent is to the dispersed field of a mathematical language in place of the unity of a single mental construct.

In that sense House VI is the first of Eisenman's buildings to break completely with an idea of meaning that is essentially formalist. When Sartre speaks of the monolith of Mallarmé's "but" he is pointing to the isolation of that word at the beginning of a poetic line, an isolation that permits one to taste for oneself "the irritating flavors of disjunction." "Disjunction" is the abstract unity to which the word *but*, made formally opaque, gives rise. Formalist opacity depends on the isolation of the signifier (the work, the pictorial element, the architectural member) in order that it become a cognitive object. But the abstract meaning, which it then yields, takes on the quality of an isolated mental entity. From what has been said up to now about the Saussurian analysis of language and the insistence that meaning takes place only through an opposition of terms rather than the perception of those terms as absolutes, it is clear that formalist assumptions are difficult to maintain in relation to a linguistic model. It is structuralism which, by embracing that model, posits an entirely different ground for meaning, insisting on the notion of a limitless field of oppositions or differences. In this view, if there can be anything like "the irritating flavors of disjunction," it is because Mallarmé's "but" emerges from a system that also contains "and" and "therefore"; and its meaning is only understood in opposition to those other two. If we have been characterizing formalism as a strategic conversion of transparency into opacity, we must understand the structuralist procedure as one that performs a very different conversion: the dispersal of unities into a field of differences.

House X, Eisenman's most recent work, is totally involved with this process of dispersal. There, for example, one encounters it in rooms with transparent (glass) floors and ceilings, and opaque (windowless) walls. The plane on which openings normally occur is thus transposed to the planes that are expected to be visually solid. And the effect of this transposition is twofold. The first is that a certain kind of somatic shock is delivered to the viewer. He is made to experience, through his own body, the fundamental opposition in an architectural language between closed and open fields. The second effect is the view of other parts of the same building produced by the transparent planes themselves, in which other sets of oppositions are manifested. The space in which the viewer finds himself is, then, one whose perspectives run vertically and diagonally through the system of the house rather than horizontally in relation to the viewer's normal plane of vision. Through this changed perspective, the occupant is forced to experience the space as a linked set of opposing terms—to encounter "the room" less as an entity than as one part of a system of differences.

To consider a phenomenon as seemingly perverse as this room, it is useful to acknowledge this space as a peculiar conversion, or rotation, of the 1914 Dom-ino diagram through which Le Corbusier had articulated the premises of architectural modernism. The Dom-ino diagram pictures a one-room structure, defining it with two horizontal slabs (floor and ceiling), supported by a columnar system pulled in from the room's perimeter. The diagram makes clear that any vertical plane that might be added to this space—wall partition, window panel—is utterly independent from this structural skeleton. Implicit in this diagram are some of the standard features of modern architecture as we have known it: the free plan, the curtain wall. What is also implicit is that inside this space, the occupant inhabits the conceptual center of a three-dimensional lattice. As he stands inside and looks about, he is therefore given the structure as pure diagram, as the bodying forth of a system that is transparent to his ability to think. The rational premises of this space are decipherable. The aesthetic pleasure it affords is tied to the pleasure of decipherment.

No matter what we understand the work of art to be, clearly one of its functions is to create an image of its perceiver—the one who looks at it or reads it. If we speak of, say, Renaissance art, we are not just referring to objects that look different from the ones that preceded (or followed) them by virtue of a transformed set of organizing rules. We are speaking as well of a different conception of a viewer and where he stands (spiritually, intellectually, politically, perceptually) vis-à-vis the object. The work of art pictures more than just its own contents; it also pictures its beholder. In addressing the subject of modernism, I used the example of Tolstoy's journal entry to describe this concern for the condition of the viewer, to raise the issue of the artist's sense that that condition must be attended to or revised. The man for whom everything is transparent, who is not forced to reflect upon his experience, who is not brought up short by it as if blocked for a moment by a wall, is, according to this parable of the dusted/undusted sofa, not someone who has seen more of his life, but experiences less. Now, if a shade is pulled down over a window, preventing one from automatically using the opening to look through, one might be forced—depending on the nature of the shade—to ask fundamental questions about the structure, purpose, and *meaning* of windows. The modernist shade was intended as a stimulus for such questions, and as the viewer responded to this stimulus he became the originator of a set of replies, definitions, and interpretations. Shklovsky's formalism was put into place in the service of creating, or elaborating, the terms of this situation. Formalism was the theoretical working-out of this modernist demand that consciousness become reflexive, examining the grounds of its own access to knowledge. But as I have said, the results of this reflection were to define consciousness as a generator or producer of meaning. Formalism's pulled-down shade may have made the real window opaque for its viewer, but the aesthetically conditioned obstacle set up a new transparency in which ideas (interpretations) appear to be transparent to the mind that thinks them. Structuralism is an attack on this second-order transparency, on the idealism inherent in this cognitive "shade."

It is in the light of this attack that we can understand the rooms in House X that turn the Dom-ino diagram on its ear, making the solid horizontals into clear surfaces and the verticals into opaque slabs. For it is the viewer's relationship to the house as a model of his own capacity to conceptualize which is also stood on its ear. The diagram is no longer oriented to the viewer as the center of a perspective system, a system measured out on the horizontal ground on which he stands, stretching away toward his horizon. That horizon is blocked by the windowless walls, and that ground, by being transparent, is no longer predicated on the orientation of his body. The viewer may stand in the middle of the rooms of House X, but he is no longer their center. This shade, which is pulled down over his view, is not one that returns it to him in the Dom-ino guise of a set of theorems—about pure forms, organizational transparency, or Cartesian lattices.

This is a different kind of shade. It functions in terms of an absolute binarism. It marks surfaces as "transparent" or "nontransparent"; and it does so without returning the originating source of the meaning of this distinction to the perceived subject. If there is anything to be read in this room, it is not a set of small-scale clues that will assist one to project for oneself the image of the house in its entirety as the theoretical extension of a root idea. Instead, it is simply the code "opaque/transparent," which one knows to be part of a larger code, that is in itself boundless. Through the glass of the floor and ceiling one can see other parts of House X. But this seeing is not the same as the "view" one had in perspective taken as a system of knowledge and prediction. This seeing is more a process of acknowledging the simple extension of the code: that it exists beyond this room and that one will in the course of one's own movements come into contact with further aspects of it.

This discussion began with the claim that insofar as Eisenman's work has been predicated on a linguistic model it has had to move further and further away from the formalist conditions expressed by modernism. The fragmentation and dispersal that occurs in House X relates to that linguistic model in a way that incorporates the notion of difference at a very deep level. When Saussure maintains that "in language there are only differences," he adds: "Even more important: a difference generally implies positive terms between which the difference is set up: but in language there are only differences *without* positive terms. Whether we take the signified or the signifier, language has neither ideas nor sounds that existed before the linguistic system, but only conceptual and phonic differences that have issued from the system. The idea or phonic substance that a sign contains is of less importance than the other signs that surround it. Proof of this is that the value of a term may be modified without either its meaning or its sound being affected, solely because a neighboring term has been modified."[15]

In this sense of language as a system without positive terms—moreover, a system fully formed prior to any one speaker's participation in it—that has made language a model for the post-modernist (or structuralist) redefinition of man as a knowing-subject. "In achieving a position of mastery over the man," Edward Said writes, "language has reduced his to a discursive function. The world of activity and of human experience stands silently aside while language constitutes order and legislates discovery. When Lévi-Strauss says that 'language, and unreflecting totalization, is human reason which has its reason and of which man knows nothing,' he is stating the condition with which serious intellectual work must reckon. Nearly every one of the structuralists acknowledges a tyrannical feedback system in which man is the speaking subject whose actions are always being converted into signs that signify him, which signs he uses in turn to signify other signs, and so on to infinity."[16] That this attitude displaces man from his position as originating subject occurs "when language is no longer thought of as a kind of secondary transparency through which shines Being."[17]

The formalist interest in the work of art as a moment through which experience is thickened and rendered opaque must be viewed in the light of this structuralist critique. For the formalist, opacity is, ultimately, "a kind of secondary transparency through which shines Being." It is a way of using the object as a lever on reality in order to essentialize a certain part of it. It is a moment of essentialization or reduction back to an ontological absolute. If the structuralists think of the work of art as opaque, that is because it is a fragment—the partial articulation of an extended field of signs, one of the terms in a system of differences. The energy of the work of art is therefore seen as centrifugal, rather than reductive. It drives the perceiver's attention outward, away from itself into the vast institution of language systems that have made it possible and to which it refers. Eisenman's ambition is to articulate the system of differences through which architecture functions as a language. To do this he has had to take the position that architectural elements express differences *without positive terms*—whether functional, symbolic, or cognitive. His architecture has assumed the conditions of post-modernism.

[1] Jean Paul Sartre, *What is Literature?* (New York: Harper and Row, 1965), 7.

[2] Sartre, 11.

[3] Quoted by Viktor Shklovsky in "Art as Technique," in *Russian Formalist Criticism*, ed. Lee T. Lemon and Marion J. Reis (Lincoln: University of Nebraska Press, 1965), 12.

[4] Clement Greenberg, "Modernist Painting," in *The New Art*, ed. Gregory Battcock (New York: Dutton, 1966), 102.

[5] "Text" is being used here neither in the sense of iconographic program nor in the sense in which semiologists invoke it—that is, as a nexus of cultural signs. Rowe is focusing on the abstract nature of the text, like that of a musical score, to be deciphered for its formal structure and thematic interrelationships.

[6] Colin Rowe and Robert Slutzky, "Transparency: Literal and Phenomenal," in *The Mathematics of the Ideal Villa and Other Essays* (Cambridge, Mass.: MIT Press, 1976), 170. Reprinted from *Perspecta* (1964) and appearing in the present volume starting on page 91.

[7] Rowe and Slutzky, 170.

[8] Colin Rowe and Robert Slutzky, "Transparency: Literal and Phenomenal . . . Part II," *Perspecta* 13 (1971): 296. Reprinted in this volume starting on page 103.

[9] Peter Eisenman, "Introduction to Cardboard Architecture," *Casabella* 174 (1973): 24.

[10] Maurice Merleau-Ponty, *Signs* (Cleveland: Northwestern University Press, 1964), 39.

[11] Ferdinand de Saussure, *Course in General Linguistics* (New York: McGraw-Hill, 1966), 53–64.

[12] Under this view the referent of the conceptual structure is the transformational process itself—that is, rotation. It should be noted here the importance, often cited by Eisenman himself, of Noam Chomsky's notion of transformational grammar on Eisenman's thinking at the time. He has discussed the influence of Chomsky's division of syntax into surface and deep structure, the two levels mediated by rules of transformation.

[13] See Peter Eisenman, "Notes on Conceptual Architecture," *Casabella* 359 (1971): 48–57.

[14] Marcia Tucker, *Robert Morris* (New York: Whitney Museum of American Art, 1970), 25.

[15] Saussure, *General Linguistics*, 120.

[16] Edward W. Said, *Beginnings, Intention, and Method* (New York: Basic Books, 1975), 283.

[17] Said, 302.

Assemblage 12 (1990)

The following letter was written in October 1989 in lieu of Derrida's presence at the conference "Postmodernism and Beyond: Architecture as the Critical Art of Contemporary Culture," organized by J. Hillis Miller at the University of California, Irvine. – Eds.

A Letter to Peter Eisenman
Jacques Derrida

My dear Peter,

I am simultaneously sending this letter, with the cassette that accompanies it, to Hillis, who must talk with us over the course of the anticipated meeting. As he must also moderate and enliven it, but for other reasons as well, Hillis is therefore, along with you, the first addressee of these questions. He understands better that any other the labyrinth, as we all know. And what I am going to say to you will probably reverberate in a sort of labyrinth. I am entrusting to the recording of the voice or the letter that which is not yet visible to me and cannot guide my steps toward an end/exit, that can barely guide them toward an "issue." I am not even sure myself whether what I am sending you holds up. But that is perhaps by design, and it is of this I plan to speak to you. In any case, I very much regret the necessity of depriving myself of this meeting with you, the two of you, all of you.

But now, do not worry, I am not going to argue with you. And I am not going to abuse my absence, not even to tell you that you perhaps believe in it, absence, too much. This reference to absence is perhaps one of the things (because there are others) that has most troubled me in your discourse on architecture, and if that were my first question you could perhaps profit from my absence to speak about it a little, about absence in general, about the role that this word *absence* will have been able to play at least in what you believed you could *say* if not *do* with your architecture. One could multiply examples, but I am limiting myself to what you say about the presence of an absence in *Moving Arrows Eros and Other Errors,* which concerns Romeo's chateau, "a palimpsest and a quarry," etc. This discourse on absence or the presence of an absence perplexes me not only because it bypasses so many tricks, complications, traps that the philosopher, especially if he is a bit of a dialectician, knows only too well and fears to find you caught up in again, but also because it has authorized many religious interpretations, not to mention vaguely judeo-transcendental ideologizations, of your work. I suspect a little that you liked and encouraged these interpretations even as you discreetly denied it with a smile, which would make a misunderstanding a little more or a little less than a misunderstanding. My question has to do not only with absence or the presence of absence, but with God. Voilà, if I did not come it is not just because I am tired and overworked, held up in Paris, but precisely to have the opportunity to ask you directly a question about God that I would never have dared to do in Irvine if I had been present in person; instead, I am glad that this question comes to you by way of this voice, that is to say, on tape. The same question brings up others, a whole group of closely related questions. For example, at the risk of shocking you: Whether it has to do with houses, museums, or the laboratories of research universities, what distinguishes your architectural space from that of the temple, indeed of the synagogue (by this word I mean a Greek word used for a Jewish concept)? Where will the break, the rupture have been in this respect, if there is one, if there was one, for you and for other architects of this period with whom you feel yourself associated? I remain very perplexed about this subject and if I had been there I would have been a difficult interlocutor. If you were to construct a place of worship, Buddhist, for example, or a cathedral, a mosque, a synagogue (hypotheses that you are not obliged to accept), what would be your primary concern today? I will make allusion shortly to Libeskind's project in Berlin for a Jewish museum. We spoke about this the other morning in New York, but let us leave that behind for the moment.

Naturally, this question concerns also your interpretation of *chora* in "our" "work," if one can say in quotations our work "in common." I am not sure that you have detheologized and deontologized *chora* in as radical a way as I would have wished (*chora* is neither the void, as you suggest sometimes, nor absence, nor invisibility, nor certainly the contrary from which there are, and this is what interests me, a large number of consequences). It is true that for me it was easier, in a certain way. I did not have anything to "do" with it and would not have been able to do anything with it, that is, for the city of Paris, for La Villette, the little city; you see what I mean (and the whole difference is perhaps between us). But I would like you to say something to our friends in Irvine, while speaking to them of the difference between our respective relations to discourse, on the one hand, and to the operation of architecture, to its putting into action, on the other hand. Profit from my absence in order to speak freely. But don't just say whatever, because as everything is being recorded today, and memory, always the same, not being at all the same, I will know all that you will have said publicly. I had the feeling, and I believe that you said it somewhere, that you have judged me to be too reserved, in our "choral work," a little bit absent, entrenched in discourse, without obliging you to change, to change place, without disturbing you enough. It is doubtless true that there would be a great deal to say about this subject, which is complicated because it is that of the place (*chora*) and of displacement itself. If I had come, I would have spoken perhaps of my own displacement in the course of "choral work" but here it is you who must speak. Therefore tell me whether after *Choral Work* (as you yourself said in Irvine in the spring) your work took, in effect, a new direction and engaged itself in other paths. What has happened? What for you is this period? this history? How does one determine the boundaries of it or put rhythm into it? When did we begin to work together, had we never done so, on this *Choral Work* that is not yet constructed but that one sees and reads everywhere? When will we stop?

This all brings me directly to the next question. It also concerns a certain absence. Not my absence today in Irvine where I would have so much liked to see you again along with other friends, even more so since I was one of those who had wished for and prepared this meeting (and I must ask you to forgive me and to make others forgive me); but absence like the shadowed sound of the voice—you see what I mean by this. What relations (new or archi-ancient, in any case different) does architecture, particularly yours, carry on, must it carry on, with the voice, the capacity of voice, but also therefore with telephonic machines of all sorts that structure and transform our experience of space every day? The question of the nearly immediate telephonic address, certainly *nearly* immediate, and I underline, but also the question of telephonic archivation, as is the case right here, with the spacing of time that telephonic archivation at once supposes and structures. If one can imagine a whole labyrinthlike history of architecture, guided by the entwined thread of this question, where would one be today and tomorrow, and you?

This question of history, as the history of spacing, like the spacing of time and voice, does not separate itself from the history of visibility (immediately mediate), that is to say, from all history of architecture; it is so great that I will not even dare to touch upon it, but will "address" this question, as you say in English, through economy and through metonymy, under the form of a single word, glass (*glas, glass*).

What is there of glass in your work? What do you say about it? What do you do with it? How does one talk about it? In optical terms or in tactile terms? Regarding tactility, it would be good if, continuing what we were saying the other morning in New York, you would speak to our friends of the erotic tricks, of the calls of desire, do I dare say, of the sex appeal of the architectural forms about which you think, with which you work, to which you give yourself up. Whether its directions are new or not, does this seduction come as supplement, into the bargain, as precisely the "subsidy/bonus of seduction" or "subsidy/ bonus of pleasure"? Or is it essential? Isn't the subsidy/bonus essential, at least? But, then, what would the subsidy/bonus *itself* be? Subsidy/Bonus? For the author of *Moving Arrows Eros and Other Errors,* what is the relation between subsidy/bonus and the rest in the calculations and the negotiations of the architect? As my American students sometimes disarmingly ask me, Could you elaborate on that? I return now to my question, after this long parenthesis on your desire, my question about glass that is not perhaps so far off. What terms do we use to speak about glass? Technical and material terms? Economic terms? The terms of urbanism? The terms of social relations? The terms of transparency and immediacy, of love or of police, of the border that is perhaps erased between the public and the private, etc.? *Glass* is an old word, and am I wrong if I believe that you are interested in glass, that you perhaps even like it? Does it only have to do with new materials that resemble glass but are no longer it, and so on? Before letting you speak about glass, I bring up a text by Benjamin, *Erfahrung und Armut,* which I'm sure you know (it also concerns architecture and was published in 1933, which is not just any date, in Germany or elsewhere). From it I extract at the outset only the following, on which our friends will certainly like to hear you comment.

But Scheerbart—to return to him—most values that his people, and according to their model, his fellow citizens, live in apartments that correspond to their rank: in houses of moving and slippery glass, such as those that Loos and Le Corbusier have since erected. It is not for nothing that glass is such a hard and smooth material upon which nothing attaches itself. Also a cold and concise material. Things made of glass have no "aura" [Die, Dinge aus Glas haben keine "Aura"]. In general, glass is the enemy of secrecy. It is also the enemy of possession. The great poet André Gide once said, "Each thing that I wish to possess becomes opaque for me."

(Here we return to the question of desire and glass, of the desire of glass: I have elsewhere tried to follow this experience of desire as the experience of glass in Blanchot, especially in *La Folie du jour* and in *L'Arrêt de mort*.)

Do people such as Scheerbart dream of glass masonry [Glasbauten] in order to have recognized a new poverty [Bekenner einer neuen Armut]? But perhaps a comparison here will reveal more than the theory. Upon entering a room of the eighties, and despite the "comfortable intimacy" ["Gemütlichkeit"] that perhaps reigns there, the strongest impression will be, "You have nothing to look for here." You have nothing to look for here because there is no ground here upon which the inhabitant would not have already left his trace: by knickknacks on shelves, by doilies on the armchair, by the sheer curtains at the windows, or by the fire screen in front of the fireplace. A beautiful word from Brecht here helps us go far, farther: "Erase your traces!" [Verwisch die Spuren!], so says the refrain of the first poem in Anthologie pour les habitants des villes. . . . *Scheerbart and his glass and the Bauhaus and its steel have opened the way: they have created spaces in which it is difficult to leave traces. "After all that has been said," declares Scheerbart twenty years later, "we can easily speak of a 'culture of glass' ['Glaskultur']. The new environment of glass will completely change man. And the only thing left to hope for now is that the new glass culture will not encounter too many opponents."*

What do you think, Peter, of these propositions? Would you be an "opponent," a supporter? Or, as I suppose, but perhaps wrongly, neither one nor the other? In any case, could you say something about it and why?

Benjamin's text speaks, as you have seen, of a "new poverty" (homonym if not synonym for a new expression, a new French concept, to designate a wandering group of poor people, indeed, of the "homeless," which is irreducible to categorizations, classifications, and former localizations of marginality or of the social ladder: the low income, the proletariat as a class, the unemployed, etc.). And the new poverty, the one about which Benjamin speaks, and none other, should be "our" future, already our present. From this fascinating text that is politically ambiguous and that must not be too fragmented, I extract the following:

Scheerbart is interested in the question of knowing what our telescopes, our airplanes, and our rockets do to men of the past in transforming them into completely new creatures, worthy of notice and affection. Furthermore, these creatures already speak in an entirely new language. And what is Decisive [das Entscheidende] in this language is the tendency toward the Arbitrary Construct [zum willkürlichen Konstruktiven], a tendency that particularly resists the organic. It is through this tendency that the language of these men, or rather of Scheerbart's people, cannot be confused with any other; because these people object to this principle of humanism that calls for the correspondence with humans. Even up to their proper names. . . . Poverty of experience [Erfahrungsarmut]: one must not understand by this that these men desire a" New Experience." No, they want to liberate themselves from experience, they want a world in which they can make their poverty be recognized—the exterior and eventually also the interior—in such a pure and distinct way that something decent comes of it. And they are not always ignorant and inexperienced. One can say the opposite: they have consumed [gefressen] all of that, "culture" and "man" until they are satiated and tired. . . . We have become impoverished. We have abandoned one piece after another of the heritage of humanity and often we should have wagered it to Mont-de-Piété [the Mount of Piety] for a hundredth of its value, in order to receive as an advance the few coins of the "Present" [des "Aktuellen"]. In the door stands economic crisis, behind her a shadow, the war to come. Today, to attach oneself to something has become the business of the small number of the powerful, and God knows whether they are not more human than the majority; for the most part more barbarous, but not in the good sense [nicht auf die gute Art]. The others, however, must settle in once again and with Little. They relate it to the men who created the Fundamentally New [das von Grund auf Neue zu ihrer Sache gemacht], and who founded it upon understanding and self-denial. In its buildings [Bauten], its paintings, and its histories, humanity prepares itself to outlive [überleben], if necessary, culture. And most important, humanity does this while laughing. Perhaps this laughter here and there sounds barbarous. Good [Gut]. Therefore let he who is an individual [der Einzelne] occasionally give a little humanity to the mass, which one day will return it to him with interest. (trans. by P. Beck and B. Stiegler)

What do you think of this text, Peter, in particular of a poverty that *should* not cause another one to be forgotten? What do you think of these two barbarities that must not be confused and as much as possible—is it possible?—must not be allowed to contaminate each other? What do you think of what Benjamin called the "present" and of his "few coins"? What, for you, would be "good" barbarity in architecture and elsewhere? And the "present"? I know that there is a present that you do not want, but what best breaks (today? tomorrow?) with this present? And you who want to abstract architecture in proportion to man, in pro-portion even to his scale, how do you understand this "destructive," in Benjamin's sense, discourse in the mouth of "these people [who] object to this principle of humanism that calls for [architecture's] correspondence with humans. Even up to their proper names."?

Therefore, Peter, I would like, and your listeners in Irvine, I imagine, will perhaps like, to hear you speak about the relations between architecture today and poverty. All poverties, the one about which Benjamin speaks and the other; between architecture and capital (the equivalent today of the "economic crisis" occurring in 1930 *"in der Tur,"* in the "opening of the door"); between architecture and war (the equivalent today of the "shadow" and of what "comes" with it); the scandals surrounding social housing, "housing" in general (not without recalling what we have both said, which is a little too complicated for a letter, of the habitable and the inhabitable in architecture), and the "homeless," "homelessness" today in the United States and elsewhere.

This letter is already too long. I shall speed up a little to link schematically other questions or requests to the preceding ones. I cited this text by Benjamin, among other reasons, to lead you to ruin and to destruction. As you know, what he says about "aura" destroyed by glass (and by technology in general) is articulated in a difficult discourse on "destruction." In the *Trauerspiel* (and certainly elsewhere but I don't remember where anymore), Benjamin talks about the ruin, especially about the "baroque cult of the ruin," "the most noble matter of baroque creation." In the photocopied pages I am sending you, Benjamin declares that for the baroque "the ancient inheritance is comparable, in each one of its components, to the elements from which is concocted the new totality. No, they build it. Because the achieved vision of this new thing is that: the ruin. . . . The work [of art] confirms itself as ruin. In the allegoric edifice of the *Trauerspiel,* these ruined forms of the salvaged work of art clearly have always already come unfastened." I will say nothing about Benjamin's concept of the ruin, which is also the concept of a certain mourning in affirmation, indeed the salvation of the work of art; I will, however, use this as a pretext to ask you the following.

First, is there a relationship between your writing of the palimpsest, your architectural experience of memory (in *Choral Work,* for example, but also everywhere else), and "something" like the ruin that is no longer a thing? In what way would you say, and would you say it, is your calculation, reckoning, of memory—not baroque in this Benjaminian sense, despite some appearances? Second, if all architecture is finished, if therefore it carries within itself the traces of its future destruction, the already past future, future perfect, of its ruin, according to methods that are each time original, if it is haunted, indeed signed, by the spectral silhouette of this ruin, at work even in the pedestal of its stone, in its metal or its glass, what would again bring the architecture of "the period" (just yesterday, today, tomorrow; use whatever words you want, modern, postmodern, post-postmodern, or amodern, etc.) back to the ruin, to the experience of "its own" ruin? In the past, great architectural inventions constituted their essential destructability, even their fragility, as a resistance to destruction or as a monumentalization of the ruin itself (the baroque according to Benjamin, right?). Is a new image of the ruin to come already sketching itself in the design of the architecture that we would like to recognize as the architecture of our present, of our future, if one can still say that, in the design of your architecture, in the past future, the future perfect, of its memory, so that it already draws and calculates itself, so that it already leaves its future trace in your projects? Taking into account what we were saying previously about Man (and God), will we again be able to speak of "the memory of man," as we say in French, for this architecture? In relation to the ruin, to fragility, to destructability, in other words, to the future, could you return to what we were talking about the other morning in New York, about excess and "weakness"? Every time that excess presents itself (it never presents itself except above and beyond ontological oppositions), for my part, I hesitate to use words of force or of weakness. But it is certainly inevitable as soon as there is announcement. This is nothing more than a pretext so that *you* talk about it, Hillis and you.

Finally, from fragility I turn to ashes, for me the other name or the surname for the essence (not the essential) of the step, of the trace, of writing, the place without place of deconstruction. There where deconstruction inscribes itself. (In "Feu la cendre"—excuse my reference to something that dates from nearly twenty years ago—this conception of ashes, as the trace itself, was principally reserved for, or rather entrusted to, the "burn everything" and to the "holocaust.") To return to our problem and to hear again the fragile words of "fragility," of "ashes," of "absence," or "invisibility," of "Jewish" or not "Jewish" architectural space, what do you think of the Berlin Museum competition, about which we also spoke the other morning in New York? In particular, what do you think of the words of Libeskind, the "winner" of the "competition," as printed in a recently published interview with him in the newsletter of the architecture school at Columbia? Here I must content myself with quoting:

And in turn the void materializes itself in the space outside as something that has been ruined, or rather as the solid remainder of an independent structure, which is a voided void. Then there is a fragmentation and a splintering, marking the lack of coherence of the museum as a whole, showing that it has come undone in order to become accessible, functionally and intellectually. . . . It's conceived as a museum for all Berliners, for all citizens. Not only those of the present, but those of the future and the past who must find their heritage and hope in this particular form, which is to transcend passive involvement and become participation. With its special emphasis on housing the Jewish Museum, it is an attempt to give a voice to a common fate—to the contradictions of the ordered and disordered, the chosen and the not chosen, the vocal and the silent. In that sense, the particular urban condition of Lindenstrasse, of this area of the city, becomes the spiritual site, the nexus, where Berlin's precarious destiny is mirrored. It is fractured and displaced, but also transformed and transgressed. The past fatality of the German Jewish cultural relation to Berlin is enacted now in the realm of the invisible. It is this invisibility which I have tried to bring to visibility. So the new extension is conceived as an emblem, where the invisible, the void, makes itself apparent as such. . . . It's not a collage or a collision or a dialectic simply, but a new type of organization which is really organized around a void, around what is not visible. And what is not visible is the collection of this Jewish Museum, which is reducible to archival material, since the physicality of it has disappeared. The problem of the Jewish Museum is taken as the problem of Jewish culture itself—let's put it this way, as the problem of an avant-garde of humanity, an avant-garde that has been incinerated in its own history, in the Holocaust. In this sense, I believe this scheme joins architecture to questions that are now relevant to all humanity. What I've tried to say is that the Jewish history of Berlin is not separable from the history of modernity, from the destiny of this incineration of history; they are bound together. But bound not through any obvious forms, but rather through a negativity; through an absence of meaning and an absence of artifacts. Absence, therefore, serves as a way of binding in depth, and in a totally different manner, the shared hopes of people. It is a conception that is absolutely opposed to reducing the museum to a detached memorial.

Once again void, absence, negativity, in Libeskind as in you. I leave you alone to deal with these words, dear Peter, dear Hillis; I will tell you what I think some other time, but I suggested what I think at the beginning. Once again I have spoken too much and naturally I abuse my absence. I admit it as a sign of love. Forgive me, Hillis and you, and ask our friends, your listeners, to forgive me for not being there to speak with them and to listen to you.

Affectionately,

Jacques

P.S. 1. This tape was recorded and this transcription finished when I read, at the end of an interview (in the special edition of the Spanish magazine *Arquitectura* devoted to "Deconstruction" [270]—it's the title of the introduction), the following lines from you that were already anticipating my questions: "I never talk about deconstruction. Other people use that word because they are not architects. It is very difficult to talk about architecture in terms of deconstruction, because we are not talking about ruins or fragments. The term is too metaphorical and too literal for architecture. Deconstruction is dealing with architecture as a metaphor, and we are dealing with architecture as a reality. . . . I believe poststructuralism is basically what I mean by postmodernism. In other words, postmodernism is poststructuralism in the widest sense of the word." I certainly believe that I would *not* subscribe to *any* one of these statements, to *any* one of these 7 sentences, neither to 1 nor to 2 nor to 3 nor to 4 nor to 5 nor to 6 nor to 7. But I cannot explain it here and I, truly, never talk much *about* deconstruction. Not spontaneously. If you wish, you could display 1, 2, 3, 4, 5, 6, 7 before the listeners and try to convince them by refuting the contrary propositions or you could let this postscript fall to the side.

P.S. 2. I was certainly forgetting the fundamental question. In other words, the question of foundation, of what you do at the foundation of the foundation or at the foundation of the foundation in your architectural design. Let's talk fundamentally about Earth itself. I have questioned you in a noncircuitous fashion about God and Man. I was think-ing about the Sky and the Earth. What does architecture, and primarily yours, have to see and do with *experience,* that is to say, with the voyage that makes its way outside of Earth? Then, if we don't give up architecture, and I believe that we are not giving it up, what are the effects on "design" itself of terrestrial architecture, of this possi-bility? Of this definite possibility from now on of leaving the terrestrial soil? Will we say that the architecture of a rocket and of astronomy in general (already announced by literature, at least, and long before becoming "effec-tive"), that they dispense with foundations and thus of "standing up," of *the* "standing up," of the *vertical* stance of man, of the building in general? Or do these architectures (of rockets and astronomy in general) recalculate foun-dations and does the calculation remain a terrestrial *difference,* something which I somewhat doubt? What would be an architecture that, without holding, without standing upright, vertically, would not fall again into ruin? How do all these possibilities and even questions (those of holding up, holding together, standing or not) record themselves, if you think that they do? What traces do they leave in what you would build right now in Spain, in Japan, in Ohio, in Berlin, in Paris, and, tomorrow, I hope, in Irvine?

Post/El Cards: A Reply to Jacques Derrida

Peter Eisenman

Dear Jacques,

After many months I find the time and the calm distance to reply to your extraordinary letter. I was pleased that you would take the time to write a letter of such energy and length, but also disturbed by what I perceived as an implied criticism in your words. I was also quite literally left speechless by your questions, questions that I could not answer personally, questions that, indeed, must be directed to architecture for a reply.

Why was I so stunned, so taken aback? Perhaps, on first thought, because I felt in your criticism a rejection of my work. However, after many re-readings, I no longer feel that same rush of defensiveness but rather a certain exhilaration, a certain sense of an *other* freedom. Why? Because in a way you are right. Perhaps what I do in architecture, in its aspirations and in its fabric, is not what could properly be called deconstruction. But things are not quite so simple: if my work is not something, then it raises questions as to what it is not. In attempting to interrogate what it is not, I will not give answer to all of your questions. Indeed, I do not think that the spirit of your letter was one of inquisition. Rather, your questions seem to outline a provocative framework for thinking about architecture. So I will attempt to follow suit, to elaborate through questions yet another framework, or perhaps a post/work, for architecture.

A question, in one sense, is a frame for an answer, a frame for a discourse that may not be the discourse of the reply. Thus I will use your three numbered questions (only two of which are actually numbered, question 3 beginning instead with the word *finally*) as posts to support me (or perhaps as the cards I might play). Indeed, knowing your fondness for precision and numbers, should I inquire further as to what happened to the missing 3, which is, after all, a reflection of the letter *E?*

How, for example, does one respond to such questions as "Do you believe in God?" or "What do you think of a culture of glass?" or "What about the homeless?" without sounding either evasive or irrelevant? How does one assert that certain urgent problems such as homelessness or poverty are no more questions of architecture than they are of poetry or philosophy without sounding callous? These are indeed human problems, but architecture, poetry, and philosophy are not the domains in which they will be solved. In that sense, such issues are no more relevant than my inquiring about your own domestic, suburban home in relationship to your work. Yet, if I fail to answer, others will ask why. No answer will be interpreted as an answer: as a refusal to answer or an inability to answer or a lack of concern to answer, but never the real answer. The real answer: that to answer is impossible either in the medium of letter or of glass.

Your questions probably require a volume, several volumes, inscribed for you. Perhaps with that you, too, would be led to "ruin and destruction." But if I do not answer some of your questions, it is not through lack of time, interest, or compassion, but rather because the questions, perhaps, cannot be answered in architecture.

I publish this letter with yours because I think that every architect should witness philosophy against the wall, should have to answer, for themselves, some of your questions. And possibly some day you, too, will problematize architecture in your discourse and thus be forced to answer these same questions. I wonder in passing if the fact of your questions points to problems that architecture poses for something that is now named deconstruction and for the "you" that may now have become the aura of Jacques Derrida. Therefore my response may be less to answer to the specific questions, frames, frame-ups that you have proposed than to place my cards on the table, cards that, perhaps, cause you some fraction of dis/ease.

Jacques, you ask me about the *supplement* and the *essential* in my work. You crystallize these questions in the term/word/material *glas/s*. You glaze over the fact that your conceptual play with the multifaceted term *glas* is not simply translatable into architectural glass. One understands that the assumption of the identity of the material glass and your ideas of *glas*, in their superficial resemblance of letters, is precisely the concern of literary decon-struction; but this becomes a problem when one turns to the event of building. This difference is important. For though one can conceptualize in the building material glass, it is not necessarily only as you suggest—as an absence of secrecy, as a clarity. While glass is a literal presence in architecture, it also indexes an absence, a void in a solid wall. Thus glass in architecture is traditionally said to be both absence and presence.

Yes, I am preoccupied by absence, but not in terms of this simple presence/absence dialectic, as you might think. For me as an architect, each concept, as well as each object, has all that it is *not* inscribed within it as traces. I am preoccupied with absence, not voids or glass, because architecture, unlike language, is dominated by presence, by the real existence of the signified. Architecture requires one to detach the signified not only from its signifier but also from its condition as presence. For example, a hole in a plane, or a vertical element, must be detached not only from its signifier—a window or a column—but also from its condition of presence—that is, as a sign of the possibility of light and air or of structure—without, at the same time, causing the room to be dark or the building to fall down. This is not the case in language where you and I can play with *glas* and *post, gaze* and *glaze,* precisely because of the traditional dialectic of presence and absence.

It is improbable to effect in architecture what you do in language. Opacity is the possibility of the poetic in language. It screens the distance between sign and signifier. Opacity and density are possible in glass, even in clear glass, which, in your quotation, is "the enemy of secrecy." The textuality of glass in architecture is different from the textuality of *glas,* the letters *g, l, a, s.* Modes of translation from one language to another, from one syn-tax to another, can do things with the word *glass* that architecture cannot. For that matter, the hinge between Derridean thought and architecture is in neither glass nor ash (gash or ass may be better). It would be naïve to think so, particularly in the face of your work. It is no longer possible to simply accept naïveté in your thought about architecture or in thought in general about architecture. One may have started there. Yet that *there,* which is not the there of my architecture, is difficult because it is dominated by what is already there in architecture another tradi-tion of sign and signified. Your idea of glass is eminently utilitarian and transparent; whereas there is no trans-parency in your *glas,* perhaps only *verre* and no truth, no *(-)itas.* Wordplay which produces both opacity and trans-parency in language has no easy equivalent in architecture. The closest, perhaps, is the classical ideal of virtual space, or the Gestalt of figure-ground. Even so, neither of these concepts moves architecture from its belief in the theory of origins to something *other.* Only when the thought-to-be-essential relationship of architecture to func-tion is undermined, that is, when the traditional dialectical, hierarchical, and supplemental relationship of form to function is displaced, can the condition of presence, which problematizes any possible displacement of architec-ture, be addressed. It is not that there is no possibility of deconstruction in architecture, but it cannot simply take issue with what you have called the metaphysics of presence. In my view, your deconstruction of the pres-ence/absence dialectic is inadequate for architecture precisely because architecture is not a two-term, but a three-term system. In architecture, there is another condition, which I call *presentness,* that is neither absence nor presence, form nor function, neither the particular use of a sign nor the crude existence of reality, but rather an excessive condition between sign and the Heideggerian notion of being: the formation and ordering of the discursive event that is architecture. As long as there is a strong bond between form and function, sign and being, the excess that contains the possibility of presentness will be repressed. The need to overcome presence, the need to supplement an architecture that will always be and look like architecture, the need to break apart the strong bond between form and function, is what my architecture addresses. In its displacement of the traditional role of function it does not deny that architecture must function, but rather suggests that architecture may also function without necessarily symbolizing that function, that the presentness of architecture is irreducible to the presence of its functions or its signs.

All of these issues lead into our differences on the question of aura. You want no aura, or the deconstruction of aura, and I want this aura that is the aura of the third—this excess that is presentness. My architecture asks, Can there be an *other* in the condition of aura in architecture, an aura that both is secret and contains its own secret, the mark of its absent openness? This may involve the difference between the thing as word, and the thing as object, between language and architecture. Unlike language, which is understandable through the gaze alone, in architecture there is no such thing as the sign of a column or a window without the actual presence of a column or a window. Both the gaze and the body are implicated by the interiority of architecture. This interiority, this necessity to enclose, is not found in language or even in painting or sculpture. Thus, you may be right that architecture strives for an aura, one having nothing to do with text, or good or bad, or truth or God, but, nevertheless, with something that needs to be explained. Presentness is the possibility of another aura in architecture, one not in the sign or in being, but in a third condition. Neither nostalgic for meaning or presence nor dependent on them, this third, non-dialectical condition of space exists only in an excess that is more, or less, than the traditional, hierarchical, Vitruvian preconditions of form: structure, function, and beauty. This excess is not based on the tradition of plenitude. This condition of aura is perhaps something that also remains unproblematized in your work, despite your protestations to the contrary. I believe that by virtue of architecture's unique relationship to presence, to what I call presentness, it will always be a domain of aura. After all, aura is presence of absence, the possibility of a presentness of something else. It is this *else* that my architecture attempts to reveal.

I say this because when I read your work on Valerio Adami, I am fascinated by your discourse, yet when I look at the painting, I find it lacking: it lacks the aura possible in marking a surface with lines, paint, color, texture, etc. I feel the same way about psychoanalysts who put symbolic and ritualistic drawings and paintings in frames on the walls of their offices and think of them (because they are framed) as art. While these works may have psychological content and intent, they are, for me, illustrated psychology, not art, because they do not establish a critical relationship to traditional art. They are not analytic or critical in the terms of their own medium, either painting or drawing. They do not take into account the history and specificity of painting. No matter how important your thoughts on Adami are, he remains uninteresting to me as an artist because of this very lack of aura. Now you probably believe that this painterly aura I speak of is one of secrecy and distance, a traditional aura of an original work ripe for deconstruction. But I am not talking about this kind of Benjaminian aura—the aura of metaphysical fullness—but rather of an *other* aura evolving from the remainder of the here and now after its deconstruction: presentness, not the presence, of the work. Traditional architecture collapses presentness into presence and has always viewed their separation as dangerous. In my view, the most virulent translation of undecidability in architecture rests on this point.

My architecture holds that architecture could write something else, something other than its own traditional texts of function, structure, meaning, and aesthetics. So, as you have observed, it always has strived, implicitly, for this other aura. Now, it is one thing to speak theoretically about these matters and it is another thing to act on them. You see, Jacques, when you leave your own realm, when you attempt to be consistent, whatever that might mean in architecture, it is precisely then that you do not understand the implications for deconstruction in architecture—when deconstruction leaves your hands. For me to toe the party line is useless; for in the end, Jacques, you would be more unhappy with an architecture that illustrates deconstruction than with my work, wherein the buildings themselves become, in a way, useless—lose their traditional significance of function and appropriate an other aura, one of excess, of presentness, and not presence. No amount of talking about absence, or of wordplay between *presence* and *present* can create such an aura that distances architecture in building from the past and future of building.

In the end, my architecture cannot be what it should be, but only what it can be. Only when you add one more reading of my work alongside your reading of it in pictures and texts—that is, a reading in the event of a building—only there will you see the play between presence and presentness, only then will you know whether I have been faithful.

Yet, I remain yours faithfully,

Peter Eisenman

62 Paul Cézanne, *Mont Sainte-Victoire*, 1904–6. Oil on canvas.
Philadelphia Museum of Art, Philadelphia.

63 Pablo Picasso, *Man with a Clarinet*, 1911. Oil on canvas.
Museo Thyssen-Bornemisza, Madrid.
64 Georges Braque, *The Portuguese*, 1911. Oil on canvas.
Offentliche Kunstsammlung, Basel.

65

66

67

65 Robert Delauney, *Simultaneous Windows*, 1911. Oil on canvas.
Kunsthalle, Hamburg.
66 Juan Gris, *Still Life*, 1912. Oil on canvas. Kunstmuseum, Bern.
67 László Moholy-Nagy, *La Sarraz*, 1930. Oil on canvas.
Private collection.

68 Fernand Léger, *Three Faces*, 1926. Oil on canvas.
Kunstmuseum, Bern.
69 Pablo Picasso, *L'Arlésienne*, 1911–12.
Oil on canvas. W.P. Chrysler Collection, New York.

Walter Gropius, Bauhaus, Dessau, Germany, 1925–26.
[inte]rior view.
[L]e Corbusier, Villa Stein de Monzie, Garches, France, 1925–26.
[Vue] en facade.

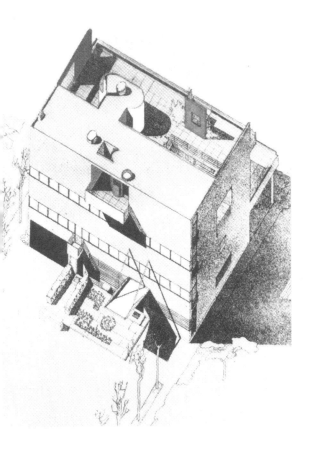

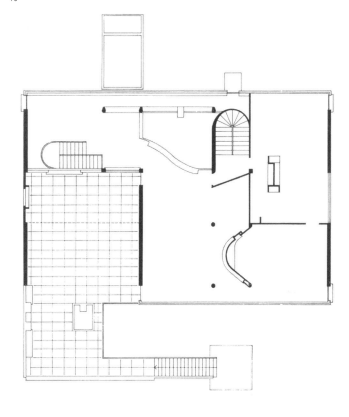

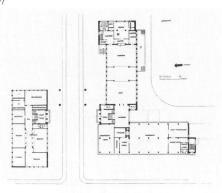

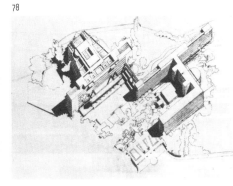

Le Corbusier, Villa Stein de Monzie, Garches, France, 1925–26.
et facade.

Walter Gropius, Bauhaus, Dessau, Germany, 1925–26.
of workshop wing.

74 Le Corbusier, Villa Stein de Monzie, Garches, France, 1925–26.
Axonometric.

75 Le Corbusier, Villa Stein de Monzie, Garches, France, 1925–26.
Main floor plan.

76 Walter Gropius, Bauhaus, Dessau, Germany, 1925–26. First-floor plan.

77 Walter Gropius, Bauhaus, Dessau, Germany, 1925–26.
Ground-floor plan.

78 Le Corbusier, League of Nations (project), Geneva, Switzerland,
1927. Axonometric.

79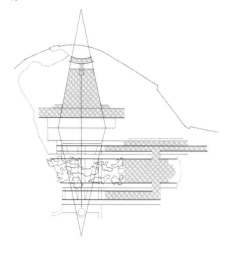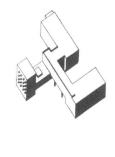

81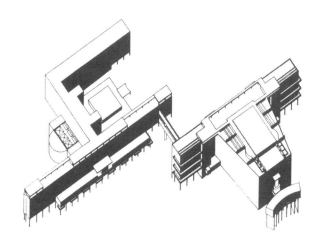

80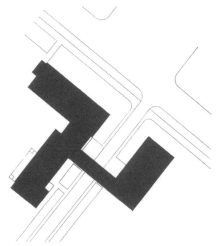

82

79 Le Corbusier, League of Nations (project), Geneva, Switzerland, 1927. Analytical diagram.
80 Walter Gropius, Bauhaus, Dessau, Germany, 1925–26. Site plan.

81 Bauhaus and League of Nations. Axonometrics.
82 Le Corbusier, Skyscraper of the Quartier de la Marine (project), Algiers, Algeria, 1938–42. Perspective.

84

3 Pietro Belluschi, Equitable Life Insurance Building, Portland, Ore.,
945–48. Exterior view.
4 I.M. Pei, Mile High Center, Denver, Colo., 1954–59. Exterior view.

85

86

85 Giacomo Vignola, Villa Farnese, Caprarola, Italy, 1560.
Exterior view.
86 Cathedral of St. Denis, near Paris, c.1140. Exterior view.

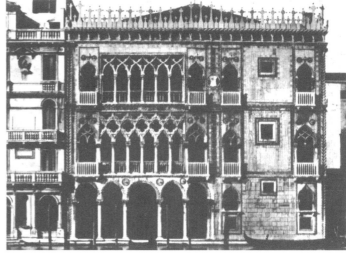

87 Palazzo Mocenigo, Venice, Italy.
88 Ca d'Oro, Venice, Italy.

89

90

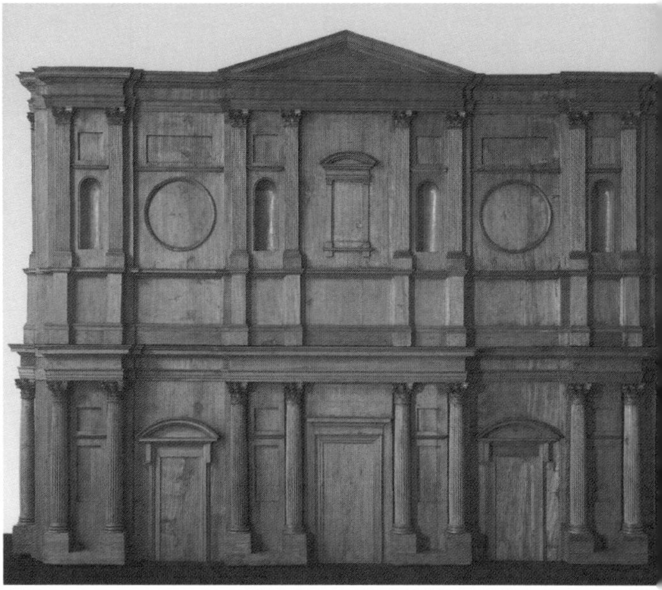

91a 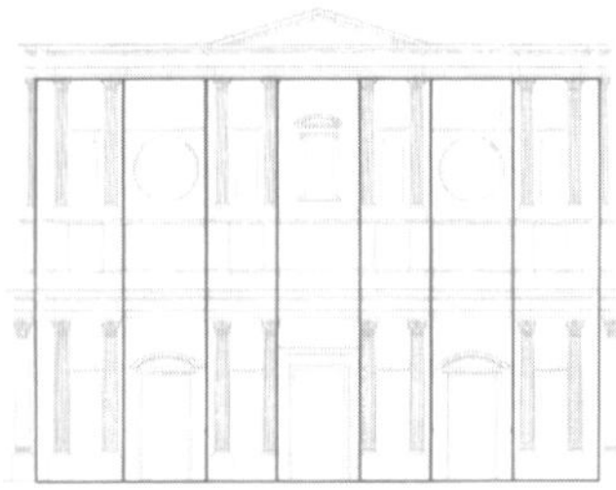   b 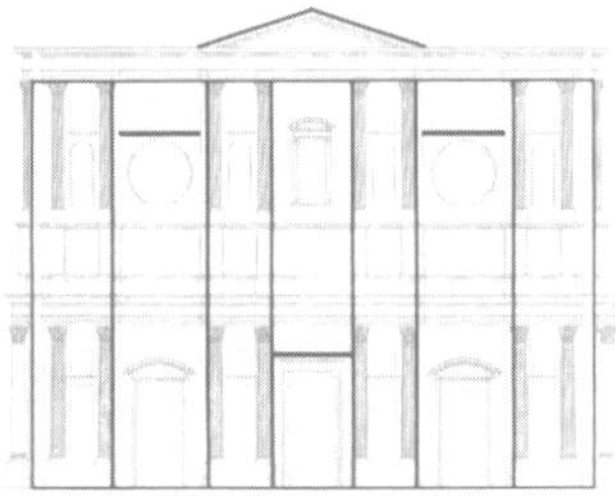   c 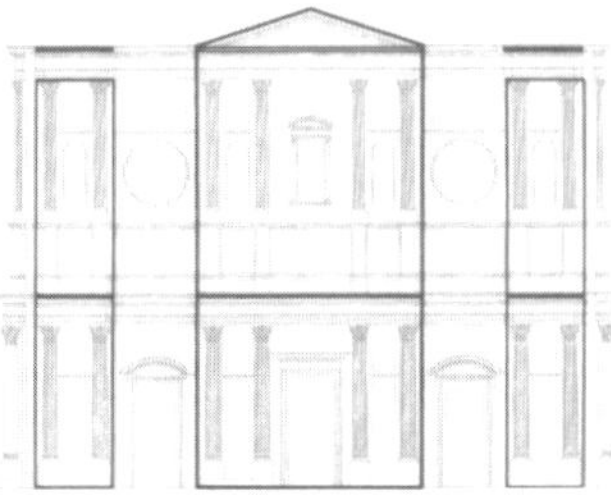   d

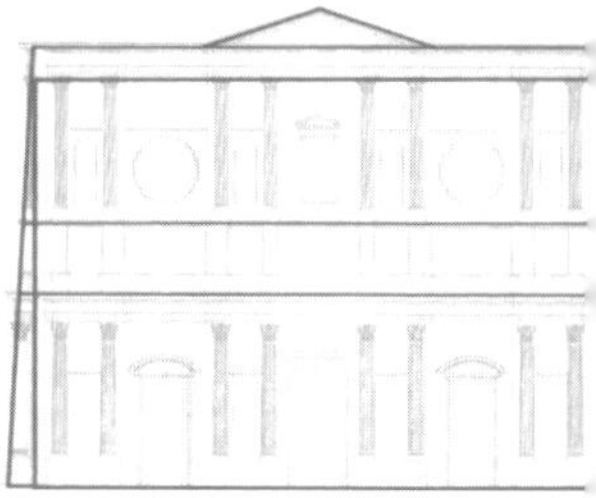

e 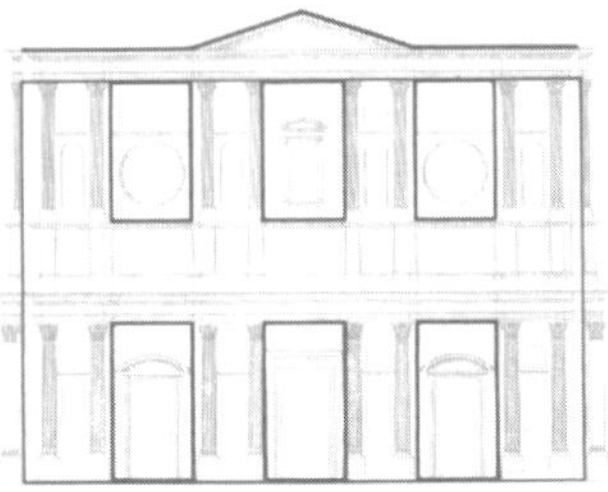   e 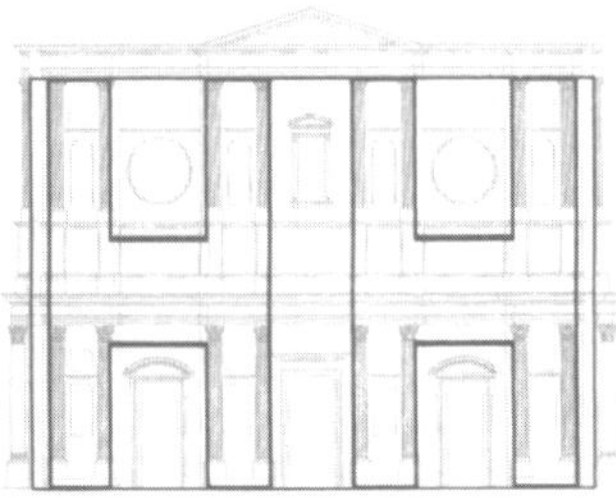   e 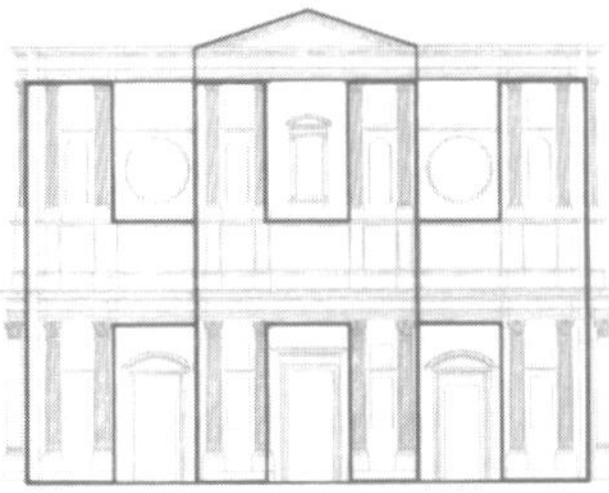   e

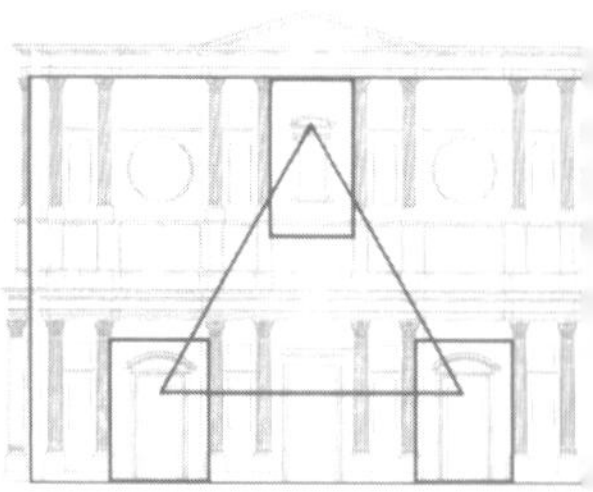

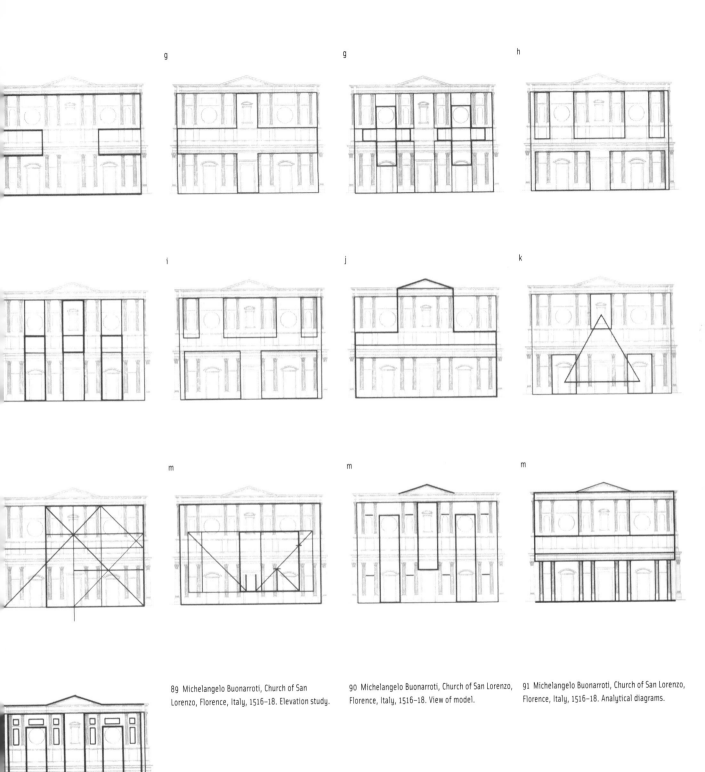

g   g   h

i   j   k

m   m   m

89 Michelangelo Buonarroti, Church of San Lorenzo, Florence, Italy, 1516–18. Elevation study.

90 Michelangelo Buonarroti, Church of San Lorenzo, Florence, Italy, 1516–18. View of model.

91 Michelangelo Buonarroti, Church of San Lorenzo, Florence, Italy, 1516–18. Analytical diagrams.

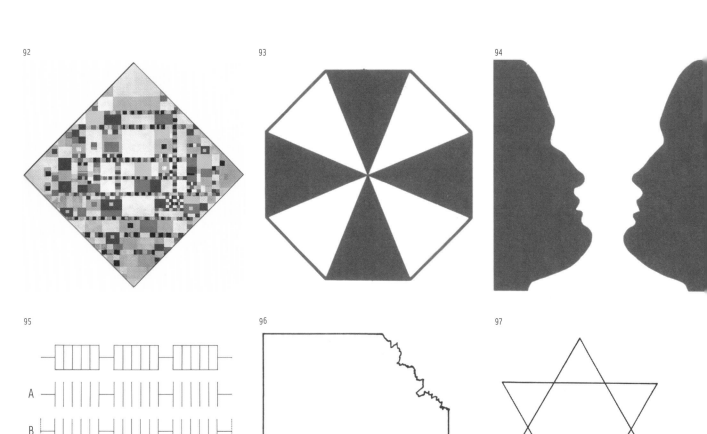

92

93

94

95

A

B

C

96

97

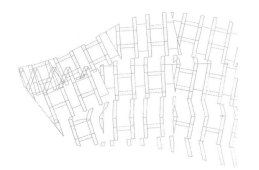

98

99

92 Piet Mondrian, *Victory Boogie Woogie*, 1943–44. Oil on canvas.
93 Gestalt diagram.
94 Gestalt diagram.

95 Gestalt diagram.
96 Gestalt diagram.
97 Gestalt diagram.

98 Peter Eisenman, Rebstockpark (project), Germany, 1990.
Plan diagram.
99 John Hejduk, *French/American/Consulates*, detail of a page
in the *Vladivostok* sketchbook, 1985.

101

Le Corbusier, Villa Savoye, Poissy, France, 1929–30. Interior view. Le Corbusier, *Still Life for the Pavillon de l'Esprit Nouveau*, 1924, dation Le Corbusier, Paris.

102 Hans von Marées, *The Courtship II*, 1885–87, Mixed media on wood. Bayerische Staatsgemäldesammlungen, Munich.

103 Adolf Hildebrand, *Courting*, 1880. Marble relief. Brewster Peploe Collection, Villa San Francesco, Florence.

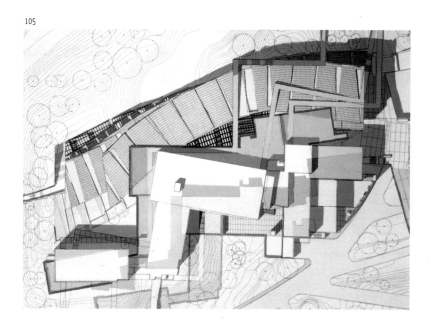

104 Peter Eisenman, DAAP (Aronoff Center for Design and Art),
Cincinnati, Ohio, 1988–93. Exterior view.
105 Peter Eisenman, DAAP (Aronoff Center for Design and Art),
Cincinnati, Ohio, 1988–93. View of model.
106 Peter Eisenman, DAAP (Aronoff Center for Design and Art),
Cincinnati, Ohio, 1988–93. Interior view.
107 Peter Eisenman, DAAP (Aronoff Center for Design and Art),
Cincinnati, Ohio, 1988–93. Interior view.

108 Peter Eisenman, House I, Hardwick, Vt., 1969–70. Exterior view.
109 Peter Eisenman, House III, Lakeville, Conn., 1969–71. Exterior view.
110 Volker Giencke, Odörfer Showroom and Warehouse, Klagenfurt, Austria, 1991.
111 Volker Giencke, Odörfer Showroom and Warehouse, Klagenfurt, Austria, 1991. Exterior view.
112 Volker Giencke, Odörfer Showroom and Warehouse, Klagenfurt, Austria, 1991. Exterior view.
113 Volker Giencke, Odörfer Showroom and Warehouse, Klagenfurt, Austria, 1991. Interior view.

Gianloranzo Bernini, *The Ecstasy of Saint Teresa*, 1645–52.
ed marble, Church of Santa Maria Vittoria, Rome, Italy.
Michelangelo Buonarotti, *Atlas (Il Prigione)*, c. 1519,
ed marble, Accademia Museum, Florence, Italy.

116 Volker Giencke, Botanical Gardens, Graz, Austria, 1995.
 Exterior view.

117 Volker Giencke, Botanical Gardens, Graz, Austria, 1995.
Aerial view.

118 Volker Giencke, Botanical Gardens, Graz, Austria, 1995.
Detail of aluminum construction.

This is the second in a series of lectures about quantum electrodynamics, and since it's clear that none of you were here last time (because I told everyone that they weren't going to understand anything), I'll briefly summarize the first lecture.

We were talking about light. The first important feature about light is that it appears to be particles: when very weak monochromatic light (light of one color) hits a detector, the detector makes equally loud clicks less and less often as the light gets dimmer.

The other important feature about light discussed in the first lecture is partial reflection of monochromatic light. An average of 4% of the photons hitting a *single* surface of glass is reflected. This is already a deep mystery, since it is impossible to predict which photons will bounce back and which will go through. With a *second* surface, the results are strange: instead of the expected reflection of 8% by the two surfaces, the partial reflection can be amplified as high as 16% or turned off, depending on the thickness of the glass.

This strange phenomenon of partial reflection by two surfaces can be explained for intense light by a theory of waves, but the wave theory cannot explain how the detector makes equally loud clicks as the light gets dimmer. Quantum electrodynamics "resolves" this wave-particle duality by saying that light is made of particles (as Newton originally thought), but the price of this great advancement of science is a retreat by physics to the position of being able to calculate only the *probability* that a photon will hit a detector, without offering a good model of how it actually happens. In the first lecture I described how physicists calculate the probability that a particular event will happen. They draw some arrows on a piece of paper according to some rules, which go as follows:

GRAND PRINCIPLE: The probability of an event is equal to the square of the length of an arrow called the "probability amplitude." An arrow of length 0.4, for example, represents a probability of 0.16, or 16%.

GENERAL RULE for drawing arrows if an event can happen in alternative ways: Draw an arrow for each way, and then combine the arrows ("add" them) by hooking the head of one to the tail of the next. A "final arrow" is then drawn from the tail of the first arrow to the head of the last one. The final arrow is the one whose square gives the probability of the entire event.

There were also some specific rules for drawing arrows in the case of partial reflection by glass. All of the preceding is a review of the first lecture.

What I would like to do now is show you how this model of the world, which is so utterly different from anything you've ever seen before (that perhaps you hope never to see it again), can explain all the simple properties of light that you know: when light reflects off a mirror, the angle of incidence is equal to the angle of reflection; light bends when it goes from air into water; light goes in straight lines; light can be focused by a lens, and so on. The theory also describes many other properties of light that you are probably not familiar with. In fact, the greatest difficulty I had in preparing these lectures was to resist the temptation to derive all the things about light that took you so long to learn about in school—such as the behavior of light as it goes past an edge into shadow (called diffraction)—but since most of you have not carefully observed such phenomena, I won't bother with them. However, I can guarantee you (otherwise, the examples I'm going to show you would be misleading) that *every* phenomenon about light that has been observed in detail can be explained by the theory of quantum electrodynamics, even though I'm going to describe only the simplest and most common phenomena.

We start with a mirror, and the problem of determining how light is reflected from it (see 1). At S we have a source that emits light of one color at very low intensity (let's use red light again). The source emits one photon at a time. At P, we place a photomultiplier to detect photons. Let's put it at the same height as the source—drawing arrows will be easier if everything is symmetrical. We want to calculate the chance that the detector will make a click after a photon has been emitted by the source. Since it is possible that a photon could go straight across to the detector, let's place a screen at Q to prevent that.

Now, we would expect that all the light that reaches the detector reflects off the middle of the mirror, because that's the place where the angle of incidence equals the angle of reflection. And it seems fairly obvious that the parts of the mirror out near the two ends have as much to do with the reflection as with the price of cheese, right?

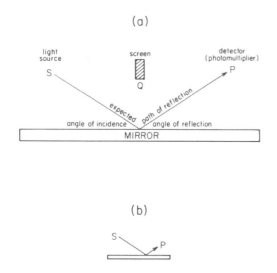

1 The classical view of the world says that a mirror will reflect light where the angle of incidence is equal to the angle of reflection, even if the source and the detector are at different levels, as in (b).

Although you might *think* that the parts of the mirror near the two ends have nothing to do with the reflection of the light that goes from the source to the detector, let us look at what quantum theory has to say. Rule: The probability that a particular event occurs is the square of a final arrow that is found by drawing an arrow for each way the event could happen, and then combining ("adding") the arrows. In the experiment measuring the partial reflection of light by two surfaces, there were two ways a photon could get from the source to the detector. In this experiment, there are millions of ways a photon could go: it could go down to the left-hand part of the mirror at A or B (for example) and bounce up to the detector (see 2); it could bounce off the part where you think it should, at G; or, it could go down to the right-hand part of the mirror at K or M and bounce up to the detector. You might think I'm crazy, because for most of the ways I told you a photon could reflect off the mirror, the angles aren't equal. But I'm *not* crazy, because that's the way light really goes! How can that be?

To make this problem easier to understand, let's suppose that the mirror consists of only a long strip from left to right—it's just as well that we forget, for a moment, that the mirror also sticks out from the paper (see 3). While there are, in reality, millions of places where the light could reflect from this strip of mirror, let's make an approximation by temporarily dividing the mirror into a definite number of little squares, and consider only one path for each square—our calculation gets more accurate (but harder to do) as we make the squares smaller and consider more paths.

Now, let's draw a little arrow for each way the light could go in this situation. Each little arrow has a certain length and a certain direction. Let's consider the length first. You might think that the arrow we draw to represent the path that goes to the middle of the mirror, at G, is by far the longest (since there seems to be a very high probability that any photon that gets to the detector must go that way), and the arrows for the paths at the ends of the

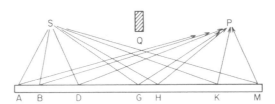

2 The quantum view of the world says that light has an equal amplitude to reflect from every part of the mirror, from A to M.

3 To calculate more easily where the light goes, we shall temporarily consider only a strip of mirror divided into little squares, with one path for each square. This simplification in no way detracts from an accurate analysis of the situation.

mirror must be very short. No, no; we should not make such an arbitrary rule. The right rule—what actually happens—is much simpler: a photon that reaches the detector has a nearly equal chance of going on *any* path, so all the little arrows have nearly the same length. (There are, in reality, some very slight variations in length due to the various angles and distances involved, but they are so minor that I am going to ignore them.) So let us say that each little arrow we draw will have an arbitrary standard length—I will make the length very short because there are many of these arrows representing the many ways the light could go (see 4).

Although it is safe to assume that the length of all the arrows will be nearly the same, their directions will clearly differ because their timing is different—as you remember from the first lecture, the direction of a particular arrow is determined by the final position of an imaginary stopwatch that times a photon as it moves along that particular path. When a photon goes way off to the left end of the mirror, at A, and then up to the detector, it clearly takes more time than a photon that gets to the detector by reflecting in the middle of the mirror, at G (see 5). Or, imagine for a moment that you were in a hurry and had to run from the source over to the mirror and then to the detector. You'd know that it certainly isn't a good idea to go way over to A and then all the way up to the detector; it would be much faster to touch the mirror somewhere in the middle.

To help us calculate the direction of each arrow, I'm going to draw a graph right underneath my sketch of the mirror (see 6). Directly below each place on the mirror where the light could reflect, I'm going to show, vertically, how much time it would take if the light went that way. The more time it takes, the higher the point will be on the graph. Starting at the left, the time it takes a photon to go on the path that reflects at A is pretty long, so we plot a point pretty high up on the graph. As we move toward the center of the mirror, the time it takes for a photon to go

4 Each way the light can go will be represented in our calculation by an arrow of an arbitrary standard length, as shown.

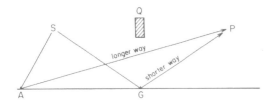

5 While the length of each arrow is essentially the same, the direction will be different because the time it takes for a photon to go on each path is different. Clearly, it takes longer to go from S to A to P than from S to G to P.

the particular way we're looking at goes down, so we plot each successive point lower than the previous one. After we pass the center of the mirror, the time it takes a photon to go on each successive path gets longer and longer, so we plot our points correspondingly higher and higher. To aid the eye, let's connect the points: they form a symmetrical curve that starts high, goes down, and then goes back up again.

Now, what does that mean for the direction of the little arrows? The direction of a particular arrow corresponds to the amount of time it would take a photon to get from the source to the detector following that particular path. Let's draw the arrows, starting at the left. Path A takes the most time; its arrow points in some direction (see 6). The arrow for path B points in a different direction because its time is different. At the middle of the mirror, arrows F, G, and H point in nearly the same direction because their times are nearly the same. After passing the center of the mirror, we see that each path on the right side of mirror corresponds to a path on the left side whose time is exactly the same (this is a consequence of putting the source and the detector at the same height, and path G exactly in the middle). Thus the arrow for path J, for example, has the same direction as the arrow for path D.

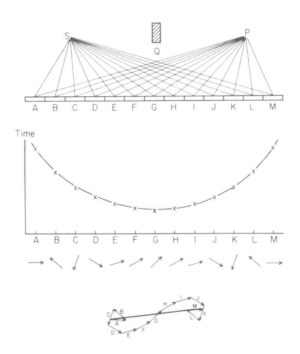

6 Each path the light could go (in this simplified situation) is shown at the top, with a point on the graph below it showing the time it takes a photon to go from the source to that point on the mirror, and then to the photomultiplier. Below the graph is the direction of each arrow, and at the bottom is the result of adding all the arrows. It is evident that the major contribution to the final arrow's length is made by arrows E though L, whose directions are nearly the same because the timing of their paths is nearly the same. This also happens to be where the total time is least. It is therefore approximately right to say that light goes where the time is least.

Now, let's add the little arrows (see 6). Starting with arrow A, we hook the arrows to each other, head to tail. Now, if we were to take a walk using each little arrow as a step, we wouldn't get very far at the beginning, because the direction from one step to the next is so different. But after a while the arrows begin to point in generally the same direction, and we make some progress. Finally, near the end of our walk, the direction from one step to the next is again quite different, so we stagger about some more.

All we have to do is draw the final arrow. We simply connect the tail of the first little arrow to the head of the last one, and see how much direct progress we made on our walk (see 6). And behold—we get a sizable final arrow! The theory of quantum electrodynamics predicts that the light does, indeed, reflect off the mirror.

Now, let's investigate. What determines how long the final arrow is? We notice a number of things. First, the ends of the mirror are not important: there, the little arrows wander around and don't get anywhere. If I chopped off the ends of the mirror—parts that you instinctively knew I was wasting my time fiddling around with—it would hardly affect the length of the final arrow.

So where is the part of the mirror that gives the final arrow a substantial length? It is the part where the arrows are all pointing in nearly the same direction—because their *time* is almost the *same*. If you look at the graph showing the time for each path (see 6), you see that the time is nearly the same from one path to the next at the bottom of the curve, where the *time is the least*.

To summarize, where the time is least is also where the time for the nearby paths is nearly the same; that's where the little arrows point in nearly the same direction and add up to a substantial length; that's where the probability of a photon reflecting off a mirror is determined. And that's why, in approximation, we can get away with the crude picture of the world that says that light only goes where the *time is least* (and it's easy to prove that where the time is least, the angle of incidence is equal to the angle of reflection, but I don't have the time to show you).

So the theory of quantum electrodynamics gave the right answer—the middle of the mirror is the important part for reflection—but this correct result came out at the expense of believing that light reflects all over the mirror, and having to add a bunch of little arrows together whose sole purpose was to cancel out. All that might seem to you to be a waste of time—some silly game for mathematicians only. After all, it doesn't seem like "real physics" to have something there that only cancels out!

Let's test the idea that there really *is* reflection going on all over the mirror by doing another experiment. First, let's chop off most of the mirror, and leave about a quarter of it, over on the left. We still have a pretty big piece of mirror, but it's in the wrong place. In the previous experiment the arrows on the left side of the mirror were pointing in directions very different from one another because of the large difference in time between neighboring paths (see 6). In this experiment I am going to make a more detailed calculation by taking intervals on that left-hand part of the mirror that are much closer together—fine enough that there is not much difference in time between neighboring paths (see 7). With this more detailed picture, we see that some of the arrows point more or less to the right; the others point more or less to the left. If we add *all* the arrows together, we have a bunch of arrows going around in what is essentially a circle, getting nowhere.

But let's suppose we carefully scrape the mirror away in those areas whose arrows have a bias in one direction—let's say, to the left—so that only those places whose arrows point generally the other way remain (see 8). When we add up only the arrows that point more or less to the right, we get a series of dips and a substantial final arrow—according to the theory, we should now have a strong reflection! And indeed, we do—the theory *is* correct! Such a mirror is called a diffraction grating, and it works like a charm.

Isn't it wonderful—you can take a piece of mirror where you didn't expect any reflection, scrape away part of it, and it reflects![1] The particular grating that I just showed you was tailor-made for red light. It wouldn't work for blue light; we would have to make a new grating with the cut-away strips spaced closer together because, as I told you in the first lecture, the stopwatch hand turns around faster when it times a blue photon compared to a red photon. So the cuts that were especially designed for the "red" rate of turning don't fall in the right places for blue light; the arrows get kinked up and the grating doesn't work very well. But as a matter of accident, it happens that if we move the photomultiplier down to a somewhat different angle, the grating made for red light now works for blue light. It's just a lucky accident, a consequence of the geometry involved (see 9).

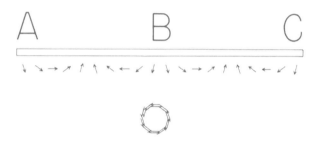

7 To test the idea that there is really reflection happening at the ends of the mirror (but it is just canceling out), we do an experiment with a large piece of mirror that is located in the wrong place for reflection from S to P. This piece of mirror is divided into much smaller sections, so that the timing from one path to the next is not very different. When all the arrows are added, they get nowhere: they go in a circle and add up to nearly nothing.

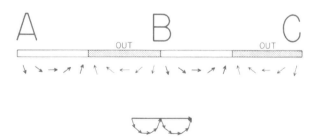

8 If only the arrows with a bias in a particular direction—such as to the right—are added, while the others are disregarded (by etching away the mirrors in those places), then a substantial amount of light reflects from this piece of mirror located in the wrong place. Such an etched mirror is called a diffraction grating.

If you shine white light down onto the grating, red light comes out at one place, orange light comes out slightly above it, followed by yellow, green, and blue light—all the colors of the rainbow. Where there is a series of grooves close together, you can often see colors—for example, when you hold a phonograph record (or better, a videodisc)—under a bright light at the correct angles. Perhaps you have seen those wonderful silvery signs (here in sunny California they're often on the backs of cars): when the car moves, you see very bright colors changing from red to blue. Now you know where the colors come from: you're looking at a grating—a mirror that's been scratched in just the right places. The sun is the light source, and your eyes are the detector. I could go on to easily explain how lasers and holograms work, but I know that not everyone has seen these things, and I have too many other things to talk about.[2]

So a grating shows that we can't ignore the parts of a mirror that don't seem to be reflecting; if we do some clever things to the mirror, we can demonstrate the reality of the reflections from all parts of the mirror and produce some striking optical phenomena (see 10).

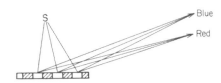

9 A diffraction grating with grooves at the right distance for red light also works for other colors, if the detector is in a different place. Thus it is possible to see different colors reflecting from a grooved surface—such as a phonograph record—depending on the angle.

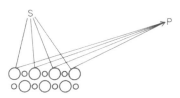

10 Nature has made many types of diffraction gratings in the form of crystals. A salt crystal reflects X rays (light for which the imaginary stopwatch hand moves extremely fast—perhaps 10,000 times faster than for visible light) at various angles, from which can be determined the exact arrangement and spacings of the individual atoms.

More important, demonstrating the reality of reflection from *all* parts of the mirror shows that there is an amplitude—an arrow—for *every way* an event can happen. And in order to calculate correctly the probability of an event in different circumstances, we have to add the arrows for *every way* that the event could happen—not just the ways we think are the important ones!

Now, I would like to talk about something more familiar than gratings—about light going from air into water. This time, let's put the photomultiplier underwater—we suppose the experimenter can arrange that! The source of light is in the air at S, and the detector is underwater, at D (see 11). Once again, we want to calculate the probability that a photon will get from the light source to the detector. To make this calculation, we should consider all the ways the light could go. Each way the light could go contributes a little arrow and, as in the previous example, all the little arrows have nearly the same length. We can again make a graph of the time it takes a photon to go on each possible path. The graph will be a curve very similar to the one we made for the light reflecting off a mirror: it starts up high, goes down, and then back up again; the most important contributions come from the places where the arrows point in the same direction (where the time is nearly the same from one path to the next), which is at the bottom of the curve. That is also where the time is the least, so all we have to do is find out where the time is the least.

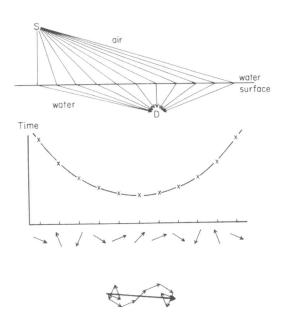

11 Quantum theory says that light can go from a source in air to a detector in water in many ways. If the problem is simplified as in the case of the mirror, a graph showing the timing of each path can be drawn, with the direction of each arrow below it. Once again, the major contribution toward the length of the final arrow comes from those paths whose arrows point in nearly the same direction because their timing is nearly the same; once again, this is where the time is the least.

It turns out that light seems to go slower in water than it does in air (I will explain why in the next lecture), which makes the distance through water more "costly," so to speak, than the distance through air. It's not hard to figure out which path takes the least time: suppose you're the lifeguard, sitting at S, and the beautiful girl is drowning, at D (see 12). You can run on the land faster than you can swim in the water. The problem is, where do you enter the water in order to reach the drowning victim the fastest? Do you run down to the water at A, and then swim like hell? Of course not. But running directly toward the victim and entering the water at J is not the fastest route, either. While it would be foolish for a lifeguard to analyze and calculate under the circumstances, there is a computable position at which the time is minimum: it's a compromise between taking the direct path, through J, and taking the path with the least water, through N. And so it is with light—the path of least time enters the water at a point between J and N, such as L.

Another phenomenon of light that I would like to mention briefly is the mirage. When you're driving along a road that is very hot, you can sometimes see what looks like water on the road. What you're really seeing is the sky, and when you normally see sky in the road, it's because the road has puddles of water on it (partial reflection of light by a single surface). But how can you see sky on the road when there's no water there? What you need to know is that light goes slower through cooler air than through warmer air, and for a mirage to be seen, the observer must

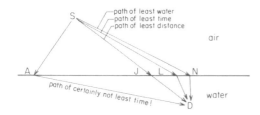

12 Finding the path of least time for light is like finding the path of least time for a lifeguard running
and then swimming to rescue a drowning victim: the path of least distance has too much water in it;
the path of least water has too much land in it; the path of least time is a compromise between the two.

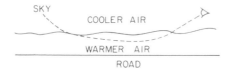

13 Finding the path of least time explains how a mirage works. Light goes faster through warm air
than through cool air. Some of the sky appears to be on the road because some of the light from the
sky reaches the eye by coming up from the road. The only other time sky appears to be on the road
is when water is reflecting it, and thus a mirage appears to be water.

be in the cooler air that is above the hot air next to the road surface (see 13). How it is possible to look *down* and see the sky can be understood by finding the path of least time. I'll let you play with that one at home—it's fun to think about, and pretty easy to figure out.

In the examples I showed you of light reflecting off a mirror and light going through air and then water, I was making an approximation: for the sake of simplicity, I drew the various ways the light could go as double straight lines—two straight lines that form an angle. But we don't have to *assume* that light goes in straight lines when it is in a uniform material like air or water; even *that* is explainable by the general principle of quantum theory: the probability of an event is found by adding arrows for *all* the ways the event could happen.

So for our next example, I'm going to show you how, by adding little arrows, it can appear that light goes in a straight line. Let's put a source and a photomultiplier at S and P, respectively (see 14), and look at *all* the ways the light could go—in all sorts of crooked paths—to get from the source to the detector. Then we draw a little arrow for each path, and we're learning our lesson well!

For each crooked path, such as path A, there's a nearby path that's a little bit straighter and distinctly shorter— that is, it takes much less time. But where the paths become nearly straight—at C, for example—a nearby, straighter path has nearly the same time. That's where the arrows add up rather than cancel out; that's where the light goes.

It is important to note that the single arrow that represents the straight-line path, through D (see 14), is not enough to account for the probability that light gets from the source to the detector. The nearby, nearly straight paths—through C and E, for example—also make important contributions. So light doesn't *really* travel only in a straight line; it "smells" the neighboring paths around it, and uses a small core of nearby space. (In the same way, a mirror has to have enough size to reflect normally: if the mirror is too small for the core of neighboring paths, the light scatters in many directions, no matter where you put the mirror.)

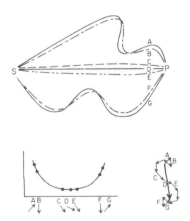

14 Quantum theory can be used to show why light appears to travel in straight lines. When all possible paths are considered, each crooked path has a nearby path of considerably less distance and therefore much less time (and a substantially different direction for the arrow). Only the paths near the straight-line path at D have arrows pointing in nearly the same direction, because their timings are nearly the same. Only such arrows are important, because it is from them that we accumulate a large final arrow.

Let's investigate this core of light more closely by putting a source at S, a photomultiplier at P, and a pair of blocks between them to keep the paths of light from wandering too far away (see 15). Now, let's put a second photomultiplier at Q, below P, and assume again, for the sake of simplicity, that the light can get from S to Q only by paths of double straight lines. Now, what happens? When the gap between the blocks is wide enough to allow many neighboring paths to P and to Q, the arrows for the paths to P add up (because all the paths to P take nearly the same time), while the paths to Q cancel out (because those paths have a sizable difference in time). Thus the photomultiplier at Q doesn't click.

But as we push the blocks closer together, at a certain point the detector at Q starts clicking! When the gap is nearly closed and there are only a few neighboring paths, the arrows to Q *also* add up, because there is hardly any difference in time between them, either (see 16). Of course, both final arrows are small, so there's not much light either way through such a small hole, but the detector at Q clicks almost as much as the one at P! So when you try to squeeze light too much to make sure it's going in only a straight line, it refuses to cooperate and begins to spread out.[3]

So the idea that light goes in a straight line is a convenient approximation to describe what happens in the world that is familiar to us; it's similar to the crude approximation that says when light reflects off a mirror, the angle of incidence is equal to the angle of reflection.

Just as we were able to do a clever trick to make light reflect off a mirror at many angles, we can do a similar trick to get light to go from one point to another in many ways.

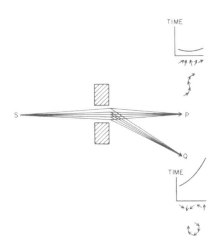

15 Light travels in not just the straight-line path, but in the nearby paths as well. When two blocks are separated enough to allow for these nearby paths, the photons proceed normally to P, and hardly ever go to Q.

First, to simplify the situation, I'm going to draw a vertical dashed line (see 17) between the light source and the detector (the line means nothing; it's just an artificial line) and say that the only paths we're going to look at are the double straight lines. The graph that shows the time for each path looks the same as in the case of the mirror (but I'll draw it sideways this time): the curve starts at A, at the top, and then it comes in, because the paths in the middle are shorter and take less time. Finally, the curve goes back out again.

Now, let's have some fun. Let's "fool the light," so that *all* the paths take exactly the same amount of time. How can we do this? How can we make the shortest path, through M, take exactly the same time as the longest path, through A?

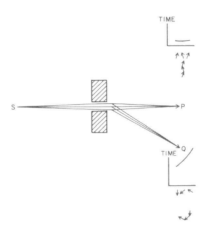

16 When light is restricted so much that only a few paths are possible, the light that is able to get through the narrow slit goes to Q almost as much as to P, because there are not enough arrows representing the paths to Q to cancel each other out.

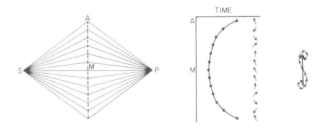

17 Analysis of all possible paths from S to P is simplified to include only double straight lines (in a single plane). The effect is the same as in the more complicated, real case: there is a time curve with a minimum, where most of the contribution to the final arrow is made.

Well, light goes slower in water than it does in air; it also goes slower in glass (which is much easier to handle!). So, if we put in just the right thickness of glass on the shortest path, through M, we can make the time for that path exactly the same as for the path through A. The paths next to M, which are just a little longer, won't need quite as much glass (see 18). The nearer we get to A, the less glass we have to put in to slow up the light. By carefully calculating and putting in just the right thickness of glass to compensate for the time along each path, we can make all the times the same. When we draw the arrows for each way the light could go, we find we have succeeded in straightening them all out—and there are, in reality, *millions* of tiny arrows—so the net result is a sensationally large, unexpectedly enormous final arrow! Of course you know what I'm describing; it's a focusing lens. By arranging things so that all the times are equal, we can focus light—we can make the probability very high that light will arrive at a particular point, and very low that it will arrive anywhere else.

I have used these examples to show you how the theory of quantum electrodynamics, which looks at first like an absurd idea with no causality, no mechanism, and nothing real to it, produces effects that you are familiar with: light bouncing off a mirror, light bending when it goes from air into water, and light focused by a lens. It also produces other effects that you may or may not have seen, such as the diffraction grating and a number of other things. In fact, the theory continues to be successful at explaining *every* phenomenon of light.

I have shown you with examples how to calculate the probability of an event that can happen in *alternative ways*: we draw an arrow for each way the event can happen, and add the arrows. "Adding arrows" means the arrows are placed head to tail and a "final arrow" is drawn. The square of the resulting final arrow represents the probability of the event.

In order to give you a fuller flavor of quantum theory, I would now like to show you how physicists calculate the probability of compound events—events that can be broken down into a series of steps, or events that consist of a number of things happening independently.

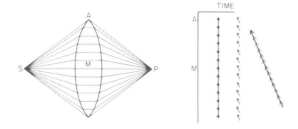

18 A "trick" can be played on Nature by slowing down the light that takes shorter paths: glass of just the right thickness is inserted so that all the paths will take exactly the same time. This causes all the arrows to point in the same direction, and to produce a whopping final arrow—lots of light! Such a piece of glass made to greatly increase the probability of light getting from a source to a single point is called a focusing lens.

An example of a compound event can be demonstrated by modifying our first experiment, in which we aimed some red photons at a single surface of glass to measure partial reflection. Instead of putting the photomultiplier at A (see 19), let's put in a screen with a hole in it to let the photons that reach point A go through. Then let's put in a sheet of glass at B, and place the photomultiplier at C. How do we figure out the probability that a photon will get from the source to C?

We can think of this event as a sequence of two steps. Step 1: a photon goes from the source to point A, reflecting off the single surface of a glass. Step 2: the photon goes from point A to the photomultiplier at C, reflecting off the sheet of glass at B. Each step has a final arrow—an *"amplitude"* (I'm going to use the words interchangeably)—that can be calculated according to the rules we know so far. The amplitude for the first step has a length of 0.2 (whose square is 0.04, the probability of reflection by a single surface of glass), and is turned at some angle—let's say 2 o'clock (see 19).

To calculate the amplitude for the second step, we temporarily put the light source at A and aim the photons at the layer of glass above. We draw arrows for the front and back surface reflections and add them—let's say we end up with a final arrow with a length of 0.3, and turned toward 5 o'clock.

Now, how do we combine the two arrows to draw the amplitude for the entire event? We look at each arrow in a new way: as instructions for a *shrink* and *turn*.

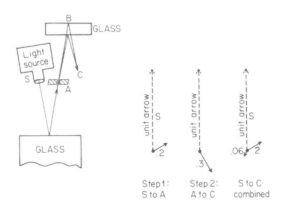

19 A compound event can be analyzed as a succession of steps. In this example, the path of a photon going from S to C can be divided into two steps: (1) a photon gets from S to A, and (2) the photon gets from A to C. Each step can be analyzed separately to produce an arrow that can be regarded in a new way: as a unit arrow (an arrow of length 1 pointed at 12 o'clock) that has gone through a shrink and turn. In this example, the shrink and turn for Step 1 are 0.2 and 2 o'clock; the shrink and turn for Step 2 are 0.3 and 5 o'clock. To get the amplitude for the two steps in succession, we shrink and turn in succession: the unit arrow is shrunk and turned to produce an arrow of length 0.2 and turned to 2 o'clock, which itself is shrunk and turned (as if it were the unit arrow) by 0.3 and 5 o'clock to produce an arrow of length 0.06 and turned to 7 o'clock. This process of successive shrinking and turning is called "multiplying" arrows.

In this example, the first amplitude has a length of 0.2 and is turned toward 2 o'clock. If we begin with a "unit arrow"—an arrow of length 1 pointed straight up—we can *shrink* this unit arrow from 1 down to 0.2, and *turn* it from 12 o'clock to 2 o'clock. The amplitude for the second step can be thought of as shrinking the unit arrow from 1 to 0.3 and turning it from 12 o'clock to 5 o'clock.

Now, to combine the amplitudes for both steps, we shrink and turn *in succession*. First, we shrink the unit arrow from 1 to 0.2 and turn it from 12 to 2 o'clock; then we shrink the arrow further, from 0.2 down to three-tenths of that, and turn it by the amount from 12 to 5—that is, we turn it from 2 o'clock to 7 o'clock. The resulting arrow has a length of 0.06 and is pointed toward 7 o'clock. It represents a probability of 0.06 squared, or 0.0036.

Observing the arrows carefully, we see that the result of shrinking and turning two arrows in succession is the same as adding their angles (2 o'clock + 5 o'clock) and multiplying their lengths (0.2 x 0.3). To understand why we add the angles is easy: the angle of an arrow is determined by the amount of turning by the imaginary stopwatch hand. So the total amount of turning for the two steps in succession is simply the sum of the turning for the first step plus the additional turning for the second step.

Why we call this process "multiplying arrows" takes a bit more explanation, but it's interesting. Let's look at multiplication, for a moment, from the point of view of the Greeks (this has nothing to do with the lecture). The Greeks wanted to use numbers that were not necessarily integers, so they represented numbers with lines. Any number can be expressed as a *transformation* of the unit line—by expanding it or shrinking it. For example, if Line A is the unit line (see 20), then line B represents 2 and line C represents 3. Now, how do we multiply 3 times 2? We apply the transformations *in succession*: starting with line A as the unit line, we expand it 2 times and then 3 times (or 3 times and then 2 times—the order doesn't make any difference). The result is line D, whose length represents 6. What about multiplying 1/3 times ?? Taking line D to be the unit line, now, we shrink it to ? (line C) and then to 1/3 of that. The result is line A, which represents 1/6.

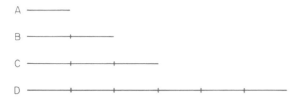

A ————
B ———————
C —————————
D ————————————————————

20 We can express any number as a transformation of the unit line through expansion or shrinkage. If A is the unit line, then B represents 2 (expansion), and C represents 3 (expansion). Multiplying lines is achieved through successive transformations. For example, multiplying 3 by 2 means that the unit line is expanded 3 times and then 2 times, producing the answer, an expansion of 6 (line D). If D is the unit line, then line C represents 1/2 (shrinkage), line B represents 1/3 (shrinkage), and multiplying 1/2 by 1/3 means the unit line D is shrunk to 1/2 and then to 1/3 of that, producing the answer, a shrinkage of 1/6 (line A).

Multiplying arrows works the same way (see 21). We apply transformations to the unit arrow in succession—it just happens that the transformations of an *arrow* involves *two* operations, a shrink and turn. To multiply arrow V times arrow W, we shrink and turn the unit arrow by the prescribed amounts for V, and then shrink it and turn it the amounts prescribed for W—again, the order doesn't make any difference. So multiplying arrows follows the same rule of successive transformations that work for regular numbers.[4]

Let's go back to the first experiment from the first lecture—partial reflection by a single surface—with this idea of successive steps in mind (see 22). We can divide the path of reflection into three steps: (1) the light goes from the source down to the glass, (2) it is reflected by the glass, and (3) it goes from the glass up to the detector. Each step can be considered as a certain amount of shrinking and turning of the unit arrow.

You'll remember that in the first lecture, we did not consider *all* of the ways that light could reflect off the glass, which requires drawing and adding lots and lots of little tiny arrows. In order to avoid all that detail, I gave the impression that the light goes down to a particular point on the surface of the glass—that it doesn't spread out. When light goes from one point to another, it does, in reality, spread out (unless it's fooled by a lens), and there is some shrinkage of the unit arrow associated with that. For the moment, however, I would like to stick to the simplified view that light does *not* spread out, and so it is appropriate to disregard this shrinkage. It is also appropriate to assume that since the light doesn't spread out, every photon that leaves the source ends up at either A or B.

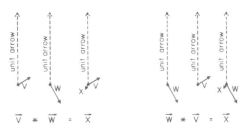

$\overrightarrow{V} \ast \overrightarrow{W} = \overrightarrow{X}$ $\overrightarrow{W} \ast \overrightarrow{V} = \overrightarrow{X}$

21 Mathematicians found that multiplying arrows can also be expressed as successive transformations (for our purposes, successive shrinks and turns) of the unit arrow. As in normal multiplication, the order is not important: the answer, arrow X, can be obtained by multiplying arrow V by arrow W or arrow W by arrow V.

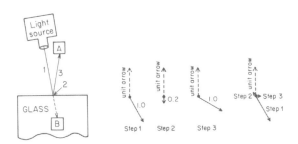

22 Reflection by a single surface can be divided into three steps, each with a shrink and/or turn of the unit arrow. The net result, an arrow of length 0.2 pointed in some direction, is the same as before, but our method of analysis is more detailed now.

So: in the first step there is no shrinkage, but there is turning—it corresponds to the amount of turning by the imaginary stopwatch hand as it times the photon going from the source to the front surface of the glass. In this example, the arrow for the first step ends up with a length of 1 at some angle—let's say, 5 o'clock.

The second step is the reflection of the photon by the glass. Here, there is a sizable shrink—from 1 to 0.2—and half a turn. (These numbers seem arbitrary now: they depend upon whether the light is reflected by glass or some other material. In the third lecture, I'll explain them, too!) Thus the second step is represented by an amplitude of length 0.2 and a direction of 6 o'clock (half a turn).

The last step is the photon going from the glass up to the detector. Here, as in the first step, there is no shrinking, but there is turning—let's say this distance is slightly shorter than in step 1, and the arrow points toward 4 o'clock.

We now "multiply" arrows 1, 2, and 3 in succession (add the angles, and multiply the lengths). The net effect of the three steps—(1) turning, (2) a shrink and half a turn, and (3) turning—is the same as in the first lecture: the turning from steps 1 and 3—(5 o'clock plus 4 o'clock) is the same amount of turning that we got then when we let the stopwatch run for the whole distance (9 o'clock); the extra half turn from step 2 makes the arrow point in the direction opposite the stopwatch hand, as it did in the first lecture, and the shrinking to 0.2 in the second step leaves an arrow whose square represents the 4% partial reflection observed for a single surface.

In this experiment, there is a question we didn't look at in the first lecture: What about the photons that go to B—the ones that are transmitted by the surface of the glass? The amplitude for a photon to arrive at B must have a length near 0.98, since 0.98 x 0.98 = 0.9604, which is close enough to 96%. This amplitude can also be analyzed by breaking it down into steps (see 23).

The first step is the same as for the path to A—the photon goes from the light source down to the glass—the unit arrow is turned toward 5 o'clock.

The second step is the photon passing through the surface of the glass: there is no turning associated with transmission, just a little bit of shrinking—to 0.98.

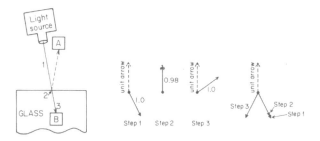

23 Transmission by a single surface can also be divided into three steps, with a shrink and/or turn for each step. An arrow of length 0.98 has a square of about 0.96, representing a probability of transmission of 96% (which, combined with the 4% probability of reflection, accounts for 100% of the light).

The third step—the photon going through the interior of the glass—involves additional turning and no shrinking.

The net result is an arrow of length 0.98 turned in some direction, whose square represents the probability that a photon will arrive at B—96%.

Now let's look at partial reflection by two surfaces again. Reflection from the front surface is the same as for a single surface, so the three steps for front surface reflection are the same as we saw a moment ago (see 22).

Reflection from the back surface can be broken down into seven steps (see 24). It involves turning equal to the total amount of turning of the stopwatch hand timing a photon over the entire distance (steps 1, 3, 5, and 7), shrinking to 0.2 (step 4), and two shrinks to 0.98 (steps 2 and 6). The resulting arrow ends up in the same direction as before, but the length is about 0.192 (0.98 x 0.2/0.98), which I approximated as 0.2 in the first lecture.

In summary, here are the rules for reflection and transmission of light by glass: (1) reflection from air back to air (off a front surface) involves a shrink to 0.2 and half a turn; (2) reflection from glass back to glass (off a back surface) also involves a shrink to 0.2, but no turning; and (3) transmission from air to glass or from glass to air involves a shrink to 0.98 and no turning in either case.

Perhaps it is too much of a good thing, but I cannot resist showing you a cute further example of how things work and are analyzed by these rules of successive steps. Let us move the detector to a location below the glass, and consider something we didn't talk about in the first lecture—the probability of *transmission* by two surfaces of glass (see 25).

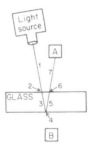

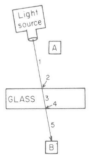

24 Reflection from the back surface of a layer of glass can be divided into seven steps. Step 1, 3, 5, and 7 involve turning only; steps 2 and 6 involve shrinks to 0.98, and step 4 involves a shrink to 0.2. The result is an arrow length of 0.192—which was approximated as 0.2 in the first lecture—turned at an angle that corresponds to the total amount of turning by the imaginary stopwatch hand.

25 Transmission by two surfaces can be broken down into five steps. Step 2 shrinks the unit arrow to 0.98, step 4 shrinks the 0.98 arrow to 0.98 of that (about 0.96); steps 1, 3, and 5 involve turning only. The resulting arrow of length 0.96 has a square of about 0.92, representing a probability of transmission by two surfaces of 92% (which corresponds to the expected 8% of reflection, which is right only "twice a day"). When the thickness of the layer is right to produce a probability of 16% reflection, with a 92% probability of transmission, 108% of the light is accounted for! Something is wrong with this analysis!

Of course you know the answer: the probability of a photon to arrive at B is simply 100% minus the probability to arrive at A, which we worked out beforehand. Thus, if we found the chance to arrive at A is 7%, the chance to arrive at B must be 93%. And as the chance for A varies from zero through 8% to 16% (due to the different thickness of glass), the chance for B changes from 100% through 92% to 84%.

That is the right answer, but we are expecting to calculate *all* probabilities by squaring a final arrow. How do we calculate the amplitude arrow for transmission by a layer of glass, and how does it manage to vary in length so appropriately as to fit with the length for A in each case, so the probability for A and the probability for B always add up to exactly 100%? Let us look a little into the details.

For a photon to go from the source to the detector below the glass, at B, five steps are involved. Let's shrink and turn the unit arrow as we go along.

The first three steps are the same as in the previous example: the photon goes from the source to the glass (turning, no shrinking); the photon is transmitted by the front surface (no turning, shrinking to 0.98); the photon goes through the glass (turning, no shrinking).

The fourth step—the photon passes through the back surface of the glass—is the same as the second step, as far as shrinks and turns go: no turns, but a shrinkage to 0.98 of the 0.98, so the arrow now has a length of 0.96.

Finally, the photon goes through the air again, down to the detector—that means more turning, but no further shrinking. The result is an arrow of length 0.96, pointing in some direction determined by the successive turnings of the stopwatch hand.

An arrow whose length is 0.96 represents a probability of about 92% (0.96 squared), which means an average of 92 photons reach B out of every 100 that leave the source. That also means that 8% of the photons are reflected by the two surfaces and reach A. But we found out in the first lecture that an 8% reflection by two surfaces is only

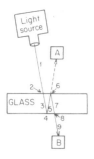

26 Another way that light could be transmitted by two surfaces must
be considered in order to make the calculation more accurate. This
path involves two shrinks of 0.98 (steps 2 and 8) and two shrinks of
0.2 (steps 4 and 6), resulting in an arrow of length 0.0384 (rounded
off to 0.04).

right sometimes ("twice a day")—that in reality, the reflection by two surfaces fluctuates in a cycle from zero to 16% as the thickness of the layer steadily increases. What happens when the glass is just the right thickness to make a partial reflection of 16%? For every 100 photons that leave the source, 16 arrive at A and 92 arrive at B, which means 108% of the light has been accounted for—horrifying! Something is wrong.

We neglect to consider *all* the ways the light could get to B! For instance, it could bounce off the back surface, go up through the glass as if it were going to A, but then reflect off the front surface, back down toward B (see 26). This path takes nine steps. Let's see what happens successively to the unit arrow as the light goes through each step (don't worry; it only shrinks and turns!).

First step—photon goes through the air—turning; no shrinking. Second step—photon passes through the glass— no turning, but shrinking to 0.98. Third step—the photon goes through the glass—turning; no shrinking. Fourth step— reflection off the back surface—no turning, but shrinking to 0.2 of 0.98, or 0.196. Fifth step—photon goes back up through the glass—turning; no shrinking. Sixth step—photon bounces off front surface (it's really a "back" surface, because the photon stays *inside* the glass)—no turning, but shrinking to 0.2 of 0.196, or 0.0392. Seventh step— photon goes back down through glass—more turning; no shrinking. Eighth step—photon passes through back sur- face—no turning, but shrinking to 0.98 of 0.0392, or 0.0384. Finally, the ninth step—photon goes through air to detector—turning; no shrinking.

The result of all this shrinking and turning is an amplitude of length 0.0384—call it 0.04, for all practical pur- poses—and turned at an angle that corresponds to the total amount of turning by the stopwatch as it times the photon going through this longer path. The arrow represents a *second* way that light can get from the source to B. Now we have two alternatives, so we must *add* the two arrows—the arrow for the more direct path, whose length is 0.96, and the arrow for the longer way, whose length is 0.04—to make the final arrow.

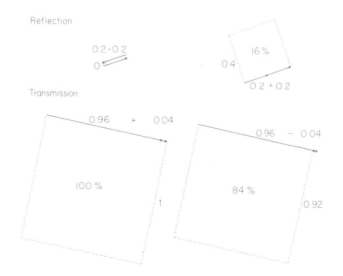

27 Nature always makes sure 100% of the light is accounted for. When the thickness is right for the transmission arrows to accumulate, the arrows for reflection oppose each other; when the arrows for reflection accumulate, the arrows for transmission oppose each other.

The two arrows are usually not in the same direction, because changing the thickness of the glass changes the relative direction of the 0.04 arrow to the 0.96 arrow. But look how nicely things work out: the extra turns made by the stopwatch timing a photon during steps 3 and 5 (on its way to A) are exactly equal to the extra turns it makes timing a photon during steps 5 and 7 (on its way to B). That means when the two reflection arrows are canceling each other to make a final arrow representing zero reflection, the arrows for transmission are reinforcing each other to make an arrow of length 0.96 + 0.04, or 1—when the probability of reflection is zero, the probability of transmission is 100% (see 27). And when the arrows for reflection are reinforcing each other to make an amplitude of 0.4, the arrows for transmission are going against each other, making an amplitude of length 0.96–0.04, or 0.92—when reflection is calculated to be 16%, transmission is calculated to be 84% (0.92 squared). You see how clever Nature is with her rules to make sure that we always come out with 100% of the photons accounted for (see 28)![5]

Finally, before I go, I would like to tell you that there is an extension to the rule that tells us when to multiply arrows: arrows are to be multiplied not only for an event that consists of a succession of steps, but also for an event that consists of a number of things happening concomitantly—independently and possibly simultaneously. For example, suppose we have two sources, X and Y, and two detectors, A and B (see 29), and we want to calculate the probability for the following event: after X and Y each lose a photon, A and B each gain a photon.

In this example, the photons travel through space to get to the detectors—they are neither reflected nor transmitted—so now is a good time for me to stop disregarding the fact that light spreads out as it goes along. I now present you with the *complete rule* for monochromatic light traveling from one point to another through space—there is nothing approximate here, and no simplification. This is all there is to know about monochromatic light going through space (disregarding polarization): the *angle* of the arrow depends on the imaginary stopwatch hand, which rotates a certain number of times per inch (depending on the color of the photon); the *length* of the arrow is inversely proportional to the distance the light goes—in other words, the arrow shrinks as the light goes along.[6]

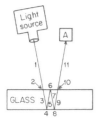

28 Yet other ways the light could reflect should be considered for a more accurate calculation. In this figure, shrinks of 0.98 occur at steps 2 and 10; shrinks of 0.2 occur at steps 4, 6, and 8. The result is an arrow with a length of about 0.008, which is another alternative for reflection, and should therefore be added to the other arrows which represent reflection (0.2 for the front surface and 0.192 for the back surface).

Let's suppose the arrow for X to A is 0.5 in length and is pointing toward 5 o'clock, as is the arrow for Y to B (see 29). Multiplying one arrow by the other, we get a final arrow of length 0.25, pointed at 10 o'clock.

But wait! There is another way this event could happen: the photon from X could go to A. Each of these subevents has an amplitude, and these arrows must also be drawn and multiplied to produce an amplitude for this particular way the event could happen (see 30). Since the amount of shrinkage over distance is very small compared to the amount of turning, the arrows from X to B and Y to A have essentially the same lengths as the other arrows, 0.5, but their turning is quite different: the stopwatch hand rotates 36,000 times per inch for red light, so even a tiny difference in distance results in a substantial difference in timing. The amplitudes for each way the event could happen are added to produce the final arrow. Since their lengths are essentially the same, it is possible for the arrows to cancel each other out if their directions are opposed to each other. The relative directions of the two arrows can be changed by changing the distance between the sources or the detectors: simply moving the detectors apart or together a little bit can make the probability of the event amplify or completely cancel out, just as in the case of partial reflection by two surfaces.[7]

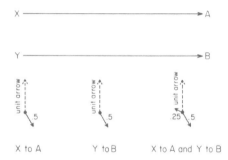

29 If one of the ways a particular event can happen depends on a number of things happening independently, the amplitude for this way is calculated by multiplying the arrows of the independent things. In this case, the final event is: after sources X and Y each lose a photon, photomultipliers A and B make a click. One way this event could happen is that a photon could go from X to A and a photon could go from Y to B (two independent things). To calculate the probability for this "first way," the arrows for each independent thing—X to A and Y to B—are multiplied to produce the amplitude for this particular way. (Analysis continued in 30).

In this example, arrows were multiplied and then added to produce a final arrow (the amplitude for the event), whose square is the probability of the event. It is to be emphasized that no matter how many arrows we draw, add, or multiply, our objective is to calculate a *single final arrow for the event*. Mistakes are often made by physics students at first because they do not keep this important point in mind. They work for so long analyzing events involving a single photon that they begin to think that the arrow is somehow associated with the photon. But these arrows are probability amplitudes, that give, when squared, the *probability* of a complete event.[8]

In the next lecture I will begin the process of simplifying and explaining the properties of matter—to explain where the shrinking to 0.2 comes from, why light appears to go slower through glass or water than through air, and so on—because I have been cheating so far: the photons don't really bounce off the surface of the glass; they interact with the electrons *inside* the glass. I'll show you how photons do nothing but go from one electron to another, and how reflection and transmission are really the result of an electron picking up a photon, "scratching its head," so to speak, and emitting a *new* photon. This simplification of everything we have talked about so far is very pretty.

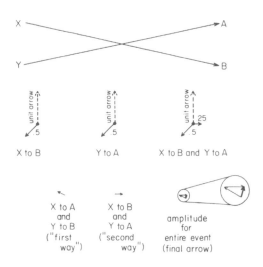

30 The other way the event described in Figure 29 could happen—a photon goes from X to B and a photon goes from Y to A—also depends on two independent things happening, so the amplitude for this "second way" is also calculated by multiplying the arrows of the independent things. The "first way" and "second way" arrows are ultimately added together, resulting in the final arrow for the event. The probability of an event is always represented by a *single final arrow*—no matter how many arrows were drawn, multiplied, and added to achieve it.

[1] The areas of the mirror whose arrows point to the left also make a strong reflection (when the areas whose arrows point the other way are erased). It's when both left-biased and right-biased areas reflect together that they cancel out. This is analogous to the case of partial reflection by two surfaces: while either surface will reflect on its own, if the thickness is such that the two surfaces contribute arrows pointing in opposite directions, reflection is canceled out.

[2] I can't resist telling you about a grating that Nature has made: salt crystals are sodium and chlorine atoms packed in a regular pattern. Their alternating pattern, like our grooved surface, acts like a grating when light of the right color (X rays, in this case) shines on it. By finding the specific locations where a detector picks up a lot of this special reflection (called diffraction), one can determine exactly how far apart the grooves are, and thus how far apart the atoms are (see 10). It is a beautiful way of determining the structure of all kinds of crystals as well as confirming that X rays are the same thing as light. Such experiments were first done in 1914. It was very exciting to see, in detail, for the first time, how the atoms are packed together in different substances.

[3] This is an example of the "uncertainty principle": there is a kind of "complementarity" between knowledge of where the light goes between the blocks and where it goes afterwards—precise knowledge of both is impossible. I would like to put the uncertainty principle in its historical place: When the revolutionary ideas of quantum physics were first coming out people still tried to understand them in terms of old-fashioned ideas (such as: light goes in straight lines). But at a certain point the old-fashioned ideas would begin to fail, so a warning was developed that said, in effect, "Your old-fashioned ideas are no damn good when . . ." If you get rid of all the old-fashioned ideas and instead use the ideas that I'm explaining in these lectures—adding *arrows* for all the ways an event can happen—there is no need for an uncertainty principle!

[4] Mathematicians have tried to find all the objects one could possibly find that obey the rules of algebra (A + B = B + A, A x B = B x A, and so on). The rules were originally made for positive integers, used for counting things like apples or people. Numbers were improved with the invention of zero, fractions, irrational numbers—numbers that cannot be expressed as a ratio of two integers—and negative numbers, and continued to obey the original rules of algebra. Some of the numbers that mathematicians invented posed difficulties for people at first—the idea of half a person was difficult to imagine—but today, there's no difficulty at all: nobody has any moral qualms or discomforting gory feelings when they hear that there is an average of 3.2 people per square mile in some regions. They don't try to imagine the 0.2 people; rather, they know what 3.2 means: if they multiply 3.2 by 10, they get 32. Thus, some things that satisfy the rules of algebra can be interesting to mathematicians even though they don't always represent a real situation. Arrows on a plane can be "added" by putting the head of one arrow on the tail of another, or "multiplied" by successive turns and shrinks. Since these arrows obey the same rules of algebra as regular numbers, mathematicians call them numbers. But to distinguish them from ordinary numbers, they're called "complex numbers." For those of you who have studied mathematics long enough to have come to complex numbers, I could have said, "The probability of an event is the absolute square of a complex number. When an event can happen in alternative ways, you add the complex numbers; when it can happen only as a succession of steps, you multiply the complex numbers." Although it may sound more impressive that way, I have not said any more than I did before—I just used a different language.

[5] You'll notice that we changed 0.0384 to 0.4 and used 84% as the square of 0.92, in order to make 100% of the light accounted for. But when *everything* is added together, 0.0384 and 84% don't have to be rounded off—all the little bits and pieces of arrows (representing all the ways the light could go) compensate for each other and keep the answer correct. For those of you who like this sort of thing, here is an example of another way that the light could go from the light source to the detector at A—a series of three reflections (and two transmissions), resulting in a final arrow length 0.98 x 0.2 x 0.2 x 0.2 x 0.98, or about 0.008—a very tiny arrow (see 28). To make a complete calculation of partial reflection by two surfaces, you would have to add in that small arrow, plus an even smaller one that represents five reflections, and so on.

[6] This rule checks out with what they teach in school—the amount of light transmitted over a distance varies inversely as the square of the distance—because an arrow that shrinks to half its original size has a square one-fourth as big.

[7] This phenomenon, called the Hanbury-Brown-Twiss effect, has been used to distinguish between a single source and a double source of radio waves in deep space, even when the two sources are extremely close together.

[8] Keeping this principle in mind should help the student avoid being confused by things such as the "reduction of a wave packet" and similar magic.

POPPAEA'S VEIL

Jean Starobinski

The hidden fascinates. "Why did Poppaea conceive the idea of masking the beauties of her face, except to make them dearer to her lovers?" (Montaigne). In dissimulation and absence there is a strange force that compels the spirit to turn toward the inaccessible and, for the sake of conquest, to sacrifice all it possesses. Fairy tales, works of realism as far as the mechanism of desire is concerned, know only hidden treasures, concealed in some dark depth. If these treasures must belong to someone, they will go to the one who has renounced everything, even the hope of becoming their master. The essence of mystery is to compel us to regard as worthless and tiresome anything that does not make it more easily accessible. Yes, the shadow has the power to make us release all our prey simply because it is shadow and provokes in us a nameless anticipation. Fascination persuades us, so that we may belong to it, to give up everything, even concern for our own lives. It takes all we have simply by promising everything we want. At first we were able to dream of laying hold of what lay hidden, but the roles were quickly reversed: all at once we found ourselves passive and paralyzed, having renounced our will and allowed ourselves to be inhabited by the imperious call of absence.

Moralists, of course, have deemed this sacrifice outrageous. What! Lose all that one has for an illusion! Allow oneself to be robbed of the present and to live forever after in destructive ecstasy? Scorn visible beauty for love of what does not exist? The passion for the hidden has not lacked critics, who reproved it sometimes for concealing the allure of the devil, sometimes that of God. But what we need is an explanation of the passion not unduly hasty to dismiss it as a mystification.

The hidden is the other side of a presence. The power of absence, if we attempt to describe it, leads us to the power possessed in varying degrees by certain real objects. These objects point beyond themselves toward a magical space. They are indices of something they are not. Obstacle and interposed sign, Poppaea's veil engenders a perfection that is immediately stolen away, and by its very flight demands to be recaptured by our desire. Thus the impediment created by the obstacle gives rise to a vast profundity, which is mistaken for essential. The fascination emanates from a real presence that obliges us to prefer what it hides, to prefer something remote, which it prevents us from attaining even as it offers itself. Our gaze is irresistibly drawn into the vertiginous void that forms in the object of fascination: an infinity opens up, devouring the real object by which it made itself sensible. In truth, if the object of fascination calls for the abdication of our will, it is because that object itself is annihilated by the absence it provokes. This strange power in a way stems from a lack, an insufficiency in the object. Rather than hold our fascination, it allows itself to be transcended in a perspective of the imagination, an obscure dimension. But objects can seem insufficient only in response to an exigency in our gaze, which, awakened to desire by an allusive presence and finding no employment for all its energies in the visible thing, transcends it and loses itself in an empty space, headed for a beyond from which there is no return. Poppaea runs the risks that her face, unveiled, will disappoint her lovers, or that her eyes, wide open and beckoning, will seem still covered by a dark veil: desire can no longer cease to search elsewhere.

To be fascinated is the height of distraction. It is to be prodigiously inattentive to the world as it is. But this inattention in a way rests upon the very objects it neglects. Having responded too impetuously to the veiled seductress, our gaze hurtles beyond the possessable body and is captured by the void and consumed in the night. Poppaea Sabina (in the "portrait" of her painted by an unknown master of the School of Fontainebleau) allows her body to be glimpsed beneath the gauze, and smiles: she is not culpable. Her lovers do not die for her; they die for the promises she does not keep.

If one looks at the etymology, one finds that to denote directed vision French resorts to the word *regard* (gaze), whose root originally referred not to the act of seeing but to expectation, concern, watchfulness, consideration, and safeguard, made emphatic by the addition of a prefix expressing a redoubling or return. *Regarder* (to look at, to gaze upon) is a movement that aims to recapture, *reprendre sous garde* (to place in safekeeping once again). The gaze does not exhaust itself immediately. It involves perseverance, doggedness, as if animated by the hope of adding to its discovery or reconquering what is about to escape. What interests me is the fate of the impatient energy that inhabits the gaze and desires something other than what it is given. It lies in wait, hoping that a moving form will come to a standstill or that a figure at rest will reveal a slight tremor, insistent on touching the face behind the mask, or seeking to shake off the bewildering fascination with depths in order to rediscover the shimmering reflections that play on the water's surface.

Some, invoking the example of Greece, have argued that the realm of the visible, the realm of light, was also the realm of measure and order: figures circumscribed by their forms, space made rhythmic by a harmonious module, by a law granting to each vantage an empire at once sovereign and precarious. But there is a hidden extravagance in the apparent triumph of measure. The will to delineate, geometrize, and fix stable relationships implies a violence beyond the natural experience of the gaze. The space of geometrical measurement is the product of a vigilant effort, which, compass in hand, revises the affective prejudices to which living space owes its "deformations." It is hard to deny that in this there is extravagance of the second degree, which consists in seeking equilibrium by rejecting the spontaneous extravagance of desire and anxiety.

It is difficult for the gaze to limit itself to ascertaining appearances. By its very nature it must ask for more. In fact, this impatience inhabits all the senses. Beyond the usual synesthesias, each sense aspires to exchange its powers with the others. In a celebrated *Elegy* Goethe said: the hands want to see, the eyes want to caress. We may add: the gaze wants to speak. It is willing to give up the faculty of immediate perception in exchange for the gift of fixing more permanently whatever flees its grasp. By contrast, speech often seeks to efface itself in order to clear the way for pure vision, for intuition perfectly oblivious of the noise of words. In each realm the highest powers are apparently those that impose a sudden, overwhelming substitution. And do not forget that the night of the blind is replete with unfulfilled gazes or, rather, gazes diverted toward the hands, converted into gropings. In the absence of a visual function, the gaze, an intentional relation with others and with the horizon of experience, may assume compensatory forms, proceeding by way of an attentively cocked ear or through the fingertips. For by gaze in this context I mean not so much the faculty of collecting images as that of establishing a relation.

Of all the senses, sight is the one most obviously ruled by impatience. A magical wish, never entirely fulfilled yet never discouraged, accompanies each of our glances: to seize, to undress, to petrify, to penetrate: to fascinate—that is, to illuminate the flame of the hidden in an immobile pupil. All are implicit actions, which do not always remain mere intentions. By revealing the intensity of desire, sometimes the gaze produces real effects. "How many children if looks could impregnate! How many dead if looks could kill! The streets would be filled with corpses and pregnant women." Can it be that Valéry did not notice all the corpses and pregnant women in our streets?

If not betrayed by an excess or want of light, the gaze is never satisfied. It opens the way to an unrelenting assault. Intelligence, cruelty, and tenderness only begin to tell the tale. They remain unappeased, unslaked. These passions awaken in the gaze and grow through the act of vision, in which, however, they find too little to satisfy them. Sight opens all space to desire, but desire is not satisfied with seeing. Visible space attests to both my power to discover and my powerlessness to attain. Everyone knows how sad the concupiscent gaze can be.

Seeing is a dangerous act. It is the passion of Lynceus, but Bluebeard's wives die of it. On this point there is striking unanimity in myth and legend. Orpheus, Narcissus, Oedipus, Psyche, and Medusa teach us that the soul that seeks to extend the scope of its vision is destined to blindness and night: "Truly, the dagger fell from her hands, but not the lamp. She had too much to do, and had not yet seen all there was to see" (La Fontaine). The burning of the oil (or of the gaze) awakens the sleeping god and brings about Psyche's dizzying fall into the desert.

The gaze, which enables consciousness to escape from the place occupied by the body, is an *excess* in the strict sense of the word. Whence the severity of the Church Fathers: of all the senses, sight is the most fallible, the most naturally culpable—"Do not fix your eyes on an object that pleases them, and remember that David perished by a glance" (Bossuet). The "concupiscence of the eyes" includes and epitomizes all others: it is the quintessential evil. "Under the eyes all the other senses are in some way included. And in common parlance to feel and to see are often the same thing." Here Bossuet is merely repeating Saint Augustine. Our hunger to see is perpetually subject to frivolous curiosity, idle distraction, and cruel spectacle. The least pretext is enough to capture our eyes, to lure our spirit from the path of salvation. Augustine found it most difficult to deny himself the pleasures of the circus. But the arena is not the only place where animals devour one another, and everything becomes theater for the ascetic unfaithful to his resolutions: "When I sit at home and watch a lizard catching flies or a spider wrapping insects that fall into its web, is not my attention conquered?"

Yet the very same people who castigate the indiscretion and dispersion of the worldly gaze invoke the same power to direct it toward "supernatural light" and intelligible forms. What they see as the natural extravagance of the gaze ceases to be culpable if directed beyond this world. Augustine, wresting himself free of the temptations of light, "that queen of colors," hopes that darkness will favor the advent of a new light, this time spiritual, invisible to the eye of the flesh. Access to the *idea*, whose very name refers to the act of seeing, is "like a vision emancipated from the limitations of sight" (Maurice Blanchot). In carnal curiosity as well as spiritual intuition, the will-to-see claims second sight as its right.

It is my hunger to see more, to repudiate and transcend my provisional limits, that impels me to question what I have already seen, to hold that it is a misleading decor. Thus begins the strange rebellion of those who, in order to grasp reality beyond appearances, make themselves enemies of what is immediately visible: they denounce the illusion of appearances without suspecting that by revoking the privileges of first sight they leave second sight little hope, in their impatience reducing the admirable theater of vision to ruins. Probably they have no choice. In the exigent gaze lies a whole critique of the primary data of vision. This critique cannot avoid *discourse* in one of its many forms: geometry, with its logical arguments, corrects the vague apprehensions of the eye with the purity of the abstract; poetic language seeks to transpose visible appearance into a new essence, because to speak, to name things, tends to prolong (if not complete) the work of safekeeping that in the gaze remains forever incomplete and precarious. The extremity of the gaze is already something more than gaze, and pursues its aim in the act whereby vision renounces and sacrifices itself. Yet criticism, having condemned deceptive appearances, is not incapable of turning on itself. If a little reflection takes us away from the sensible world, a more demanding philosophy brings us back—as if, having braved the limits of the horizon and traversed the void, the gaze had no alternative but to return to immediate evidence: everything recommences *here*. Montaigne, in this view, would have proposed the most aggressive critiques of appearance in the name of a truth to be unveiled, a fascination to be conjured away, attacking masks and shams only to arrive in the end at a wisdom that would allow itself to be "molded by appearances" and would accept the veil by means of which Poppaea is able to arouse in us such delicious discomfort and impatience. Skepticism first warns us against universal deception, then leads us very gently to the idea of recommencing knowledge with a wisdom that, under the protection of the *reflexive* gaze, trusts in the senses and in the world the senses reveal.

My studies here are all concerned in one way or another with literary works that deal with the pursuit of a hidden reality, a reality temporarily dissimulated yet within the grasp of anyone who knows how to force it out of hiding and compel its *presence*. What was needed, accordingly, was to retrace the history of a gaze lured by desire from discovery to discovery. It was also necessary to show, in a variety of circumstances, how the pursuit of what lies hidden, being an exorbitant ambition, poses the risk of failure and disappointment.

This book is much less and much more than a systematic exploration of a theme. Much less, because I felt no need to catalog all the expressive means (physiognomy, seduction, language of signs) and perceptual devices (world view, interplay of surfaces and depths) involved in the exercise of vision. Much more, because by consistently attending to the fate of the demand implicit in the gaze and unsatisfied by first appearances, I was obliged to trace an adventure that was almost always played out in the *interval* between the intended prey and the eye that wished to subdue it. The gaze was the living link between the person and the world, between self and others: the writer's every glance questions anew the status of reality (and of literary realism) as well as the status of communication (and of human community). Hence I am not dealing with an artificially isolated theme of literature. In this inquiry I try to understand what constitutes the *necessity* of the works studied.

For writers—and also, despite appearances, for painters—the adventure continues beyond the first view, even if unsatisfied desire must later, after losing contact with the sensible, return us there. In these essays my aim is to describe a language that begins with a glance, at times dazzled, at times lustful, at times defiant, and then proceeds along other, often deviant paths in pursuit of what it finds lacking in its original vision. To have declined to follow the same path (or absence of a path), to have shunned its risks, would have been to flout the underlying law of the gaze, which refuses to be satisfied with what it is offered initially. Full knowledge of vision's excess is required, full understanding of the extravagance that causes the gaze to overstep its bounds and risk blindness.

By refocusing on distant objects (whose fate is often merely to be glimpsed) consciousness begins by transforming itself. Its own tension, its own desire, undergoes metamorphosis. Hence these essays seek not so much to describe the specific world of sight as to retrace the shifting fate of the *libido sentiendi* in its relation to the world and to other human consciousnesses.

In Corneille everything begins in dazzlement. But dazzlement is a precarious thing, which lasts only a fleeting instant. Drawn to brilliant objects, the Cornelian hero struggles against falling adoringly into their clutches. The bedazzled consciousness throws off passivity and seeks to effect a reversal of roles. It aspires to be dazzling itself, to achieve the power that comes with brilliance. It claims this privilege first of all through the language of generosity. But glorious speeches are not enough. It is necessary to proceed to action–to action promised, perhaps imprudently, in language. Boasts of valor bind the hero and make inevitable the decision that consecrates his greatness. Thus is man born to the admirable destiny that he has invented for himself: he offers himself triumphant to the world's gaze. His greatest happiness lies neither in the act of seeing (*voir*) nor in the energy of doing (*faire*) but in the complex act of demonstrating (*faire voir*). What exploit, what wish will reveal the hero's everlasting brilliance and spread his renown? The one effective course of action, the one certain to produce the desired "effect," is self-sacrifice, in which the individual turns all his energy against himself, denying himself so completely as to be reborn for all eternity in the eyes of generations called to witness. In this way the hero establishes an immortal name. For this, however, he requires the consent and vigilant complicity of crowds of onlookers: if doubt is cast on human memory and the endurance of renown, everything crumbles in obscurity and vanity, leaving nothing but a dusty stage set; the generous hero becomes nothing but a parody of himself, a ridiculous actor in a "comic illusion."

In Racine passion and desire control everything. A strange weakness, a fatal blindness, prevents Racine's heroes from fully dominating their actions. An obscure and wicked force dictates their crimes, subjects them to misfortune, and exposes them to our piteous regard. They are beset by bewildering uncertainties that reason is unable to surmount. Though not incapable of recognizing their downfall, critical awareness does not prevent them from hastening to their ruin. Full lucidity comes to them only when it is too late, and the clarity of tragic knowledge coincides with a feeling of total impotence in the face of irrevocable misfortune.

An attentive reading of Racine's plays, a methodical analysis of his expressive means, reveals that the gaze takes the place of theatrical gesticulation and becomes the act par excellence. It expresses the pained keenness of a desire that knows in advance that possession equals destruction but is unable to renounce either one. For Racine the tragic is not associated exclusively with either the structure of the plot or the fatality of its outcome. It is the very heart of the human condition that is condemned, since every desire is caught in the inevitable failure of the gaze. No one accepts this failure. Racine's characters struggle in vain, which only compounds their guilt. Voyeurism–the desire to possess solely through sight, to wound through the act of looking–is exacerbated– by the feeling that it must remain forever unsatisfied. In the cruelest scenes, in which the power to torture is expressed exclusively in the gaze, the frustrated torturer suffers as much as his victims. In the very heart of desire, in the intense glow of visual lust, we can thus make out a desperate, self-consuming flame. Incapable of obtaining the desired object, desire can transcend its suffering only by choosing catastrophe, only by dying in darkness. The hero plunges into the abyss, while in a heaven filled with light the implacable gods bear sovereign witness to a disaster that exalts their omnipotence.

For Rousseau the happiness of childhood lay in living a carefree life under the gaze of a witness raised to the level of benevolent deity. But soon this benevolence gave way to a sense of all-enveloping hostility. From then on it became impossible to desire publicly even the most innocent of pleasures without incurring criticism or ironic comment. Shamefaced desire was forced to beat a retreat, give up the idea of possession, and resort to the clandestine glance. Now we can understand why Rousseau exhibits such clear signs of voyeurism and exhibitionism. Fearful of guilty contacts or initiatives, he contents himself, from a distance, with seeing and being seen. At first these predilections take perverse forms, but later they are disguised and transformed through sublimation: in *La Nouvelle Héloïse* Wolmar, the virtuous atheist, proclaims his desire to become pure vision, a "living eye." In *Emile* the preceptor finds moral pretexts for observing his pupils' most intimate caresses. The "ridiculous object" is exhibited once again, albeit in novel fashion, in the virtuous cynicism of total confession. But to see and be seen is still too much. The hostility is too great, and Rousseau, incapable of combatting it head on, generally prefers to concede defeat and to retreat into a more secret realm. Desire, once manifest, becomes a latent power. It renounces all external objects. Reveling in itself, it exposes itself to neither error nor punishment. But this inward retreat, with its concomitant dissimulation of desire, is compensated by a discovery that reveals what had remained hidden since the inception of civilization: neglected nature and natural man. This is a most important discovery, since it establishes a norm against which existing societies can be properly judged and a more equitable community can be imagined.

Both the man of sentiment and the child are gripped by a quite irrational conviction, that to avoid looking at external temptations and to abandon hope of external conquest is to avoid being looked at in return, hence a way of escaping hostile scrutiny and warding off persecution. At the center of a world of enchanted fictions, Rousseau reconciles the innocence of time's beginning with love's most searing pleasures. He invents a bewildering and loving spectacle in which nothing prevents him from participating in person. Nothing intervenes to compromise the transparency of happiness regained. As in his child's paradise, his ego binds itself to benevolent counterparts through trusting dialogue: avoiding the misunderstandings inherent in speech, they communicate through the language of signs and understand one another at a glance.

Yet beyond this spectacle of the imagination and by dint of the enthusiasm that overcomes him, Rousseau attains an extreme of ecstasy, a pure sentiment of existence, in which all images disappear. The dreamer's inward gaze having exhausted the pleasures of fictive celebration, desire wants to know a still higher degree of satisfaction, and it succeeds in doing so. At this moment all vision is abolished, replaced by a voluptuous stupefaction that is both total light and absolute darkness.

More than anyone else, Rousseau forces us to acknowledge that the gaze, from the moment of its first awakening, bears within it a strange power of separation. It discovers objective space, but only at the price of acquiescing in distance. It obliges us to see things as distinct—distinct from us and distinct from one another. Thus it disrupts a prior unity, a unity originally enjoyed by being (*l'être*) in its blind self-absorption. When gaze becomes reflection this loss of unity is further accentuated, for to reflect is to relinquish contact with the immediate and to sink ever more deeply into the misfortune of separate existence. Discursive reason, insofar as it is a product of reflexive thought, marks the utmost estrangement from primitive unity. But the trial of division ignites and fans the flames of a desire to regain the lost unity: enduring loss leads to discovery of the need for communication, which will repair the fragmentation of reality. Logical reflection must not be banished. To be rid of it one must follow it unflinchingly to its ultimate conclusion. When speech, having done its job, falls silent, consciousness enlightened by reason returns to the law of sentiment and to the undivided unity of the beginning. A cycle is completed: separate vision and the evil of reflection lead consciousness down a path that returns to the original happiness.

Rousseau is far from an irrationalist, but his rationalism goes along with the conviction (shared by the romantics) that "existential" truth belongs to the realm of time—or of the instant—and not to the realm of objective space subject to the quantitative operations of reason. Don't forget that this adventure of consciousness, whose goal is to transcend the servitude of conventional language, is presented to us entirely through the vehicle of language. If the reflexive gaze, rigorously pursued, can lead beyond the misfortune of reflection, then perfected language (that is, poetry or opera) seeks and finds an analogous power to transcend. It seems clear that Rousseau made a decisive contribution to the revelation of this power.

Stendhal, like Rousseau, began by experiencing a sudden shock of shame when confronted by the ironic gaze of others. But with Stendhal the feeling of guilt was less onerous. This accounts for the extraordinary vivacity of his riposte. How should one respond to a hostile gaze? By becoming someone else, transforming or masking oneself. Stendhal responds to an external affront by mounting a disciplined counteroffensive. His metamorphoses only appear to be escapes. One problem preoccupies him constantly: how to portray himself, how to influence the situation in such a way that his enemies, vanquished, cease to fight and unwittingly become allies in his own projects, auxiliaries in his pursuit of happiness. In extreme cases he would have to make himself fascinating by means of magic. Stendhal dreamed of this, not without self-indulgence. For a long time he believed that with logic, lessons from professional actors, and his knowledge of Destutt de Tracy he would be able to create a seductive and triumphant character for himself. The society in which he lived was so vile that anyone who hoped to succeed required a mask. Direct energy and strength of character were regarded as suspect. Stendhal played the game well enough, though he expressed nostalgia for those times and places when men won power and esteem through noble deeds. Why didn't he settle for what he had? What dissatisfaction drove him to ask for more? In the end he required nothing less than literature, which he saw as a game of chance. He created characters who lived lives different from his own but in whom he could feel himself living. He looked to the future to provide his audience. Above all, he transformed himself through the effect that the written work had upon his life.

And what about reading? What about the critical gaze? The exigencies that animate it are not unlike the ones we find in the creators. Sight is asked to lead the mind beyond the realm of vision into that of *meaning*. The critical gaze deciphers words in order to intuit their full meaning: this perception is a visual act only in the metaphorical sense. Thus the critical gaze *loses itself* in the meaning it awakens. It blazes a trail, but only to make pure pleasure possible without laborious access (Mallarmé's "*pur plaisir sans chemin*"). It transforms the written signs on the page into living speech and, beyond that, establishes a complex world of images, ideas, and feelings. This absent world was waiting for help, anxious for protection. Once awakened, however, this imaginary world requires the reader to make an absolute sacrifice: it no longer allows him to keep his distance. It demands contact and involvement; it imposes its own rhythm and its own destiny.

The critic is a person who, while consenting to the fascination of the text, nevertheless seeks to maintain his *right of scrutiny*. He desires greater penetration: beyond the manifest sense that is revealed, he perceives a latent significance. Beyond the initial "sight reading," further vigilance is necessary if he is to advance toward a *second meaning*. Do not overestimate that term, however: unlike medieval exegesis, modern criticism is interested not in deciphering an allegorical or symbolic equivalent of the original text but in revealing the vaster life or transfigured death inherent in it. Frequently the search for what is most remote leads to what is nearest at hand: to what was obvious at first glance, the forms and rhythms that seemed merely to hold the promise of a secret message. After a long detour we come back to the words themselves, where meaning chooses to reside, and that gleaming mysterious treasure we had felt compelled to seek in a "deeper dimension."

The truth is that the critical gaze is drawn toward two opposing possibilities, neither of which can be fully achieved. The first is to lose oneself in intimate intercourse with the fabulous consciousness glimpsed in the work: comprehension then becomes a matter of progressive pursuit of total complicity with the creative subjectivity, a passionate participation in the sensual and intellectual experience unfolded in the work. Yet no matter how far he goes in this direction, the critic can never stifle the conviction that he possesses a separate identity, the banal but insistent certainty that he is not one with the consciousness with which he desires union. Even assuming that it is possible for him to utterly confound himself with that consciousness, the result, paradoxically, would be loss of his own voice. He would inevitably fall silent. Through sympathy and mimicry the perfect critical discourse would give the impression of the most complete silence. Unless he manages in some way to break the pact of solidarity that ties him to the work, the critic is capable only of paraphrase or pastiche. One must *betray* the ideal of identification in order to acquire the power to speak of this experience and to describe, in a language other than that of the work, the life one has found there. Thus, in spite of our desire to drown in the vital depths of the work, we are obliged to stand at a distance if we are to speak of it at all. So why not deliberately establish a distance capable of revealing in a panoramic view the *surroundings* with which the work is organically associated? We might attempt to identify certain significant relations unnoticed by the writer; to interpret his unconscious motives; to understand the complex interactions between, on the one hand, a life and a work and, on the other hand, their social and historical circumstances.

This second possible mode of critical interpretation I shall call the *panoramic gaze*. The eye wishes to lose none of the patterns revealed by distance. In this expanded field of view, the work is of course the primary focus, but it is not the only object that commands attention. It is defined by other, nearby objects and makes sense only in relation to its context. There's the rub: the context is so vast, the number of relations so large, that vision succumbs to a secret despair. The whole picture consists of so many elements that the single gaze can never gather them all in. What is more, the moment one decides to situate a work in terms of historical coordinates, the scope of the inquiry can be limited only by an arbitrary decision. It could in principle be expanded to the point where the literary work ceases to be the primary focus, now reduced to one of many manifestations of an era, a culture, or a "world view." As the gaze expands to embrace more and more correlative facts in the social world or the author's life, the work vanishes. Hence the triumph of the panoramic gaze is also a kind of failure. The panoramic gaze causes us to lose sight of the work and its meanings by trying to give us the world in which it is immersed.

Perhaps the most comprehensive criticism is that which aims at neither totality (the panoramic view) nor intimacy (intuitive identification). It is the product of a gaze that can be panoramic or intimate by turns, knowing that truth lies in neither one nor the other but in the ceaseless movement between the two. Neither the vertigo of distance nor that of proximity is to be rejected. One must aim for that double excess in which the gaze is always close to losing its power entirely.

Yet criticism is wrong, perhaps, to seek to discipline its gaze in this way. Often it is better to forget oneself and make room for surprise. We may then be rewarded by the feeling that the work is developing a gaze of its own, directed toward us, a gaze that is not only a reflection of our interrogation. An alien consciousness, radically other, seeks us out, fixes us, summons us to respond. We feel *exposed* by its probing. The work interrogates us. Before speaking for ourselves, we must lend our voice to the strange power that queries us. Yet docile as we may be, there is always the risk that we will prefer comforting tunes of our own invention. It is not easy to keep our eyes open, to welcome the gaze that seeks us out. But surely for criticism, as for the whole enterprise of understanding, we must say: "Look, so that you may be looked at in return."

LIGHTNESS

Italo Calvino

I will devote my first lecture to the opposition between lightness and weight, and will uphold the values of light-ness. This does not mean that I consider the virtues of weight any less compelling, but simply that I have more to say about lightness.

After forty years of writing fiction, after exploring various roads and making diverse experiments, the time has come for me to look for an overall definition of my work. I would suggest this: my working method has more often than not involved the subtraction of weight. I have tried to remove weight, sometimes from people, sometimes from heavenly bodies, sometimes from cities; above all I have tried to remove weight from the structure of stories and from language.

In this talk I shall try to explain—both to myself and to you—why I have come to consider lightness a value rather than a defect; to indicate the works of the past in which I recognize my ideal of lightness; and to show where I situate this value in the present and how I project it into the future.

I will start with the last point. When I began my career, the categorical imperative of every young writer was to represent his own time. Full of good intentions, I tried to identify myself with the ruthless energies propelling the events of our century, both collective and individual. I tried to find some harmony between the adventurous, picaresque inner rhythm that prompted me to write and the frantic spectacle of the world, sometimes dramatic and sometimes grotesque. Soon I became aware that between the facts of life that should have been my raw materials and the quick light touch I wanted for my writing, there was a gulf that cost me increasing effort to cross. Maybe I was only then becoming aware of the weight, the inertia, the opacity of the world—qualities that stick to writing from the start, unless one finds some way of evading them.

At certain moments I felt that the entire world was turning into stone: a slow petrification, more or less advanced depending on people and places but one that spared no aspect of life. It was as if no one could escape the inexorable stare of Medusa. The only hero able to cut off Medusa's head is Perseus, who flies with winged sandals; Perseus, who does not turn his gaze upon the face of the Gorgon but only upon her image reflected in his bronze shield. Thus Perseus comes to my aid even at this moment, just as I too am about to be caught in a vise of stone—which happens every time I try to speak about my own past. Better to let my talk be composed of images from mythology.

To cut off Medusa's head without being turned to stone, Perseus supports himself on the very lightest of things, the winds and the clouds, and fixes his gaze upon what can be revealed only by indirect vision, an image caught in a mirror. I am immediately tempted to see this myth as an allegory on the poet's relationship to the world, a lesson in the method to follow when writing. But I know that any interpretation impoverishes the myth and suffocates it.

With myths, one should not be in a hurry. It is better to let them settle into the memory, to stop and dwell on every detail, to reflect on them without losing touch with their language of images. The lesson we can learn from a myth lies in the literal narrative, not in what we add to it from the outside.

The relationship between Perseus and the Gorgon is a complex one and does not end with the beheading of the monster. Medusa's blood gives birth to a winged horse, Pegasus—the heaviness of stone is transformed into its opposite. With one blow of his hoof on Mount Helicon, Pegasus makes a spring gush forth, where the Muses drink. In certain versions of the myth, it is Perseus who rides the miraculous Pegasus, so dear to the Muses, born from the accursed blood of Medusa. (Even the winged sandals, incidentally, come from the world of monsters, for Perseus obtained them from Medusa's sisters, the Graiae, who had one tooth and one eye among them.) As for the severed head, Perseus does not abandon it but carries it concealed in a bag. When his enemies are about to overcome him, he has only to display it, holding it by its snaky locks, and this bloodstained booty becomes an invincible weapon in the hero's hand. It is a weapon he uses only in cases of dire necessity, and only against those who deserve the punishment of being turned into statues. Here, certainly, the myth is telling us something, something implicit in the images that can't be explained in any other way. Perseus succeeds in mastering that horrendous face by keeping it hidden, just as in the first place he vanquished it by viewing it in a mirror. Perseus's strength always lies in a refusal to look directly, but not in a refusal of the reality in which he is fated to live; he carries the reality with him and accepts it as his particular burden.

On the relationship between Perseus and Medusa, we can learn something more from Ovid's *Metamorphoses*. Perseus wins another battle: he hacks a sea-monster to pieces with his sword and sets Andromeda free. Now he prepares to do what any of us would do after such an awful chore—he wants to wash his hands. But another problem arises: where to put Medusa's head. And here Ovid has some lines (IV:740–52) that seem to me extraordinary in showing how much delicacy of spirit a man must have to be a Perseus, killer of monsters: "So that the rough sand should not harm the snake-haired head (*anquiferumque caput dura ne laedat harena*), he makes the ground soft with a bed of leaves, and on top of that he strews little branches of plants born under water, and on this he places Medusa's head, face down." I think that the lightness, of which Perseus is the hero, could not be better represented than by this gesture of refreshing courtesy toward a being so monstrous and terrifying yet at the same time somehow fragile and perishable. But the most unexpected thing is the miracle that follows: when they touch Medusa, the little marine plants turn into coral and the nymphs, in order to have coral for adornments, rush to bring sprigs and seaweed to the terrible head.

This clash of images, in which the fine grace of the coral touches the savage horror of the Gorgon, is so suggestive that I would not like to spoil it by attempting glosses or interpretations. What I can do is to compare Ovid's lines with those of a modern poet, Eugenio Montale, in his "Piccolo testamento," where we also find the subtlest of elements—they could stand as symbols of his poetry: "traccia madreperlacea di lumaca / o smeriglio di vetro calpestato" (mother-of-pearl trace of a snail / or mica of crushed glass)—put up against a fearful, hellish monster, a Lucifer with pitch-black wings who descends upon the cities of the West. Never as in this poem, written in 1953, did Montale evoke such an apocalyptic vision, yet it is those minute, luminous tracings that are placed in the foreground and set in contrast to dark catastrophe—"Conservane la cipria nello specchietto / quando spenta ogni lampada / la sardana si farà infernale" (Keep its ash in your compact / when every lamp is out / and the sardana becomes infernal). But how can we hope to save ourselves in that which is most fragile? Montale's poem is a profession of faith in the persistence of what seems most fated to perish, in the moral values invested in the most tenuous traces: "il tenue bagliore strofinato / laggiú non era quello d'un fiammifero" (the thin glimmer striking down there / wasn't that of a match).[1]

In order to talk about our own times I have gone the long way around, calling up Ovid's fragile Medusa and Montale's black Lucifer. It is hard for a novelist to give examples of his idea of lightness from the events of every-day life, without making them the unattainable object of an endless quest. This is what Milan Kundera has done with great clarity and immediacy. His novel *The Unbearable Lightness of Being* is in reality a bitter confirmation of the Ineluctable Weight of Living, not only in the situation of desperate and all-pervading oppression that has been the fate of his hapless country, but in a human condition common to us all, however infinitely more fortunate we may be. For Kundera the weight of living consists chiefly in constriction, in the dense net of public and private constrictions that enfolds us more and more closely. His novel shows us how everything we choose and value in life for its lightness soon reveals its true, unbearable weight. Perhaps only the liveliness and mobility of the intelligence escape this sentence—the very qualities with which this novel is written, and which belong to a world quite different from the one we live in.

Whenever humanity seems condemned to heaviness, I think I should fly like Perseus into a different space. I don't mean escaping into dreams or into the irrational. I mean that I have to change my approach, look at the world from a different perspective, with a different logic and with fresh methods of cognition and verification. The images of lightness that I seek should not fade away like dreams dissolved by the realities of present and future . . . . .

In the boundless universe of literature there are always new avenues to be explored, both very recent and very ancient, styles and forms that can change our image of the world. . . . . . But if literature is not enough to assure me that I am not just chasing dreams, I look to science to nourish my visions in which all heaviness disappears. Today every branch of science seems intent on demonstrating that the world is supported by the most minute entities, such as the messages of DNA, the impulses of neurons, and quarks, and neutrinos wandering through space since the beginning of time . . . . .

Then we have computer science. It is true that software cannot exercise its powers of lightness except through the weight of hardware. But it is software that gives the orders, acting on the outside world and on machines that exist only as functions of software and evolve so that they can work out ever more complex programs. The second industrial revolution, unlike the first, does not present us with such crushing images as rolling mills and molten steel, but with "bits" in a flow of information traveling along circuits in the form of electronic impulses. The iron machines still exist, but they obey the orders of weightless bits.

Is it legitimate to turn to scientific discourse to find an image of the world that suits my view? If what I am attempting here attracts me, it is because I feel it might connect with a very old thread in the history of poetry.

The *De Rerum Natura* of Lucretius is the first great work of poetry in which knowledge of the world tends to dissolve the solidity of the world, leading to a perception of all that is infinitely minute, light, and mobile. Lucretius set out to write the poem of physical matter, but he warns us at the outset that this matter is made up of invisible particles. He is the poet of physical concreteness, viewed in its permanent and immutable substance, but the first thing he tells us is that emptiness is just as concrete as solid bodies. Lucretius's chief concern is to prevent the weight of matter from crushing us. Even while laying down the rigorous mechanical laws that determine every event, he feels the need to allow atoms to make unpredictable deviations from the straight line, thereby ensuring freedom both to atoms and to human beings. The poetry of the invisible, of infinite unexpected possibilities—even the poetry of nothingness—issues from a poet who had no doubts whatever about the physical reality of the world.

This atomizing of things extends also to the visible aspects of the world, and it is here that Lucretius is at his best as a poet: the little motes of dust swirling in a shaft of sunlight in a dark room (II.114–24); the minuscule shells, all similar but each one different, that waves gently cast up on the *bibula harena*, the "imbibing sand" (II.374–76); or the spiderwebs that wrap themselves around us without our noticing them as we walk along (III.381–90).

I have already mentioned Ovid's *Metamorphoses*, another encyclopedic poem (written fifty years after Lucretius's), which has its starting point not in physical reality but in the fables of mythology. For Ovid, too, everything can be transformed into something else, and knowledge of the world means dissolving the solidity of the world. And also for him there is an essential parity between everything that exists, as opposed to any sort of hierarchy of powers or values. If the world of Lucretius is composed of immutable atoms, Ovid's world is made up of the qualities, attributes, and forms that define the variety of things, whether plants, animals, or persons. But these are only the outward appearances of a single common substance that—if stirred by profound emotion—may be changed into what most differs from it.

It is in following the continuity of the passage from one form to another that Ovid displays his incomparable gifts. He tells how a woman realizes that she is changing into a lotus tree: her feet are rooted to the earth, a soft bark creeps up little by little and enfolds her groin; she makes a movement to tear her hair and finds her hands full of leaves. Or he speaks of Arachne's fingers, expert at winding or unraveling wool, turning the spindle, plying the needle in embroidery, fingers that at a certain point we see lengthening into slender spider's legs and beginning to weave a web.

In both Lucretius and Ovid, lightness is a way of looking at the world based on philosophy and science: the doctrines of Epicurus for Lucretius and those of Pythagoras for Ovid (a Pythagoras who, as presented by Ovid, greatly resembles the Buddha). In both cases the lightness is also something arising from the writing itself, from the poet's own linguistic power, quite independent of whatever philosophic doctrine the poet claims to be following.

From what I have said so far, I think the concept of lightness is beginning to take shape. Above all I hope to have shown that there is such a thing as a lightness of thoughtfulness, just as we all know that there is a lightness of frivolity. In fact, thoughtful lightness can make frivolity seem dull and heavy.

I could not illustrate this notion better than by using a story from the *Decameron* (VI.9), in which the Florentine poet Guido Cavalcanti appears. Boccaccio presents Cavalcanti as an austere philosopher, walking meditatively among marble tombs near a church. The *jeunesse dorée* of Florence is riding through the city in a group, on the way from one party to another, always looking for a chance to enlarge its round of invitations. Cavalcanti is not popular with them because, although wealthy and elegant, he has refused to join in their revels—and also because his mysterious philosophy is suspected of impiety.

Ora avvenne un giorno che, essendo Guido partito d'Orto San Michele e venutosene per lo Corso degli Adimari infino a San Giovanni, il quale spesse volte era suo cammino, essendo arche grandi di marmo, che oggi sono in Santa Reparata, e molte altre dintorno a San Giovanni, e egli essendo tralle colonne del porfido che vi sono e quelle arche e la porta di San Giovanni, che serrata era, messer Betto con sua brigata a caval venendo su per la piazza di Santa Reparata, vedendo Guido là tra quelle sepolture, dissero: "Andiamo a dargli briga"; e spronati i cavalli, a guisa d'uno assalto sollazzevole gli furono, quasi prima che egli se ne avvedesse, sopra e cominciarongli a dire: "Guido, tu rifiuti d'esser di nostra brigata; ma ecco, quando tu avrai trovato che Idio non sia, che avrai fatto?"

A' quali Guido, da lor veggendosi chiuso, prestamente disse: "Signori, voi mi potete dire a casa vostra ciò che vi piace"; e posta la mano sopra una di quelle arche, che grandi erano, sí come colui che leggerissimo era, prese un salto e fusi gittato dall'altra parte, e sviluppatosi da loro se n'andò.

One day, Guido left Orto San Michele and walked along the Corso degli Adimari, which was often his route, as far as San Giovanni. Great marble tombs, now in Santa Reparata, were then scattered about San Giovanni. As he was standing between the porphyry columns of the church and these tombs, with the door of the church shut fast behind him, Messer Betto and his company came riding along the Piazza di Santa Reparata. Catching sight of Guido among the tombs, they said, "Let's go and pick a quarrel." Spurring their horses, they came down upon him in play, like a charging squad, before he was aware of them. They began: "Guido, you refuse to be of our company; but look, when you have proved that there is no God, what will you have accomplished?" Guido, seeing himself surrounded by them, answered quickly: "Gentlemen, you may say anything you wish to me in your own home." Then, resting his hand on one of the great tombs and being very nimble, he leaped over it and, landing on the other side, made off and rid himself of them.

What interests us here is not so much the spirited reply attributed to Cavalcanti (which may be interpreted in the light of the fact that the "Epicurianism" claimed by the poet was really Averroism, according to which the individual soul is only a part of the universal intellect: the tombs are your home and not mine insofar as individual bodily death is overcome by anyone who rises to universal contemplation through intellectual speculation). What strikes me most is the visual scene evoked by Boccaccio, of Cavalcanti freeing himself with a leap "sí come colui che leggerissimo era," a man very light in body.

Were I to choose an auspicious image for the new millennium, I would choose that one: the sudden agile leap of the poet-philosopher who raises himself above the weight of the world, showing that with all his gravity he has the secret of lightness, and that what many consider to be the vitality of the times—noisy, aggressive, revving and roaring—belongs to the realm of death, like a cemetery for rusty old cars.

I would like you to bear this image in mind as I proceed to talk about Cavalcanti as the poet of lightness. The dramatic personae of his poems are not so much human beings as sighs, rays of light, optical images, and above all those nonmaterial impulses and messages he calls "spirits." A theme by no means "light," such as the sufferings of love, is dissolved into impalpable entities that move between sensitive soul and intellective soul, between heart and mind, between eyes and voice. In short, in every case we are concerned with something marked by three characteristics:

1. it is to the highest degree light
2. it is in motion
3. it is a vector of information

In some poems this messenger-cum-message is the poetic text itself. In the most famous one—"*Per ch'i' no spero di tornai giammai*" (Because I never hope to return)—the exiled poet addresses the ballad he is writing and says: "*Va' tu, leggera e piana, / dritt' a la donna mia*" (Go, light and soft, / straight to my lady). In another poem it is the tools of the writer's trade—quills and the knives to sharpen them—that have their say: "*Noi sián le triste penne isbigottite / le cesoiuzze e'l coltellin dolente*" (We are the poor, bewildered quills, / The little scissors and the grieving penknife). In sonnet 13 the word *spirito* or *spiritello* appears in every line. In what is plainly a self-parody, Cavalcanti takes his predilection for that key word to its ultimate conclusion, concentrating a complicated abstract narrative involving fourteen "spirits," each with a different function, and all within the scope of fourteen lines. In another sonnet the body is dismembered by the sufferings of love, but goes on walking about like an automaton "*fatto di rame o di pietra o di legno*" (made of copper or stone or wood). Years before, Guinizelli in one of his sonnets had transformed his poet into a brass statue, a concrete image that draws its strength from the very sense of weight it communicates. In Cavalcanti the weight of matter is dissolved because the materials of the human simulacrum can be many, all interchangeable. The metaphor does not impress a solid image on us, and not even the word *pietra* (stone) lends heaviness to the line. Here also we find the equality of all existing things that I spoke of in regard to Lucretius and Ovid. The critic Gianfranco Contini defines it as the "*parificazione cavalcantiana dei reali*," referring to Cavalcanti's way of putting everything on the same level.

The most felicitous example of Cavalcanti's leveling of things we find in a sonnet that begins with a list of images of beauty, all destined to be surpassed by the beauty of the beloved woman:

Biltà di donna e di saccente core
e cavalieri armati che sien genti;
cantar d'augelli e ragionar d'amore;
adorni legni 'n mar forte correnti;

aria serena quand'apar l'albore
e bianca neve scender senza venti;
rivera d'acqua e prato d'ogni fiore;
oro, argento, azzuro 'n ornamenti

Beauty of woman and of wise hearts,
and gentle knights in armor;
the song of birds and the discourse of love;
bright ships moving swiftly on the sea;

clear air when the dawn appears,
and white snow falling without wind;
stream of water and meadow with every flower;
gold, silver, azure in ornaments.

   The line "*e bianca neve scender senza venti*" is taken up with a few modifications by Dante in *Inferno* XIV:30: "*Come di neve in alpe sanza vento*" (As snow falls in the mountains without wind). The two lines are almost identical, but they express two completely different concepts. In both, the snow on windless days suggests a light, silent movement. But here the resemblance ends. In Dante the line is dominated by the specification of the place ("*in alpe*"), which gives us a mountainous landscape, whereas in Cavalcanti the adjective *bianca*, which may seem pleonastic, together with the verb "fall"—also completely predictable—dissolves the landscape into an atmosphere of suspended abstraction. But it is chiefly the first word that determines the difference between the two lines. In Cavalcanti the conjunction *e* (and) puts the snow on the same level as the other visions that precede and follow it: a series of images like a catalogue of the beauties of the world. In Dante the adverb *come* (as) encloses the entire scene in the frame of a metaphor, but within this frame it has a concrete reality of its own. No less concrete and dramatic is the landscape of hell under a rain of fire, which he illustrates by the simile of the snow. In Cavalcanti everything moves so swiftly that we are unaware of its consistency, only of its effects. In Dante everything acquires consistency and stability: the weight of things is precisely established. Even when he is speaking of light things, Dante seems to want to render the exact weight of this lightness: "*come di neve in alpe sanza vento.*" In another very similar line the weight of a body sinking into the water and disappearing is, as it were, held back and slowed down: "*Come per acqua cupa cosa grave*" (Like some heavy thing in deep water; *Paradiso* III.123).
   At this point we should remember that the idea of the world as composed of weightless atoms is striking just because we know the weight of things so well. So, too, we would be unable to appreciate the lightness of language if we could not appreciate language that has some weight to it.

We might say that throughout the centuries two opposite tendencies have competed in literature: one tries to make language into a weightless element that hovers above things like a cloud or better, perhaps, the finest dust or, better still, a field of magnetic impulses. The other tries to give language the weight, density, and concreteness of things, bodies, and sensations.
   At the very beginnings of Italian, and indeed European, literature, the first tendency was initiated by Cavalcanti, the second by Dante. The contrast is generally valid but would need endless qualification, given Dante's enormous wealth of resources and his extraordinary versatility. It is not by chance that the sonnet of Dante's instilled with the most felicitous lightness ("*Guido, i' vorrei che tu e Lapo ed io*") is in fact addressed to Cavalcanti. In the *Vita nuova* Dante deals with the same material as his friend and master, and certain words, themes, and ideas are found in both poets. When Dante wants to express lightness, even in the *Divina Commedia*, no one can do it better than he does, but his real genius lies in the opposite direction—in extracting all the possibilities of sound and emotion and feeling from the language, in capturing the world in verse at all its various levels, in all its forms and attributes, in transmitting the sense that the world is organized into a system, an order, or a hierarchy where every thing has its place. To push this contrast perhaps too far, I might say that Dante gives solidity even to the

most abstract intellectual speculation, whereas Cavalcanti dissolves the concreteness of tangible experience in lines of measured rhythm, syllable by syllable, as if thought were darting out of darkness in swift lightning flashes.

This discussion of Cavalcanti has served to clarify (at least to myself) what I mean by "lightness." Lightness for me goes with precision and determination, not with vagueness and the haphazard. Paul Valéry said: *"Il faut être léger comme l'oiseau, et non comme la plume"* (One should be light like a bird, and not like a feather). I have relied on Cavalcanti for examples of lightness in at least three different senses. First there is a lightening of language whereby meaning is conveyed through a verbal texture that seems weightless, until the meaning itself takes on the same rarefied consistency. I leave it to you to find other examples of this sort. Emily Dickinson, for instance, can supply as many as we might wish:

A sepal, petal and a thorn
Upon a common summer's morn—
A flask of Dew—A Bee or two
A Breeze—a caper in the trees—
And I'm a Rose!

Second, there is the narration of a train of thought or psychological process in which subtle and imperceptible elements are at work, or any kind of description that involves a high degree of abstraction. To find a more modern example of this we may turn to Henry James, opening any of his books at random:

It was as if these depths, constantly bridged over by a structure that was firm enough in spite of its lightness and of its occasional oscillation in the somewhat vertiginous air, invited on occasion, in the interest of their nerves, a dropping of the plummet and a measurement of the abyss. A difference had been made moreover, once for all, by the fact that she had, all the while, not appeared to feel the need of rebutting his change of an idea within her that she didn't dare to express, uttered just before one of the fullest of their later discussions ended. ("The Beast in the Jungle," chap. 3)

And third there is a visual image of lightness that acquires emblematic value, such as—in Boccaccio's story—Cavalcanti vaulting on nimble legs over a tombstone. Some literary inventions are impressed on our memories by their verbal implications rather than by their actual words. The scene in which Don Quixote drives his lance through the sail of a windmill and is hoisted up into the air takes only a few lines in Cervantes's novel. One might even say that the author put only a minimal fraction of his resources into the passage. In spite of this, it remains one of the most famous passages in all of literature.

I think that with these definitions I can begin to leaf through the books in my library, seeking examples of lightness. In Shakespeare I look immediately for the point at which Mercutio arrives on the scene (I.iv. 17–18): "You are a lover; borrow Cupid's wings / And soar with them above a common bound." Mercutio immediately contradicts Romeo, who has just replied, "Under love's heavy burden do I sink." Mercutio's way of moving about the world is plain enough from the very first verbs he uses: to dance, to soar, to prick. The human face is a mask, "a visor."

Scarcely has he come on stage when he feels the need to explain his philosophy, not with a theoretical discourse but by relating a dream. Queen Mab, the fairies' midwife, appears in a chariot made of "an empty hazelnut":

Her wagon-spokes made of long spinners' legs,
The cover, of the wings of grasshoppers;
Her traces, of the smallest spider web;
Her collars, of the moonshine's wat'ry beams;
Her whip, of cricket's bone; the lash, of film

And let's not forget that this coach is "drawn with a team of little atomies"—in my opinion a vital detail that enables the dream of Queen Mab to combine Lucretian atomism, Renaissance neo-Platonism, and Celtic folklore.

I would also like Mercutio's dancing gait to come along with us across the threshold of the new millennium. The times that form a background to *Romeo and Juliet* are in many respects not unlike our own: cities bloodstained by violent struggles just as senseless as those of the Montagues and Capulets; sexual liberation, as preached by the Nurse, which does not succeed in becoming the model for universal love; ventures carried out in the generous optimism of "natural philosophy," as preached by Friar Laurence, with unsure results that can yield death as much as life.

The age of Shakespeare recognized subtle forces connecting macrocosm and microcosm, ranging from those of the Neo-Platonic firmament to the spirits of metal transformed in the alchemist's crucible. Classical myths can provide their repertory of nymphs and dryads, but the Celtic mythologies are even richer in the imagery of the most delicate natural forces, with their elves and fairies. This cultural background—and I can't help thinking of Frances Yates's fascinating studies on the occult philosophy of the Renaissance and its echoes in literature—explains why Shakespeare provides the fullest exemplification of my thesis. And I am not thinking solely of Puck and the whole phantasmagoria of *A Midsummer Night's Dream* or of Ariel and those who "are such stuff / As dreams are made on." I am thinking above all of that particular and existential inflection that makes it possible for Shakespeare's characters to distance themselves from their own drama, thus dissolving it into melancholy and irony.

The weightless gravity I have spoken of with regard to Cavalcanti reappears in the age of Cervantes and Shakespeare: it is that special connection between melancholy and humor studied by Raymond Klibansky, Erwin Panofsky, and Fritz Saxl in *Saturn and Melancholy* (1964). As melancholy is sadness that has taken on lightness, so humor is comedy that has lost its bodily weight (a dimension of human carnality that nonetheless constitutes the greatness of Boccaccio and Rabelais). It casts doubt on the self, on the world, and on the whole network of relationships that are at stake. Melancholy and humor, inextricably intermingled, characterize the accents of the Prince of Denmark, accents we have learned to recognize in nearly all Shakespeare's plays on the lips of so many avatars of Hamlet. One of these, Jacques in *As You Like It* (IV.i. 15–18), defines melancholy in these terms: "But it is a melancholy of mine own, compounded of many simples, extracted from many objects, and indeed the sundry contemplation of my travels, which, by often rumination, wraps me in a most humorous sadness." It is therefore not a dense, opaque melancholy, but a veil of minute particles of humors and sensations, a fine dust of atoms, like everything else that goes to make up the ultimate substance of the multiplicity of things.

I confess that I am tempted to construct my own Shakespeare, a Lucretian atomist, but I realize that this would be arbitrary. The first writer in the modern world who explicitly professed an atomistic concept of the universe in its fantastic transfiguration is not found until some years later, in France: Cyrano de Bergerac.

An extraordinary writer, Cyrano, and one who deserves to be better known, not only as the first true forerunner of science fiction but for his intellectual and poetic qualities. A follower of Gassendi's "sensism" and the astronomy of Copernicus, but nourished above all by the natural philosophy of the Italian Renaissance—Cardano, Bruno, Campanella—Cyrano is the first poet of atomism in modern literature. In pages where his irony cannot conceal a genuine cosmic excitement, Cyrano extols the unity of all things, animate or inanimate, the combinatoria of elementary figures that determine the variety of living forms; and above all he conveys his sense of the precariousness of the processes behind them. That is, how nearly man missed being man, and life, life, and the world, the world.

Vous vous étonnez comme cette matière, brouillée pêle-mêle, au gré du hasard, peut avoir constitué un homme, vu qu'il y avait tant de choses nécessaires à la construction de son être, mais vous ne savez pas que cent millions de fois cette matière, s'acheminant au dessein d'un homme, s'est arrêtée à former tantôt une pierre, tantôt du plomb, tantôt du corail, tantôt une fleur, tantôt une comète, pour le trop ou le trop peu de certaines figures qu'il fallait ou ne fallait pas à désigner un homme? Si bien que ce n'est pas merveille qu'entre une infinie quantité de matière qui change et se remue incessamment, elle ait rencontré à faire le peu d'animaux, de végétaux, de minéraux que nous voyons; non plus que ce n'est pas merveille qu'en cent coups de dés il arrive un rafle. Aussi bien est-il impossible que de ce remuement il ne se fasse quelque chose, et cette chose sera toujours admirée d'un étourdi qui ne saura pas combien peu s'en est fallu qu'elle n'ait pas été faite. (Voyage dans la lune, 1661, Garnier-Flammarion edition, pp. 98–99)

You marvel that this matter, shuffled pell-mell at the whim of Chance, could have made a man, seeing that so much was needed for the construction of his being. But you must realize that a hundred million times this matter, on the way to human shape, has been stopped to form now a stone, now lead, now coral, now a flower, now a comet; and all because of more or fewer elements that were or were not necessary for designing a man. Little wonder if, within an infinite quantity of matter that ceaselessly changes and stirs, the few animals, vegetables, and minerals we see should happen to be made; no more wonder than getting a royal pair in a hundred casts of the dice. Indeed it is equally impossible for all this stirring not to lead to something; and yet this something will always be wondered at by some blockhead who will never realize how small a change would have made it into something else.

By this route Cyrano goes so far as to proclaim the brotherhood of men and cabbages, and thus imagines the protest of a cabbage about to be beheaded: *"Homme, mon cher frère, que t'ai-je fait qui mérite la mort?. . . Je me lève de terre, je m'épanouis, je te tends les bras, je t'offre mes enfants en graine, et pour récompense de ma courtoisie, tu me fais trancher la tête!"* (Man, my dear brother, what have I done to you, to deserve death?. . . I rise from the earth, I blossom forth, I stretch out my arms to you, I offer you my children as seed; and as a reward for my courtesy you have my head cut off!).

If we consider that this peroration in favor of truly universal *fraternité* was written nearly one hundred and fifty years before the French revolution, we see how the sluggishness of the human consciousness in emerging from its anthropocentric parochialism can be abolished in an instant by poetic invention. And all this in the context of a trip to the moon, in which Cyrano's imagination outdistances his most illustrious predecessors, Lucian of Samosata and Ludovico Ariosto. In my discussion of lightness, Cyrano is bound to figure chiefly because of the way in which (before Newton) he felt the problem of universal gravitation. Or, rather, it is the problem of escaping the force of gravity that so stimulates his imagination as to lead him to think up a whole series of ways of reaching the moon, each one more ingenious than the last—for example, by using a phial filled with dew that evaporates in the sun; by smearing himself with ox marrow which is usually sucked up by the moon; or by repeatedly tossing up a magnetized ball from a little boat.

As for the technique of magnetism, this was destined to be developed and perfected by Jonathan Swift to keep the flying island of Laputa in the air. The moment at which Laputa first appears in flight is one when Swift's two obsessions seem to cancel out in an instant of magical equilibrium. I am speaking of the bodiless abstraction of the rationalism at which his satire is aimed and the material weight of the body: "And I could see the sides of it, encompassed with several gradations of galleries, and stairs at certain intervals, to descend from one to the other. In the lowest gallery I beheld some people fishing with long angling rods, and others looking on." Swift was a contemporary and adversary of Newton. Voltaire was an admirer of Newton, and he imagined a giant called Micromégas, who in contrast to Swift's giants is defined not by his bulk but by dimensions expressed in figures, by spatial and temporal properties enumerated in the rigorous, impassive terms of scientific treatises. In virtue of this logic and style, Micromégas succeeds in flying through space from Sirius to Saturn to Earth. One might say that, in Newton's theories, what most strikes the literary imagination is not the conditioning of everything and everyone by the inevitability of its own weight, but rather the balance of forces that enables heavenly bodies to float in space.

The eighteenth-century imagination is full of figures suspended in air. It is no accident that at the beginning of that century Antoine Galland's French translation of the *Thousand and One Nights* opened up the imagination of the West to the Eastern sense of marvel: flying carpets, winged horses, genies emerging from lamps. In this drive to make the imagination exceed all bounds, the eighteenth century reached its climax with the flight of Baron von Münchausen on a cannonball, an image identified forever in our minds with the illustrations that are Gustave Doré's masterpiece. These adventures of Münchausen, which—like the *Thousand and One Nights*—may have had one author, many authors, or none at all, are a constant challenge to the laws of gravity. The baron is carried aloft by ducks; he pulls up himself and his horse by tugging at the pigtail of his wig; he comes down from the moon on a rope that during the descent is several times cut and reknotted.

These images from folk literature, along with those we have seen from more learned literature, are part of the literary repercussions of Newton's theories. When he was fifteen years old, Giacomo Leopardi wrote an amazingly erudite *History of Astronomy*, in which among other things he sums up Newton's theories. The gazing at the night skies that inspires Leopardi's most beautiful lines was not simply a lyrical theme: when he spoke about the moon, Leopardi knew exactly what he was talking about. In his ceaseless discourses on the unbearable weight of living, Leopardi bestows many images of lightness on the happiness he thinks we can never attain: birds, the voice of a girl singing at a window—the clarity of the air—and, above all, the moon.

As soon as the moon appears in poetry, it brings with it a sensation of lightness, suspension, a silent calm enchantment. When I began thinking about these lectures, I wanted to devote one whole talk to the moon, to trace its apparitions in the literatures of many times and places. Then I decided that the moon should be left entirely to Leopardi. For the miraculous thing about his poetry is that he simply takes the weight out of language, to the point that it resembles moonlight. The appearances of the moon in his poetry do not take up many lines, but they are enough to shed the light of the moon on the whole poem, or else to project upon it the shadow of its absence.

Dolce e chiara è la notte e senza vento
e queta sovra i tetti e in mezzo agli orti
posa la luna, e di lontan rivela
serena ogni montagna.
. . . . .

O graziosa luna, io mi rammento
che, or volge l'anno, sovra questo colle
io venia pien d'angoscia a rimirarti:
e tu pendevi allor su quella selva
siccome fai, che tutta la rischiari.
. . . . .

O cara luna, al cui tranquillo raggio
danzan le lepri nelle selve. . .
. . . . .

Giá tutta l'aria imbruna,
torna azzurro il sereno, e tornan l'ombre
giu' da' colli e da' tetti,
al biancheggiar della recente luna.
. . . . .

Che fai tu, luna, in ciel? Dimmi, che fai,
silenziosa luna?
Sorgi la sera e vai,
contemplando i deserti, indi ti posi.

Soft and clear is the night and without wind, and quietly
over the roofs and in the gardens rests the moon, and far
away reveals every peaceful mountain.
. . . . .

252

O gentle, gracious moon, I remember now, it must be a
year ago, on this same hill I came to see you; I was full of
sorrow. And you were leaning then above that wood just as
now, filling it all with brilliance.

. . . . .

O cherished moon, beneath whose quiet beams the hares
dance in the woods . . .

. . . . .

Already all the air darkens, deepens to blue, and shadows glide
from roofs and hills at the whitening of the recent moon.

. . . . .

What do you do there, moon, in the sky? Tell me what you
do, silent moon. When evening comes you rise and go
contemplating wastelands; then you set.

Have a great number of threads been interwoven in this lecture? Which thread should I pull on to find the end in my hand? There is the thread that connects the moon, Leopardi, Newton, gravitation, and levitation. There is the thread of Lucretius, atomism, Cavalcanti's philosophy of love, Renaissance magic, Cyrano. Then there is the thread of writing as a metaphor of the powder-fine substance of the world. For Lucretius, letters were atoms in continual motion, creating the most diverse words and sounds by means of their permutations. This notion was taken up by a long tradition of thinkers for whom the world's secrets were contained in the combinatoria of the signs used in writing: one thinks of the *Ars Magna* of Raymond Lully, the Cabala of the Spanish rabbis and of Pico della Mirandola . . . . . Even Galileo saw the alphabet as the model for all combinations of minimal units . . . . . And then Leibniz . . . . .

Should I continue along this road? Won't the conclusions awaiting me seem all too obvious? Writing as a model for every process of reality . . . . . indeed the only reality we can know, indeed the only reality *tout court* . . . . . No, I will not travel such roads as these, for they would carry me too far from the use of words as I understand it— that is, words as a perpetual pursuit of things, as a perpetual adjustment to their infinite variety.

There remains one thread, the one I first started to unwind: that of literature as an existential function, the search for lightness as a reaction to the weight of living. Perhaps even Lucretius was moved by this need, perhaps even Ovid: Lucretius who was seeking—or thought he was seeking—Epicurean impassiveness; and Ovid who was seeking—or thought he was seeking—reincarnation in other lives according to the teachings of Pythagoras.

I am accustomed to consider literature a search for knowledge. In order to move onto existential ground, I have to think of literature as extended to anthropology and ethnology and mythology. Faced with the precarious existence of tribal life—drought, sickness, evil influences—the shaman responded by ridding his body of weight and flying to another world, another level of perception, where be could find the strength to change the face of reality.

In centuries and civilizations closer to us, in villages where the women bore most of the weight of a constricted life, witches flew by night on broomsticks or even on lighter vehicles such as ears of wheat or pieces of straw. Before being codified by the Inquisition, these visions were part of the folk imagination, or we might even say of lived experience. I find it a steady feature in anthropology, this link between the levitation desired and the privation actually suffered. It is this anthropological device that literature perpetuates.

First, oral literature: in folktales a flight to another world is a common occurrence. Among the "functions" catalogued by Vladimir Propp in his *Morphology of the Folktale* (1968), it is one of the methods of "transference of the hero," defined as follows: "Usually the object sought is in 'another' or 'different' realm that may be situated far away horizontally, or else at a great vertical depth or height." Propp then goes on to list a great number of examples of the hero flying through the air: on horseback or on the back of a bird, disguised as a bird, in a flying boat, on a flying carpet, on the shoulders of a giant or a spirit, in the devil's wagon.

It is probably not pushing things too far to connect the functions of shamanism and witchcraft documented in ethnology and folklore with the catalogue of images contained in literature. On the contrary, I think that the deepest rationality behind every literary operation has to be sought out in the anthropological needs to which it corresponds.

I would like to end this talk by mentioning Kafka's "Der Kübelreiter" (The Knight of the Bucket). This is a very short story written in 1917 in the first person, and its point of departure is plainly a real situation in that winter of warfare, the worst for the Austrian Empire: the lack of coal. The narrator goes out with an empty bucket to find coal for the stove. Along the way the bucket serves him as a horse, and indeed it takes him up as far as the second floor of a house, where he rocks up and down as if riding on the back of a camel. The coal merchant's shop is underground, and the bucket rider is too high up. He has a hard time getting his message across to the man, who would really like to respond to his request, but the coal merchant's wife wants nothing to do with him. He begs them to give him a shovelful of even the worst coal, even though he can't pay immediately. The coal merchant's wife unties her apron and shoos away the intruder as if he were a fly. The bucket is so light that it flies off with its rider until it disappears beyond the Ice Mountains.

Many of Kafka's short stories are mysterious, and this one is particularly so. It may be that Kafka only wanted to tell us that going out to look for a bit of coal on a cold wartime night changes the mere swinging of an empty bucket into the quest of a knight-errant or the desert crossing of a caravan or a flight on a magic carpet. But the idea of an empty bucket raising you above the level where one finds both the help and the egoism of others; the empty bucket, symbol of privation and desire and seeking, raising you to the point at which a humble request can no longer be satisfied—all this opens the road to endless reflection.

I have spoken of the shaman and the folktale hero, of privation that is transformed into lightness and makes possible a flight into a realm where every need is magically fulfilled. I have spoken of witches flying on humble household implements, such as a bucket. But the hero of Kafka's story doesn't seem to be endowed with the powers of shamanism or witchcraft; nor does the country beyond the Ice Mountains seem to be one in which the empty bucket will find anything to fill it. In fact, the fuller it is, the less it will be able to fly. Thus, astride our bucket, we shall face the new millennium, without hoping to find anything more in it than what we ourselves are able to bring to it. Lightness, for example, whose virtues I have tried to illustrate here.

[1] The English translation of these lines from Montale's "Little Testament" has been provided by Jonathan Galassi.

ART AND OSCILLATION
Gianni Vattimo

As in the whole of modernity,[1] it may be that the distinctive character of existence, or in Heidegger's terms the "meaning of being" in our epoch, appears first and most clearly in aesthetic experience. It therefore deserves special attention, if we wish to understand what is to become not only of art in late modernity, but more generally of being.

The problem of art in a society of generalized communication was decisively addressed by Walter Benjamin in his 1936 essay "The Work of Art in the Age of Mechanical Reproduction"[2]—a text that is still relevant today and one we should keep going back to, for in my view it has never been properly assimilated and "digested," so to speak, by subsequent research in aesthetics. In fact, it has generally been understood as nothing more than a straightforward sociological account of the new conditions under which contemporary art operates. As such, it has been used either as an instrument of polemic against the art market or as the theoretical basis for a reflection on all artistic phenomena located outside the traditional institutions of art (outside the theater, as in the "happening" [in English in the original—Trans.]; outside the museum and the gallery, as in various forms of performance art, landscape art, etc.). Alternatively, it has been dismissed as expressing an illusion, namely that the technical reproduction of art might offer a positive opportunity for its rejuvenation, whereas in reality, as Adorno maintained, the standardized civilization he experienced in America is a long way from realizing Benjamin's utopia, and reflects instead the total uniformity all art acquires through the manipulation of consensus by the mass media. Yet these various readings of Benjamin's essay seem broadly inadequate. We need to go back to this essay and reflect on its central intuition, namely, the idea that the new conditions of artistic production and appreciation that obtain in the society of mass media substantially modify the essence of art, its *Wesen* (a term we shall use in the Heideggerian sense: not the eternal nature of art, but its way *of giving itself* in the present epoch).

Neither Adorno, in his radical critique of reproduction, nor any of the sociological interpretations (which even go so far as to hope, like Marcuse, for an aesthetic reconciliation of existence), have added anything new, or even of the same stature, to Benjamin's remarks on this change of essence. When Adorno denies that art can (or should) actually lose the *aura* that isolates the work from the everyday, he defends the critical power of the work with respect to existing reality, whilst also adopting and maintaining the traditional conception of art as a place of harmony and perfection that runs throughout Western metaphysics from Aristotle to Hegel. That the harmony is utopian and belongs within the realm of appearance, as Adorno underlines in an opportune deployment of Kant against Hegel, does not mean a true change in essence, however, but only its location in an indefinite future, where its role remains that of a regulative ideal. This point warrants our attention, even at a time of renewed interest in Adorno's aesthetics and the thought of Ernst Bloch, above all in France (a little later than in other cultural circles, such as Italy).

Benjamin's comments open the way for a reflection on the new *Wesen* of art in late-industrial society that overcomes the traditional metaphysical definition of art as a place of harmony, correspondence between inside and outside, catharsis. These points can be developed satisfactorily on the basis of an analogy that looks paradoxical at first sight, and which to my knowledge has still not been remarked upon. Benjamin's essay was written in 1936, the same year another key text for contemporary aesthetics was born, namely, Heidegger's essay "Der Ursprung des Kunstwerkes" (The origin of the work of art).[3] This is the text in which Heidegger elaborates his central notion of the work of art as the "setting-into-work of truth" arising in the strife between the work's two constitutive elements: the setting up of the world and the setting forth of the earth. Heidegger defines the effect on the observer of such a work by the term *Stoss*—literally, a blow. Although the basis and meaning of the theory we find in Benjamin's essay appear to be quite different, it describes the effect of cinema, as the art-form most characteristic of the age of technical reproduction, precisely in terms of *shock*. The view I wish to put forward is that by developing the analogy between Heidegger's *Stoss* and Benjamin's *shock,* we shall be able to assemble the essential features of a new "essence" of art in late-industrial society, features that have eluded even the most acute and radical reflections on contemporary aesthetics, including those of Adorno.

Technical reproduction seems to work in exactly the opposite sense to *shock.* In the age of reproduction, both the great art of the past and new media products reproducible from their inception, such as cinema, tend to become common consumer objects and consequently less and less well defined against the background of intensified communication. This growing psychological dullness could be put down to symbols being transmitted and multiplied too quickly and "wearing themselves out." But this is not the only way that the technical means of reproduction tend to level out works. No matter how perfect, such means end up picking out and accentuating those characteristics of the work most "visible" to them, or else forcing the work within limits set by the means themselves. Adorno, for example, objected strongly to the distortions of musical tempi that can result from pieces being squeezed onto record.

Of course, this conflict between the work's "being in itself" and its adaptation to the means of reproduction only arises if—like Adorno—one still distinguishes between a work's ideal "use value" and its alienated and degenerate "exchange" value (linked to market conditions, fashions, etc.), As we know, in his 1936 essay Benjamin on the contrary welcomed as a decisive and positive step the change brought about by technical reproduction, whereby the "cult" value of a work gave way entirely to its "exhibition" value. This amounted to saying that the work has no "use value" apart from its exchange value, or that its entire aesthetic significance is inseparable from the history of its *Wirkung,* of its fate, appreciation, and interpretation in culture and society. (This, incidentally, is not the same as advocating the purely hermeneutic nihilism expressed in the words of Valéry, *"mes vers ont le sens qu'on leur prête"*; individual interpretations are not weighed up in a vacuum, but are linked to all other interpretations, to the global *Wirkungsgeschichte,* or "effective history" of the work in a way that is not only historico-factual, but also normative.[4])

But the problem of the relation between cult value—or "aural" value, in Benjamin's sense—and exhibition value can only be resolved if the implications of the theory of *shock* are followed through to the end. As long as the appreciation of the work of art is thought of in terms of the appreciation of formal perfection and the experience of satisfaction at this perfection, it will be impossible to accept that, as we have said, use value dissolves into exchange value, or that cult value gives way to exhibition value.

In Benjamin's essay, the shock-effect is presented as characteristic of the cinema, which in this respect had been anticipated by Dada. The Dadaist work of art is actually conceived as a projectile launched at the spectator, at his every security, sensory expectation, and perceptual habit. The cinema too is made up of projectiles, of projections: as soon as an image is formed, it is replaced by another to which the spectator's eye and mind must readapt. In a note to the essay, Benjamin explicitly compares the perceptual competence required when watching a film with that of a pedestrian (or, we might add, a driver) in the midst of traffic in a big modern city. "Film," writes Benjamin "is the art that is in keeping with the increased threat to life which modern man has to face."[5] It is as if we read here, albeit curiously demythologized and scaled down to everyday life (the risks of traffic), what Heidegger thematizes in his essay "The Origin of the Work of Art" with the notion of *Stoss*. In a sense distinct from Benjamin's, yet perhaps profoundly close to it, Heidegger too takes the experience of the *shock* of art to be concerned with death—not so much with the risk of being run over by a bus, as with death as a possibility that is constitutive of existence. In the experience of art, according to Heidegger, it is the very fact of the work's being-there rather than not that gives rise to the *Stoss*.[6] The fact of a thing's being-there, its *Dass*, as readers of *Being and Time* will recall,[7] is also at the root of the existential experience of anxiety. In section 40 of *Being and Time* anxiety is described as the mood of *Dasein* (human being) when confronted with the naked fact of its being thrown into the world. Whilst single things belong to the world insofar as they are inserted in a referential totality of significance (each thing is referred to others, as effect, cause, instrument, sign, etc.), the world as such and as a whole does not refer and thus has no significance. Anxiety is a mark of this insignificance, the utter gratuitousness of the fact that the world is. The experience of anxiety is an experience of "uncanniness" (of *Un-heimlichkeit,* or *Un-zu-Haus-sein).*[8] The analogy of the *Stoss* of art with this experience of anxiety may be appreciated if one recalls that the work of art does not allow itself to be drawn back into a pre-established network of significance, at least insofar as it cannot be deduced as a logical consequence. Moreover, it does not simply slot into the world as it is, but purports to shed new light upon it. As Heidegger describes it, the encounter with the work of art is like an encounter with someone whose view of the world is a challenge to our own interpretation. It is above all in this sense that one must understand the Heideggerian thesis according to which the work of art *founds* a world by presenting itself as a new historical event or "opening" of Being. Although the *Stoss* seems to be described in more "positive" terms than anxiety in *Being and Time,* which always concerns *Stimmungen* like fear, preoccupation, etc., its meaning is essentially the same: that of suspending the familiarity of the world, of stimulating a preoccupied wonder at the fact, in itself insignificant (strictly speaking, since it refers to nothing, or refers to the nothing), that the world is there.

To what extent is this notion of *Stoss* actually related, other than terminologically, to the *shock* spoken of by Benjamin in connection with the media of reproduction? Heidegger seems to link the *Stoss* of the work of art to its "setting-into-work of truth"; that is, to its being a new ontologico-epochal opening. In this sense, one should speak of *Stoss* only in reference to the great works that present themselves as decisive points in a culture's history, or at least in the experience of individuals: the Bible, the Greek tragedies, Dante, Shakespeare, and so on. Benjamin's *shock* seems instead to be something much simpler and more familiar, such as the rapid succession of projected images whose demands on a viewer are analogous to those made on a driver in city traffic. Yet the two conceptions, Heidegger's and Benjamin's, have at least one feature in common: their insistence on disorientation. In each case, aesthetic experience appears to be an experience of estrangement, which then requires recomposition

259

and readjustment. However, the aim of this is not to reach a final recomposed state. Instead, aesthetic experience is *directed toward keeping the disorientation alive.* For Benjamin, given his chosen example of the cinema, it is all too clear that we cannot regard the experience of film as fulfilled when it is reduced to a single still frame. For Heidegger, the experience of disorientation that belongs to art is in opposition to the familiarity of the object of use, in which the enigmatic character of the *Dass* (the "that-it-is") dissolves in usability. One cannot attribute to Heidegger the view that the experience of aesthetic disorientation "concludes" in a recuperation of familiarity and obviousness, almost as though it were ultimately the destiny of the art-work to transform itself into a simple object of use. The state of disorientation, for both Heidegger and Benjamin, is constitutive and not provisional. This is precisely what is most radically new about these aesthetic positions compared with both traditional reflections on the beautiful and the survival of this tradition in the aesthetic theories of this century. From the Aristotelian doctrine of catharsis to the free play of the Kantian faculties, to the beautiful as the perfect correspondence of inside and outside in Hegel, aesthetic experience seems always to have been described in terms of *Geborgenheit*—security, "orientation" or "reorientation."

The novel element in the positions of Heidegger and Benjamin, by virtue of which they break with every conception of aesthetic experience given in terms of *Geborgenheit,* may be identified via the notion of oscillation. This calls for a shift in emphasis with respect to the usual interpretation of Heidegger's aesthetics. For if the "founding" role art plays in relation to the world is overstated, one ends up with a view heavily laden with romanticism. To be sure, this refrain too is there in Heidegger: "Poets alone ordain what abides," to cite the line he often recalls from Hölderlin, meaning that the decisive turns of language, which is the "house of Being," the place where the fundamental coordinates of every possible experience of the world are delineated, occur in poetry.

Yet Heidegger's concern, and this comes to light in many passages of the 1936 essay and in his readings of the poets, is not to give a positive definition of the world that poetry opens and founds, but rather to determine the significance of the "unfounding"[9] which is always an inseparable part of poetry. Foundation and unfounding are the meaning of the two features Heidegger identifies as constitutive of the work of art, namely, the setting up (*Aufstellung*) of the world and the setting forth (*Her-stellung*) of the "earth." The world is set up as the system of significations it inaugurates; the earth is set forth by the work insofar as it is put forward, shown, as the obscure and thematically inexhaustible depths in which the world of the work is rooted. If, as we have seen, disorientation is essential to aesthetic experience, and not merely provisional, it owes far more to earth than to world. Only because the world of significance unfolded in the work seems to be obscurely rooted (hence not logically "founded") in the earth can the effect of the work be one of disorientation. Earth is not world. It is not a system of signifying connections: it is other, the nothing, general gratuitousness and insignificance. The work is a foundation only insofar as it produces an ongoing disorientation that can never be recuperated in a final *Geborgenheit.* The work of art is never serene, never "beautiful" in the sense of a perfect harmony between inside and outside, essence and existence, etc. It may have something of Aristotelian catharsis about it, but only if catharsis is understood as an exercise in finitude, a recognition of the insuperable terrestrial limits of human existence; not perfect purification, but rather *phronesis.* Thus, it is not so much in terms of founding as of unfounding that an analogy may be drawn between the Heideggerian *Stoss* and the shock to which Benjamin refers. The analogy will elude us and seem absurd if we contrast the apparent insignificance of Benjamin's shock with too inflated a view of the work of art as an inauguration and foundation of historico-cultural worlds. But to read Heidegger's theory in this way is still to interpret it in a metaphysical, or in Heidegger's terms, ontical form, such that the *Stoss* would depend on the weight and distinctive proportions of the new world inaugurated and founded by the work. To interpret and appreciate the work would mean to establish oneself in this world and its new manner of signifying. It becomes clear, however, that, as with anxiety, what interests Heidegger about the *Stoss* is its disorienting effect with regard to any world whatsoever—whether the given world or that set out in positive terms by the work.

"Film," writes Benjamin, "is the art that is in keeping with the increased threat to life." But in the context of his essay as a whole, it is also the art that realizes the late-modern essence of every art, and in whose light alone aesthetic experience as such—even of art-works from the past—is now possible. This experience can no longer be characterized as a kind of *Geborgenheit,* a security and harmony. Rather, it is essentially precarious, linked not only to the risk of accident run by the pedestrian, but to the precarious structure of existence in general. The *shock* characteristic of new forms of reproducible art is simply the expression in our own world of Heidegger's *Stoss,* the essential oscillation and disorientation constitutive of the experience of art. In Benjamin's essay, one perceives a generally positive evaluation of technology. For him, the end of the cult and aural value of the work of art represents a clear opportunity of liberating ourselves from the art of superstition and alienation, and ultimately from the chains of metaphysics. In contrast, Heidegger seems to be a harsh judge of modern existence, not least because the increasingly banal character of language in the society of generalized communication destroys the very possibility of the work existing *qua* work, flattening it into insignificance. Yet it is hard to present Heidegger as a theoretician of the work of art as a cult item—as if he saw the aesthetic value of the work in the *hic et nunc* of its presence *qua* successful and perfect form, produced by the artist as a creative genius. These are all categories that, although essential to the cult conception of the work of art, are radically foreign to Heidegger, for whom the work is the "setting-into-work of truth" precisely insofar as it is always more than art, more than an accomplished and perfect form, more than the result of mastery or a creative act. The work functions as an opening of the truth because it is an "event" (*Ereignis*) of being, which has its essence as event in being over-turned and "expropriated" in the "mirror-play of the world" (as Heidegger says in his essay "The Thing"[10]).

However, it is more important here to pursue the other problem, namely Heidegger's approach to human existence in the technical world. In clarifying this problem we may uncover something of importance regarding the disorientation and oscillation intrinsic to aesthetic experience in late modernity, and this may help us to develop those elements in Benjamin's proposals that have so far remained implicit. (In passing, we might note that both Heidegger and Benjamin draw on Georg Simmel's description of human existence in the modern metropolis.[11] If we go back to the passages of *Identity and Difference* and *The Question Concerning Technology* where Heidegger illustrates his notion of *Ge-stell*,[12] we find that he uses this term, roughly translatable as "enframing," to characterize the whole apparatus of modern technology. This may in general be thought as a *Stellen,* a "setting up": man sets up things as objects of his manipulation, but he is in turn forever called upon to meet new demands, such that *Ge-stell* is a kind of continual and frantic reciprocal provocation on the part of man and being. But the essence of modern technology defined in this way is not only the highest point of the metaphysical oblivion of being. For Heidegger, *Ge-stell* is also "a first, oppressing flash of *Ereignis,*"[13] that is, of the event of being, beyond the metaphysical oblivion of being.[14] Precisely in the *Ge-stell,* that is, in the society of technology and total manipulation, Heidegger sees an opportunity of overcoming the oblivion and metaphysical alienation in which Western man has lived until now. The *Ge-stell* can offer such an opportunity because it is defined in almost identical terms to those used by Benjamin in speaking of *shock.*

In fact, in the *Ge-stell,* Heidegger writes, "Our whole human existence everywhere sees itself challenged—now playfully and now urgently, now breathlessly and now ponderously—to devote itself to the planning and calculating of everything."[15] The provocation to which the existence of modern man is subject is analogous to the condition of Benjamin's pedestrian, for whom art can only be *shock,* continual disorientation, and ultimately an exercise in mortality. The opportunity of overcoming metaphysics offered by the *Ge-stell* is linked to the fact that in it man and being lose "those qualities with which metaphysics has endowed them."[16] Nature is no longer the place of necessary law and the "positive sciences," whilst the human world—itself rigorously subjected to technologies of manipulation—is no longer the complementary and diametrically opposed realm of freedom, the field of the "human sciences." Accordingly, in this reshuffle, as the theater of metaphysics with its well-defined roles wanes, so an opportunity for a new advent of being dawns.

Is the aesthetic terminology at our disposal, the concepts that recur again and again in different forms whenever we talk of art (of its production or appreciation), adequate for thinking aesthetic experience as disorientation, oscillation, unfounding, and shock? An indication to the contrary may be seen in the fact that aesthetic theory has yet to do justice to the mass media and the possibilities they offer. It is as if it were always a matter of "saving" some essence of art (creativity, originality, appreciation of form, harmony, etc.) from the menace the new existential state of mass society presents not only to art, it is said, but also to the very essence of man. Reproducibility is thought to be irreconcilable with the seemingly indispensable demands for creativity in art. This is due only in part to the fact that the rapid diffusion of information tends to render every message immediately banal (indeed, in order to keep the media satisfied, such messages are banal from birth). Above all, it is because the reaction to this depletion of symbols is the invention of "novelties" that, like those of fashion, have none of the radicality seemingly necessary to the work of art. They are presented as superficial games; indeed, everything sent out by the mass media is imbued with a strange air of fragility and superficiality. This clearly clashes with the preconceptions of an aesthetic that draws its inspiration more or less explicitly from the ideal of the art work as a *momentum aere perennius,* and of the deep and authentic involvement of the subject in aesthetic experience, either as creator or as spectator. A stability and permanence in the work, a depth and authenticity in the aesthetic experience of creation and appreciation, are things we can no longer expect from late-modern aesthetic experience, dominated as it is by the power (and impotence) of the media. In opposition to the nostalgia for eternity (in the work) and authenticity (in experience), it must be clearly recognized that *shock* is all that remains of the creativity of art in generalized communication. And *shock* is defined by the two characteristics we have singled out with the help of Benjamin and Heidegger: fundamentally, it is nothing but metropolitan man's nervous and intellectual inconstancy and hypersensitivity. The focal point for art corresponding to this excitability and hypersensitivity is no longer the *work,* but *experience,* where this is thought of in terms of a minimal and continual variation (exemplified by watching film). These issues have often been treated by nineteenth- and twentieth-century aesthetic theory, though their consequences have never been fully worked out: for example, Heidegger draws our attention to them—polemically—in Nietzsche's theory of art.

The second feature constitutive of *shock* as the sole remnant of creativity in late-modern art is what Heidegger thinks via the notion of *Stoss,* namely the disorientation and oscillation connected with anxiety and the experience of mortality. The phenomenon Benjamin describes as shock, then, does not concern only the conditions of perception, and nor is it simply to be entrusted to the sociology of art. Rather, it is the manner of the work of art's actualization as conflict between world and earth. *Shock–Stoss* is the *Wesen,* the essence, of art in the two senses this expression has in Heidegger's terminology. It is the way in which aesthetic experience presents itself in late modernity, and it is also that which appears to be essential for art *tout court;* that is, its occurrence as the nexus of foundation and unfounding in the form of oscillation and disorientation—and ultimately as the task of mortality.

Is this to offer too hasty an apology for mass culture, as though it were redeemed of all the alienating characteristics so tellingly identified by Adorno and critical sociology? The equivocality of this sociology in our own day seems to arise from a failure to distinguish between the conditions of political alienation proper to society as total organization and the novel elements implicit in late-modern existence. As a result of this equivocality, the perversity of standardization and total organization has often been condemned in the name of humanistic values whose critical significance was due entirely to their being anachronistic. In fact, such values pre-date the metaphysics whose outcome, as Heidegger saw very clearly, has been the total organization of society. Perhaps we have now reached the stage where we can recognize that the superficiality and fragility of aesthetic experience in late-modern society do not necessarily have to be signs and symptoms of alienation linked to the dehumanizing aspects of standardization.

Contrary to what critical sociology has long believed (with good reason, unfortunately), standardization, uniformity, the manipulation of consensus and the errors of totalitarianism *are not* the only possible outcome of the advent of generalized communication, the mass media and reproduction. Alongside these possibilities—which are objects of political choice—there opens an alternative possible outcome. The advent of the media enhances the inconstancy and superficiality of experience. In so doing, it runs counter to the generalization of domination, insofar as it allows a kind of "weakening" of the very notion of reality, and thus a weakening of its persuasive force. The society of the spectacle spoken of by the situationists is not simply a society of appearance manipulated by power: it is also the society in which reality presents itself as softer and more fluid, and in which experience can again acquire the characteristics of oscillation, disorientation, and play.

The ambiguity many contemporary theories take to be characteristic of aesthetic experience is not provisional: it is not a matter of mastering language in general more completely—as subjects—by the freer and less automated use of language found in poetry. This would merely be to use poetic ambiguity as a means toward the fuller appropriation of language by the subject. As such, it would be a matter of an intentional disorientation aiming at an ultimate reorientation still hostage, if not to the category of "work," then certainly to the corresponding category of "subject." On the contrary, art is constituted as much by the experience of ambiguity as it is by oscillation and disorientation. In the world of generalized communication, these are the only ways that art can (not *still,* but perhaps *finally*) take the form of creativity and freedom.

1. Cf. Chapter 6 of my *End of Modernity* (1985), trans. J. Snyder (Cambridge: Polity Press, 1988).

2. Published in English in W. Benjamin, *Illuminations*, trans. H. Zohn, ed. H. Arendt (London: Jonathan Cape, 1982).

3. M. Heidegger, "The Origin of the Work of Art," in *Poetry, Language, Thought*, trans. A. Hofstadter (New York: Harper and Row, 1971).

4. This is one of the central themes of contemporary hermeneutic debate. Cf. H. G. Gadamer, *Truth and Method* (1960) (London: Sheed and Ward, 1975), 305 ff.

5. W. Benjamin, "The Work of Art," 252 (note 19).

6. Heidegger, *Poetry, Language, Thought*, 65–66.

7. M. Heidegger, *Being and Time* (1927), trans. J. Macquarrie and E. Robinson (Oxford: Basil Blackwell, 1980).

8. Heidegger, *Being and Time* (1927), 233–34.

9. ["sfondamento." In Italian, the addition of an "s" to an existing word: e.g. *contento* (happy)–*scontento* (unhappy), *fondare* (to found), *sfondare* (to break through or knock the bottom (*fondo*) out of something). In general, then, the term *sfondamento* means "breaking." However, it could also be taken as "non-foundation," the contrary to *fondamento*. This sense is clearly implicit in Vattimo's use of the term. In addition, Vattimo plays on the word's connection with *sfondo*, which generally means "background" (but which could also be read as the contrary of *fondo*, which means bottom, end, or base), thereby suggesting a further sense of "setting a thing in place against a background." Vattimo mentions this sense explicitly on page 73–Trans.]

10. The essay is included in Heidegger, *Poetry, Language, Thought*.

11. Cf. Georg Simmel's essay "Metropolis and Mental Life" (1902), in *Second Year Course in the Study of Contemporary Society* (Chicago: University of Chicago Press, 1936), 221–38.

12. M. Heidegger, *Identity and Difference* (1957), trans. J. Stambaugh (New York: Harper and Row, 1969); *The Question Concerning Technology and Other Essays*, trans. W. Lovitt (New York: Harper and Row, 1977).

13. Heidegger, *Identity and Difference*, 38.

14. There is a further discussion of the concept of oblivion of being proper to metaphysics, and of other terms from Heidegger's philosophy, in my *Introduction to Heidegger* (Rome/Bari: Laterza, 1982).

15. Heidegger, *Identity and Difference*, 34–35.

16. Heidegger, *Identity and Difference*, 37.

TRANSPARENCY

Anthony Vidler

Modernity has been haunted, as we know very well, by a myth of transparency: transparency of the self to nature, of the self to the other, of all selves to society, and all this represented, if not constructed, from Jeremy Bentham to Le Corbusier, by a universal transparency of building materials, spatial penetration, and the ubiquitous flow of air, light, and physical movement. As Sigfried Giedion observed in his *Bauen in Frankreich* of 1928,

The houses of Le Corbusier define themselves neither by space nor by forms; the air passes right through them! The air becomes a constitutive factor! For this, one should count neither on space nor forms, but uniquely on relation and compenetration! There is only a single, indivisible space. The separations between interior and exterior fall.[1]

Walter Benjamin, who copied this citation in his monumental compilation of quotes, the *Passagen-Werk*, heard in this urge for transparency a death knell for the ancient art of dwelling:

In the imprint of the turning point of the epoch, it is written that the knell has sounded for the dwelling in the old sense, dwelling in which security prevailed. Giedion, Mendelssohn, Le Corbusier have made the place of abode of men above all the transitory space of all the imaginable forces and waves of air and light. What is being prepared is found under the sign of transparency.[2]

On another level, transparency opened up machine architecture to inspection—its functions displayed like anatomical models, its walls hiding no secrets; the very epitome of social morality. In this vein, André Breton criticized the hermeticism of Huysmans and the interiority of symbolism:

As for me, I continue to inhabit my glass house [ma maison de verre], where one can see at every hour who is coming to visit me, where everything that is suspended from the ceilings and the walls holds on as if by enchantment, where I rest at night on a bed of glass with glass sheets, where who I am will appear to me, sooner or later, engraved on a diamond.[3]

Reading this passage, which does not entirely, as we might imagine, join Breton to his modernist contemporaries, Walter Benjamin was drawn to remark, "To live in a glass house is a revolutionary virtue par excellence. It is also an intoxication, a moral exhibitionism, that we badly need. Discretion concerning one's own existence, once an aristocratic virtue, has become more and more an affair of petit-bourgeois parvenus."[4] Such an ideology of the glass house of the soul, a psychogeographic glass house one might say, parallels the ideology of the glass house of the body—the aerobic glass house—and together the two themes inform the 1920s with dialectical vigor. No wonder that Marcel Duchamp, Man Ray, and of course Georges Bataille were all in favor of a little dust. In Bataille's ironic encomium of dust:

The storytellers have not imagined that the Sleeping Beauty would be awakened covered by a thick layer of dust; no more have they dreamed of the sinister spiders' webs that at the first movement of her brown hair would have torn. Nevertheless the sad nappes de poussière *endlessly invade earthly dwellings and make them uniformly dirty; as if attics and old rooms were planned for the next entry of obsessions, of phantoms, of larvae living and inebriated by the worm-eaten smell of the old dust. When the big girls "good for anything" arm themselves, each morning, with a big feather duster, or even with a vacuum cleaner, they are perhaps not entirely ignorant that they contribute as much as the most positive savants to keeping off the evil phantoms that sicken cleanliness and logic. One day or another, it is true, dust, if it persists, will probably begin to gain ground over the servants, invading the immense rubbish of abandoned buildings, of deserted docks: and in this distant epoch there will be nothing more to save us from nocturnal terrors.[5]*

Glass, once perfectly transparent, is now revealed in all its opacity.

Indeed, it was under the sign of opacity that the universalism of modernism, constructed on the myth of a universal subject, came under attack in the past twenty-five years. Beginning with Colin Rowe and Robert Slutzky's sly undermining of modernist simplicities in their "Transparency: Literal and Phenomenal," transparency was gradually discredited by the critique of the universal subject in politics and psychoanalysis.[6] In its place, opacity, both literal and phenomenal, became the watchword of the postmodern appeal to roots, to tradition, to local and regional specificity, to a renewed search for domestic security. A few years ago one might have concluded that, if the old art of dwelling had not been entirely revived, save in kitsch imitation, certainly transparency was dead.

Yet in the last few years, as if confirming the penchant of the century for uncanny repetition, we have been once again presented with a revived call for transparency, this time on behalf of the apparently "good modernism," patronized by the French state in its Parisian *grands projets. La transparence* is now the rage in France, represented by the winning schemes for the new national library and the Palais des Expositions near the Eiffel Tower, reopening questions originally posed in the context of the first of François Mitterand's monuments—the pyramid of the Louvre. But what seemed, in the case of the pyramid, to be an ostensibly practical problem of making a new monument disappear in relation to its context has been raised to the status of principle. Transparency, in the form of the four towers proposed for the book stacks of Dominique Perrault's library and the three box-shaped pavilions for the expo building, is now, at least in the minds of Mitterand, his administration, the juries and apologists for the schemes, and, of course, the architects themselves, firmly identified with progressive modernity. And is thus posed against what is regarded as a regressive postmodern tendency of historical atavism. The association is made confidently, with the apparent faith of the first avant-gardes of the 1920s.

On one level, the connection transparency/modernity is easy enough to understand. Following a decade of historical and typological exploration of "false walls" and fake stones, postmodernism, the argument goes, has been seen for what it was—the Potemkin City of the present—to be purified only by a renewed adhesion to the spirit of the age. In France at least, the spirit of the age is still haunted by the ghosts of technocratic "rational" architecture from Durand and Viollet-le-Duc to Pierre Chareau, continued in the 1960s with the technological expressionism of the Centre Pompidou, and, more recently, Norman Foster's Town Hall for Nîmes, next door to the Maison Carrée.

Literal transparency is of course notoriously difficult (as Pei himself admitted) to attain; it quickly turns into obscurity (its apparent opposite) and reflectivity (its reversal). Despite all the research of the Saint-Gobain glass company, the pyramid remains a glass pyramid, no more or less transparent than Bruno Taut's glass block pavilion of 1914. As for the library, the claim of transparency—books exposed to the world as symbols of themselves—was quickly suppressed in the face of professional librarians asking simple questions. The solution has been twofold: either to "fake" transparency—a falsely lit wall beyond the walls protecting the stacks from daylight—or to embrace its mirror image, so to speak, reflectively.

Why then transparency in the first place? To make huge cubic masses, monumental forms, urban constructions of vast scale—disappear? A crisis of confidence in monumentality? Certainly it seems significant that the projects were selected from models, without structure or scale—and conceptual models at that, where the expo "boxes" seem (and are) like giant perspex boxes. The conclusion would be that to work effectively, the ideology of the modern, either as *bête noire* of the postmodern or its recent replacement, would have to be a fiction in practice. Public monumentality would then be in the same position as in the 1940s when Giedion posed the question of whether a "new monumentality" was indeed possible in modern materials.

We are presented with the apparently strange notion of a public monumentality that is more than reticent—indeed wants literally to disappear, be invisible—even as it represents the full weight of the French state. And perhaps the underpinnings of the present revival should indeed be sought in the difficult area of representation, one that is no doubt joined to the problematic outlined by Gianni Vattimo, that of a "weak" or background monumentality, but also, and perhaps more fundamentally, to the self-perceived role of architecture in the construction of identity. For if it was in the task of constructing a new and modern subject that transparency in architecture was first adduced, the present passion for see-through buildings is indubitably linked to the attempt to construct a state identity of technological modernity against a city identity (Paris, Chirac) enmeshed in the tricky historicism of preservation.

Yet, coupled with this tendency, we may begin to discern the emergence of a more complex stance, one that, without rejecting the technological and ideological heritage of modernism, nevertheless seeks to problematize its premises, recognizing that the "subject" of modernity has indeed been destabilized by its worst effects. In this vein, the cube of glass envisaged by Rem Koolhaas in his competition entry for the French national library, with its internal organs displayed, so to speak, like some anatomical model, is at once a confirmation of transparency and its complex critique. For here the transparency is conceived of as solid, not as void, with the interior volumes carved out of a crystalline block, so as to float within it, in amoebic suspension. These are then represented on the surface of the cube as shadowy presences, their three-dimensionality displayed ambiguously and flattened, superimposed on one another, in a play of amorphous densities. Transparency is thus converted into translucency, and this into darkness and obscurity. The inherent quality of absolute transparency to turn into its opposite, reflectivity, is thrown into doubt; the subject can no longer lose itself in *l'espace indicible* of infinite reason or find itself in the narcissism of its own reflection. Rather, it is suspended in a difficult moment between knowledge and blockage, thrust into an experience of density and amorphism, even as it is left before an external surface that is, to all intents and purposes, nothing more than a two-dimensional simulacrum of interior space.

The qualities of estrangement that result are, on one level, similar to the uncanny effects of all mirroring, apparent to writers from Hoffmann to Maupassant. In the latter's story "Le Horla" (1887), which served as an exemplary model for Otto Rank in his book *The Double*, the narrator is tormented by the thought that he is ever accompanied by an invisible other, a spirit that he cannot see but that nevertheless resides in his house, drinks his wine, controls his actions and thoughts; he is obsessed with the idea of catching it out, often running into his room in order to seize his mysterious double and kill it. Once, on an impulse, he turned around quickly, to face a tall wardrobe with a mirror; but, as he recalled, "I did not see myself in my mirror. The glass was empty, clear, deep, brightly lit, but my reflection was missing, though I was standing where it would be cast." Then, after gazing at this large clear mirrored surface from top to bottom for some time, he was terrified, for "suddenly I saw myself in a mist in the center of the mirror, through a sort of watery veil; and it seemed to me as if the water were slipping very slowly from left to right." Convinced he had seen his double, he develops a case of what, in the context of our analysis, might be called advanced agoraphobia: barricading the windows and doors of his room with iron; leaving and setting fire to the room in order to kill the apparently trapped other. But beset with doubts as to whether he had actually killed this invisible specter, he was finally forced to kill himself.[7]

Such themes of mirror reflection and its uncanny effects were noted by Freud, who tells the amusing but disturbing story of sitting alone in his compartment in a *wagon lit* [sleeping car], when a jolt of the train caused the door of his washing cabinet to swing open; "an elderly gentleman in a dressing gown and traveling cap came in." Jumping up angrily to protest this unwonted intrusion, Freud at once realized to his dismay "that the intruder was nothing but my own reflection in the looking glass of the open door. I can still recollect that I thoroughly disliked his appearance" (U 244). Interpreting this scene, Sarah Kofman has concluded:

Repetition, like repression, is originary, and serves to fill an originary lack as well as to veil it: the double does not double a presence but rather supplements it, allowing one to read, as in a mirror, originary "difference," castration, death, and at the same time the necessity of erasing them.[8]

The psychoanalyst Mahmoud Sami-Ali has gone further in explaining this association of the uncanny with reflection, taking Lacan's notion of the mirror stage and arguing that the proximity, noted by Freud, of the familiar and the strange causes "a profound modification of the object, which from the familiar is transformed into the strange, and as strange something that provokes disquiet because of its absolute proximity." Sami-Ali proposes that space itself is de-formed by this experience. If, as Freud had implied, "the feeling of the uncanny implies the return to that particular organization of space where everything is reduced to inside and outside and where the inside is also the outside," then the space of the mirror would precisely meet this condition: a space of normal binocular, three-dimensional vision, modified by being deprived of depth. This would lead to the conflation, on the same visual plane, of the familiar (seen) and the strange (projected). In the case of the mirror stage, this would involve a complex superimposition of the reflected image of the subject and, conflated with this, the projected image of the subject's desire—the other: "Being simultaneously itself and the other, familiar and nevertheless strange, the subject is that which has no face and whose face exists from the point of view of the other."[9]

But, while the presence of such an uncanny in Koolhaas's library project is undeniable, we have yet to account for its equally evident refusal of mirroring, its absorbency to both interior representation and external reflection. Here the unexpected manifestation of this as yet undefinable condition, erupting suddenly out of an apparently simple play of transparencies, should be distinguished from the qualities of reflectivity found in modernism as well as from any "postmodern" surface play of simultaneity and seduction. The architect allows us neither to stop at the surface nor to penetrate it, arresting us in a state of anxiety.

This condition seems to approximate not the mirror stage itself but that moment, described by Lacan, of the *accomplishment* of the stage. "This moment in which the mirror stage comes to an end inaugurates, through identification with the *imago* of the counterpart and the drama of primordial jealousy . . . the dialectic that will henceforth link the *I* to socially elaborated situations." Such socially elaborated situations were, he concluded, characterized by "paranoiac alienation, which dates from the detection of the specular *I* into the social *I.*"[10]

With this swerve from the self to the social, the subject is no longer content to interrogate its face in the mirror in the search for transparency of the soul but, following Lacan's deliberately chosen metaphor, desires to stage its self in its social relations. Here two-dimensional physiognomy, the representation of the "face," is transformed into the three-dimensional space of subjectivity, place for the staging of social activity. That is, the plane of the mirror becomes the space of a theater: "The *mirror stage* is a drama," asserts Lacan.[11]

In Lacan's wordplay, the mirror stage is staged, or, following the connotations of the French, the *stade* (or biological stage) acts in the space of a *stade* (or stadium):

The formation of the I is symbolized oneirically by a fortified camp, a stadium indeed—establishing, from the interior arena to its outer enclosure, its periphery of rubbish and marshes, two opposed fields of struggle where the subject is caught up in the quest for the lofty and distant chateau, whose form (sometimes juxtaposed in the same scenario) symbolizes the id in a striking fashion. And in the same way we find realized, here on the mental level, those structures of the fortified work the metaphor of which rises up spontaneously, and as a result of the very symptoms of the subject, to designate the mechanisms of inversion, of isolation, of reduplication, of annulation, of displacement, of obsessional neurosis.[12]

In this image of the self, fortified and surrounded by garbage dumps, staged in an arena, is established the parameters of what Victor Burgin in a recent article also following Lacan has termed "paranoiac space."[13]

In the light of Rem Koolhaas's preoccupation, outlined in *Delirious New York*, with the "paranoid critical method" of Salvador Dalí, a method that anticipates Lacan's first publications on paranoia, we might be tempted to apply such a designation to the facade of the Koolhaas library project. The paranoiac space of the library would then be that which is staged through the anxiety instigated at its surface.

In his seminar on *angoisse* conducted between 1962 and 1963, Lacan himself tied anxiety directly to the experience of the uncanny, claiming, indeed, that it was through the very structure of the *unheimlich* that anxiety might be theorized. The "field of anxiety" is framed by the uncanny, so to speak, even as the uncanny itself is framed as a sudden apparition seen, as it were, through a window: "The horrible, the suspicious, the uncanny, everything by which we translate as we can into French this magisterial word 'unheimlich,' presenting itself through the skylights [*lucarnes*] by which it is framed, situates for us the field of anxiety": The notion of "suddenness," of the "all at once," is fundamental for Lacan in setting this scene of uncanny anxiety: "You will always find this term at the moment of entry of the phenomenon of the *unheimlich!*" In this space of the sudden, as in "that brief, quickly extinguished moment of anxiety" before the curtain goes up in the theater—the moment of the three taps of the conductor's baton—anxiety is framed; it is for a moment collapsed into waiting, preparation, "a state of alert." But, beyond the frame, anxiety is, in a real sense, in the frame; it is something already known, and therefore anticipated: "Anxiety is when, in this frame, something appears that was already there, much closer to the house, the *Heim*: the host." The host, suddenly appearing at the door of the home or on the scene of the stage, is both expected and hostile, foreign to and yet embedded in the house: "It is this rising up of the *heimlich* in the frame that is the phenomenon of anxiety."[14]

The anxiety of the subject confronted with the "soft" space of Koolhaas's surfaces is then the manifestation of an uncanny based on the newly formulated conditions of interiority and exteriority, where the "ghosting" of the functionalist interior on the exterior mirrors not the outward appearance of the subject but its own, now-transparent biological interior. Paranoiac space is transformed then into panic space, where all limits become blurred in a thick, almost palpable substance that has substituted itself, almost imperceptibly, for traditional architecture.

[1] Sigfried Giedion, *Bauen in Frankreich* (Leipzig: Klinkhardt and Biermann, 1928), 85, quoted in Benjamin, *Passagen-Werk,* 533.

[2] Walter Benjamin, "Die Wiederkehr des Flaneurs," in *Gesammelte Schriften,* 7 vols., ed. Rolf Tiedemann and Hermann Schweppenhauser (Frankfurt am Main: Suhrkamp Verlag, 1972ff.), 3:168.

[3] André Breton, *Nadja* (Paris: Gallimard, 1964), 18–19.

[4] Benjamin, "Surrealism," in *Reflections: Essays, Aphorisms, Autobiographical Writings,* ed. Peter Demetz, trans. Edmund Jephcott (New York: Harcourt Brace Jovanovich, 1978), 180.

[5] Bataille, *Oeuvres complètes*, 1:197.

[6] Colin Rowe and Robert Slutzky, "Transparency: Literal and Phenomenal," in *The Mathematics of the Ideal Villa* (Cambridge, Mass.: MIT Press, 1976), 160–76. Reprinted in this volume starting on page 91.

[7] Guy de Maupassant, "Le Horla," in *Le Horla et autres contes d'angiosse* (Paris: Garnier-Flammarion, 1984), 77–80.

[8] Sarah Kofman, *The Childhood of Art: An Interpretation of Freud's Aesthetics*, trans. Winifred Woodhull (New York: Columbia University Press, 1988), 128.

[9] Mahmoud Sami-Ali, "L'espace de l'inquiétante étrangeté," *Nouvelle Revue de Psychanalyse* 9 (Spring 1974): 33, 43.

[10] Jacques Lacan, *Ecrits, a Selection*, trans. Alan Sheridan (New York: Norton, 1977), 5.

[11] Lacan, *Ecrits*, 4.

[12] Jacques Lacan, "Le Stade du miroir," in *Ecrits,* 2 vols. (Paris: Seuil, 1966), 1:94.

[13] Victor Burgin, "Paranoiac Space," *New Foundations* 12 (Winter 1990): 61–75.

[14] Jacques Lacan, unpublished seminar, "L'Angoisse," December 19, 1962.

THE GLAZE: PHANTASM AND MODERN ARCHITECTURE

Eeva-Liisa Pelkonen

The demand for ambiguity and the fictional seems to be a common dominator in all the operational moves discussed in this chapter. It gains its ultimate expression in glass, which has dominated modern architecture ever since the erection of the Crystal Palace (figs. 59 and 60) for the 1851 world exhibition. Glass has become a mythic trope for the subject matter of modern architecture: technology, openness, harmony with nature. The typical building types that were born with glass architecture—the glasshouse, the railway station, the exhibition hall, the gallery—are also sites for the ultimate modern experience: the urban stroll, the *dérive*, a moment when we willingly surrender ourselves to the sensuous stimulus that enters our consciousness without control, and the most urban experience of all, the seductive opportunity to look and be looked at. Early glass architecture was meant for transient purposes, for acts experienced by the masses, rather than as places for individual contemplation. It created scenes of desire, power, and collective experience.[1]

Glass also takes architecture back to the early modern era by emphasizing spiritual, visual, and social qualities. According to Scheerbart, it brings a completely new mode of life into being. He reveals his spiritual motivation: "Glass architecture makes homes into cathedrals, with the same effects."[2] Glass also was to represent the shock of the new, having an almost hypnotizing power over the spectator. Underlying its use was the will for change, change that could not be preprogrammed in terms of a definite goal. The elusiveness of glass and its ability to enter into a reciprocal relationship with its environment by means of light became the perfect symbol for change and the new, still devoid of any singular meaning.

Glass architecture has gone through many phases since Paxton's Crystal Palace. It began with glasshouses and orangeries that were conceived as arenas for the fantastic and exotic gathered from all over the world. Therefore its origins were in travel, commodity fetishism, and the longing for paradise, which had as their source the desire for the new and fantastic. All that changed in the late 1920s.

Twentieth-century mainstream modernism found glass attractive for quite different reasons. It emphasized either the romantic and sentimental belief in the continuity between humans and nature with the flow of spaces between the inside and outside of a building, or the pragmatic advantages of maximum penetration of light in terms of hygiene.[3] It reduced glass to a mere transparent material, something one sees through. Yet it is the mythic in the early modern tradition that serves as a point of reference for contemporary architects who seem obsessed by glass as an embodiment of the subtle complexities of their poetic and symbolic language.

Glass is the emblem of the modern in the sense that it amalgamates even opposites into a symbolic unity. Hugo von Hofmannstahl's description of the experience at the turn of the last century seems appropriate: "Today, two things seem to be modern: the analysis of life and the flight from life. . . . One practices anatomy on the inner life of one's mind, or one dreams. Reflection or fantasy, mirror image or dream image."[4] As discussed by James

McFarlane, the modern is understood as a combination of two *Weltanschauungen*: the mechanistic and the intuitive. Hofmannstahl notes that "modern" at the turn of the century meant a coalescence and fusion of dream and reality to the point of indistinguishability. For him as well as for Simmel[5] and other contemporaries it meant that humans had partly lost control over the stimuli produced by technology and life in a metropolis. To lose control and to deal with ambiguities and discontinuities became part of the modern experience; therefore, fragment and the particular gain importance over abstraction and the generalization.

By virtue of its elusive materiality glass can blur the line between nature and technology, between inside and outside, between the real and the imaginary. It plays with notions of the ephemeral and the permanent, as well as with those of the real and the imaginary. By adding to the real a quality of the imaginary, and to the imagined a possibility of transformation into the real, what was considered permanent becomes transient. Glass rotates images between the two, adding an ephemeral quality to real objects and places and obscuring the real and turning it into a dream vision. Its inherent qualities are wish and potentiality. Glass is an antonym for ruin: it means not-yet, whereas ruin implies no-more. By enacting a wish, it suggests transformation.[6]

Adding Taut's and Scheerbart's visionary glass utopias to our discussion, it seems that early glass architecture always aimed at exceeding mere architecture; it attempted to change life by constituting new realities. There is something magical about the space of glass that produces moments of self-transcendence understood as typically modern, and urban experience per se. Glass has two main qualities that support this idea of something greater than reality-yet-present. First, as Benjamin noted, it is the enemy of recollections and possessions because it is perpetually new, and second, due to its obvious tie to modern technology, glass architecture always promises to create something not-yet-present (Bloch). Conceived as such it becomes the emblem of what Walter Benjamin calls a wish-image. In disguise, overtly present through reflection, or transparent, which is its most harmonious of incarnations, glass always seems to play with perceivers by manipulating what we consider real.

The return to the beginning of modern (glass) architecture of the mid-nineteenth century can be explained by the fact that utopian images, which are always accompanied by the emergence of the new, reach back to the Ur-past, as Susan Buck-Morss discusses in her study of Benjamin's *Passagenwerke*. Thus it returns to its origin, as enlightenment visionaries turned to the *Urhütte*. This reflection makes the contemporary mythic through the tradition it follows, and it is exactly the mythic and symbolic quality that activates the utopian impulse. Contemporary glass architecture reassesses the myth of the modern by recalling its own tradition.[7]

The utopian impulse relies on the ability of glass architecture to appropriate the relationship between architecture and technology. Through technology, architecture participates in industrial production, which constantly transforms reality. As Benjamin discussed in his famous article "Art in the Age of Mechanical Reproduction," only by using new methods of production can art have an impact on the masses, albeit also an alarming impact. Through the symbolic liaison between technology and nature, art anticipates the production and change of reality that only technology seems to have mastered. Glass architecture participates in this production of reality by means of a shock that, quoting Giorgio Agamben, "appropriates unreality."[8] Agamben thus refers to the late-nineteenth-century ideas of modernity in his discussion about the reassessment of art in the era of industrial revolution. Recalling Benjamin, he writes:

Baudelaire understood that if art wished to survive industrial civilization, the artist had to attempt to reproduce that destruction of use-value and traditional intelligibility that was at the origin of the experience of shock. In this way the artist would succeed in making the work the vehicle of the unattainable and would restore in unattainability itself a new value and a new authority. . . . Without the personal experience of the miraculous ability of the fetish object to make the absence present through its own negation, he would perhaps not have dared to assign to art the most ambitious task that any human being has ever entrusted to one of his or her creations: the appropriation of unreality.[9]

There are countless examples of the use of glass in contemporary European architecture, yet few demonstrate the sensibilities that make it perhaps the most powerful fiction of modernity. The excessive use of glass in Volker Giencke's showroom and warehouse in Klagenfurt (figs. 110–13) reveals some of the ideas that address the quintessentially modern sensibilities that the material engages. It is the ambiguity of the material, its malleability, its changing incarnations that become the subject matter.

Commissioned by the firm Odörfer, and often referred to as such, the building occupies a site by the ring road through the industrial zone near Klagenfurt. It is dominated by a sixty-five-meter-long tilted glass roof; or maybe it is more appropriate to define it as a wall that has become a roof. This roof-wall rises from the ground at a slight angle. The ambiguous relationship between building and ground demonstrates that the building wants to be more than a mere inanimate object; it wants to become part of the real by raising itself from the ground, simulating animation by the combination of a wall turning into a roof and back into a wall when viewed in motion, and by the way glass changes character in this situation. Our attention is drawn first of all to this fragment from which the building later unfolds. The eye seems to stay on the surface rather than look through. "Like all desire, vision should be conceived from the beginning in relation to lack, a drift from metaphor to metaphor, an infinite chain of difference."[10] The showroom becomes vaguely visible when the roof is seen at a right angle.

The long glass surface is parallel to the road, and sometimes in late summer it is almost invisible from farther than a few hundred meters away due to the high cornfield that surrounds the site. The uncanniness of the roof is due to its sudden appearance. Seeing is not simultaneous with recognition: viewed sideways, the roof reflects the sky melting into it to the point of absolute disappearance. A few seconds later one grasps the physical reality and presence of the building. At first one imagines a totally different material for the roof. Only later, when the reflection turns it transparent, does the surface reveal its materiality. This happens when one is level with the building and the roof starts suddenly to change both its form and incarnation: the tilted reflective or opaque (depending on the light) surface suddenly becomes a semitransparent wall. It is hardly surprising that the glass roof almost caused a few car accidents; we actually thought about erecting a traffic sign with the text *"Achtung Architektur!"* One becomes aware of the building at the moment when the reflection becomes transparent. Having given us no chance of visual control and adjustment, the building's presence comes as an absolute surprise.

The second level of confrontation happens afterward when perception has yielded to an after-image, a dream-like vision that allows an allegorical reading. It is this prolongation of the actual confrontation by means of the image that stays with the perceiver and exceeds what might otherwise be an isolated experience. The image again looks for the material emblem of the "involuntary beauty of the ephemeral"[11]—the veil. The use of glass in Odörfer reminds me of Christo's wrappings, which also rely on the singularity of instant confrontation. The unreal quality of the glass surface, at first opaque and reflecting, then transparent, similarly suggests an act of unfolding, unveiling.

Most critics still talk about architecture's will for disappearance, transparency, and dematerialization. I suggest it is the ability of glass to transform itself into three incarnations, the transparent, opaque, and reflecting, while remembering the moments of transformation in between, that reveals its ambiguous quality. The element of surprise, the game of hide and seek, and the metamorphosis from one incarnation to another make the discovery of boundary, of material surface, an arrival. Conceived as such, glass seems to be as much about appearance and materialization—unfolding—as it is about disappearance and dematerialization. Architecture devoid of metaphysics turns into an object of desire that has its own animated presence. Glass's gaze (glaze) explains something about the will "to deprive the external world of the privilege of being inanimate."[12] The animation is based on the ability of glass to react to changes of light conditions as well as to the position of the spectator. Reflection and opacity conceal and force the eye to wander in search of revelation and arrival, whereas the transparent condition embodies the final bliss by revealing the materiality of glass, and allowing the spectator to know the interior.

A curtain and a mirror play with the idea of simultaneous concealing and revealing. Glass reveals something before it is available and tangible, sustains things as objects of desire that are not yet there to be possessed or, in the case of architecture, spaces not yet accessible. In Odörfer the tease reaches its climax when the glass louvers of the roof open: the ultimate exhibitionist act. This ability to move and to react to outer stimuli defines the skin of Odörfer as an "osmotic membrane," a zone of "transference between two milieus, two substances" that Paul Virilio talks about—an invisible difference.[13]

Glass architecture has traditionally been employed to emphasize different aspects, mainly continuity and vastness, as the conceptions of modern architectural space. Contemporary glass architecture, on the contrary, seems to prove the impossibility (even immorality) of representing space as a hierarchically defined structure. Examples demonstrate this by emphasizing the ambiguity, not elimination, of the boundary of space. The veiling turns spatiality into temporality, the most subjective element of human experience according to Merleau-Ponty. The process of unveiling makes time into both a visual and a sensuous element.

[1] Cf. Susan Buck-Morss, *The Dialectics of Seeing: Walter Benjamin and the Arcades Project* (Cambridge: MIT Press, 1989), 129–30.

[2] Paul Scheerbart, *Glass Architecture* (New York: Praeger Publishers, 1972), 72. See Scheerbart's essay starting on page 345 of this volume.

[3] Here I refer to Reyner Banham's comment that glass architecture represents "the aseptic side of modern architecture." See his *Theory and Design in the First Machine Age* (London: Architectural Press, 1960), 266.

[4] James McFarlane, "The Mind of Modernism," in *Modernism*, ed. Malcolm Bradbury and James McFarlane (London: Penguin Books, 1985), 71. (*Heute sheinen zwei Dinge modern zu sein: die Analyse des Lebens und die Flucht aus dem Leben.. . . . Man treibt Anatomie des eigenen Seelenlebens, oder man träumt. Reflexion oder Phantasie, Spiegelbild oder Traumbild.*)

[5] Cf. Georg Simmel, "Metropolis and Mental Life," in *Georg Simmel: On Individuality and Social Forms* (Chicago: University of Chicago Press, 1985).

[6] See Buck-Morss's chapter "Mythic Nature: Wish Image," in *The Dialectics of Seeing*, 110–58.

[7] Buck-Morss "Mythic Nature: Wish Image," 116.

[8] Giorgio Agamben, *Stanzas; Word and Phantasm in Western Culture* (Minneapolis: University of Minnesota Press, 1993), 42–43.

[9] Agamben, *Stanzas; Word and Phantasm in Western Culture*, 42–43.

[10] Birgit Pelzer, "Vision in Process," in *October* 10 (Fall 1979): 115. Here Pelzer participates in the discussion that started to reassess vision and criticize Western oculocentrism in the end of the 1970s using psychoanalytic methods. The following sentence sums up her argument: "Vision, naturally associated with the order of consciousness (witness the triumph of geometrical perspective contemporaneous with Descartes' postulates), belongs less to that order than that of desire."

[11] Dominique G. Laporte, *Christo* (New York: Pantheon Books, 1986), 28.

[12] Elaine Scarry, *The Body in Pain: The Making and Unmaking of the World* (Oxford: Oxford University Press, 1985), 285.

[13] Paul Virilio, "The Overexposed City," in *The Lost Dimension* (New York: Semiotext(e), 1991), 17.

THE VEIL: ARCHITECTURE WITHOUT ORGANS
Eeva-Liisa Pelkonen

Didi-Huberman's view of detail collides with the aim of a good part of the twentieth-century avant-garde: the elimination of representation, of mimesis, of the duality between signifier and signified, of form and content. When evaluating this shift, the question becomes whether or not the move away from hermeneutic reading to hermetic text is, as Renato Poggioli suggests, a social task.

The new sensibility toward materiality and structure, which has been set free from functional ordering principles, liberates architecture from its traditional modes of representation based on the interdependence of form and content. Architecture comes rather to be defined as a physical object characterized by the transmission of a certain character and ambience, as a physical condition marked by a human act and attitude.[1] We can call such a physical demonstration a gesture. We can therefore continue to ask how architecture is able to sustain this attitude, this gesture, as a fetish is able to sustain a memory of an act.

Gesture refers to movements and attitudes of the body, not the functioning of the body. A gesture can be understood as an "outward physical expression of the inward soul."[2] Agamben writes, "What characterizes gesture is that in it there is neither production nor enactment, but undertaking and supporting. In other words, gesture opens the sphere of *ethos* or the most fitting sphere of the human."[3]

Therefore, to understand how architecture can make a statement, as the avant-garde has tried to do, we have to reassess the analogy between body and architecture in the light of gesture. Just as we imagine the body being a transmitter of what lies within, architecture can function as a transmitter of the ethical in its thinking. Central is that a gesture is an act, a movement that is not motivated by the body's needs or its functioning, but by its desires and attitudes. The traditional understanding of the body as the abode of the soul has to be reassessed; consciousness, or soul if you wish, is rather to be understood as "consciousness of something," as Sartre observed, always directed out toward something, without having a content in itself.

To clarify this analogy between body and architecture, I quote Bachelard:

The phenomenology of the poetic imagination allows us to explore the being of man considered as the being of a surface, of the surface that separates the region of the same from the region of the other. It should not be forgotten that in this zone of sensitized surface, before being, one must speak, if not to others, at least to oneself. . . . It would be contrary to the nature of my inquiries to summarize them by means of radical formulas, by defining the being of man, for example, as the being of an ambiguity. I only know how to work with a philosophy of detail. Then, on the surface of being, in that region where being wants to be both visible and hidden, the movements of opening and closing are so numerous, so frequently inverted, and so charged with hesitation, that we could conclude on the following formula: man is a half-open thing.[4]

Pursuing the analogy of body and architecture through gesture and ambiguity, we arrive at the envelope itself, the surface of the boundary as the most decisive architectural element. The boundary is where different intensities, including attitudes, unfold, and therefore is the most ambiguous element of all, the one that has the capacity to reveal and to conceal. It belongs to neither the interior nor the exterior and has, by its very nature, the power to question this preliminary segregation in architecture: inside versus outside, form versus content, body versus soul. The boundary is therefore the political architectural element per se.

The boundary finally decides what becomes visible and what stays concealed. Lefebvre writes: "Consider the great power of a facade, for example. A facade admits certain acts to the realm of what is visible, whether they occur on the facade itself (on balconies, window ledges, etc.) or are to be seen from the facade (processions in the street, for example). Many other acts, by contrast, it condemns to obscenity: these occur behind the facade. All of which already seems to suggest a 'psychoanalysis of space.'"⁵ Here we should keep in mind Loos's architecture, in which facade simply segregates and conceals, and therefore insists on the segregation of private and public, as well as on social integrity and status quo. What is at stake in the contemporary view of facade is that it always carries a promise of revelation and of breaking boundaries.

What Lefebvre calls the "psychoanalysis of space" and the politics of concealing versus revealing finally leads to questions about the erotics of architecture. "In the figurative arts, eroticism appears as a relationship between clothing and nudity. Therefore, it is conditional on the possibility of movement—transit—from one state to the other,"⁶ writes Mario Perniola, and " transit does exist between the visible and the invisible, between clothing and what it covers."⁷

In this context, transit becomes a condition that is emblematic of the whole avant-garde tradition; a transit between the promise and its delivery, between the idea and its realization, between the real and the unreal, between individual and community. Curiously literal translations of this understanding of the transit zone are made when the boundary begins to show signs of animation.

Traces of Austria's baroque heritage are preserved in contemporary sensibilities of the boundary. Perniola discusses the baroque view of what he calls the erotic transit as follows: "The transit [movement] established between clothing and nudity shows up in two fundamental ways: in the use of the erotics of drapery or attire, as we see in Bernini, and in the depiction of the body as a living garment, as we see in anatomical illustrations."⁸ Two kinds of elements are at stake: the veil and the skin.

Perniola elaborates on erotic transit:

It is necessary to keep these premises in mind in order to fully understand the extraordinary erotic magic of Bernini's masterpiece, the Ecstasy of Saint Teresa *[fig. 114], made for the Cornaro chapel in the Church of Santa Maria della Vittoria in Rome. Its magic does not depend simply upon the angel's splendor, the evident sexual symbolism of the arrow, or upon the expression that crosses the saint's lovely face, clearly indicating that she is about to faint, but mostly on the fact that Saint Teresa's body disappears in the drapery of her tunic. It has undergone a transformation that has emancipated it from human form, while it still projects all the impetuous and vibrant shuddering of a body in ecstasy. . . . By conceding less to the formal unity of the work, it accentuates the essen-*

tial: the transit between body and clothes, the displacement of what lies beneath the drapery. . . . The sacramental
presence is a living presence; it is "an ever renewed motion. . . that sees clearly how form is only one aspect
of what exists." It does not find peace, rest or repose in a pleasing surface, nor in a spiritual marriage nor in
theatricality as an end in itself. Rather, it tirelessly and continually flows, ebbs, moves and shifts.[9]

When discussing the contemporary concepts of enclosure and boundary one can find architectural translations of both of them introduced by Perniola: the skin and the veil. They require two structural approaches as well as two strategies. The skin implies a boundary suspended between inside and outside; it requires a certain tension. The veil on the other hand implies wrapping that can be removed. It suggests secrecy yet promises revelation.

Let us look at examples. As discussed in previous chapters, the botanical garden by Volker Giencke (figs. 116–18) is an ultimate example of the skin. Whereas the body conceived as a half-open thing negates the notion of an enclosed or unified entity, the skin must form an adaptable and elastic surface. The acrylic skin in the botanical garden reflects this view of an adaptable surface. It appears as if in tension and it adapts to the conditions of breathing, the requirements of ventilation and exit, in a flexible manner. We might as well accept a slip into the figurative reading. The building reminds us of dinosaurs. Conceived as a skin, the boundary becomes a kind of "osmotic membrane" (Virilio): a zone between two atmospheres, between two intensities.[10]

Whereas the skin marks a difference, the veil always implies covering something. Concealment and disappearance of a veiled object can mean two things: "plus value of loss, of absence," as proposed by Dominique Laporte in discussing Christo's wrappings,[11] or what Derrida calls the "subsidy/bonus of seduction," that is, seduction understood as a supplement.[12] The former implies obtrusiveness, where what is covered gains its true nature only by being absent. The latter, on the other hand, means that the act of concealment, the tease, is itself a productive act that triggers desire. The veil has to have a life of its own, it has to fluctuate and tremble, and most of all, it has to promise the act of unveiling.

In Odörfer the veil recalls the sensuality of something wrapped around the body. The act of wrapping is exaggerated by separating the glazing from the carrying construction; hangers made of bent wire convey the image of a cloth or a curtain hung from the structure: something extra. During construction the "something put in front" became a culmination point: the glass made the expressive and dynamic steel structure appear more subtle and ambiguous and lose its functional meaning. The glass surface added a new dimension (supplement) to the structure by the simultaneous act of veiling the functional and unveiling the ambiguous material image.

The structure—the naked truth—is made ambiguous through veiling. The veil prevents the architecture from turning into an ontological stasis, from reaching the limit that is found in structure, which can be said to represent only itself through ordering. The glass surface wrapped around the construction itself represents this limit condition: the veil, as Perniola writes, "is not a mere obstacle to seeing with a naked eye, but actually the condition that makes vision possible."[13] Unlike the modernist conception of glass architecture, the act of disappearance is the reverse. Normally, an opaque surface is visible and transparency is invisible, but the glass roof of Odörfer challenges our habitual ways of seeing: the transparent (uncovered) state makes possible the presence of the ultimate architectural, the structure, by revealing its own limit condition.

The new glass architecture is generally more about this ability to avoid stasis by suspending the moment prior to unveiling than it is about transparency and revelation. Tied to the economics of desire, like the body that is both veil and veiled, it becomes a transit zone that cannot be possessed, but signifies a way to architecture, its rediscovery. Therefore glass can hardly be reduced to continuity or clarity, but should be considered as veiling, the most ambiguous gesture that modern architecture has yet produced: the erotic transit that promises the possibility of movement from one state to another. Transit, or Heideggerian unfolding, is based on the tension between the veil and that which it covers, between the visible and the invisible. Perceived as such, architecture is able to fuse and condense meaning rather than separate and clarify it, and thus evoke the symbolic and poetic within the modern tradition.

1 The section heading refers to the chapter "How to Make Yourself a Body Without Organs," in Gilles Deleuze and Felix Guattari, *A Thousand Plateaus* (Minneapolis: University of Minnesota Press, 1987), 149–66. The following paragraph is relevant to the move I am making, which implies dissolving of the primacy of form and spatial closure: "BwO is made in such a way that it can be occupied, populated only by intensities. Only intensities pass and circulate. . . . The BwO causes intensities to pass, it produces and distributes them in a spatium that is itself intensive, lacking extension. It is not space, nor is it in space; it is matter that occupies space to a given degree— to the degree corresponding to the intensities produced" (153).

2 Jean-Claude Schmitt, "The Ethics of Gesture," in *Fragments for a History of the Human Body*, ed. Michel Feher (New York: Zone Books, 1989), 130.

3 Agamben, *Infancy and History* (New York: Verso Books, 1996), 140.

4 Gaston Bachelard, *The Poetics of Space* (Boston: Beacon Press, 1958), 222.

5 Lefebvre, *The Production of Space* (Oxford: Blackwell Publishers, 1991), 99.

6 Mario Perniola, "Between Clothing and Nudity," in *Fragments for a History of the Human Body* (New York: Zone Books, 1989), 237.

7 Perniola, "Between Clothing and Nudity," in *Fragments for a History of the Human Body*, 242.

8 Perniola, "Between Clothing and Nudity," in *Fragments for a History of the Human Body*, 253.

9 Perniola, "Between Clothing and Nudity," in *Fragments for a History of the Human Body*, 254–55.

10 Similar ideas occur in many of other projects by Giencke, including Benedek House. Several of his unbuilt projects explore the notion even further by putting both structure and material in constant tension, as in *Judohalle* and the carpentry school.

11 Dominique Laporte, *Christo* (New York: Pantheon Books, 1986), 69.

12 Jacques Derrida, "Letter to Peter Eisenman," in *Assemblage* 12 (Cambridge, Mass.: MIT Press, 1990), 9.

13 Perniola, "Between Clothing and Nudity," 246–48.

119

120

121

122

119 Hans Scharoun, *Three by Three Dimensional House*, 1920.
120 Hermann Finsterlin, *Interior*, 1921.
121 Bruno Taut, *Crystal House in the Mountains*, 1919.
122 Bruno Taut, *Crystal House in the Mountains*, 1919.

123 Peter Behrens, frontispiece, *Feste Lebens und der Kunst*, 1900.
124 Peter Behrens, decorative illustration, 1901.
125 Bruno Taut, Glass Pavilion, Cologne, Germany, 1914. Interior view.

126 Bruno Taut, Glass Pavilion, Cologne, Germany, 1914. Interior view.

DER FELS MATTERHORN < < <

DIE BERGNACHT ·

SCHEINWERFER UND LEUCHTENDE BAUTEN

runo Taut, *The Matterhorn Studded with Crystal Ornaments,*

128 Bruno Taut, *Illuminated Glass Architecture Floodlit at Night by Colored Beacons,* 1919.

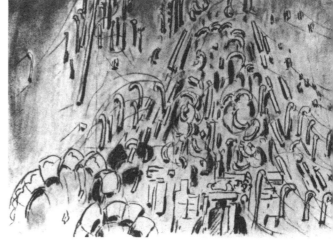

129 Bruno Taut, *The Unfolding of Space*, 1920.
130 Bruno Taut, *The Collapse of Forms*, 1920.
131 Lyonel Feininger, *The Cathedral of Socialism*, 1919. Woodcut.

132

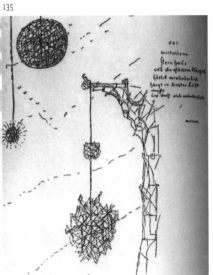

133

134

135

136

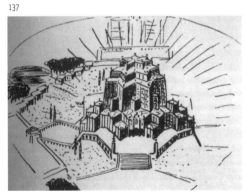

137

132 Wenzel Hablik, *Fantasy*, 1920.
135 Carl Krayl, *The Crystalline Star House and the Glass Sphere*, 1920.

133 Carl Krayl, *Rock Castle*, 1920.
136 Bruno Taut, *The Rotating House*, 1920.

134 Carl Krayl, *The Gleaming House on the Swing*, 1920.
137 Bruno Taut, *House of Heaven*, 1920.

138

139

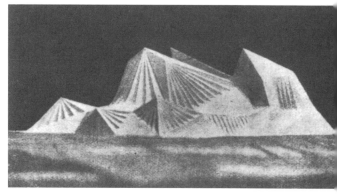

140

141

142

143

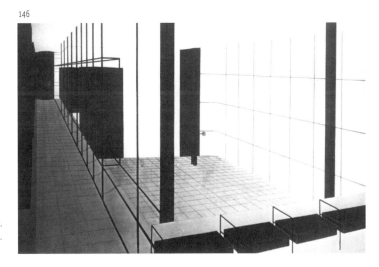

Wassili Luckhardt, untitled, 1920.

Wassili Luckhardt, *Cinema*, 1920.

Hans Scharoun, *Communal House*, 1920.

Walter Gropius, Memorial to the March Victims, Weimar,
any, 1922. View.

Philip Johnson and John Burgee, Pennzoil Place, Houston, Tex.,
Exterior view.

Philip Johnson and John Burgee, Crystal Cathedral, Garden Grove
nunity Church, Garden Grove, Calif., 1980.

Oskar Kokoschka, *Portrait of Paul Scheerbart*, 1915.

Pierre Chareau, Maison de Verre, Paris, France, 1932. Interior view.

Pierre Chareau, Maison de Verre, Paris, France, 1932. Perspective.

147

148

147 Pierre Chareau, Maison de Verre, Paris, France, 1932. Perspective.

148 Pierre Chareau, Maison de Verre, Paris, France, 1932.
Interior view.

149 Ludwig Mies van der Rohe, Friedrichstrasse Skyscraper (project), Berlin, Germany, 1920. Perspective.
150 Kurt Schwitters, Mertzbau, Hanover, Germany, 1920–26. Interior view.

151 Edvard Munch, *The Scream*, 1895. Woodcut.
152 Eric Mendelsohn, Schocken Department Store, Stuttgart, Germany, 1926–27. Exterior view.

153

154

153 George Grosz, *Friedrichstrasse*, 1918. Lithograph.

154 Ludwig Mies van der Rohe, Friedrichstrasse Skyscraper (project),
Berlin, Germany, 1920. Perspective.

Ludwig Mies van der Rohe, Glass Skyscraper (project),
–21. View of model.

156

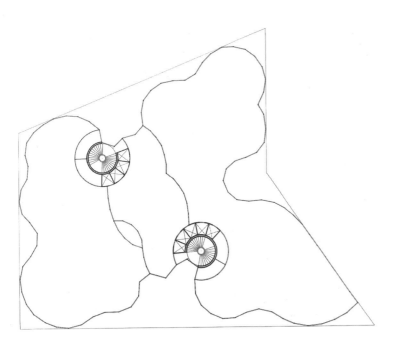

157

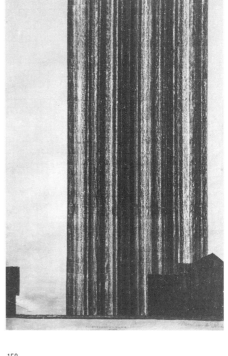

158

159

160

156 Ludwig Mies van der Rohe, Glass Skyscraper (project), 1920–21. Plan.
157 Ludwig Mies van der Rohe, Glass Skyscraper (project), 1920–21. Elevation.
158 Ludwig Mies van der Rohe, Alexanderplatz (project), Berlin, Germany, 1928. Perspective.
159 Ludwig Mies van der Rohe, Alexanderplatz (project), Berlin, Germany, 1928. Perspective.

160 Ludwig Mies van der Rohe, Alexanderplatz (project), Berlin, Germany, 1928. Perspective.
161 Ludwig Mies van der Rohe, Barcelona Pavilion, Barcelona, Spain, 1929. Exterior view.
162 Ludwig Mies van der Rohe, Barcelona Pavilion, Barcelona, Spain, 1929. Plan.

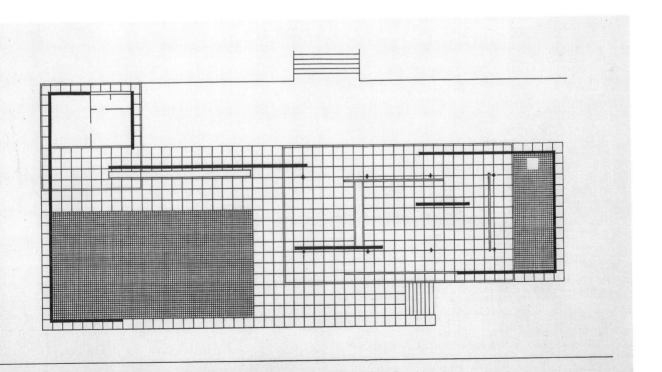

163

164

165

166

163 Ludwig Mies van der Rohe, Barcelona Pavilion, Barcelona, Spain, 1929. Interior view.
164 Ludwig Mies van der Rohe, Barcelona Pavilion, Barcelona, Spain, 1929. Interior perspective.

165 Ludwig Mies van der Rohe, Barcelona Pavilion, Barcelona, Spain, 1929. Interior view.
166 Ludwig Mies van der Rohe, Barcelona Pavilion, Barcelona, Spain, 1929. Interior view.

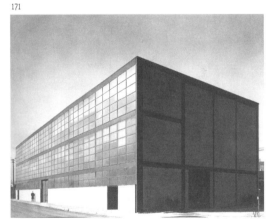

168

170

171

Ludwig Mies van der Rohe, Barcelona Pavilion, Barcelona, Spain,
9. Interior view with George Kolbe's *The Dancer*.
Ludwig Mies van der Rohe, Barcelona Pavilion, Barcelona, Spain,
9. Interior view with George Kolbe's *The Dancer*.

169 Max Ernst, "Tous les vendredis, les Titans parcourront
nos buanderies," from *La Femme 100 Têtes*, 1929.

170 Ludwig Mies van der Rohe, Illinois Institute of Technology,
Chicago, Ill., 1939. Aerial collage.
171 Ludwig Mies van der Rohe, Illinois Institute of Technology,
Chicago, Ill., 1939. View of Minerals and Research Building.

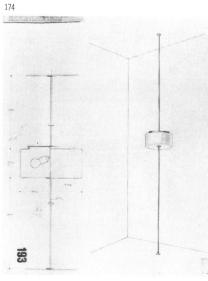

172 Ludwig Mies van der Rohe, Barcelona Pavilion, Barcelona, Spain, 1929. Exterior view.

173 Ludwig Mies van der Rohe, Barcelona Pavilion, Barcelona, Spain, 1929. Interior view.

174 Ludwig Mies van der Rohe, Tugendhat House, Brno, Czech Republic, 1928–29. Lamp placed on rod stretched from floor to ceiling. Perspective and section.

175 Ludwig Mies van der Rohe, Barcelona Pavilion, Barcelona, Spain, 1929. View.
176 Ludwig Mies van der Rohe, 860 Lake Shore Drive, Chicago, Ill., 1948–51. Exterior view.

177

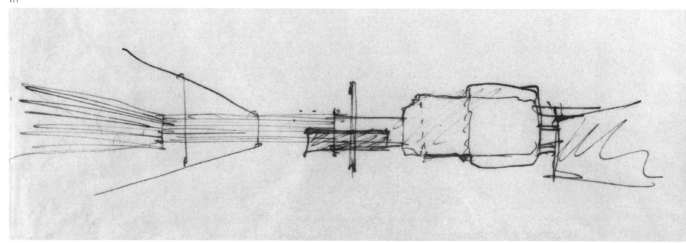

178

177 Ludwig Mies van der Rohe, Court House (project),
c.1931. Perspective.
178 Sir Joshua Reynolds, *Self Portrait*, 1747. Oil on canvas,
National Portrait Gallery, London.
179 Ludwig Mies van der Rohe, Barcelona Pavilion, Barcelona,
Spain, 1929. Interior view.
180 Ludwig Mies van der Rohe, Barcelona Pavilion, Barcelona,
Spain, 1929. Exterior view.
181 Jean Dubreuil, Prismatic anamorphosis to reduce six heads
to two profiles, from *Perspective pratique*, 1651.

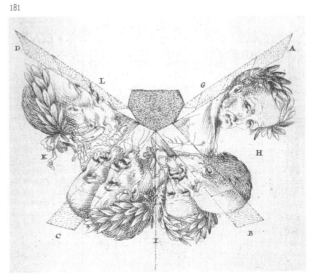

182 Ludwig Mies van der Rohe, Barcelona Pavilion, Barcelona, Spain, 1929. The small pool court. Four kinds of reflective symmetry can be observed here. The pool court itself is bilaterally symmetrical. When reflected in the green-tinted glass wall (left), it is duplicated into quadrilateral symmetry. The horizontal symmetry is emphatic. The pool makes another reflection, below, from the resulting eight-part symmetry.

183 Toyo Ito, White U, Tokyo, Japan, 1976. Interior view.

184 Toyo Ito, ITM Building, Matsuyama, Japan, 1993. Interior view.

185 Toyo Ito, University of Paris Library (project), Paris, France, 1992. View of model.

186 Toyo Ito, University of Paris Library (project), Paris, France, 1992. View of model.

187 Herzog and de Meuron, Ricola Europe Factory and Storage Building, Mulhouse-Brunnstatt, France, 1992–93. Exterior view.

188 Herzog and de Meuron, Ricola Europe Factory and Storage Building, Mulhouse-Brunnstatt, France, 1992–93. Interior view.

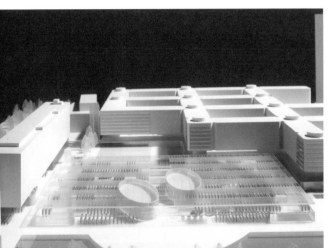

186

188

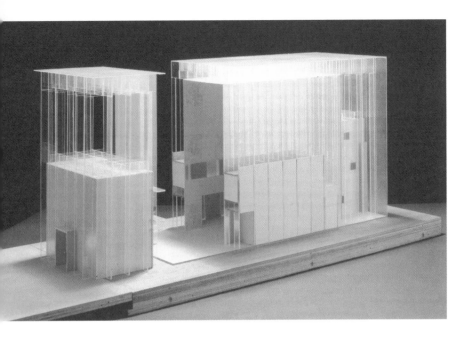

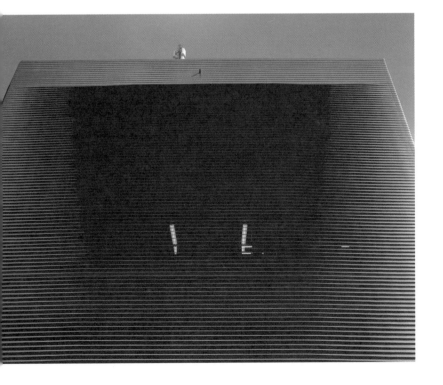

Herzog and de Meuron, Goetz Collection, Munich, Germany, 2. Interior view.

190 Herzog and de Meuron, Greek Orthodox Church (project), Zurich, Switzerland, 1989. View of model.
191 Herzog and de Meuron, Signal Box auf dem Wolf, Basel, Switzerland, 1995. Exterior view.

192 Tattoo Art.
193 Ludwig Mies van der Rohe, Barcelona Pavilion, Barcelona, Spain, 1929. Interior view.

Journal of the Society of Architectural Historians
40, no. 1 (March 1981)

THE INTERPRETATION OF THE GLASS DREAM:
EXPRESSIONIST ARCHITECTURE AND
THE HISTORY OF THE CRYSTAL METAPHOR

Rosemarie Haag Bletter

Expressionist architecture is well known for its lack of constraints and its freedom from traditional norms. In Expressionist design the basic orthogonal system that underlies most of Western architecture is mainly ignored. Like Wassily Kandinsky's introduction of abstract forms in painting, Expressionism brought to architecture a nonobjective approach. But just as we know today that Kandinsky's presumed abstractions retained a variety of allusions to representational art, so too in Expressionist architectural design it can be shown that ancient images lurk beneath the surface impression of totally revolutionary forms.[1]

Most Expressionist projects were produced after World War I by a group of architects belonging to the circle around Bruno Taut and the Arbeitsrat für Kunst (Work Council for the Arts), loosely based on the workers' soviets active in Germany during the November Revolution of 1918. Members of the Arbeitsrat had welcomed the overthrow of the Prussian Empire. And although few architectural commissions were to be had during the immediate postwar years because of a disastrous economy, these architects were euphoric about architectural experimentation possible under the new regime. At the inception of the Weimar Republic both its supporters and detractors assumed that a full-fledged socialist revolution had taken place, one that at the time seemed comparable in its impact to the Russian Revolution of the previous year. The architects' fervent belief in a new society at a time when they were without meaningful work led to a paradoxical union of intense optimism coupled with a feeling of impotence. The result can be seen in the uninhibited, free-form sketches produced by both the Arbeitsrat and by members of the Gläserne Kette (Glass Chain), an offshoot of the former group. These sketches show a frenetic attempt both to challenge and conquer at once. The style of these drawings is not easily categorized: precisely because traditional norms had been abandoned and the general preference for abstraction does not allow for the establishment of new rules, Expressionist design does not seem to have a characteristically consistent language of forms. Soft, amorphous shapes, as in Hermann Finsterlin's *Interior* (fig. 120), can be found alongside raw, jagged sketches, as in Hans Scharoun's "Glass House" (fig. 119). Or even within the work of one architect, Taut (in two designs for a *Crystal House in the Mountains*), the building is expressed on the one hand in gentle, arcuated forms (fig. 121), and, on the other, is has sharp faceted excrescences (fig. 122). The best one can say in defining the Expressionist style in terms of its forms is that no inhibiting principles seem to have been adopted. It appears to be the first style without at least a few rules. This freedom—or what some might characterize as lawlessness—in Expressionism is conventionally assumed to be an indication of extreme self-expression. The variety of forms found in both Expressionist painting and architecture are ascribed to a kind of artistic self-indulgence, as it were.[2]

A definition of style, however, cannot simply be made on the basis of characteristic forms, but must include shared attitudes and common intentions. An iconographic analysis of Expressionist design reveals a widespread adoption of specific symbolic images that belies its formal open-endedness and abstraction. Many Expressionist projects have in common the use of glass or crystal as proposed construction material. The fact that glass is a viscous material that can be molded into any desired shape leads us to assume that it might have been chosen as the perfect embodiment of Expressionism's idiosyncratic forms. Concrete, however, could also have been used to do the same job. Hence another property of glass, aside from its malleability, must have been the reason for its frequent use. A recurring motive in many of these designs (in addition to glass and crystal as material) is transparency and flexibility. Such projects, had they been built, would have produced a rich, shimmering, and illusory world of reflections. This extraordinarily unstable conception of architecture would have further enhanced the incomprehensible and abstract quality of Expressionist design. But behind such intentionally disorienting and novel forms lies an extended, if not always continuous, history of glass and crystal symbolism. Bruno Taut's statement "The Gothic cathedral is the prelude to glass architecture" and one of the couplets written by the poet Paul Scheerbart for Taut's Glass House of 1914, "Light seeks to penetrate the whole cosmos / And is alive in crystal,"[3] give a clearer indication than the designs themselves of the mystical tradition behind this imagery. That the wild, exuberant Expressionist projects quite consciously allude to a traditional, if esoteric, iconography is remarkable for a style whose formal framework seems so rebellious.

Wolfgang Pehnt in his *Expressionist Architecture* of 1973 writes correctly that the use of the crystalline imagery is a characteristic motive of Expressionism. He even cites several sources for this iconography, but then obscures its meaning by saying that Taut used crystal in a "vague, ecstatic sense."[4] Numerous statements by Expressionist architects, artists, and writers make it clear that the Expressionist crystal-glass metaphor represents a twentieth-century reincarnation, with only a few changes, of an ancient and specific iconography. If we look at the Expressionists in isolation, their preference for glass and crystal does indeed appear as a vague motive, like the preference for the S curve in Art Nouveau, for example. But it is only when we examine closely the checkered history of this symbol that we can understand its exact significance in Expressionism.

Isolated fragments of this iconographic tradition are known from medieval and Moslem architecture. Paul Frankl in his *The Gothic: Literary Sources and Interpretations through Eight Centuries* cites numerous legends containing descriptions of fantastic glass buildings, but he discusses them only in relation to the use of Gothic form and stained glass.[5] Concerning Moslem architecture, Frederick P. Bargebuhr in *The Alhambra: A Cycle of Studies on the Eleventh Century in Moorish Spain* cites many Arabic myths that allude to mysterious and powerful glass structures that might have been an inspiration for the first Alhambra palace.[6] Neither Frankl nor Bargebuhr attempt to deal with the meaning of glass imagery outside their own areas of specific interest. The significance of this iconography has never been looked at in a wider historical context. Such a comparative analysis is a necessary first step in proposing links between cultures and epochs. It is meant to be suggestive, not exhaustive.

One of the main reasons why the iconography of glass and crystal has not been traced before is that its most frequent manifestation by far has occurred in architectural fantasies largely as written proposals. These proposals represented idea constructs. And because of the preciousness of glass in preindustrial periods, coupled with its structural weakness, such projects usually remained in the realm of wishful thinking. Diaphanous structures so easily conjured up in a literary format did, nevertheless, eventually affect built form. In any case, the architectural drawings and even executed buildings can speak to us only indirectly through their forms, while myths concerning architecture are often more explicit.

The source for the earliest known versions of the glass metaphor is in the Old Testament, specifically in the person of that great mainstay of arcane wisdom, King Solomon. The biblical description of Solomon's construction of his Great Temple was to become the nucleus of later fanciful Jewish and Arabic legend concerning his architectural feats. The Old Testament story does not actually include a building of glass, but the materials that are mentioned, gold and water, will be found in close association with the later glass symbolism, forming a kind of iconographic constellation. Possibly the reflective qualities of gold and water led in the later apocrypha to their being misinterpreted as, or intentionally magnified into, translucent buildings of glass.

According to 1 Kings 6:30, the original inspiration for most of the subsequent architectural glass fantasies, the whole floor of Solomon's Temple was overlaid with gold. In 1 Kings 7:23–25 a round "molten sea" (a font) of brass resting on figures of twelve oxen is described. The long-lasting influence of such brief passages on later myths and actual buildings is not due to the architectural brilliance of these references, but to the forceful representation of King Solomon as a figure of both tremendous secular and spiritual power: he "exceeded all the kings of the earth for riches and for wisdom" (1 Kings 10:23) and the Lord himself in an apparition approved the construction of the Temple (1 Kings 9:3), making Solomon and his architecture an example well worth following.

These biblical descriptions contain only the germ of the allegorical tradition that concerns us here. The apocrypha surrounding the figure of Solomon, however, has a closer bearing on the development of architectonic symbols of glass. In a number of Jewish legends and subsequent Arabic stories inspired by them, King Solomon is said to have built a palace of glass (with glass floors) to reveal to him whether the visiting Queen of Sheba was a real woman or, as was suspected, a genie. Genies were rumored to have hairy legs and the glass floors were intended to settle that question. The Queen of Sheba, not familiar with the illusory effects of glass architecture, upon entering Solomon's palace (as the legend would have it) believed that the king was sitting in the midst of water. To step over to him across the imagined pool, she lifted her skirts to keep them dry, but thereby exposed her hairy legs.[7]

In this particular Solomonic legend, the meaning of glass architecture and its suggestion of shimmering water is quite direct and literal: it helps to reveal what would otherwise remain hidden—the true supernatural nature of Sheba.[8] In any case, the allusion to a glass floor suggesting a watery surface is most probably a coalesced vestige of the golden, reflecting floor of the biblical passage, and the "sea," or font of Solomon's Temple. The legend was then codified in Moslem tradition: a reference to Solomon's glass palace occurs in the Koran (chapter 27).[9]

In Arabic legends of the early Middle Ages, Solomon's role as patron of glass architecture expands to truly fantastic proportions. He is said to have commanded genies to construct for him an underwater dome of glass and an aerial palace or city of crystal. The following account by Abu Mansur was written approximately in the tenth century:

Solomon sees rising from the bottom of the sea a pavilion, tent, tabernacle, or tower, vaulted like a dome, which is made of crystal and is beaten by the waves. . . . The aerial city is erected by the genii at the order of Solomon, who bids them build him a city or palace of crystal a hundred thousand fathoms in extent and a thousand storeys high, of solid foundations but with a dome airy and lighter than water; the whole to be transparent so that the light of the sun and the moon may penetrate its walls.[10]

Crystal and water here have replaced the glass of the earlier story as the imagery of translucence. In later allegories these materials—glass, crystal, and even water—will be used almost interchangeably. King Solomon is also no longer just a wise and wealthy ruler, but a man imbued with supernatural powers. He has become lord of sea and air. In fact, he seems to have taken on those very powers of sorcery attributed to the Queen of Sheba in the Judeo-Christian tradition (it is as if in unmasking her, he was able to acquire her magic for himself). Solomon as a figure of supernatural powers was to influence the mystical, esoteric side of the glass metaphor during the later Middle Ages.

Of greater real consequence for the later dissemination of Solomonic architectural lore were the echoes of these legends in the built architecture of Islam. For example, the first Alhambra Palace of the eleventh century clearly evoked biblical as well as apocryphal Solomonic architecture. The Alhambra was not, of course, a glass palace, but it was intended as an analogue both to Solomon's palace described in the Old Testament and to his Koranic glass palace.

The eleventh-century Alhambra was erected for Yusuf ibn Naghralla, who was a Jew and the powerful chancellor to the Zirid kings of Granada. The fact that he belonged to a Jewish minority within a Moslem culture made the selection of a meaningful architectural prototype quite a delicate task. Solomon, whose attributes in the Moslem tradition belonged largely to the fantastic realm of magic, but who could at the same time evoke visions of a Solomonic kingdom for the Jews, provided a generally acceptable paragon. Yusuf's father, Ismail ibn Naghralla, had been chancellor before his son. Both father and son were not merely important statesmen, but also intellectuals who surrounded themselves with poets and philosophers. Both were intent on a romantic revival of the Solomonic age.[11]

Ismail ibn Naghralla had been interested in the creation of fantastic structures. This is attested by a poem he wrote describing a fountain he had built in his house:

Tell me what is the torch upon the lamp
that spouts its crystals onto a crystal base?
A stream that will not kill fire in its midst,
its waters standing like a wall and missiles,
A sky encrusted with an onyx skin
stretched over a ground of bdellium. [12]

Ismail's equation of water with crystal, and his reference to onyx and bdellium (a biblical name for rock crystal, carbuncles, or pearls) as part of the building materials for his imagined structure, bear a striking resemblance to later medieval Christian legends about the Holy Grail. The poem's architectural metaphors were based on the features of an actual fountain. Yusuf, who collected his father's poems, verified the accuracy of the images in an editorial note which precedes the poem:

The poem describes a fountain which was in his house; from its head, water poured forth and fell in the form
of a dome upon a floor of alabaster and marble; lights were set inside this "dome" and were thus covered by it;
there was also a wax light on top.[13]

The combination of glass, water, and light to form a playful architectural effect was not exceptional in Islamic court architecture of that period. A glass pavilion reportedly built for Yahya ibn Ismail al-Mamun, King of Toledo, also dates from the eleventh century:

The King of Toledo constructed in the Middle [of his palace area] a lake, in the center of which lake he built a pavilion of stained glass, and encrusted with gold. The water was caused to rise to the top of the pavilion, owing to an artful device invented by his engineers, so that the water used to descend from the summit of the pavilion, encompassing it, the various streams uniting themselves with one another. In this fashion the glass pavilion was within a sheet of water which was shed across the glass, and which was flowing incessantly while al-Mamun sat within the pavilion without being in the least touched by the water; and even torches could be lighted in it, producing, thereby, an astonishing and marvelous spectacle.[14]

This report of the King of Toledo's glass and water pavilion may be partly imaginary, but it illustrates at least that the creation of an architecture having a dematerialized and fluid nature was found desirable.

Yusuf ibn Naghralla, inspired by his father's interest in the creation of a fairy-tale architecture, had as a youth engaged in the design of elaborate water gardens.[15] And the father's vision of a new Solomonic kingdom was realized in part when Yusuf built his own palace on the Alhambra hill. Today this structure can be appreciated only indirectly (the portion of the Alhambra we see today dates from the fourteenth century) through a panegyric poem by the Hebrew poet and Neoplatonist Solomon ibn Gabirol, one of Yusuf's circle. The poem is addressed to Yusuf and contains references to his new mansion. A paraphrase of Solomon's Song of Songs, it reads in part:

The dome is like the Palanquin of Solomon
hanging above the rooms' splendours,
That rotates in its circumference, shining like
bdellium and sapphire and pearls
Thus it is in the daytime, while at dusk it looks
like the sky whose stars form constellations.

And there is a full "sea," matching Solomon's Sea,
yet not resting on ox;
But there are ions, in phalanx on its rim
seeming to roar for prey. . . .[16]

The poem's allusion to a dome which rotates and appears to be made of precious materials is almost certainly allegorical in this context. Nevertheless, the rotating dome has a long tradition in visionary architecture which may have its source in the legendary rotating dome in Nero's Domus Aurea. In Yusuf's palace the rotation was probably only implied by means of small oculus placed in the dome which would have cast fleeting light across the ceiling during the course of a day. A more direct model for such an apparently moving dome would have been the Hall of Caliphs in the palace of Abd ar-Rahman III, the tenth-century caliph of Cordoba:

The ceiling, which was made of gold and dull alabaster, was within the hall's bright-colored body of various colors. . . . .In its center the pearl was placed which the "King of Constantinople," Leo, had presented to an-Nasir. The roof tiles [visible from within the hall] of this palace were of gold and silver. In the middle of this majlis *[audience hall] was a huge cistern filled with quicksilver. On each side of this* majlis *were eight doors filled joined to [vaulting] arches of ivory and ebony, encrusted with gold and various kinds of jewels, and which rested upon columns of colored alabaster and clear beryl. Whenever the sun entered these doors, and whenever its rays struck the ceiling and the walls of the* majlis, *then a light would be created which would suspend eyesight. Whenever an-Nasir wished to awe a man present in his . . . company, he would signal one of his Slav slaves to put in motion that quicksilver, thereby light would be produced like lightning flashes which would arrest the hearts of those assembled, until it would appear to all in the* majlis, *as long as the quicksilver was in motion, that the place was rotating about them. It was said that this* majlis *circled and oriented itself toward the sun.[17]*

The later fourteenth-century Alhambra palace clearly continued the spirit of Yusuf's Solomonic fantasies. For instance, a fourteenth-century inscription at the Alhambra speaks of "that palace of glass, whoever saw it, thinks it is a body of water"[18] and another one speaks of the "palace of crystal,"[19] all references to the Koranic passage about Solomon's glass palace. And, as in some of the earlier legends, glass, crystal, and water are used as synonymous images. Because an actual glass or crystal palace was not technically feasible, the semblance of such a building was attained through allusion: water and light were used to suggest a dissolution of solid materials into a fleeting vision of disembodied, mobile architecture.

Although no other Moslem palace emulated the Solomonic legends as closely as did the Alhambra, strong evidence indicates that this grand example influenced later Moslem architecture. Even in the sixteenth century we find echoes of this tradition in the great palaces of the Mogul emperors; with their pools and water channels (which in illuminated manuscripts are often reproduced in silver like the quicksilver pool of the Hall of Caliphs) and with semiprecious stones and mirrors inlaid into their walls, those buildings still participate fully in this Solomonic fairy-tale architecture.

The second element of the tradition that will help in understanding the meaning of the later glass-crystal symbolism comes from the New Testament: the Revelation of St. John. This aspect of the iconography is better known than the Moslem strand, and at least its importance for medieval Grail legends and the Gothic cathedral has generally been acknowledged. But that the Revelation of St. John contains a number of vestiges of Solomonic legends needs to be pointed out.

In John's vision of the Lamb he sees in front of the throne "a sea of glass like unto crystal" (Revelation 4:6). This is presumably a pastiche of the biblical references to Solomon's "molten sea" and the apocryphal story in which Sheba sees Solomon enthroned in his glass-floored palace and is misled into thinking that he is sitting in water. And in this passage from Revelation, glass is again likened to crystal, an identification which had also occurred in the earlier Solomonic legends.

John's vision of the New Jerusalem, too, points up the interchangeability of light, glass, crystal, precious stones, and gold as metaphors of a transcendent life. St. John writes of the New Jerusalem, " and her light was like unto a stone most precious, even like a jasper stone, clear as crystal" (Revelation 21:11). After describing the city's foundations, measurements, and number of gates, John goes on to some of the building materials used:

And the building of the wall of it was of jasper: and the city was pure gold, like unto clear glass.

And the foundations of the wall of the city were garnished with all manner of precious stones. The first foundation was jasper; the second, sapphire; the third, a chalcedony; the fourth, an emerald;

The fifth, sardonyx; the sixth, sardius; the seventh, chrysolite; the eighth, beryl; the ninth, topaz; the tenth, a chrysoprasus; the eleventh, a jacinth; the twelfth, an amethyst.

And the twelve gates were twelve pearls; every several was one of pearl: and the street of the city was pure gold as it were transparent glass (Revelation 21:18–21).[20]

The city and its streets of gold are apparently another echo of the golden floor of King Solomon's Temple. The reflective intensity of the gold is compared to glass ("pure gold, as it were transparent glass"). Such an analogy may explain the origin of the legends of Solomon's glass structures. The gilt temple described in the Old Testament may have been compared to glass in its general effect, as is done in John's vision of the New Jerusalem. At some later point this purely metaphorical use of glass was probably misinterpreted as a reference to real glass. In any case, the association of light, gold, precious stones, crystal, and glass with the New Jerusalem, the supernatural city inhabited by the saved, was to be of tremendous importance to the conception of the Gothic cathedral and its stained-glass program as it was for the further evolution of the glass myth during the Middle Ages.

In the Middle Ages of the Old Testament, Moslem and New Testament traditions finally coalesce into a single highly eclectic whole: the apocrypha of Solomonic architecture, which had become separated into two distinct strands— a Judeo-Christian—one and an Arabic one—are reunited because of the increased contacts between the Moslem world and the West. Indeed, in the many legends surrounding the Holy Grail this syncretism is quite complex, for often Solomonic fantasies are superimposed on those connoting the New Jerusalem. From the Old Testament was taken the concept of the priest-king, from the Koran and Moslem legends the idea of a transparent and sometimes mobile structure created by magic powers, and from Revelation the notion of edifices of precious materials as an architecture of spiritual salvation and transcendence. As is to be expected, the most fantastic examples are again to be found in literary works, not in built architecture.

For example, the *Letter of Prester John* of 1165 describes the palace of a priest-king that has at its apex a carbuncle that shines at night. Outside the building, next to an arena with an onyx floor, a giant mirror reveals approaching dangers to the ruler inside.[21] The onyx floor and the mirror suggest both Solomon's glass floor and his magic powers. Nearly a century later, ca. 1250, a scribe added to the *Letter of Prester John* what appears to be the description of a building in the tradition of mobile Solomonic glass architecture: he details a *Capella vitrea*, a magic glass chapel which automatically expands to accommodate as many worshippers as enter it.[22]

One of the Grail legends, Wolfram van Eschenbach's *Parzifal*, written in 1205–14, is even more directly inspired by Islamic culture. It depicts the Holy Grail as a precious stone, dislodged from the crown of God by Lucifer's lance when he was cast out of Paradise. According to this story, the divine gem is then preserved inside a cave by Adam.[23] Most legends surrounding the Grail have at least some Near Eastern sources. Wolfram van Eschenbach's version specifically was inspired by a Provençal poet who in turn had derived his own story from an Arabic manuscript.[24] *Parzifal* bears Gnostic and alchemical overtones in its allusion to the holy stone containing the spark of divine light, hidden in the bowels of a dark cave. In this instance the Grail story suggests a dualistic image of light and dark—the Grail and the cave—a contrast also implied by the very names of the protagonists, Lucifer (bearer of light) and Adam (earth), a mystical usage that will recur in later alchemical lore.

In another legend about the Grail, Albrecht von Scharfenberg's *The Younger Titurel* of about 1270, Montserrat near Barcelona, in this story portrayed as a cliff of onyx, is chosen to bear the Holy Grail.[25] Titurel is instructed to polish the onyx cliff, after which a building plan miraculously appears on the polished surface of the rock. The exterior of this divinely designed sanctuary for the Grail is like a gigantic crown, encrusted with jewels, with a roof of gold and enamel that sparkles in the sun. At night, glowing rubies atop subsidiary towers and the light of a carbuncle at the apex of the central tower help to guide the way of the Templars to the shrine. The windows and interior are jeweled also, and the floor is described as a "crystal sea" through which one can see, as through a layer of clear ice on a lake, water and fish. This reference to the floor as a "crystal sea" betrays the origin of at least this aspect of the story as deriving from Solomonic legends.[26] The bejeweled exterior of the Grail temple, on the other hand, seems to be related to the vision of the New Jerusalem.

Whereas the earlier Grail legends may have affected Gothic architecture, later Grail stories in turn were as much influenced by the visual experience of Gothic architecture. The jeweled interior and in particular the jeweled windows of the Grail temple in the *Younger Titurel* suggest that Albrecht von Scharfenberg had in mind a temple suffused with light where a mystical union with God is made tangible through an apparently bodiless colored light, an effect comparable to the Gothic cathedral with its profusion of stained-glass windows.

Precious metals and stones were considered the best carriers of divine light. From Abbot Suger's description of his building program at St. Denis, we know that such materials were used extensively for reliquaries, crosses, and small liturgical utensils.[27] Although these same materials would have been desirable for the large window of the cathedrals, it is obvious that this was impracticable. A plausible substitute for the translucence of precious stone was stained glass. That Gothic stained-glass windows often alluded to the precious stones is revealed by the names given in the Middle Ages to various stained-glass colors; i.e., "ruby glass" or "sapphire glass."[28] The true function of stained glass was within the scope of a mystical, transcendent light: a light that illuminates the soul of the worshipper.

The religious import accorded precious materials and glass naturally affected the secular imagery of the Middle Ages as well. Luminosity became an important attribute in the definition of beauty in the twelfth and thirteenth centuries. In philosophical and courtly literature, the most commonly used adjectives of beauty were "lucid," "luminous," and "clear."[29] While the Gothic cathedral's stained-glass program continued the Biblical and Koranic traditions in which translucent and reflective materials symbolize transcendence, spiritual light, or divine wisdom, we begin to find in the secular literature of the later Middle Ages new meanings in the iconography of glass and crystal: the imagery reveals more private and personal attitudes, a change in meaning that will gradually affect its outward form.

Gottfried von Strassburg's *Tristan* of the early thirteenth century contains a description of a grotto that houses a bed of crystal. Significantly, in an appended allegorical interpretation of *Tristan* this crystalline bed is said to stand for pure and transparent love.[30] A further association between translucent matter and love made in Chaucer's poem *House of Fame* of ca. 1381, which relates that the temple of Venus appears as if it were a temple of glass. And a similar theme is versified in *Temple of Glass* by John Lydgate, a Chaucer imitator.[31] On the other hand, folk legends from around 1300 onward, usually attributed to the minnesinger Tannhäuser, depict the abode of Venus as the interior of a mountain.

The crystal bed and grotto, still found in association in *Tristan* and quite comparable to the light/earth metaphors of the Grail inside the cave of *Parzifal*, are separated into two seemingly opposing ideas in the legends surrounding the goddess of love and become a glass temple in Chaucer or the interior of a mountain in the legends attributed to Tannhäuser. Such a drastic division between the abodes of Venus, the temple of glass or the *Venusberg*, may well allude to the segregated concepts of pure and earthly love.

In the troubadour or minnesinger tradition of the thirteenth and fourteenth centuries, glass and crystal are secularized. They now symbolize pure love. More important, glass and crystal no longer solely represent the upward movement toward a transcendent realm, as the Grail legends had suggested. In larger terms, the trend may be regarded as a movement away from the extreme spirituality of the earlier Middle Ages toward a concept of man which includes both his spiritual *and* earthly manifestations. In this context it is extremely significant that in literature from about 1410 onward the site of the Holy Grail and the *Venusberg* become one and the same.[32] The quest for god and love could now be undertaken simultaneously!

Nearly all the medieval literary traditions of the glass-crystal symbolism covered to this point are summarized in a Renaissance work, Francesco Colonna's *Hypnerotomachia Poliphili* (*The Dream of Poliphilo*). In highly syncretistic fashion, the book unites the metaphors of religious mysticism and of courtly love poetry. It is interesting that *The Dream of Poliphilo* was regarded from the Renaissance until the seventeenth century as a great model for classical forms by both architects and sculptors. That they could mistake the book's mystical-medieval references for actual descriptions of ancient structures makes it clear that its symbolic language, containing the kind of spiritual message well known in the Middle Ages, had fallen into disuse. Its appeal for the post-Renaissance period lay primarily in its rich architectural fantasy, which is of interest to us also, though not because of its "classicism."[33]

In this work Poliphilo, in his quest for his ideal love, Polia, encounters Queen Eleuterilida's palace, the roof of which consists of vines and honeysuckle made of gold and precious stones. One of Queen Eleuterilida's gardens is similarly a faithful copy of nature in gold and glass. It is a world in which all of nature has been transmuted into what mystics regarded as higher forms of matter. Later in the book, when Poliphilo is reunited with Polia, they arrive at an amphitheater on the island of Cythera. Its bases and beams are made of copper gilt, and the rest of the building is a single piece of Indian alabaster which is as transparent as glass. The floor of the amphitheater's interior is a single block of polished black obsidian, reminiscent of the *Younger Titurel*'s Holy Grail site. When Poliphilo enters the building his senses are confused by the reflective floor and, believing that he is falling into a black abyss, he stumbles. But by keeping his eyes on the surrounding walls, he regains his balance and sees that the sky, the clouds, and the colonnades visible through the transparent alabaster are reflected in the polished black floor as if in a calm sea. The translucence and reflection of clouds in the obsidian floor produces a sensory dislocation which is close in spirit to the legendary encounter of Sheba with Solomon in his glass-floored palace. The fountain of Venus is in the center of this amphitheater and is, like the floor, of black obsidian. Seven columns of precious stones support a canopy of pure crystal on whose summit is a carbuncle as large as an ostrich egg, the last perhaps another echo of the *Younger Titurel*'s Grail building. In the center of this fountain Venus is revealed standing half submerged in water.[34]

The amphitheater's floor, which appears to be a sea, and the crystal-roofed fountain seem like a double reflection of the Solomonic glass legends. While *The Dream of Poliphilo* borrows quite heavily from the imagery of the Grail stories, it seems at the same time indebted to the source for earlier glass mythologems, the Solomon and Sheba story. Like Sheba, who had been deceived into lifting her skirts by being made to think that Solomon was enthroned in water, so Poliphilo encounters a metaphorical "sea" which makes him believe he is falling. But, in addition, the inner sanctum in *The Dream of Poliphilo*, its Venusberg, so to speak, is a crystal-topped fountain in which Venus is immersed, transforming the original "as if" conditions of the Solomon and Sheba myth into something more palpable. This reference, in what might be called a back-formation from all the Grail legends, is apt in the Poliphilo-Venus context, since the Solomon and Sheba story had always contained greater erotic possibilities than the rarefied, masculine world of the Holy Grail. In any case, as in the earlier medieval courtly love literature, the primary intention of *The Dream of Poliphilo* is to signify transformation from base instinct to purified love.[35]

The symbolism of transmutation suggested through glass, crystal, water, precious stones, and gold in the later Middle Ages is not only kept alive through its partial secularization in the minnesinger tradition, but is also retained as a quasi-religious, though now highly subjective, image of alchemy. The exact origins of alchemy are not known. More sources connect it to the late Hellenistic world and specifically to Gnostic ideas. Alchemical beliefs were transmitted to the West via Arabic writings and the Jewish Kabbala. Through both these sources, the wisdom of Solomon became an important inspiration for the medieval alchemist.

The basic desire of all adherents of alchemy consisted in wanting to transmute base matter into a noble material, variously called simply the *lapis*, the philosopher's stone, or *elixir vitae*. Gold, but particularly the diamond—because of its fire, transparency, and hardness—often appear as the specific carriers of this symbolism.[36] For the alchemist the search for this *lapis*, a kind of personalized Grail, was a mystical quest for gnosis and transubstantiation. Like the Grail, the philosopher's stone of the alchemist is frequently equated with Christ's transfigured body.

Despite its original spiritual intent, alchemy retains few of the altruistic principles associated with the quest for the Holy Grail. The finding of the Grail had suggested communal salvation—according to most Grail legends, the finding of the Grail promised not just the salvation of the knight who found it, but spiritual renewal for the whole realm. In the later alchemical tradition, by contrast, the quest for the Stone of Wisdom leads only to self-knowledge and individual metamorphosis. Because the Stone of Wisdom is only a symbol of the self, the crystal imagery loses all its earlier architectural dimensions. That is, when this metaphor of transformation, whether spiritual or secular, implies a general social change, it takes on architectural form, but when it stands for individual gnosis alone, the image is reduced to the shape of a stone. Gnosis and immortality, with the *lapis* as the image of the transmuted self, are discovered within oneself, and consequently introspection and self-searching attitudes become the hallmarks of the alchemist. It was precisely this egocentric mysticism that was to appeal to the sensibilities of the Romantics later on.[37] For it was basically in the hermetic form of the alchemists, as the *lapis*, that the cryptic meaning of crystal and glass was transmitted to the nineteenth century. And though the crystal metaphor during this period is stripped of its older architectonic, i.e., social, connotation, even in its reduced, vestigial form as the Stone of Wisdom the image retains the idea of transcendence and metamorphosis.

Given the esoteric nature of alchemy, it is appropriate that the alchemists chose as their guiding spirit not the biblical Solomon, but the master sorcerer of Arabic legends with power over air and land. Alchemy's uneasy balance between religious gnosis and occult science makes it clear that it could easily be debased into black magic. The metaphoric transformation of base matter into gold could be presented by the unscrupulous alchemist as a distinct possibility. The fortune-teller's crystal ball is another mongrelized form of the philosopher's stone. Because of the abuses of the pseudo-alchemists, but more because of the increasing secularization of society in the later Middle Ages, the mystic unity of alchemy broke apart into two separate strands: on the one hand, divested of its mystic import, it gave rise to such modern science as chemistry and geology. On the other hand, retaining its hermetic, occult elements, it affected the Rosicrucian movement of the seventeenth century, as well as Freemasonry.[38]

The overt crystal and glass symbolism of the Middle Ages that had become highly esoteric and had gone underground during the post-Renaissance period was consciously resurrected by writers of the Romantic age. This was usually done in an effort to bolster the quest for identity with spiritual intensity, but also to create a harmonious portrait of the past that would show an inevitable continuity between the presumed social and religious strength of the Middle Ages and the present. This was true particularly in Germany, where the lack of political unity inspired strong yearnings for a golden age, yearnings that were to increase after the Napoleonic invasion.

In the 1790s the early Romantic writer Ludwig Tieck began to renew interest in old German stories, in the legends of the Grail, and in alchemy through his own writings and through his transcription of German love poetry.[39] Sulpiz Boisserée, better known for his involvement in the completion of Cologne Cathedral, his study of Gothic architecture in general, and for his collection of old German and Netherlandish paintings (which made a deep impression on Goethe), also wrote a book about the description of the Grail temple in *Titurel*.[40] Goethe too used many elements of the Grail legend, alchemy, and Masonic imagery in a number of his works, particularly in his *Faust* and *Parable*.[41]

One of the many Romantic works,[42] Novalis's incomplete work *Heinrich von Ofterdingen* (1802) goes back most clearly to imagery of mysticism, the Grail legends, medieval love poetry, and alchemy. In this novel, the protagonist, Heinrich, encounters a palace with a crystal garden[43] comparable to the garden described in *The Dream of Poliphilo*, and is told about an even more precious garden in which silver trees with fruit of ruby stand on a crystal floor.[44] And, as in *Tristan*, Freya, the daughter of Prince Arthur, is seen on a bed of crystal,[45] echoing accurately the medieval metaphor for pure love. During Heinrich's long wanderings, as if he were in search of the Grail, he has a dream in which he sees a cave containing a fountain of trembling, moving colors. This fountain reflects a bluish light against the cave wall and water flows from the fountain into the cave's interior.[46] The dream is intended as a sign to Heinrich of his search for the true self detailed in the later sections of the novel. The metaphor of the sparkling fountain within the dark cave is similar to the Grail hidden in the cave or the alchemists' philosopher's stone or *elixir vitae* created from dark, ignoble matter. The blue color projected from the water against the cave walls prefigures the Blue Flower, a concrete symbol of Heinrich's quest for a purified identity. Indeed the Blue Flower appears to be Novalis's equivalent of the elusive *lapis*: Novalis at one point compares the Blue Flower to a carbuncle,[47] a reference that would be gratuitous without the medieval mystical background.[48]

In Novalis, then, the by now familiar imagery still carries mystical, alchemical overtones, but with this difference: the old imagery of metamorphosis is no longer introduced in conjunction with spiritual salvation. The emphasis in Novalis's exploration of dreams and the darker passages of the mind is rather on self-exploration, in finding the center of his individuality. In Novalis the dark cave and the sparkling fountain have a new coexistence. The sparkling fountain does not signify transformation of lowly matter, as it would have in the alchemical tradition, but instead, though it arises from the cave, is depicted as flowing back into the earth. This would seem to exclude any sort of spiritual transcendence. The fountain (or carbuncle) and cave here have come to stand simply for the mind in general and for the regeneration of the self specifically.

The use of mystical imagery like that found in Novalis becomes widespread in Romantic literature, but the mythological power of the older legends is usually missing. Like the mysticism of the Rosicrucians, the mystical symbolism of the Romantics loses the earlier, wider significance and becomes a language of the initiated, meaningful only to those who are already versed in it.

In the later nineteenth century this mystical tradition can still be discerned in vestigial forms. It seems to reach its most esoteric heights in Nietzsche's *Also Sprach Zarathustra*. Light/dark opposites are used to delineate Zarathustra's road to self-knowledge. He inhabits a cave on a mountain peak, a clear metaphor for the mind. The two beasts attending him, eagle and snake, are an even older variant of the ancient chthonic and celestial forces. Images of Zarathustra's self or soul are as eclectic as Nietzsche's metaphors for the struggle between earthly body and disembodied mind. Zarathustra compares his soul to a fountain,[49] a child offers him a mirror for self-reflection,[50] and he is himself addressed as the "Stone of Wisdom."[51] Alchemical metaphors of transmutation now only stand for a narcissistic self-apotheosis.

The mysticism of the Symbolist movement of the late nineteenth century brings us within the youthful experience of Expressionist architects and writers. In their attempt to redress some of the nineteenth-century excesses of scientific confidence and positivism, the Symbolists turned away from the descriptive, naturalistic style of the preceding generation and embraced a mode of expression that was tinged with Romantic sensibility, interest in the irrational, and heightened sensory awareness. Given their general anti-materialistic notions, it is fitting that the Symbolists also unearthed occult Rosicrucian symbolism. Such esoteric spiritualism must have fulfilled a quest for emotional relevance for men who might have been embarrassed to turn to any established church. This latter-day mysticism catered not merely to man's spiritual needs, but satisfied his speculative nature and his thirst for knowledge at the same time. Salvation through knowledge is a proposition of some attraction for malcontent artist-intellectuals. That the Stone of Wisdom represents the mind can only be deduced in Novalis and Nietzsche. But in a work by the Symbolist writer Alfred Jarry, in his *Exploits and Opinions of Doctor Faustroll*, written in 1895, the philosopher's stone is literally located in Vincent Van Gogh's brain.[52] The German poet Alfred Mombert and Paul Klee also identified with the brain and with images of the self.[53]

Another instance of an essentially Symbolist use of the crystal metaphor returns us to the artistic-architectural realm which is at the root of this investigation. Peter Behrens, the Jugendstil artist turned architect, presented to the assembled audience at the opening festivities of the Darmstadt Artists' Colony in 1901 a "Zeichen" (sign), which was a great crystal. Its reference to Nietzschean mysticism is clear: the last section of *Also Sprach Zarathustra*, in which Zarathustra emerges from his cave like the sun, is entitled "Das Zeichen."[54] The fact that Behrens reintegrates the image of the philosopher's stone with its older alchemical substance, crystal (something Nietzsche had not done), points to the eclectic and historicist approach of Behrens (figs. 123 and 124). He seems to return to the mystical tradition in which crystal signifies transformation. But he gives the tradition a slightly new direction: crystal stands for the metamorphosis of everyday life into a heightened artistic experience. In essence, crystal represents for Behrens an escape from reality into a world of the artist's own making, above the squalor of common life. Like Zarathustra's cave at the top of a mountain, the Darmstadt Artists' Colony, built on a height overlooking the city, suggests in clear visual terms such a stratification of society. The artist has taken up the position at the apex of the social pyramid formerly occupied by the aristocracy.[55]

Although Behrens returns the crystal imagery to an architectural setting, his specific usage is not architectonic, but is still within the Romantic literary tradition. He redefines the self-contained symbol of the philosopher's stone. It is not, of course, the Stone of Wisdom depicted in alchemical legends: Behrens's crystal Zeichen is a dramatic prop and, therefore, merely a theatrical symbol.

Not until early manifestations of Expressionism is the crystal-glass iconography again associated with architectural models. This occurs earliest, not surprisingly, in literature, in the short stories and novels of the Expressionist writer Paul Scheerbart.[56] His whimsical, witty science-fiction stories often have as their hero an architect of glass and crystal buildings. At the outset of his career in the 1890s, Scheerbart's imagery is not far removed from that of Symbolism or Jugendstil: crystalline architecture is introduced as the metaphor of individual transcendence. But in his writings of the early twentieth century (Scheerbart died in 1915) this symbolism is less solipsistic. As his proposals for glass structures grow more architectonic, there is a concurrent increase in these buildings' flexibility. Scheerbart describes a mobile glass architecture of rotating houses, buildings that can be raised and lowered from cranes, floating and airborne structures, and even a city on wheels. This interest in the literal flexibility of architecture is further augmented by the suggestion of apparent motion through the use of constantly changing lights, reflecting pools of water, mirrors placed near buildings, or glass floors which reveal the movement of waves and fish of a lake below (the last is very much like the effect of the Grail temple in the *Younger Titurel*). Such actual and apparent transformations of glass and crystal architecture—terms used interchangeably by Scheerbart—in his later works come to stand for the metamorphosis of the whole society, an anarchist society which, through its exposure to this new architecture, has been lifted from dull awareness to a higher mode of sensory experience and from political dependence to a liberation from all institutions.

Thus, the older, alchemical notion of metamorphosis, signified by the change of lowly matter into precious substance, is intensified by Scheerbart through the proposal for continually shifting forms. Although we have encountered such a conjunction of transparent materials and flexible forms in the Arabic legend concerning Solomon's airborne glass palace, in the mobile effects of Arabic architecture, or in the medieval *Capella vitrea*, whose elastic skin flexes to accommodate any number of worshippers, this heightening of images of transmutation through apparent and actual movement becomes the norm in Expressionism. The notion of a flexible, mobile architecture is used to underline the promise of the crystalline metaphor: metamorphosis and transcendence. The Expressionist architectural style is difficult to define precisely because its forms are not perceived as fixed and measurable. There is not an ideal conjunction of forms. On the contrary, if there is an ideal, it is incompletion and tension. Shifting, kaleidoscopic forms are forever moving out of chaos toward a potential perfection, a perfection which is, however, never fully attained. This is not unlike the quest for the Grail or Stone of Wisdom, which in most legends was sought but seldom or never found.

While most of Scheerbart's architectural proposals appear to spring full-fledged from his unfettered imagination, he was in reality quite aware of historical precedents. For instance, he saw his suggestions for glass architecture as improvements on nineteenth-century botanical gardens and on Joseph Paxton's Crystal Palace in particular. But he considered the mystic effect of Gothic stained glass with its suffused, colored light more suitable as a model for the synaesthetic experience he himself wished to achieve than the clear glass of nineteenth-century industrial architecture. Most important, Scheerbart had thoroughly studied Arabic culture and Sufi mysticism, and because he regarded the Near East as the cradle of glass architecture, he always held Moslem traditions in the greatest esteem. As a case in point, he regarded the dematerialized effects of the Alhambra's honeycomb vaults a worthwhile prototype for his ethereal glass architecture. Even though it is not clear whether Scheerbart knew that the Alhambra was meant to allude to Solomon's glass palace, he seems to have been aware of the general intentions behind it.

Around 1912, in the circles of Herwarth Walden's periodical *Der Sturm*, Scheerbart met the young architect Bruno Taut, who was to become one of the central figures of Expressionist architecture. During Scheerbart's few remaining years their friendship became truly symbiotic. Scheerbart dedicated his book *Glass Architecture* of 1914 to Taut, and Taut that same year dedicated to Scheerbart his Glass House, a pavilion at the German Werkbund Exhibition in Cologne (figs. 40, 125, and 126).[57] In the Glass House, the literary fantasies about glass architecture are, for the first time since Gothic architecture, again reinstated as built form.

This gemlike Glass House, with its colored glass dome set in a concrete frame, is a replica of Scheerbart's architectural ideas. Its small scale is reminiscent of late Gothic chapels and its pear-shaped dome recalls Moslem architecture. The exterior aspect of the Glass House is curious and insignificant, except for the glass spheres resembling crystal balls placed mysteriously around its base. The progression through the building was carefully controlled. From the entrance two curving stairs of luxfer prisms (fig. 125) led up to the space under the dome, the "cupola room." This cupola room was enclosed by a double skin of colored glass, one of Scheerbart's proposals to avoid the tremendous heat loss from which glazed botanical gardens suffered. This uppermost space under the dome was bathed in light, but no visual contact was possible with the outside world. From the cupola room a second set of curving stairs led back to the interior of the middle level, the level of the entrance. This circular space was enclosed by a wall of translucent silvered glass set between larger stained-glass panels created by several Expressionist painters, including Max Pechstein (fig. 126).[58] The real centerpiece of this room was a sparkling fountain, which was surrounded by a glass mosaic floor in a white, blue, and black pattern. Red case glass and gilded glass tiles covered a conical ceiling leading up to a circular opening directly above the pool of water. The light admitted through this oculus from the brighter cupola room above produced a flickering, disorienting impression as it was reflected by the fountain and the glazed surfaces. From the fountain room a water cascade flanked by two stairs led to the semidarkness of the basement. The walls enclosing the cascade stairwell were covered with polychrome glass mosaics. This display of sound, light, and color was further enhanced by long chains of glass pearls placed in the water and lit dramatically from below by lights situated under the water basins of the cascade. At the lowest level a dark tunnel, lined in soft purple velvet, led to a cave-like, completely dark "kaleidoscope room" in which abstract patterns of colored light were projected onto an opaque screen.

A walk through this building was like an alchemical rite of passage: it began in an aura of crystalline lightness, but the most intense experience occurred, paradoxically, at the end of a long, dark corridor. In Novalis-fashion the kaleidoscope inside the Glass House was hidden in the darkest recess of a cave. The primary impression of the building was theatrical, synaesthetic, and mystical. The contemporary architectural critic Adolf Behne, a friend of Taut, clearly understood the mystical intention behind the Glass House when he wrote:

The longing for purity and clarity, for glowing lightness, crystalline exactness, for immaterial lightness, and infinite liveliness found in glass a means of its fulfillment—in its most bodiless, most elemental, most flexible, material, richest in meaning and inspiration, which like no other fuses with the world. It is the least fixed of materials transformed with every change of the atmosphere, infinitely rich in relations, mirroring the "below" in the "above," animated, full of spirit and alive!

The thought of the beautiful cupola room which was vaulted like a sparkling skull, of the unreal, ethereal stair, which one descended as if walking through pearling water, moves me and produces happy memories.[59]

Although the Glass House was one of the earliest executed Expressionist buildings, to the degree that it stood for a "sparkling skull," it also clung to the Romantic-Symbolist tradition in which the crystalline *lapis* was identified with the self or brain. Another key to the hermetic nature of this building was provided by couplets composed by Scheerbart for the Glass House, such as "Light seeks to penetrate the whole cosmos / And is alive in crystal" or "Colored Glass / Destroyed Hatred."[60] These were inscribed on the fourteen-sided concrete band under the dome.

The Glass House and the Werkbund Exposition were closed prematurely in August of 1914 because of the outbreak of World War I. Paul Scheerbart died in 1915. His ideas were transmitted to the postwar generation of young architects by Taut. Because few architectural commissions could be had during and immediately after the war, Taut turned to the publication of books, pictorial treatises about glass architecture as the ideal of a utopian, generally anarchist society. In his *Alpine Architektur*, published in 1919,[61] Taut was able to respond to Scheerbart's proposals even more directly than was the case with the Glass House. Functional requirements for the Glass House had been minimal because it was an exhibition pavilion. But in his utopian tracts Taut could approach design with absolute freedom. Any limits imposed by site, materials, or economic factors were now totally absent. In *Alpine Architektur*, as if it were some megalomaniac earth art, whole mountain ranges are recut and peaks are decorated with colored glass (fig. 127). Crystal houses high up in the mountains are for quiet contemplation (fig. 121), and sparkling mountain lakes are embellished with floating, ever-changing glass ornaments. The idea of transparency, transformation, and movement is achieved by means of an illuminated glass architecture, floodlit at night by colored light beacons (fig. 128). This notion of constant change and dissolution was to become even more graphic in Taut's *Der Weltbaumeister* (*The World Architecture*) of 1920,[62] in which structures, like a kaleidoscope, form an impermanent architecture, only to dissolve and to regroup into new configurations (figs. 129 and 130).

The cyclopean reconstruction of nature in *Alpine Architektur* has no utilitarian purpose. Its sole function is to edify and to bring peace. The very process of construction is meant to serve a social, if highly Romantic, purpose: these alpine constructions are to be built communally by the masses in the same way Taut assumed Gothic cathedrals had been built. The general pacifist intent is clear from the following passage:

PEOPLES OF EUROPE!
CREATE FOR YOURSELF SACRED POSESSIONS—BUILD!

The Monte Rosa and its foothills down to the
green plains is to be rebuilt.
Yes, impracticality and without utility!
But have we become happy through utility?
Always utility and utility, comfort and convenience—
good food, culture—knife, fork, trains, toilets and yet also—
cannons, bombs, instruments of murder!
To want only the utilitarian and comfortable without
higher ideals is boredom. Boredom brings quarrel, strife, and war . . .
Preach the social idea . . .
Engage the masses in a great task, which fulfills everyone,
from the humblest to the foremost . . . Each sees in the great
communality clearly the work of his own hands: each builds—
in the true sense. . . . [63]

Taut's own evolution in giving the crystal-glass metaphor architectural form leads him from the egocentric image of the crystal brain as used in the Glass House to the utopian socialism of *Alpine Architektur*. Glass, transparency, and flexibility all signify here a purified, changed society. This new attitude was no doubt a reaction to the devastation of the war.

In 1920 Taut published another visionary tract, *Die Auflösung der Städte* (*The Dissolution of the Cities*).[64] In this text his Romantic preoccupation with the reworking of mountain ranges for a consummate society is replaced by his concern for more existential conditions. The general social structure is totally anarchist: no governments, schools, or institutions such as marriage. There are no cities, but only some small, nearly self-sufficient communes. Glass architecture is no longer as ubiquitous as it was in *Alpine Architektur*. Glass structures in *Auflösung der Städte* are centralized and few: they function as communal gathering points. In this they are the visible symbol of these anarchist communities.[65] Thus, as the notion of a perfect society is objected to at least a modicum of political reality, the proposed change is for a new kind of social nucleus rather than for the heady idealism of *Alpine Architektur*. Hence the glass structures become more programmatically focused in this later book. Taut's social concepts are elaborated on in a series of mostly socialist and anarchist quotations, listed at the end of the book, by such men as Rousseau, Lenin, Engels, Kropotkin, and also Scheerbart. The crystalline house in *Die Auflösung der Städte* concretizes for Taut the kind of unstructured society he envisioned. Glass is here no longer the carrier of spiritual or personal transformation but of a political metamorphosis.

Aside from publishing these utopian tracts, Taut also became the initiator of several working groups after the November Revolution of 1918. One of these, the Arbeitsrat für Kunst, produced manifestoes in which were debated hypothetical architectural questions inspired by the rise of a socialist government. Among many other matters discussed were the place of architectural education in the new society, whether decisions on architectural commissions should be controlled by professionals alone or whether they should be shared by laymen, and the place of architects in fostering public awareness of architecture, which was presumed to play a leading role in the reconstruction of country. Several exhibitions of architectural designs were held, some in the workers' districts of Berlin. By the spring of 1919 the Arbeitsrat had become too large and unwieldy for Taut—by 1919 it had grown to over one hundred members from its initial membership of just over fifty. Some of the better-known members of the Arbeitsrat in 1919 were the architects Otto Bartning, Paul Gösch, Walter Gropius, Ludwig Hilberseimer, Carl Krayl, Hans and Wassili Luckhardt, Paul Mebes, Eric Mendelsohn, Adolf Meyer, Hans Poelzig, Max and Bruno Taut; the painters Heinrich Campendonck, Viking Eggeling, Lyonel Feininger, Hermann Finsterlin, Wenzel Hablik, Erich Heckel, César Klein, Ludwig Meidner, Otto Muller, Emil Nolde, Max Pechstein, Christian Rohlfs, and Karl Schmidt-Rottluff; the sculptors Rudolf Belling, Bernhard Hoetger, Georg Kolbe, and Gerhard Marcks; and the critics and historians Adolf Behne, Paul Cassirer, Karl Ernst Osthaus, Wilhelm Valentiner, and Paul Zucker. Although Taut stayed on as a member, the leadership was passed on to Walter Gropius in February 1919. Gropius, however, left for Weimar shortly thereafter to become the director of the Bauhaus. Taut continued to proclaim the virtues of Scheerbart's writings in his own books as well as in the publications of the Arbeitsrat. Indeed, Gropius seemed to have read Scheerbart with great interest,[66] for the Scheerbartian crystal iconography becomes incorporated into the text of Gropius's opening manifesto for the Bauhaus of April 1919:

Together let us desire, conceive, and create the new structure of the future, which will embrace architecture and sculpture and painting in one unity and which will one day rise toward heaven from the hands of a million workers like the crystal symbol of a new faith.[67]

The text by Gropius at the same time reveals an almost medieval model of handicrafts and communal work (the interest in creating prototypes for industry, for which the Bauhaus is better known, did not become part of its curriculum until about 1923). The same attitude is borne out in Lyonel Feininger's woodcut, *The Cathedral of Socialism*, made to illustrate the manifesto by Gropius: sparkling faceted objects are affixed to the towers of a Gothic church like some visual palimpsest of the Grail temple's carbuncles and the Gothic cathedral (fig. 131).

While still a member of the Arbeitsrat, Taut had formed a small working group in late 1919, called Gläserne Kette (Glass Chain), which continued most clearly the Scheerbartian tradition of glass architecture in both its statements and designs.[68] Many of the Gläserne Kette projects were later published in Taut's magazine *Frühlicht* (*Dawn*), which appeared from 1920 through 1922, and which was the only Expressionist periodical dealing exclusively with architecture. The designs of the group of mostly architects (a few were painters who during this period turned to architectural drawing) show just how much their conceptions were indebted to the crystal-glass iconography. There are floating crystalline forms and crystalline extrusions by Wenzel Hablik (fig. 132)[69] and Carl Krayl (fig. 133) reminiscent of Scheerbart and Taut. Such drawings, which are at best proto-architectural, demonstrate how the general interest in crystallinity as a metaphor could also become the inspiration for specific architectural form. In the pages of *Frühlicht* appeared design that further clarified the association of crystal and glass with transformation, expressed in some instances quite directly as actual movement. Krayl's proposal for a swinging house, whose forms and movements are mirrored in a pool of water (fig. 134), and his design for a "crystalline star house" which rotates and which is precariously suspended in midair (fig. 135), both reflect similarly fanciful suggestions by Scheerbart. Taut's design for a revolving house of colored glass and iron is the least fantastic of these (fig. 136).[70] It looks almost like a mobile version of the Glass House of 1914. Other proposals that demonstrate the influence of the crystal metaphor on architectural conception are designs by Taut (fig. 137), by Wassili Luckhardt (figs. 138 and 139), and by Hans Scharoun (fig. 140). This relationship between meaning, the symbolic content of crystallinity, and its expressed form was not always made explicit, however. Gently undulating forms, as long as they were meant to be executed in glass, could also be carriers of this iconography. Most of Finsterlin's designs fall into this less clearly stated category (fig. 120).

Despite the use of untraditional forms, the meaning of the crystal-glass imagery can be seen as basically tradition, though pointed in a slightly new direction. Especially in Taut's hands the metaphor signifies change and transformation, but it is given a somewhat more political turn. The revival of this metaphoric tradition did not only occur through the inspiration of Scheerbart's writings, which went back to its Moslem and Gothic aspects. The Expressionist architects around Taut seemed to have been quite aware of many of the older forms of this tradition as well. In *Frühlicht*, together with designs and essays on contemporary issues, is a description of the version of the Flemish medieval mystic, Sister Hadewich, who had a Grail-like revelation in which precious stones were the carriers of the divine presence. Equally mystifying, without an understanding of the meaning of this metaphor, is the quotation, also in *Frühlicht,* of John's vision of the New Jerusalem.[71] The vision of the New Jerusalem is especially significant, for its contains elements of the crystal-glass metaphor. But more important, in contrast to an image such as the philosopher's stone, the vision of the New Jerusalem is an urban vision, not a garden of paradise, but the city of the saved. One could say that for Taut it represented the salvation of society.

By around 1920 the most intense visionary planning for glass architecture diminished. The country was still in a state of near civil war, with frequent street battles between left- and right-wing factions and a large number of political murders. The political weakness of the young Weimar Republic was becoming abundantly clear during these immediate postwar years.[72] Along with political disillusionment came the gradual demythification of the crystal metaphor. Echoes of the Expressionist crystal-glass metaphor continued after 1920, but such instances become much rarer. Most often architects either turned away from glass as the suggested building material or, when glass was still suggested, the forms of Expressionism were recollected without their metaphoric content.

One example of the former is Walter Gropius's Memorial to the March Victims in Weimar (fig. 141). This memorial was dedicated to workers who had been killed in Weimar during riots following the right-wing Kapp Putsch in March 1920. The local Trades Council commissioned this memorial and it was inaugurated in May 1922.[73] This monument is of concrete and would seem to have little to do with the iconography of glass. But when the writer Johannes Schlaf discussed the memorial in *Frühlicht* shortly after its completion, he explained its meaning in terms of crystalline transformations that to him suggested a change from inorganic to organic forms, from death to life.[74] Hence, even though the building material is not transparent, the basic meaning of the crystal is maintained.

On the other hand, in the same issue of *Frühlicht* in which the Weimar monument by Gropius was published, there appeared a brief illustrated essay by Ludwig Mies van der Rohe on his designs for glass skyscrapers (figs. 154–57).[75] Mies apparently was affected by the abstract forms of Expressionism in these proposals: both crystalline and curving forms are present and the use of glass is more extensive than it had been in any previous skyscraper design. Mies wrote that new problems cannot be solved with traditional forms and that the acutely angular plan of the Friedrichstrasse project (fig. 154) was determined by the triangular site. But despite Mies's basic pragmatism, one can say that he was, at least superficially, influenced by Expressionist designs. For he wrote further that in using glass, the forms should not be conditioned so much by the effects of light and shade as by the interplay of reflected light. This belief, more than the specific configuration of any site, explains Mies's use of unorthodox forms. The full metaphoric content of earlier Expressionist glass architecture, however, is not alluded to.

Expressionist forms, stripped of their original meaning, still affect contemporary architecture. Reyner Banham, in an article of 1959, "The Glass Paradise,"[76] for the first time called attention to Paul Scheerbart, who had been forgotten in the histories of the modern movement. Banham pointed to the connection between the visionary proposals of Scheerbart and Taut and their eventual fulfillment in Mies's Seagram Building. Today this connection seems even clearer: it can be extended to Philip Johnson's recent faceted glass buildings, such as the IDS Center in Minneapolis of 1973 with its Crystal Court, Pennzoil Place in Houston of 1976 (fig. 142), and the "Crystal Cathedral" of the Garden Grove Community Church of 1980 (fig. 143). Johnson's inspiration seems to have come not so much from the Seagram Building, on whose design he had collaborated with Mies, but straight from Mies's earlier

Expressionist glass-skyscraper designs.[77] This revival of Expressionism is, of course, interesting, but it is a continuity of forms only. One might compare this with the fate of the International Style when it was promulgated in this country in the 1930s (in which Philip Johnson also played a role). The formal characteristics of the style were praised without much discussion of the social reforms with which they had for the most part been associated. Numerous versions of faceted, crystalline designs have proliferated, especially in recent American skyscrapers. The stated justification for such forms is that they are more interesting than monotonous slabs. Changes in meaning from the Expressionist association of crystallinity could be expected in a different setting more than fifty years later. No new associations seem to have evolved, however, and any relationship to Expressionism is one of outward form, not content.

For Bruno Taut, who became one of the most important architects of workers' housing after 1923 when Germany's rampant inflation had come to a halt and building resumed, the utopian social ideal of his Expressionist phase continued in surprisingly pragmatic ways. The crystal-glass metaphor disappeared from his executed architecture at this time. First of all, glass was simply too expensive a material to use extensively. To be sure, there were indirect references to stained glass in the vividly colored stucco Taut used for most of his housing schemes. It must be said, though, that color was used not just as an aesthetic or metaphoric device, but to give visual and urbanistic coherence to large groups of buildings, resulting in a fair balance between the utopian and the down-to-earth sides of his architecture. Secondly, once Taut was engaged in large-scale social housing programs—he was responsible for about ten thousand dwelling units during the 1920s in Berlin—the yearning for a transformed society no longer seemed necessary. The crystal image, symbol of the new society for Taut, had become obsolete: the change had taken place.

Within the glass and crystal tradition, then, the imagery of transcendence and metamorphosis has itself undergone a transformation. Beginning with the Solomonic legends, continuing in the Revelation of John, Moslem architecture, Grail legends, the Gothic cathedral, and culminating in that late echo of the Middle Ages, Colonna's *Hypnerotomachia Poliphili*, the glass-crystal metaphor had generally been expressed through more or less architectonic concepts. But with alchemy and later the Romantic and Symbolist movements, the imagery of transformation shed most of its architectural manifestation. It became a rudimentary pebble, an image of the soul or brain as this symbol became identified solely with the transformation of the self. The return in the early twentieth century to the older, more architectonic format in the works of Scheerbart, Taut, and a large number of other Expressionists signified a turning away from introspection toward a search for social identity and community. Though this metaphor was often a rather cryptic sign, it could be adapted from a religious to a personal and finally to a social context. Looking at the whole iconography of glass, one can no longer insist that Expressionist architecture constitutes mere idiosyncratic self-expression. Those very aspects of Expressionist design that appear on first glance to be its most revolutionary ones—transparency, instability, and flexibility—on closer examination turn out to be its most richly traditional features.

1 The basic outline of this paper was presented in a talk to the New York chapter of the Society of Architectural Historians in February 1968. In its current form it is an abbreviated and adapted version of chapter 4 of my dissertation "Bruno Taut and Paul Scheerbart's Vision: Utopian Aspects of German Expressionist Architecture," Columbia University, 1973. For help with the dissertation I am indebted to George R. Collins, Edgar Kaufmann, Jr., my sponsors, and Theodore Reff. For helpful advice on the present manuscript I wish to thank Richard Brilliant and François Bucher.

2 Such an attitude is implied in W. Pehnt, *Expressionist Architecture,* trans. J. A. Underwood and E. Küstner (New York: Praeger Publishers, 1973). See my review of this book in *JSAH* 37 (1978): 131–33.

3 B. Taut, *Glashaus–Werkbund-Ausstellung Cöln* (Berlin, 1914), motto drawing of Glass House. Scheerbart's aphorisms for the Glass House appear in a letter to Taut of February 10, 1914, which is reprinted in "Glashausbriefe," *Frühlicht,* supplement of *Stadtbaukunst Alter und Neuer Zeit* 3 (1920): 45–48.

4 Pehnt, *Expressionist Architecture,* 37–41. The Song of Songs, cited by him as a source, does not contain any reference to this imagery. Though he mentions Ernst Toller's play *Die Wandlung* (The Transformation), he overlooks the clue to the meaning of the crystal iconography contained in its very title.

5 P. Frankl, *The Gothic: Literary Sources and Interpretations through Eight Centuries* (Princeton, N.J.: Princeton University Press, 1960).

6 F. P. Bargebuhr, *The Alhambra: A Cycle of Studies on the Eleventh Century in Moorish Spain* (Berlin: de Gruyter, 1968).

7 Ginzberg, *The Legends of the Jews* (Philadelphia: Jewish Publication Society of America, 1954 and 1946), 4: 145 and 6: 289.

8 However, Solomon's apparent immersion in water also has erotic implications: Sheba's Arabic name is Bilkis, which seems to be related to the Hebrew word for concubine (Ginzberg, *Legends,* 6: 289).

9 F. P. Bargebuhr, "The Alhambra Palace of the Eleventh Century," *Journal of the Warburg and Courtauld Institutes* 19 (1956): 229.

10 Bargebuhr, "The Alhambra Palace of the Eleventh Century," 116, 257–58 n. 116.

11 Bargebuhr, "The Alhambra Palace of the Eleventh Century," 197.

12 Bargebuhr, "The Alhambra Palace of the Eleventh Century," 212.

13 Bargebuhr, "The Alhambra Palace of the Eleventh Century," 211–12.

14 Bargebuhr, "The Alhambra Palace of the Eleventh Century," 248 n. 60.

15 Bargebuhr, "The Alhambra Palace of the Eleventh Century," 211.

16 Bargebuhr, "The Alhambra Palace of the Eleventh Century," 199. Bargebuhr uses the reference to the lion fountain as major evidence that the fourteenth-century Alhambra was based on and continued many of the ideas introduced by Yusuf's palace. Further evidence is in the typical Zirid construction (horizontal lines of bricks inserted between oblong patches of small, usually round unshaped stones), found in the lower walls of the Alhambra, which Bargebuhr believes to be remains of Yusuf's palace.

17 Bargebuhr, "The Alhambra Palace of the Eleventh Century," 228–29.

18 Bargebuhr, "The Alhambra Palace of the Eleventh Century," 229.

19 Bargebuhr, "The Alhambra Palace of the Eleventh Century," 117, 268 n. 117.

20 Revelation was also influenced by Ezekiel's vision, in which the splendor of the spiritual realm in associated with precious stones. However, the meaning of the crystal metaphor is not as lucid as in Revelation, as can be seen in these passages from Ezekiel:

And the likeness of the firmament upon the heads of the living creatures was as the color of the terrible crystal, stretched forth over their heads above. (1:22)

And above the firmament that was over their heads was the likeness of a throne, as the appearance of a sapphire stone; and upon the . . . throne was . . . the appearance of a man. . . . And I saw as the color of amber, as the appearance of fire round about within it from the appearance of his loins even upward, and from the appearance of his loins even downwards, I saw as it were the appearance of fire, and it had brightness round about. (1:26–27)

Later Jewish commentaries on the Scriptures also refer to crystal and precious materials in describing paradise (Midrash Konen and the midrash attributed to Rabbi Joshua ben Levi, for example). Though they are claimed to be old texts, they were most likely written in the early Middle Ages. See *The Jewish Encyclopedia,* ed. I. Singer (New York, 1964) 9:516.

[21] Frankl, *The Gothic*, 168–69.

[22] Frankl, *The Gothic*, 175.

[23] Wolfram von Eschenbach, *Parzifal*, trans. H. M. Mustard and C. E. Passage (New York: Vintage, 1961); *Wolfram von Eschenbach's Parzifal und Titurel*, 4th ed., ed. K. Bartsch, (Leipzig, 1927); Frankl, *The Gothic*, 177–79.

[24] Wolfram von Eschenbach's own claim as the Arabic source of his material is discounted by R. S. Loomis in his "The Origin of the Grail Legends," *Arthurian Literature in the Middle Ages* (Oxford: Clarendon Press, 1959) 292–93. Loomis believes that the origin of the Grail legends must be sought in Welsh and Irish lore. See also A. C. L. Brown's similar attitude in *The Origin of the Grail Legend* (New York: Russell and Russell, 1966). Indeed a number of motives in Welsh and Irish stories would seem to justify this contention. Several of the legends include references to a city of glass, to a castle of glass, island of glass, glass pillars, etc., associated with fairy-tale settings originally, but very early on confused with the Land of the Dead (Brown, *Origin of the Grail Legend*, 89). The meaning of such references is, therefore, not very clear, and, in any case, citations of glass imagery are quite cursory and certainly not as fully developed as glass architecture is in the Arabic tradition. Interestingly, F. Anderson in *The Ancient Secret–In Search of the Holy Grail* (London: Gollancz, 1953) has suggested that Celtic folktales were influenced by Solomonic legends (see particularly her chapter 12, "The Sea of Glass"). In any case, many architectural motives in the Grail legends indicate a quite direct connection with the Solomonic tradition. Near Eastern and Solomonic sources for the Grail legends are discussed by L. I. Ringbom, *Graltempel und Paradies; Beziehungen zwischen Iran und Europa im Mittelalter* (Stockholm, 1951). and F. Kampers, *Das Lichtland der Seelen und der heilige Gral* (Cologne, 1916). Frankl also believes that the source for *Parzifal* is an Arabic one (*The Gothic*, 179), though it must be said that the variously proposed influences on the Grail legends are not necessarily mutually exclusive.

[25] B. Röthlisberger, *Die Architektur des Graltempels im Jüngeren Titurel* (Bern, 1917); G. Trendelenburg, *Studien zum Gralraum im Jüngeren Titurel* (Göppingen, 1972); and Frankl, *The Gothic*, 176, 180–82.

[26] Such a figure of speech depends probably on Solomon's "molten sea" and its mongrelization in later legends to a glass floor.

[27] *Abbot Suger on the Abbey Church of St. Denis and Its Art Treasures*, ed., trans., and annotated by E. Panofsky (Princeton: Princeton University Press, 1946). For the influence of reliquaries on architectural conceptions see F. Bucher's "Micro-Architecture as the 'Idea' of Gothic Theory and Style," *Gesta*, 15 (1976): 71–89.

[28] J. R. Johnson, *The Radiance of Chartres* (New York: Random House, 1964), 53–66.

[29] O. von Simson, *The Gothic Cathedral* (New York: Pantheon Books, 1956), 50.

[30] Frankl, *The Gothic*, 173. See also *The "Tristan and Isolde" of Gottfried von Strassburg*, trans. and annotated by E. H. Zeydel, (Princeton: Princeton University Press, 1948).

[31] Frankl, *The Gothic*, 194.

[32] Frankl, *The Gothic*, 194–95. Though Frankl cites these examples and describes architectural references contained in them, he does not discuss the meaning of these legends.

[33] For Colonna's influence on post-Renaissance architecture see M. S. Huper, *The Architectural Monuments of Hypnerotomachia Poliphili* (Ann Arbor: University Microfilms, 1956); and A. Blunt, "The Hypnerotomachia Poliphili in Seventeenth-Century France," *Journal of the Warburg Institute* 1 (October 1937): 117–37. Frankl, who is only concerned with the Gothic quality of Colonna's architectural descriptions, does not relate this work to the Solomonic tradition.

[34] For a mystical, alchemical interpretation of this work see L. Fierz-David, *The Dream of Poliphilo*, trans. M. Hottinger (New York: Pantheon Books, 1950).

[35] Similar glass and water images together with architectural fantasies can also be found in Hieronymus Bosch's *Garden of Earthly Delights*. The general theme here, however, no longer refers to the gentle courtly troubadour tradition, but it is shown is a more earthly manifestation, lust. Thus the ladies depicted half-submerged in a circular pool of water and the couples enclosed in glass spheres are not transmuted by their environment, but are trapped as in prisons. This is comparable to the depiction of the original fairyland as a nether world in Celtic folktales (see n. 24).

[36] C. G. Jung, *Psychologie und Alchemie* (Zurich: Rascher Verlag, 1944), 574.

[37] According to C. G. Jung, alchemy was based on fantasy and illusion, but at the same time served a psychotherapeutic function in that it projected the psychic process of individuation onto chemical transformations. In Jung's opinion this represents the emerging conflict between individuality and collectivism, between the self and society, a conflict which does not fully surface until the nineteenth and twentieth centuries (*Psychologie and Alchemie*, 644).

38 M. Eliade, *The Forge and the Crucible*, trans. S. Corrin (New York: Harper and Row, 1962); G. H. Hartlaub, *Alchemisten und Rosenkreuzer* (Willsbach and Heidelberg, 1947); W. E. Peuckert, *Die Rosenkreuzer; Zur Geschichte einer Reformation* (Jena, 1928); F. L. Pick and G. N. Knight, *The Pocket History of Freemasonry* (London, 1963). In addition to the better-known rose and cross, the Rosicrucians also used the crystal as a symbol. Rosicrucians and Freemasons claimed ancient Arabic origins. The Freemasons, in particular, used the Temple of Solomon as an archetypal model. What interested them, however, was not so much Solomon's biblical attributes, but more his prowess as a sorcerer associated with him in Arabic lore.

39 In Tieck's story "Dr getreue Eckart und der Tannenhäuser" (1799), for instance, the medieval story of the Venusberg served as inspiration. Also, in his "Runenberg" (1802) crystal imagery is used in connection with a supernatural, seductive woman, comparable to Tannenhäuser's Venus (*Märchen und Geschichten*, ed. P. Ernst (Munich and Berlin, n.d.), 1:121.

40 S. Boisserée, *Über die Beschreibung des Temples des Heiligen Grales in dem Heldengedicht: Titurel*, Vol. 3 (Munich, 1834).

41 A. R. Raphael, *Goethe and the Philosopher's Stone; Symbolic Patterns in "The Parable" and the Second Part of "Faust"* (London, 1965). Goethe's *The Parable* of 1795 is also discussed by E. A. Santomasso ("Origins and Aims of German Expressionist Architecture: An Essay into the Expressionist Frame of Mind in Germany, Especially as Typified in the Work of Rudolf Steiner," dissertation, Columbia University, 1973) as one of the sources for Wenzel Hablik's use of crystalline forms in his drawings. Though Goethe's story is full of alchemical and Masonic images—there is gold hidden in a cave and there is a crystalline bridge as in some Grail legends—the temple described by Goethe is not "crystalline," as claimed in Santomasso (150). Goethe's use of the crystal metaphor is basically Romantic; i.e., nonarchitectural. Santomasso's inclusion of *The Parable*, together with medieval and later sources, as a precedent for Hablik's use of crystallinity to signify very broadly a paradisaic setting or the presence of divine will is, however, appropriate, because Hablik himself seldom transformed the crystal imagery into anything more than proto-architectural conceptions (see also n. 69).

42 The resurrection of alchemical lore is by no means confined to works of the German Romantic period. For instance, there is the early Romantic tale *Vathek* by William Beckford, the patron of Fonthill Abbey, that well-known example of Neogothic taste (W. Beckford, *Vathek*, with an introduction by R. Garnett [London: Lawrence and Bullen, 1924]. This book was first published in the 1780s in English and French editions). The metaphors of alchemy are commingled with those of romantic love. *Vathek* contains the description of a labyrinthine subterranean palace in which the hero encounters the king and prophet Soliman. Soliman's heart, enveloped in flames, is visible through his bosom, which is "transparent as crystal" (166).

43 Novalis, *Schriften*, ed. E. Heilborn (Berlin, 1901), 1, 126.

44 Novalis, *Schriften*, 89.

45 Novalis, *Schriften*, 121.

46 Novalis, *Schriften*, 7.

47 Novalis, *Schriften*, 191.

48 The general association of diamond and Blue Flower is also mentioned by Jung (*Psychologie und Alchemie*, 151). In addition to such an esoteric symbol as the Blue Flower, Novalis also makes use of the better-known alchemical imagery; the search of the philosopher's stone is symbolized more generally by a miner who searches for gold in the bowels of the earth (Novalis, *Schriften*, 72).

49 F. Nietzsche, *Thus Spake Zarathustra*, trans. T. Common (New York: Modern Library, 1917), 117.

50 Nietzsche, *Thus Spake Zarathustra*, 95.

51 Nietzsche, *Thus Spake Zarathustra*, 165.

52 *Selected Works of Alfred Jarry*, ed. R. Shattuck and S. W. Taylor (New York, 1965), 236. Jarry's *Dr. Faustroll* was published in part in 1895; the complete work was published posthumously in 1911—Jarry had died in 1907. During Faustroll's travels in search of knowledge, the hero encounters nearly all the symbols of spiritual transformation current at one time or another. Jarry's eclecticism takes us all the way back to the probable origins of this mythology, Solomon's glass palace, as is clear from this passage:

His female retainers, whose dresses spread out like the ocelli of peacocks' tails, gave us a display of dancing on the glassy lawns of the island: but when they lifted their trains and walked upon this sward less glaucous than water, they evoked the image of Balks, summoned from Sheba by Solomon, whose donkey's feet were betrayed by the hall's crystal floor, for at the sight of their capripede clogs and their fleece skirts we were seized with fright and flung ourselves into the skiff lying at the foot of the jasper landing-steps. (*Selected Works*, 209–12)

Jarry's work was better known in the early twentieth century than it is today. Marinetti in his proto-Futurist periodical *Poesia*, for example, published Jarry alongside the German poets Arno Holz and Richard Dehmel, both friends of Peter Behrens and Paul Scheerbart.

[53] Mombert, whose intensity and gnostic imagery make him a forerunner of Expressionist poetry, as early as 1896 had identified the crystal with the self in his poem "Der Glühende" (The glowing). See A. Mombert, *Dichturgen* (Munich, 1963), 90. The crystal becomes totally identified with the brain in his poem "Der Held der Erde" (The world of hero) of 1914:

Felsen aus Opal, aus Bergkristall.
Die hüten das Obere.
Sie sammeln das Welt-Licht. Und senken es
Grünbläulich, schillernd, herunter ins Haus –
Purpur; Gold; violette Bläue – :
Hereunter in mein kristallen Hirn.

Rocks of opal, of rock-crystal.
They protect the higher.
They gather the world-light. And lower it
Green-blue, scintillating, down into the house – :
Purple; gold; violet blueness – :
Down into my crystal brain.
(*Dichtungen*, 471; my translation)

Paul Klee also identified the crystal metaphor with the self, as is clear from this phrase used in his *Diaries* in 1915: "I thought I was dying, war and death. But can I really die, I crystal" (V. Miesel, ed., *Voices of German Expressionism* [Englewood Cliffs, N.J.: Prentice Hall, 1970], 80).

[54] S. O. Anderson, "Peter Behrens and the New Architecture of Germany—1900–1917" (dissertation, Columbia University, 1968), 47–67. Anderson's thesis contains a detailed discussion of Behrens's dependence on Nietzschean imagery. He also explains Behrens's use of the crystal as a symbol for transformation:

The symbolism of the crystal relies on a metaphorical relationship between transformations which take place at the micro- and macro-cosmic levels; for example, just as mere carbon under tense conditions assumes a particular crystal structure and becomes prized diamond, so the power of art may transform everyday life into a resplendent life filled with meaning. ("Peter Behrens," 24)

A briefer discussion of Behrens and the Darmstadt Artists' Colony appears in S. Anderson, "Behrens' Changing Concept," *Architectural Design*, 39 (February 1969): 72–78.

[55] The new social order suggested by this undertaking is made even more explicit by the fact that the artists' colony was financed and supported by the ruler of Hesse, the Grossherzog Ernst Ludwig, whose palace in the city was in a real sense below the artists' settlement overlooking the city. Wassily Kandinsky in his *Concerning the Spiritual in Art*, first published in 1912, was to speak of a similar social pyramid with the artist at its apex (trans. M. Sadleir, F. Golffing, and H. Osertag [New York: Wittenborn, Schultz, 1947]).

[56] See my "Paul Scheerbart's Architectural Fantasies," *JSAH*, 34 (May 1975): 83–97. Scheerbart had been using crystal imagery long before 1901, and because he was a close friend of the writers Richard Dehmel, Otto Julius Bierbaum, and Otto Erich Hartleben, who had all been associated with Peter Behrens at the Darmstadt Artists' Colony, it is quite possible that Behrens's overt use of the crystal was influenced by Scheerbart.

[57] P. Scheerbart, *Glasarchitektur* (Berlin, 1914). This has been republished (Munich, 1971), with a postscript by W. Pehnt and with a Scheerbart bibliography. An English translation can be found in *Glass Architecture by Paul Scheerbart and Alpine Architecture by Bruno Taut*, ed. D. Sharp, trans. J. Palmes and, S. Palmer (New York: Praeger, 1972). Taut's Glass House was discussed and illustrated in P. Jessen, "Die Deutsche Werkbund-Ausstellung Köln, 1914," *Jahrbuch des Deutschen Werkbundes* (1915): 1–42; and in F. Stahl, "Die Architektur der Werkbundausstelung," *Wasmuths Monatshefte für Baukunst* 1 (1914–15): 200.

[58] At the time Taut was engaged in the design of the Glass House he published an essay "Eine Notwendigkeit" (A necessity) in *Der Sturm*, 4 (February 1914): 174–75, which contains his proposal for an ideal building in which all the arts would be unified. This essay reveals his awareness of the work of Kandinsky and other Expressionist artists and sculptors.

[59] A. Behne, "Gedanken über Kunst und Zweck dem Glashaus gewidmet," *Kunstgewerbeblatt* 27 (October 1915): 4; my translation.

[60] The whole set of aphorisms composed by Scheerbart for the Glass House—not all were used because the building was not big enough—are listed in Scheerbart, "Glashausbriefe," 45–48. An English translation appears in *Glass Architecture*, ed. D. Sharp.

[61] B. Taut, *Alpine Architektur* (Hagen, I. W., 1919). A poor English translation of this appears in F. Borsi and G.K. König, *Architettura dell'Espressionismo* (Genoa, 1967). A better translation can be found in *Glass Architecture*, ed. D. Sharp, though the claim made in the introduction that Taut was an untrained architect is not correct.

62 B. Taut, *Der Welbaumeister–Architektur-Schauspiel für Symphonichemusik* (Hagen, I. W., 1920). All illustrations and an inferior English translation of the captions appear in Borsi and König, *Architettura dell'Espressionismo*, 246–55.

63 Taut, *Alpine Architektur*, plate 16; my translation.

64 B. Taut, *Die Auflösung der Städte* (Hagen, I. W., 1920). All illustrations and an English translation of the captions can be found in Borsi and König, *Architettura dell'Espressionismo*, 276–87. The quotations by other writers and political theorists at the end of the book, however, are not reproduced in Borsi and König.

65 This notion of the glass structure as the focus of society is stated even clearer in Taut's *Die Stadtkrone* (The City's Crown) (Jena, 1919). A few of its illustrations appear in Borsi and König, *Architettura dell'Espressionismo*, 273–75, but without the supporting text. *Die Stadtkrone*, though published in 1919, was begun in early 1916 and completed in early 1918; i.e., it was written before the Revolution (see Junghanns, *Bruno Taut–1880–1938*) and to this extent reflects earlier attitudes to city planning. *Walter Gropius and the Creation of the Bauhaus in Weimar–The Ideals and Artistic Theories of its Founding Years* (Urbana: University of Illinois Press, 1971), 124 n. 93.

66 M. Franciscono, *Walter Gropius and the Creation of the Bauhaus in Weimar–The Ideals and Artistic Theories of its Founding Years*, 124 n. 93.

67 H. M. Wingler, *The Bauhaus*, trans. W. Jabs and B. Gilbert (Cambridge, Mass., 1969), 31.

68 *Die Gläserne Kette, Visionäre Architekturen aus dem Kreis um Bruno Taut 1919–1920, Ausstellung im Museum Leverkusen, Schloss Morsbroich, und in der Akademie der Künste* (Berlin, 1963).

69 Hablik seems to have been the only one of these designers whose crystal imagery derived form an interest in crystals in nature. He began to design in aerial, mobile colonies as early as 1908 and continued such projects into the mid-1920s. These flying settlements were not usually of glass or crystal, however. On the other hand, when he discussed the use of crystal and glass, as late as 1922, it was done in terms of the older Romantic and Symbolist manner: he writes of changing the darkness of houses, hearts, and brains into transparent glass (W. A. Hablik, "Die Freitrangende Kuppel," *Frühlicht*. 3 (Spring 1922): 94-98. For further discussion of Hablik see also Santomasso, *Origins and Aims of German Expressionist Architecture*, 129 ff.

70 According to the index in *Stadtbaukunst*, of which *Frühlicht* was a supplement in its first year of publication, this is a design by Bruno Taut. Pehnt in *Expressionist Architecture*, fig. 377, and D. Sharp in *Modern Architecture and Expressionism* (New York, 1966), 69, attribute this design to Max Taut. In the republication of *Frühlicht* (*Bruno Taut–Frühlicht*), ed. U. Conrads, Ullstein Bauwelt Fundamente 8, Berlin, 1963. (17,68) the same design is attributed to Hablik. The handwriting seems to be that of Bruno Taut, however. The caption states that it was to be built in 1914 for a Mr. Mendthal.

71 "Aus den Visionen der Schwester Hadewich," *Frühlicht* 11 (1920): 188. Revelation, chapter 21, is cited in *Frühlicht* 8 (1920): 125. In the slightly abridged republication of *Frühlicht* most of these references to the older mystical tradition have been left out.

72 For a general history of this period see A. J. Ryder, *Twentieth Century Germany: From Bismarck to Brandt* (New York, 1973); and F. Stern, *The Failure of Illiberalism: Essays on the Political Culture of Modern Germany* (New York: A.A. Knopf, 1972).

73 The dating of this memorial varies widely from publication to publication. The Bauhaus leaflet reproduced by J. Willett, *Art and Politics in the Weimar Period–The New Sobriety, 1917–1933* (New York: Pantheon Books, 1978), 50, however, states that the inauguration took place in May 1922.

74 J. Schlaf, "Das Neue Denkmal in Weimar," *Frühlicht* 4 (Summer 1922): 107.

75 [L.] Mies van der Rohe, no title, *Frühlicht* 4 (Summer 1922) 122–24.

76 R. Banham, "The Glass Paradise," *Architectural Review* 125 (February 1959): 87–89.

77 See for instance pp. 38, 226, and 271 in *Writings / Philip Johnson*, forward V. Scully, intro. P. Eisenman, commentary R. A. M. Stern (New York: Oxford University Press, 1979).

Architecture Review
No. 745 (February 1959)

THE GLASS PARADISE
Reyner Banham

The public were less surprised by Lever House (fig. 61) than was the architectural profession—and this was logical, for had not a massive body of opinion-making machinery been telling them, since the mid-1920s, that modern architecture was just a lot of glass boxes? Architects, on the other hand, knew that between the glass legend and the concrete fact there was a great gulf fixed—a gulf forty years wide and as deep as the building industry.

In spite of near-misses like Gropius's *Faguswerke*, and any number of exhibition buildings, in spite of Mies van der Rohe, Lever House was still the first of the glass towers to realize a seminal concept that has lurked in the mind of the Modern Movement since before the First World War. The reasons for this extraordinary lack of phasing may be traced back to the movement's own view of itself, and particularly to its tendency to try to tidy up its own history as it goes along.

The respectable genealogy of the glass legend is primarily the work of two men: one was Herman Muthesius, father of the *Deutscher Werkbund*, who wrote in his *Stilarchitektur und Baukunst* of 1902 of the beauties of the Crystal Palace (figs. 59 and 60) and the Galerie des Machines, station halls, covered markets, and most of the totemic objects of the glass dream—a pioneer reassessment of the nineteenth century. The other is Sigfried Giedion, whose *Bauen in Frankreich* of 1928 related the architecture of his contemporaries back to Muthesius's canon of nineteenth-century masterpieces, and interpolated, with a great historical subtlety and erudition, a philosophy common to both. His contemporaries were, of course, delighted to find that they were following such distinguished precedents, most of which were unknown to them until they opened the book.

But if these precedents were, in practice, unknown to them, what precedents did they follow, what motives drove them? What, in fact, had been said and done to further the glass dream between 1902, when Muthesius pointed the way, and 1929, when Giedion's book was shortly followed by others by, e.g., Artur Korn or Konrad Werner Schulz, which dealt specifically and exclusively with glass in building?

One can point first to two respectable contributions, Meyer's *Eisenbauten*, before the First World War, and the *Ingenieurbauten* of Lindner and Steinmetz after it, which both drew attention to buildings of the type originally praised by Muthesius, but were not particularly slanted toward glass. One also sees that Bauhaus teaching, and the example of the Bauhaus buildings in Dessau must have turned men's minds in the direction of transparent membranes, even though Le Corbusier's first *pans de verre* were still, so to speak, around the corner of a white rendered wall. But in all these there is no sign of the singing tones of prophecy, the incantatory repetitions that give a material those symbolic powers, over and above the recommendations of reason, that make it a live component in architecture.

It is to Germany, in the months immediately preceding and immediately following the First World War, that we have to turn to find that prophetic tone, to the period bracketed by the completion of the glass wall of *Faguswerke*, late in 1913, and the second 1920, glass-tower project of Mies van der Rohe (figs. 155–57). Both of these are accounted works of the party of reason, yet both, on examination, are found to have some curious cousins. Mies's glass towers have been justly called Expressionist, while their contemporaries, from Gropius's side, include the first Bauhaus proclamation with its gushing rhetoric about buildings "like crystal symbols," and a three-spired Gothic cathedral on its cover.

All this is commonly written off as an aberration due to "Post-war Berlin." But if it was, then it was an aberration that gripped a generation, and must have been more in it than meets the eye. In fact, there is a great deal in it, a great deal of the Modern Movement's disreputable ancestry, but as far as the glass legend is concerned, there are two dominant strains, both traceable back to the Werkbund's exhibition in Cologne in 1914. The importance of that exhibition for the glass dream is known, and acknowledged in every history by an illustration of one of the staircases of Gropius's office block in its glass hemicylinder. But that is only half the story.

There was also at Cologne for that exhibition a pavilion devoted to the glory of glass exclusively, a pavilion that demonstrably had a far greater immediate effect on the imagination of German architects than Gropius's did, for sundry descendants of it can be identified in designs done after the war, including Mies's first, faceted design for the Friedrichstrasse skyscraper. The pavilion cannot be comfortably fitted into the history of the Modern Movement—particularly if that history, like Giedion's, is slanted for continuity—because it is so wrong for its time: a primitive geodesic dome of steel and glass, raised on a drum of glass bricks containing staircases with glass treads and glass risers, a design imbued with the homogeneity and visual certainty that Gropius's office block so conspicuously lacks, even allowing for differences in function and form.

The Glass Pavilion (figs. 40, 125, and 126) was the work of Bruno Taut, and so far exceeds every other design from his drawing board that one may properly inquire what lies behind it. The clue is given by Konrad Werner Schulz: it was *Paul Scheerbart gewidmet*, and this Paul Scheerbart was *der literarischer Vorläufer und Anreger moderner Glasarchitektur*. Now, the statement that the literary forerunner and instigator of modern glass architecture was Paul Scheerbart will probably come as a complete surprise to English-speaking readers and to many German-speaking readers as well. In German architectural literature his name is unknown outside the works of Schulz, Platz (two brief references in *Baukunst der neuesten Zeit*), and some forgotten books by Bruno Taut. In English, there is a glancing reference in Giedion's *Walter Gropius: Work and Teamwork*, but not a word in *Space, Time and Architecture*.

The oblivion into which Scheerbart's name has fallen suggests—and how rightly—that he is not to be numbered among Modern Architecture's respectable ancestors. Handbooks of German literature, unanimously unaware of his architectural interests, record an almost spherical bohemian layabout—and Kokoschka's portrait (fig. 144) confirms this—a fringe-member of the Futurist-Expressionist *Sturm* group, born in 1863 and dead in 1915, the author of fascinating novels, mostly short and decorated by his own hand in Yellow Book style. Many of these novels can best be described as contra-science-fiction, astral pantomimes, moon romances, astral novelettes, and what-have-you. Beyond this, his output included appendices to the Munchausen legend, Harem romances, an *Eisenbahnroman* that appears to be the pioneer of that genre of literature whose chief ornament is the *Madonna of the Sleeping Cars*, a "Hippopotamus" novel (of which more in due course), and a telegraphic romance called *The Mid-ocean Hay-fever Sanatorium*, in whose very title one perceives something of the vein of practical logic that runs through his one work specifically devoted to the arts of building, *Glasarchitektur*, published in 1914.

Dedicated, as one might have guessed, to Bruno Taut, it is a slim, soberly presented volume, quite unlike his novels in typography and format, and runs about a chapter to a page—some of the chapters no more than single thoughts noted in a couple of sentences—for 125 pages. These chapters are only loosely connected, though not much more loosely than those of Le Corbusier's *Vers une architecture*, and like that work they expound an unpredictable mixture of uninhibited vision and sharp practicality. Both the vision and the practicality draw their strength from the things that Scheerbart knew at first hand or had seen with his own eyes—glazed verandas, palm-houses, public halls, searchlights, zeppelins, sanatoria, mirror-paneled café interiors, theosophist publications, the Cologne pavilions of Taut (explicitly) and Gropius (by inference), and much more besides. The vision he offers is a compound of all these, torn from their contexts, and reassembled by a mind unrestrained by conventional ideas and received opinions, but buttressed by a shrewd idea of what will, and what won't work.

The vision of a glass world

. . . as entirely delectable as the gardens of the Arabian Nights. . . a paradise on earth. . . we shall show no longing for the paradise of heaven

begins with something that was common knowledge to Scheerbart and most of his readers, the glazed conservatory. This he envisaged becoming even larger and more important until it had to be emancipated from the house, and set up independently in the garden. The glass-world citizen then abandons his old house and moves into the conservatory, which is aesthetically linked to the garden (floodlit at night) by glass walls and screens that extend its structure into its surroundings. As a habitable environment, the conservatory-house, which Scheerbart seems to envisage as something like Taut's glass pavilion, has double walls of colored glass carried in a reinforced concrete frame clad in mother-of-pearl or mosaic. Its floors were to be of colored ceramic tiling, its furniture of glass with brightly enameled steel legs and upholstery of glistening glass-fiber cloth. Artificial light was to enter the rooms from sources between the double glazing, and from hanging lamps of oriental style, the heating under the floor.

The landscape in which the jewel-like house and its floodlit garden is situated is to be a diffuse metropolis, with air-navigation beacons winking from the tops of its taller buildings. Illuminated trains, cars, and motorboats, like blazing jewels, traverse the night scene, while overhead, zeppelins, brightly lit themselves, and shedding light over the land, cruise toward an air-terminal in a park of experimental glass buildings, one of which is a hangar whose roof-space is occupied by an exhibition of models of historic airships, all with their own miniature lights ablaze. The shore line of the Swiss lakes, the outlines of the smaller Alps are picked out in brilliantly lit glass hotels, the summits of the higher peaks are floodlit in color. Venice—or a new moveable Venice—is a cluster of huge pyramidal buildings, glazed and illuminated and doubled by their reflections in the calm sea. Tourists, no longer hurrying from distraction to distraction, move calmly from the contemplation of one glass wonder to another.

About this vision certain things need to be said. Its inspiration was certainly personal—Scheerbart, it appears, was often poor, cold, and miserable in squalid surroundings, and had an acquired hatred of the ill-lit and oppressive atmosphere of congested masonry cities. Hence the diffuse planning of the glass dream-world, the gardens and the greenery. Hence, too, the dedicatory motto he pronounced at Taut's Cologne Pavilion

Das Glas bringt uns die neue Zeit
Backsteinkultur tut uns nur Leid

(Glass brings us the new age
Brick culture does us only harm)

and his insistence that the "metropolis in our sense" must be dissolved. But Scheerbart, unlike some of the glass-enthusiasts of later generations, was under no illusion that glass was in itself a universal panacea. He had too much practical sense for that, and he knew the weakness and side effects of its use. He knew that it was all too pervious to heat, and insists frequently on the need for double glazing. He knew also of the greenhouse effects it can produce, and insisted that glass architecture was for the temperate zones, and not the tropics nor the polar regions. He knew that his call for *Mehr Farbenlicht!*—More colored light!—that runs through the whole book could only reasonably be answered when electricity was more cheap and plentiful than at the time he wrote. When hydroelectric power came in, he prophesied, then even private persons will have floodlighting in their gardens. He knew from Taut that the making of convincing models of glass buildings awaited more tractable materials than the picture-glass and brass strip then in use, and looked forward to developments in transparent plastics (he names a forgotten proprietary product: Tektorium). Beyond that again, he looked forward to even better materials than glass for full-sized buildings, and identified laminated glass (*zwischen zwei Glasplatten eine Zelluloïdplatte*), which had only just come in, as an example of what should be looked for from a lively and developing technology, for

We stand at the beginning, not the end, of a culture-period.
We await entirely new miracles of technology and chemistry.
Let us never forget it.

This optimistic view of technology puts him at one with the Futurists, whose works he certainly knew, and in this, as in his long-range prophecies, he is clearly of the party of progress, a member of the mainstream of modern architectural thought. Where he is conspicuously outside that mainstream is in the detail aesthetics of his vision. Whether or not he knew any Tiffany interiors, he certainly knew and admired individual pieces of Tiffany glass, and its aesthetics, notably the nuanced colors that he calls *die Tiffany-Effekte*, inform many of his visualizations. To this must be added an insistence on ornament based on mineral forms and vegetation—perhaps like Louis Sullivan's—and a strong strain of conscious orientalism that directs his thoughts on light fittings, cloths and fabrics, floor coverings, tile-work, and so forth.

Here, in fact, we see him headed against the supposed tide of Modern Movement ideas. As Charles Mitchell pointed out some time ago, the idea of good modern design for which we have settled is a profoundly classical idea, in opposition to the anti-classicism of much of the nineteenth-century thought. Scheerbart was no classicist, and for an entirely logical reason: *Hellas ohne Glas*—Greece without Glass. Equally logical, he admired those cultures that delighted in colored glass, in the Orient and in Gothic Europe. Equally logical again, he combated the classicist polemics of Adolf Loos (by implication if not by name) against ornament.

But—and still perfectly consistent—he also saw Gothic architecture as the true forerunner of the great glass and iron structures of the nineteenth century that he admired quite as much as Muthesius ever did, and in this linking back of the *Grands Constructeurs* to the Gothic spirit, he is at one with the French Rationalist tradition from Viollet-le-Duc to Auguste Choisy, the tradition that produced most of the buildings that were featured in *Bauen in Frankreich*. Again, his orientalisms, gothicisms, his interest in theosophy and light-mysticism, which all seem a mile away from mainstream Modern Movement ideas, are no distance at all away from the frame of mind in which Johannes Itten created one of the greatest glories of the Modern Movement, the Bauhaus preliminary course. The Bauhaus connection cuts even closer than this—much of the text of the first proclamation, where it deals with eliminating the barriers between brain-worker and artisan, directly echoes the apocalypse of Scheerbart's *Immer Mutig* (the Hippopotamus novel referred to above) where

Kings walk with beggermen, artisans with men of learning

and the three-spired cathedral in Lyonel Feininger's woodcut (fig. 131) on the cover is now seen to be topped, not—as has been supposed—by three stars of Bethlehem, but by three navigation lights for zeppelins.

One could pursue the matter further, into the ever-ramifying but ever more attenuated influence of Scheerbart as it runs into the 1920s—including perhaps the glass towers of Le Corbusier's *Plan Voisin de Paris*, for they are close cousins to Mies's Friedrichstrasse project, and their form with emphatic vertical accents was later written off by Le Corbusier as a mistake peculiar to German architecture. But the mere pursuit is not the point—it is the necessity and attractions of the pursuit that are the point. Why, in a word, do we have to rewrite the history of the Modern Movement?

Not because that history is wrong; simply because it is less than life-size. The official history of the Modern Movement, as laid out in the late 1920s and codified in the 1930s, is a view through the marrow-hole of a dry bone—the view is only possible because the living matter of architecture, the myths and symbols, the personalities and pressure-groups, have been left out. The choice of a skeletal history of the movement with all the Futurists, Romantics, Expressionists, Elementarists, and pure aesthetes omitted, though it is most fully expressed in Giedion's *Bauen in Frankreich*, is not to be laid to Giedion's charge, for it was the choice of the movement as a whole. Quite suddenly modern architects decided to cut off half their grandparents without a farthing.

In doing so, modern architecture became respectable and gutless; it entered on what Peter Smithson has justifiably called its Academic phase, when it became a style with books and rules, and could be exported to all parts of the Western world. But having set itself up as something more than a style, as a discipline of pure reason, it had to double-talk fast and frequently to explain its obsession with certain materials, particularly glass and that smooth white reinforced concrete that never existed outside architects' dreams and had to be faked in reality with white rendering. Clearly, these materials were symbolic, they were totemic signs of power in the tribe of architects. But while concrete has never lacked respectable medicine-men, from Auguste Perret to Pierluigi Nervi, to maintain its *mana*, the image of Gropius as the official witch-doctor had never looked very convincing. On the other hand, the fanaticism of a Bruno Taut possessed by the spirit of Paul Scheerbart, as by a voodoo deity, has much more the air.

This is not to say that we now throw away the history of glass in modern architecture as it has been established so far—the position of Muthesius and Gropius among its prophets is not demolished, only diminished. We have to find some space for Scheerbart, as Giedion now clearly recognizes. The problem, which is not to be settled by a single article, is—how much space? As to his right to that space there can be no further doubt, for if one applies to him the normal test for missing pioneers, that of prophecy uttered in the right ears at the right time, he scores more heavily than many other writers of his day. Not only were his architectural writings known and in varying degrees influential among the generation of Gropius and Mies van der Rohe, but at a time when many spoke of steel and glass, he also spoke of water as the natural complement of glass, of the need to temper the white glare of light through glass by the use of colored tinting, when he spoke of America as the country where the destinies of glass architecture would be fulfilled, and he spoke of the propriety of the "Patina of bronze" as a surface. In other words, he stood closer to the Seagram Building than Mies did in 1914. To put him back into the history of modern architecture is to shed upon it precisely what he would have us shed upon it—*Mehr Farbenlicht!*

GLASS ARCHITECTURE
Paul Scheerbart

Honi soit qui mal y pense.
Dedicated to Bruno Taut

1 ENVIRONMENT AND ITS INFLUENCE ON THE DEVELOPMENT OF CULTURE

We live for the most part in closed rooms. These form the environment from which our culture grows. Our culture is to a certain extent the product of our architecture. If we want our culture to rise to a higher level, we are obliged, for better or for worse, to change our architecture. And this only becomes possible if we take away the closed character from the rooms in which we live. We can only do that by introducing glass architecture, which lets in the light of the sun, the moon, and the stars, not merely through a few windows, but through every possible wall, which will be made entirely of glass—of colored glass. The new environment, which we thus create, must bring us a new culture.

2 THE VERANDA

Obviously the first thing to tackle is something quickly done. To start with, therefore, the veranda can be trans-formed. It is easy to enlarge it, and to surround it on three sides with double glass walls. Both these walls will be ornamentally colored and, with the light between them, the effect of the veranda in the evening, inside and out, will be most impressive. If a view of the garden is to be provided, this can be achieved by using transparent window-panes. But it is better not to fit window-type panes. Ventilators are better for admitting air.

In a modest way, it is thus comparatively easy for any villa-owner to create "glass architecture." The first step is very simple and convenient.

3 THE BOTANICAL GARDENS AT DAHLEM

We already have glass architecture in botanical gardens. The Botanical Gardens at Dahlem near Berlin show that very imposing glass palaces have been erected. But—color is missing. In the evening sunlight, however, the Palm House and the Cold House look so magnificent that one has a good idea of what could be achieved if color were exploited. The Palm House is particularly interesting: outside, the seemingly unsupported iron* construction; inside, the framework of wood glazing bars, so that no rust-water accumulates and the iron can be repainted again and again. Wood, because of its impermanence, is not an impressive material. The worst thing, though, is that the glass walls are single and not double; in consequence, the expenditure on winter heating is simply enormous. In one of its guidebooks, the management recounts with unjustified pride that in winter, in a single day with a temperature at 8:00 A.M. of -10 degrees centigrade, a load of 300 centners** of best Silesian coal is consumed. That, it will be conceded, is rather excessive and not a fit source of pride. Heating expenses of this sort should have been coun-tered with double glass walls.

*Throughout the translation of *Glasarchitekur* the German word *Eisen* is given as "iron."
**About 15 tons.—Ed.

4 DOUBLE GLASS WALLS, LIGHT, HEATING AND COOLING

As air is one of the worst conductors of heat, the double glass wall is an essential condition for all glass architecture. The walls can be a meter apart—or have an even greater space between. The light between these walls shines outward and inward, and both the outer and the inner walls may be ornamentally colored. If, in so doing, too much light is absorbed by the color, the external wall may be left entirely clear; it is then advisable simply to provide the light between the walls with a colored glass shade, so that the wall light in the evening does not dazzle on the outside.

To place heating and incandescent elements between the walls is in most cases not to be recommended, since by this means too much warmth or cold is lost to the outer atmosphere. Heating and cooling elements, however, can be suspended like lamps in the interior, where all hanging lights are to some extent superfluous, since light is distributed by the walls.

In the first instance it is clearly advisable to build glass houses only in the temperate zones, and not in the equatorial and polar regions as well; in the warmer climates one could not do without a white reinforced concrete roof, but in temperate zones this need does not arise. To provide floor heating and cover, electrically heated carpets are recommended.

5 THE IRON SKELETON AND THE REINFORCED CONCRETE SKELETON

An iron skeleton is of course indispensable for glass architecture. This will inevitably stimulate an extraordinary upsurge in heavy industry. How to protect iron from rust has not yet been solved in a satisfactory manner. There are many methods of counteracting rust, but so far we do not know which is the best. The simple protective coating, long in vogue, leaves much to be desired aesthetically. The glass architect must surely think of something better to offer. But we can confidently leave this to future developments.

If we are ready to allow larger dimensions to the structural frame, for not every particle of the glass house has to be of glass, a reinforced concrete skeleton is well worth thinking about, for it has proved itself so admirably as a building material that nothing more need be said about its merits here. Reinforced concrete can also be handled artistically—either with color or to aesthetic effect by designs cut with the chisel.

6 THE INNER FRAMEWORK OF GLASS SURFACES

The iron or reinforced concrete skeleton virtually frames the glass, but the glazed surfaces must have another smaller inner frame. For this purpose in the Botanical Gardens, as already mentioned, impermanent wood was used. Instead of wood a durable material must now be found. Iron is certainly more lasting, but has to be protected against rust, which can be done by nickelling or coating with paint. The latter, as has been said before, is aesthetically displeasing and has to be renewed often. Perhaps reinforced concrete is an ideal building material here, as it does not take up so much surface.

Various other new building materials might be considered, but these have not yet been sufficiently tested for them to be thought of as entirely credible materials suitable for framing glazed surfaces. It is the technical man's problem, and he will surely find the right answer. In any case, only very strong and rust-free materials are potentially appropriate; wood is not durable and in iron constructions should only be used as a last resort. Wood is no longer used in bridges either; they are built entirely of iron and reinforced concrete. Similarly, glass architecture is half-iron architecture. Heavy industry has consequently won a completely new market, which is bound to raise the consumption of iron tenfold.

7 THE AVOIDANCE OF WOOD IN FURNITURE AND INTERIOR DECORATION

Inside the glass house, too, wood is to be avoided; it is no longer appropriate. Cupboards, tables, and chairs must be made of glass if the whole environment is to convey a sense of unity. This will naturally be a grievous blow to the wood industry. Nickel-steel would, of course, have to be decorated with enamel and niello, so that the furniture may create a striking aesthetic effect—like extremely fine wood-carving and wooden cabinets inlaid with other woods. Wood is to be avoided, because of its impermanence, but the use of iron in iron-glass construction lies along the natural line of development.

8 THE FURNITURE IN THE MIDDLE OF THE ROOM

It will surely appear self-evident that the furniture in the glass house may not be placed against the precious, ornamentally colored glass walls. Pictures on the walls are, of course, totally impossible. Given the highest intentions, this revolution in the environment is inevitable. Glass architecture will have a tough fight on its hands, but force of habit must be overcome. Ideas derived from our grandparents must no longer be the deciding influence in the new environment. Everything new has to wage an arduous campaign against entrenched tradition. It cannot be otherwise, if the new is to prevail.

9 THE LARGER VERANDA AND ITS INDEPENDENCE OF THE MAIN BUILDING

Whoever has provided his veranda with color-ornamented glass on three sides will soon want to have more glass architecture. One thing leads to another, and to stop the process is unthinkable. So the veranda continues to grow; in the end it emancipates itself from the main building, and may become the main building itself. To promote this evolution of the veranda will be the chief task of every glass architect.

10 GARDEN HOUSE AND PAVILIONS

The ancient Arabs lived far more in their gardens than in their castles. For this reason garden houses and kiosks were very quickly developed by them. Unluckily, since perishable wood was their constant choice of building material, nothing remains of this Arabian garden architecture.

The task of the modern architect, therefore, is to use only the best iron and reinforced concrete materials for garden houses and pavilions, and to encourage double color-ornamented glass walls everywhere in the garden. In introducing glass architecture, it is best to begin with the garden; every owner of a large garden will want to have a glass garden house.

11 STONE FLAGS AND MAJOLICA ON GARDEN PATHS

In their gardens, the Arabs had patterned floors of stone and majolica; they thus transferred their taste for carpets to their gardens. The Dutch have copied this from the Arabs.

Modern glass architects will be well advised to pave their garden paths with stone and majolica tiles, for in this way the splendor of the glass palaces will be worthily framed.

12 MAGNESITE AND THE PERFECT FLOOR COVERING FOR THE HOUSE

We can now hardly avoid considering many new building materials, but only by way of suggestion. Jointless magnesite floors have much to recommend them; but whether they are equally suited to the house, with its colorful glass walls, is not so easily decided. In any case, many other materials obviously come into the picture as the perfect floor covering—even stone "parquet," consisting of stones arranged like mosaic. But magnesite should be very durable, and therefore good. Inside the house one will have to be sparing with color for the floor, in order to achieve a contrasting effect with the walls.

13 THE FUNCTIONAL STYLE

The reader might gain the impression that glass architecture is rather cold, but in warm weather, coolness is not unpleasant. Anyhow, let me make it clear that colors in glass can produce a most glowing effect, shedding perhaps a new warmth. What has been said up to now takes on a somewhat warmer atmosphere. I should like to resist most vehemently the undecorated "functional style,"* for it is inartistic. It has often been adopted before in other contexts, and this is happening once again.

For a transition period, the functional style seems to me acceptable; at all events it has done away with imitations of older styles, which are simply products of brick architecture and wooden furniture. Ornamentation in the glass house will evolve entirely of its own accord—the oriental decoration, the carpets, and the majolica will be so transformed that in glass architecture we shall never, I trust, have to speak of copying. At least, let's hope so!

14 THE CLADDING OF BUILDING MATERIALS AND ITS JUSTIFICATION

A housefront faced with perishable plaster is clearly reprehensible, and a single coat of paint, which is not weatherproof, is obviously not permissible. Architects have therefore declared any cladding unjustifiable and display the brick front completely naked. A ghastly sight! Brick is only effective if it has weathered and has the character of a ruin—when it looks like a ruin. The ancient Egyptians faced their brick pyramids with smooth granite slabs. These have not been destroyed, but stolen. If the latter occurs, preservation is naturally out of the question. A cladding of an inferior material is, in my opinion, fully justified.

Since, nowadays, there are very many buildings which cannot be replaced in a day by glass structures, we may reasonably give some thought to durable facing materials for factories, harbor installations, etc. Enameled panels of iron and majolica are particularly suitable. Old walls, brick "fences," stables, and so on can be clad in this way. Houses, too, can be given a passable veneer with roof-gardens, if large numbers of glass pavilions are erected in them.

---

* The German word here is *"Sachstil"* (author's quotes).—Ed.

15 THE FINISHING AND PLASTIC TREATMENT OF REINFORCED CONCRETE

Reinforced concrete is a building material which is very strong and weather-resistant. It has been rightly acclaimed by architects as the ideal material. A pity that it is not transparent: only glass is.

But reinforced concrete is unsightly if left in its natural state. A smooth finish to reinforced concrete, which is perfectly feasible, is therefore much to be recommended; the finish should also be able to take weather-proof color. In addition, reinforced concrete should be provided with plastic decoration; it is as easy to work with the chisel as granite. Granite is not exactly easy to work, but it can be done.

16 ENAMEL AND NIELLO APPLIED TO METAL PANELS ON REINFORCED CONCRETE

If thin metal panels can be pressed into the surface of reinforced concrete during casting, these can be given an enamel coating—possibly one of transparent *cloisonné* enamel.* Small surfaces can also be hollowed out and filled with niello,** although lacquered niello is only suitable for interiors. Externally, metal niello would be very effective, but only precious metals should be used; the patina of bronze would also be suitable. Glass mosaic, too, is an obvious possibility.

17 GLASS FIBERS IN APPLIED ART

It has been forgotten by many that glass can be developed as fibers which can be spun. The story goes back more than forty years, perhaps further. I am not sure. These glass fibers may lead to a whole new industry in applied art; divan covers, chair arms, etc., can be made of them.

18 THE BEAUTY OF THE EARTH, WHEN GLASS ARCHITECTURE IS EVERYWHERE

The face of the earth would be much altered if brick architecture were ousted everywhere by glass architecture. It would be as if the earth were adorned with sparkling jewels and enamels. Such glory is unimaginable. All over the world it would be as splendid as in the gardens of the Arabian Nights. We should then have a paradise on earth, and no need to watch in longing expectation for the paradise in heaven.

19 GOTHIC CATHEDRALS AND CASTLES

Glass architecture is unthinkable without Gothic. In the days when Gothic cathedrals and castles were rising, an architecture of glass was also tried. It was not completely realized, because iron, the indispensable material, was not yet available, and this alone enables the totally glass room to be constructed. In Gothic times, glass was entirely unknown in most private houses. Today it is a principal factor in the architecture of every house. But it still lacks color. Color, however, will come.

20 ANCIENT GREECE WITHOUT GLASS, THE EAST WITH AMPULLAE AND MAJOLICA TILES

In ancient Greece glass was almost unknown. But before the Hellenic civilization there were already many colorful glass ampullae and lustrous majolica tiles in the countries bordering the Euphrates and Tigris, a thousand years before Christ. The Near East is thus the so-called cradle of glass culture.

*A pattern of raised metal strips, filled in with transparent enamel.
**A black compound worked into a pattern cut into the surface.

21 GLASS, ENAMEL, MAJOLICA, AND PORCELAIN

All building materials which are durable and obtainable in weather-resistant colors have the right to be used. Brittle brick and inflammable wood have no such right; a brick building is also easy to shatter by explosives, which endanger the whole building equally. This is not the case in a glass-iron building; only partial destruction can be induced by explosives in the latter.

Wherever the use of glass is impossible, enamel, majolica, and porcelain can be employed, which at least can display durable color, even if they are not translucent like glass.

22 THE EFFECTS OF TIFFANY

The famous American Tiffany, who introduced the "Tiffany glass," has by this means greatly stimulated the glass industry; he put colored clouds into glass. With these clouds the most marvelous effects are feasible—and the walls acquire an entirely new charm, which admittedly puts the decoration into the background, but in particular situations is quite practicable.

23 THE AVOIDANCE OF THE QUICKSILVER EFFECTS OF MIRRORS

If the dangers of Tiffany effects may not be wholly ignored—they are only dangerous, after all, in inartistic hands—one should only allow the quicksilver effects of mirrors a utilitarian existence in the dressing-room. In the other rooms of the house mirror-effects, which continue to reflect their surroundings again and again in a different light, disturb the general architectural impression, for they do not last. When kaleidoscopic effects are wanted, they are perfectly justified. Otherwise it is best to do without the quicksilver-mirror; for it is dangerous—like poison.

24 THE AVOIDANCE OF FIGURE REPRESENTATION IN ARCHITECTURE

While architecture is spatial art, figure-representation is not spatial art and has no place in architecture. The animal and human body is made for movement. Architecture is not made for movement, and is concerned with formal composition and ornament. Only the plant and mineral kingdoms should be exploited—better still the whole repertoire of free invention—one should not think of the animal and human body as a design element. The fact that the ancient Egyptians did so is no reason at all for doing so today; we no longer associate our gods with the bodies of animals and humans.

25 THE LANDSCAPE ARCHITECT AND THE TREE AND PLANT WORLD IN THE ROCOCO PERIOD

The Rococo period treated trees and plants as if they were moldable clay; to create perspective effects trees were shaped like walls and yew hedges clipped into geometrical figures. At the same time, the architect ruled the garden, which he should do today. But such laborious treatment of plant and tree material does not pay—because of the changing seasons and transitory results.

More glass walls in the garden would give it quite a different aspect, linking the garden to the architecture of the house, if the latter is glass architecture. It is scarcely imaginable what wonderful effects could be achieved in this way. An occasional mirror-wall close to pools is worth considering. But not too many.

26 THE DOOR

In our technical age developments occur rapidly; we often forget this. There is no reason to think that they will suddenly slow down. Fifty years ago there was not a single town in Germany with main water and drainage. Fifty years later one cannot imagine a home without a vacuum cleaner. And there will be many other things which now strike us as utopian, although those which are now feasible, like glass architecture, should never be so described.

The door in the glass house, for example, will be unlike those most commonly found today in brick houses. Self-closing doors are commonplace nowadays, but self-opening doors will be equally common soon. The outside doors do not need to open by themselves, but if the inside ones are self-opening, it is like a friendly gesture by the householder, although he does not have to make any movement with his hands. The mechanism is actuated by treading quite lightly on a sensitive plate. It already exists in Berlin pubs, and has been fully worked out and patented. The idea can be extended; rotating crystal elements—or flashing lights—can be set in motion in doors; a friendlier greeting than that of a liveried supercilious servant.

The doors can be made of transparent glass with crystal effects, and of ornamentally colored glasses. To every room, then, its own particular entrance. This should create a more festive atmosphere. The outside doors can also be of glass.

Cities in their present form are not yet fifty years old. They can vanish as quickly as they came. Even the permanent way of the steam railway is not immortal.

27 THE CHAIR

The most complicated item in the whole of applied art is the chair. The steel chair seems to be an aesthetic impossibility, yet steel can be made so splendid with enamel and niello that it need not fear comparison with the finest Venetian carving. The prices of enamel and niello chairs are far from being higher than those for carved wood chairs, for which 400–500 marks are willingly paid. Enamel work is so cheap that enameled chairs can be produced very well for 100 marks apiece.

Of course, an industry which turns out identical chairs by the score will have to be disregarded. But one can reasonably expect that an industry which wants to satisfy artistic requirements will stop the indiscriminate production of identical objects. The industry of the future will also turn eagerly to glass fibers. For only fire-resistant materials will be used—both for divans and for flooring, where glass fibers will prove the most important material.

28 METAL IN ART AND APPLIED ART

It seems to me that habit lies like a heavy lead weight upon art and applied art. Because in grandfather's time most furniture and artifacts were made of wood, they must continue to be made of wood. But this should not be so. Glass architecture is also a compelling influence on applied art and art in general. We shall therefore be obliged to give preference in all fields to metal. The aestheticians will naturally try to counteract this, and the threatened timber industry will mobilize them.

There will be a lot of talk about the valuable associative ideas inherent in wood. I believe, however, that all the associative ideas inherent in wood can be transmitted to metal—by developing the artistic potentialities of metal—as I have already indicated many times. Metal is supposed to be cold, whereas wood is supposed to be warm. These are notions born of habit: we found glazed tiles cold before the existence of the tiled stove. Majolica only became warm to us because of this association. The same thing may occur with metal.

29 HOLLOW GLASS ELEMENTS IN EVERY POSSIBLE COLOR AND FORM AS A WALL MATERIAL (THE SO-CALLED GLASS BRICK)

So-called glass bricks make a wall material which may well become an interesting specialty of glass architecture. Large industrial undertakings have been formed already which could have a big future. Everything fire-proof and transparent is aesthetically justifiable as a wall material. Glass bricks should make many iron skeletons superfluous.

30 ASCHINGER'S BUILDINGS IN BERLIN, 1893

If ideas are to be productive, they must really be "in the air"—in very many heads at the same time—even if in a distorted form. This became clear to me in 1893 or a little later. Franz Evers was editing the theosophist journal *Sphinx,* and in consequence was overwhelmed with theosophist, spiritualist, and other such literature; in this wilderness there was a lot to make one laugh. One gentleman, whose name escapes me, asserted that glass was the source of all salvation; that one must always have a glass crystal near one on the writing table, and sleep in a room of mirrors, etc., etc. It all sounded crazy. But Aschinger's beer halls, with their frightful mirrors, seemed to me an echo of that theosophist publication about mirrored bedrooms. At any rate some telepathic influence was at work. I am convinced that every constructive idea will appear in many heads at the same time and quite irrationally; one should therefore not speak carelessly about the seemingly confused and crazy; it generally contains the germ of reason. In the East the madman is left at liberty and honored as a prophet. But that is by the way.

31 GLASS MOSAIC AND REINFORCED CONCRETE

It must be emphasized that reinforced concrete with a glass mosaic skin is probably the most durable building material which we have so far discovered. People are always so afraid that glass may be shattered by some malicious hand. Now, cases of windows being broken by stones thrown from the street are probably infrequent nowadays; stones are far more often thrown at a man's head than at a window-pane. But I have never heard of stones being thrown at glass mosaic.

During the last century, when telegraph wires were introduced, it was thought that they should all be laid underground for fear of the rude populace. Today nobody thinks of destroying the overhead wires. Therefore there is no need to fear that glass houses would be destroyed by stones flung by the lower orders. But that, too, is by the way.

32 HEATING AND COOLING APPLIANCES IN SPECIAL COLUMNS, VASES, SUSPENDED ELEMENTS, ETC.

Although the electric light commands the room from between the double walls, this is not the place for the heating and cooling because, as already stated, half the warm and cold air is uselessly dissipated.

For this reason the heating can be installed in columns, vases, and suspended elements, and their outer shells can be designed, like the oriental ampulla, as delightful decoration.

33 LIGHTING BETWEEN THE DOUBLE WALLS (WHICH DOES NOT EXCLUDE SUSPENDED FITTINGS IN THE ROOM)

I have so often said that the double walls are there, not merely to maintain the temperature of the room, but to accommodate the lighting elements. I must ask to be forgiven for repetition but I want to stress and underline it.

With this type of lighting the whole glass house becomes a big lantern which, on peaceful summer and winter nights, shines like fire-flies and glow-worms. One could easily become poetic. But lighting can also be installed inside the room. This interior lighting also illuminates the walls—if not so strongly as the light between the double walls.

34 THE VACUUM-CLEANER—IN THE PARK, TOO—ALSO AS AN INSECT-EXTERMINATOR
In the near future the vacuum-cleaner will seem as important as main water, and it will be used in parks, for the inlaid paths must be kept free of "dust." The vacuum-cleaner will naturally be needed as an insect-exterminator. It is absolutely horrifying that today it is still not used for this purpose. That the vacuum-cleaner has already been employed for getting rid of street dust, I take to be a known fact.

35 VENTILATORS, WHICH ARE OUSTING THE CUSTOMARY WINDOWS
It will seem very natural that ventilators should have a principal part to play in a glass house, and will supplant everything window-like. When I am in my glass room, I shall hear and see nothing of the outside world. If I long for the sky, the clouds, woods and meadows, I can go out or repair to an extra-veranda with transparent glass panes.

36 LIGHT COLUMNS AND LIGHT TOWERS
Hitherto, columns have served only as supports. Iron construction needs fewer supports than masonry; most of them are superfluous in the glass house. In order to make the columns in larger glass buildings lighter, they can be equipped with light elements behind a completely glass surround, so that the light columns do not give the impression of supporting, and the entire architectural effect seems much more free—as if everything were self-supporting; glass architecture will acquire an almost floating quality with these light columns.

Towns and other places should always be distinguished by towers. Every effort must naturally be made to lend enchantment to towers by night. Under the rule of glass architecture, therefore, all towers must become towers of light.

37 DIRECTION-FINDING FOR AERONAUTICS
Aeronautics will undoubtedly be determined to conquer the night. All towers must therefore become towers of light. And—to simplify navigation—every light tower will be built differently, emit a different light, and be fitted with glass elements of widely differing form. Uniformity in light towers is consequently out of the question. The signaling impulse can be so simple, and the tower itself must be so different from any other, that the aeronaut will immediately be informed where he is.

38 UKLEY MOTHER-OF-PEARL ON THE CONCRETE WALL
Naturally, transparent walls are not possible everywhere, in particular because the householder may not always want to sit or lie down between transparent walls. For such rooms, however, wallpapers and wall-fabrics are to be avoided because of fire risks, and wood-paneling is no longer appropriate—it is as impermanent as paper and fabrics, encourages woodworm, and is potentially inflammable.

Another wall cladding material must now be found. Reinforced concrete is not easy to handle artistically; it is as hard as granite, and enamel and niello are not all that cheap, anyway. Imitation pearls are coated with Ukley mother-of-pearl. This coating is perhaps to be recommended for walls as well. It could easily be embellished with semi-precious stones and glass brilliants.

But it is quite possible that a mother-of-pearl coat, applied to an uneven surface, could do the job alone. Whether this artificial mother-of-pearl retains its color when daylight is kept away from it would have to be tested.

Dome-like undulating bulges may be very effective if they occur regularly and symmetrically.

39 WIRED GLASS

For the walls, a good glass material is still, of course, the most worthwhile. After glass mosaic, however, the most durable glass material is the fairly familiar wired glass, which is particularly suitable for the external wall. Nowadays, wired glass can be handled in such a way that the wire mesh is scarcely visible. In the external wall the mesh does not matter because to an outside viewer it is practically invisible.

40 THE VERTICAL IN ARCHITECTURE, AND HOW TO OVERCOME IT

The brick architecture of the past often overcame the problem of the vertical by domes, but to escape from the vertical in walls seemed impossible. In glass architecture it is quite different. The large Palm House in the Botanical Gardens in Berlin no longer has vertical walls; the upward curve begins at a height of three meters.

41 THE DEVELOPMENTS MADE POSSIBLE BY IRON CONSTRUCTION

Iron construction permits walls of any desired form. Vertical walls are no longer inevitable. The developments made possible by iron construction are thus quite unlimited. One can shift the overhead dome effects to the sides, so that, sitting at a table, one only has to glance up sideways to appreciate them. Curved surfaces are also effective for the lower parts of walls—it is especially easy to get results in smaller rooms which are even less tied to verticals. The importance of the ground-plan in architecture will be reduced by such means; the building's silhouette will now be more significant than it used to be.

42 MOVABLE PARTITIONS IN THE HOME AND THE PARK

The Japanese constantly changes his living space by dividing it into smaller areas by partition-screens. Different silk materials are laid over these screens from time to time, so that the smaller "room" can have a frequently varying appearance. The same can be done in the living-rooms of glass houses by mobile and sliding glass partitions.

If one introduces movable glass walls, which of course do not have to be vertical, into a park, one can create wonderful perspectives, and a very delicate architecture of higher wall-screens could give the park a new architectural significance. This novelty would be perpetually flexible.

43 OVERCOMING THE DANGER OF FIRE

After what has been said, it is probably obvious that glass architecture makes fire-protection superfluous. By avoiding all inflammable materials fire insurance can be abolished. But the exclusion of fire risks should always be borne in mind in architecture; in the applied arts and interior decoration, only materials which do not burn should be permitted.

44 VANQUISHING VERMIN

That in a glass house, if properly built, vermin must be unknown, needs no further comment.

45 FLOODLIGHTS IN THE PARK, ON TOWERS AND HOUSE-ROOFS

As colored glass greatly softens the strength of light, we have far too little electric light at the present time. But we should have a thousand times as much, if, wherever there is running water, we installed turbines, as is feasible. Given adequate light, we can have far more floodlights than before, and night can become day. The night, indeed, can be more glorious than the day, quite independently of the splendor of the starlit sky, which, when it is clouded, is invisible to us anyway.

Even the private citizen will have his "park" flood-lit, and there will be floodlights on all roof constructions and roof-gardens. And a tower without floodlights will then be entirely unfamiliar and look unnatural. Aeronauts will show their indignation at unlit towers.

46 GETTING RID OF THE USUAL ILLUMINATION EFFECTS

Glass architecture will be scornfully called "illuminations architecture" by its opponents, who naturally should not be ignored. This contempt is unjustifiable, for nobody will want to illuminate a glass house the way a brick house is lit up today; when it is lighted inside the glass house is in itself an illumination element. When there are many such elements, the effect cannot be so harsh as the primitive elements of present-day illumination. By manipulating mobile reflectors, the floodlights can project a thousand beams of every conceivable color into the sky. Mirrors (used with discretion) and floodlights together will oust the usual illumination. The new illumination will be essentially for airship travel, to guide the aeronaut.

47 THE END OF THE WINDOW; THE LOGGIA AND THE BALCONY

With the introduction of electricity for cooking and heating, the chimney must unquestionably be abolished. People claim that such an introduction would be expensive, but forget that the tempo of technical development is continually quickening. Admittedly, this happens in the workshop and the expert's room, where talking a lot about oneself is frowned upon. But the enthusiasm is no less.

When glass architecture comes in, there will not be much more talk of windows either; the word *window* will disappear from the dictionaries. Whoever wants to look at nature can go onto his balcony or into his loggia, which of course can be arranged for enjoying nature as before. But then it will not be spoilt by hideous brick houses.

These are visions of the future which we must nonetheless keep in mind if the new age is ever to come about.

48 STONE MOSAIC AS PAVING

Up to now, we have not adequately discussed how to pave the surface underfoot. Stone flags are recommended for all paths and paved areas in gardens, but inside the house only magnesite has been mentioned for floors, in rooms of secondary importance. For better rooms, stone mosaic alone is advisable. Of course, the colors of the floor must be made to match the glass walls or to contrast with them. Perhaps a fiber-glass carpet would also be practicable. But inflammable materials must be rejected, and carpets of materials not fire-proofed, even if this is difficult.

49 MODELS FOR GLASS ARCHITECTURE

The most important objective would be for a number of models of glass architecture to be exhibited. Let us hope this happens at the 1914 Werkbund Exhibition at Cologne, for which Bruno Taut has built a glass house, in which the entire glass industry is to be represented. It does not seem right to me to produce models of glass architecture of pasteboard and selenite, but brass and glass models would not be cheap. A new model-building industry ought to be created to make models only for glass architecture, including church buildings, from good materials. Perhaps it would be advisable to use a different imitation-glass for larger models. About twenty years ago there was a substance called Tektorium—it was a transparent, colored, leather-like material on wire-netting. For model purposes it would be admirable, but for buildings it would not be durable enough, although it could always be mended.

50 MOUNTAIN ILLUMINATION

So much sounds fantastic, which actually is not fantastic at all. If one suggests applying mountain illumination to the Himalayas, this is just a ridiculous fantasy outside the realms of practical discussion. Illuminating the mountains near the Lake of Lugano is quite another thing. There are so many hotels there which would like to be part of the scenery, that they would be well disposed to glass architecture, if the proposition were not beyond their means. Their means are not inconsiderable, and the illumination of the mountains by illuminating the hotels, if these were built of glass, can no longer be described as fantastic. The rack-railway, which ascends the Rigi, could also be illuminated very easily and effectively by floodlights.

When aeronautics have conquered the dark, the whole of Switzerland will have her mountains colorfully lit up at night by glass architecture. We constantly forget how many things have changed in the last century. In the 1830s the aged Goethe did not see the coming of the railways. Less than a hundred years have passed since then, and the whole earth is encompassed by steel rails. Mountain illumination, which today still seems a fantasy to many, can develop just as quickly.

51 PARK ILLUMINATION

But park illumination will develop sooner than mountain illumination. If only we have more electric light, much will evolve of its own accord. Above all, we should consider towers of various forms in the parks for guiding airships (as already discussed).

A glass tower should not only be equipped with floodlights; many of the glass surfaces could be made to move and so bring about kaleidoscopic effects. Here also the possibilities are boundless.

52 GHOSTLY ILLUMINATION

When we speak of light, we are generally thinking of the glaring light of gas and electricity. In the past fifty years light has progressed quite surprisingly. It is all happening so quickly that one can hardly keep up. But if we had light in greater quantity (and this is perfectly feasible by using more turbines and dynamos), it would not have to be harsh in its effect and could be softened by color. It can be so reduced by color that it looks ghostly, which to many people would perhaps seem sympathetic.

53 THE SOLID WALL AS BACKGROUND FOR SCULPTURE

Where one either cannot or will not remove a solid non-transparent wall, it may perhaps be suitable as background for plastic art. This need not be statuary. Ornamental work stands out very effectively against a wall, and plant motifs are also simple to apply. But painting should not be used. In any case, it detracts from the architectural unity of a building.

54 CARS, MOTOR BOATS, AND COLORED GLASS

Now let us transfer glass architecture to the world of movement—to cars and motor boats. In this way the landscape will become quite different; it has already been permanently transformed by the steam train—so transformed that for decades people could not grow used to the change. The colored automobile, with its glossy glazed surfaces, and the glass motor boat, however, will alter the landscape so pleasantly that mankind, let us hope, should adjust itself to the change more quickly.

55 THE STEAM AND ELECTRIC RAILWAY LIT UP IN COLOR

When glass architecture has successfully captured the car and the motor boat, there will naturally be no course open to the other vehicles, especially those which scorch along rails, except to accommodate themselves to it. We shall then enjoy a wonderful impression, if we see an express illuminated in color speeding by day or by night through the countryside. The railway, greeted so sourly by sensitive natures to start with, will in the end reach a level of artistic charm beyond our present powers of description.

56 NATURE IN ANOTHER LIGHT

After the introduction of glass architecture, the whole of nature in all cultural regions will appear to us in quite a different light. The wealth of colored glass is bound to give nature another hue, as if a new light were shed over the entire natural world. There will be no need to look at nature through a colored piece of glass. With all this colored glass everywhere in buildings, and in speeding cars and air- and water-craft, so much new light will undoubtedly emanate from the glass colors that we may well be able to claim that nature appears in another light.

57 REINFORCED CONCRETE IN WATER

Reinforced concrete, as is well known, has proved itself in water; it is practically indestructible. It is therefore suitable for a new Venice, which must have foundations that are non-transparent, stable, rust-free, and indestructible. Upon this sound base the most colorful glass architecture can rise and be reflected in the water. A new Venice in this style will eclipse the old one. Water, because of its intrinsic capacity to reflect, belongs to glass architecture; the two are almost inseparable, so that in future water will be introduced wherever there is none at the moment. If, after the example of the old Venice, a "colony" were to be laid out with canal-streets, the traditional Venetian facade-architecture would have to be renounced from the outset; it does not agree with glass buildings which, when they are to be several storeys high, have in any case to be built in pyramid shape with terraces; otherwise too few of the glass walls come in contact with the daylight.

Should the individual sites be very close to one another, care must be taken over suitable boundaries. These can be walls of reinforced concrete, perhaps sheltering a covered way, open on one side. But they could be made in plenty of other ways. Anyone can develop the theme further, even a non-architect.

58 FLOATING ARCHITECTURE

If reinforced concrete, as has often been asserted in many quarters—even by the State Material-Testing Commission*—cannot be attacked by water, then it is capable of carrying the largest building, like a ship. We can talk in all seriousness of floating architecture. For this, of course, everything which was said in the previous chapter holds good. The buildings can obviously be juxtaposed or moved apart in ever changing patterns, so that every floating town could look different each day. The floating town could swim around in regions of large lakes—perhaps in the sea too. It sounds most fantastic and utopian, but it is far from being so, if reinforced concrete, shaped to the form of an indestructible vessel, carries the architecture. Indestructible boats have already been built out of reinforced concrete in German New Guinea. We must learn to accept that new building materials, when they really are of unrivalled strength and free from rust, can guide the architecture of the whole world into new paths. Reinforced concrete is one such material.

59 RIVER AND LAKE SHIPPING IN COLORED LIGHTING

As soon as there is floating glass architecture, ships—both great and small—will be fitted out in glass. The rivers, lakes, and seas will then become very gay. It does not take much perspicacity to predict this development in lake and river shipping, once a floating building is erected and is imitated.

60 AIRCRAFT WITH COLORED LIGHTS

It is generally known that the aeronauts would like to take over the night. That they have not so far done so is easily explained; on the earth the night is not yet light enough. But when, thanks to glass architecture, it has become light down below, it will also be light up in the air; the aircraft will be equipped to project colored lights, which will also form the vocabulary of a signal-language, understood everywhere by the light-projecting stations of the earth-towers and giving a practical value to the color display both above and below. Here the elements of progress fit smoothly together and are slowly but steadily completely transforming life on the surface of the earth. The changes brought about by the steam train have not been so significant and far-reaching as those which glass and iron construction is bound to produce. The crucial factor in this is undoubtedly reinforced concrete.

61 REINFORCED CONCRETE AND THE ARCHITECTURE OF FENCES

Reinforced concrete can be a few centimeters thick, and is very convenient to use for fences. If it is treated artistically, with enamel and glass mosaic or embellished with niello ornamentation, areas with such concrete boundary fences can easily be converted into places of recreation. In the architecture of fences reinforced concrete has a great part to play.

62 TERRACES

In higher glass buildings, when there are several storeys, the terrace-form is beyond question a necessity, for otherwise the glazed surfaces do not touch the sunlit air but can only fulfill their purpose at night and not by day. These terrace-form storeys will naturally oust the tedious facade-architecture of brick houses.

*The German here is *staatliche Matarialprufungskommission*.—Ed.

63 VIEW-POINTS

One imagines the view-points, from which nowadays we can survey a town or landscape. These view-points will show us quite different pictures, when glass architecture has become general and all vehicles (even the flying ones) reveal the full possibilities of colored glass. One must simply try to make such view-points clear to visualize. It is not easy, but the imagination soon adapts itself in the end to giving more than isolated details.

64 GLASS IN FACTORY BUILDINGS

To have a comprehensive picture of the glass-architecture world, it is essential also to think of factory buildings in glass. There will be no question of immediately destroying brick structures everywhere, but at first the brick will be faced with glass materials and glazes—and glass garden pavilions will be put on roofs, etc.

65 MARKET HALLS ENTIRELY OF GLASS AND IRON

It is well known that market halls are already being built entirely of glass and iron. Missing only are the double walls and ornamental color. It is not fanciful, however, to assume that both these will come soon. A total architecture of glass and iron cannot be far off.

66 CHURCHES AND TEMPLES

In Europe the larger church buildings are very well planned and executed as a result of the unnatural concentration of people in the larger towns. Whether it will be possible in this field to impose a purely glass and iron architecture in individual cases by rejecting brick, I do not know. But I do know well that the greater cheapness of glass and iron building must help toward success; we shall only have this greater cheapness when a larger number of firms are in competition—and for that we must wait. The free churches of America may well be the first to build glass temples, thus making a good step forward for glass architecture in the religious sphere. It ought to be stressed here that the whole of glass architecture stems from the Gothic cathedrals. Without them it would be unthinkable; the Gothic cathedral is the prelude.

67 CLUB AND SPORTS BUILDINGS

Club and sports buildings are today being erected in large numbers. As these are almost always the concern of well-to-do societies, glass architects would do well to pay closer attention to them; the advantages of glass architecture for rooms mainly used for social occasions are obvious.

68 MILITARISM AND BRICK ARCHITECTURE

So often only the obnoxious side of militarism is alluded to; but there is also a good one. It consists in the fact that, with the significant advent of the "dirigible" aerial torpedo, it inevitably draws attention to the dangers of brick architecture; if a brick church tower is struck low down by a torpedo, it will in every case collapse, kill many people, and reduce an entire group of buildings to rubble.

If, therefore, militarism evolves logically, it is bound to bring our brick culture into disrepute; this is its good side, and one constantly emphasized, especially by those tired of living as "brick-dwellers." A glass tower, when it is supported by more than four metal piers, will not be destroyed by an aerial torpedo; a few iron members will be bent, and a number of glass panels will have holes or cracks, but such damage is simple to repair.

69 PARLIAMENT BUILDINGS

What has just been said about glass towers applies also to parliament buildings built entirely of steel and glass. In wartime these, too, are much more resistant to damage than the old parliament buildings of brick faced with sandstone. To many this claim will seem very paradoxical, but it is quite logical. Dynamite can only damage a glass house partially; in relation to the whole it is fairly harmless. It needs a hailstorm of dynamite bombs to destroy a larger building complex made of glass and iron.

70 RESTAURANTS, CAFÉS, HOTELS, AND SANATORIA

It seems to me beyond question that restaurants, cafés, and hotels will be the first to show an interest in glass architecture, in order to attract a larger public, who always have plenty to spend on anything new. Sanatoria also will want glass buildings; the influence of splendid glass architecture on the nerves is indisputable.

71 TRANSPORTABLE BUILDINGS

Transportable glass buildings can be produced as well. They are particularly suitable for exhibition purposes. Transportable buildings of this type are not easy to make.

But one must not forget that, in a new movement, the most difficult step is often the first.

72 THE FUTURE INVENTOR, AND THE MATERIALS WHICH COULD COMPETE WITH GLASS

To earn a lot of money by inventions is not exactly easy. All the same, as I am bound to concede at once, the number of inventors grows daily; while many inventors lose all their goods and chattels and achieve nothing, the others are not deterred. Despite everything, however, the amply provided inventor is, in the long run, a very rare exception. Failure has its humorous side, and, so long as this is so, things are not so bad. But that is by the way. Nevertheless, it cannot be doubted that inventors—for their number, as we have said, is constantly growing— could or should have a great future.

Materials will be invented able to compete with glass. I am thinking of those which are elastic, like rubber, and transparent. The previously mentioned Tektorium is one already invented; but it is only too easily broken— and that, after all, is a defect. However, the outcome may be different. Materials may be invented combining transparency with durability. With the ever increasing number of inventors everything possible is indeed ultimately possible.

73 THE TIMELESSNESS OF ORNAMENTAL GLASS AND GLASS MOSAIC

Meanwhile, since we do not yet have the better, we must put up with the good, and this good is glass and ornamental glass mounted in lead, glass mosaic, and enamel. These glorious materials have not been outmoded by time; they have survived hundreds and thousands of years. It is regrettable that they have not been protected from infamous hands, but tough granite, which was used to face Egyptian pyramids, has fared no better and has also been stolen.

But this is no place for lamentations; our hope is that glass architecture will also improve mankind in ethical respects. It seems to me that this is a principal merit of lustrous, colorful, mystical, and noble glass walls. This quality appears to me not just an illusion, but something very real; the man who sees the splendors of glass every day cannot have ignoble hands.

74 EXHIBITION BUILDINGS IN AMERICA AND EUROPE

In the past twenty years we in Europe have frequently heard fabulous tales of American glass buildings. In part, these have certainly been only the idle fancies of reporters, but there may well be a grain of truth in them. Tiffany plays a great part in America, and the Americans are very well disposed to glass things. It would be very interesting to know what is planned in glass for the World Exhibition of 1915 in San Francisco.

In my opinion the exhibition buildings in America must differ considerably from those in Europe. The American bridge constructions at Niagara Falls are at all events so magnificent that an exhibition hall, if it is built of iron and glass, should also reveal impressive dimensions. Whether it will be double-walled with colored decoration, we do not yet know.

America is also the chief country for impressive giant buildings: the Pan-American Railroad, which is intended to protect the North and South against military attacks from East and West, is at present probably the greatest engineering work on earth.

A hope lies here that America might also tackle the greatest architectural work on earth. May it be composed of iron with glass of every color.

Europe is too conservative and slow.

75 EXPERIMENTAL SITE FOR GLASS ARCHITECTURE

Glass-painters never fix the glass pieces with lead without first testing the effect experimentally. This is done with all new designs. The full effect cannot be appreciated in the imagination. For the same reason, experiment is also essential for glass buildings. We need an experimental site for the purpose. It would be advisable for such a site to be provided by private enterprise rather than by the state. The latter brings in its official architects, who unhappily are rarely artists and are incapable of becoming so overnight.

76 A PERMANENT EXHIBITION OF GLASS ARCHITECTURE

A glass architecture exhibition would have to be linked to the experimental site, and it would have to be permanent. Glass architecture can only be effectively promoted if every new idea can be exhibited at the same time, and all those interested can constantly order or buy on the spot whatever is best or newest.

77 THE CRYSTAL ROOM ILLUMINATED BY TRANSLUCENT FLOORS

At the exhibition, particular attention would have to be given to lighting tests. We do not yet know, for example, what the effect would be of a room lit by translucent floors. One could discuss lights forever, but things like flooring, and many other ideas, would have to be tested. In my view a Glass Building Association would have to make capital available for the site and exhibition. If the interest were general, the association would soon be formed.

78 METAL FILIGREE WITH ENAMEL INLAY AND HUNG IN FRONT OF CRUDE REINFORCED CONCRETE

Many experiments could be imagined; the choice is almost unlimited. Particular thought must be given to overcoming the crudeness of reinforced concrete: filigree ornament with enamel inlay is perhaps worth considering. It would look like a piece of jewelry, on a large scale. Much of glass architecture concerns the jeweler, and jewels should be transposed from necks and arms onto walls. For the time being, ladies are not going to allow this because they are afraid of losing their share of adornment. It is one of the most unpleasant things about many new movements, that the first thing everybody asks is: Can it be harmful to me? The old fear of competition is in all things a far from pleasant phenomenon, even in art. The oil-color manufacturers are undoubtedly opponents of glass-painting, because they cannot make anything out of it.

79 THE AERONAUT'S HOUSE WITH AIRSHIP MODELS ON THE ROOF

Let's turn to something pleasanter! In my opinion, air-navigation will be eager to build an aeronaut's house in the restaurant garden of the exhibition, with airship models projecting little mobile lights fixed to the domed roof. This would be a variant of the *Seeschifferhaus* at Bremen. To immortalize aircraft models in this way would be of great interest to the aeronautical profession, and would lie very close to its heart.

80 SOFT LIGHTING

It must be repeated that efforts should not be directed toward achieving greater brightness in lighting, for we have got that already. We should think all the time of the softening of light in choosing colors.

81 TWILIGHT EFFECTS

Incidentally, we should consider introducing light behind colored glass panels into a few corners, even in bright sunshine. It produces wonderful twilight effects during the dusk and dawn hours. A great many lighting experiments will, of course, be necessary.

82 LIGHTHOUSES AND SHIPPING

When new lighthouses have to be built, the glass architect must see to it that in the immediate future glass architecture is adopted on a large scale. Since lighthouses generally stand on high eminences, it is undoubtedly cheaper than designs in brick, where the frightful labor of lifting such materials to the site disqualifies them. Building will unquestionably be cheaper with the simple equipment needed for carrying up metal and glass. This must be repeatedly emphasized.

83 AIRPORTS AS GLASS PALACES

For the building of airports, also, glass-iron construction has much to recommend it; airports must be visible and identifiable from far off and this is best achieved by colored ornamental glass. This will reach its full effect at night, when the entire building is crowned by a diadem of projected lights, delighting not only the aeronauts, but also people who have no airship at their bidding.

84 LIGHT NIGHTS, WHEN GLASS ARCHITECTURE COMES

It seems easy to say that something is indescribable, but of those light nights, which glass architecture must bring us, there is nothing else left for us to say except that they are truly indescribable. One thinks of the lights shining from all the glass towers and in every aircraft, and one thinks of these lights in all their many colors. One thinks of the railway trains all gaily lighted, and one adds the factories in which at night, too, the light shines through colored panes. Then one thinks of the great palaces and cathedrals of glass and the villas of glass, and of the town-like structures, on solid land and in the water—often in movement—and of ever more water in ever different colors. On Venus and Mars they will stare in wonder and no longer recognize the surface of the earth.

Perhaps men will live more by night than by day. Astronomers will erect their observatories in quiet mountain ravines and on peaks, because the huge sea of colored light may disturb the study of the heavens.

All this is not a modern concept—the great Gothic master-builders thought of it first. We must not forget that.

85 THE BRILLIANT (DIAMOND) EFFECT IN ARCHITECTURE

Brilliants are treasured on the hands and neck, but in architecture the diamond effect is by no means prized. I suggest that this only happens because the brilliant is too small and architecture is too big. Large glass brilliants, however, can be produced of pumpkin size, without becoming too expensive. Will architecture despise the brilliant effect, when glass can be seen everywhere in large quantities? That seems to me unlikely. It is no argument against colored glass that primitive people and small children are enraptured by it.

86 THREE-DIMENSIONAL AND TWO-DIMENSIONAL ORNAMENT IN ARCHITECTURE

In the Alhambra, we mostly find three-dimensional ornament, but of perishable plaster-work. Glass architecture can also use such ornament, but of imperishable glass materials. The most delicate blown decoration is made of glass, even of frosted and filigree glass. This kind of plastic art for the ornamental glass wall should admittedly only be considered for formal rooms; there it is entirely feasible and not merely a figment of the imagination. Venice is no longer the pinnacle of glass culture, although it has contributed much that often obliges one to return to it later. I do not recommend copies, but it certainly seems to me that the splendors of Venetian glass, as reflected in particular by the palaces of Isola Bella, are valuable sources of inspiration. One often forgets that present-day Italy, without glass, really has very little attraction.

87 THE TRANSFORMATION OF FIREWORKS

When there is more glass everywhere, fireworks will be transformed; thousands of reflection effects will be possible. But this chapter must wait until pyrotechnics have been further developed.

88 COLOR-LIT POOLS, FOUNTAINS, AND WATERFALLS

This chapter shall be left to the landscape architects. They will tackle the job with great enthusiasm and be determined to offer more than the Rococo period offered us.

89 THE DISCOVERY OF THE BRICK BACILLUS

Brick decays. Hence fungus. The discovery of the brick bacillus is no great discovery, but now the doctor also has a major interest in finally ousting the cult of brick.

In the cellars of brick houses the air is always full of brick bacilli; glass architecture needs no cellars beneath it.

90 THE NERVOUS EFFECT OF VERY BRIGHT LIGHT UNSOFTENED BY COLOR

We have to thank very bright lights, in part, for the nervous ailments of our time. Light softened by color calms the nerves. In many sanatoria it is recommended by nerve doctors as beneficial.

91 RAILWAY STATIONS AND GLASS ARCHITECTURE

For station premises, which have to be screened at least partially against wind and rain, glass architecture is so appropriate that nothing further needs to be said about it.

92 UNIFORM STREET-LAMPS AND THEIR ELIMINATION

If we must mention something detestable, this is, in my view, those street lamps which in every town look so alike that one cannot help wondering how mankind can be capable of such monotonous repetition. Happily, this repetition can be quickly eliminated by combinations of colored glass hanging-lamps, which are adaptable to a vast number of forms. This elimination will of course come very soon.

93 PRESENT-DAY TRAVEL

Today people travel from nervous habit: they want to have something different, and although they know that all hotels and towns, mountain villages, and health resorts have a dreadful sameness, they travel there just the same. They travel, knowing well that they will find nothing better wherever they go.

94 FUTURE TRAVEL

In the future, people will travel in order to look at new glass architecture, which will differ widely in various parts of the world. To travel for the sake of glass architecture has at all events a meaning; one may surely expect new glass effects in other places. One may also assume that nine-tenths of the daily press will report only on new glass effects. The daily press wants novelty—so it will not be unfriendly to glass.

95 THE DOPPLER AND THE ZEEMAN EFFECT

It has often been said that glass is not a "precious" commodity. In contrast to this, remember Frauenhofer's lines of the glass spectrum. In addition, Christian Doppler discovered that light, when it approaches or recedes, breaks up Frauenhofer's lines into infra-red and ultra-violet. By using photography it has been possible to measure this, and from these measurements we know precisely whether stars of weak luminosity are approaching us or receding, and at what speed. Without glass the Doppler effect would not be discernible; I should think that this speaks volumes for the importance of glass.

The Zeeman effect occurs through the action of a magnetic field and a flame; the spectrum then shows Frauenhofer's lines suddenly triplicated. From these "triplets" one can determine the existence of magnetic fields, which are detectable in sun-storms and explain the constitution of sun-spots. I believe that the Zeeman effect also speaks volumes for the importance of glass.

Thus one can no longer be permitted to describe glass as of little value; whoever does that has no right to be considered an educated person.

96 WHICH SPHERES OF INTEREST ARE FOSTERED OR ENDANGERED BY GLASS ARCHITECTURE

The livelihood of masons and carpenters—from what has been said above—is clearly threatened; also that of the whole timber industry, joiners, turners, etc. But the process will not be so rapid that it will be impossible to assimilate those affected into other trades; they will have plenty of time to transfer to the metal and glass industries. Very many new skills are required, and nothing stands in the way of the change.

Admittedly, many locksmiths say that a mason could never become a locksmith; the locksmith only says this because he fears competition.

But the spheres which will inevitably be stimulated by glass architecture are principally heavy industry, the chemical dye industry, and the glass industry.

97 HEAVY INDUSTRY

The introduction of iron into house-building will, beyond question, bring so many new orders to heavy industry that it could continue to exist even if all cannon-making were stopped. Accordingly, heavy industry would be well advised not to take the ideas discussed in this book too lightly; they will bring it great pecuniary advantages. In any case, heavy industry should note that there will be many new potential clients because of glass architecture.

98 THE CHEMICAL DYE INDUSTRY

The same thing applies to the color industry. Glass architecture will consume vast quantities of color.

99 THE GLASS INDUSTRY

It is undeniable that the glass industry has the lion's share in glass architecture. The present scale of the industry, however, is inadequate for the greater demand; it must expand in proportion. The financial success which will result from this is quite incalculable.

100 THE INFLUENCE OF COLORED GLASS ON THE PLANT WORLD

Glass architecture will also exercise an influence on botanical gardens; entirely colorless, plain glass will be gradually abandoned. Colored glass will only be used externally, where it does not absorb too much light. The plants will then be exposed experimentally to colored light, and the experts may well have some surprises. The experiments should not be carried out in haste.

101 ART IN BRIDGE-BUILDING

There have been times when the engineer has had the upper hand over the architect; not unnaturally, for the engineer was more needed.

Today the engineer no longer wants to stuff all the fees into his pocket; he gladly allows half to the architect. This will soon be apparent in bridge-building, where there are high artistic ambitions. One could wish that these related to glass architecture.

102 THE TRANSFORMATION OF THE EARTH'S SURFACE

So many ideas constantly sound to us like a fairytale, when they are not really fantastic or utopian at all. Eighty years ago, the steam railway came and undeniably transformed the face of the earth. From what has been said so far the earth's surface will once again be transformed, this time by glass architecture. If it comes, a metamorphosis will occur, but other factors must naturally be taken into consideration, which cannot be discussed here.

The present brick "culture" of the city, which we all deplore, is due to the railway. Glass architecture will only come if the city as we know it goes. It is completely clear to all those who care about the future of our civilization that this dissolution must take place. To labor the point is useless.

We all know what is meant by color; it forms only a small part of the spectrum. But we want to have that part. Infra-red and ultra-violet are not perceptible to our eyes—but ultra-violet is perceptible to the sensory organs of ants. If we cannot at the moment accept that our sensory organs will develop appropriately overnight, we are justified in accepting that we should first reach for what is within our grasp—i.e., that part of the spectrum which we are able to take in with our own eyes—in fact, the miracles of color, which we are in a position to appreciate ourselves. In this, only glass architecture, which will inevitably transform our whole lives and the environment in which we live, is going to help us. So we must hope that glass architecture will indeed transform the face of our world.

103 THE TRANSFORMATION OF THE OFFICIAL ARCHITECT

When the private client wants to build, he looks for the best architect. When the state wants to build, government architects are at its disposal—not the best architects, who are generally freelancers. This is a deplorable situation, and it is the state that one chiefly deplores. These official architects, who are always hamstrung by bureaucracy (hence their inhibitions and conservatism), must once again become free; otherwise they will hinder future architectural progress. One sees from the buildings produced by official architects that they are scared of color; scared of ridicule. This remarkable color-shyness stems from old Peter Cornelius, who would have nothing to do with color.

In the Botanical Gardens at Dahlem there is as yet no orchid house. This is bound to be a glass palace. Its construction must be already assigned to government architects. I am curious to see the result. Heating by (ceramic) stoves has been proposed, for they are supposed to be better suited to orchids than central heating; I do not know whether the construction of the stoves is being entrusted to a government master-potter.

104 THE PSYCHOLOGICAL EFFECTS OF THE GLASS ARCHITECTURAL ENVIRONMENT

The peculiar influence of colored glass light was already known to the priests of ancient Babylon and Syria; they were the first to exploit the colored-glass hanging lamp in the temples, and the colored-glass ampulla was later introduced into churches throughout Byzantium and in Europe. From these were developed the stained-glass windows of the Gothic period; it is not to be wondered at that these make an especially festive impression, but such an impression from colored glass is inevitably inherent in glass architecture; its effect on the human psyche can accordingly only be good, for it corresponds to that created by the windows of Gothic cathedrals and by Babylonian glass ampullae. Glass architecture makes homes into cathedrals, with the same effects.

105 A COMPOSED AND SETTLED NATION, WHEN GLASS ARCHITECTURE COMES

When home life has reached the stage where even the wildest fancies appear to be realized, the longing for something different ceases; people will travel only to learn about a particular type of glass art and possibly to bring it home—to be able to reproduce it in a similar design.

Perhaps somewhere one may discover the art of making glass fibers like brocade, so that the fibers, viewed from different angles, will show different color effects. Perhaps somewhere they can make a lace-like fabric from glass fibers and fix it to a darker glass wall of one color; an intimate effect might result, and this would make for a homely atmosphere, which one would leave reluctantly; a curtain effect would be created. Perhaps then one would only travel to find out about new glass crafts; much that was new might emerge from old designs. But the entirely new is also to be expected from the great inventors of our own and future times.

106 MORE COLORED LIGHT!

We must not strive to increase the intensity of light—today it is already too strong and no longer endurable. But a gentler light is worth striving for. Not more light!—"more colored light!" must be the watchword.

107 THE MAIN ENTRANCE

The pyramids are monumental. Cologne cathedral, too, is monumental—the Eiffel tower is also often so described nowadays, but the idea of what is monumental will be changed by glass architecture. Glass towers will be built deep in the sea, creating a special kind of luxury architecture, cool and very peaceful. Many people might think of giant windmills, with sails over a hundred meters long; but town hall and powder-magazine towers might not be suitable for windmill purposes; brick architecture would not stand up to a severe storm.

108 THE MONUMENTAL

In my opinion, the entrance to a great palace should always be an open hall of many glass walls, gathered together one upon another like the petals of an exquisite flower. The best architects should devote themselves particularly to entrance-hall construction, and then invite the interior designers to surpass the complicated architectonic effects. This should create a splendid challenge; and it would simply be necessary for the client to bear the cost and not come to the end of his financial resources too quickly.

109 STREETS AND HIGHWAYS AS LIGHT-COLUMN AVENUES

The verges of streets and highways will no longer be planted with trees, which are not high enough for the purpose, but columns of light, provided with festoons of lights and shedding constantly changing colored light, would be highly appropriate for verges.

110 CHEMISTRY AND TECHNICS IN THE TWENTIETH CENTURY

We are not at the end of a cultural period—but at the beginning. We still have extraordinary marvels to expect from technics and chemistry, which should not be forgotten. This ought to give us constant encouragement. Unsplinterable glass should be mentioned here, in which a celluloid sheet is placed between two sheets of glass and joins them together.

111 GLASS CULTURE

After all the above, we can indeed speak of a glass culture. The new glass environment will completely transform mankind, and it remains only to wish that the new glass culture will not find too many opponents. It is to be hoped, in fact, that glass culture will have ever fewer opponents; to cling to the old is in many matters a good thing; in this way at any rate the old is preserved. We, too, want to cling to the old—the pyramids of ancient Egypt should most certainly not be abolished. But we also want to strive after the new, with all the resources at our disposal; more power to them!

MODERN MONUMENTS

Reyner Banham

In many an attempt to make learned (as opposed to common) sense of the new Lloyds Building, and other examples of High Tech architecture, one will read references to some mysterious *Maison de Verre*. But what "House of Glass" is meant? Everybody knows that Modern Architecture is "just a bunch of glass boxes," so it could be anything or nothing. Or is it perhaps a Platonic ideal; some pure conception of the ultimate glass box that has been trying to get itself built ever since Modernism came in?

Retrospectively it almost is just that—if you look for a comprehensive prototype for all the mechanistic romanticism and engineer-styling that comes with recent British High Tech buildings, you are liable to find yourself falling backwards through time until you soft-land in the late 1920s, touching down in the *Septième Arondissement* of Paris, outside an uninformative gate in an equally anonymous standard Rive Gauche facade, where you have to address an electronic squawk box to be admitted.

Inside, you confront a wall of glass bricks set in concrete in a black steel frame at the back of a standard Paris-type courtyard, with two steel ladders flying up on either side, and some massive floodlamps carried on clever steel brackets (fig. 12). Even if you know it from photographs, the physical presence is still a shock in that traditional-type context. This is not modern architecture as it is generally understood; not the modern architecture of Gropius, or Le Corbusier, yet it is unmistakably "modern" in its materials, its aesthetics, the kind of earnest life-style it implies.

It's as if its architects, the French Art-Deco superstar Pierre Chareau, and the Dutch modernist Bernard Bijvoët, had invented an alternative Modernism to the one that is in all the books, and that is why the *Maison* isn't in those books; not in Giedion, not in Pevsner (which is probably why it isn't in Banham, either; I caught up with it later), not in Hitchcock, nor all those lay-person's "introductions" to modern architecture. It appears briefly in Tafuri's revisionist *Modern Architecture,* and in William Curtis's equally revisionist text under the same title. But—sensationally—it's not in Frampton's *Modern Architecture: A Critical History,* even though he has made himself the world expert on the house. Known and admired, it is still "unassimilated to the canon."

In a way, it almost threatens the canon, which is probably why it is so much in vogue at present. The interior, in particular, is not only a knockout, but it suggests even more forcibly than the facade how Modern might have been quite different. On the ground floor are doctor's consulting rooms but they are not in the standard chrome-and-glass iconography of Modernist hygiene; there's wood, and the metal is black. Everything is rational but different; sliding doors rotate on hidden pivots, screens concertina away on curved tracks.

From the consulting level you go upstairs—at a low angle on a light-metal open-riser staircase that is mounted on a hinge at the top and sliders at the bottom, with low handrails spread so wide that they seem intended only to catch you if you fall off!—and at the top you come into what must be one of the greatest rooms of the twentieth century, irrespective of style or period (fig. 148). It is two storeys high behind that wall of glass bricks, which becomes a wall of light when seen from inside (fig. 145). Photographs make the room look too tall and too dark, whereas the reality is marvelously luminous and spacious in all directions.

The furniture is stolidly well-made Art Deco wood, but everything else is strictly "Machine Age." The original rubber floor is still in place and intact, though it looks its age; exposed steel columns rise through the space, jointed with dozens of hefty nuts and bolts—but partly clad in expensive marble! Electrical conduitry and switchgear are all in view but the main light-fittings are partly concealed and heating comes out of metal grilles in the floor and every cubic inch of wooden cabinet work is carried in skinny black metal framing that is a continuation of the handrails around balconies and stairs. And it is all lovingly handcrafted, as if even the metal was cabinetmakers' work. It shows how good modern architecture might have been if it had been properly made!

And, looking at all that neat black metal, some of it perforated even, you can see only too clearly where so much current black and perforated High Tech furniture (the stuff you see in Astrohome in Covent Garden) had its origins. The wheel of fashion has creaked around, and the house that didn't fit the canon a decade ago is now the house that everyone wants to see. Which is very tough on doctors trying to practice on the ground floor and the descendants of Dr. Dalsace (who built it), trying to live on the upper floors.

This happens to all inhabitants of great modern architecture, of course—some owners of houses by Frank Lloyd Wright in Chicago suburbs really do keep a sawn-off shotgun handy, because their openlawned front yards don't give any protection against marauding architecture buffs.

This whole issue of public access to private dwellings that are monuments in the history of culture is something you don't have to be called Bedford or Bath to know about, but there is a twist in the case of the *Maison de Verre*: Can a work of such determined Modernism be *historic,* a *monument*? It is surely a contradiction of the intentions and nature of Modernism for its products to stand around long enough to become monuments anyhow, even if some of the exhibits in the Museum of Modern Art in New York are *over a hundred years old!* I still get a funny feeling whenever I write a phrase like "the modern tradition" even though I know it stands for something real, and I think that at least one of the reasons why we have been having the "crisis of modernism" that gets academics so excited at conferences is that we are faced with the problem of forcing a lot of anti-historical material into historical categories that it was deliberately designed not to fit.

The problem is worse when the monument in question is as private unto itself, as independent of the institutionalized movement of Modernism, as the *Maison de Verre.* You can see this clearly enough if you contrast its case with that of Weissenhof Siedlung, in the suburbs of Stuttgart. Built in 1927 as a public demonstration of modern housing, master-planned by Mies van der Rohe, it is not so much "assimilated to the canon," it *is* the canon. Its white-walled, flat-roofed buildings by Le Corbusier, Mies himself, Gropius, J. J. P. Oud, Peter Behrens, and others, including mystery men like Mart Stam and rank expressionists like Hans Scharoun, represented the first major rally of modernist architects, the first all-modern community whose townscape one could walk about in.

This past summer, at my third visit, there was nothing casual, disregardful, or bashed up about the Weissenhof scene as there had been when I first visited it after the war. The great German *Kulturschutzmaschine* has taken over; all is now neat and tidy, the buildings put back like 1927. All that saved it from being completely mummified and spooky was that the restoration work was not absolutely completed; the famous apartment block by Mies van der Rohe was only half done, and one could sneak into the unfinished parts where the crews were still at work, and see original structural steel exposed, original brass handrails, even original bathroom tiling, and those horizontal strip windows that still give such spectacular panoramic views over the ring of mountains that frames the city below.

What else saved it from being a total mausoleum was that people actually live in it, hang ludicrous chandeliers in their living rooms, put cheerfully wrong curtains in the windows, hang surprisingly provocative underwear out to dry, and generally behave like living *Volk*. The effect, for me, was very strange; it is good to see quality buildings being given the upkeep they deserve but is the embalmed result *modern* anymore?

I think not—unless you treat Modern as just another historical style, like Rococo or Flamboyant, which is very definitely not how any self-respecting modern architect, dead or alive, has ever regarded it. The problem seems worse in architecture than in the non-constructive arts—*Finnegans Wake,* for instance, has been procrusted into the canon of great literature it set out to mock rotten—but the persistence of the classic (oh?) monuments of architectural modernism is of a different order, and they defy "interpretation" in ways that other arts do not.

Great works of architecture—and ancient ones tend to be as resistant as modern ones—seem to populate the history of Western culture in a nonconforming mode and on a different time-scale that together make nonsense of the seamless web of *Zeitgeist.* Impressionist painting, impressionist literature, impressionist music, even impressionist sculpture—but impressionist building? Only at the expense of voiding the word of usable meaning. Could it be the same with Modern, and that the "permanent masterpieces" of modern architecture operate under a different rule book in which the canon is almost irrelevant, so that the houses on the hill of Weissenhof can sit around being public, canonical, and *kulturgeschichtlich,* and the *Maison de Verre* can go on being private, uncanonized, and category-proof, without being any the less significant for being so unconformable?

Or will the *Maison de Verre* turn out to be the basis of an alternative canon? More and more architecture pundits have lately been running this up the proverbial flagpole to see if anyone else is paying attention. The usual format of the argument, made explicit in the catalogue of the massive exhibition "Vision der Moderne, das Prinzip Konstruktion," at the Deutsches Architektur Museum in Frankfurt this year, is that historian-propagandists of modern architecture got the *Zeitgeist* twisted, and propagandized a style (that was to become canonical) of closed volumes, simple geometrical forms, and smooth surfaces, while offering to trace its ancestry from objects like the Crystal Palace and the Eiffel Tower, that were open-work, complicated, and less smooth than rugged.

If High Tech is that ancestry reasserting itself (and Lloyds looks very much like it) over the established canon, then the *Maison de Verre* has its uneasy place as the first example of a modern architecture true to its claimed parentage. But does even that make it a permanent monument, like, say, Stonehenge?

PIERRE CHAREAU: AN ECLECTIC ARCHITECT
Kenneth Frampton

It is the paradoxical lot of certain gifted people that they never find their real profession, so that all through their lives they seem haunted by the thought of other careers that they could have chosen. Pierre Chareau seems to have been such a character. Studying at the Paris Ecole des Beaux Arts from 1900 to 1908, he divided his time between painting, music, and architecture before he finally decided on the profession of décorateur, becoming an apprentice at the relatively late age of twenty-five in the decoration department of the Paris branch of the English firm Waring and Gillow. This was the beginning of a long and thorough apprenticeship, which lasted from 1908 until the beginning of the First World War.

Chareau's career was in many respects inseparable from the life of a young couple, Jean and Annie Dalsace, who were in the end to be the clients of the Maison de Verre. It was they who entrusted him with his first private commission, the decoration of their two-room apartment at Saint Germain des Près, which was completed at the end of 1918. This commission led Chareau and his loyal collaborator, the metal-worker Louis Dalbet, to design and execute a bed and a desk which were subsequently exhibited at the Salon d'Automne of 1919. These objects established Chareau's reputation as a "decorative artist," and were sufficiently admired to entitle him to membership of the prestigious Société des Artistes Décorateurs.

While he was immediately accepted by his peers, particularly as the creator of well-designed and finished furniture, his reputation as an *ensemblier* was to remain slightly marginal in relation to the canon of quality established by French decorative art after 1925. Chareau's distance from the mainstream can be measured by the fact that Charles Moreau, in his *Interieurs Français au Salon des Artistes Décorateurs*, only chooses him three times for inclusion in the annual selection in the ten years from 1926 to 1936. Each time he seems to have been retained not for his inventive ingenuity and his ability as an architect but above all for his precious and prestigious furniture around which he composed interiors to suit the taste of progressive bourgeoisie. This divide, between inventiveness on the one hand, and taste on the other, is already suggested in the Dalsace apartment of 1918 and appears again in the furnishings of his own apartment on the rue Nollet in Paris. In both cases, a tension is created between the high-quality finish of the specially designed wooden pieces and the somewhat austere, poetic "brutality" of the metal-framed screens and the various folding devices (permanent fixtures) which Chareau used to fit out his interiors. Where the former perpetuate the bourgeois sense of quality (an interior within an interior), the latter convey a somewhat utopian ideal of invention, as if these new devices in themselves heralded a new style of life. At the same time, it would be wrong to assume that Chareau's work was entirely separate from the triumph of French decoration which followed the celebrated Exposition des Arts Décoratifs of 1925, Chareau having taken quite as much part as any artist in the evolution of certain aspects of this Art Déco style.

Chareau remained at variance with the total Art Déco aesthetic, as can be seen from his own contribution to the Exposition des Arts Décoratifs, for example, the "Study-library of a French embassy," which was entirely lined in palm wood. In its overall atmosphere it is comparable to later interiors, furnished entirely in wood to the designs of such fashionable decorators as Lucie Renaudot, Josef Frank, and Gabriel Guévrékian. In this respect, Chareau appeared as a precursor: what was to be decisive here from an architectural point of view was that the woodwork was on the scale of the entire suite, focused about a desk at the center which was the masterpiece of the composition. The work should, however, be judged in terms of taste and invention rather than architecture: the first quality derives above all from the rich hermeticism of the wood paneling; second results from the revolving cylindrical shutter used to transform the cupola of the ambassador's office from the unfolded position (day) to the folded position (night). In this work two characteristics are noticeable which we will observe on a larger scale in the Maison de Verre: the tendency to design an introverted interior, without regard to context (however appropriate it might have been in the circumstances), together with a tendency to bring dualities into play in the form of surprising and ambiguous reciprocal effects. This tendency appears clearly in the operation of the revolving and folding palm wood shutter, which, when it is totally unfolded, completes the hermeticism of the wood-sealed interior. The shutter had, of course, to be folded away (closed up like a Japanese fan) to reveal the indirectly lit ceiling at night. In fact, there is the suggestion that this reflected, artificial light is in some way natural, because the shutter folds up in front of the source of light, almost like a curtain in front of a window, so that when it is completely closed, it is possible to imagine that above this seal there is a glass cupola opening to the sky. This ambiguous arrangement harks back once again to Chareau's obsessional preference for enclosed spaces, a preference shared by J. K. Huysmans's character, Des Esseintes, who was convinced that the exterior world was less real and more remote than the interior one.[1]

A further feature of Chareau's particular sensibility appears in this context. The shutter was a useless mechanism, because clearly the strength of the light could have been altered more effectively by a dimmer switch than by a fan shutter. It is difficult to judge from the existing photographs, which always show the shutter folded up and the ceiling open, what effects could have been obtained by partially opening the shutter. But, apart from the uneven lighting conditions which would inevitably have been the result, there is every reason to think that, when completely unfolded, the shutter must have been far less efficient from the point of view of space. In other words, we are faced with a modifiable object, where the only possible modification is paradoxically "negative" in its effect.

We can see from the example of this embassy interior that Chareau would readily comply with an established style, with the requirements of a general level of refinement and decorum, just as he would reject it the instant that he sensed that certain details were dictated by considerations of fashion or by the Art Déco tendency toward an over-aestheticized *Gesamtkunstwerk*.* In other words, while he wished to create a hermetic environment, he firmly resisted the temptation to abandon himself to a desultory style. Apart, then, from the curtains and carpet by Hélène Henry, a Jacques Lipschitz sculpture, and some Cubist-inspired wall lights in alabaster and metal, designed by Chareau, there is not much here of the Art Déco style, in the sense in which Robert Mallet-Stevens or Louis Süe would have understood it, and least of all in the main pieces of furniture designed by Chareau—the wood-framed armchairs, covered with velvet (which evoke the "gondola" style of chairs by Ruhlmann and Van de Velde, more than the abstract manner of Mallet-Stevens), and the extendable desk, made of mahogany and oak, covered with Macassar ebony. Even this last, where the values of grand bourgeois decoration are clearly apparent in the costly finish, hardly escapes Chareau's disjunctive impulse. This disjunction can be seen in the tubular metal drawer-handles which are closer to the anonymity of American mass-produced office furniture (compare the modern idea of office furniture in Ronéo metal which Le Corbusier discusses in his 1925 polemic against Art Déco, "L'art Décoratif d'aujourd'hui"[2]) than to the cabinet-making tradition to which the object, in the main, clearly belongs.

Chareau's first foray into the field of architecture, in the proper sense, was the only detached building of his career in France apart from the Djemil Anik House of 1937. This was the reinforced concrete club-house designed in collaboration with the Dutch architect Bernard Bijvoët and completed at Beauvallon (near Saint Tropez) in 1928. From an architectural point of view, the principal anomaly of this work is that it looks like an unfinished Cubist com- position. From whichever side it is approached, it is always off balance, as if its maker was in some way confused by the need for an exterior form. This last is composed of two main elements: a double-height club-room with a bar and a covered outside terrace, with an assembly of small service rooms situated to the rear (kitchen, cloakroom, etc.). Awkward in its external appearance, this building does not even succeed in achieving one of those dynamic spatial relationships that we have come to expect from three-dimensional Cubism, so that the main interest lies, once again, in the furnishing of its volumes. Photographs of the period bring out the curiously disjointed effects achieved by the furnishing and the eccentric treatment of architectural details: the contrast, say, between the exte- rior treatment of the chimney, and the interior hearth which is built partly from brick and partly from plastered reinforced concrete.

Similar inconsistencies are to be found in the interiors that Chareau and Bijvoët designed in the same years for the Grand Hôtel de Tours (designed by Maurice Boille, 1928–31), which included a large ballroom, a smoking room, a bar, and a large variety of smaller areas reserved for rest and reading. Here, the Cubist style of the period finds an unequivocal expression in the glyptic surfaces, the unornamented planes of the mezzanine balcony, and the orderly concrete beams which flank the three-story-high ballroom on every side. However, this first manner is departed from, if not utterly rejected, by the non-architectonic way in which the space is detailed. The rest of the work reverses to Cubism in the surface decoration of certain areas, in the abstract, orthogonal design of the marquetry, floor and in the neo-plastic mosaic decoration of certain columns in the adjoining spaces.

Elsewhere, the tone and the syntactic repertoire owe more to principles borrowed directly from the anonymous tradition of shop fitting or other discrete forms of quality carpentry. For instance, the wood panels which encase the ballroom as far as the level of the cornice are held in place by continuous bands of chrome steel, while the areas of uncovered plaster above are animated by a sprinkling of randomly arranged invisible "luminous stars." This mixed aesthetic seems to swing oddly between the antithetical poles of a post-*Jugendstil* Viennese manner: on the one hand, the deconstructed decorative style crystallized by Josef Hoffmann; on the other, the "silent" interiors of Adolf Loos. The anonymous tradition of shop fitting, as found in Loos's Knize shop of 1910, sets the tone for the remaining areas, with glass screens framed by black-painted, light metal, with marquetry on nearly all the available wall sur- faces, while versions of the English club chair, in the form of a truncated chaise lounge without armrests, uphol- stered in leather, serve to maintain an aura of luxurious austerity. Such, in substance, is the basic interior syntax which was to be adopted two years later in the furnishing details of the Maison de Verre. Other pieces of furniture should, however, be noted in passing, which serve to forestall the already somewhat attenuated elegance of the hotel bar and smoking room. These are the bar stools, summarily built of tubes of encased metal, and the strange high bar tables designed to go with them. One has the feeling that when Chareau designed these pieces of furniture in 1925 he was momentarily more concerned with experimental construction than aesthetic refinement. Whether this peculiar combination of furniture was intentional or not, the effect was the same, namely, a lapse into a kind of "styleless" style, combined with a strange discrepancy between the apparent dimensions of the various pieces of furniture—the stools appear almost too tall and the chairs too low. Taken together, these discordances in style and scale have a Surrealist feel to them, and this characteristic in Chareau's work was pointed out by Paul Nelson in one of the first studies on the Maison de Verre.[3]

In the Maison de Verre (figs. 12, 145–48), designed in collaboration with Bijvoët and under construction from 1928 to 1932, this disjunctive tendency is resolved at once by a clearly marked opposition between the taste governing the choice of furnishings, whether bought or specially created, and the inventiveness of the house as a whole. This separation between furniture and permanent fixtures was henceforth to be the norm. It is, clearly, close to the distinction made by Adolf Loos when he stated that furniture should never be designed by architects but rather created by craftsmen and arranged by the client according to his taste. Loos claimed that the influence of the architect should not extend beyond permanent fixtures. Chareau could accept responsibility for both sides of this argument, because he was, in a sense, at the same time craftsman and architect. The Maison de Verre is capable of adapting to different types of furniture without compromising its technical and architectural syntax in any way. It is as if this house was suffused with some kind of benevolent mechanism capable of assimilating entirely different works—an antique dining table and chairs, a suite by Chareau, or a decorative tapestry by Jean Lurçat—without its character, or technical qualities, being compromised or contradicted.

It is important to recall the special circumstances which prevailed at the time of the house's construction. In 1928, Madame Dalsace's father bought an eighteenth-century *hôtel particulier* in Paris, at 31 rue Saint Guillaume. The site was enclosed on all sides by party walls of varying heights and contained, besides the three-floor *hôtel particulier*, a forecourt and a garden at the rear. The clients intended to demolish the existing building and build from scratch, but the presence of a protected tenant on the second floor obliged clients and architect to envisage another solution. Out of this came the decision to underpin the second floor with steel and to demolish the unoccupied floors beneath, keeping only the existing access staircase. The resulting volume was sufficiently spacious to make room for three new floors of normal height, each level being set aside for a different purpose: the first floor to the practice of medicine; the second floor to daily living; and the third for sleeping quarters. A narrow service wing of three floors was built as an extension on one side of the forecourt to house the kitchen, a work room, and a maid's room, etc. Once this idea had been perfected and the steel frame erected, all that was needed was to enclose the house in a protective envelope and to furnish the interior. In this respect it was not unlike the embassy exhibited by Chareau in 1925, in that the latter was conceived as an exhibit of permanent fixtures of an exceptional size and complexity, constructed within an enclosing volume provided by an existing site. Dr. Dalsace was to write on this subject:

In order to spare an old lady who didn't want to leave her dingy second-floor apartment, Pierre Chareau has performed the extraordinary feat of building three floors full of light, in the ground and first floor of a small hôtel particulier. . . . The light circulates freely through this block, the first floor of which is devoted to medicine, the second floor to social life and the third to nighttime privacy. The problem this raised was enormously difficult to resolve. Interconnecting rooms, certain of which occupy two floors, make the problem of soundproofing very difficult. . . . The first floor, the professional section of the building, facilitates work and, with their initial uneasiness overcome, calms the patients down considerably. The whole house has been created under the influence of friendship, in complete affectionate understanding.[4]

From the first perspective sketches of the interior (the only drawings which remain) it may be deduced that the subdivisions and fittings were worked out little by little, as the work proceeded. These rather hasty drawings are the only evidence existing of the methodology of the project and construction. And thus, once the main idea had been laid down, the entire operation unfolded like a montage, bit by bit. In fact, we know that no working drawings in the general sense of the term were done.[5] On the contrary, the procedure usually consisted of moving from on-site drawings and sketches straight to fabrication as the craftsman Dalbet was on hand to build the prototypes and execute the final work. A rather crude model exhibited in 1931 shows the basic volume of the house after the structural work. It also shows the floors in place and the glass block curtain walls which comprised the two façades of the house. Site photographs taken in 1930 show more or less the same state of affairs.

Chareau used this commission to invent and perfect new prototypes of components, and in a sense the creator of the Maison de Verre seems to have regarded the work as a laboratory for the development of a hypothetical industrial architecture. Materials and techniques were either derived from industrial practice or from new combinations which were rich with industrial possibilities when the ideas were new. Chareau evidently had a passion for new materials, as is clearly seen in the first perspective sketches. In this context, it is quite characteristic that bent duraluminum sheeting was the first material considered for the balustrade of the main staircase. Even though this deployment was, in the end, reduced to a low, psychologically reassuring, tubular-steel guard-rail, bent duraluminum was to reappear in the cylindrical broom cupboard placed behind the staircase and in the freestanding clothes closet designed for the master bathroom.

In spite of the one-off experimental objects which abound throughout, the Maison de Verre is also built along rational lines. Thus, because of the standardization of its components, the house was to take on a wealth of implications which place it beyond the limits of a bourgeois domestic space. Although by definition limited in its realization to specialized craftsmen (it is almost unthinkable that the house could have been built without the many talents of Dalbet) it postulated nonetheless, by virtue of its modular nature, to a form of high-quality mass-production. Doors, stair rails, bookshelves, and cupboards as well as the curtain wall fenestration are treated like the modular components of a grid which crosses the entire house from back to front and, to a certain extent, from side to side.

Apart from this industrial potential, which even today remains largely unexploited in society as a whole, the Maison de Verre was the total machine object, elegantly conceived and executed with precision. In many instances, in line with the economical spirit of the French construction industry, the resistance of a material or a given component was pushed to its limits, as illustrated by the rolling-sliding mobile library ladder which moves on a carriage made from a single piece of bent tubing. It is significant that the railway carriage windows, made of vertically sliding plate glass, the clerestorys and remote-control ventilation shutters are, apart from the side-hung doors, the only openings of the outer envelope. From this we can conclude that the concept of "mobility" impregnated nearly all the details of the house, from sliding or swiveling windows to detachable staircases, from rotating cupboards to pivoting bidets, from sliding partitions to rotating screens.

In this respect the Maison de Verre is the transformable plan par excellence, to the extent that the ultimate motive of each transformation can appear completely variable, passing from necessity in one case to convenience in the next, or let us say this "poetry of equipment" has a more overtly symbolic significance in one instance than in another. The glass door pivoting on its axis on the first-floor landing of the main staircase is necessary to separate the social areas from the medical premises, and vice versa, while the service hatch for serving tea in Madame

Dalsace's boudoir may be viewed as a straightforward convenience. Similarly, the hinged, perforated, zinc screens which are attached to the pivoting glass door can be regarded as pure "poetry of equipment," in opposition, say, to the play between fixed and folding staircases at the rear of the house which have to be seen as having certain mythical connotations—to which we will return. Differences of this sort are clearly presented as concrete phenomena. In fact, the Maison de Verre appears to be organized homologically so that paired oppositions and reciprocal relations are found at every instance (compare the analysis of the Berber house by Pierre Bourdieu).[6] This is nowhere more pronounced than in the treatment of light, in which natural is noticeably opposed to *artificial* light, *translucent* to *transparent*, and so on. Depending on the hour of day, the light is now natural, now artificial; and the house is now illuminated externally or is itself the source of light. This homology appears in the course of time as a circumstantial sequence in which the components and the positions change place reciprocally. In the first case, the house is lit from the outside by the natural light penetrating to the interior through a translucent enclosure. In the second, the house is lit from inside by artificial lighting, some of which filters out through the glass-block facades, so that the house glows like a Chinese lantern. In the third case, the house is lit from outside by the artificial light, penetrating to the interior through these same facades—the house now being lit from the front and back by floodlights mounted on cantilevered brackets and freestanding ladders.

A homology of a similar, though less complex, nature may be observed in the interior fittings; specifically in the correspondence established between the layout of the library staircase (the mind) and the layout of the serving hatch from the kitchen to the dining area (the body). On the whole, this structural homology predominates in the design of all the mechanical services. For instance, throughout the house, all the electric cabling and interconnections run in separate vertical tubes which rise from one floor to another. At suitable points, these tubes are fitted with steel-covered consoles on which are placed all the necessary switches and sockets, so that the walls are kept clean. While energy and communication are conveyed in vertical tubes which cross the body of the house like a grid, heat in the form of air-conditioning circulates in ducts. In the first instance, invisible, modern energy is transported vertically and rendered visible; in the second, palpably antique energy (Roman) is conveyed horizontally and rendered, almost inevitably it seems, invisible. Essentially, the adjustable polished-metal vents, set in black lacquered manifolds are the only signs of the presence of this channeled air.

The Maison de Verre was recognized in its day as a functionalist work and as an integral part of the avant-garde of the Modern Movement, especially by Alberto Sartoris in his book *Gli elementi dell' architettura funzionale*—published in 1931, the year of the Maison de Verre's completion. Otherwise, it has in the main been left out of general works which discuss the Modern Movement, with the exception of the French edition of my book *Modern Architecture: A Critical History*.[7] The reasons for this strange omission are not hard to find. On one hand, its functionalism exceeded the minimum necessary to satisfy certain material requirements, leading to a certain redundancy in terms of both form and mechanical device. On the other, it was furnished in such a way as to exemplify the homogeneity of the interior and its capacity to assimilate different components of varied origin. In this respect, one would have no doubt mistrusted the non-transparent, but translucent walls and the taste for highly upholstered interiors as in the curtained walls of Dr. Dalsace's study. All these ambiguous characteristics would surely have been anathema to the fresh-air and hygiene cult of the mainstream Modern Movement.[8]

In fact, the Maison de Verre is just as difficult to classify according to accepted genres or common ideologies as is Marcel Duchamp's equally atypical work, *Le Grand Verre*, his famous glass construction created during the years 1915–23, more accurately known as *The Bride Stripped Bare by her Bachelors, even*. This comparison goes much further than the seemingly trivial fact that the two works were based on an obsessional and superfluous use of glass, since the two objects break all the classificatory rules which accord with a traditional understanding of their respective disciplines. Similar problems of classification abound in each. Should the Maison de Verre be looked on as architecture or as a furnishing operation on a large scale? Should *Le Grand Verre* be seen as a painting or a relief construction? In both cases, the works are unclassifiable in any conventional sense; they are "other" in the deepest sense of the word and this "strangeness" is a consequence of their opposition to the mainstream of Western art after the Renaissance. In this respect, both are "anti-" works, the Maison de Verre being a piece of anti-architecture and *Le Grand Verre* an anti-painting. The more or less continuous translucent covering of the Maison de Verre at one stroke does away with the counterpoint between solid and void which one finds in all architecture including the Modern Movement. The same is true for *Le Grand Verre*, which utterly undermines all established ideas on the fundamental nature of painting, that is to say, that it is about an image and a surface to be looked at, rather than looked through. As Duchamp was to say,"'retained in glass' doesn't mean 'painting on glass.' It is simply a means for no longer regarding the thing in question as a painting."[9]

But the comparison does not stop there, because the two works are homologically structured in a way that has more to do with pre-Renaissance magic or alchemic culture than with the Cartesian civilization. Of course, this is not to pretend that the conceptual structure of *Le Grand Verre* and the Maison de Verre are in any way identical, or that there is any proof of a direct influence by the one on the other. But nevertheless, in the two works, certain common themes become apparent which are worth noting. In the first place, the two works display in different ways a sort of excessive and needless mechanization; secondly, the two works are arranged in ways which, to some extent, at least, have erotic or sexual implications. In the case of *Le Grand Verre*, all this is well established and generally accepted; in the case of the Maison de Verre, we have little data except that the plan of the house lends itself to a reading which makes it appear as a "bachelor machine," according to the definition that Michel Carrouges has given of these contrivances:

To the contrary of real machines and even the larger part of imaginary but rational and useful machines such as Jules Verne's Nautilus or the rockets of science fiction, the bachelor machine appears first and foremost as a machine that is impossible, useless, incomprehensible, delirious. . . .

Each bachelor machine is a system of images composed of two equal and equivalent ensembles. One of these is the sexual ensemble. By definition this is comprised of two elements: masculine and feminine. . . .

The other part is the mechanical ensemble, also composed of two mechanical elements, which correspond respectively to the two masculine and feminine components of the sexual ensemble.

This duality and correspondence appear very distinctly in Duchamp's Le Grand Verre *which places the "bride" alone at the top, while the masculine "bachelor machine" is isolated at the bottom.*[10]

With the gynecological suite entirely occupying the first floor, the scheme of the Maison de Verre corresponds rather paradoxically with the first condition of this definition, and not only as far as the first floor is concerned, since the second and third floors follow a similar hierarchical order. In this way, the first floor can legitimately be analyzed as the "bachelor" or male part of the house, above all because it is in fact Dr. Dalsace's sacred domain and necessarily consecrated to celibacy; the third floor, which is that of the family bedrooms, can be taken as the "bride's" domain or the feminine area. Between these two floors, of course, lies the complex interface of the *piano nobile*, which is in part public and social, and in part private and intimate, and it is a fact that the second floor seems to comply with this code on more than one level.

This second floor is divided, quite intentionally, it would seem, into two sections. The eastern section combines the privacy of the boudoir, the domestic space of the kitchen, and the sociability of the dining area and can therefore conventionally be considered as the domain of the bride. The western section combines the privacy of the study and the public status of the drawing room and, as such, is under the conventional sign of the bachelor. While it is quite reasonable to suggest that this layout simply responded to functional needs as expressed in the project, the way in which these divisions are coded homologically by the varied floor coverings and by mechanical devices, such as the service stairs, only goes to demonstrate the mythic status of the house as a bachelor machine.

First, the rubber tiling of the first-floor gynecological suite continues via the main staircase to become the floor covering of the lounge and is further prolonged along an inconvenient, almost inelegant route which stops at the threshold of the boudoir. This coding is completed by the use of different floor coverings in other areas. Both the boudoir (female) and the study (male) are distinguished as intimate spaces by a flooring of matte black ceramic tiles, while the dining room and the service passage which leads to the kitchen are finished in parquet flooring, the warmth of the wood indicating their obvious character as domestic spaces.

Second, the "mechanical" side appears in the reciprocal disposition of the service staircases, which set up a discreet but precise relationship between the intimate spaces of the second floor—the boudoir and the study— and the respective spheres of the male and the female on the other floors, the bride being above and the bachelor below. The specific form of the stairs is not without significance in this regard. First, because the bride's staircase is quite explicitly a mechanical device, an open ladder that can be lowered and retracted into the soffit of the ceiling separating the boudoir from the main bedroom above, which is evidently the bride's domain; and second because the bachelor's staircase is fixed although still mechanical in that it winds around a telephone cabin as it descends from the study to the medical suite. This implicit movement is emphasized by the way in which the handrail in tubular steel climbs in an unbroken zigzag from the ground to the *piano nobile*.

The homologous disposition of the private areas in the bride's and bachelor's domains on the first floor reads then as follows: the boudoir (the bride) is linked by a detachable "rising" staircase to the main bedroom above, while the study (the bachelor) is linked by a fixed "descending" staircase to the gynecologist's consulting room below. An indication of this homology is encountered in the same area of interface in plan, as an exchange, so to speak, between the coding of the second and third floors. This exchange transpires between the study and the boudoir on the one hand, and the bathroom and the main bedroom on the other. In the first case, a double set of staggered sliding doors, set at right angles, creates a valvular passage between the study and the boudoir. In the second, a similarly valvular arrangement is involved in the division of the main bathroom into a male and a female zone: between the rectangular bath (female) and the circular shower cubicle (male) situated on opposite sides of the bathroom. The fact that these different arrangements conform to Madame and Dr. Dalsace's respective preferences for ablution reinforces rather than undermines the symbolic organization of the Maison de Verre according to the myth of the bachelor machine.

Such a combination is further confirmation of the astonishing intimacy, "the friendship, the complete affectionate understanding," which existed at the creation of the Maison de Verre. It is clear that, as in all first-rate houses, the client shares the responsibility equally with the architect. In fact, there are times when the entire work seems to be an exact reflection of the personality of Annie Dalsace: a subtle homage that Chareau pays to his client. Subtly, but with a curious insistence, the house appears to be dedicated again and again to the "bride," from the gynecological suite itself to the multiplicity of bidets arranged on the bedroom floor. Moreover, in spite of the functional motifs, a dominant feminine image (which is nevertheless paradoxically submissive) is twice placed at the panoptic center of a space; the first in the axis of the entrance hall, which appropriately falls under the eye of the nurse who supervises the medical floor, the second on the third floor, where the maid's work and control room looks down on the entire volume of the lounge. It may be added that these two panoptic control positions are assumed by the servants of the "bachelor" and "bride" respectively.

Although the relationship (or rather the absence of relationship) between *Le Grand Verre* and the Maison de Verre must almost certainly remain as one of the enigmas of twentieth-century avant-garde culture, a comparison of this sort cannot completely ignore the consideration of certain specific correspondences between the two works. For instance, we can ask ourselves whether there is not some justification in comparing the detachable staircase of the Maison de Verre with the *panda female* ("swinging this way and that") of *Le Grand Verre*, or if it is not correct to see the staccato climb of the study staircase or the revolving clothes cupboard of the main bathroom as transpositions of Duchamp's *Chocolate Grinder* of 1914, of which he was to write in *La Boîte Verte*, 1934: "The bachelor grinds his chocolate himself."[11]

The thing which is clear in all this is that Chareau was perfectly *au fait* with the vicissitudes of Cubism and Futurism and must therefore without any doubt have had knowledge of Duchamp's *Le Grand Verre* and the different paintings in his production from which it was derived. Moreover, it is significant that Chareau resorted to Cubist devices—changes of level and of material—to differentiate the areas of the various floors. These differences were juxtaposed in a way which strongly recalls Synthetic Cubism, above all the Cubist collage, and marked, as we have seen, changes in the real and mythic status of the volumes.

Throughout his career, at least until the Maison de Verre, the work of Chareau wavered continually between the cult for the "ready-made," which he owed in part to the influence of Dadaism, and the standards of quality craftsmanship of the Salon des Artistes Décorateurs. There is without doubt only one work from his period of greatest activity in which this opposition is for a moment abandoned in favor of a normative, functional approach that is entirely rational. This is the offices for the LTT Telephone Company in Paris (1931–32), which was notably the only commission in Chareau's career that was not a domestic but a utilitarian building. Of a mechanical precision throughout, with its concrete mosaic floors, tubular-steel chairs, standardized steel office furniture, glass-tiled partitions, mirror screens, and metal windows, the interior of the LTT was a tour de force in steel and glass construction. This austere work was illuminated by large windows and sparkling with light. In it Chareau seems finally to have abandoned his predilection for enclosed interiors. Under the influence of International Constructivism, via his daily dealings with Bernard Bijvoët, he comes closer than ever in this work to the hyper-functionalism of the Neue

Sachlichkeit.* Indeed, two years later, he was to choose an even more "sachlich" approach in the project for a boat cabin, an exhibition piece destined for the fifth exhibition of the Union des Artistes Modernes as part of the Salon d'Automne.[12]

The swan song of Chareau's career in France was the little weekend house that he built for the dancer Djemil Anik in the Paris suburbs in 1937.[13] This work seems to announce a fundamental break in the nature of Chareau's approach, a break as definitive as that undergone by Francis Picabia in his career as a painter, after 1924. While such ruptures were not in themselves connected in any way, they are comparable in the sense that after having reached a certain pinnacle of success, the work of each of the artists was irremediably changed. In the case of Picabia, it is the set designs for *Relâche* and *Entr'acte*, both of 1924, which seem to have been the decisive factors; in Chareau's case it is the completion of the Maison de Verre. The rupture between the Maison de Verre and the Anik house is so complete that René Herbst chose to exclude any illustration of it in his monograph of 1954 in memory of Chareau, even though his text proves that he knew of its existence.[14] It is equally significant and even understandable that Herbst should have discriminated between Chareau's work in France, which is well represented, with large photographs, and his production in America, to which he accords only small illustrations as pointers.

Apart from the Depression and the further shock of the Second World War, which obliged him to exile himself in the United States, not to mention the modest sums that were subsequently placed at his disposal, there seem to be only two plausible explanations for this sudden change in his work. The first is that Chareau was psychologically burnt out after the energy spent on the Maison de Verre. The second is that, in the middle of the 1930s, he lost his principal collaborators, Bijvoët, who returned to Holland in 1935, and Dalbet, who was left exhausted and ruined after the work on the Maison de Verre. At any event, Chareau seems to have consciously decided that a certain epoch had come to an end and that there was no other alternative but to continue a kind of *degré zero* architecture. Partly from necessity, partly from choice, after 1932 Chareau opted for ordinary, low-cost constructions, in which the only poetic qualities that could be found came from subtle inflections imposed on the common necessities of everyday life.

Influenced possibly by the house that Le Corbusier built at Mathes in 1935, the Anik house is an attempt to return to a modern rustic style, the architectural emphasis passing from the body of the house to the structure, and to a deliberate interplay between two gently sloping roofs which were to cover respectively the main dwelling and the outhouse with the toilets, etc. Chareau seems to have attempted to accentuate the rustic effect by giving these roofs different slants. In other respects, the organization of the house could hardly be simpler, the first floor being given over to a garage and a shower room, and the second floor consisting of a large room facing west over a covered access gallery. The only interruption in the main volume was a steep staircase climbing to two attic bedrooms and a small enclosed kitchen. The structure consists of a three-story framework set on low stone walls and pillars. Above this stone base, the building is covered with panels of heraclite. Something of Chareau's fondness for the Japanese attention to detail (clearly apparent in the steel objects lacquered in black and painted with red oxide of the Maison de Verre) is again present here, above all in the naive orientalism of the revealed wooden skeleton. In other respects, the woodwork is typically Western with bolted, centered window frames. Little, in fact, remains of the inventiveness that was peculiar to Chareau and still less of his taste, except perhaps for the metal grill balustrade in the gallery and the portholes which light the garage. In the main, the Anik house seems like a disenchanted reflection on the impossibility of preserving architectural culture, a sort of compensatory worship of "the dumb and the ordinary" thirty years *avant la lettre*.

* Die Neue Sachlichkeit: the new objectivity. Exhibition organized from June 14 to September 13, 1925, at the Kunsthalle in Mannheim. This movement particularly influenced the painters (for example, Christian Schad, Otto Dix) and the photographers (for example, Albert Renger-Patzch, August Sander).

This feeling undoubtedly persisted in the American houses that Chareau designed at the end of his life, the house and studio built for the painter Robert Motherwell in corrugated-metal shells of military quonset huts, and in the rather anonymous one-story house built for himself on the same East Hampton site. In these simple buildings, and in a scarcely more important work built in New York State for Germaine Monteux and Nancy Laughlin, and known as *La Colline*, neither invention nor taste really survive, because the whole thing was reduced to variations on an American pseudo-vernacular. Everything about these houses was decided either by the tightness of the budget or by the prevailing circumstances, so that all that remained was a hidden nostalgia, expressed in crude material, which brought back in one way or another the memory of the lost glories of the Maison de Verre. This nostalgia appears perhaps even more poignantly in the mezzanine of the Motherwell house, where the floor is covered in sawn-off logs set in concrete and where once again there is a metal grill balustrade, even though, unlike in the Anik house, the grill is the cheapest kind of chicken wire. In the Motherwell house, the Maison de Verre is still present in the exposed columns and the steel I-beams supporting the upper floor, in the collapsible canvas canopy and the continuous flower box which both occupy and articulate the space between the fenestration of the long greenhouse window and the semicircular structure of the hut itself. At East Hampton, everywhere there are brief flashes of the old mastery: the sliding entrance door, the open plan, the freestanding fireplace of the Motherwell house, and in the strange doors and oblique windows of Chareau's own one-story house. But in the main he had thrown in his hand and little remained to be done in the last decade of his life, in those twilight years in New York where he worked on the exhibitions that he was asked to present for the French Cultural Center. He surely knew what was lost when he wrote to René Herbst a few months before his death: "I cannot tell you the emotion which I feel from a distance at all the touching gestures and expressions of friendship. I feel it all the more because I am certain of your support in the pursuit of my duties here. I would give so much for us to meet before long, what can you do, I have to choose to be of some use and I believe that I am."

These laconic words testify more than anything else, perhaps, to Chareau's stoicism and modesty: the architect as bricoleur before the deluge.

[1] J. K. Huysmans, *A Rebours* (Paris, 1884).

[2] Le Corbusier, "L'Art Décoratif d'aujourd'hui" in *L'Esprit nouveau* (Paris, 1959).

[3] Paul Nelson, "Maison de Verre," in *L'Architecture d'Aujourd'hui* 9 (November–December 1933), 9.

[4] Cited by René Herbst in *Un Inventeur, l'architecte Pierre Chareau* (Paris, 1954), 7 and 8.

[5] In an interview with Robert Vickery in 1965 Bernard Bijvoët stated that no real working drawings were ever done for the house.

[6] Pierre Bourdieu, "La Maison ou le monde renversé," in *Esquisse d'une théorie de la pratique précédé de trois études d'ethnologie Kabyle* (Paris, 1972).

[7] Kenneth Frampton, *Modern Architecture: A Critical History* (London: Thames and Hudson, 1980).

[8] For some, the house was too functional. See the account by Julien Lepage in *L'Architecture d'Aujourd'hui* 9, (November–December 1933): 14–15.

[9] Marcel Duchamp, *La Boîte Verte* (New York, 1960).

One may equally refer to another text by Duchamp where he writes: "This is no longer a painting: the transparent surface of the glass ceases to play the role of an imaginary screen; the erotic machinery operates in empiric space."

[10] Michel Carrouges, "Mode d'emploi," in *Les Machines célibataires* (Venice, 1975), 21.

[11] Duchamp, *La Boîte Verte*.

[12] L'Union des Artistes Modernes (UAM) was founded by René Herbst; the first executive committee in 1930 was composed of the following: Hélène Henry, René Herbst, Francis Jourdain, Robert Mallet-Stevens, Raymond Templier. Pierre Chareau appeared as a "guest member" in 1930.

[13] See Phillippe Bourgeois, Jean-Marc Dutrevis, Robert Ecoiffier, and Rémi Leberre, "Un Projet inédit de Pierre Chareau," in *Architecture, Mouvement, Continuité* 51 (December 1980): 45–54.

[14] Herbst, *Un Inventeur*.

Perspecta 21: The Yale Architectural Journal
34)

CRITICAL ARCHITECTURE: BETWEEN CULTURE AND FORM

K. Michael Hays

That architecture, as activity and knowledge, is fundamentally a cultural enterprise may hardly seem a contentious proposition. And yet questions concerning the precise nature of the reciprocal influences between culture and architectural form bring opposing theories of architecture and its interpretation into forceful play.[1]

In this essay I shall examine a critical architecture, one resistant to the self-confirming, conciliatory operations of a dominant culture and yet irreducible to a purely formal structure disengaged from the contingencies of place and time. A reinterpretation of a few projects by Mies van der Rohe will provide examples of a critical architecture that claims for itself a place *between* the efficient representation of preexisting cultural values and the wholly detached autonomy of an abstract formal system. The proposition of a critical realm between culture and form is not so much an extension of received views of interpretation as it is a challenge to those views that claim to exhaust architectural meaning in considerations of only one side or the other. It will be helpful, therefore, to begin with a brief review of two prevalent interpretive perspectives that make just such a claim.

ARCHITECTURE AS AN INSTRUMENT OF CULTURE

The first position emphasizes culture as the cause and content of built form; the task of the interpreter, then, becomes the study of objects and environments as signs, symptoms, and instruments of cultural values. In this view architecture is essentially an epiphenomenon, dependent on socioeconomic, political, and technological processes for its various states and transformations. Moreover, as a functional support for human institutions and as a reification of a collective volition, architecture ennobles the culture that produces it; architecture reconfirms the hegemony of culture and helps to assure its continuity. Accordingly, the optimum relationship to be established between culture and form is one of correspondence, the latter efficiently representing the values of the former.

The temporal convention of interpretation is, in this view, retrospective. Architecture is seen as already completed; the critic or historian attempts to restore an architectural object to its original meaning. Misunderstanding is presumed to arise naturally because of the changes in architecture, language, and worldview that have taken place in the time separating the architectural object from the interpreter; the meaning must therefore be recovered by a disciplined reconstruction of the cultural situation in which the object originated. Starting from the documents, recorded actions, and artifacts which are the base material of the historical world, understanding is seen as essentially a self-transposition or imaginative projection backward in time. When this historical method is of sufficient fidelity, an *objective* and *true* explanation of the object in question results. It is supposed that the only alternative to the strict methodological recovery of the cultural situation at the time of the object's origin is the denial of any historical objectivity and capitulation to the idea that all schemes of interpretation are hopelessly subjective.[2]

The opposite position begins with the assumption that the only alternative to a strict, factual recovery of the originating situation is the renunciation of a single *truth*, and advocates a proliferation of interpretations based solely
on form. Interpretations made from this second position are characterized by the comparative absence of historical
concerns in favor of attention to the autonomous architectural object and its formal operations—how its parts have
been put together, how it is a wholly integrated and equilibrated system that can be understood without external
references, and as important, how it may be reused, how its constituent parts and processes may be recombined.

The temporal convention of interpretation here is that of an ideal moment in a purely conceptual space; architectural operations are imagined to be spontaneous, internalized—that is, outside circumstantial reality—and
assimilable as pure idea. Architectural form is understood to be produced in a particular time and place, of course,
but the origin of the object is not allowed to constrain its meaning. The intent is precisely to dismiss any of the
worldly, circumstantial, or socially contaminated content of history, because such subject matter would necessarily
impinge upon the intellectual liberty of criticism and the availability of the formal strategies for reuse. Architectural
form can be read and interpreted, of course, yet misreadings and misunderstandings are understood to occur rou-
tinely, and with benefit. In any case, there is a conscious avoidance of any historical or material fact other than
those of a dislodged formal system. The way in which a building as a cultural object in time is possessed, rejected,
or achieved is not addressed.[3]

Such an approach has not been entirely unhealthy for architectural interpretation. It has done away with testi-
monials rhetorically proclaiming a work's greatness and humanistic worth on the basis of its accurate representation
of the dominant culture. It has developed a specialized vocabulary enabling critics to talk seriously, technically,
and precisely about the architectural object as distinct from other kinds of objects. Furthermore, so long as we con-
strue architecture as essentially dependent on or representative of something else, we cannot see what it does
itself; so long as we expect to understand architecture in terms of some anterior process, we cannot see an architecture that is, paradoxically, both the end of representation and the beginning of something quite its own.

Nevertheless, the absolute autonomy of form and its superiority over historical and material contingencies
is proclaimed, not by virtue of its power in the world, but by virtue of its admitted powerlessness. Reduced
to pure form, architecture has disarmed itself from the start, maintaining its purity by acceding to social and
political inefficacy.

Moreover, this formalist position risks collapsing into an interpretive scientism not unlike the one it seeks
to criticize. If attempts to recover "history as it really happened" display a quite overt emulation of the positivist
methodology of the natural sciences, the formalist attitude too often falls unwittingly into its own scientism as
formal categories become more rigidly defined and entrenched. When priority is ascribed to formal categories and
operations that claim to be free of history and circumstance, interpretive analysis risks simply reaffirming what its
formal categories predict. The supposed universality of any one kind of formal analysis obscures the fact that critical methods are formed through examination of a necessarily limited set of exemplars, and that these paradigms
emanate from a specific culture—they do not come to us untainted. It also obscures the fact that the methods of
study of these objects are themselves part of a larger complex ensemble of relationships, are contaminated by their

own worldliness, and are legitimized by some other cultural authority. A perhaps unforeseen consequence of this idealization of object and method is that architecture is denied its special status as a cultural object with a causation, presence, and duration of its own.

THE WORLDLINESS OF ARCHITECTURE

The two positions sketched above are symptomatic of a pervasive dichotomy in architectural theory and criticism. One side describes artifacts as instruments of the self-justifying, self-perpetuating hegemony of culture; the other side treats architectural objects in their most disinfected, pristine state, as containers of a privileged principle of internal coherence. An alternative interpretive position which cuts across this dichotomy would bear not only a more robust description of the artifacts, but also the more intricate analysis demanded by artifacts situated explicitly and critically *in the world*—in culture, in theories of culture, in theories of interpretation itself.

A discussion of a few projects by Mies van der Rohe will draw attention to the fact that an architectural object, by virtue of its situation in the world, is an object whose interpretation *has already commenced* but is *never complete*. Historical contingency and circumstantiality, as well as the artifact's persisting sensuous particularity, must all be considered as incorporated in the architectural object; they saturate the very essence of the work. Each architectural object places itself in a specific situation in the world, so to speak, and its manner of doing this constrains what can be done with it in interpretation. The particular works by Mies to be examined are those I would describe as *critical*. They might also be called *resistant* and *oppositional*. This is an architecture that cannot be reduced either to a conciliatory representation of external forces or to a dogmatic, reproducible formal system. If a critical architecture is to be worldly and self-aware simultaneously, its definition is in its difference from other cultural manifestations and from a priori categories or methods.

THE CRITICAL ARCHITECTURE OF MIES VAN DER ROHE

Among the principal problems the intellectual faced in the first half of the twentieth century was the acute anxiety that derived from the chaotic metropolitan experience. In the essay "The Metropolis and Mental Life," the sociologist and philosopher Georg Simmel described this condition as "the intensification of nervous stimulation" resulting from the "the rapid crowding of changing images, the sharp discontinuity in the grasp of a single glance, and the unexpectedness of onrushing impressions. These are the psychological conditions which the metropolis creates." The typical consequence of this *nervenleben,* according to Simmel, is a blasé attitude—a blunting of discrimination, an indifference to value, a languid collectivity. "In this phenomenon the nerves find in the refusal to react to their stimulation the last possibility of accommodating to the contents and forms of metropolitan life. The self-preservation of certain personalities is bought at the price of devaluating the whole objective world, a devaluation which in the end unavoidably drags one's own personality down into a feeling of the same worthlessness."[4]

The problem for the intellectual, then, was how to oppose this debilitating dismay, but first how to reveal it—how to provide a cognitive mechanism with which to register the intense changes continually experienced in the modern city. Many of the century's early artistic experiments, from the woodcuts of Edvard Munch (fig. 151) to the novels of Franz Kafka, may be seen as attempts to articulate the abject despair of the individual caught by impersonal and incomprehensible forces. The *reklamearchitektur* (advertising architecture) of Eric Mendelsohn and the factories of Hans Poelzig made manifest, as if to pin down and contemplate, the dynamism, the contradictions, and the disjunctures in the processes and reasoning of commerce and industry. On the other hand, Dada's ferocious nihilism was an explicit attempt to demonstrate the futility of conventional modes of reasoning in the face of the chaotic city. As Jean Arp put it, "Dada wished to destroy the hoaxes of reason and to discover an unreasoned order."[5] And Mondrian named the city itself as the ultimate form toward which de Stijl tended. "The genuinely Modern artist sees the metropolis as Abstract living converted into form; it is nearer to him than nature."[6] It is against this metropolitan predicament that the early work of Mies van der Rohe should be seen.

The rather startling image of the 1922 skyscraper project (fig. 155), published in the second issue of *G*, comprises two architectural propositions. One, a result of experiments already begun in Mies's Friedrichstrasse project (fig. 154), is a building surface qualified no longer by patterns of shadow on an opaque material but by the reflections and refractions of light by glass. The other, a radical departure from even the earlier skyscraper studies, is a building form conceived not in terms of separate, articulated masses related to one another by a geometrically derived core, but as a complex unitary volume that does not permit itself to be read in terms of an internal formal logic. With these two related propositions Mies confronted the problem of physically and conceptually relating the architectural object to the city. The glass curtain wall—alternately transparent, reflective, or refractive depending on light conditions and viewing positions—absorbs, mirrors, or distorts the immediate images of city life. The convex, faceted surfaces are perceptually contorted by the invasion of circumstantial images, while the reflection each concavity receives on its surface is that of its own shadow, creating gaps which exacerbate the disarray.

These surface distortions accompany and accentuate the formal inscrutability of the volumetric configuration. In classically derived form, the viewer can grasp an antecedent logic of the object, deciphering the relationships between its parts and connecting every part to a coherent formal theme; the alternative posited by Mies is an object intractable to decoding by formal analysis. It is impossible, for example, to reduce the whole to a number of constituent parts related by some internal armature or transformed through some formal operation; indeed, no such compositional relationships exist. Neither is it possible to explicate the object as a deflection from some type; Mies has rejected the meanings that such classical design methods tend to promote. Instead he has invested meaning in the sense of surface and volume that the building assumes in a particular time and place, in a contextually qualified moment.

Mies insists that an order is immanent in the surface itself and that the order is continuous with and dependent upon the world in which the viewer actually moves. This sense of surface and volume, severed from the knowledge of an internal order or a unifying logic, is enough to wrench the building from the atemporal, idealized realm of autonomous form and install it in a specific situation in the real world of experienced time, open to the chance and uncertainty of life in the metropolis.[7] Mies here shares with Dada an antagonism against a priori and reasoned order; he plunges into the chaos of the new city and seeks another order within it through a systematic use of the unexpected, the aleatory, the inexplicable.[8]

This solicitation of experience is intrinsic to the meaning of the work; it serves to identify and individuate the work itself as an event having sensuous particularity and temporal duration, both of which are infrangible to its capacity for producing and conveying meaning. Nevertheless, Mies's skyscraper project is not conciliatory to the circumstances of its context. It is a critical interpretation of its worldly situation.

In the skyscraper project of 1922 Mies approached a radically new conception of reciprocity between the corporeality of the architectural object and the images of culture that surround it; by 1928—in projects like the Adam building on the Leipzigerstrasse in Berlin, the bank in Stuttgart, and the competition for the Alexanderplatz in Berlin (figs. 159 and 160)—he seems to have diverted his efforts. These projects abstain from any dialogue with the physical particularities of their contexts; as peremptorily demonstrated in the drawings, the glass-walled blocks could be reproduced on any site with no significant manipulation of their form. Though each building unit has been adapted to the shape and size of its own lot (for example, the Alexanderplatz project), the relentless sameness of the units and their undifferentiated order tend to deny the possibility of attaching sig-nificance to the placement or arrangement of the forms. But the repudiation of a priori formal logic as the primary locus of meaning is precisely what is at issue; it is this repudiation that links the projects of 1928 to the research of 1922. Meaning is made a function of impersonal productive systems rather than of formal operations or of repre-sentational devices.

Here we must take Mies at his word. "We refuse to recognize problems of form, but only problems of building. Form is not the aim of our work, but only the result. Form by itself does not exist. Form as an aim is formalism; and that we reject."[9] As hypothesized by Mies, modern building production requires that each building unit be complete in itself yet identical to all others, disallowing either hierarchical relationships among units or predetermined points of focus or termination. Rejecting the specifications of the Alexanderplatz competition, for instance—which favored a curved, peripheral building that would enclose and centralize the space of the preexisting traffic circle—Mies's objects are disposed in such a way that no resolute center can be found. Across the *Platz* or across the inter-vals of space between the serial building units, each glass-walled block confronts and recognizes nothing but its double. Like two parallel mirrors, each infinitely repeats the other's emptiness. The space is duplicitous, but the motivation is inescapable. Mies's achievement was to open up a clearing of implacable silence in the chaos of the nervous metropolis; this clearing is a radical critique, not only of the established spatial order of the city and the established logic of classical composition, but also of the inhabiting *nervenleben*. It is the extreme depth of silence in this clearing—silence as an architectural form all its own—that is the architectural meaning of this project.

Both conceptions of the architectural object—as the efficient embodiment of a dominant system of values, and as the uncircumstanced existence of autonomous form—are seriously challenged, if not defeated, by the way in which this silent clearing claims a place in the world. First there is the recognition of the reciprocity between the culturally qualified, empirical conditions of building production and the practice of architecture. Mies's obdurate refusal to manipulate his objects to conform to any a priori formal logic has the effect of repudiating internal formal operations as a source of the objects' meaning. Second, though Mies succeeds in directing the architectural mean-ing to the outside—to what might be called cultural space—there is the insistence that architecture does not *honestly* represent the technical, social, or economic conditions that produced it. Indeed, Mies's architecture conceals the *real* origins of its formation by displacing them with a material substitute—an irreducibly architectural object. It effectively cancels the complex network of colliding forces in which architecture originates to present us with the silent fact of its existence. "Since the facts have the floor, let anyone who has anything to say come forward and keep his mouth shut," wrote Karl Kraus.[10] Mies's silent architecture, following Kraus's dictum, comes forward to occupy its cultural space actively; it displaces what would have been in its place. Critical architecture pushes aside other kinds of discourse or communication in order to place before the world a culturally informed product, part of whose self-definition includes the implication of *discontinuity* and *difference* from other cultural activities.

Distinguishing architecture from the forces that influence architecture—the conditions established by the market and by taste, the personal aspirations of its author, its technical origins, even its purpose as defined by its own tradition—became the objective of Mies. To achieve this, he placed his architecture in a critical position between culture as a massive body of self-perpetuating ideas and form supposedly free of circumstance.

Our observations can be verified against the masterwork of Mies's early career, the 1929 German Pavilion in Barcelona (figs. 161-68, 172, 173, 175, 179, and 182). With respect to our analysis thus far, this project initially appears polemical and self-critical. The pavilion has been widely regarded as the most immaculate transcription of the modern spatial conception: a synthesis of Wright's horizontal planes and the abstract compositions of the Suprematist-Elementarists; with honorific nods to the walls of Berlage ("let alone from floor to cornice"), the materials of Loos, and the podium and columns of Schinkel; all processed through the spatial conceptions of de Stijl. This seems to claim for the pavilion a rarefied spatial order that presents itself as an a priori mental construct rather than a palpable worldly object.

However, this is precisely *not* the order of Mies: "The idealistic principle of order. . . with its over-emphasis on the ideal and formal, satisfies neither our interest in simple reality nor our practical commonsense."[11]

The Barcelona Pavilion begins with a horizontally extended space which is described by the uninterrupted roof slab, its relation to the columns and walls, and the corresponding constancy of section and volume implied by the floor plane. Space is, quite literally, continuous between the pavilion and the plaza in front of the Palace Alfonso XIII. The pavilion more specifically engages its site through the careful contrast between the long travertine walls, the roof slab, and the unbroken palace wall. All this solicits the viewer to walk through the building, but the limpid harmony of the exterior is confounded in the experience of the spatial succession of the interior.

There is no prescribed logic of passage; the composition is neither a relational hierarchy of component parts nor a series of identical units repeated in a potentially endless chain. What is presented instead is an assemblage of different parts of disparate materials: the travertine pavement and walls surrounding the large pool, the marble walls facing the court, tinted glass diaphragms, the onyx slab and light wall, the chromium columns and glazing bars. The relationships among these parts are in constant flux as one moves through the building. Because there is no conceptual center to organize the parts or transcend our perception of them, the particular quality of each material is registered as a kind of absolute; space itself becomes a function of the specificities of the materials.

The normal system of expectations about materials, however, is quickly shattered as materials begin to contradict their own nature. Supporting columns dissolve in an invasion of light on their surfaces; the highly polished green Tinian marble reflects the highlights of the chromium glazing bars and seems to become transparent, as does the onyx slab; the green-tinted glass, in turn, becomes an insuperable mirrored screen; the pool in the small court—shielded from the wind and lined in black glass—is a perfect mirror, in which stands George Kolbe's *Dancer*. The fragmentation and distortion of the space is total. Any transcendent order of space and time that would confer an overarching unity onto this assemblage is systematically and utterly dispersed. Mies has constructed a labyrinth that denies us access to the ideal moment of organization lying beyond the actual experience of this montage of contradictory, perceptual facts. The work itself is an event with temporal duration, whose actual existence is continually being produced.

What should strike us forcibly, then, is that the artifact is nothing less than a *winning of reality*.[12] Though it exists to a considerable extent by virtue of its own formal structures, it cannot be apprehended only formally. Nor does it simply represent a preexisting reality. The architectural reality takes its place *alongside* the real world, explicitly sharing temporal and spatial conditions of that world, but obstructing their absolute authority with an alternative of material, technical, and theoretical precision. A participant in the world and yet disjunctive with it, the Barcelona Pavilion tears a cleft in the continuous surface of reality.

A brief analogy will perhaps afford these points added clarity. In 1929 Max Ernst published his pictorial novel, *La Femme 100 Têtes* (The hundred headless woman, fig. 169), a purely metropolitan inspiration comprising a series of collages made from scenes gathered from popular nineteenth-century illustrated books and magazines onto which Ernst grafted objects or occupants foreign to them. What results in such collages as "Tous les vendredis, les Titans parcourront nos buanderies" (Every Friday, the Titans will invade our laundry) is a laconic display of two incommensurable experiences interlocked across the surface of the work. Like Ernst, Mies was able to see his constructions as the place in which the motivated, the planned, and the rational are brought together with the contingent, the unpredictable, and the inexplicable. This vision persisted even in Mies's later works. The campus of IIT (fig. 170), for example, can be construed as a redistribution of some of the design strategies of the Alexanderplatz project and the Barcelona Pavilion—a subtle grafting of an alternative reality onto the chaos of Chicago's South Side.

AUTHORSHIP AS A RESISTANT AUTHORITY

From the skyscraper project of 1922 to the Barcelona Pavilion, Mies's architectural program was a persistent rewriting of a few themes. Beginning with a set of arbitrary propositions, Mies rationalized his initial choice of themes by demonstrating the range of their applicability. He reused them in changing circumstances; he modified and refined them over time. This sort of repetition renders the issue of origins or first causes unproblematic, one arbitrary *cantus firmus* being imitated and repeated so many times as to lose its primacy.

Though the beginning of his authorship is arbitrary, repetition demonstrates the consistency of Mies's authorial motivation; it establishes the constancy of his intent. A persistently rearticulated intent accumulates knowledge—more specific and more precise—of the general architectural program and allows the growth of that knowledge according to its own special beginnings and conventions rather than according to those derived from some prior authority. Mies does not accept a preexisting frame of reference; he represents neither an authoritative culture nor an authoritative formal system.

Repetition thus demonstrates how architecture can resist, rather than reflect, an external cultural reality. In this way authorship achieves a *resistant authority*—an ability to initiate or develop cultural knowledge whose absolute authority is radically nil but whose contingent authority is a quite persuasive, if transitory, alternative to the dominant culture. Authorship can resist the authority of culture, stand against the generality of habit and the particularity of nostalgic memory, and still have a very precise intention.

One crucial issue remains unclear: What is the precise realm of theoretical interest in a critical architecture? How does one define or demarcate the spatial or temporal interval that is the focus of a critical examination of architecture? This discussion of Mies suggests that the realm of interest is in the distance established between architecture and that which is *other* than architecture.

No single building—neither the most distinguished nor the most pedestrian—can reflect a preexistent cultural reality with perfect fidelity. To the extent that a work is architecture, it differs qualitatively both from a representation of reality and from a reduplication of other cultural activities. But the difference carries ideological motivation; it produces knowledge both about culture and about architecture. It should be possible to recognize both the means by which architecture maintains its distance from all that is outside architecture and the conditions that permit the existence of that distance.

The kind of theoretical study suggested here does not assume the prior existence of unchanging principles for interpreting architecture. Instead what is assumed is a specific situation from which came the decision to make architecture. This means that each architectural object places restraints upon interpretation, not because the situation is hidden within the object as a puzzle, but rather because contingent and worldly circumstances exist at the same level of surface particularity as the object itself. Interpretive inquiry lies in an irreducibly architectural realm between those conditions that seem to generate or enable the architect's intention to make architecture and those forms in which the intention is transcribed.[13]

The contingent authority of the individual architect exists at a sensitive nodal point. The individual consciousness is a part of and is aware of the collective historical and social situation. Because of this awareness, the individual is not a mere product of the situation but is a historical and social actor in it. There is choice and, therefore, the responsibility of a critical architecture.

But what, then, is the responsibility of architectural criticism or of critical historiography? Is it to teach and to disseminate information about the monuments of culture? Is it to deliver technical insights and opinions about the capabilities of the architect or the form of the building? Or is it, as has been suggested here, to concentrate on the intrinsic conditions through which architecture is made possible? In order to know all we can about architecture we must be able to understand each instance of architecture, not as a passive agent of culture in its dominant ideological, institutional, and historical forms, nor as a detached, disinfected object. Rather we must understand it as actively and continually occupying a cultural place—as an architectural intention with ascertainable political and intellectual consequences. Criticism delimits a field of values within which architecture can develop cultural knowledge.

Architectural criticism and critical historiography are activities continuous with architectural design; both criticism and design are forms of knowledge. If critical architectural design is resistant and oppositional, then architectural criticism—as activity and knowledge—should be openly contentious and oppositional as well. We must seek alternatives to entrenched modes of operation and canonical forms. We must strive to invest critical discourse with something more than compensatory, appreciative reflections or methods of formal analysis for objects whose cultural meaning is thought to be undecidable. It is precisely the responsibility of criticism that this cultural meaning be continually decided.

I have benefited from the questions and criticisms of RSID students who participated in my seminar "Interpretations of Modern Architecture," where many of the ideas presented here were formulated; and from the responses of colleagues who read earlier versions of the paper. I especially wish to thank Stanford Anderson and Rodolfo Machado for their continued support and encouragement.

1. By culture, as I shall use the term here, I understand a conceptual unity comprising, on the one hand, those theoretical and practical systems which authorize, promote, or constrain the production and use of ideas and objects and by which a society or a place differentiates itself and maintains its hegemony; and on the other hand, the artifacts and environments which endure as resourceful physical precedents or exemplars of systems of production and become transmitters of culture. Thus, it is in the purview of culture that the production of architecture is overseen from above by a dominant system of values saturating downward, and generated or validated at its base by normative standards of practice and methodologies which may themselves become cultural agents.

2. The historicism of this position has been criticized by numerous authors, most notably Stanford Anderson, Colin Rowe, and David Watkin. Watkin uses a Popperian argument against historicism without holding Anderson's earlier study "Architecture and Tradition" in *The History, Theory, and Criticism of Architecture*, ed. Marcus Whiffen (Cambridge, Mass.: MIT Press, 1965).

Watkin does mention in a different context Anderson's review of Pevsner's *Source s. . .* in *Art Bulletin* 53 (Sept. 1971): 274-75. I shall not rehearse these criticisms here. For a recent discussion of interpretations that emphasize the object's origins see S. Anderson, "A Presentness of Interpretation and of Artifacts: Toward a History for the Duration and Change of Artifacts," in *History in, of, and for Architecture*, ed. John E. Hancock (Cincinnati: University of Cincinnati Press, 1981).

3. The unfortunate oversimplification, packaging, and consumption of Colin Rowe's *Collage City* approach by various epigones is indicative of the prevalence of this attitude. Though Rowe could not be fitted easily into the architecture-as-autonomous-form mould, such statements as the following are often misleading to those inclined toward uncritical consumption of images of the past: "It should be obvious by this point that present arguments have little to do with 'history.' 'History,' so far as we are aware, relates to concatenation of events and their stylistic profile. In the framework of this discussion it can only interest us very little; and, if we are interested in the usefulness of particular morphologies, we are correspondingly unconcerned with the provenance of specific models." Fred Koetter and Colin Rowe, "The Crisis of the Object: the Predicament of Texture," *Perspecta* 16 (1980): 135 and note 15.

4. "The Metropolis and Mental Life" (English translation of "Die Grosstadt und das Geistleben" [Dresden, 1903]) in *The Sociology of Georg Simmel*, trans. and ed. Kurt H Wolff (New York: Free Press, 1950), 415.

5. Jean Arp, *On My Way: Poetry and Essays, 1912–1916* (New York: Wittenborn, 1948), 91.

6. Piet Mondrian, *De Stijl*.

7. Rosalind Krauss makes a distinction between what she calls analytic or narrative time—in which the viewer encounters form open to change and circumstance. The development of each in modern sculpture is discussed in *Passages in Modern Sculpture* (New York: Viking Press, 1977).

8. Mies's well-known friendship with the Dadaists Kurt Schwitters and Hans Richter and his collaboration with the editors of *G* support this reading of the 1922 skyscraper. The implications of Mies's involvement with the Dadaists have yet to be fully explored.

9. In Philip Johnson, *Mies van der Rohe* (New York: Museum of Modern Art, 1947).

10. Karl Kraus quoted by Walter Benjamin in *Reflections*, trans. Edmond Jephcott (New York: Harcourt Brace Jovanovich, 1978), 243.

11. Johnson, *Mies van der Rohe*, 194. Also see Mies's disavowal of de Stijl in Peter Blake, "A Conversation with Mies," in *Four Great Makers of Architecture*, ed. G. M. Kallman (New York: Da Capo Press, 1970), 93 ff.

12. Stanford Alexander uses the phrase *the winning of reality* to emphasize the reciprocity between an object, its creation, and its interpretation. The phrase captures the notion that the understanding of a building unfolds and changes through time. See Anderson, "A Presentness of Interpretations and of Artifacts."

13. I owe my understanding of intention—as all that which follows from a special beginning—to Edward Said, *Beginnings, Intention, and Method* (Baltimore: Johns Hopkins University Press, 1975).

MIES VAN DER ROHE'S PARADOXICAL SYMMETRIES

Robin Evans

Buildings are not always better than pictures show them to be, nor are they necessarily more significant than the theories that spring up around them. It all depends. One of Mies van der Rohe's most famous works, the Barcelona Pavilion of 1929, has been used to illustrate this point. In his study of its critical history, Juan Pablo Bonta showed why the actual pavilion came a poor third against photographs of it and writings about it. The pavilion's existence had been brief—only six months—and it had received modest coverage by the press; yet, more than a quarter of a century after being dismantled, it was raised to the status of masterpiece—mostly by critics who had never seen it. Bonta then asked two very pertinent questions: Why had it taken so long, and in the absence of the pavilion itself, on what basis were judgments being made? After reading Bonta's book, I began to see the pavilion as a mere phantom, its reputation built on the flimsy evidence of a few published photographs and an inaccurate plan (fig. 162).[1] Then I visited the building after it had been reconstructed on the original site in 1985–86.

ASYMMETRY

If one thing lay beyond dispute, it was the pavilion's asymmetry. This may be understood as a response to its site, which was at the end of a long plaza, the major lateral axis in a vast array of monumental and asymmetrically disposed buildings erected for the 1929 Barcelona Exposition.[2] The asymmetrical pavilion straddled this axis, canceling the symmetry at precisely the point where affirmation was demanded. Corresponding to it, at the other end of the plaza, was the stolidly symmetrical facade of the pavilion representing Barcelona. We know that Mies chose this site in preference to the one originally offered. Though it was on the main thoroughfare, the first site was not implicated in the axial layout of the exposition. Mies deliberately placed his building on the axis, sliding it in between two existing elements of the symmetrical scenery: a screen of Ionic columns in front, and a flight of steps behind. As he developed the design, he kept drawing the axial line through the plan of the pavilion, measuring the asymmetries against it.[3] The flight of steps leading up the steep slope immediately beyond gave dramatic emphasis to the local obliteration of symmetry, since anyone descending it would be presented with an axial view along the full extent of the plaza, and their eye-level raised above Mies's floating and displaced roofs and walls in the foreground.

Few modern buildings have been so deliberately antagonistic toward their surroundings. Loos's unadorned Michaelerplatz block, confronting the Imperial Palace in Vienna, alone stands comparison. Observation of the Barcelona Pavilion *in situ* indicates that it is related to its context by being at odds with it. In these circumstances the asymmetry must be considered aggressive, not accommodating. Yet Bonta has shown that, at the time, the pavilion's asymmetry was associated with the conciliatory political stance of the Weimar Republic.

There is another, more recent political interpretation of Mies's *Repräsentationspavillon* for the German Reich. Much has been written about his willing collaboration with the Nazis between 1933 and 1937.[4] Although exoneration has been attempted (he was just a man who loved his country, he was not interested in politics), some of the mud sticks.[5] But does it stick to his buildings? This is where Mies's silence is so hard to interpret. Is it a refusal to give in, or a failure to respond? Giedion describes Mies as standing quiet but firm in his enlightened modernity, as night descended around him,[6] but Jose Quetglas, in a clever piece of writing that makes it seem almost as if the Barcelona Pavilion itself precipitated the Third Reich, identifies its useless, silent, marmoreal, vacant qualities as "premonitory symbols of Prussian militarism—medium of the Hitlerian hordes who will begin to operate immediately after the crisis of 1929."[7] But how was the pavilion premonitory? Did it help give rise to the Hitlerian hordes, or is it just that, after they arrived, the pavilion would call them to mind?

As to the former question, such a thing is possible. A climate of opinion and a climate of desire may arise from the cumulative effect of unstated suggestions, and from the subliminal promptings of what is seen and felt; therefore, a building could, whether intentionally or not, be an agent of political indoctrination. But any mute influence from the Barcelona Pavilion that might have inclined toward Nazism would surely have been trifling in comparison with what inclined toward the opposite direction. Hitler certainly did not like this building.[8]

The asymmetry, the tranquil horizontal disposition, the absence of insignia (Mies refused to put the German eagle on the green marble wall facing the axis) are suggestive less of chauvinism than of its deliberate effacement. Writing in 1929, Rubio Tuduri paraphrased the speech made at the opening ceremony by the German Kommissar, Georg von Schnitzler:

Here you see the spirit of the new Germany: simplicity and clarity of means and intentions all open to the wind, as well as to freedom—it goes straight to our hearts. A work made of honesty, without pride. Here is the peaceful house of an appeased Germany![9]

Adamant in its denial of the accepted means of establishing monumental order, the pavilion, read as a metaphor for a nation's disposition, turned something all too readily associated with humiliation into a thing of disarming beauty. The Weimar Republic's stance of conciliation toward the other nations of Europe was expressed in a violent repudiation of symmetry, because symmetry was an architectural convention associated with imperiousness, authority, and national aggrandizement. The result: belligerent tranquility, an architectural oxymoron. Mies liked that kind of thing (less is more).

Five months later, in October, the end of the Weimar Republic was in sight. This was the period when few things roused Nazi ire more than the supine posture of Germany in the international community, especially the Weimar government's continuing acceptance of disarmament and reparations.[10]

As to the latter question—if the Barcelona Pavilion calls to mind anything that followed, it would be a small-town American drive-in bank, not Hitler's hordes. There is more to say about the politics of the pavilion, but let us put aside the subject for now.

In the meantime it would be useful to know a bit more about the nature and extent of the pavilion's asymmetry. A lot depends on how you define symmetry. The architectural conception of symmetry is quite restricted in scope. Architects do not normally entertain the physicist's conception of it, which can be exemplified in things which display no visible symmetry. As it happens, there is a rare exception within easy reach of Barcelona: Gaudí's Colonia

Güell Chapel. Although the chapel lacks formal regularity, it was designed to accord with certain equations in statics. We are talking, therefore, of the type of symmetry which can exist in a principle.[11] Architectural usage also customarily excludes Vitruvius's more general concept of symmetry, Hambidge's "dynamic symmetry," as well as serviceable varieties of symmetry dealt with in mathematics, such as rotational symmetry. What architects mean, when they talk about symmetry, is reflective symmetry, also called mirror symmetry. In spite of its restricted definition, this kind of symmetry is remarkably pervasive, and almost impossible to eradicate from modern buildings. There are multitudes of reflective symmetries in the Barcelona Pavilion. In fact, every component—walls, pools, windows, paving slabs, and roof-plates (all rectangular)—has at least three planes of reflective symmetry.

The asymmetry of the pavilion resides in the overall composition of its components, not in the components themselves, which are rather more symmetrical and homomorphic than is usual in a building. One kind of order is substituted for another. Hitchcock and Johnson recognized this in 1932, when they proposed regularity as a substitute for symmetry. Standardization, they wrote, "gives automatically a high degree of consistency in the parts. Hence modern architects have no need of the discipline of bilateral or axial symmetry to achieve aesthetic order. Asymmetrical schemes of design are actually preferable aesthetically as well as technically. For asymmetry certainly heightens the general interest of the composition."[12] According to them, asymmetry was a reaction not so much against classical architecture as against modern architecture itself, which was already endowed with an overwhelmingly repetitive order in its components. In the Barcelona Pavilion reactions against both classical and modern occur simultaneously and *in extremis,* as if David had set out to behave more casually while slaying Goliath.

RATIONAL STRUCTURE

Symmetry came and went in Mies's work, so it could be argued that neither symmetry nor asymmetry is central to an understanding of his development. His lifelong concern was with the logic of structure and its expression. Were we to look in this direction, we might find fewer paradoxes, and all those epithets like universal, clear, rational, etc., might more easily fall into place.

Mies later recalled that he first realized the wall could be freed of the burden of the roof while designing the Barcelona Pavilion. The function of the column was to support the building; that of the wall was to divide space. Logic at last, of a sort.[13] The plan shows this clearly: eight columns, symmetrically arranged in two rows, support the roof slab, while the asymmetrically disposed walls slide away from the columns, away from each other, and out of alignment within the orthogonal matrix. A principle turns into a fact.

Well, this is not *actually* true, nor is it *apparently* true, except in the plan. Pass over the decided lack of candor in the construction, with its brick vaults beneath the podium and its armature of steel concealed in the roof slab and the marble walls—walls which give a tell-tale hollow ring when tapped. Ignore this, because, whenever such an observation is made about any of Mies's buildings, it always elicits the same response: Mies was not just interested in the truth of construction, he was interested in *expressing* the truth of construction. The most celebrated examples of this twice-stated truth are for the most part the later American buildings: the Lake Shore Drive apartments, Crown Hall, and so on. Should we say, then, that the Barcelona Pavilion was an early but none too successful attempt to get these two versions of structural truth to accord with each other, so that the building would express this newly discovered principle? I think not, for two reasons: first, because the principle is expressed very badly in the pavilion and, second, because the pavilion is so refined and so beautiful.

A colleague who was with me in Barcelona suggested that Mies should have left a gap between the walls and the ceiling.[14] Technical objections to one side (the roof would probably collapse), it would certainly have illustrated an idea more vividly. Frank Lloyd Wright also offered improving advice. In 1932 he wrote to Philip Johnson that he would like to persuade Mies "to get rid of those damned little steel posts that look so dangerous and interfering in his lovely designs."[15] Both of these recommendations seek to clarify what appears to be structurally ambiguous. Either the walls are interfering with the roof, or the columns are interfering with the walls. When you look at the pavilion instead of its plan, when you see those little steel posts, cruciform and cased in chrome so as to dissipate their meager substance into attenuated smears of light, you cannot seriously regard them as the sole means of support (which they are not), or even as the principal means of support (which they are). Considered thus, they do indeed look "dangerous."

Now turn to the photographs from 1929 and to the only surviving perspective from Mies's hand which is not just a sketch (fig. 164). The photographs show shimmering columns even less substantial in appearance (because more reflective) than those in the reconstruction, while in the foreground of the perspective two vertical lines that indicate a column are drawn so close together that they look more like a stretched cord than a compressed column—wherein lies a clue.

One of the light fittings designed for the Tugendhat House in 1930 is mounted on a strand of cable stretched between floor and ceiling (fig. 174). Imagined in this way, the columns of the Barcelona Pavilion make more sense. All but one are located near a wall. The walls appear to rest on the podium, and the roof appears to rest on the walls. The elements are assembled, but not held together. The columns appear to perform this task, like bolts tying the roof to the floor and clamping the walls tightly in between. This intuited structural relation between the parts is not, I would maintain, entirely imaginary (in high winds the columns may indeed perform in tension, as bolts do), but its relation to the truth is less significant than its coherence as a fiction.

Considered in the light of the explanation offered by Mies and his Chicago School followers, the Barcelona Pavilion structure is at once deceitful and nonsensical. A principle was discovered and then obscured, which does not sound particularly rational or particularly expressive. The structure can make apparent sense, but only if we relinquish the official explanation. The columns hold the roof down onto the walls, as if it were in danger of flying away. They hold it down more surely than they hold it up. Even the redoubtable rationalist Hilberseimer needed miracles to help sustain his friend Mies's structures, which he held to be rational in the same way that Hagia Sophia was rational. In this fine work of engineering, he wrote, the dome seems "to hang on golden ropes from heaven." He was quoting Procopius, a firm enough historical foundation, but where is the rational foundation for this effect?[16]

There are two reasons why we may think the Barcelona Pavilion is a rational structure: Mies said it was, and it looks as if it is. It looks rational because we know what rationality looks like: precise, flat, regular, abstract, bright, and, above all, rectilinear. This image of rationality is unreliable, however. The Güell Chapel has none of these attributes, yet it is consistent and logical in structure and construction. The entire chapel was to have been scaled up from an inverted funicular model made of wires draped with paper and fabric. Gaudí spent ten years, from 1898 to 1908, developing this model, which hung from the ceiling of a workshop. Each of the funicular wires represented an arch. As they intersected, these arches changed shape. The model grew into an elaborate, distended web of tensile force vectors, each modified by all the others. Gaudí tinkered with it until the whole thing was tantamount to a continuous surface. The model was wholly in tension. Turned upside down, it would produce a structure wholly

402

in compression, thus avoiding persistent tension, against which masonry has little resistance.[17] This is a rational structure. By contrast, the structure and construction of the Barcelona Pavilion is piecemeal and inchoate.

We believe that Mies's buildings exhibit a sublime rationality because so many people have reported seeing it there. These sightings are only rumors. The whole matter resides in recognition. I recognize plant life when I see it, and I recognize rationality in architecture when I see it, because I begin to understand, after much practice, what the word is applied to. I am then tempted to think that all things bearing the same name, whether or not they are architecture, must share an essential property, but this is not necessary, nor, in this instance, is it likely. We may choose to believe that squarish, simple things are tokens of rationality in some wider sense, and that curvaceous, complicated things are tokens of irrationality, but our highly developed powers of visual recognition are exercising no more than a prejudice when we go out hunting for items to pin these terms onto. Yet, while prejudices may be without foundation, they are not without consequence. The belief that we can identify rational structure by these vital signs has rendered us insensitive to the two incomparable ideas of structure, both of which we think we see. Within the word *structure* is a latent oxymoron. In Mies's architecture this trivial confusion of thought is turned into an incredible apparition.

The structure of a sentence is not the same sort of thing as the structure of a building. I have been treating the Barcelona Pavilion structure as a means of holding its own weight off the ground. This kind of structure is about gravitation, mass, and the transmission of loads through solids; it is concerned with concrete, physical things, even though our understanding of it is achieved by means of abstractions such as vectors and numbers. The other kind of structure is also present. We refer to the pavilion's gridded structure or its orthogonal structure, and yet these structures have nothing to do with material or weight. They refer to organizing formats which may be imposed upon, or discovered in, material objects, but which remain conceptual, like the structure of a sentence.

"The language of architects is notorious for its imprecision, pretentiousness, and addiction to cliché," admits Peter Gay, in a last-ditch attempt to gain us some sympathy.[18] Architectural critics are just as guilty. I have sometimes wondered whether these failings conceal some advantages. "Great things are never easy," mutters the oracular Mies, quoting Spinoza.[19] Take the two distinct ideas in the word *structure*, and then make a building in which they appear to blend together as effortlessly as they do on the page. That is a way of taking advantage. It is not easy. Is it great?

At Barcelona, Mies could have divorced the structure from the enclosure in accordance with the well-known principle. He did not do so. Instead, everything in the pavilion gives the impression of being implicated in the transmission of structural forces. We begin to lose track of what does what, and already the building refuses to declare the downward thrust of its own mass.

Look at the Lake Shore Drive apartments (1941–51), where, twenty years later, every effort was made to deny that structure has anything to do with weight, heaviness, crushing, distension, or bending (fig. 176). The towers do not stand there. They hang. Not even that. I am searching for a word that does not convey any idea of gravitation. There are plenty of words that suggest lightness and there are plenty of buildings that do the same. Lightness implies dynamic, but only partial, escape from ponderous immobility. The towers at Lake Shore Drive do not represent a remission of mass. They do not rise against the pull of gravity; gravity does not enter into it. They make you believe, against reason, that they do not partake of that most pervasive and relentless of all natural forces. So the result is not the exhilarating levitation of an object (a familiar effect), but a gentle, dreamy disorientation in the observer.

The steelwork is painted matte black. It does not look like steel. It does not even look like paint. It just looks black. Black things ought to look heavy, but this one doesn't. The twelve black pillars around the open perimeter under the towers seem uninvolved in the business of support, because they end in a milk-white soffit, giving no indication that they penetrate through it. The soffit, uncannily bright even in the dullest weather because it picks up the reflection of the sky from the travertine pavement, terminates every load-bearing member from both directions, leaving them eccentrically connected by the thickness of a flange (a hair's breadth), and reveals the situation in luminous high contrast. Of course these are load-bearing structures, but it has been made to look as if that were a scurrilous libel.

Since the mechanical structure of a building is nothing but a response to gravity, any architectural expression of mechanical structure would surely declare the transmission of load, not conceal it. Yet conceal it Mies does—always and in all ways. How, then, have his buildings maintained their reputation as expressions of structural truth and structural rationality? We need only return to the double meaning to find this out: as the buildings suppress all association with the stresses and strains of load-bearing structure, they begin to look more like conceptual structures. Conceptual structures are notable for their independence from material contingency. Think of a mathematical grid: it is not subject to gravity. Any substance, even the most adamantine, changes shape when a force passes through it. A mathematical grid, on the other hand, cannot change shape in any circumstances. The two kinds of structure could never be exactly identical. In order to look like a conceptual structure, a load-bearing structure must brazenly deny the fact of its burden. "To me," said Mies, "structure is something like logic"[20]: a flaccidly ambiguous statement from a man whose buildings are taut with the same ambiguity.

If Mies adhered to any logic, it was the logic of appearance. His buildings aim at effect. Effect is paramount. In the period between its being dismantled and its resurrection, the Barcelona Pavilion was renowned for the transcendent logic of its determining grid. Yet, as Wolf Tegethoff ably demonstrated, even before the rebuilding had taken place, the basic 110-centimeter-square paving looks regular, but in fact it adapts to local events. Varying between 81.6 centimeters and 114.5 centimeters, it adjusts to the dimensions of the very elements it supposedly ordains.[21] Tegethoff discovered this from a drawing made by the pavior, which had dimensions on it. Nobody sees the difference. The unyielding abstraction was secretly tailored, and measured equality was sacrificed for the sake of apparent consistency.

The very word *apparent* still languishes in the shadow of Plato's disdain.[22] We tend to assume that appearance lies some distance from the truth. But the grid of the pavilion suggests that there might be circumstances in which appearance is the final arbiter. If what we seek is appearance, then appearance must be the measure of truth, at least temporarily. That is what happens when things are made to be looked at. Appearance is never the whole truth, but it is true to itself, and it is made more evidently so by the visual arts, especially when they play tricks with sight. Plato was wrong. These tricks do not deceive us; they sharpen our perceptions. Our perceptions of appearance are remarkably stable, so much so as to be virtually moribund. Visual art strives to tease them back to life. Language, too, is stable, but not completely so. Mies's pavilion suggests how, in this constant effort at resuscitation, vision can be revived by means of an elixir concocted from prosaic ambiguities—the ambiguities of everyday language.

Those of us who are wary of words would judge the excellence of a work of visual art by the degree to which it is unsullied by them. This cannot be right. It simply reverses a recurrent phobia, well expressed by St. Augustine when he lamented the domination of thought by images, noting that, while no one says they listen to a picture, everyone says, when they understand something that has been spoken, that they see what is meant.[23] Attempts to prove either that the visual arts are languages or that they are independent of language are equally wide of the mark. In the whole gamut of art, only vision and language count for much, and each is deeply imbued with the other. If we wish to find a zone of sense that is uninflected by words, we should not look to vision. Any other sense— sound, the medium of speech, even smell—would serve better. And, while we are on the subject of words, why call the Barcelona Pavilion a pavilion? Caroline Constant makes a convincing case that it is more like a landscape than a pavilion.[24] Regarded as a landscape, the Barcelona Pavilion is small, she writes, although it appears to be large. But Christian Devillers believes that this is not just a matter of appearance: it is much larger—175 feet long—than you would think.[25] How big it is depends partly on what you call it. Rubio Tuduri was surprised, in 1929, to find a national pavilion that did not look like a giant, inflated monument. He thought it looked more like a domestic build-ing.[26] If that is how it is seen, it surely is a rather large house. At the same time, it is, as Constant maintains, a very small landscape.

EXTREMES OF VISION

Yet its uncertain size is not due only to its uncertain title. "His powerful drive toward universality had produced an almost unprecedentedly generalized open plan," Franz Schulze writes of Mies's brick country house of 1924.[27] This remark could also apply to the Barcelona Pavilion. If we turned it upside-down and said that his powerful drive toward particularity had produced a closed plan, it should prove false; if it does not, we have another paradox on our hands. Yet Quetglas has described the pavilion as being confined—well on the way to the "obstinate closure" of the later courtyard houses. He claims that "With Mies we find a constant desire to construct segregated, closed spaces, defined only by the horizontal planes."[28] The problem is that we are being offered two extreme options: either the vertigo of universal extension, or the claustrophobia of living in a crack.

The plan looks extensive. The section looks compressed. The building gives the impression of being neither. Vistas along the length of the pavilion are bracketed at both ends by walls. From within, you get diagonal glimpses of the foliage on the hillside though tinted glass, on which, as Quetglas notices, the scene seems to impinge like a picture, pulling it closer still (fig. 175). The only extensive view would have been down the plaza, but in 1929 this was seen through a row of Ionic columns a few yards away. Vision is not so much confined as impeded. The dark glass of the pavilion prevents you from seeing clearly beyond. Add to this a floor and a ceiling, and you are left with a variegated, horizontal strip in middle ground, sandwiched between two broad, blank bands above and below. Mies is often criticized for pressing architectural space between flat, horizontal sheets. That is all he ever did.

During the 1920s Dr. Marius von Senden was gathering evidence to prove that the congenitally blind have no conception of space. He obtained statements from congenitally blind persons who had been operated on and were thus able to see. One of the respondents described his extreme perplexity on looking upward. Von Senden's opinion notwithstanding, this respondent must have had, it seems to me, a highly developed sense of space when blind. He had understood it to extend wherever he could walk. It was sheath-like, defined horizontally by the limits of his own locomotion, and vertically by the extent of his own body.[29] What dismayed and disturbed him, when he was able to see, was the realization that space carried on upward, vertiginously, far beyond his reach. Mies's spaces are practically indistinguishable from this blind man's sheath of space.

There is another way to describe this same geography. The conventional gesture for signifying the act of peering at a remote horizon is an arm raised, with the hand flattened just above the eyes (an almost instinctive response to glare) (fig. 178): that is, in order to see at a distance we create a version of the Miesian horizontal slice. Oddly, the shape of sightless space and the shape of space made for extended vision are nearly the same, and this is the source of yet another group of paradoxes in Mies's work. Whether seascape, prairie, or desert, a vast and vacant scene tends to concentrate visual interest on the horizon. The same thing happens in the Barcelona Pavilion, as it does in many of Mies's buildings.[30] The scene is quite intimate, but there is always a presentiment of great distance, evoked by this subtle but powerful affinity with a broad landscape (fig. 177). The effect is enhanced by the unexpected brightness of the ceiling, achieved by exactly the same means as at Lake Shore Drive.

Mies dismissed the observation made by Patrick Barr in 1936, and often repeated since, that his plans of the 1920s tended to resemble De Stijl paintings, such as Van Doesburg's *Rhythm of a Russian Dance,* with the comment that architecture is not the same as painting.[31] Certainly his plans do sometimes look like a composition by Van Doesburg, but this likeness is visible only in these abstract documents. No such resemblance would strike a person wandering around the pavilion, because the De Stijl configuration is experienced from within the picture plane, so to speak. What Mies said about architecture being different is indubitably true. If a composition derived from a painting were laid flat, as if it were the plan of a building, its intelligibility would be reduced, and in all likelihood it would turn into something different.

Such is the case at Barcelona. The interesting thing is that, while the result is in some degree painterly, it is the abstractions of an earlier age that are recalled, not ours. The horizon line became prominent in perspective drawing. Alberti's own demonstrations of the technique, which he was the first to describe, included a seascape, presumably because it revealed the recession of the idealized ground plane into this idealized line. The basic elements of Alberti's perspective were planes pointing toward the horizon: "I say that some planes are thrown back on the earth and lie like pavements on the floors of buildings; others are equidistant to these. Some stand propped up on their sides like wall."[32]

From this statement alone, we can see that the Miesian "free" plan, as experienced, has far more to do with the compositional discoveries of perspective painting than the anti-perspectival ambitions of the De Stijl artists.

Alberti made his scenic perspective demonstrations inside boxes.[33] He maintained that "if the sky, the stars, the sea, mountains and all bodies should become—should God so will—reduced by half, nothing would appear to be diminished in any part to us."[34] However; to propose a connection between the ideas of Alberti and the Barcelona Pavilion is not to accuse Mies of historicism, for no such exploration of the horizon, or of relative scale, ever occurred in Renaissance architecture.

Another aspect of the pavilion that is reminiscent of a De Stijl painting is its color. It took Mondrian twenty years of painstaking subtraction to get from landscape painting to the purity of his mature canvases. His ambition was to remove all contingency. Mies took the painted planes of primary color that were left and reinvested them with— I was going to say as many contingencies as he could muster, but it would be more accurate to say *half* as many. Panels of blue, yellow, and red on a white ground would turn into panels of dark green verd-antique marble; fili- greed grey-green Tinian marble; and grotesquely varicose orange onyx dorée, on a ground of creamy, pock-marked travertine.

The potential humor in this is heightened by another diverting maneuver. Let's assume that it was in the cause of honesty and of truth to materials that Mies rejected painted surfaces of pure color in a building that had been commissioned, after all, by Georg von Schnitzler, director of a paint and dyestuffs cartel.[35] When the Bauhaus fun- damentalist Hannes Meyer encouraged architects to paint "without a brush," using the colors of the materials them- selves,[36] I doubt that he had in mind sheets of luxurious ornamental stone hung on steel trellises—although it could be said that this was just another way of applying a decorative coat. What Mies did with color destroyed "ideas" and "influences" with a parodist's precision. So is the pavilion a joke at the expense of both realism and idealism, since its architecture implies neither? This seems unlikely. Mies's behavior has the same pattern as humor, consid- ered in context, but it is not funny. What it shares with humor is the element of the unexpected.

Western tradition and modernist polemics have together conspired to convince us that abstraction is achieved by the removal of corporeal properties. That is why Arthur Drexler conjured up Plato to help explain why Mies's architecture seeks "an absolute and unvarying principle, assumed to be independent of the senses through which its manifestations are perceived."[37] Mies's own statements lend further credibility to this view, as do drawings and photographs of his buildings. Experienced directly, they could hardly be said to draw attention to their own solidity. It is nevertheless quite false to portray their physical incarnation as merely the sign of something beyond.

Some material properties of the Barcelona Pavilion, such as mass, are suppressed, but others are accentuated to the point of sense saturation. This need not surprise us. Kasimir Malevich pointed out that, as things become simpler, emptier, the mind dwells on the little that remains. He wanted to create a "desert" in which all attention would be focused on this remainder. Figures like the square and the circle, and colors like black and white, were admissible precisely because they were of little intrinsic interest.[38] What is left, wrote Malevich, is feeling. The materialists among us might say that what is left, in his work, is paint—deftly applied, feathery strokes of paint that is now cracking (never evident in photographic reproductions). The effort to eliminate sensual properties makes one hypersensitive to their presence. That is why twentieth-century abstract painting has oscillated between glorification of the material surface and denial of it; between Pollock and Mondrian. But there are a large number of works, the Barcelona Pavilion among them, that belong to another class. They adopt the procedure of abstraction in order to reveal properties that are neither formal nor material. They do this by accentuating color, luminosity, reflectiveness, and absorption of light.[39]

Light is physical, but it has no mass; gravity has barely any grasp on it. Light has provided a major escape route from the hylomorphism that dominates so much of our thinking and perception, by limiting our consciousness of physical reality to two principles: form and matter.

The most striking properties of the pavilion have to do with the perception of light and depth. That is one reason why the drawn elevations give no idea of what it is like, and that in turn is one reason why it was a surprise to find, right in the middle of the pavilion, a slim, opalescent, luminous box of glass (fig. 179).[40] Bonta found a first-hand description that said it felt gloomy under the canopy, and he agreed that anyone could see, from a cursory look at the drawings, that it would be.[41] Despite its brightness, the luminous box is surrounded by obscurity. Where is it in the photographs, descriptions, and drawings of 1929? There is enough information to confirm that it was constructed, but evidence of it was then minimized. Mies, reportedly unhappy with the shadows it cast, turned off the electric light inside it during the opening ceremony.[42] What the photographs show is that the slot in the roof, which let in such a quantity of daylight, was also screened. But then Mies made a similar luminous wall behind the dining alcove of the Tugendhat House.[43] Now, in the reconstruction, it looks like a vacant body-light for advertising, a premonition of American commercialism, signage with no sign, augury of Midwestern pathos; it is beautiful (again).

Both the forms and the materials of the pavilion are merely instruments for the manipulation of light and depth. The combination of polished marbles, chrome, and tinted glass—all smooth and highly reflective—denies access to the solids beneath. So it is appropriate that the walls of the pavilion ring hollow to the knuckles.

Of these, the onyx wall was the most exotic, improbable, and expensive (fig. 173). Many critics regard it as a centerpiece but, according to Mies, the choice of onyx was accidental. In direct consequence of this chance event, another decision was taken which, I maintain, did more to establish the paradoxical coherence of the whole than anything else. Thirty years later, Mies recalled:

When I had the idea for this building I had to look around. There was not much time, very little time in fact. It was deep in winter, as you cannot move marble in from the quarry in winter because it is still wet inside and would easily freeze to pieces. So we had to find dry material. I looked round the huge marble depots, and in one I found an onyx block. This block had a certain size and, since I had only the possibility of taking this block I made the pavilion twice that height.[44]

Although it had been earmarked for vases in a luxury liner, he persuaded the management to set it aside for him by paying for it on the spot. To judge from his comment about it, Mies had only a casual interest in the height of the ceiling—though he chose, at much the same time, an almost identical height for the Tugendhat House, and for quite a few projects thereafter.

Perusing the slides I had taken of the reconstructed pavilion, I found it difficult to decide which way up they went—an artifact of photography, no doubt. Then I changed my mind. It was not an artifact of photography, but a property of the pavilion itself, a property of which I had not been conscious while there. The photographs had made it easier to discern. Soon after, I was looking at some student sketches of the pavilion, and I discovered that someone else had experienced the same difficulty. He had inadvertently begun to caption his drawing the wrong way up.

Disclosed in our pictures was something quite different from the effect noticed by Kandinsky, and exploited by cartoonists ever since, that non-figurative forms have no privileged orientation. At Barcelona the reversibility derives from the most unlikely source: symmetry. It is unexpected because Mies had gotten rid of vertical bilateral symmetry (the kind we expect), making a conspicuous show of its absence. He then reintroduced it, in quantity, in another dimension, where no one would think of looking for it: horizontally. Horizontal symmetry is inadmissible in classical architecture. There is parity between right and left, and there is disparity between up and down. Things should not look the same when up-ended. The world turned upside-down is an image of disorder, domestic or political.[45] We understand these metaphors, but what kind of world is it, we might ask, that could be turned upside-down without our noticing? This is the most serene of derangements.

Although incomplete, the horizontal symmetry of the Barcelona Pavilion is very powerful. Its overwhelming strength is attributable to one simple fact: the plane of symmetry is very close to eye-level. For a person of average height, the dividing line between the onyx panels is indistinguishable from the horizon line. If we believe Mies's recollections, then we must accept that this is a coincidence. There is, however, some evidence to suggest that Mies was soon aware of the implications of his choice, and that it altered his perception of what he was doing.[46]

Alberti called the horizon line the centric line, a term he also used to describe the diameter of a circle. This indicates that he envisaged it as cutting the field of vision into two equal parts, at eye-level.[47] The plane of symmetry constructed this way, in this dimension, is far harder to escape than is vertical symmetry. The dead-center, frontal view of a vertically symmetrical object is privileged, but occasional; most of the time we see such symmetries from oblique angles, and so the retinal images of the two sides are not actually the same size. In Mies's pavilion the plane of symmetry is almost impossible to escape. The eyes are delivered into it by virtue of normal ambulant posture, and so the retinal images of the lower and upper halves are rendered equal. The only way to avoid this is to stoop, sit, or squat. I have since looked at as many photographs as I could find of both the original and the reconstructed pavilion. They show that, although nobody ever mentions the commanding plane, most people (and their cameras) occupy it. If the photographs contain figures, notice how their eyes hover around the horizontal joint between the onyx slabs. If not, notice, first, how many elements reflect across this line, then look at the receding contours of obliquely viewed surfaces and notice how nearly identical are the angles from floor and ceiling to the horizon—a property of all perpendicular, rectangular planes in perspective, viewed from mid-height. Notice the difficulty of distinguishing the travertine floor, which reflects the light, from the plaster ceiling, which receives it. If the floor and the ceiling had been of the same material, the difference in brightness would have been greater. Here, Mies used material asymmetry to create optical symmetry, rebounding the natural light in order to make the ceiling more sky-like[48] and the ambience more expansive.

The only carefully constructed perspective drawing of the pavilion which survives (fig. 164) indicates that Mies was conscious of this property. It shows the onyx wall divided exactly in half by the horizon. Turned sideways, the drawing reveals a bilaterally symmetrical outline. Such also is the case with Mies's perspective of the Tugendhat living room, although in that house he used three bands of onyx paneling in the freestanding wall, so that the horizon line would not be visible to advertise the equality of upper and lower portions, as it was at Barcelona. Observers will be more likely to notice what is happening to their vision when their eyes scan this line (all the other marbles at Barcelona were also laid in three bands). The accidental source, and sole measure, of the powerful but subliminal symmetry was thus erased in the Tugendhat house, which Mies built slightly later. The Barcelona Pavilion has 312 centimeters of headroom; the Tugendhat house has 317.5 centimeters. The Esters/Lange house, begun in 1927, had a similar ceiling height (306.25 centimeters), but did not exploit horizontal symmetry, while perspectives for a number of subsequent projects show it clearly and consistently, including the Gericke house, the Ulrich Lange house, the Hubbe house, and the three courtyard houses. In the drawings, Mies was more inclined to incorporate figurative sculpture than human figures. Often the eye-level of the statue is removed from the horizon line, either by overscaling, as with the Kolbe statue at Barcelona, or because of its recumbent posture. Mies never acknowledged his interest in this phenomenon. It is significant, however, that Le Corbusier, who proclaimed the horizontal line of vision to be an essential feature of man, disallowed the double Modulor height (366 centimeters) for interiors, explaining that he wished to avoid the equalization of floor and ceiling.[49]

The implications of this reestablishment in one plane of a property so completely eradicated in another are not immediately obvious, but it is reminiscent of other tergiversations practiced by Mies. Abstraction, materiality, spirit, structure, symmetry, asymmetry—no concept was safe in his hands. Bonta, studying the critical fortunes of the original pavilion, reached the conclusion that it was only an "idea" that had been promoted to greatness. But what I saw in the reconstruction was a building that ate ideas.

REFLECTIONS ON THE CRITICAL FUNCTION

It ate new ideas as well as old ones. The reflective properties of the Barcelona Pavilion have been for the most part treated as incidental. One writer even complained that they had "frequently blinded critics to the significant architectural values of his [Mies's] work."[50] By contrast, Manfredo Tafuri, Michael Hays, and Jose Quetglas have recently given more emphasis to reflectiveness in their analyses of Mies's buildings, especially the pavilion. They see it as an aspect of Mies's buildings' obdurate silence. A reflective building is an echo, not a statement. In "Fear of Glass" Quetglas dramatizes the plight of a lone occupant of the Barcelona Pavilion, displaced into his own virtual images.[51] In "Critical Architecture" Hays presents reflection as the key to the pavilion. Elaborating ideas put forward in more general terms by Tafuri,[52] he discusses the way reflections confuse the picture of reality. The virtual and the real become hard to distinguish, thus exemplifying the immanent chaos of modern life. For Hays and Tafuri reflectiveness is the means by which Mies creates a silent theater of the world, while maintaining critical distance from it. For all three, reflections break up the calm and isotropic space of ordinary perception. "The fragmentation and distortion of the space is total. Any transcendent order of space and time that would confer an overarching unity onto this assemblage is systematically and utterly dispersed,"[53] writes Hays of this "montage of contradictory, perceptual facts." While I would certainly endorse this shift of attention, I find myself disagreeing with these critics' interpretations of the pavilion's reflectiveness.

Reflections are often a source of confusion, and numerous works of art and architecture, including certain projects by Mies, have exploited this: the Glass Skyscrapers of 1922 for instance,[54] and the glass exhibit for the *Deutsches Volk/Deutsche Arbeit* Exposition of 1934 (the one project Mies built for the Nazi government). Cylinders of glass stood in serried ranks, refracting images of each other and of their background, as they became lens-like. Extruded reflections bounced all over the place. In certain circumstances the play of light in the Barcelona Pavilion can also be confusing (fig. 180). But can the pavilion as a whole be described in terms of ruptures and dislocations? Perhaps only the columns can—the columns that hold it up, or down.[55]

Mirrors can destroy coherence, but they can also reveal it. There were numerous demonstrations of this capability in the seventeenth century. They combined anamorphosis (the projection of distorted and illegible images) with catoptrics (the study of mirrors). By placing a cylindrical or conical mirror over the center of the projection, the warped image would be restored to its proper shape. Most of these tricks transformed continuous distortions into recognizable images by means of curved mirrors, but in Jean Dubreuil's *Perspective pratique* (1651) a prismatic mirror was used.[56] The plane surfaces of the prism reflected only certain parts of the image on which it stood. Dubreuil used this device to change a medley of heads turned at various angles into a single pair of profiles, transforming the multiform into the binary (fig. 181). The purpose of the anamorphic projection was to obscure the image; the purpose of the mirror was to permit its retrieval. The mirror finds what is hidden. That is why many of the surviving examples of anamorphosis portray secret or illicit subject-matter—sexual, political, or religious.[57] Reflected images in the Barcelona Pavilion work in a similar fashion: they restore a secret that has been erased from the tangible form of the building.

It must be admitted that the usual effects of reflection are disruptive and confusing. However, when a construction reflects itself more than it reflects its surroundings and where, moreover, these reflections are always into plane surfaces parallel or perpendicular to one another, the result is quite different. In such circumstances an asymmetrical arrangement becomes virtually symmetrical, like Siamese twins, whenever a reflective plane cuts through it.

One example of this pairing provides evidence that Mies took advantage of the effect I have described, while he was designing the pavilion. Viewed from the northeast, the podium—a podium we are so often told is never overridden by the walls that rest on it—appears as no more than a thin strip along the front of the building (fig. 172). Beyond this, the Tinian marble enclosing the small pool cuts straight into the ground. Something left incomplete? Another accident? Mies repeatedly drew the rim of the podium so that it extended around the entire perimeter of the building, he approved a much later redrawing that showed it thus, and he drew it that way for publication in 1929 (fig. 162).[58] But the second preliminary scheme[59] indicates that, even in the early stages of design, Mies was thinking of it much as built, except that he first drew the spur of the podium so that it returned much further round the corner of the Tinian wall.

The view from the northeast contains one of several "Siamese twins" created by the pavilion's reflections of itself. The two halves straddle a shining vertical plane of grey-green marble, extended into panels of glazing. Three white elements cling to this surface: a narrow, U-shaped bracket at the far end of the site, contrasted against the dark wall of the exhibition hall; a long wing-like strip balanced on top of the knife-edge of the reflective wall surface; and, below this, the stranded spur of the podium. The wall is inset to the depth of one travertine paving slab. The line of slabs doubles itself in reflection. Because the continuation of the spur beyond the end of the wall is also two slabs wide, the mirror symmetry of these three pieces—half real, half vertical—is perpetrated beyond the end of the reflective plane.[60] The illusion of symmetry extends a little way into reality—a triumph of the optical over the planimetric. Mies made this adjustment later on. The drawings suggest that initially he introduced the discontinuous podium for its own sake, then adjusted the projecting spur of the podium in order to pick up the symmetry. First, symmetry is eliminated (in the composition of plan and elevation), then it is smuggled in sideways as an optically constructed symmetry between floor and ceiling, and finally it is readmitted in its normal orientation as a family of fictions (in reflections). Mies did not dispense with symmetry in his radical European works, only to restore it later in the United States. Symmetries were never present in greater strength and numbers than they were in the Barcelona Pavilion, which turns out to be a veritable Trojan horse filled with them (fig. 182). The presence of symmetry in, say, a paving slab can be so obvious as to be beyond recognition; its presence across the optical horizon of the pavilion can be so unexpected as to be also beyond recognition. Thus symmetry in the Barcelona Pavilion is utterly prosaic, or nearly inconceivable. Removed from its normal, normative middle ground, it is harder to recognize, impossible to avoid.

According to Tafuri and Hays, Miesian reflections are a way of breaking things up; according to me, a way of creating coherence. Both kinds of reflection occur in the Barcelona Pavilion. Which prevails? For the sake of argument, assume the latter. What, then, happens to the idea, promoted so forcefully by Tafuri and Hays, that Mies's architecture takes a critical stance by dismembering our too coherent picture of reality? It would not apply, but this does not necessarily mean that the building is not critical. It may be critical in other ways.

Then, again, it may not. In some circles the critical function of art is now taken for granted: a work of art is judged to be good in so far as it is critical. This somewhat uncritical acceptance is facilitated by assuming that any difference between one thing and another can be formulated as an applied criticism, and indeed it can. It can equally well be called an accident, an instance of plurality or contrast. Any work of art or architecture may be surrounded by critical intentions. It may also elicit critical responses that would never otherwise have occurred. For all that, it may yet be possible to show that a work of art cannot be essentially critical. While it need not negate, it must affirm—even if all it affirms is its worthiness to enter our consciousness. However, if the critical function is taken to be the measure of art, then art blends into commentary and, once again, the analogy with language steals in. The Barcelona Pavilion is not analogous to language. Its relationship to language is predatory, not mimetic.

Art has so often been portrayed as being against the world, because it is obliged to affirm by being untypical or unreal. Ordinary existence seems bland by comparison. That is why criticism, disappointment, frustration, disdain, repugnance can frequently be inferred from the affirmative work. And that is why the pavilion, full of positive attributes, may still cast a long negative shadow. In their interpretation of Mies, Tafuri and Hays have taken the old idea of aesthetic distance and reformulated it as critical distance.[61] The two kinds of distance may be described in similar terms, but they originate in opposite tendencies. Critical distance is maintained for the purpose of scrutiny; aesthetic distance is maintained for the purpose of adulation. Critical distance reveals blemishes; aesthetic distance is prophylactic. Let us return now to the politics of the pavilion's beauty. I would argue that Mies is holding the world at arm's length, less to contemplate its absurdity than to avoid its odor.

Alberti thought it prudent to build beautiful buildings, because beauty preserves things from assault. He asks, "Can any Building be made so strong by all the Contrivance of Art, as to be safe from Violence and Force?" and he answers that it can, since "Beauty will have such an effect even upon an enraged Enemy, that it will disarm his Anger, and prevent him from offering it any Injury: Insomuch that I will be bold to say, that there can be no greater Security to any Work against Violence and Injury, than Beauty and Dignity."[62] Beauty turns vulnerability into impregnability, and it is easy to see from this example that the beauty and dignity of buildings was the same kind of beauty and dignity that women were supposed to have, and probably for much the same reason. Alberti implies that an army regards a monument like a man regards a woman, and not much separates Alberti's views on the subject from those of Jean-Paul Sartre five hundred years later. In *The Psychology of Imagination* Sartre explains how beauty puts things out of reach, prompting feelings of "sad disinterest." "It is in this sense that we may say that great beauty in a woman kills the desire for her. . . . To desire her we must forget she is beautiful, because desire is a plunge into the heart of existence, into what is most contingent and absurd."[63]

Although the terms *attractive* and *beautiful* are considered almost synonymous, beauty, as described by Alberti and Sartre, is not attractive; it is, to coin a word, "distractive." The kind of beauty that dominates Western consciousness quells desire for a thing by diverting attention from the thing's use (or abuse) to its appearance. The beauty of the Barcelona Pavilion is also distractive, but it is not diverting attention from its own vulnerability; the Barcelona Pavilion distracts the entranced observer from what is troubling elsewhere. This is the architecture of forgetting.

From what is Mies's architecture distracting us? The question is almost meaningless. The abstraction, the silence, the vacancy of the pavilion makes it hard to determine what has been removed. Isn't this the point? If we could easily tell, then the effort of escape would have been worthless. Even if we could delve into Mies's personality in order to discover what his architecture allowed him to forget, it wouldn't necessarily tell us what it allows us to forget, or what it will allow others to forget. The question is almost meaningless—but not quite. Forgetting is a social activity. Ignorance can be constructed socially, just as knowledge can. The collective practice of forgetting produces innocence—the kind that we construct to protect ourselves from others, and others from ourselves, not the kind that is lost.

I would make two guesses about what the Barcelona Pavilion helped Mies and his contemporaries forget: politics and violence. Thucydides, who actually fought in the wars he chronicled, said he preferred the art of forgetting to the art of memory. His preference for amnesia has a psychological explanation. As a situation gets worse, attention is either completely engaged by it, or completely withdrawn. Thus John Willett writes of artists in Weimar Germany: "Even at the calmest and apparently sanest moments of the mid-1920s the more sensitive amongst these people reflected an uneasy precariousness which was often electrifying. 'I felt the ground shaking beneath my feet,' wrote George Grosz in his autobiography many years later, 'and the shaking was visible in my work.'"[64] But it was not visible in Mies's architecture. Insulated from seismic disturbance, the pavilion gives no indication of it, and therefore the tremors seem not to exist.

History tells us that much was at stake. To forget too much in Weimar Germany was to open the door to barbarism, in the effort to escape knowledge of the threat. No doubt there was a lot of this kind of forgetting. It is all too clear that art can soothe a troubled conscience. What I am trying to suggest is that there is another kind of collective forgetting, potentially constructive, which has been conveniently forgotten in twentieth-century accounts of art—although much of modernism exemplifies it. Suppose I were to claim that the distractions supplied by art have been essential to the development of our equilibrium, our humanity, our enlightenment. Would I be claiming too much? I doubt it. Art always presents a challenge, but not every challenge leads to exposure or revelation. Forgetting can also be a challenge. This is the message of the Eumenides.

By virtue of its optical properties, and of its disembodied physicality, the pavilion always draws us away from consciousness of it as a thing, and draws us toward consciousness of the way we see it. Sensation, forced into the foreground, pushes consciousness into apperception. The pavilion is a perfect vehicle for what Kant calls aesthetic judgment, where consciousness of our own perception dominates all other forms of interest and intelligence. But, he insists, out of this apparently purposeless activity, we construct our own destiny. Take away five and add ten. Oblivious to the tremors that beset the present, we intimate a pattern for a potential future. Distraction is not amnesia, it is displacement.

However, it might seem that Mies was more intent on displacement into the past than into the future. Colin Rowe interpreted the more explicit symmetry in Mies's later work as a return to the conventions of classicism.[65] Several of the ways the pavilion encourages the conscious savoring of our own perception involve symmetries which go unnoticed. Does this not suggest that Mies, who was certainly a master of equivocation, covertly reintroduced the hieratic formation of bilateral symmetry to counteract the freedom and democracy signified by the pavilion's asymmetry? The Trojan horse introduces foreign troops by stealth. This subterfuge fits in with everything so far said about Mies's predilection for conflating opposites, and confirms that a profound authoritarianism lurks just beneath the bright surface.

It is generally believed that bilateral symmetry asserts unity by emphasizing the center. Monumental architecture has been demonstrating this for millennia. Hegel declared that symmetry is the primordial manifestation of symbolic art, the first embodiment of the human spirit in sensuous form. By its symmetry, "architecture prepared the way for the inadequate actuality of God," he wrote.[66] The social order of theocracy, tyranny, and aristocracy seems locked into this formal arrangement. Bruno Zevi speaks for generations of modern critics when he claims that "Once you get rid of the fetish of symmetry, you will have taken a giant step on the road to a democratic architecture."[67] Our idea of bilateral symmetry comes from familiar examples: from the great architectural monuments of the past and also, according to Blaise Pascal, from the human face. The king's portal and the mouth have a lot to answer for. Both, sitting astride the plane of symmetry, tend to obscure the fact that the production of bilateral symmetry is a twinning operation, not a centralizing activity. There is nothing hierarchical in bilateral symmetry; quite the reverse. Only by adding a third term between the duplicated halves do we turn the equalization into a graduated hierarchy. This term is an inessential extra, which is why Siamese twins or a pair of semi-detached houses better illustrate bilateral symmetry than do the human face or the Palace of Versailles. The transformation of bilateral symmetry in monumental architecture is a spectacular instance of the mute politics embodied in appearances.

When we have rid ourselves of the prejudices established over the centuries by means of architecture, we may recognize that bilateral symmetry is a way of creating equivalence, not privilege. The hidden symmetries of the Barcelona Pavilion will then appear in a different light. Most are bipartite. None emphasize the center. Maybe that is why they had to be hidden. If the symmetries had been identified and named, this might have led to a false insinuation, and might have obscured the properties of the thing it was meant to describe. The building that ate so many words would have fallen victim to a word.

The symmetries in the Barcelona Pavilion are of an entirely different order to those of monumental classicism. To appreciate them we must revise our understanding of the word *symmetry*. Pascal summed up the classical view in a single sentence: "Symmetry is what we see at a glance, based on the fact that there is no reason for any difference, and based also on the face of a man: whence it happens that symmetry is only worked in breadth, not in height or depth."[68] The symmetries in the Barcelona Pavilion are not seen at a glance; there are good reasons for their presence; they are not like the face of a man; and they are worked in other dimensions than breadth.

POSTSCRIPT

I refrain from commenting on the reconstruction of the pavilion, except to applaud those responsible. Others regard the issues of its authenticity and reproducibility as significant, but I am unable to see why.

[1] Juan Pablo Bonta, *Architecture and Its Interpretation* (New York: Rizzoli, 1979), 131–224.

[2] Ibid. 171–74, and Wolf Tegethoff, *Mies van der Rohe: The Villas and Country Houses* (New York and Cambridge, Mass.: MoMA/MIT Press, 1985), 72–73.

[3] MoMA, *Mies van der Rohe Archive*, part 1, vol. 2. In plan 14.2, the axial line is used as a datum from which to measure the different length of the pavilion podium extending in either direction; in 14.3 a plinth for sculpture is aligned on it; in 14.7 and 14.20 it is integrated as the center-line of the paving grid.

[4] Sybil Moholy-Nagy, "The Diaspora," *Journal of the Society of Architectural Historians* 24, no. 1 (March 1965): 24–26; Elaine Hochman, *Architects of Fortune* (New York: Weidenfeld and Nicolson, 1989).

[5] Howard Dearstyne, letter in response to the article by S. Moholy-Nagy, *JSAH* 24, no. 3 (October 1965): 256.

[6] S. Giedion, *Space, Time, and Architecture* (Cambridge, Mass.: Harvard University Press, 1954), 548.

[7] Jose Quetglas, "Fear of Glass," in *Architectureproduction, Revisions,* ed. B. Colomina and M. Hays (New York: Princeton Architectural Press, 1985), 150.

[8] Hochman, *Architects of Fortune*, 203.

[9] "Voilà l'esprit de l'Allemagne nouvelle: simplicité et clarté de moyens et d'intentions tout ouvert au vent, comme à la franchise— rien ne ferme l'accès à nos coeurs. Un travail honnêtement fait, sans orgueil. Voilà la maison tranquille de l'Allemagne apaisée!" (Bonta, *Architecture and Its Interpretation*, 155). For Nicholas M. Rubio Tuduri, see "Le Pavillon d'Allemange à l'Exposition de Barcelona par Mies van der Rohe," *Cahiers d'art* 8–9 (1929): 409–11. Reprinted in Fundació Publica del Pavelló Alemany, *El Pavelló Alemany de Barcelona de Mies van der Rohe* (Barcelona, 1987), 42.

[10] Peter Gay, *Weimar Culture* (New York: Harper and Row, 1970), 139.

[11] Herman Weyl, *Symmetry* (Princeton, N.J.: Princeton University Press, 1952), 77. Commenting on Kepler's search for order manifest in forms, Weyl writes: "We still share his belief in a mathematical harmony of the universe. . . . But we no longer seek this harmony in static forms like the regular solids, but in dynamic laws."

[12] H. R. Hitchcock and Philip Johnson, *The International Style* (New York: W. W. Norton and Company, 1966), 59–60.

[13] It is difficult to understand why this realization of 1929 should so often be cited, as if Mies had achieved some completely new insight. The principle had been announced some years earlier by Le Corbusier.

[14] Jonathan Greigg.

[15] Franz Schulze, *Mies van der Rohe: A Critical Biography* (Chicago: University of Chicago Press, 1985), 158.

[16] Ludwig Hilberseimer, *Mies van der Rohe* (Chicago: Paul Theobald, 1956), 16. The quote was taken from Procopius, *Buildings*, I, i, 46. Adrian Gale, who worked with Mies toward the end of his career, observes a similar effect in the American work. He describes how the interior space of Crown Hall seems to be gripped within the vice-like external frame, which threatens to pull the roof down to the floor. The threat requires preventive resistance, and the only force the mind can introduce to keep them apart is in the sandwiched space itself, as if it were substantial and elastic. A. Gale, "Mies: An Appreciation," in *Mies van der Rohe: European Works,* AD Architectural Monograph no. 11 (London, 1986), 96.

[17] Isidre Puig Boada, *L'Església de la Colonia Güell* (Editorial Lumen, 1976).

[18] Gay, *Weimar Culture*, 101.

[19] Acceptance speech on receiving the AIA Gold Medal, 1960. See Peter Serenyi, abstract, *JSAH* 30, no. 3 (October 1971): 240.

[20] Peter Blake, "A Conversation with Mies," in *Four Great Makers,* 93.

[21] Tegethoff, *Mies,* 81–82.

[22] Plato, *The Republic,* book 10, sec. 1.

[23] St. Augustine, *Confessions,* book 10, sec. 35.

[24] Caroline Constant, "The Barcelona Pavilion as Landscape Garden: Modernity and the Picturesque," *AA Files* 20 (Fall 1990): 46–54.

[25] In conversation.

[26] See note 9.

[27] Schulze, *Mies,* 116.

[28] Quetglas, "Fear of Glass," 133.

[29] Marius von Senden, *Space and Sight: The Perception of Space and Shape in the Congenitally Blind before and after Operation,* trans. P. Heath (Glencoe, Ill.: Free Press, 1960).

[30] MoMA, *Mies Archive,* part 1, vol. 2, 2.320-23.

[31] Patrick H. Barr Jr., *Cubism and Abstract Art* (reprint New York: Museum of Modern Art, 1986), 156–57. Barr notes the similarity in their "broken, asymmetrical" character.

[32] Leon Battista Alberti, *On Painting,* trans. Spencer (New Haven: Yale University Press, 1966), 52.

[33] M. Boscovits, "Quello ché dipinturi oggi dicono prospettiva," *Acta Historiae Artium* (Budapest: Akadémiai Kiadó, 1962), vol. 8, 246.

[34] Alberti, *On Painting,* 54.

[35] *Mies van der Rohe: European Works,* 39. Georg von Schnitzler, Commissioner General of the Reich, who picked Mies to design the pavilion, was a director of the IG Farben cartel.

[36] "The New World" (1926), in *Hannes Meyer: Buildings, Projects and Writings,* ed. Claude Schnaidt, 95. Quoted by Michael K. Hays in "Reproduction and Negation: The Cognitive Projects of the Avant-Garde," in *Architectureproduction, Revisions,* p. 161.

[37] Arthur Drexler, *Ludwig Mies van der Rohe* (New York: G. Braziller, 1960), 9.

[38] Kasimir Malevich, *The Non-Objective World,* trans. Dearstyne (Chicago, 1959).

[39] The most modern works of this type tend to be sculptures and installations from the 1960s onward. Mies's efforts are therefore remarkable on three counts; for being early, for being architecture, and for exploiting far more subtle optical phenomena than other artists, such as László Moholy-Nagy, who were working with light and reflection in the 1920s and 1930s.

[40] Constant regards it as vying for centrality with the onyx wall (the traditional candidate); Quetglas, as part of a binary centrality that circulates round the black carpet as well as the light wall. It would be wrong to give the pavilion a center it does not want, but there is one characteristic, other than its odd brightness, that makes the luminous wall more prominent than the onyx wall: it is the only surface, other than the two "brackets" at either extremity, which is transverse. All the others are oriented along the length of the pavilion. The long view down the building, from end to end, is decidedly dominant, once the visitor mounts the podium. The luminous wall is therefore turned into the field of vision, filling it far more extensively for far more of the time than any other single element. By comparison, one has to make an effort to face the onyx wall. For me, this effort was prompted by the knowledge that it was indeed of central importance. Its reputation had preceded it.

[41] Bonta, *Architecture and Its Interpretation,* 145. The observation was made by Platz in 1930.

[42] *Mies van der Rohe: European Works,* 69. I am indebted to Matilda McQuaid, of the MoMA Mies van der Rohe Archive, for information on the construction of the light wall in 1929.

[43] MoMA, *Mies Archive,* part 1, vol. 2, 2.320-23.

[44] Onyx quote: Bonta, *Architecture and Its Interpretation,* 151, but cited from Peter Carter, 1961.

[45] See, for example, Christopher Hill, *The World Turned Upside Down: Radical Ideas during the English Revolution* (Harmondsworth, New York: Penguin Books, 1975).

[46] MoMA, *Mies Archive.*

[47] Alberti, *On Painting,* 44, 58.

[48] Often Mies's ceilings seem to get light from nowhere. In the exhibit for the glass industry at Stuttgart in 1927, Mies, using many of the materials he would use again at Barcelona, installed a false ceiling of taut strips of white fabric sewn together. This was top-lit to create a luminous surface.

[49] Conversation with Jerzy Soltan, 1989.

[50] Peter Carter, *Mies van der Rohe at Work* (New York: Praeger, 1974), 24.

[51] Quetglas, "Fear of Glass," 128-31.

[52] Manfredo Tafuri, *Architecture and Utopia,* trans. B. L. La Penta (1979), pp. 148-49; Tafuri, *The Sphere and the Labyrinth,* trans. P. d'Acierno and R. Connolly (Cambridge, MA: MIT Press, 1987), 111-12, 174-75. K. Michael Hays, "Critical Architecture: Between Culture and Form," *Perspecta* 21 (1981).

[53] Hays, "Critical Architecture," 11.

[54] This property was noticed early on. Arthur Korn in *Glass in Modern Architecture,* first published in 1929, although giving preference to sparse, rectilinear examples, remarks that "Glass is noticeable yet not quite visible. It is the great membrane, full of mystery delicate yet tough. It can disclose and open spaces in more than one direction. Its peculiar advantage is in the diversity of the impressions it creates." (Introduction to the first edition.)

[55] The glass doors also add to the confusion, but Mies removed them for the opening ceremony. It is significant that the columns, which are supposed to ensure the stability of the pavilion, are the only elements rendered unstable by their reflectiveness.

[56] Jean Dubreuil, *Perspective pratique,* 2nd ed. (Paris, 1651), 144-46.

[57] Jurgis Baltrusaitis, *Anamorphic Art,* trans. W. J. Strachan (Cambridge, 1977).

[58] The redrawing was done by Werner Blaser. The drawing for publication in 1929 is illustrated in MoMA, *Mies Archive,* part 1, vol. 2, 14.6.

[59] MoMA, *Mies Archive,* part 1, vol. 2, 14.2.

[60] There is a slight difference between the depth of the reflection and the depth of the projecting spur, arising from the need to accommodate the thickness of the Tinian wall.

[61] K. Gilbert and H. Kuhn, *A History of Esthetics* (London: Thames and Hudson, 1956), 269-70.

[62] Leon Battista Alberti, *The Ten Books of Architecture,* trans. Bartoli/Leoni, ed. Rykwert (Tiranti, 1955), book vi, ch. 2, 113.

[63] Jean-Paul Sartre, *The Psychology of Imagination* (New York: Citadel Press, 1961), conclusion, 282.

[64] John Willett, *The New Sobriety: Art and Politics in the Weimar Period* (London, 1978), 16.

[65] Colin Rowe, "Neo-'Classicism' and Modern Architecture I and II," in *The Mathematics of the Ideal Villa* (Cambridge, Mass.: MIT Press, 1982), 119–58.

[66] H. Paolucci and F. Ungar, eds., *Hegel on the Arts* (New York: Ungar, 1979), 64.

[67] Bruno Zevi, *The Modern Language of Architecture* (Seattle: University of Washington Press, 1978), 15.

[68] Blaise Pascal, *Pensées* (London, 1940), no. 28.

ANY Magazine 5 (1994)

A GARDEN OF MICROCHIPS:
THE ARCHITECTURAL IMAGE
OF THE MICROELECTRONIC AGE
Toyo Ito

THE VISUAL IMAGE OF THE MICROELECTRONIC AGE

The 1990 exhibit entitled "Information Art: The Diagramming of Microchips" at the Museum of Modern Art in New York was an event of great significance for the world of architecture and design. I did not see the exhibit, but according to the catalog it consisted of many enlarged photographs of microchips; that is, diagrammatic images of integrated circuits that are used in computers.

These microchips resemble finely woven textiles. They have grid patterns in beautiful colors applied to silicon, and each diagrammed image is different. On a chip shown in the catalog a striped pattern is repeated. Another features a patchwork, with each patch having a different color and texture. Many of the chips have borders, and these square, cell-like shapes are arranged like buildings on a map. Still another chip has a complex diagram in which a mesh of organic form like the nervous system of the human body is superimposed on a grid pattern.

These microchip patterns suggest not only electronic fabrics but maps for the contemporary city. A chip so tiny that it must be enlarged several hundred times to be identifiable to the naked eye can contain millions, and more recently tens of millions, of transistors. By the turn of the century the development of a chip with a billion transistors is expected. The seemingly flat patterns are really three-dimensional compositions with ten to twenty-five layers.

The MoMA exhibit was significant because these photographs of microchips presented in clear visual images an aesthetic for the microelectronic age. It was the first convincing presentation of a new aesthetic that will supplant the machine-age aesthetic of the twentieth century. Nearly half a century has already passed since the invention of the transistor, and rapid progress was made back in the 1960s in high-performance, mainframe computers. Some might ask, Why this talk now of a microelectronic age, when the transition from the mechanical to the electronic was in fact made long ago? Certainly the Japanese were introduced to the computerized reservation system for the Shinkansen around the time of the 1964 Tokyo Olympics and were made to realize that computer technology would lead to decisive changes in society.

However, despite advances in microelectronics, we have been unable to develop clear visual images for the machine age. In the field of architecture and design, we ultimately depend on visually expressive forms, even when we attempt to depict a futuristic society.

In the 1960s, the Archigram Group captivated young architects and students with a succession of architectural and urban images. Projects like Plug-in City (1964) and Instant City (1969) by Peter Cook and Walking City (1964) by Ron Herron were visualizations of a technological utopia in which human beings disported with computers in a man machine system. Yet these future cities, though fantastically drawn, were still grounded in a machine aesthetic. The cities were collages of mechanical objects such as huge cranes, space frames, rocket launching pads, and lunar landing crafts. Looking back, it was only Dennis Crompton who presented in his Computer City project (1964) a different kind of image, one based on a gridded network suggesting the nervous system. However, even that project seems to have involved just the substitution of an enlarged integrated circuit for the physical network of the city. That is, the urban framework was based on a simple visual analogy.

That points out the reason why we have been unable to create an aesthetic of the microelectronic age. In the machine age, the forms of machines, such as airplanes, ships, and automobiles, and machine parts, like engines, screws, and plugs, were themselves the inspiration for visual imagery, but in the electronic age, we have not been able to discover visual forms that can serve an iconic purpose.

There is a causal relation, however ambiguous, between the form of a mechanical object and the performance and function of that object. In the case of vehicles, dynamic forms such that offer the least resistance to air or water are expressive of speed. The myth that the most functional forms are the most beautiful prevailed in the design world in the twentieth century. However, there is no such causal relation between form and function in electronic objects. Even the forms of objects such as audiovisual equipment that produce sounds and images do not suggest their workings. The enormous capacity of computers to retain information or to compute does not evoke formal images. We see only the data to be fed into the computer and the results that the computer produces. We cannot begin to imagine the flow of electricity of the speed and the immense quantities involved between input and output. That is why in trying to visualize images of the electronic age we have continued to rely on mechanical imagery.

However, the microchips clearly evoke images that are different from those of mechanical objects. These images are not so much of forms as of a space in which invisible things flow. One might describe that space as a transparent field in which diverse phenomenal forms emerge as the result of flow. What is important here is not so much the expressed forms as the image of a space that makes the expression of those forms possible.

It is often pointed out that recent car designs in Japan are products of the electronic age. They do not have immediately recognizable forms as well-known European cars like Porsche and Mercedes-Benz do. Instead they are as subtle and elusive as the shimmer of hot air. Though they may express a sense of speed, these Japanese cars do not necessarily have aerodynamic forms. They give the impression of having been designed to run soundlessly in an airless world. The transparent electronic space symbolized by the microchip probably accounts for such Japanese cars. Like images in that transparent space that appear for an instant only to fade in the next, these elusive forms represent products of phenomenal design.

THE CITY IS A GARDEN OF MICROCHIPS

An enlarged photograph of a microchip is like a computerprocessed bird's-eye view of a city. When converted by means of an effector, an aerial photograph of an urban area can be a highly abstract diagram showing just the outlines of buildings and civil engineering works or a diagram filled with colorful points of light. Urban space loses substance and begins to look just like a photograph of a microchip.

The emergence of another city, that is, the city as microchip, when the substance of urban space is erased, is symbolic, because the city not only is diagrammatically similar to the microchip but shares with the microchip certain attributes.

Their common attributes are (1) fluidity; (2) multiple layers; and (3) phenomenality.

I have pointed out on previous occasions that urban space is composed of not only immovable objects such as buildings but various things in flow such as water and air, human beings and automobiles stirred by diverse activities, and different kinds of energy and information.

The Japanese city originally developed as the superimposition of a man-made network of roads and canals on a highly undulating natural terrain through which rivers coursed. Edo in particular featured attractive urban spaces in which the man-made network was skillfully wedded to natural topography. "Bushu Toyoshima-gun Edo shozu," considered the oldest surviving published map of Edo, is said to show Edo in the middle of the seventeenth century. It depicts a network of rivers, canals, and roads centered on Edo castle that spirals outward in a dynamic fashion. The road grid, which one might expect to be rectilinear, is distorted and warped under the influence of its spiral pattern, and changes into a quite organic, fluid space. The result is a space entirely different from the urban space of the West, where geometrical patterns are rigorously imposed on natural terrain.

The "Edo ikkenzu byobu," said to have been painted in the early nineteenth century, by Kuwagata Isaitsuguzane, shows the spiral quality of the space even more clearly. The screen is a bird's-eye view from somewhere above Fukagawa, looking in the direction of Edo Castle and Mt. Fuji. Areas of abundant greenery, rivers, and canals wind their way past daimyo residences and the houses of the townspeople. A lively urban space with a dynamic quality that is scarcely imaginable from present-day Tokyo once existed.

Hidenobu Jinnai describes the beautiful garden-like city in which buildings, greenery, and water were skillfully joined as the product of a compromise between the will to plan, so evident in castle towns, and the desire to respond flexibly to the undulating natural topography of the Musashino plateau. "[The authorities] did not create a clear structure to which the entire city has to conform. On the contrary, the subtle underlying topography was carefully studied and the urban organization arranged bit by bit to create a mosaic pattern that was in harmony with the land."[1]

In this garden city called Edo, man-made elements such as buildings, roads, and canals blended with nature on every level. The result was a unified space. That is, technology and nature were integrated into one consistent system, from the macro-scale of the master plan to the micro-scale of residential and garden design.

Beginning in the Meiji era, man-made elements such as transportation systems were forcibly introduced into this beautiful space that had blended the artificial with the natural, and the equilibrium that had been maintained was upset. In particular, the introduction of a network of expressways and the enormous increase in the scale of structures in the postwar period of intensive economic growth proved decisive in destroying the natural system.

It is easy to point out the violence done by technology and the confusion wrought by the overlapping of heterogeneous systems in Tokyo today. However, I believe it is far more meaningful to search for new ways to make today's urban space attractive than to bemoan the wretched condition of Tokyo and indulge in nostalgia for the garden city of the past.

Tokyo has lost much of dynamic flow of greenery and water that Edo possessed. As I have already stated, the loss has been in inverse proportion to the increase in the flow of man-made things. In central Tokyo numerous transportation networks are stacked one on top of the other, from a level of several meters below ground to up in the air. Each layer has an extremely complex horizontal network of its own, and these layers are linked by vertical transportation systems. Throughout the city there are spaces in which networks are layered in a way that would have been unimaginable in the Edo period.

People and cars are not the only moving objects. The flow of diverse forms of energy and information has increased at a tremendous rate, and indeed the flow of such invisible things is coming to dominate urban space. However, we cannot conjure up an image of an information space because information does not give rise to a physical network. It only takes a terminal to retrieve information.

Urban space becomes phenomenal as the flow of electronic things, including information, increases. That is, another, phenomenal city of lights, sounds, and images is superimposed on the tangible urban space of buildings and civil engineering works. This city as phenomena takes may different guises, from space created directly by lights and images to abstract spaces woven from signs that fall into the category of the media. In any event, the city as phenomena is a space of ephemeral effects born of the invisible electronic flow. It does not express itself in form. The phenomenal city alters the surface of the tangible city into a city of lights, sounds, and images or a city of illusion enveloped in signs. If the tangible portion of the city were removed, the network of energy and electronic flow that manipulates those illusions would no doubt become apparent.

Thus the spaces of the contemporary city are characterized by fluidity, multiple layers, and phenomenality. These also happen to be characteristics of microchips.

However, to call this city a "garden of microchips" may be to unduly idealize it. The presence of man-made things introduced in the process of modernization is oppressive. Like archaeologists excavating a ruin, we must now dig up the subtle network of flow that Edo possessed—the network erased when various transportation systems that did not take the existing topography into consideration were introduced, canals were filled in, and huge buildings that completely disregarded the flow of nature were constructed.

Might it not be possible to discover historical ruins and the flow of nature amid the constructs of the machine age, and superimposing the network of the electronic age, effect their rebirth, at least as phenomenal space? This city will become a true "garden of microchips" only when the network of new technologies and the basic flow of nature overlap and begin to work together.

What bearing does this development of spaces in the contemporary city into gardens of microchips have on architectural design? Is it possible to translate such phenomenal spaces into actual works of architecture?

I have always thought of my architecture as being inseparable from gardens. By that I mean that I have always thought of my architecture as being itself a garden, not that my aim has been necessarily to create an architecture integrated with the landscape. To be sure, in the last several years I have tried to diminish the apparent size of buildings and establish an active relationship between buildings and exterior space by selectively removing or adding earth. I have found such work very stimulating and believe inserting an artificial "natural" environment between buildings is an effective stratagem in Japanese urban spaces where no context is easily discovered.

However, when I speak of architecture as a garden, the architecture I am imagining is one that is fluid and phenomenal as urban space. It is not an architecture whose overall image is made apparent in an instant. The people who experience architecture connect in their minds the phenomenal spaces that different scenes give rise to, and it is only as the sum of such spaces that an overall image emerges. Instead of scenes that are clearly articulated, like rooms in a building, I am trying to create scenes that shift imperceptibly from one to the next, as in a motion picture in which fade-ins and fade-outs are repeated.

An architecture that involves such temporal sequences is not so much visual as aural. That is, the space is close to being a space of sounds—a space in which countless sounds are afloat. These sounds of course are not the randomly transmitted sounds typical of urban noise. They are selected so that they enter into relationships, yet the whole is not governed by one form as in classical music or a Japanese tour-style garden. The people who experience the architecture are free to choose which sounds to connect. A musical space from which a score can be created exists, but the score itself as a sequence of sounds in time is different for each individual. When I refer to an architecture that is a garden, I am imagining such an aural space.

However, White U (fig. 183), my first attempt to create a work of architecture that is a garden, did possess a space similar to that of a tour-style garden. A "garden of light" was created between two walls curved in a U shape. A space of variegated light was produced by natural light introduced from the top and the side of this pure white tubular ring. The phenomenon of light was used to give birth to a space that flows and eddies. People within the space may linger here and there, but they have no choice with respect to their path. They can only circle the central courtyard. The space is powerful because the scheme is clear and simple, but like a tour-style garden it is a world that is complete in itself.

The recently completed ITM Building in Matsuyama (fig. 184) might also be called a "garden of light." Whereas the space of White U is enclosed in concrete, here a space filled with soft light has been created by means of translucent glass on which a film has been applied to control the amount of light. The various architectural elements arranged within this volume of soft light suggest extension in the horizontal and vertical directions even as they are loosely related like sounds that drift in the air.

Horizontal and vertical relationships are maintained, but "up" and "down" have practically no meaning here. That is, those architectural features that derive their significance from their relationship to gravity such as floors, walls, and ceilings have disappeared. If the space were to be flipped over 90 degrees or 180 degrees, the meaning of this space would change very little.

Architectural elements like slabs, stairs, and partitions are designed with translucent panels so that light will penetrate anywhere. Not bound by gravity, people stroll through this new "garden of light," free to select sounds (i.e., architectural elements) and put together their own scores. If White U and the ITM Building in Matsuyama are "gardens of light," then Silver Hut and the Yatsushiro Municipal Museum are "gardens of wind." In each of these two projects the roof is a series of thin, lightweight vaults of steel frame truss, supported on freestanding columns, around which are open spaces. The spaces are a garden through which air flows as in the woods. In the case of Yatsushiro, there is continual change of scene, from the curved bridge built over the green berm, the space under the vaults that affords a "hilltop" view, the exhibition space with supports that suggest a grove of trees growing randomly, to the open-air exhibition area that offers a space completely different in character from the main approach to the museum. This building is ostensibly a museum, but above the exhibition space provided to serve that specific function a garden that includes both outdoor and indoor space is created. Visitors sense the air flowing and eddying. They stroll and linger, weaving a "garden of wind." I began to take an interest in electronic phenomena with the Tower of Winds in Yokohama in 1986. That project is not truly a work of architecture, but it anticipated a series of works in which lights and images are used. The intention was to extract the flow of air (wind) and noise (sound) from the general flow of things in the environment of the project and to transform them into light signals; that is, visual information.

The exact same intention, to convert the environment into information, was behind the project entered in the Yokohama Urban Ring Exhibit of 1992. There the aim was to convert information related to Yokohama Harbor into a visual and aural space through lights, sounds, and images. The resulting space, a sort of "media park," is a space of phenomenal water superimposed on actual water. Thus the project involves simultaneously both the conversion of the environment into information and the conversion of information into an environment.

In what way is this information to be converted into an environment to create an architecture that is a "garden of microchips"? An act of architecture represents the creation of a new environment that is both physical and phenomenal through the introduction of information into an existing environment. Architecture becomes a device for both the transmission and the retention of information. That is, instead of being an assertive physical form, architecture ought to be a device for producing a phenomenal form; that is, an environment.

In the Project for a Library for the University of Paris (figs. 185 and 186) last year the goal was to make architecture a device for controlling the environment. First, a large oval place (center) was established in an open area surrounded by three buildings. This place is a center of information that will join the three buildings and convert what has been a negative space into a positive space. Specifically, it is a space whose main function is to serve as the reading area for the library; that is, it is a device for the retention and transmission of information and a domain of highly concentrated information, serving as a center of communication for students and faculty. Next, two layers of striped slabs were introduced in this oval space. These are not only floor and roof elements but also environmental control devices for regulating light, sound, and heat. It is by means of these two layers of horizontally arranged louvers that a pleasant, artificially controlled place for reading is created inside the oval. These louvers are devices for passing through light and air in controlled amounts. The two layers of slabs are intended not to separate the outdoors from the indoors but to produce an outdoor-like environment that is more comfortable than outdoors. Thus the concept of a facade is irrelevant to this building. The outdoors and the indoors are given equal weight in this project: though separated by glass, visitors feel them to be one continuous space. On the one hand, this is a device for the retention and transmission of information; on the other, it is a filtering device for light, heat (air), and sound, a place where the natural flow undergoes a conversion. These two aspects of the project are represented respectively by the oval and the stripes, which are superimposed to form a layered space. This project is the realization in architecture of a "garden of microchips" in that it is characterized by fluidity, multiple layers, and phenomenality. Moreover, these attributes are embodied in architectural elements, namely the slabs and the screens.

The two projects currently in progress for a fire station and a home for the elderly in Yatsushiro City are similarly composed of layered spaces. The intention is to satisfy the specific functional requirements of a fire station and a home for the elderly while creating garden-like places that are open to the environment. Layered spaces here are not just a matter of physical composition. In the case of the fire station, the aim is to superimpose its specific function as a fire station on its more ambiguous function as a garden and to cause these functions to interact so as to produce a garden that is unique to a fire station. An interaction, that is, a transparent relationship of two social functions, must be achieved through the actual architecture. The same is true for the home for the elderly.

Projects like the Rejuvenation Project for Antwerp and the Shanghai Luijiazui Central Area International Planning and Urban Design Consultation Project are also intended to create "microchip gardens." Because these projects are on an urban scale, actual urban spaces can more readily serve as reference. That is because new gardens emerge whenever the layered networks that real urban spaces possess are coordinated and transparent relationships established among them.

In any case, visualizing an image for the microelectronic age is for me a task consistent with trying to achieve a "garden of microchips." It is an attempt to create an electronic eddy in the electronic flow; that is, an attempt to give rise to a place of information where in the past there was a *genius loci*.

[1] Hidenobu Jinnai, *Tokyo no kukan jinruigaku* (The spatial anthropology of Tokyo) (Chikuma Shobo Publishing Co.).

El Croquis 84 (1997)

THE CUNNING OF COSMETICS:
A PERSONAL REFLECTION ON THE ARCHITECTURE
OF HERZOG AND DE MEURON

Jeffrey Kipnis

During the toasts celebrating the opening of Light Construction, *the deep-seated tension . . . broke out in a bristling exchange between Herzog and Koolhaas.*
   El Croquis 79

How long now—six years? eight?—since I tossed off my first snide dismissal of the work of Herzog & de Meuron. Of course, for a critic such as I, advocate of the architectural avant-garde, intellectual apologist for the extreme, the exotic, the subversive, was it not *de rigueur* to scorn the superficial propositions of HdM? While one branch of the avant-garde proposed exotic form as a vector of architectural resistance, HdM offered flagrantly simple Cartesian volumes. While another branch cultivated event-theory into seditious programming techniques, HdM indulged contentedly in expedient, reductive planning. HdM's fixation on the cosmetic, on fastidious details, eye-catching materials and stunning facades appeared frivolous in comparison with those other more overtly radical experiments. Even worse, the overall cast of their work seemed complicit, if not aligned, with the taste for Neo-Modern Confections that had already begun to emerge as the hallmark of the reactionary New Right in Europe and elsewhere.

   The question more to the point, then, is when exactly did my infatuation with HdM's work begin? When did I start returning to publications to gape secretly, furtively, at the Goetz Gallery (figs. 8 and 189), the Signal Box (figs. 17 and 191), Ricola Europe (figs. 187 and 188), or the sublime Greek Orthodox Church (fig. 190), like a schoolboy ogling soft porn? Did my longing for the work grow over time, or was I beguiled from the outset, my oafish snubs but the hackneyed disavowals of one discomforted by the throws of forbidden desire?

   In any case, it was not until March 1996 that the utter cunning of HdM's project dawned on me in its full dimension. By then, I had already realized that their architecture's ability to insinuate itself into my psyche was a powerful effect that, like it or not, must be taken seriously. All the more so, when it occurred to me that HdM's work did not, by virtue of any polemic, force itself on me against my will; rather, like a computer virus, it slipped into my consciousness through my will, eluding any and all resistance as it began to reprogram my architectural thoughts and feelings.

   In March 1996 I encountered an *Arch-Plus* special issue on HdM. What shocked me into a new awareness was not any particular essay in the issue, though it contained several excellent ones.[1] Rather, the agent of my epiphany was the unceremonious cover title: *Herzog et de Meuron: Minimalismus und Ornament.* As soon as I saw it, I knew something was wrong, very wrong; I could feel it, though I could not quite put my finger on it.

Thumbing through the magazine, I found that Nikolaus Kuhnert had, without comment, separated the firm's work into two sections: *Ornament* held all of the projects with printed surfaces, *Minimalism* everything else—a brute act of blunt taxonomy. The source of the uneasiness spawned by the cover title became apparent. How could such a coherent collection of works by one architectural intelligence lend itself so easily to partitioning into such antagonistic categories as Minimalism and Ornament?

At first glance, the division seemed quite sensible but, as might be expected, it did not sustain closer inspection. For example, Kuhnert placed the Signal Box—a key work in the HdM oeuvre—in the Minimalist section, no doubt in respect of the simple form, the monolithic uniformity effected by the copper banding system, and the functional role attributed. On the other hand, does not the luxurious field of copper bands also fit any non-trivial definition of architectural ornament, even, as we shall see, if it also undermines the concept of ornament at the same time? After all, each band was painstakingly warped to engender a mesmerizing, ephemeral gesture in light, shadow, and form over a large area of the skin, one much larger than required to admit natural light to the few interior spaces. And the functional rationalization of the system as a Faraday Cage is merely a smokescreen.[2] My point, however, is not to contest the details of Kuhnert's partitioning; rather, it is to admire the insidious guile of an architecture able to infiltrate so effortlessly such irreconcilable categories, and, in doing so, begin to dismantle and reform them.

Already I have touched on the most potent characteristics of HdM's architecture: an urbane, cunning intelligence and intoxicating, almost erotic allure. It is these traits that enable it to go anywhere, to go everywhere, into site and psyche alike, to appear ever fascinating yet ever harmless even as it plies its undermining subterfuges and sly deceits. And while this constellation of themes and its attendant techniques are ancient indeed,[3] the most precise placement of HdM's work in contemporary architecture is simply that it is the coolest architecture around. All that remains for us, then, is to watch it in action, to speculate a bit on its methods, and to begin an audit of its gains and losses.

Let us return to the Signal Boxes. Would it be too much to liken them to sirens, to temptresses that lure the unsuspecting into dangerous territory? The sirens of the *Odyssey*, if I remember correctly, charmed sailors into hazardous waters with the sheer beauty of their voices, voices that sang but said nothing, meant nothing, promised nothing. Do you not feel the song of the Signal Box? Are you not enticed by it, drawn to a distant train yard to drink in its presence with your eyes? What pulls you there? And why go, when the only thing certain is that there is absolutely nothing for you there, save, perhaps, peril?

In its single-minded obsession with Unspeakable Beauty, the Signal Box series is exemplary of the HdM project at its most radical. To achieve its edgy *à la mode*, HdM brushed aside the Big Questions that such a project would, today, customarily trigger. HdM ignores the fact that the signal station belongs to remote networks and inter-urban infrastructures and, therefore, that its architecture should be conceived more in terms of flows and intensities than in terms that might be likened to the visual niceties that have come to appoint bourgeois travel. Nor does HdM give a moment's thought to the inappropriateness of High Design in the harsh, dirty reality of the site, though the shrill understatement of the Signal Box is as hip to its surroundings as a gangster in colors is to South Central L.A. In that regard, the Signal Box raises doubts about the subtly patronizing fantasy of a context so brutal, so unrelentingly utilitarian that it cannot even broach the cloying frippery of design.

Make no mistake about it, these are not just hypothetical interrogations made in the name of the infrastructuralists and dirty realists. In his published comments to HdM, Rem Koolhaas first remarks on the undeniable beauty of the firm's facades. Then, on the way to framing his final indictment as a question, "Is architecture reinforcement therapy or does it play a role in redefining, undermining, exploding, erasing? [sic]," he begins to signal his misgivings by asking HdM, "Does every situation have a correct architecture?" no doubt with the Signal Box in mind.[4]

For the proponents of exotic form, the signal station series would have been an opportunity of another ilk. Largely free from the demands of human program, unencumbered by historical or formal typology, unobligated to a prevailing contextual language of architectural merit, the signal station offered an ideal prospect to experiment with the very limits of form. Furthermore, because several would be built, the morphological research could have been extended to the fascinating question of non-prototypical serialization. That HdM should adhere so closely to the box, that they should even consider developing a prototype was anathema. To this group of architects, the appearance in the second Signal Box of warped surfaces will surely seem a tacit admission of the futility of the original prototypical ambition and the inadequacy of the Cartesian box. As we shall see, however, nothing could be further from the truth.

In brief, the design of the Signal Box shows no concern whatsoever for flows or event-structures, for realism or new form. Its architecture is entirely a matter of cosmetics, a hypnotic web of visual seductions that emanate entirely from the copper band system, a system, it should be said, that is in fact not the building's actual skin, which lies just beneath; it only poses as the building's skin.

The point here, however, is not to diminish the architectural import of the Signal Boxes by relegating them to cosmetic, but to embrace their irresistible intrigue, to acknowledge their vitality, and in doing so, to assert the transformative power of the cosmetic. Some care must be taken here, for the *cosmetic* is not just another member of the family of decorative architectural appurtenances collectively known as ornamentation. The field of effects of the cosmetic is quite different from those of its relatives, and it is precisely in those differences that HdM's contemporary project is born.

Ornaments attach as discreet entities to the body like jewelry, reinforcing the structure and integrity of the body as such. Cosmetics are indiscreet, with no relation to the body other than to take it for granted. Cosmetics are erotic camouflage; they relate always and only to skin, to particular regions of skin. Deeply, intricately material, cosmetics nevertheless exceed materiality to become modern alchemicals as they trans-substantiate skin into image, desirous or disgusting. Where ornaments retain their identity as entities, cosmetics work as fields, as blush or shadow or highlight, as aura or air. Thinness, adherence, and diffuse extent are crucial to the cosmetic effect, which is more visceral than intellectual, more atmospheric than aesthetic. Virtuosity at ornamentation requires balance, proportion, precision; virtuosity at cosmetics requires something else, something menacing: paranoid control, control gone out of control, schizo-control.

Though the cosmetic effect does not work at the level of the body, nevertheless, it requires a body—or at least a face—as a vehicle. Like veal for the saucier, or the gaunt, featureless visage of choice recently for make-up artists, the ideal vehicle for the extreme cosmetician is a body, face, or form denuded of its own ability to engender affect. These days, the effects of form as such are just too obtuse to be cool.

If the attitude of the cosmetician toward the body is a minimalism, then it is of a very different sort than the Minimalism spawned by the art world more than two decades ago. While the two share a desire to collapse the time of impact of a work to the immediate, the former pursued that goal by distilling form and material into an essence that radiated (spiritual) affect through unmediated presence. The reductions of cosmetic minimalism, on the other hand, are anorexic, a compulsion to starve the body until it dissolves into pure (erotic) affect, like a Cheshire cat in heat. Witness the necrophilic charge of the anemic Kantonsspital Pharmacy, or speculate on the rejection of HdM's dazzling Greek Orthodox Church by the bishop. Was it because he grasped the conversion of its space from the spiritual to the erotic?

Thus, Kuhnert's bipartite distribution missed the decisive achievement of HdM's work thus far, the sublimation of the antithesis between ornamentalism and minimalism into a new coherence. The most famous example of this synthesis to date is Ricola Europe, with its renowned flourish, walls patterned with translucent tiles silk-screened with leaf images. When backlit, as seen in the interior during the day, the leaf pattern takes on an empty, numbing, camp fascination of a Warholian wallpaper. On the exterior, the images are rarely visible, emerging only fleetingly as hallucinations when hit at exactly the right angle by glancing light. Photos (actually, photographers) of this building tend to exaggerate the leaf image to the point of kitsch; its presence on the exterior is actually much rarer and more ephemeral. But in any case, this slick, eye-catching device belies the range and depth of technique HdM exercised in realizing the full cosmetic sophistication of the work.

As usual, the form is starved to skin and bones and gutted of any distracting conceit in plan. The silk-screened panels tile the two long walls; starting on the underside of the cantilevered awning, the strip paneling turns to wrap down the wall. The effect of the wrap is to subvert the integrity of the two distinct formal elements of the building, the facade and the soffit, blurring them into a single field. Ironically, this leaves the thin strip of clear glass revealing the terminal truss of the roof extensions as, strictly speaking, the only actual facade.

To further distance the thin, weightless leaf field from a wall, even a curtain-wall, it is edged like a draped veil. The edging causes the long, thin strips to seem to stream from the top to the ground, trickling so gently that the slight thickness of the upper track of the horizontal glass doors breaks the flow.

This streaming illusion on the panels blurs the front, translucent fields into the side concrete walls. On those sides, roof water flows over the concrete, causing it to reflect like glass when wet and leaving a field of parallel vertical tracks, the residue of evaporated flow. In the same device at the wraith-like echo of Ricola Europa, the Remy Zaugg studio, iron on the roof dyes the rainwater rust red to create a more dramatic if somewhat disconcerting effect. At Ricola Europe, these flow tracks and the pattern of widths they delimit reiterate uncannily the field of translucent tiles and seams in form and proportion.

For all of its modes of assertiveness, its blatant use of images, its indulgence in materiality, and the bluntness of its form, the genius of the Ricola Europa is that the building, in itself and as such, is never there. Its promise of stark presence withdraws to leave pure allure, a tour de force of architectural cosmetics.

As with other critical treatment of HdM's work, e.g., as neo-modernism or as applied minimal art, the question of cosmetics with all of its allusions to make-up and scents, to skins and bodies, would have only the force of analogy were it not for the matter of HdM's technique.

With form, planning, structure, and construction, even with materials, HdM's technique is architectural to the point of fanaticism. In the firm's entire body of work to date, there is not a single use of form, structure, or material that does not belong to the strictest canon of the architectonic. Every experiment is an effort to reanimate and update that canon, never to augment it with new entries, certainly not with new forms or programs, but not even with new materials. Even the stained water tracks and the algae, lichens, and molds that grow on old surfaces have belonged to the canon, albeit as nuisances, for centuries.

What makes the firm so interesting is that, unlike the avant-garde, HdM derives its critical edge from an assumption of architecture's basic adequacy and an ease with the controversial proposition that architecture has no other more profound project than to fabricate a new sensibility from its own palette. In that it pursues the new not as a matter of ideology or as a condition of marginality, but as a forthright, even aggressive assertion of the center, it is perhaps the most *au courant* practice.

If the notion of the cosmetic has any deeper purchase for HdM than mere analogy, it is because the firm does not apply cosmetics to architecture as theory or borrowed practice. HdM unleashes the destabilizing power of the cosmetic as a moment and a movement already residing within architecture's orthodoxy. In so doing, it often accomplishes timely effects *en passant* that other practices grounded more in applied theory have pursued with less success.

By working steadfastly within the protocols of architectural materiality, HdM achieves a far more convincing realization of architectural dematerialization than Peter Eisenman, who has pursued that idea in his architecture for over two decades. Eisenman, steeped in a post-structural account of architecture as an endless system of references by immaterial signs, theorized that the tradition of materiality in architecture was a perversion manifest either as fetishism or nostalgia. Accordingly, he sought to render his forms as pure signs by constructing them as empty shades in indifferent materials, e.g., EIFS or gyp-board. As a result, more often than not, his buildings fail to insist themselves and are easily dismissed as irreal, like stage sets or amusements parks.[5]

By beginning with more traditional and tactile material such as glass, wood, or concrete and then manipulating them in non-traditional ways, HdM is able to insist on the reality of the building while never allowing it to settle as a reliable and persistent presence. In other words, they do not dematerialize a concrete form by replacing the concrete; they dematerialize the concrete itself.

The forthcoming Kunstkiste Museum for the Grohte Collection should provide an acute study in this aspect of HdM's work. As published, the project promises to be nothing short of an essay in extreme concrete, one whose rude materiality should make Ando's renowned use of the material seem hopelessly genteel, as the building will certainly do to the saccharine confections by Schultes and Peichl nearby.

The top-heavy proportions of the vertical slab make the form of the Kuntskiste seem poised to topple, the threat further intensifying the insistent weight of the materiality. But the roof water, now destined to stain every surface with its vertical striations of rust and algae, will transform the appearance of the concrete box into that of a viscous liquid in an aquarium, the image confirmed by the blackened windows floating at random like objects at neutral buoyancy. Heavy or light? Solid or liquid? Essential presence or imagistic illusion?

But as intriguing as the project is in its published form, Jacques Herzog reveals that HdM entertained an even more astonishing thought for the project. At one point they considered printing exactly positioned, full-scale photo-images of the interior of the galleries on the concrete. The photo-printing surfaces would, in effect, make the concrete appear transparent! As if the phenomenal dislocation were not enough, the idea also carried a deconstructive implication, perhaps its downfall. The photographer would have been a young artist of note from Berlin, whose presence on the surfaces would have marked his absence from the collection and raised questions about the collection itself. For whatever reason, the idea seems to have been abandoned. Nevertheless, it was a brilliant thought, and one that indicates just how aware HdM is of the eruptive force of their cosmetic techniques.

[1] *Arch-Plus* 129–30 (December 1995). Included in the volume is a reprint of Alejandro Zaera's excellent "Between the Face and the Landscape," from the first *El Croquis* (no. 60, 1993) on HdM, and Rem Koolhaas's "Architectures of Herzog and de Meuron," republished in *Arch-Plus* under the new title "New Discipline," as well as insightful comments by Mark Taylor, Terry Riley, and Hans Frei.

[2] The electronic equipment in all facilities such as switching stations is adequately shielded interference. Thus, though the copper banding system does indeed technically produce a Faraday Cage, it is far from a functional necessity.

[3] Cf. M. Detienne and J.P. Vernant, *Ruses de l'intelligence: la métis des Grecs*, (Paris: Flammarion, 1974), translated into English as *Cunning Intelligence*.

[4] From *Arch-Plus,* 129–30.

[5] Cf. my remarks in the recent *El Croquis* volume on Peter Eisenman (no. 83, 1997).

AFTERWORD

Terence Riley

Getting the chance to add in two more cents worth, after having had all the opportunity in the world to make your point initially, is more than a curator should hope for. But having been given the opportunity, I'd like to address a few points.

Under the category of "I wish I had said that" is Mark Taylor's aside in the symposium at Columbia, unfortunately unrecorded, where he compared "Light Construction" to a concurrent exhibition—"Pierced Hearts and True Love"—at the Drawing Center. While "Light Construction" was, of course, an exhibition about architecture, "Pierced Hearts" presented a century of drawings for tattoos. I tried to make a number of references in the catalogue that might tie the show more tightly to contemporary culture—and less tightly to the somewhat hermetic world of architecture—but none were as enlightening as Taylor's observation that both shows were about information in the skin. Taylor's observation did more than provide a pop metaphor though. I had previously thought of Kolbe's statue in Mies's reconstructed Barcelona Pavilion as a collage-like presence within the otherwise abstract space, a phenomenon repeated through its reflection on the building's reflective surfaces. Taylor's remarks helped me understand the reflections as being *in* the surface rather than *on* the surface. (figs. 192, 193).

The *New York Times* architecture critic, Herbert Muschamp, jumped on the show for having too many projects, amongst other reasons, and ended his review of the exhibition by suggesting that "less 'Light Construction' would have been a whole lot more." I disagreed with him then and, after considerable hindsight, I would pass on his advice again. In fact, I really wish I had added one more project, Toyo Ito's fantastic Mediathèque in Sendai (fig. 58). The project had been in development at the time I was talking with Ito about the exhibition and visiting his projects in Japan. For whatever reason, he didn't show it to me, much to my regret. From the first time I saw the project, with its voluptuously writhing spiderwebs of support, I knew that the book would always have an inexplicable lacuna.

At the Columbia symposium, Greg Lynn and Jacques Herzog squared off, I recall, over an issue I cannot recall, and which, like Taylor's aside, is not recorded in the volume of D that documented the proceedings. Nonetheless, the result of that exchange was, I feel, a tilting of "Light Construction" into the then brewing debate between Blobs and Boxes—a tilt that was perceived as endorsing the latter over the former. Six years later, I would like to underscore that "Light Construction" was intended to be the antidote to that kind of polemic, an argument that turned on other issues than form. While no one could accuse me of antipathy to the right angle, a re-visitation of the catalogue shows a rather promiscuous attitude toward geometry; from the strictly rectilinear vocabulary of Jean Nouvel's Cartier Foundation to the limpid, if not limp, curving lines of Ito's Shimosuwa Municipal Museum (fig. 29). If people remember it otherwise, I hope this volume will further argue for an architecture that is formally plural even as it maintains a fundamentally critical position.

CONTRIBUTORS

Reyner Banham (1922–1988) was Sheldon H. Solow Professor of the History of Architecture at the Institute of Fine Arts, New York University, and before that Professor of Art History at the University of California, Santa Cruz. His many books include *Los Angeles: The Architecture of Four Ecologies, Theory and Design in the First Machine Age,* and *Concrete Atlantis: U.S. Industrial Building and European Modern Architecture.*

Rosemarie Haag Bletter is Director of the Graduate Program in Art History at the City University of New York.

Italo Calvino was born in Cuba in 1923 and grew up in Italy. He was an essayist and journalist and a member of the editorial staff of Einaudi in Turin. His books include *Marcovaldo, Invisible Cities, The Castle of Crossed Destinies, If on a Winter's Night a Traveler,* and *Mr. Palomar.* In 1973 he won the prestigious Premio Feltrinelli. He died in 1985.

Cynthia Davidson is a co-founder and editor of *ANY* magazine. She has edited a number of books, including the eleven-volume series based on the ANY architecture conferences, and *Eleven Authors in Search of a Building,* published by the Monacelli Press.

Jacques Derrida is Director of Studies at the Ecole des Hautes Etudes en Sciences Sociales in Paris.

Hugh Dutton is a structural engineer practicing in Paris.

Peter Eisenman, principal of Eisenman Architects, is the Irwin S. Chanin Distinguished Professor of Architecture at the Cooper Union. His buildings include the Wexner Center for the Arts in Columbus, Ohio, the Nunotani Office Building in Tokyo, and the Aronoff Center at the University of Cincinnati. Eisenman is a prolific writer whose criticism has been featured in many architectural journals. His study of the work of Italian Modernist Guiseppe Terragni is forthcoming from the Monacelli Press.

Robin Evans, architect, teacher, historian, and theoretician, was Visiting Professor, Graduate School of Design, Harvard University; Lecturer, University of Westminster, London; and Visiting Lecturer, Architectural Association, London. His books include *The Projective Cast* and *Translations from Drawing to Building.* He died in 1993.

Richard Feynman was Professor of Physics at the California Institute of Technology. His widely read books on physics include *QED: The Strange Theory of Light and Matter* and *Five Easy Pieces.* He died in 1988.

Kenneth Frampton is Ware Professor of Architecture at the Graduate School of Architecture, Planing and Preservation at Columbia University. He is author of a number of books, including *Modern Architecture: A Critical History* and *Studies in Tectonic Culture.*

Todd Gannon is a Lecturer in Architectural Theory and Design at the Knowlton School of Architecture at the Ohio State University and a project designer with Acock Associates Architects in Columbus, Ohio. He is co-editor, with Jeffrey Kipnis, of *Morphosis/Diamond Ranch High School,* published by the Monacelli Press.

K. Michael Hays is Professor of Architectural Theory at Harvard's Graduate School of Design and Curator of Architecture at the Whitney Museum of American Art in New York. He is the founding editor of *Assemblage* and is editor of *Architecture Theory since 1968*.

Toyo Ito is principal of Toyo Ito and Associates, Architects, in Tokyo. He has lectured extensively throughout Japan, the United States, and Europe and his work has appeared in numerous international exhibitions. Recent projects include the Yatsushiro Fire Station and the Sendai Mediathèque.

Jeffrey Kipnis, Professor of Architecture at the Knowlton School of Architecture and Curator of Architecture at the Wexner Center for the Arts, was formerly Director of the Graduate Design Program at the Architectural Association in London. He is co-editor of *Chora L Works* and a contributor to *Autonomy and Ideology: Positioning an Avant-Garde in America*, both published by the Monacelli Press.

Rosalind Krauss is Professor of Art History at Columbia University and a founding editor of the journal *October*. Her books include *The Optical Unconscious* and *Passages in Modern Sculpture*.

Greg Lynn is principal of the Los Angeles–based architecture firm Greg Lynn FORM. His writings have appeared in numerous architectural journals and his books include *Animate Form*, and *Folds, Bodies and Blobs: Collected Essays*. Lynn has taught throughout the United States and Europe and is currently Assistant Professor at the University of California, Los Angeles.

Detlef Mertins is an architect, historian, and critic teaching at the University of Toronto. He is co-curator of *Toronto Modern: Architecture 1945–1965* and editor of *The Presence of Mies*. Recent essays have appeared in *Assemblage*, *ANY*, *AA Files*, *Alphabet City*, *Monolithic Architecture*, and *Architecture and Cubism*.

Herbert Muschamp is an architecture critic for the *New York Times*.

Guy Nordenson has a structural engineering practice in New York and is Associate Professor of Architecture at Princeton University. He designed the 480-meter cable-stayed Rio Grande de Loiza Bridge in Carolina, Puerto Rico, and has collaborated on a number of important buildings, including Richard Meier's Chiesa di Anno 2000 in Rome.

Joan Ockman is Assistant Professor of Architecture and Director of the Buell Center of the Study of American Architecture at Columbia University's Graduate School of Architecture, Planning and Preservation. A graduate of Harvard University and the Cooper Union School of Architecture, she writes on the history and theory of modern architecture. She has edited many architectural publications, including *Oppositions*, Oppositions Books, the Revisions series, and *Architecture Culture 1943–1968*.

Eeva-Liisa Pelkonen teaches architectural design and theory at the Yale University School of Architecture. From 1988 to 1992 she collaborated with architect Volker Giencke in Graz, Austria. She is author of *Achtung Architektur! Image and Phantasm in Contemporary Architecture* and is a partner, with Turner Brooks, in Brooks + Pelkonen architects.

Terence Riley is Chief Curator of Architecture at the Museum of Modern Art in New York. He studied architecture at the University of Notre Dame and Columbia University and since 1984 has been in private practice with John Keenen. He has curated a number of shows at MoMA, including "Light Construction," "The Un-Private House," and exhibitions on Bernard Tschumi, Rem Koolhaas, and Frank Lloyd Wright. Riley is a frequent visiting critic and lecturer at universities in the United States and abroad.

Colin Rowe was Professor Emeritus at Cornell University School of Architecture and a 1995 RIBA Gold Medalist. His numerous works of architectural criticism include *The Mathematics of the Ideal Villa and Other Essays*, *Collage City* (with Fred Koetter) and the three-volume collection of essays, *As I Was Saying*. Rowe died in 2000.

Paul Scheerbart (1863–1915) was a German novelist and poet based in Berlin. Called "the literary forerunner and instigator of modern glass architecture" by German historian Konrad Werner Schulz, his many books include *Glasarchitektur*, *Rakkox, per Billionär*, and *The Emperor of Utopia*.

Robert Slutzky is a painter, critic, and professor at the University of Pennsylvania.

Robert Somol teaches design and theory in the Department of Architecture and Urban Design at the University of California, Los Angeles, and is a member of the editorial board of *ANY* magazine. He is a frequent contributor to architectural journals and is editor of *Autonomy and Ideology: Positioning an Avant-Garde in America*, published by the Monacelli Press. Somol also maintains a design practice in Los Angeles with Linda Pollari.

Jean Starobinski is Professor Emeritus, University of Geneva. His books in English include *Jean-Jacques Rousseau, Montaigne in Motion*, and *The Emblems of Reason, 1789*.

Mark Taylor teaches Humanities at Williams College in Williamstown, Massachusetts. His books include *Disfiguring: Art, Architecture, Religion*, *Nots*, and *Imagologies: Media Philosophy*.

Bernard Tschumi is principal of Bernard Tschumi Architects in New York and Paris and Dean of the School of Architecture, Planning and Preservation at Columbia University. He is the architect of several award-winning projects, including Parc de la Villette in Paris, and is the author of *Manhattan Transcripts*, *Architecture and Disjunction*, and *Event Cites 1&2*.

Gianni Vattimo is professor of theoretical philosophy at the University of Turin. He is author of a number of books, including *The End of Modernity* and *The Transparent Society*.

Anthony Vidler is Professor of Art History and Architecture at the University of California, Los Angeles. His recent books include *The Architectural Uncanny* and *Warped Space*.

ILLUSTRATION CREDITS

All reasonable efforts have been made to trace the copyright holders of the visual material reproduced in this book. The publisher and the Knowlton School of Architecture apologize to anyone who has not been reached.

1 © Michael Van Valkenburgh Associates, Inc.

2 Photo by Richard Payne, FAIA.

3 Shinkenchiku-sha.

4 Shinkenchiku-sha.

5 Photo by Toshiharu Kitajima.

6 Courtesy of Fumihiko Maki.

7 © 2001 Artists Rights Society (ARS), New York / VG Bild-Kunst, Bonn. Image courtesy of the Museum of Modern Art, New York, gift of the architect.

8 Photo by Margherita Spiluttini.

9 Photo by Philippe Ruault. © 2001 Artists Rights Society (ARS) New York / ADAGP, Paris.

10 Courtesy of OMA/Rem Koolhaas.

11 © 2001 Artists Rights Society (ARS), New York, ADAGP, Paris / Estate of Marcel Duchamp.

12 Reproduced from *Pierre Chareau: Architect and Craftsman, 1883–1950* (New York: Rizzoli, 1986).

13 Photo by Atelier Kim Zwarts.

14 Courtesy of OMA/Rem Koolhaas.

15 © Steven Holl Architects.

16 Photo by Paul Warchol.

17 Photo by Margherita Spiluttini.

18 Reproduced from *El Croquis* 88/89 (Madrid: El Croquis Editorial, 1998).

19 Courtesy of Harry C. Wolf.

20 Reproduced from Terence Riley, *Light Construction* (New York: Museum of Modern Art, 1995).

21 Photo by Jussi Tiainen.

22 Reproduced from Terence Riley, *Light Construction* (New York: Museum of Modern Art, 1995). After Allessandro Parronchi, *Studi su la dolce prospettive* (Milan: A. Martello, 1964), fig. 91.

23 Photo by Bill Jacobson, courtesy of Dia Center for the Arts.

24 Reproduced from *Abalos and Herreros* (Barcelona: GG, 1993). Photo by Emilio Izquierdo.

25 Courtesy of Bernard Tschumi Architects.

26 Yoshio Hata.

27 Photo by Don F. Wong.

28 Photo by George Stowell, Nicholas Grimshaw and Partners.

65 Reproduced from Colin Rowe, *The Mathematics of the Ideal Villa* (Cambridge: MIT Press, 1992).

66 © 2001 Artists Rights Society (ARS) New York / ADAGP, Paris. Kunstmuseum, Bern.

67 Private collection.

68 © 2001 Artists Rights Society (ARS) New York / ADAGP, Paris. Kunstmuseum, Bern.

69 © 2001 Estate of Pablo Picasso / Artists Rights Society (ARS) New York.

70 Courtesy of The Walter Gropius Archive, Busch-Reisinger Museum, Harvard University. Gift of Walter Gropius. Photographic Services. President and Fellows of Harvard University.

71 © 2001 Artists Rights Society (ARS) New York / ADAGP, Paris / FLC.

72 © 2001 Artists Rights Society (ARS) New York / ADAGP, Paris / FLC.

73 Courtesy of The Walter Gropius Archive, Busch-Reisinger Museum, Harvard University. Gift of Ise Gropius. Photographic Services. President and Fellows of Harvard University.

74 © 2001 Artists Rights Society (ARS) New York / ADAGP, Paris / FLC.

75 © 2001 Artists Rights Society (ARS) New York / ADAGP, Paris / FLC.

76 Courtesy of The Walter Gropius Archive, Busch-Reisinger Museum, Harvard University. Gift of Walter Gropius. Photographic Services. President and Fellows of Harvard University.

77 Courtesy of The Walter Gropius Archive, Busch-Reisinger Museum, Harvard University. Gift of Walter Gropius. Photographic Services. President and Fellows of Harvard University.

78 © 2001 Artists Rights Society (ARS) New York / ADAGP, Paris / FLC.

79 Reproduced from Colin Rowe, *The Mathematics of the Ideal Villa and Other Essays* (Cambridge, MA: MIT Press, 1976), 183.

80 Courtesy of The Walter Gropius Archive, Busch-Reisinger Museum, Harvard University. Gift of Walter Gropius. Photographic Services. President and Fellows of Harvard University.

81 Reproduced from Colin Rowe, *The Mathematics of the Ideal Villa and Other Essays* (Cambridge: MIT Press, 1976), 173.

82 © 2001 Artists Rights Society (ARS) New York / ADAGP, Paris / FLC.

83 Reproduced from *Perspecta* 13/14: The Yale Architectural Journal. 1971.

84 Photo by Ezra Stoller. © Esto. All rights reserved.

85 Photo by Todd Gannon.

86 Reproduced from *Perspecta* 13/14: The Yale Architectural Journal. 1971.

87 Reproduced from *Perspecta* 13/14: The Yale Architectural Journal. 1971.

88 Reproduced from *Perspecta* 13/14: The Yale Architectural Journal. 1971.

89 Scala/Art Resource, NY.

90 Reproduced from H. Millon and V. Lampugnani, eds., *The Renaissance: From Brunelleschi to Michelangelo* (Milan: Bompiani, 1994).

91 Reproduced from *Perspecta* 13/14: The Yale Architectural Journal. 1971.

92 © 2001 Artists Rights Society (ARS), New York / Beeldrecht, Amsterdam.

93 Reproduced from *Perspecta* 13/14: The Yale Architectural Journal. 1971.

94 Reproduced from *Perspecta* 13/14: The Yale Architectural Journal. 1971.

95 Reproduced from *Perspecta* 13/14: The Yale Architectural Journal. 1971.

96 Reproduced from *Oppositions* 13, Summer 1978.

97 Reproduced from *Oppositions* 13, Summer 1978.

98 Courtesy of Eisenman Architects.

99 John Hejduk Archive. Collection Centre Canadien d'Architecture / Canadian Centre for Architecture, Montreal.

100 © 2001 Artists Rights Society (ARS) New York / ADAGP, Paris / FLC.

101 © 2001 Artists Rights Society (ARS) New York / ADAGP, Paris / FLC.

102 Reproduced from *AA Files* 32.

103 Courtesy of Conway Library, Courtauld Institute of Art, London.

104 Courtesy of Eisenman Architects. Photo by Jeff Goldberg – ESTO.

105 Courtesy of Eisenman Architects. Photo by Jeff Goldberg – ESTO.

106 Courtesy of Eisenman Architects. Photo by Jeff Goldberg – ESTO.

107 Courtesy of Eisenman Architects. Photo by Jeff Goldberg – ESTO.

108 Courtesy of Eisenman Architects. Photo by Dick Frank.

109 Courtesy of Eisenman Architects. Photo by Dick Frank.

110 Archiv Atelier Giencke. Reproduced from *Volker Giencke: Projekte-Projects* (New York: Springer, 2001).

111 Photo by Paul Ott. Reproduced from *Volker Giencke: Projekte-Projects* (New York: Springer, 2001).

112 Photo by Paul Ott. Reproduced from *Volker Giencke: Projekte-Projects* (New York: Springer, 2001).

113 Photo by Paul Ott. Reproduced from *Volker Giencke: Projekte-Projects* (New York: Springer, 2001).

114 Erich Lessing/Art Resource, NY.

115 Scala/Art Resource, NY.

116 Archiv Atelier Giencke. Reproduced from *Volker Giencke: Projekte-Projects* (New York: Springer, 2001).

117 Archiv Atelier Giencke. Reproduced from *Volker Giencke: Projekte-Projects* (New York: Springer, 2001).

118 Photo by Hans Georg Tropper. Reproduced from *Volker Giencke: Projekte-Projects* (New York: Springer, 2001).

119 Reproduced from *Staadtbaukunst-Frülicht*, no.10, 158.

120 Reproduced from *Frülicht*, no. 2 (Winter 1921–22): 34.

121 Reproduced from Bruno Taut, *Alpine Architektur*, Hagen i.W. (1919), 3.

122 Reproduced from *Die Auflösung der Städte*, Hagen, i.W., (1920), 26.

123 © 2001 Artists Rights Society (ARS), New York / VG Bild-Kunst, Bonn. Reproduced from Peter Behrens, *Feste Lebens und der Kunst*, Leipzig, 1900, frontispiece.

124 © 2001 Artists Rights Society (ARS), New York / VG Bild-Kunst, Bonn. Reproduced from *Ein Dokument deutscher Kunst: Die Austellung der Künstler-Kolonie in Darmstadt–1901*, Munich (1901), 4.

125 Reproduced from *Jahrbuch des Deutschen Werkbundes* (1915), 82.

126 Reproduced from *Jahrbuch des Deutschen Werkbundes* (1915), 79.

127 Reproduced from Bruno Taut, *Alpine Architektur*, Hagen, i.W. (1919), 20.

128 Reproduced from Bruno Taut, *Alpine Architektur*, Hagen, i.W. (1919), 21.

129 Reproduced from *Der Weltbaumiester,* Hagen, i.W. (1920), n.p.

130 Reproduced from *Der Weltbaumiester,* Hagen, i.W. (1920), n.p.

131 © 2001 Artists Rights Society (ARS), New York / VG Bild-Kunst, Bonn. Reproduced from *Das Bauhaus 1919-33: Idee und Wirklichkeit*, Berlin, 1965, fig. 1.

132 Reproduced from *Ruf zum Bauen*, Berlin, 1920, n.p.

133 Reproduced from *Staadtbaukunst-Frülicht*, no. 3 (1920): 48.

134 Reproduced from *Staadbaukunst-Frülicht*, no. 10 (1920): 157.

135 Reproduced from *Staadbaukunst-Frülicht*, no. 8 (1920): 124.

136 Reproduced from *Staadbaukunst-Frülicht*, no. 2 (1920): 31.

137 Reproduced from *Staadbaukunst-Frülicht*, no. 7 (1920): 109.

138 Reproduced from *Staadbaukunst-Frülicht*, no. 4 (1920): 61.

139 Reproduced from *Ruf zum Bauen*, Berlin, 1920, fig. 14.

140 Reproduced from *Ruf zum Bauen*, Berlin, 1920, fig. 34.

141 Courtesy of The Walter Gropius Archive, Busch-Reisinger Museum, Harvard University. Gift of Walter Gropius. Photographic Services. President and Fellows of Harvard University.

142 Photo by Richard Payne, FAIA.

143 Photo by Richard Payne, FAIA.

144 © 2001 Artists Rights Society (ARS), New York / ProLitteris, Zürich. Reproduced from *Der Sturm*, no. 15/16, 1915.

145 Reproduced from *Pierre Chareau: Architect and Craftsman, 1883–1950* (New York: Rizzoli, 1986).

146 Reproduced from *Pierre Chareau: Architect and Craftsman, 1883–1950* (New York: Rizzoli, 1986).

147 Reproduced from *Pierre Chareau: Architect and Craftsman, 1883–1950* (New York: Rizzoli, 1986).

148 Reproduced from *Pierre Chareau: Architect and Craftsman, 1883–1950* (New York: Rizzoli, 1986).

149 © 2001 Artists Rights Society (ARS), New York / VG Bild-Kunst, Bonn. Image courtesy of the Museum of Modern Art, New York, gift of the architect.

150 © 2001 Artists Rights Society (ARS), New York / VG Bild-Kunst, Bonn. Reproduced from *Perspecta* 21: The Yale Architectural Journal.

151 © 2001 The Munch Museum / The Munch-Ellingsen Group / Artists Rights Society (ARS), New York.

152 Reproduced from R. Stephan, ed., *Erich Mendelsohn: Architecture 1910–1953* (New York: Monacelli Press, 1999).

153 © 2001 Artists Rights Society (ARS), New York / VG Bild-Kunst, Bonn.

172 © 2001 Artists Rights Society (ARS), New York / VG Bild-Kunst, Bonn. Photo by Robin Evans. Courtesy of the Robin Evans Archive, The Architectural Association, London.

173 © 2001 Artists Rights Society (ARS), New York / VG Bild-Kunst, Bonn. Photo by Robin Evans. Courtesy of the Robin Evans Archive, The Architectural Association, London.

174 © 2001 Artists Rights Society (ARS), New York / VG Bild-Kunst, Bonn. Image courtesy of the Museum of Modern Art, New York, gift of the architect.

175 © 2001 Artists Rights Society (ARS), New York / VG Bild-Kunst, Bonn. Photo by Robin Evans. Courtesy of the Robin Evans Archive, The Architectural Association, London.

176 © 2001 Artists Rights Society (ARS), New York / VG Bild-Kunst, Bonn. Photo by Robin Evans. Courtesy of the Robin Evans Archive, The Architectural Association, London.

177 © 2001 Artists Rights Society (ARS), New York / VG Bild-Kunst, Bonn. Image courtesy of the Museum of Modern Art, New York, gift of the architect.

178 Courtesy of the National Portrait Gallery, London.

179 © 2001 Artists Rights Society (ARS), New York / VG Bild-Kunst, Bonn. Photo by Robin Evans. Courtesy of the Robin Evans Archive, The Architectural Association, London.

180 © 2001 Artists Rights Society (ARS), New York / VG Bild-Kunst, Bonn. Photo by Robin Evans. Courtesy of the Robin Evans Archive, The Architectural Association, London.

181 Reproduced from Jean Dubreuil, *Perspective pratique*, 1651.

182 © 2001 Artists Rights Society (ARS), New York / VG Bild-Kunst, Bonn. Photo by Robin Evans. Courtesy of the Robin Evans Archive, The Architectural Association, London.

183 Photo by Koji Taki.

184 Photo by Tomio Ohashi.

185 Courtesy of Toyo Ito.

186 Shinkenchiku-sha.

187 Photo by Margherita Spiluttini.

188 Photo by Margherita Spiluttini.

189 Photo by Margherita Spiluttini.

190 Courtesy of Herzog and de Meuron.

191 Photo by Margherita Spiluttini.

192 Reproduced from *Pierced Hearts and True Love: A Century of Drawings for Tattoos* (New York: Drawing Center, 1995).

193 2001 Artist Rights Society (ARS), New York/ VG Bild-Kunst, Bonn.